Adaptation and Human Behavior

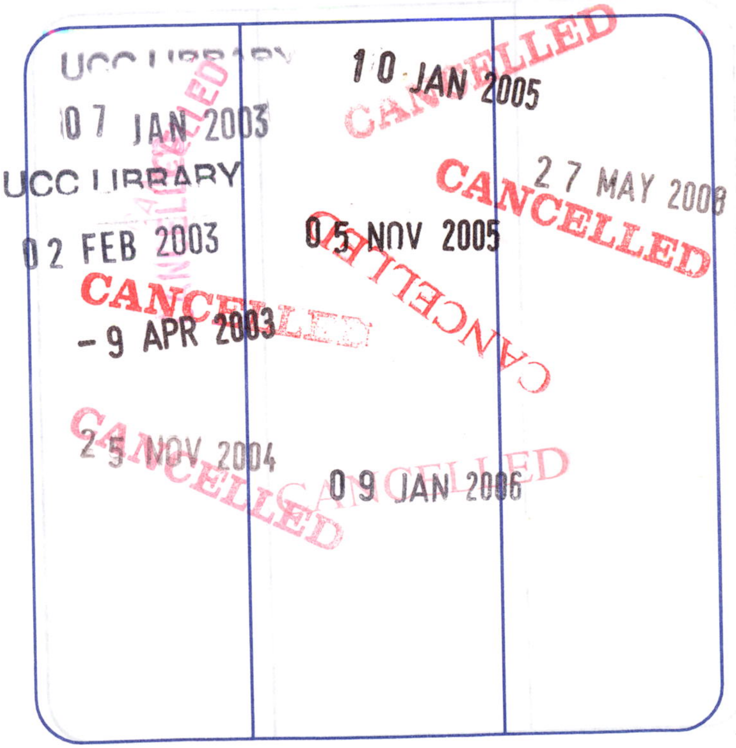

EVOLUTIONARY FOUNDATIONS OF HUMAN BEHAVIOR

An Aldine de Gruyter Series of Texts and Monographs

EDITED BY

Monique Borgerhoff Mulder, *University of California, Davis*
Marc Hauser, *Harvard University*

Richard D. Alexander, **The Biology of Moral Systems**

Laura L. Betzig, **Despotism and Differential Reproduction: A Darwinian View of History**

James S. Chisholm, **Navajo Infancy: An Ethological Study of Child Development**

Russell l. Ciochon and John G. Fleagle (eds.), **Primate Evolution and Human Origins**

G.A. Clark and C.M. Willermet (eds.), **Conceptual Issues in Modern Human Origins Research**

Lee Cronk, Napoleon Chagnon, and William Irons (eds.), **Adaptation and Human Behavior: An Anthropological Perspective**

Martin Daly and Margo Wilson, **Homicide**

Irenäus Eibl-Eibesfeldt, **Human Ethology**

Richard J. Gelles and Jane B. Lancaster (eds.), **Child Abuse and Neglect: Biosocial Dimensions**

Kathleen R. Gibson and Anne C. Petersen (eds.), **Brain Maturation and Cognitive Development: Comparative and Cross-Cultural Perspectives**

Frederick E. Grine (ed.), **Evolutionary History of the "Robust" Australopithecines**

Barry S. Hewlett (ed.), **Father-Child Relations: Cultural and Biosocial Contexts**

Kim Hill and A. Magdalena Hurtado, **Ache life History: The Ecology and Demography of a Foraging People**

Warren G. Kinzey (ed.), **New World Primates: Ecology, Evolution, and Behavior**

Jane B. Lancaster, Jeanne Altmann, Alice S. Rossi, and Lonnie R. Sherrod (eds.), **Parenting across the Life Span: Biosocial Dimensions**

Jonathan Marks, **Human Biodiversity: Genes, Race, and History**

Lewis Petrinovich, **The Cannibal Within**

Richard B. Potts, **Early Hominid Activities at Olduval**

Eric Alden Smith, **Inujjuamiut Foraging Strategies: Evolutionary Ecology of an Artic Hunting Economy**

Eric Alden Smith and Bruce Winterhalder (eds.), **Evolutionary Ecology and Human Behavior**

Barbara Boardman Smuts, **Sex and Friendship in Baboons**

Patricia Stuart-Macadam and Susan Kent (eds.), **Diet, Demography, and Disease: Changing Perspectives on Anemia**

Wenda R. Trevathan, **Human Birth: An Evolutionary Perspective**

James W. Wood, **Dynamics of Human Reproduction: Biology, Biometry, Demography**

Adaptation and Human Behavior

An Anthropological Perspective

Editors

Lee Cronk

Napoleon Chagnon

William Irons

ALDINE DE GRUYTER
NEW YORK

ABOUT THE EDITORS

Lee Cronk is Associate Professor of Anthropology at Rutgers University, New Brunswick, New Jersey.
Napoleon Chagnon is Professor of Anthropology, Emeritus, at the University of California, Santa Barbara, California.
William Irons is Professor of Anthropology at Northwestern University, Evanston, Illinois.

ALDINE DE GRUYTER
A division of Walter de Gruyter, Inc.
200 Saw Mill River Road
Hawthorne, New York 10532

This publication is printed on acid free paper ♾

Library of Congress Cataloging-in-Publication Data
Adaptation and human behavior : an anthropological perspective /
[edited by] Lee Cronk, Napoleon Chagnon, and William Irons.
p. cm. — (Evolutionary foundations of human behavior)
Includes bibliographical references.
ISBN 0-202-02043-6 (cl. : alk. paper). — ISBN 0-202-02044-4 (pa. : alk. paper)
1. Sociobiology. 2. Human behavior. 3. Social evolution. 4. Human evolution. 5. Human ecology. I. Cronk, Lee. II. Chagnon, Napoleon A., 1938– . III. Irons, William. IV. Series.
GN365.9.A33 1999
304.5—dc21 99-26821
CIP

Manufactured in the United States of America

10 9 8 7 6 5 4 3 2 1

In memoriam

W. D. Hamilton (1936–2000)
Late Royal Society Research Professor in Zoology
Oxford University
without whose new insights
into the behavior of all organisms
this volume and the paradigm it explores
would never have been possible

CONTENTS

Part I Some Statements of Theory

Part II Mating

Preface

Edited volumes play an important role in modern scholarship. Often, they serve to alert researchers to the arrival of new and promising approaches in their fields. That was the case in 1979 when Duxbury press published *Evolutionary Biology and Human Social Behavior: An Anthropological Perspective*, edited by Napoleon A. Chagnon and William Irons. The publication of that book, the first collection of empirical tests of hyphotheses about human behavior derived from recently developed ideas in evolutionary biology, was a watershed event for the emerging field of human behavioral ecology.

The 1979 volume grew out of two sessions organized by Chagnon and Irons at the 1976 annual meetings of the American Anthropological Association. In 1995, with this still fresh and rapidly growing approach about to enter its third decade, the three editors of the present volume thought that it would be a good time to take stock, to see how far we have come, and how far we have yet to go. With that in mind, we organized two long sessions at the 1996 annual meetings of the American Anthropological Association in San Francisco. The sessions, which were invited by the Council for General Anthropology and the Biological Anthropology Section of the AAA, were very successful, and, as in 1976, we decided to use some of the papers presented there as the core of a new volume of empirical studies in human behavioral ecology.

The chapters in this volume cover a wide range of societies and topics organized into six sections. The first section includes two chapters that provide some historical background on the development of human behavioral ecology and compare it to two complementary approaches in the study of evolution and human behavior, evolutionary psychology, and dual inheritance theory. The second section includes five studies of mating effort in a variety of societies from South America and Africa. The third section covers parenting, with five studies on societies from Africa, Asia, and North America. The fourth section breaks somewhat with the tradition in human behavioral ecology by focusing on one particularly problematic issue, the demographic transition, using data from Europe, North America, and Asia. The fifth section includes studies of cooperation and helping behaviors, using data from societies in Micronesia and South America. The sixth and final section consists of a single chapter that places the volume in a broader critical and comparative context.

Lee Cronk
Napoleon Chagnon
William Irons

Acknowledgments

This volume would not have been possible without the help of a great many people. Wenda Trevathan, 1996 program chair for the Biological Anthropology Section, and Dan Moerman, 1996 program chair for the Council for General Anthropology, guided us through the process of setting up the original sessions that eventually led to this book. The chapter authors, of course, deserve the greatest credit for all of the effort they put into their contributions and for giving us the privilege of including their work in this collection. Each of the chapters went through a rigorous process of anonymous peer reviews, and we would like to sincerely thank all of those scholars who so generously contributed their time to give us their insightful and constructive comments on the manuscripts. The reviewer's comments were extremely helpful to us as editors and to the authors of the various chapters, and it is fair to say that virtually every chapter was greatly improved as a result of their input. Although we would like to be able to thank them all by name, in keeping with our commitment to respect their anonymity, we must settle for a generic statement of thanks. A number of people at Aldine de Gruyter also were essential to the success of this project. The series editors, Monique Borgerhoff Mulder and Marc Hauser, supported this project from its inception; our editor, Richard Koffler, his assistant Sissy Girard, managing editors Arlene Perazzini and Mai Shaikhanuar-Cota, and copyeditor June-el Piper were all extremely helpful, and, above all, patient, in shepherding this book to completion.

Contributors

Helen Alvarez	Department of Anthropology, University of Utah
Nicholas G. Blurton Jones	Departments of Anthropology, Education, Psychiatry University of California–Los Angeles
Monique Borgerhoff Mulder	Department of Anthropology and Graduate Group in Ecology, University of California–Davis
Richard Chacon	Division of Behavioral and Social Sciences, El Camino College
Napoleon A. Chagnon	Department of Anthropology, University of California–Santa Barbara
Eric L. Charnov	Department of Biology, University of New Mexico
Lee Cronk	Department of Anthropology and Center for Human Evolutionary Studies, Rutgers University
J. Patrick Gray	Department of Anthropology, University of Wisconsin–Milwaukee
Raymond Hames	Department of Anthropology, University of Nebraska
Kristen Hawkes	Department of Anthropology, University of Utah
Barry S. Hewlett	Department of Anthropology, Washington State University
William Irons	Department of Anthropology, Northwestern University
Doug Jones	Department of Anthropology, University of Utah
Hillard S. Kaplan	Department of Anthropology, University of New Mexico
Michael E. Lamb	Section on Social and Emotional Development, National Institute of Child Health and Human Development

Jane B. Lancaster	Department of Anthropology, University of New Mexico
Birgit Leyendecker	Martin-Luther University, Halle, Germany
Bobbi S. Low	School of Natural Resources and Environment, University of Michigan
Barney Luttbeg	National Center for Ecological Analysis and Synthesis, University of California–Santa Barbara
Ruth Mace	Department of Anthropology, University College, London
Marc Mangel	Department of Environmental Studies, University of California–Santa Cruz
Frank W. Marlowe	Department of Anthropology, Harvard University
James F. O'Connell	Department of Anthropology, University of Utah
John Q. Patton	Department of Anthropology, Washington State University
Axel Schölmerich	Ruhr University, Bochum, Germany
Daniel W. Sellen	Department of Anthropology, Emory University Department of International Health, Rollins School of Public Health Public Health Nutrition Unit, London School of Hygiene and Tropical Medicine
Daniela F. Sieff	Real World Pictures, Priory House, London SW8 2PD
Eric Alden Smith	Department of Anthropology, University of Washington
Richard Sosis	Department of Anthropology, University of Connecticut
Beverly I. Strassmann	Department of Anthropology, University of Michigan
Lawrence S. Sugiyama	Department of Anthropology and Institute of Cognitive and Decision Sciences, University of Oregon

PART I

SOME STATEMENTS OF THEORY

1

Two Decades of a New Paradigm

WILLIAM IRONS and LEE CRONK

This book is a collection of state-of-the-art empirical studies in a paradigm that has become known as human behavioral ecology. The emergence of this approach in anthropology was marked by the publication in 1979 of another collection of studies entitled *Evolutionary Biology and Human Social Behavior: An Anthropological Perspective* (Chagnon and Irons 1979). During the two decades that have passed since then, the approach has matured and expanded into new areas. This chapter describes the origins of the approach, its early reception, and its subsequent development.

We use the phrase "human behavioral ecology" chiefly because it is the label used most often by those doing similar work on nonhumans, thereby accentuating the fact that this approach has its roots in animal behavior studies or ethology. It also has the advantage of avoiding notions of genetic determinism that are commonly (though mistakenly) associated with the term "sociobiology." In addition, it serves to differentiate this approach from other, complementary approaches such as evolutionary psychology and cultural transmission theory (see Smith, chapter 2, this volume). However, it should be kept in mind that not everyone working within this approach uses this same label and that other labels, including human evolutionary ecology, human ethology, human socioecology, and human sociobiology, are also commonly used.

THE ORIGINS OF HUMAN BEHAVIORAL ECOLOGY

The 1960s and the 1970s witnessed some very significant advances in evolutionary theory, especially theory relevant to the evolution of individual behavior. William D. Hamilton's theory of kin selection and inclusive fitness was published in 1964, followed by his important work on senescence (1966), sex ratios (1967), and herding behavior (1971). In 1966, George C. Williams's watershed book *Adaptation and Natural Selection* clarified a number of issues, especially the question of the level in the hierarchy of life (gene, individual, population, species, ecosystem) at which adaptations are most likely to evolve. That same year, Robert H.

MacArthur and Eric Pianka (1966) laid the foundations for the development of optimal foraging theory and the now widespread use of economic models in animal behavior studies. Robert L. Trivers presented the theory of reciprocal altruism in his classic 1971 paper, which was followed soon afterward by his theoretical papers on parental investment and sexual selection (1972; see also Trivers and Willard 1973) and parent-offspring conflict (1974; see also Trivers and Hare 1976).

These theoretical ideas formed a coherent perspective that viewed organisms as products of natural selection favoring phenotypes that enhanced the representation in future generations of the genes that coded for them. This approach is sometimes labeled "adaptationism" and "selectionist thinking" (Gray, chapter 21, this volume; see also Daly and Wilson 1988:2–5), but of course an understanding of natural selection and its role in designing adaptations had been around for a long time. What was new was the focus on behavior as something that, like physiology, may be subject to the forces of natural selection. With these theoretical developments in hand, animal behaviorists soon conducted a flurry of new field studies on a wide variety of taxa, including, to name just a few, arthropods, fish, birds, rodents, carnivores, and primates. Because primatology has long been an accepted branch of anthropology, it formed a bridge between anthropology and animal behavior studies in general, and primatologists such as Jeanne Altmann, Irven DeVore, Sarah Blaffer Hrdy, Joan Silk, Barbara Smuts, and Richard Wrangham played an important role in introducing the insights of Hamilton, Trivers, and Williams to anthropology. Their long-term, detailed observational studies of animal behavior also drew on the ethological tradition of researchers such as Niko Tinbergen and Konrad Lorenz. At about the same time, a variety of anthropologists and others, including Earl Count, Robin Fox, Derek Freeman, Robert Hinde, Nicholas Humphrey, Desmond Morris, and Lionel Tiger, were beginning to use evolutionary theory to study human behavior, while human ethologists like Irenäus Eibl-Eibesfeldt and Nicholas Blurton Jones began to give the field an empirical base, and economists like Gary Becker pioneered the application of optimization models to noneconomic behavior.

The stage was set for the extension of the new refinements of evolutionary theory to the study of the human species. In 1974, University of Michigan zoologist Richard Alexander published a classic paper summarizing the evolutionary theory of sociality and making numerous specific suggestions about how this theory might enhance our understanding of human social behavior. In 1975, Harvard biologist E. O. Wilson published a large volume entitled *Sociobiology: The New Synthesis,* which summarized the evolutionary theory of social behavior and reviewed much of the evidence supporting this perspective from studies of social behavior of a wide range of animal taxa. In the final chapter of *Sociobiology,* Wilson suggested that this perspective could shed light on human social behavior and outlined some of what he thought this new insight might be. In 1976, Richard Dawkins published his classic popularization of the new approach entitled *The Selfish Gene,* which explained with unusual clarity the theoretical perspective underlying the work of Hamilton, Williams, and Trivers. Like Alexander and Wilson, Dawkins also suggested that evolutionary theory might shed light on human behavior, though he advocated an emphasis on the role of culturally rather than genetically inherited information in shaping behavior.

EARLY ATTEMPTS AT ANTHROPOLOGICAL APPLICATION

In 1974 and 1975, Napoleon Chagnon and William Irons were involved in an ongoing discussion about the use of these new refinements of evolutionary theory in anthropology, especially cultural anthropology. At that time they were both in the Anthropology Department at Pennsylvania State University; both had extensive fieldwork experience; and both were convinced that selectionist thinking would enrich their ethnographic research. After absorbing the works of Alexander, Hamilton, Trivers, Williams, and Wilson, they decided to organize two symposia on the use of evolutionary theory in anthropology for the 1976 annual meeting of the American Anthropological Association to present to the discipline their attempts to incorporate selectionist thinking into their ethnographic research. Eventually their symposia were coordinated with two symposia on the same topic organized by Irven DeVore of Harvard University. These symposia formed the basis for the edited volume *Evolutionary Biology and Human Social Behavior: An Anthropological Perspective* (Chagnon and Irons 1979).

The research presented in those contexts focused on traditional anthropological topics such as kinship, marriage, infanticide, and social stratification, and the methods and data were also largely of traditional anthropological varieties. The novel element was the use of such data to test hypotheses derived from the theoretical expectation that human social behavior would reflect strategies that would enhance inclusive fitness in environments similar to those of past human evolution. The questions asked were derived in straightforward ways mainly from the work of Alexander, Hamilton, and Trivers: Do human beings tend to be more helpful to genetic kin than non-kin, and more competitive in dealing with non-kin than kin? Can such a tendency influence family and village formation in traditional societies? Do parents manipulate sex ratios in ways that increase the number of their grandchildren? Can status striving be seen as means to reproductive success? Although not everyone working in this area was included either in the 1976 symposia or the 1979 volume, these fora did serve to mark the beginning of a new school of thought in anthropology by bringing together a large number of empirical studies that used ethnographic data to test hypotheses about human behavior derived from evolutionary theory.[1]

The year 1979 was a productive year for the new paradigm in other ways as well. Two journals that deal extensively with the use of evolutionary theory in the study of human social behavior, *Ethology and Sociobiology* (recently renamed *Evolution and Human Behavior*) and the *Journal of Social and Biological Structures* (now the

Journal of Social and Evolutionary Systems), began publication, and the journal *Behavioral Ecology and Sociobiology,* which focuses primarily on nonhumans but which has also included some work on humans, first appeared. In that same year, two important theoretical books were published, Alexander's *Darwinism and Human Affairs* and Donald Symons's *The Evolution of Human Sexuality,* while E. O. Wilson's *On Human Nature* had appeared the year before.

THE RECEPTION BY CULTURAL ANTHROPOLOGY

At the same time that this new field was rapidly developing, a number of extraordinarily hostile attacks upon it soon appeared. The gist of these attacks was almost always twofold. First, it was argued that the theoretical perspective represented by Hamilton, Trivers, Williams, Alexander, and Wilson could easily be shown to be totally indefensible on both logical and empirical grounds. Second, it was argued that the perspective tends to justify an oppressive status quo by encouraging racism, sexism, elitism, and imperialism.

A general hostility to the new approach developed especially early and intensely among cultural anthropologists. At the 1976 meeting of the American Anthropological Association at which the symposia organized by Chagnon and Irons were held, a motion was introduced at the business meeting to condemn "sociobiology." The motion was hotly debated, but it was finally defeated by a narrow margin. Interestingly, several people who debated against the motion were also opposed to sociobiology itself. Marshall Sahlins, for example, argued that passage of the motion would tend to strengthen sociobiology by making its supporters look like martyrs, and Margaret Mead argued that the motion, if passed, could be misconstrued as condemning any use of Darwinian theory. It is interesting to speculate whether the motion would have passed had it not been for these arguments from leaders of the profession who were already on record as being sharply critical of "sociobiology." At about the same time, the journal of the American Anthropological Association, *American Anthropologist,* published very negative reviews of the first watershed books presenting the approach that was to become human behavioral ecology. For example, John Buettner-Janusch (1978) described Richard Dawkins's *The Selfish Gene* as "an example of the silliness that can result from an Oxbridge education" based on his misbelief that Dawkins attributed conscious intentions to "selfish genes." Elliot Chapple's (1976) review of E. O. Wilson's *Sociobiology* in the *American Anthropologist* said that it "clearly wins the prize as the worst book in biology for 1975."

At the time of the 1976 anthropology meetings, Marshall Sahlins's book *The Use and Abuse of Biology* was freshly in print. In this book, a recognized leader among cultural anthropologists unequivocally condemned sociobiology as logically and empirically indefensible and politically dangerous. At the time, the book sold well and convinced a great many anthropologists that the new approach was both bad science and politically dangerous. When, as a freshman at Northwestern University, Cronk let it be known that he had read Wilson's and Dawkins's books while still a high school student and was interested in the new paradigm, he was instructed by an anthropology faculty member to read Sahlins's book as a purgative. Sahlins's book is still in print and is still cited favorably by anthropologists and other social scientists (e.g., Bodley 1994:66; Ohnuki-Tierney 1994; Rosenblatt 1997; Schubert 1991; Schultz and Lavenda 1995a:83, 1995b:224), suggesting that a significant number of people are still sympathetic to its arguments. Because of the continuing impact of Sahlins's arguments, we will use part of this chapter to explain why we and other behavioral ecologists do not find them persuasive.

Part of Sahlins's critique was the common theme that sociobiology justifies free markets and the oppression that many people believe such markets necessarily entail. He said that this was an example of culture doing what cultures always do, in other words, inventing an ideology that justifies the culture itself. In Western society, he argued, oppression is a manifestation of the capitalist system, and that system has somehow generated sociobiology as a projection of the capitalist ethic of competition onto the natural world to encourage the idea that capitalism is somehow natural and therefore inevitable. In his own words, "What is inscribed in the theory of sociobiology is the entrenched ideology of Western society: the assurance of its naturalness and the claim of its inevitability" (1976:101). This is a hard argument to take seriously. The fact that neither Sahlins nor anyone else has offered an alternative approach to the evolution of life that does not include the differential reproduction of competing genotypes as a central element suggests that any similarity between the logic of capitalism and the logic of natural selection is coincidental. Furthermore, the overwhelming evidence supporting the theory of evolution by natural selection would make it appear that it maintains its currency not because of its supposed usefulness as an ideological tool but rather because of its success in explaining why organisms are the way they are.

This ideological attack was especially surprising to the many early sociobiologists who were committed to political and economic change and enhanced social justice and who bridled at the accusation that they were unwitting propagandists for any particular political or economic system. Unlike Sahlins, they understood that a central tenet of modern evolutionary theory is that no argument about the naturalness of a behavior can be used as a moral justification of that behavior. To do otherwise is to commit what is well known in the field as "the naturalistic fallacy" (Moore 1903; see also Hume 1739/1740). They also understood that the ideas of Hamilton and Trivers have as much or more to do with cooperation than with competition among organisms. Evolutionary biologist David Queller (1995:488) notes that his own work on social insects "emphasizes altruistic behavior, focuses on females rather than the males, and suggests that collective worker interests are crucial determinants of advanced insect societies." He asks, "Does this make me a good guy, a nurturing feminist, and a stalwart of the working class?"

A large part of Sahlins's attempt at a scientific argument against sociobiology focused on kinship: "The issue between sociobiology and social anthropology is decisively joined on the field of kinship" (1976:18). He claimed that the most elementary anthropological knowledge, "Anthropology 101," decisively refutes sociobiology's claim that human kinship is shaped by kin selection because in no society do kinship categories correspond with genealogical relatedness as measured by the proportion of genes individuals share by recent common descent, commonly represented as *r*. For instance, husbands of one's parents' sisters ($r = 0$) may be lumped together with one's parents' brothers ($r = .25$), or full brothers ($r = 0.5$) may be lumped with male parallel cousins ($r = 0.125$ for first cousins). Furthermore, he pointed out, households routinely contain people who are related in a wide variety of ways to a wide variety of degrees.

The problem is that Sahlins had derived a prediction from kin selection theory that no one who really understands evolutionary theory would ever make. No one expects that an individual will be more closely related to everyone in her household than to everyone outside of the household. The formation of a household represents a compromise between several competing goals. In an outbreeding sexual species, such as humans, individuals need to find mates who are not closely related. Inbreeding depression lowers fitness, and therefore close kin do not make good mates. Thus it is not surprising that people marry distant or non-kin and that one or both parties move after marriage so that typically one has a distantly related or unrelated spouse in one's household and full siblings who have taken up residence elsewhere. It is also the case that cooperating with an unrelated brother-in-law who is the father of one's nieces and nephews is not a violation of kin selection theory because affinal kin share a genetic interest in their common descendants (Alexander 1979:159–160; Dow 1984). Furthermore, human kinship systems are almost certainly based on a combination of kin altruism and reciprocal altruism (Trivers 1971).

Sahlins also argued that the whole project is flawed from the start by the fact that many other societies lack words for fractions and hence cannot calculate genealogical relatedness, adding as a side note that the obvious inability of animals to calculate fractions "introduces a considerable mysticism" to sociobiological theory (1976:45). Among animal behaviorists this has become known as "Sahlins's Fallacy," and it is considered a real howler. Dawkins (1979, 1989:291–292) points out that "A snail shell is an exquisite logarithmic spiral, but where does the snail keep its log tables?" and "How do 'green plants' figure out the formula for chlorophyll?" Similarly, although we may need differential equations in order to describe the trajectory of a baseball, that does not mean that an outfielder needs to solve any equations in order to catch one (Dawkins 1976:103–104, 1989:96). In short, although our understanding of many behaviors and biological processes is enhanced by mathematical models, this does not mean that organisms themselves need any understanding of mathematics in order to develop or behave.

A pioneering example of the use of inclusive fitness theory to shed light on human behavior was Chagnon and Bugos's (1979) analysis of a Yanomamö ax fight that was included in *Evolutionary Biology and Human Social Behavior*. The fight had been filmed and photographed (Asch and Chagnon 1975; Biella, Chagnon, and Seaman 1997; Chagnon 1997), and Chagnon had a complete set of genealogies for the participants. The data were used to test the prediction that the participants in the fight would tend to take sides with closer kin against more distant kin. Since almost everyone in the village was related to almost everyone else in the village, there was no question of taking sides with or against non-kin. The data indicated that those who chose to fight together were on average more highly related to one another than the village average. It also showed that those they chose to fight against were less related to them than the village average. Had the participants in the fight chosen sides without regard to genealogical distance, the expected result would be that average relatedness to their own faction and to their opposing faction would be the same as their average relatedness to the entire village. In this analysis, Chagnon and Bugos predicted that genealogical relatedness would be one factor, but not the only one, influencing individuals' choices of sides. Other factors considered include affinal ties and lineage affiliations. Judging from his discussion in *The Use and Abuse of Biology,* Sahlins's prediction regarding the ax fight would have been that the members of each faction would all be more closely related to all the members of their faction than to any members of the other faction. This would be reasonable only if kinship were the only factor influencing the choice of sides.

Another position taken by Sahlins (1976:84) was that if human behavior toward kin is thought of as being influenced by reciprocity as well as a tendency toward nepotism then the resulting model would be unfalsifiable: "If ego is good to his kinsmen, it benefits his own inclusive fitness; if on the other hand, he aids a stranger rather than a kinsman, it also comes back to his advantage in the form of reciprocal altruism." To behavioral ecologists, these are fighting words. Behavioral ecologists are committed to scientific methods and build their research around falsifiable theories and hypotheses. They find it especially annoying to be told their theories are unfalsifiable by a cultural anthropologist, a representative of a subdiscipline whose practitioners rarely concern themselves with the unfalsifiability of their own assertions. Fortunately, research on kin and reciprocal altruism has clearly shown that Sahlins has this wrong. Susan Essock-Vitale and Michael McGuire (1980), for example, did exactly what Sahlins said was impossible: they made falsifiable predictions based on Hamilton's theory of kin selection and on Trivers's theory of reciprocal altruism, analyzing fifteen studies from various societies in terms of a set of five predictions derived from the hypothesis that both genealogical relatedness and reciprocity would make various forms of altruism more probable. Because the data available did not allow each hypothesis to be tested in each of the fifteen societies, they were able to conduct a total of thirty tests of their predictions. Twenty-seven predictions were confirmed, one was disconfirmed, and in two cases the data were insufficiently clear to allow a decision of whether the data confirmed or disconfirmed a particular prediction. If we assume as a null hypothesis that nepotism and reciprocity have no effect on the occurrence of altruism, then we can estimate the chance of getting Essock-Vitale and McGuire's results simply by sampling error. We can do this by assuming that each prediction was as likely to be disconfirmed as confirmed. The conservative way to do this would be to count the questionable cases as disconfirmation. Thus the null hypothesis suggests a binomial distribution with a probability of .5 for both confirmation and disconfirmation in each test. The likelihood of getting this result, given the assumptions of this null hypothesis, would be roughly two in a thousand. The important point here is that the expectations of behavioral ecologists are statistical. They expect some cases will not fit their expectations, and the validity of their claim can be judged only from a large number of cases. Since the publication of Essock-Vitale and McGuire's study, many more studies testing inclusive fitness theory among humans have been published, and the result is to lend support both to the notion that a nepotistic tendency is at least widespread if not universal in our species and to the broader project of the evolutionary biological study of human social behavior (see Turke 1996).

In an ironic way, human behavioral ecology owes Marshall Sahlins an intellectual debt because his confusion over the theory and its application led to some important research. For example, Joan Silk's (1980) work on adoption in Polynesia was inspired by Sahlins's claim that the practice, which is widespread in that part of the world, falsified inclusive fitness theory. Similarly, Sahlins's concerns about the lack of fit between kin terminologies and genealogical relatedness led to Kristen Hawkes's (1983) research on relatedness, kin terms, and helping among the Binumarien of New Guinea. Finally, Sahlins's concerns about how individual organisms could know the identities of their relatives have been addressed by research on kin recognition among nonhumans (e.g., Fletcher and Michener 1987; Hepper 1991). Furthermore, the enthusiastic reception given Sahlins's book by cultural anthropologists makes it clear that, as Gray notes (this volume), "sociobiology" has long had a serious public relations problem.

DECONSTRUCTING CULTURAL ANTHROPOLOGY: SOME PERSONAL OBSERVATIONS

Being cultural anthropologists gives us insights into why cultural anthropologists are suspicious of "sociobiology." In effect, we have done participant observation among cultural anthropologists. Numerous interactions with cultural anthropological colleagues over many years makes us aware of widespread beliefs among them. One such belief is that "sociobiology" encourages a long list of evil "isms": racism, sexism, elitism, imperialism, and essentialism. For some reason racism is the most frequently emphasized. Moral outrage is a salient component of the typical cultural anthropologist's reaction to "sociobiology," and the morally outrageous quality of "sociobiology" makes it unnecessary to be careful with facts and logic when attacking it (cf. Sahlins's argument about animals not knowing fractions).

Heavy-handed criticisms of this sort were not at all rare in the first decade after the appearance of *Evolutionary Biology and Human Social Behavior*. They cropped up frequently in intellectual discussions of either a formal or an informal variety. Often they involved people who were not anthropologists. Psychologists, economists, and educated non-academics often expressed very negative views of "sociobiology," often based on strange misconceptions about the nature of "sociobiology." In the 1990s, however, conversations of this sort have become much rarer *except when talking to cultural anthropologists*. Evolutionary theory is now widely accepted among psychologists and psychiatrists, and we also encounter many economists, political scientists, and other academics who are informed and interested in evolutionary theory. Biological anthropologists have always been evolutionists, and the majority of them are now well-informed about behavioral ecology and sympathetic to its scientific objectives. However, for some reason cultural anthropologists are the last-ditch defenders of the view that human behavior and culture are *not* influenced by our evolutionary history and that serious social and political harm will flow from any attempt to argue that they are. Although some cultural anthropologists are informed and sympathetic, the majority of cultural anthropologists continue to accept the broad outlines of Sahlins's argument. They see selectionist thinking (which they usually insist on labeling "sociobiology") as scientifically unsound and politically dangerous. We do not think Sahlins's book caused cultural anthropologists to have these views. Rather, Sahlins's book expressed deeply held views that the majority of cultural anthropologists already had. Sahlins's book resonated with their views and provided a seemingly authoritative support for them.

These negative views of "sociobiology" are surprisingly persistent. In 1998, a prominent and influential cultural anthropologist presented a colloquium in Irons's department on the future of anthropology. This leader of the profession warned the audience that they should not get involved in "sociobiology" and emphasized the "fact" that sociobiology has "horrendous implications for social policy." Most of Irons's cultural colleagues expressed agreement with this view, but little was supplied in the way of specifics about these policy implications. Several days after the talk, Irons asked one of his cultural colleagues what some of these "horrendous implications" were. In response, his colleague offered as an example the fact that *The Bell Curve* (Herrnstein and Murray 1994) was being taken seriously as an argument against affirmative action. For this cultural anthropologist, the distinction between behavioral ecology and the psychometrics of *The Bell Curve* was too subtle to take into account. Anything that was somehow biological and somehow evil could be conveniently lumped under the label "sociobiology." It appears to be irrelevant to such moralistic reasoning that *The Bell Curve* and behavioral ecology have next to nothing in common, as shown by the fact that the bibliographies of this volume and of *The Bell Curve* include almost none of the same sources.

As we see it, the cultural anthropological condemnation of behavioral ecology as a justification for racism, sexism, or other forms of oppression is not based on solid knowledge of the paradigm.[2] Rather it is based on a simple assumption that any attempt to argue for an evolved human nature influencing human behavior can be rejected out of hand. Such arguments can be dismissed as "genetic determinism" and thinly veiled right-wing political plots. As the majority of cultural anthropologists see it, their discipline derives much of its value from its role in discouraging racism and sexism, and condemning "sociobiology" is an important part of that role.[3]

CHANGING TIDE: GROWING ACCEPTANCE IN MANY QUARTERS

Sharply critical attacks on "sociobiology" continued in the late 1970s and early 1980s. Many of these critiques had provocative titles like *Not In Our Genes* (Lewontin et al. 1984), *Biology as a Social Weapon* (Ann Arbor Science for the People Editorial Collective 1977), and *Vaulting Ambition* (Kitcher 1985). The political motivation behind these books often was openly stated, as in the preface to *Not In Our Genes*: "We share a commitment to the prospect of the creation of a more socially just—a socialist—society. And we recognize that a critical science is an integral part of the struggle to create that society, just as we also believe that the social function of much of today's science is to hinder the creation of that society by acting to preserve the interests of the dominant class, gender and race" (Lewontin et al. 1984:ix).

Since that time, the tide appears to have shifted. Kitcher (1985) was the last widely read book to attack sociobiology. Although Kitcher's rhetoric was as negative as any of the preceding books, he conceded that nonhuman behavioral ecology was often quite sound, eventually (1990) taking the position that while "human sociobiology" was bad, "human behavioral ecology" was a promising approach. Another outsider to the approach, historian Carl Degler (1991), took a very different and much more positive view of it. Having examined the history of selectionist thinking in the social sciences since the nineteenth century, he regarded the return to this tradition in the 1970s as a corrective to an overemphasis on culture that had emerged in the early twentieth century. Furthermore, he argued that the "return of biology" did not justify racism or sexism and need not be feared on those grounds. Degler's book was something new for behavioral ecologists who had become accustomed to a degree of "biophobia" on the part of outside reviewers. The wider acceptance of this approach in the 1990s is also evident in fields such as psychology and economics, where the testing of evolutionary biological hypotheses about behavior has become not only accepted but encouraged and even institutionalized in some very progressive programs. At the same time, books like *Vaulting Ambition* have become rare, and instead we have a steady stream of popular books for the educated public that are positive about selectionist thinking by such authors as William F. Allman (1994), David Buss (1994), Helena Cronin (1991), Richard Dawkins (1976, 1982, 1986, 1989, 1995, 1996), Carl Degler (1991), Daniel C. Dennett (1995), Helen Fisher (1982, 1992), Sarah Hrdy (1999), Steven Pinker (1994, 1997), Matt Ridley (1993, 1996), Meredith Small (1995, 1998), and Robert Wright (1994).

Because most human behavioral ecologists are also anthropologists, special attention should be paid to the status of the approach within this discipline. Because they studied behavior and because behavior was traditionally dealt with by cultural anthropology, most anthropologists working in this approach in the 1970s identified themselves with that subdiscipline. At the time, most cultural anthropologists still felt themselves to be working within a scientific rather than a humanistic tradition. And at that time most biological anthropologists identified themselves as strictly *physical* anthropologists because they dealt with human physical evolution and modern human physical variation rather than with behavior. Since then things have changed considerably in both subdisciplines. Cultural anthropology has become increasingly humanistic and decreasingly scientific as it has embraced interpretive, hermeneutic, and postmodernist ideas from fields such as literary criticism. The study of behavior has largely been supplanted in cultural anthropology by the study of meaning. The continued biophobia of cultural anthropology is related, in a way, to the focus on meaning. It would be harder, we believe, to maintain biophobia while attempting to be scientific. Physical anthropologists, on the other hand, have increasingly identified themselves as *biological* anthropologists, reflecting that subdiscipline's expansion to include the study of behavior as well as physiology. The greater acceptance of behavioral ecological ideas among biological anthropologists than among cultural anthropologists was reflected in a survey conducted by Leonard Lieberman (1989). When asked, for example, whether the concept of kin selection was likely to be useful in the study of human behavior, 82% of animal behaviorists and 74% of biological anthropologists but only 35% of cultural anthropologists thought that it would. This difference between the subdisciplines is also reflected in an institutional shift that has occurred during the past twenty years. While most behavioral ecologists twenty years ago were identified by their departments as cultural anthropologists, these days it is more common to find behavioral ecologists being hired for positions in biological anthropology.

DEVELOPMENTS IN HUMAN BEHAVIORAL ECOLOGY SINCE 1979

Since the heady times of the late 1970s several things have happened in human behavioral ecology. The first and most important is that, despite its public relations problems, human behavioral ecology has become an established paradigm with a large empirical literature to its credit. While in 1976 there was one paper in print that explicitly tested a behavioral ecological hypothesis about traditional human societies (Hartung 1976), with a few more appearing in print by 1979, within a decade the number of such studies had grown dramatically. Monique Borgerhoff Mulder (1988b) did a count of all the studies she could find that met two criteria: (1) they presented a hypothesis about human social behavior derived from evolutionary theory; (2) they presented quantitative data from a traditional society to test the hypothesis. Her total count was 188. To make such a count today would be a momentous task given the enormous growth of the field during its second decade. Many of these studies have been published in the journals mentioned above, in the new journals *Human Nature* and *Evolutionary Anthropology,* and also in mainstream journals such as *Current Anthropology, Politics and the Life Sciences,* and *Behavioral and Brain Sciences.* A great many edited volumes on human behavioral ecology are also now available, including Winterhalder and Smith's collection of foraging studies (1981), Betzig, Borgerhoff Mulder, and Turke's collection of studies of reproduction (1988), Smith and Winterhalder's collection of critical reviews of major subfields within human behavioral ecology (1992), and Betzig's collection of classic articles along with critiques and updates (1997). The quality and rigor of the studies included in these various outlets is quite high, comparing extremely favorably with any of the other social and behavioral sciences and in particular with cultural anthropology. Reviews of this body of research have recently been published by Borgerhoff Mulder (1991), Cronk (1991), and Smith (1992), while Gray's 1985 book reviewing this research also remains very useful. At the same time, fields that currently lie outside behavioral ecology but that are essential to its continued development have also grown rapidly, including evolutionary psychology (see Buss 1995 for a recent review), cultural transmission or dual inheritance theory (see Smith, this volume), reproductive biology (e.g., Baker and Bellis 1995; Trevathan 1987), reproductive ecology (e.g., Ellison 1994; Wood 1994), evolutionary medicine (Nesse and Williams 1994), and behavior genetics (Plomin 1997).

Another event that marks the maturation of behavioral ecology and related approaches is the formation of the Human Behavior and Evolution Society (HBES). In October 1988 at the University of Michigan a conference was held that focused on the work of psychologists and psychiatrists. At this conference a decision was made by a number of the participants to form a society, and the name of the society was settled in an open discussion among the participants. William Hamilton was chosen as the first president and Randolph Nesse, who initiated and led the discussion, was chosen as the president elect. HBES's first annual meeting was held at Northwestern University, and meetings have been held every year since then at various universities. The society now publishes a journal *(Evolution and Human Behavior,* formerly *Ethology and Sociobiology),* and has about seven hundred members from psychology, anthropology, and a wide variety of other fields.

In addition, many human behavioral ecologists are members of the European Sociobiology Society and the International Society for Human Ethology.

At the level of theory, human behavioral ecology has also made considerable strides. One major improvement since the late 1970s is the convergence of work on mating, parenting, and social behavior, on the one hand, with work on foraging strategies on the other. In the 1970s these areas were mostly explored by different groups of researchers, whereas in the 1980s and into the 1990s the distinction between them has become increasingly blurred and both lines of thought have become enriched. This has happened as people have considered the possibility that social and reproductive goals may influence economic strategies and, conversely, that the characteristics of resources and environments may affect mating, parenting, and social behavior. Examples include Smith's analysis of forager group size (1981, 1985, 1991); Hawkes's showoff model (1990, 1991, 1993); work by Winterhalder (1986, 1990), Kaplan and Hill (1985), Kaplan, Hill, Hawkes, and Hurtado (1984), Kaplan, Hill, and Hurtado (1990), and Blurton Jones (1987b) on food sharing (see also Bliege Bird and Bird 1997); Blurton Jones's (1987a) analysis of !Kung women's foraging work and birth spacing; Borgerhoff Mulder's application of the polygyny threshold model to the mate choices of Kipsigis women (1990); and Cronk's (1989) analysis of subsistence change among the Mukogodo as a result of reproductive rather than economic considerations. This approach is also well represented in the contents of this volume (e.g., the chapters by Hames, Hewlett and colleagues, Kaplan and Lancaster, Low, Sellen and colleagues, Sosis, and Sugiyama and Chacon).

Developments in nonhuman behavioral ecology and evolutionary biology also have had an impact on human behavioral ecology. For example, a persistent bugbear of this approach in its early years was the specter of "genetic determinism." Many people outside behavioral ecology thought that in order for the theory of natural selection to be relevant to the understanding of a particular behavior, that behavior must be under strict genetic control. The posture of behavioral ecology on this issue has been clarified by Alan Grafen (1984) under the label "the phenotypic gambit." This phrase refers to the fact that behavioral ecologists focus on phenotypes, which may be influenced by many nongenetic factors such as environment and culture, rather than genotypes, and set aside the details of the heritable basis of the traits in question as neither directly relevant to the behavioral ecological project nor feasible to demonstrate in most cases (see also Smith and Winterhalder 1992:33–34). Theoretical developments in other areas, such as sexual selection (e.g., Grafen 1990a, 1990b; Hamilton and Zuk 1982; Zahavi et al. 1997), sexual attractiveness (e.g., Gangestad and Thornhill 1996), life history theory (see Hill 1993), game theoretical models (see Weibull 1995), and animal communication (see Dawkins and Krebs 1978; Hauser 1996; Johnstone 1997; Krebs and Dawkins 1984; Zahavi et al. 1997) also have had an impact on human behavioral ecology and evolutionary psychology. At the same time, human behavioral ecologists and their allies have begun to tackle problems unique to the species they study, including culture (e.g., Barkow 1989; Boyd and Richerson 1985; Cronk 1995; Durham 1991; and Irons 1979), morality (Alexander 1987; Cronk 1994a, 1994b; Frank 1988; Irons 1991, 1996; de Waal 1996), and the demographic transition (see chapters in this volume by Kaplan and Lancaster, Low, Luttbeg and colleagues, and Mace).

BACKGROUND TO THIS VOLUME

This volume was conceived of as a way both to update and to commemorate *Evolutionary Biology and Human Social Behavior: An Anthropological Perspective*. Accordingly, we thought an appropriate way to start would be with sessions at the 1996 annual meetings of the American Anthropological Association, and we eventually organized two long sessions involving a total of twenty-six papers and two discussants. As was the case with the 1976 session and the 1979 volume, the presentations at the 1996 meeting form the core of this volume.

For the most part, this volume is organized along fairly traditional lines in behavioral ecology. It begins with "Some Statements of Theory," a title borrowed from the 1979 volume. Whereas in the 1970s it was necessary to begin with chapters that introduced the general approach, its fundamental concepts, and some of its key hypotheses, twenty years later the basics of the paradigm are widely enough known and so generally agreed upon by most practitioners that restating the basics no longer seems necessary. Instead, we begin with this chapter that puts the volume in a historical context and the next chapter by Smith that compares the approach taken in most of this volume with other contemporary approaches to the evolutionary biological study of human behavior.

Behavioral ecologists think in terms of the allocation of effort, and traditionally the starting point is somatic effort, in other words, what an organism does to develop and maintain itself. Although a few years ago a book like this probably would have begun with a section on somatic behavior featuring a series of optimal foraging studies, in the 1990s most research on human foraging is being conducted not solely with an eye toward understanding diet and patch choices but rather as integral parts of examinations of reproductive and social behavior. In this volume, for example, data on food acquisition play a role in but are not the central focus of chapters by Blurton Jones and colleagues on divorce in hunting and gathering societies, by Hawkes and her coauthors on grandmothers and the origins of human females' long postmenopausal lifespans, by Sugiyama and Chacon on injury risk and foraging strategies, and by Sosis on cooperative fishing. Accordingly, although this volume contains a great deal of information about foraging, the data are distributed throughout the volume rather than collected in a single section.

Two sections of the book concern reproductive behavior, divided into the traditional categories of mating and parenting. Beverly Strassmann's chapter on the Dogon of Mali examines the costs of polygyny to women in terms of child survivorship. The chapter by Nicholas Blurton Jones, Frank W. Marlowe, Kristen Hawkes, and James F. O'Connell examines divorce rates in several hunter-gatherer societies and finds little support for the traditional paternal investment theory of human pair bonding. The chapter by Daniel W. Sellen, Monique Borgerhoff Mulder, and Daniela Sieff examines the costs and benefits of polygyny among the Eyasi Datoga of Tanzania, finding, among other things, that having a single co-wife can be costly, especially to women married to poor men, and suggesting that we need to look at the constraints on women's choices if we are to understand the maintenance of polygyny in this group. Napoleon Chagnon updates his earlier work (1988) on Yanomamö kin term manipulation as a form of reproductive competition, showing that adult males are more accurate than adult females in classifying their kin. Doug Jones combines an anthropological interest in the cultural construction of race with an evolutionary psychological interest in physical attractiveness in a study of racial categorization and attractiveness ratings by Brazilian men and women.

The next group of chapters examines why people take care of children in the ways that they do: Why do some parents invest more in their offspring than do other parents? Why do some men invest in children that are not their own? Why do some parents invest more heavily in sons while others invest more in daughters? Why do women's life histories make it possible for them to invest in their grandoffspring rather than having more offspring of their own? Barry S. Hewlett, Michael E. Lamb, Birgit Leyendecker, and Axel Schölmerich use data from foraging, farming, and industrialized societies to evaluate three adaptationist models of parental investment. Jane B. Lancaster and Hillard S. Kaplan use data from their large survey of men in Albuquerque, New Mexico, to examine the question of why men sometimes behave parentally toward children they know not to be their own offspring, finding that the child in question is usually either a relative of the investor, making the investment a form of kin altruism, or the investor's mate's child, making the investment a form of mating effort. The chapters by Lee Cronk and William Irons present tests of the Trivers-Willard hypothesis of sex-biased parental investment both in a society known for female-biased parental behavior and in one with a reputation for male favoritism. In their chapter, Kristen Hawkes, James F. O'Connell, Nicholas Blurton Jones, H. Alvarez, and E. L. Charnov propose that human females' long postmenopausal lifespans may have evolved because of the ability of older women to help their younger kin reproduce.

The next section breaks from tradition in human behavioral ecology by looking not at why or how people have so many children but rather at why in some societies they have so few. With encouragement from critics like Vining (1986), in recent years a number of behavioral ecologists have examined the problem of the demographic transition: Why have people in the wealthiest, most economically developed societies increasingly chosen to have so few offspring? Does this fact undermine and even falsify the entire behavioral ecological project, as some would argue, or is there instead an evolutionary logic behind the limitation of family size? Ruth Mace's chapter examines this question with a dynamic model of decisions about the timing of reproduction and the inheritance of wealth and finds that increases in the costs of children may be a key to the fertility reduction associated with the demographic transition. Hillard S. Kaplan and Jane B. Lancaster use data from their large survey of Albuquerque men to test their hypothesis that fertility reductions in modern societies reflect a response on the part of parents to an environment in which the wages workers receive, and hence their wealth, is directly linked to the costs of obtaining the skills necessary to be competitive in today's skills-based labor markets. Bobbi Low takes a critical look at the problem of the demographic transition, arguing that in order to solve it we need better data as well as a better understanding of the relationship between resource consumption and fertility. Finally in this section, Barney Luttbeg, Monique Borgerhoff Mulder, and Marc Mangel present the results of a dynamic model of men's decisions to take additional wives, recommending that similar modeling methods would be useful in the study of the reproductive decisions of people during the demographic transition.[4]

The chapters on sociality demonstrate the extent to which human behavioral ecologists have gone beyond simple demonstrations of nepotism to the examination of a range of other factors influencing reciprocal aid and cooperation. Lawrence Sugiyama and Richard Chacon examine the effects of pathology on the productivity of foraging among the Yora and Shiwiar of the Ecuadorian Amazon, suggesting that the need to receive aid when disabled may help explain a variety of social phenomena including group sizes and food sharing. Raymond Hames looks at food sharing among the Yanomamö, finding that it is mostly restricted to groups of households who preferentially share with each other. John Q. Patton examines the role of altruism in warfare in the Ecuadorian Amazon. Richard Sosis tests theoretical models of the emergence and stability of cooperative foraging with data on cooperative fishing and fish catch distribution from the Micronesian atoll of Ifaluk. Finally, J. Patrick Gray provides a critical and constructive commentary on the state of this approach more than two decades after it began to take off, suggesting, among other things, that in the future selectionist social science needs to do more to incorporate the concept of culture.

THE FUTURE

Explanation in biology is usually conceived of as occurring on four complementary levels: evolutionary or phylogenetic explanations that focus on the origins and evolutionary history of a trait; ultimate or distal explanations that focus on how the trait is spread and maintained through its positive effects on the inclusive fitness of its bearers; developmental or ontogenetic explanations that focus on how the trait develops during the lifetime of the individual organisms; and proximate explanations that focus on the immediate details of the trait's expression in individual organisms (based on Mayr 1961 and Tinbergen 1963). Behavioral ecology has focused primarily on ultimate or distal explanations, but we agree with Barkow (1989), Cronk (1991), and others who have called for increased vertical integration in the evolutionary study of human behavior. Major steps in this direction have already been taken, particularly in the areas of hominid evolutionary ecology (Alexander 1990; Foley 1987, 1992), evolutionary developmental psychology (e.g., Belsky, Steinberg, and Draper 1991), and the study of the proximate psychological and physiological factors influencing human behavior (e.g., Flinn and England 1995). Along with increased vertical integration, there is a need for increased horizontal integration among a variety of complementary and closely related approaches, including behavioral ecology, cultural transmission theory, evolutionary psychology, behavior genetics, and reproductive ecology. In addition, we need to improve our field methods, our models, and our methods of analysis, and we need to tackle tougher subjects that either may challenge our approach or lie outside our traditional areas of inquiry.

These tendencies are already evident in current research, and many of them are well demonstrated in this volume. A move toward a blending of behavioral ecology and evolutionary psychology is indicated by Jones's chapter on sexual attractiveness in Brazil. Improved research design and field methods are evident in many chapters, including the prospective design of Strassmann's study of Dogon polygyny and child mortality, Cronk's and Sellen and his coauthors' use of anthropometry to assess child growth performance, the systematic behavioral observations used in Strassmann's, Cronk's, and Hewlett and colleagues' chapters to assess childcare patterns, Chagnon's creative interview techniques, and the large-scale survey of Kaplan and Lancaster and Lancaster and Kaplan. More sophisticated modeling techniques are demonstrated in the chapters by Luttbeg and colleagues, Mace, and Sosis. Innovations in data analysis are exemplified by Jones's and Patton's use of multidimensional scaling techniques. Theoretical progress is evident in many chapters, including Blurton Jones and colleagues' rethinking of the nature of human pair bonding, Hawkes and colleagues' use of new developments in life history theory, Sugiyama and Chacon's insights into the influence of pathology risk on human social behavior, the distinction Hames draws between food-sharing patterns among the horticultural Yanomamö and that seen in foraging groups, and Kaplan and Lancaster's skills-based competitive labor markets theory of the demographic transition. And, finally, a willingness—indeed, an eagerness—to tackle subjects that are daunting in their complexity and that have been promoted as challenges to the entire approach (e.g., Vining 1986) is well demonstrated by the four chapters on demographic transition theory by Kaplan and Lancaster, Low, Luttbeg and colleagues, and Mace.

CONCLUSION

A legitimate question to ask of any research program is whether it has produced any new knowledge. Human behavioral ecology and closely related approaches can give a confident affirmative answer to this question. Thanks to the research that has gone on over the past twenty years, we know that human nature is not the blank slate it once was thought to be. Rather, to continue the metaphor, the slate has much written on it, and some things are much easier to write on it than others. We know for example that human beings tend to learn with ease who their relatives are and to be more cooperative and less competitive in dealing with them than with nonrelatives. We know that they tend to adjust their parenting strategies so as to be more nurturing of children of the sex with the greater reproductive potential if there is a predictable difference in reproductive opportunities. We know that although men's and women's mate preferences have considerable overlap, they also differ, on average, in a way predicted by evolutionary theory. We know that in a variety of contexts, ranging from foraging to cooperative arrangements, people tend to respond to costs and benefits as measured in terms of inclusive fitness or a good proxy currency. We know that in societies that resemble those in which humans evolved, the goals people consciously strive to achieve generally correlate with reproductive success. This accumulated knowledge represents considerable progress since the time of *Evolutionary Biology and Human Social Behavior,* when we hypothesized these tendencies but could offer only a few empirical tests of them. We now have a large body of data from many different societies, giving the field a solid foundation and setting the stage for further refinements of the approach. We hope that the readers of this volume find that the studies included here take us even further toward our goals.

SUMMARY

1. Human behavioral ecology has its theoretical roots primarily in the 1960s and early 1970s in work by W. D. Hamilton and Robert Trivers on sociality and parental investment, George C. Williams on the issues of adaptation and levels of selection, and Robert MacArthur and Eric Pianka on foraging strategies.
2. Research into the evolutionary biology of human behavior began in earnest in the 1970s and was showcased in a session organized by Napoleon A. Chagnon and William Irons at the 1976 annual meetings of the American Anthropological Association and in a subsequent edited volume, *Evolutionary Biology and Human Social Behavior: An Anthropological Perspective* (Chagnon and Irons 1979). The present volume is in part in commemoration of the twentieth anniversary of that early work.
3. Although initial reaction to this new approach was sharply critical, especially among cultural anthropologists, over the past two decades the approach has gained new adherents and has developed in terms of its empirical findings, its methods, and its theories. Its development has been aided in this by the establishment of a number of new journals and organizations dedicated to research on the evolution of human behavior.

4. Human behavioral ecology can claim to have produced a great deal of new knowledge on many fundamental issues in the evolution of human behavior. The state of the art of this new and still rapidly developing approach is exemplified by the chapters in this volume on such issues as mating, parenting, the demographic transition, and sociality.

NOTES

1. For example, Jerome Barkow, Rada Dyson-Hudson, and Eric Alden Smith presented papers at the AAA symposia that, for various reasons, were not included in the 1979 volume, Nicholas Blurton Jones and John Hartung began to publish such work at about this time, and Bruce Winterhalder (1977) had recently completed the first application of optimal foraging theory to humans.

2. Justifying oppression and describing it are not the same thing. One needs to keep the naturalistic fallacy in mind. We challenge anyone to make a good argument to the effect that any of the chapters in this volume justify, as opposed to describe, oppression.

3. For a recent example, see Dagg 1998 and the response by Silk and Stanford 1999.

4. For other evolutionary approaches to the demographic transition not included in this volume, see Bereczkei 1998; Rogers 1992; and Turke 1989.

REFERENCES

Alexander, Richard D. 1974. The evolution of social behavior. *Annual Review of Ecology and Systematics* 5:325–383.

———. 1979. *Darwinism and Human Affairs*. Seattle: University of Washington Press.

———. 1987. *The Biology of Moral Systems*. New York: Aldine de Gruyter.

———. 1990. *How Did Humans Evolve? Reflections on a Uniquely Unique Species*. Ann Arbor: Museum of Zoology, University of Michigan, Special Publication No. 1.

Allman, William F. 1994. *The Stone Age Present*. New York: Simon and Schuster.

Ann Arbor Science for the People Editorial Collective, eds. 1977. *Biology as a Social Weapon*. Minneapolis: Burgess.

Asch, Timothy, and Napoleon A. Chagnon. 1975. *The Ax Fight* (16mm film). Watertown, Massachusetts: Documentary Educational Resources.

Baker, Robin R. and Mark A. Bellis. 1996. *Sperm Competition: Copulation, Masturbation, and Infidelity*. London: Chapman and Hall.

Barkow, Jerome H. 1989. *Darwin, Sex, and Status*. Toronto: University of Toronto Press.

Belsky, Jay, L. Steinberg, and Patricia Draper. 1991. Childhood experience, interpersonal development, and reproductive strategy: An evolutionary theory of socialization. *Child Development* 62:647–670.

Bereczkei, Tamas. 1998. Kinship network, direct childcare, and fertility among Hungarians and Gypsies. *Evolution and Human Behavior* 19:283–298.

Betzig, Laura, ed. 1997. *Human Nature: A Critical Reader*. Oxford: Oxford University Press.

Betzig, Laura, Monique Borgerhoff Mulder, and Paul Turke, eds. 1988. *Human Reproductive Behaviour*. Cambridge: Cambridge University Press.

Biella, Peter, Napoleon A. Chagnon, and Gary Seaman. 1997. *Yanomamö Interactive: The Ax Fight*. Fort Worth: Harcourt Brace.

Bliege Bird, Rebecca L. and Douglas W. Bird. 1997. Delayed reciprocity and tolerated theft: The behavioral ecology of food-sharing strategies. *Current Anthropology* 38:49–78.

Blurton Jones, Nicholas G. 1987a. Bushman birth spacing: Direct tests of some simple predictions. *Ethology and Sociobiology* 8:183–204.

———. 1987b. Tolerated theft, suggestions about the ecology and evolution of sharing, hoarding and scrounging. *Social Science Information/Information sur les Sciences Sociales* 26:31–54.

Bodley, John H. 1994. *Cultural Anthropology: Tribes, States, and the Global System.* Mountain View, California: Mayfield.

Borgerhoff Mulder, Monique. 1988a. Kipsigis bridewealth payments. In *Human Reproductive Behaviour: A Darwinian Perspective,* L. Betzig, M. Borgerhoff Mulder, and P. Turke, eds. Pp. 65–82. Cambridge: Cambridge University Press.

———. 1988b. Behavioral ecology in traditional societies. *Trends in Ecology and Evolution* 3:260–264.

———. 1990. Kipsigis women's preferences for wealthy men: Evidence for female choice in mammals? *Behavioral Ecology and Sociobiology* 27:255–264.

———. 1991. Human behavioral ecology. In *Behavioral Ecology: An Evolutionary Approach,* third ed., J. R. Krebs and N. B. Davies, eds. Pp. 69–98. Oxford: Blackwell Scientific.

Boyd, Robert, and Peter J. Richerson. 1985. *Culture and the Evolutionary Process.* Chicago: University of Chicago Press.

Buettner-Janusch, John. 1978. Review of Dawkins (1976). *American Anthropologist* 80:463–464.

Buss, David M. 1994. *The Evolution of Desire: Strategies of Human Mating.* New York: Basic.

———. 1995. Evolutionary psychology: A new paradigm for psychological science. *Psychological Inquiry* 6:1–30.

Chagnon, Napoleon A. 1988. Male Yanomamö manipulations of kinship classifications of female kin for reproductive advantage. In *Human Reproductive Behaviour: A Darwinian Perspective,* L. Betzig, M. Borgerhoff Mulder, and P. Turke, eds. Pp. 23–48. Cambridge: Cambridge University Press.

———. 1997. *User's Guide to Accompany Yanomamö Interactive: The Ax Fight.* Fort Worth: Harcourt Brace.

Chagnon, Napoleon A. and Paul E. Bugos, Jr. 1979. Kin selection and conflict: An analysis of a Yanomamö ax fight. In *Evolutionary Biology and Human Social Behavior: An Anthropological Perspective,* N. A. Chagnon and W. Irons, eds. Pp. 213–238. North Scituate, Massachusetts: Duxbury Press.

Chagnon, Napoleon A. and William Irons, eds. 1979. *Evolutionary Biology and Human Social Behavior: An Anthropological Perspective.* North Scituate, Massachusetts: Duxbury Press.

Chapple, Eliot D. 1976. Ethology without biology. *American Anthropologist* 78:590–593.

Cronin, Helena. 1991. *The Ant and the Peacock.* Cambridge: Cambridge University Press.

Cronk, Lee. 1989. From hunters to herders: Subsistence change as a reproductive strategy among the Mukogodo. *Current Anthropology* 30:224–234.

———. 1991. Human behavioral ecology. *Annual Review of Anthropology* 20:25–53.

———. 1994a. Evolutionary theories of morality and the manipulative use of signals. *Zygon: Journal of Religion and Science* 29(1):81–101.

———. 1994b. The use of moralistic statements in social manipulation: A reply to Roy A. Rappaport. *Zygon: Journal of Religion and Science*. 29(3):351–355.

———. 1995. Is there a role for culture in human behavioral ecology? *Evolution and Human Behavior* 16(3):181–205.

Dagg, Anne Innis. 1998. Infanticide by male lions hypothesis: A fallacy influencing research into human behavior. *American Anthropologist* 100(4):940–950.
Daly, Martin, and Margo Wilson. 1988. *Homicide*. New York: Aldine de Gruyter.
Dawkins, Richard. 1976. *The Selfish Gene.* Oxford: Oxford University Press.
———. 1979. Twelve misunderstandings of kin selection. *Zeitschrift für Tierpsychologie* 51:184–200.
———. 1982. *The Extended Phenotype*. Oxford: Oxford University Press.
———. 1986. *The Blind Watchmaker*. New York: Norton.
———. 1989. *The Selfish Gene,* second ed. Oxford: Oxford University Press.
———. 1995. *River Out of Eden.* New York: Basic.
———. 1996. *Climbing Mount Improbable*. New York: Norton.
Dawkins, Richard, and John Krebs. 1978. Animal signals: Information or manipulation? In *Behavioural Ecology: An Evolutionary Approach,* J. Krebs and N. Davies, eds. Pp. 282–309. Sunderland, Massachusetts: Sinauer.
de Waal, Frans B. 1996. *Good Natured*. Cambridge: Harvard University Press.
Degler, Carl. 1991. *In Search of Human Nature*. Oxford: Oxford University Press.
Dennett, Daniel. 1995. *Darwin's Dangerous Idea.* New York: Simon and Schuster.
Dow, James. 1984. The genetic basis for affinal cooperation. *American Ethnologist* 11:380–383.
Durham, William H. 1991. *Coevolution: Genes, Culture, and Human Diversity*. Stanford: Stanford University Press.
Ellison, P. T. 1994. Advances in human reproductive ecology. *Annual Review of Anthropology* 23:255–275.
Essock-Vitale, Susan M. and Michael McGuire. 1980. Predictions derived from the theories of kin selection and reciprocation assessed by anthropological data. *Ethology and Sociobiology* 1:233–243.
Fisher, Helen. 1982. *The Sex Contract*. New York: William Morrow.
———. 1992. *The Anatomy of Love*. New York: Norton.
Fletcher, David J. C., and Charles Duncan Michener. 1987. *Kin Recognition in Animals*. Chichester, New York: Wiley.
Flinn, Mark V. and Barry England. 1995. Childhood stress and family environment. *Current Anthropology* 36:854–866.
Foley, Robert. 1987. *Another Unique Species*. New York: John Wiley.
———. 1992. Evolutionary ecology of fossil hominids. In *Evolutionary Ecology and Human Behavior,* Eric Alden Smith and Bruce Winterhalder, eds. Pp. 131–164. New York: Aldine de Gruyter.
Frank, Robert H. 1988. *Passions within Reason*. New York: W. W. Norton.
Gangestad, Steven W. and Randy Thornhill. 1997. Human sexual selection and developmental stability. In *Evolutionary Social Psychology,* J. Simpson and D. Kenrick, eds. Pp. 169–195. Hillsdale, New Jersey: Erlbaum.
Grafen, Alan. 1984. Natural selection, kin selection and group selection. In *Behavioural Ecology: An Evolutionary Approach,* second ed., J. R. Krebs and N. B. Davies, eds. Pp. 62–84. Oxford: Blackwell Scientific.
———. 1990a. Biological signals as handicaps. *Journal of Theoretical Biology* 144:517–546.
———. 1990b. Sexual selection unhandicapped by the Fisher process. *Journal of Theoretical Biology* 144:473–516.
Gray, J. Patrick. 1985. *Primate Sociobiology*. New Haven: HRAF Press.
Hamilton, W. D. 1964. The evolution of social behavior. *Journal of Theoretical Biology* 7:1–52.
———. 1966. The moulding of senescence by natural selection. *Journal of Theoretical Biology* 12:12–45.

———. 1967. Extraordinary sex ratios. *Science* 156:477–488.

———. 1971. Geometry for the selfish herd. *Journal of Theoretical Biology* 31(2):295–311.

Hamilton, W. D., and M. Zuk. 1982. Heritable true fitness and bright birds: A role for parasites. *Science* 218:384–387.

Hartung, John. 1976. On natural selection and the inheritance of wealth. *Current Anthropology* 17:607–622.

Hauser, Marc. 1996. *The Evolution of Communication.* Cambridge: MIT Press.

Hawkes, Kristen. 1983. Kin selection and culture. *American Ethnologist* 10:345–363.

———. 1990. Why do men hunt? Some benefits for risky choices. In *Risk and Uncertainty in Tribal and Peasant Economies,* Elizabeth Cashdan, ed. Pp. 145–166. Boulder: Westview.

———. 1991. Showing off: Tests of another hypothesis about men's foraging goals. *Ethology and Sociobiology* 11:29–54.

———. 1993. Why hunter-gatherers work: An ancient version of the problem of public goods. *Current Anthropology* 34:341–361.

Hepper, Peter G. ed. 1991. *Kin Recognition.* Cambridge: Cambridge University Press.

Herrnstein, Richard J. and Charles A. Murray. 1994. *The Bell Curve: Intelligence and Class Structure in American Life*. New York: Free Press.

Hill, Kim. 1993. Life history theory and evolutionary anthropology. *Evolutionary Anthropology* 2:78–88.

Hrdy, Sarah Blaffer. 1999. *Mother Nature: A History of Mothers, Infants, and Natural Selection.* New York: Pantheon Books.

Hume, David. 1739/1740. *A Treatise of Human Nature, Volume II, Book III: Of Morals.* Reprinted by Oxford University Press in 1966.

Irons, William. 1979. Cultural and biological success. In *Evolutionary Biology and Human Social Behavior: An Anthropological Perspective,* N. A. Chagnon and W. Irons, eds. Pp. 257–272. North Scituate, Massachusetts: Duxbury Press.

———. How did morality evolve? *Zygon: Journal of Religion and Science* 26:49–89.

———. 1996. In our own self image: The evolution of morality, deception, and religion. *Skeptic* 4:50–61.

Johnstone, Rufus A. 1997. The evolution of animal signals. In *Behavioural Ecology: An Evolutionary Approach,* fourth ed., J. R. Krebs and N. B. Davies, eds. Pp. 155–178. Oxford: Blackwell Science.

Kaplan, Hillard, and Kim Hill. 1985. Food sharing among Ache foragers: Tests of explanatory hypotheses. *Current Anthropology* 26:233–245.

Kaplan, Hillard, Kim Hill, Kristen Hawkes, and Ana Magdalena Hurtado. 1984. Food sharing among Ache hunter-gatherers of eastern Paraguay. *Current Anthropology* 25: 113–115.

Kaplan, Hillard, Kim Hill, and Ana Magdalena Hurtado. 1990. Risk, foraging, and food sharing among the Ache. In *Risk and Uncertainty in Tribal and Peasant Economies,* Elizabeth Cashdan, ed. Pp. 107–144. Boulder: Westview Press.

Kitcher, Philip. 1985. *Vaulting Ambition: Sociobiology and the Quest for Human Nature.* Cambridge: MIT Press.

———. 1990. Developmental decomposition and the future of human behavioral ecology. *Philosophy of Science* 57:96–117.

Krebs, John R. and Richard Dawkins. 1984. Animal signals: Mind-reading and manipulation. In *Behavioural Ecology: An Evolutionary Approach,* second ed. Pp. 380–402. Oxford: Blackwell Scientific.

Lewontin, Richard, Steven Rose, and Leon Kamin. 1984. *Not in Our Genes: Biology, Ideology and Human Nature*. New York: Pantheon.

Lieberman, Leonard. 1989. A discipline divided: Acceptance of sociobiological concepts in anthropology. *Current Anthropology* 30:676–682.

MacArthur, R. H., and Eric R. Pianka. 1966. On optimal use of a patchy environment. *American Naturalist* 100:603–609.

Mayr, Ernst. 1961. Cause and effect in biology. *Science* 134:1501–1506.

Moore, George Edward. 1903. *Principia Ethica.* Cambridge: Cambridge University Press.

Nesse, Randolph M. and George C. Williams. 1994. *Why We Get Sick: The New Science of Darwinian Medicine.* New York: Times Books.

Ohnuki-Tierney, Emiko. 1994. Brain death and organ transplantation: Cultural bases of medical technology. *Current Anthropology* 35:233–254.

Pinker, Steven. 1994. *The Language Instinct.* New York: William Morrow.

———. 1997. *How the Mind Works.* New York: W. W. Norton.

Plomin, Robert. 1997. *Behavioral Genetics,* third ed. New York: W. H. Freeman.

Queller, David C. 1995. The spaniels of St. Marx and the Panglossian paradox: A critique of a rhetorical programme. *Quarterly Review of Biology* 70:485–489.

Ridley, Matt. 1993. *The Red Queen: Sex and the Evolution of Human Nature.* New York: Macmillan.

———. 1996. *The Origins of Virtue: Human Instincts and the Evolution of Cooperation.* New York: Viking.

Rogers, Alan. 1992. Resources and population dynamics. In *Evolutionary Ecology and Human Behavior,* Eric Alden Smith and Bruce Winterhalder, eds. Pp. 375–402. New York: Aldine de Gruyter.

Rosenblatt, D. 1997. The antisocial skin: Structure, resistance, and "modern primitive" adornment in the United States. *Cultural Anthropology* 12:287–334.

Sahlins, Marshall. 1976. *The Use and Abuse of Biology.* Ann Arbor: University of Michigan Press.

Schubert, G. 1991. Sociobiology's bully pulpit—romancing the gene. *Behavioral and Brain Sciences* 14(4):749.

Schultz, Emily A. and Robert H. Lavenda. 1995a. *Anthropology: A Perspective on the Human Condition.* Mountain View, California: Mayfield.

———. 1995b. *Cultural Anthropology: A Perspective on the Human Condition,* third ed. Mountain View, California: Mayfield.

Silk, Joan. 1980. Adoption and kinship in Oceania. *American Anthropologist* 82:799–820.

Silk, Joan and Craig B. Stanford. 1999. Infanticide article disputed. *Anthropology News* 40(6): 29–29.

Small, Meredith. 1995. *What's Love Got to Do With It? The Evolution of Human Mating.* New York: Anchor.

———. 1998. *Our Babies, Ourselves: How Biology and Culture Shape the Way We Parent.* New York: Anchor.

Smith, Eric Alden. 1981. The application of optimal foraging theory to the analysis of hunter-gatherer group size. In *Hunter-Gatherer Foraging Strategies,* Bruce Winterhalder and Eric Alden Smith, eds. Pp. 36–65. Chicago: University of Chicago Press.

———. 1985. Inuit foraging groups. *Ethology and Sociobiology* 6:27–47.

———. 1991. *Inujjuamit Foraging Strategies: Evolutionary Ecology of an Arctic Hunting Economy.* New York: Aldine de Gruyter.

———. 1992. Human behavioral ecology, parts I and II. *Evolutionary Anthropology* 1:20–25, 50–55.

Smith, Eric Alden, and Bruce Winterhalder. 1992. Natural selection and decision-making: Some fundamental principles. In *Evolutionary Ecology and Human Behavior,* Eric Alden Smith and Bruce Winterhalder, eds. Pp. 25–60. New York: Aldine de Gruyter.

———, eds. 1992. *Evolutionary Ecology and Human Behavior*. New York: Aldine de Gruyter.

Symons, Donald. 1979. *The Evolution of Human Sexuality*. Oxford: Oxford University Press.

Tinbergen, Niko. 1963. On aims and methods of ethology. *Zeitschrift für Tierpsychologie* 20:410–433.

Trevathan, Wenda. 1987. *Human Birth: An Evolutionary Perspective*. New York: Aldine de Gruyter.

Trivers, Robert. 1971. The evolution of reciprocal altruism. *Quarterly Review of Biology* 46:35–57.

———. 1972. Parental investment and sexual selection. In *Sexual Selection and the Descent of Man,* B. Campbell, ed. Pp. 136–179. New York: Aldine de Gruyter.

———. 1974. Parent-offspring conflict. *American Zoologist* 14:249–264.

Trivers, Robert, and Hope Hare. 1976. Haplodiploidy and the evolution of social insects. *Science* 191:249–263.

Trivers, Robert, and Dan E. Willard. 1973. Natural selection of parental ability to vary the sex ratio of offspring. *Science* 179:90–92.

Turke, Paul. 1989. Evolution and the demand for children. *Population and Development Review* 15:61–90.

———. 1996. Nepotism. *Encyclopedia of Cultural Anthropology* 3:853–855. New York: Henry Holt.

Vining, Daniel R. 1986. Social versus reproductive success: The central theoretical problem of human sociobiology. *Behavioral and Brain Sciences* 9:167–216.

Weibull, Jorgen W. 1995. *Evolutionary Game Theory*. Cambridge: MIT Press.

Williams, George C. 1966. *Adaptation and Natural Selection*. Princeton: Princeton University Press.

Wilson, Edward O. 1975. *Sociobiology: The New Synthesis*. Cambridge: Harvard University Press.

———. 1978. *On Human Nature*. Cambridge: Harvard University Press.

Winterhalder, Bruce. 1977. *Foraging Strategy Adaptations of the Boreal Forest Cree: An Evaluation of Theory and Models from Evolutionary Ecology*. Ph.D. dissertation, Cornell University, Ithaca, New York.

———. 1986. Diet choice, risk, and food sharing in a stochastic environment. *Journal of Anthropological Archaeology* 5:367–392.

———. 1990. Open field, common pot: Harvest variability and risk avoidance in agricultural and foraging societies. In *Risk and Uncertainty in Tribal and Peasant Economies,* Elizabeth Cashdan, ed. Pp. 67–87. Boulder, Colorado: Westview.

Winterhalder, Bruce, and Eric Alden Smith, eds. 1981. *Hunter-Gatherer Foraging Strategies: Ethnographic and Archaeological Analyses*. Chicago: University of Chicago Press.

Wood, James W. 1994. *Dynamics of Human Reproduction: Biology, Biometry, Demography*. New York: Aldine de Gruyter.

Wright, Robert. 1994. *The Moral Animal: The New Science of Evolutionary Psychology*. New York: Pantheon.

Zahavi, Amotz, Avishag Zahavi, Naama Zahavi-Ely, and Melvin Patrick Ely. 1997. *The Handicap Principle*. Oxford: Oxford University Press.

2

Three Styles in the Evolutionary Analysis of Human Behavior

ERIC ALDEN SMITH

> A theory does not give conclusions—it directs the nature of the research, but each application of the theory demands careful research. . . . There is no way for a scientist to leap directly from genetic or evolutionary theory to conclusions about human behavior. The principal task for the scientist is the research that links theory and conclusion.
>
> —Sherwood L. Washburn (1978)

As the title indicates, my chapter is focused on the diversity contained within the field of inquiry surveyed in this volume. Specifically, I want to compare the approaches known as evolutionary psychology, behavioral ecology, and dual inheritance theory with respect to their key assumptions, explanatory goals, and realms of application. These distinct approaches to evolutionary analysis of human behavior have each crystallized during the twenty-plus years since Chagnon and Irons organized the 1976 American Anthropological Association symposia commemorated here—symposia which coincided roughly with the publication of E. O. Wilson's *Sociobiology* (1975) and Dawkins's *The Selfish Gene* (1976). After surveying the three approaches, I will consider why they have come to be seen as competing alternatives, and then explore to what extent it might make better sense to see them as complementary. Although most comparisons to date have been rather partisan or even polemical, and I myself am closely identified with one of the approaches (behavioral ecology), in this essay I do my best to provide an even-handed account.

EVOLUTIONARY PSYCHOLOGY

Evolutionary psychology (EP), as the name suggests, applies evolutionary reasoning to psychological phenomena. The goal of EP, as succinctly put by Symons (1992:137), is to uncover "the psychological mechanisms that underpin human . . . behavior, and . . . the selective forces that shaped those mechanisms."

Reviews of this approach can be found in Barkow, et al. (1992), Buss (1995), and Daly and Wilson (1997).

EP embraces several key assumptions, which I will term modularity, historicity, adaptive specificity, and environmental novelty. *Modularity* posits that human behavior is guided by specialized cognitive mechanisms performing specialized tasks rather than "general purpose" mechanisms that work across multiple behavioral domains. This assumption is taken directly from contemporary cognitive psychology, and indeed most of the evidence for it is developed in that field in nonevolutionary (i.e., standard psychological) analyses. *Historicity* refers to the EP assumption that natural selection shaped these modular cognitive mechanisms to produce adaptive behavior in the so-called EEA ("environment of evolutionary adaptedness"), meaning past environments of long duration and consistent selective pressures (Bowlby 1969; Symons 1987). *Adaptive specificity* holds that these modular products of our evolutionary history are designed to produce very specific adaptive outcomes: male preference for mates who are youthful, healthy, and beautiful, for example (Buss 1994). Finally, *environmental novelty* refers to the EP view that modern (post-Paleolithic) environments are characterized by an unprecedented degree of novelty, owing to extensive sociocultural change following the abandonment of a foraging way of life.

From these assumptions, evolutionary psychologists deduce the following consequences:

1. Valid adaptive (Darwinian) explanations of behavior must refer to genetically evolved psychological mechanisms linked to specific features of the EEA.
2. "Culture," "learning," "rational choice," and "fitness maximizing" are insufficiently modular (without further specification) to be realistic cognitive or behavioral mechanisms.
3. Contemporary human behavior often involves responses to evolutionarily novel conditions using modular cognitive mechanisms adapted to the EEA, and hence some of these responses may be maladaptive.
4. Measuring fitness outcomes or correlates of contemporary behavioral patterns is irrelevant and misleading.

To date, the great bulk of research in EP has been focused on mating behavior, particularly mate preferences (reviewed in Buss 1994). Prominent work has also been done on violence, particularly in the contexts of male-male competition, male mate-guarding, and conflicts over parental investment in dependent young (e.g., Daly and Wilson 1988; Thornhill and Thornhill 1992). Surprisingly, very little EP research has actually focused on documenting the existence of modular cognitive mechanisms, though an exception is the work of Cosmides and Tooby on reasoning concerned with detecting cheaters in social exchange situations.

This topic of social exchange will serve here as a heuristic example of differing research strategies in the three approaches. The EP approach to social exchange has of course focused on the notion that humans have a specialized cognitive mechanism for monitoring such exchange (Cosmides and Tooby 1989). The hypothesis is given an evolutionary basis by proposing that such exchanges were especially adaptive in the EEA—that is, among Pleistocene hunter-gatherers, who had both the ecological conditions favoring delayed reciprocity (particularly of hunted game) and the social and cognitive preadaptations needed to stabilize it against free riding (small groups, repeated opportunities for interaction, good memory and individual recognition) (Axelrod and Hamilton 1981; Trivers 1971).

Evidence adduced in favor of the hypothesis consists primarily of pencil-and-paper tests (based on the logic problem known as the Wason selection task) conducted among college students, although a sample of nonliterate Shiwiar Indian subjects in Amazonian Ecuador has also been tested (Tooby, personal communication).[1] The results indicate that narrative content involving social contracts and the possibility of cheating is a powerful predictor of success in these tests (Cosmides 1989; Cosmides and Tooby 1992; Gigerenzer and Hug 1992; but cf. Davies et al. 1995; Pollard 1990).

HUMAN BEHAVIORAL ECOLOGY

Behavioral ecology (BE) is the branch of evolutionary ecology concerned with tracing the link between ecological factors and adaptive behavior (Krebs and Davies 1997). This approach to the study of human populations began to appear about twenty years ago, and such studies have been reviewed several times (Borgerhoff Mulder 1991; Cronk 1991; Smith 1992; Smith and Winterhalder 1992; Winterhalder and Smith 2000).

The key assumptions of HBE (or BE in general) include its ecological selectionist logic, a "piecemeal" analytical approach, a reliance on modeling, a focus on "decision rules" or "conditional" strategies, and the so-called phenotypic gambit. *Ecological selectionism* consists of analyzing any behavioral phenomenon by asking "What are the ecological forces that select for behavior X?" The "ecological" part of this logic means that HBEs usually look to environmental features (e.g., resource density, competitor frequency) and examine the covariation in these features and the behavior of interest (e.g., territorial defense). The "selectionist" aspect means that predictions about this covariation are derived from expectations about what patterns we expect natural selection to favor. This of course sidesteps two complex issues (on which more below): Does natural selection act on this variation, and how? Do current selective forces correspond to the evolutionary past?

The *piecemeal approach* holds that complex socioecological phenomenon are fruitfully studied piece by piece—in a reductionist rather than holistic fashion. Thus, a complex problem such as explaining the marriage patterns in a population is broken down into a set of component decisions and constraints such as the female preferences for mate characteristics, male preferences, the distribution of these characteristics in the population, the ecological and historical determinants of this distribution, and so on. This piecemeal analysis relies on a series of simple and general analytical *models* (e.g., the polygyny threshold model—Borgerhoff Mulder 1990; Orians 1969); the assumption is that such models are fruitful sources of testable hypotheses (e.g., the number of wives per male will be proportional to their wealth; a female will choose to marry the male who provides the greatest expected share of resources to her, hence equilibrating female fitness across polygynous and monogamous marriages).

HBE usually frames the study of adaptive design in terms of "decision rules" (Krebs 1978) or *conditional strategies.* These are abstract and somewhat metaphorical ways of conceiving the covariation of behavior and socioecological environment, having the general form "In context X, do α; in context Y, switch to β." Thus, HBEs tend to focus on explaining behavioral *variation* as adaptive responses to environmental variation; they assume that this adaptive variation (facultative behavior, phenotypic response) is governed by evolved mechanisms that instantiate the relevant conditional strategy or decision rule. This assumption, which takes a "black-box" approach to the actual mechanisms involved, is part of what Grafen (1984) terms the *phenotypic gambit.* This means taking a calculated risk to ignore the (generally unknown) details of inheritance (genetic or cultural), cognitive mechanisms, and phylogenetic history that may pertain to a given decision rule and behavioral domain in hopes that these don't matter to the end result. Put another way, the phenotypic gambit posits that the genetic, phylogenetic, and cognitive constraints on phenotypic adaptation are minimal, and hence as a first approximation can be ignored in constructing models and generating or testing hypotheses.

Human behavioral ecologists draw several key conclusions from these assumptions, including:

1. Behavioral diversity is largely a result of diversity in the contemporary socioecological environment (rather than in contemporary variation in genes or cultural inheritance, or in past environments).
2. Adaptive relationships between behavior and environment may arise from many different mechanisms; hence HBE is generally agnostic about mechanisms (including the question of cognitive modularity).
3. Since humans are capable of rapid adaptive shifts in phenotype, they are likely to be well-adapted to most features of contemporary environments, and to exhibit relatively little adaptive lag.

These conclusions obviously conflict with some of those drawn by evolutionary psychology (EP) and dual inheritance theory (DIT), a point to which I will return.

Most HBE research has focused on subsistence and resource exchange (particularly in foraging societies), on parental investment (e.g., birth spacing, gender differences in parenting), and on reproductive strategies (e.g., polygyny vs. monogamy vs. polyandry) (reviews in Borgerhoff Mulder 1991; Cronk 1991; Smith and Winterhalder 1992; Winterhalder and Smith 2000).

As with EP, we can briefly examine the HBE analysis of social exchange as a heuristic example of this research strategy. Whereas EP has concerned itself with the cognitive mechanisms underlying social exchange, and tested for evidence of these in controlled experimental (but thus nonnaturalistic) circumstances, HBE research has focused on quantifying the behavioral occurrence, socioecological context, and fitness-correlated payoffs from food exchange in extant hunter-gatherer and horticultural populations (e.g., Berté 1988; Hames 1990, this volume; Kaplan and Hill 1985). Increasingly, this work is motivated by attempts to evaluate alternative models or hypotheses concerning the selective factors that may favor observed patterns of food transfer (Winterhalder 1996). The candidates include delayed reciprocity for risk reduction (Smith 1983, 1985, 1988; Smith and Boyd 1990; Winterhalder 1986, 1990), tolerated theft (Bliege Bird and Bird 1997; Blurton Jones 1984; Boone 1992; Hawkes 1992), trade of food for social benefits such as sexual access (Hawkes 1990, 1991, 1993; Kaplan et al. 1990), kin selection (Morgan 1979; Palmer 1991), and group selection (Wilson 1998). In light of this unresolved debate, it is interesting to note that EP analyses of social exchange assume that only the first of these mechanisms is at work and are not designed to test the competing assumptions just noted.

DUAL INHERITANCE THEORY

The dual inheritance (DIT) approach refers to studies that view culture and genes as providing separate (but linked) systems of inheritance, variation, and fitness effects—and hence of distinct but interacting evolutionary change. Reviews of this work can be found in Boyd and Richerson (1985), Durham (1990, 1991, 1992), Pulliam and Dunford (1980), and Richerson and Boyd (1992).

Key assumptions of DIT include cultural inheritance, multiple forces, population modeling, and codetermination. *Inheritance* refers to the idea that culture is information that is acquired socially—that it is a (nongenetic) system of inheritance. This is meant to contrast culture with information acquired through nonsocial learning, as well as genetically inherited information. Most DIT practitioners posit that the spread of cultural information or "memes" (Dawkins 1976) is affected by *multiple forces:* natural selection (differential fitness of culturally inherited variation), decision making (based on genetically or culturally evolved preferences and constraints, and subject to manipulation and coercion by others), and transmitter influence or prominence (since cultural "parents" need not be biological parents). These various forces or dynamics are analyzed via *modeling* that links individual characteristics (such as memes) with population-level processes (such as meme frequency), in a manner analogous to (and sometimes directly borrowed from) evolutionary population genetics. Finally, the *codetermination* assumption holds that human behavior is jointly shaped by genetic, cultural, and (nonsocial) environmental influences, thus advancing a form of explanatory pluralism notably lacking from the "purer" versions of EP and HBE.

Conclusions that DIT scholars deduce from these assumptions include the following:

1. Since culture exhibits the three characteristics required for evolution by natural selection (variation, heritability, fitness effects), cultural evolution can be analyzed using neo-Darwinian methods.
2. Since cultural inheritance differs from genetic inheritance in key ways (e.g., non-parental transmission, multiple transmission events over a lifetime), the evolutionary dynamics of culture will also differ in important but analytically understandable ways.
3. Genetically nonadaptive cultural evolution is possible, and it is more likely when the differences just referred to are most marked (e.g., modern bureaucratic societies and other hierarchical social/enculturation structures).

Thus, in contrast to classical forms of cultural evolutionism (e.g., White 1959; Sahlins and Service 1960) as well as what some term "evolutionary archaeology" (O'Brien 1996; cf. Boone and Smith 1998), DIT practitioners posit that cultural evolution is embedded in and constrained by genetically evolved psychological propensities. Indeed, one of the primary themes of DIT is the development of scenarios or models for the genetic evolution by natural selection of particular mechanisms of cultural transmission (see especially Boyd and Richerson 1985:98ff., 1995; Rogers 1988). But in contrast to classical sociobiology, or most varieties of EP and HBE, DIT holds that culture can sometimes evolve in directions quite different from what we would predict from genetic evolution alone, including genetically maladaptive directions. DIT is not, however, primarily a theory about how cultural evolution supersedes genetic evolution and takes humans down a maladaptive but independent pathway, as some of its critics as well as naive supporters too often claim. Indeed, the general thrust of both Durham's (1991) version as well as recent work by Richerson and Boyd (1998, 1999) is that mechanisms of cultural evolution often find ways of *improving* on adaptive outcomes compared to what can be achieved by ordinary genetic evolution plus phenotypic adaptation.

To date, DIT has focused primarily on mathematical modeling of various possible patterns of cultural evolution or of gene-culture coevolution. Hence it is theoretically rich and sophisticated, but empirically impoverished; indeed, the most detailed empirical studies in the DIT literature seem to converge very closely to the HBE approach (Borgerhoff Mulder and Mitchell 1994).

In parallel with my discussions of EP and HBE, we can briefly consider DIT research on social exchange. Since collective action often involves systems of widespread and indirect reciprocity (e.g., serving as a soldier on behalf of one's society is reciprocated with various kinds of rewards to the soldier or his kin), it qualifies as a form of social exchange. Boyd and Richerson (1982, 1985, 1987) have constructed models of cultural group selection of such group-beneficial behaviors. These models show that cultural inheritance plus conformity transmission ("when in Rome, do as the Romans do") can in principle create and maintain significant between-group differences despite reasonable rates of migration between these groups, thus avoiding a major obstacle facing classical forms of genetic group selection.

The mechanism of group selection most commonly proposed in this regard is group dissolution due to warfare, with refugees from defeated groups being absorbed by allied groups; if culturally transmitted traits that favor socially altruistic traits (e.g., contributing to the collective good of military defense and offense) decrease the probability of group defeat and dissolution, then these could spread by cultural group selection (Peoples 1982). However, a recent examination of empirical evidence from highland New Guinea (Soltis et al. 1995), an area of chronic between-group hostilities, indicated that historical rates of group dissolution are probably too low to make this a plausible mechanism for the generation of a substantial amount of the variation in New Guinea in group-cooperative behavior. It remains a viable hypothesis to explain slower trends in cultural evolution (e.g., the rise of urban city-states), however (Richerson and Boyd 1999).

COMPETITION OR PLURALISM?

Given the distance between Darwin's general theory of evolutionary adaptation and the specifics of human behavior (as suggested in my epigraph from Washburn), the development of divergent styles in the evolutionary analysis of human behavior was perhaps inevitable. There are many plausible ways to go about filling the chasm between general theory and empirical data, and different "schools" have coalesced around those who pioneered various tracks through this terra incognita. In addition, this divergence reflects differing research traditions and academic disciplines—ethnography, cognitive psychology, evolutionary ecology, population genetics—that predate the emergence of modern evolutionary studies of human behavior. Indeed, it may be that the three- part division is found throughout the social and behavioral sciences: approaches that see behavior as a manifestation of underlying mental structures (e.g., psychoanalytic theory, structuralism, Chomskian linguistics), those that focus on determination by supra-individual structures (e.g., classical cultural determinism, classical sociology, Foucauldian theory), and those that model behavior in terms of costs and benefits (e.g., operant conditioning, rational choice theory, social exchange theory).[2]

Yet there is more to this divergence than simple cultural inertia or division of labor, for the differences between these three approaches reflect underlying fault lines concerning fundamental questions about the explanatory logic of Darwinism as applied to human behavior. As a result, the three approaches just surveyed have been portrayed by proponents of each as self-sufficient, and as alternatives to or competitors of the other approaches. But there are good reasons to see them as complementary as well (a point also made by Blurton Jones 1990 and Borgerhoff Mulder et al., 1997).

As summarized in Table 2.1, the three approaches differ in several ways. First, although all three ostensibly share the same goal of using Darwinian theory to analyze human behavior, in fact they identify different explananda (objects of explanation). EP's explanandum is the panhuman set of genetically evolved psychological predispositions that are believed to provide the "missing link" between evolution and behavior (Cosmides and Tooby 1987). These predispositions are presumed to take the form of cognitive algorithms or decision rules, in conformity with EP's parent discipline of cognitive psychology. The primary explanandum in HBE is observable patterns of behavior, with the goal of linking these patterns to environmental conditions (as eliciting factors) and to fitness- correlated payoffs (as reinforcing outcomes). For DIT, the explananda consist of culturally and genetically inherited information (memes and genes) that are shaped by evolutionary forces and that in turn shape cognitive algorithms and behavioral responses. Thus, DIT—following the tradition of its parent discipline of evolutionary genetics—focuses on the evolutionary equilibria and dynamics of heritable information, as well as the ways in which this information is transmitted.

Table 2.1. Summary comparison of the three styles of explanation.

	Evolutionary Psychology	*Behavioral Ecology*	*Dual Transmission Theory*
Explanandum:	Psychological mechanisms	Behavioral strategies	Cultural evolution
Key constraints:	Cognitive, genetic	Ecological, material	Structural, information
Temporal scale of adaptive change:	Long-term (genetic)	Short-term (phenotypic)	Medium-term (cultural)
Expected current adaptiveness:	Lowest	Highest	Intermediate
Hypothesis generation:	Informal inference	Optimality and ESS models	Population-level models
Hypothesis-testing methods:	Survey, lab experiment	Quantitative ethnographic observation	Mathematical modeling & simulation
Favored topics:	Mating, parenting, sex differences	Subsistence, reproductive strategies	Large-scale cooperation, maladaptation

Most evolutionary social scientists and biologists would agree that complete evolutionary explanations of behavior will include *(i)* heritable information that helps build *(ii)* psychological mechanisms, which in turn produce *(iii)* behavioral responses to *(iv)* environmental stimuli, resulting in *(v)* fitness effects that shape the evolutionary dynamics of *(i)* heritable information (see Figure 2.1). DIT focuses on culturally inherited components of *(i)* and its links to *(ii)* and *(v)*; EP focuses on *(ii)* and its links to *(iii)* and especially *(iv)*; and HBE focuses on *(iii)* with attention to *(iv)* and especially *(v)*. While advocates of each approach may be all too human in claiming to have the best or only valid perspective on evolution and human behavior, a more dispassionate assessment might acknowledge that each approach contributes to understanding the entire set of relevant phenomena. Viewed in this light, a tentative case can be made for explanatory complementarity.

Second, the three approaches utilize different—but potentially complementary—methods of data collection and hypothesis testing. EP's hypothesized cognitive mechanisms are primarily inferred from questionnaires (surveys and paper-and-pencil psychological tests) and from lab experiments in which subjects interact with computer images, other subjects (or confederates), or in small groups. Again, all this conforms to the parent discipline of academic cognitive psychology. In contrast, HBE emphasizes ethnographic methods derived primarily from its parent discipline of anthropology (and secondarily from its other parent discipline of behavioral ecology).[3] DIT's methods of data collection are underdeveloped, but hypothesis testing is likely to rely upon mathematical modeling (including simulations) as well as cross- cultural tests.

Each of these methods has strengths and weaknesses, and none of them seem tied in any deep way to the approaches with which they are primarily associated. Thus, questionnaires and experiments can generate large quantities of data and address domains in which observational data are difficult to collect (such as sexu-

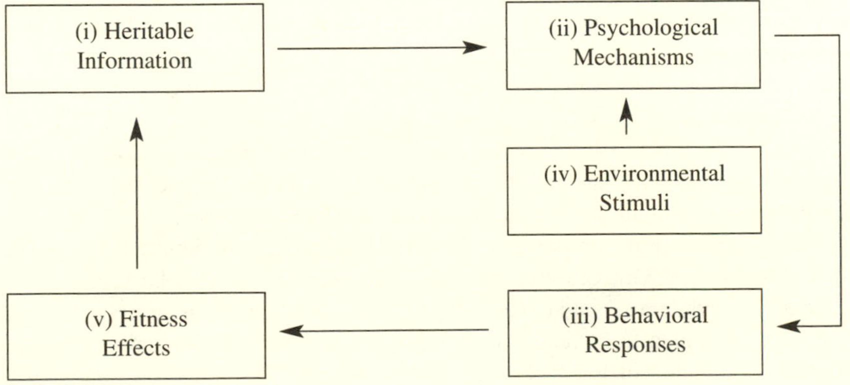

Figure 2.1. Causal foci and pathways in evolutionary analysis of behavior.

ality); on the other hand, these forms of data collection are subject to bias from deception and self-deception, and are sometimes of questionable relevance to "real-life" situations. Naturalistic observation uncovers context and provides concrete evidence of adaptive effects of phenotypic variants; yet it is vulnerable to the problems of sampling error and "phenotypic correlation" (i.e., confounding variables that mask the effects under investigation).[4] Mathematical modeling and simulation can be powerful means of revealing nonintuitive outcomes from a set of assumptions, but they can be an ambiguous basis for hypothesis testing since they illuminate causality in simplified possible worlds rather than in complex real ones. Again, I see these points as supporting the argument for complementarity of the three approaches.

A third dimension in which the differences between our three approaches can be seen as complementary is the temporal scales over which they conceive of adaptive change. EP's concern with psychological universals that evolved in past episodes of natural selection implies a longer time scale for adaptive change than that of the other two approaches. According to some of its proponents (e.g., Symons 1989; Tooby and Cosmides 1989, 1990), complex cognitive adaptations are likely to have taken shape in the Pleistocene or earlier, and to be maintained by phylogenetic inertia for millennia after the selective conditions that favored them have vanished. Although various critiques of this position have been published (e.g., Foley 1996; Irons 1990, 1998; Sherman and Reeve 1996; Turke 1990), it remains a plausible (if relatively untested) account of some patterns of human cognition and decision making.

Because HBE assumes that evolved mechanisms of phenotypic adaptation are quite flexible and broad—that we are adapted to a wide *range* of conditions rather than to a particular environmental state—its temporal scale for adaptive change is short-term, in behavioral rather than evolutionary time. Viewed this way, there should be as much complementarity as conflict between EP and HBE, despite the pronouncements of some: EP focuses on delineating adaptations that were genetically evolved in millennia past, while HBE focuses on how (at least some of) these adaptations may produce adaptive behavior in the present, responding to local and short-term environmental variation with matching phenotypic variation. The temporal scale of DIT is intermediate to these two extremes, given its focus on culturally heritable variation that is likely to evolve substantially faster than the complex cognitive mechanisms of EP but to adapt to changed conditions less quickly on average than the behavioral responses central to HBE.[5]

These complementarities between the three approaches are countered by some clear contradictions. One of these involves assumptions regarding key constraints on adaptation, while a second concerns the degree to which contemporary human behavior is predicted to be adaptive. Both of these flow quite logically from the differing explananda of the three approaches. Given EP's focus on genetically evolved cognitive mechanisms, it is no surprise that the key constraints to achieving adaptive success are seen as cognitive and genetic. If human behavior is guided by special-purpose cognitive algorithms that are genetically canalized and adapted to the EEA (see above), and if present social and natural environments are markedly different from this EEA, it follows that contemporary behavior may be frequently maladaptive. In the more extreme versions of this "adaptive lag" argument, humans in modern environments resemble computers trying to run new software on outdated operating systems. For example, men are viewed as following cognitive algorithms to pursue status and wealth which in the EEA translated into reproductive success, but now produce suboptimal fertility or sterile copulations because of contraception. (Indeed, there is some empirical support for such a view; see Kaplan et al. 1995 and Pérusse 1993.)

DIT's concern with cultural transmission and the tradeoff between acquiring adaptive feedback via trial and error versus imitating the local practices (a simple form of cultural inheritance) lead it to view key adaptive constraints as informational (how hard is it to determine the states of the environment, and the local beliefs and practices?) and structural (who are the most likely sources of cultural information, and why?). Although some extreme views in the DIT literature suggest that memes are best viewed as "mind parasites" that replicate at the expense of their human hosts (e.g., Cullen 1995; Dawkins 1993; Lynch 1996), the dominant position has been that spread of maladaptive memes is a byproduct (though a regular and predictable one) of reliance on a system of cultural inheritance that on average enhances the fitness of those who posses it (Boyd and Richerson 1985, 1995; Durham 1976, 1991).

The HBE approach identifies the key constraints to adaptation as ecological and material: unpredictable variance in ecological conditions, limitations of social institutions or technology, and phenotypic (nonheritable) differences in power or circumstance. Cognitive and genetic, or structural and informational, constraints are rarely considered in this tradition, leading some critics to charge HBE with hyperadaptationism; whether this charge is justified or not, HBE clearly takes the most optimistic view of contemporary adaptiveness of human behavior. While committed to empirical tests that can in principle falsify any particular adaptationist hypothesis, HBE practitioners generally seem to expect that maladaptation will be the exception rather than the rule.

As I've already implied, many commentators have identified the key conflict between EP and HBE as revolving around the centrality of psychological mechanisms in evolutionary (adaptive) explanations. Since much ink has already been spilled on this topic, I will simply point out that HBE's *agnosticism* regarding psychological mechanisms is not the same as a *denial* that they play a necessary role in any complete explanation of behavior. While some (e.g., Symons 1989) have seen this agnosticism as a misplaced fear of genetic reductionism, and others (e.g., Tooby and Cosmides 1992) as a variant of standard social science's naive view of cognition, I think it is better seen as a venerable tradition in adaptationist studies, part of the "phenotypic gambit" noted earlier. That is, HBE focuses on "why" questions (Why did selection design this creature to respond to environmental condition X with phenotypic adaptation a?) at the expense of considering "how" questions (What are the mechanisms that produce the phenotypic response?). If I'm correct, HBE should exhibit just as much agnosticism concerning physiological mechanisms as psychological ones—which I believe it does.[6]

The nub of the conflict between EP and DIT concerns the source of preferences and beliefs that inform adaptively significant decisions (Flinn 1997; Richerson and Boyd 1989; Rogers 1988). EP's focus on genetically evolved panhuman cognitive algorithms tends to make its practitioners relatively hostile to the DIT view that humans acquire a substantial proportion of their beliefs and preferences through cultural inheritance, and that these beliefs and preferences can change through a process of cultural evolution. In contrast, HBE's agnostic or ecumenical position regarding decision mechanisms creates less overt conflict with DIT, as does the fact that DIT practitioners are far more likely to have training and expertise in evolutionary ecology than in cognitive psychology.

But more detailed examination reveals that the HBE community is split on the issue of cultural evolution, with some granting it great importance while others express skepticism or even antipathy to the approach. Similarly, the EP community is far from monolithic in rejecting DIT. Indeed, common ground between the two approaches can be found in the fact that DIT is founded on the assumption that humans have genetically evolved psychological mechanisms to facilitate cultural adaptation, including such postulated algorithms as "conformity transmission" and "indirect bias" (Boyd and Richerson 1985). Thus, at least some DIT practitioners (Boyd and Richerson 1983, 1985; Pulliam and Dunford 1980) were doing EP before EP was cool—or had a name. Further complicating the matter is the importance that some EP practitioners ascribe to extensive cultural change (none dare call it evolution) since the time of the EEA, the source of EP skepticism concerning HBE attempts to portray post-Pleistocene behavioral innovations as adaptations. For if the divergence from the EEA is a product of cultural change, then culture is inescapably important in explaining contemporary human behavior.

In truth, the conflicts between the three approaches, so starkly drawn in some classical position papers (e.g., Durham 1979; Irons 1979; Symons 1989), are increasingly ambiguous and muted.[7] I view this as one more piece of evidence that complementarity should replace conflict as the primary view (and mode) of their relations. Ultimately, these issues will have to be worked out via empirical research and theory development, rather than through the polemical pronouncements that have thus far dominated most attempts to confront them.

True complementarity will be at hand when researchers from the three traditions conduct their investigations at a variety of levels and using a variety of techniques—when cognitive algorithms are analyzed in naturalistic settings as well as with experiments or questionnaires, when phenotypic adaptation to socioecological variation is studied experimentally as well as ethnographically, and when models of cultural evolution are operationalized and tested against empirical data on a sustained basis. Evaluation of the relative efficacy of the three styles in explaining human behavioral adaptation will be possible only when each of them has produced a substantial body of data on a single topic, so that we can compare (for example) the different predictions each generates concerning the adaptive significance of reduced family size under modernization (is it a maladaptive outcome of stone-age algorithms, a means of enhancing lineage fitness by preserving heritable wealth, or a product of cultural evolution when transmission of memes and genes is negatively correlated?).[8]

Even in areas where contradiction seems to trump complementarity, there may be considerable room for the latter. Thus, while it cannot be simultaneously true that a given instance or pattern of human behavior is a product of a genetically programmed cognitive algorithm that no longer produces adaptive results, a product of a culturally inherited meme that persists because it has high replication rate, and a product of phenotypic adaptation that is optimally geared to local environmental conditions, I see no reason to deny that each of these hypotheses could be true for *different* behavioral domains or instances.

In sum, it may turn out that each of our three approaches will have limited but significant success with different domains of human behavior. More optimistic, perhaps, is the hope that the not-too-distant future may see a synthesis of all three styles into a robust and pluralistic discipline focused on the evolutionary study of human behavior. A similar (if more elegantly phrased) prediction was in fact offered by Mel Konner (1982:xv) in *The Tangled Wing* some 15 years ago:

> We prefer simple, clear explanations. This is understandable; we are busy with other things. We need theories that . . . transcend the complexities, paring away all that is irrelevant, leaving the elegant, decisive beauty of a Euclidean proof . . .
>
> I offer no such theories. It is my belief that the failure of behavioral science up to the present day results, precisely, from the pursuit of them. Marxism, psychoanalysis, learning theory, structuralism, sociobiology—not a single one false in its essence, but each one false in its ambitions and in its condemnation of the others. A good textbook of human behavioral biology, which we will not have for another fifty years, will look not like Euclid's geometry—a magnificent edifice of proven propositions deriving from a set of simple assumptions—but more like a textbook of physiology or geology, each solution grounded in a separate body of facts and approached with a quiverful of different theories, with all the solutions connected in a great complex web.

SUMMARY

1. Three distinct approaches to evolutionary analysis of human behavior have developed in recent years: evolutionary psychology (EP), behavioral ecology (BE), and dual inheritance theory (DIT).

2. EP is based on the assumptions of modularity, historicity, adaptive specificity, and environmental specificity.

3. BE is based on ecological selectionism, piecemeal analysis, deductive modeling, conditional strategies (phenotypic adaptation), and the phenotypic gambit (ignoring the possible effects of inheritance, cognitive constraints, and phylogeny).

4. DIT assumes culture is a system of inheritance, that cultural change is affected by multiple forces (including genetically evolved psychological mechanisms), and that cultural evolution can be modeled mathematically.

5. Competition between the three approaches is fueled by differences in their assumptions, analytical methods, and alliances with other disciplines.

6. One key issue of contention is empirical: to what degree is contemporary human behavior adaptive, and what forces shape it to be adaptive or maladaptive?

7. Complementarity between the three styles may emerge from using complementary methods of investigation (e.g., observation vs. experiment), investigating different levels (e.g., psychological vs. behavioral), analyzing different constraints (cognitive, ecological, informational), examining adaptation on different time scales, or focusing on different behavioral domains.

ACKNOWLEDGMENTS

For helpful comments on drafts of this paper, I am grateful to Monique Borgerhoff Mulder, Rob Boyd, Nick Blurton Jones, Lee Cronk, Peter Richerson, Margo Wilson, Bruce Winterhalder, and a very gracious anonymous reviewer from the EP camp. Since I did not always follow the advice I was given, please do not hold any of the above responsible for what is wrong.

NOTES

1. The structure of the Wason test is as follows. There is a conditional statement of the form "If P, then Q." This statement is "conditional" in the sense that it is a claim that if condition P occurs, then result Q will occur. The statement may be true or false. The problem is to figure out if the evidence at hand supports the claim or not. The test usually involves a short narrative establishing the identity of P, Q, etc., followed by a presentation of four cards labeled with statements that signify "P," "Q," "not-P," and "not-Q" on their face, with the back of each card indicating whether the conditional rule ("If P, then Q; if not-P, then not-Q.") turned out to be true in the event or social interaction described in the narrative. The question before the subject is to decide the *minimum* set of cards that must be turned over in order to see if the rule has been violated; the solution is always to turn over *only* the cards marked "P" and "not-Q." Thus, the evidence Cosmides has assembled is that problems with a social contract narrative and rule ("If you take the benefit, then you pay the cost") are solved more readily (ca. 65–80% correct) than are problems associated with either a familiar (ca. 40%) or unfamiliar (ca. 20%) non-contract narrative.

2. I thank Lee Cronk (personal communication) for this suggestion.

3. Some HBE researchers more strongly influenced by nonhuman behavioral ecology are also motivated by a desire to make their methods and data conform to the standards set

by that field. On the other hand, the few extensions of HBE research into urban and industrialized settings (e.g., Betzig and Lombardo 1992; Kaplan et al. 1995; Pérusse 1993) have pragmatically adopted a questionnaire method of data collection reminiscent of sociological studies.

4. Phenotypic correlation occurs when a predicted effect of a determining variable on a phenotypic outcome is confounded by "uncontrolled" variables which also affect the same aspect of phenotype and are negatively correlated with the determining variable. For example, Lack's (1954) model of optimal clutch size has been used to generate the hypothesis that shorter interbirth intervals (IBI) put a strain on mother's ability to deliver food and care to her offspring, and hence increase the mortality risk for dependent children (Blurton Jones and Sibly 1978). The resultant prediction is that IBI length should be optimized to maximize the total number of surviving offspring, with most women exhibiting the optimal IBI. While data from the !Kung support this prediction (Blurton Jones 1986), data from the Ache do not (Hill and Hurtado 1996). As the latter note, the reason might well be due to phenotypic correlation: Ache mothers who for other reasons have relatively more resources at their disposal will have more resources per offspring and can thus "afford" a shorter IBI. The resultant phenotypic correlation means that short IBI can be positively (rather than negatively) correlated with offspring survival, even though Lack's tradeoff between more rapid reproduction and offspring survival applies. Indeed, Lack had to resort to some experimental manipulation of clutch size in order to counter such phenotypic correlation in his bird studies!

5. Those parts of DIT that deal with the genetic evolution of mechanisms of cultural transmission, or the coevolution of genetic and cultural variation, obviously assume a longer-term view of the evolutionary process.

6. This "physiological agnosticism" then indicates a gap to be filled, which of course has been done for a long time by biological anthropologists interested in human adaptability, including recent work in "reproductive ecology" (Ellison 1994; Wood 1994). However, in general this work does not ask questions about adaptive design informed by sociobiological theory à la Hamilton, Trivers, and Maynard Smith.

7. A parallel development is occurring in animal behavior studies; see, for example, the introductory chapter (among others) in the latest edition of Krebs and Davies (1997), or any issue of the journal *Behavioral Ecology.* However, not everyone is ready to bury the hatchet—*vide* Buss's recent (1995:9ff.) attack on Alexander, Betzig, Turke et al. under the heading "Why I am not a sociobiologist."

8. These three different predictions, generated by practitioners from each of the three schools, can be found in various sources, including Symons (1979), Rogers (1990), and Boyd and Richerson (1985).

REFERENCES

Axelrod, Robert, and William D. Hamilton. 1981. The evolution of cooperation. *Science* 211:1390–1396.

Barkow, Jerome H., Leda Cosmides, and John Tooby, eds. 1992. *The Adapted Mind: Evolutionary Psychology and the Generation of Culture.* New York: Oxford University Press.

Berté, Nancy A. 1988. K'ekchi' horticultural labor exchange: Productive and reproductive implications. In *Human Reproductive Behavior,* L. Betzig, M. Borgerhoff Mulder, and P. Turke, eds. Pp. 83–96. Cambridge: Cambridge University Press.

Betzig, Laura, and Leslie Hodgkins Lombardo. 1992. Who's pro-choice and why. *Ethology and Sociobiology* 13:49–71.

Bliege Bird, Rebecca, and Douglas Bird. 1997. Delayed reciprocity and tolerated theft: The behavioral ecology of food-sharing strategies. *Current Anthropology* 38:49–78.

Blurton Jones, Nicholas G. 1984. A selfish origin for human food sharing: Tolerated theft. *Ethology and Sociobiology* 5:1–3.

———. 1986. Bushman birth spacing: A test for optimal interbirth intervals. *Ethology and Sociobiology* 7:91–105.

———. 1990. Three sensible paradigms for research on evolution and human behavior? *Ethology and Sociobiology* 11:353–359.

Blurton Jones, Nicholas G., and R. M. Sibly. 1978. Testing adaptiveness of culturally determined behaviour: Do Bushmen women maximize their reproductive success by spacing births widely and foraging seldom? In *Human Behaviour and Adaptations,* N. G. Blurton Jones and V. Reynolds, eds. Pp. 135–157. Symposia of the Society for the Study of Human Biology, Vol. 18. London: Taylor & Francis.

Boone, James L. 1992. Conflict, competition and the emergence of hierarchies. In *Evolutionary Ecology and Human Behavior,* E. A. Smith and B. Winterhalder, eds. Pp. 301–337. New York: Aldine de Gruyter.

Boone, James L., and Eric Alden Smith. 1998. Is it evolution yet? A critique of evolutionary archaeology. *Current Anthropology* 39:5141–5173.

Borgerhoff Mulder, Monique. 1990. Kipsigis women's preferences for wealthy men: Evidence for female choice in mammals? *Behavioral Ecology and Sociobiology* 27:255–264.

———. 1991. Human behavioural ecology. In *Behavioural Ecology: An Evolutionary Approach,* third ed., J. R. Krebs and N. B. Davies, eds. Pp. 69–98. Oxford: Blackwell.

Borgerhoff Mulder, Monique, and S. D. Mitchell. 1994. Rough waters between genes and culture: An anthropological and philosophical view on coevolution. *Biology and Philosophy* 9:471–487.

Borgerhoff Mulder, Monique, Peter J. Richerson, Nancy W. Thornhill, and Eckart Voland. 1997. The place of behavioral ecological anthropology in evolutionary social science. In *Human by Nature: Between Biology and the Social Sciences,* P. Weingart, S. D. Mitchell, P. J. Richerson, and S. Maasen, eds. Pp. 253–282. Hillsdale, New Jersey: Erlbaum.

Bowlby, John. 1969. *Attachment.* New York: Basic Books.

Boyd, Robert, and Peter J. Richerson. 1982. Cultural transmission and the evolution of cooperative behavior. *Human Ecology* 10:325–351.

———. 1983. The cultural transmission of acquired variation: Effects on genetic fitness. *Journal of Theoretical Biology* 100:567–596.

———. 1985. *Culture and the Evolutionary Process.* Chicago: University of Chicago Press.

———. 1987. The evolution of ethnic markers. *Cultural Anthropology* 25:65–79.

———. 1995. Why does culture increase human adaptability? *Ethology and Sociobiology* 16:125–143.

Buss, David M. 1994. *The Evolution of Desire.* New York: Basic Books.

———. 1995. Evolutionary psychology: A new paradigm for psychological science. *Psychological Inquiry* 6:1–30.

Cosmides, Leda. 1989. The logic of social exchange: Has natural selection shaped how humans reason? Studies with the Wason Selection Task. *Cognition* 31:187–276.

Cosmides, Leda, and John Tooby. 1987. From evolution to behavior: Evolutionary psychology as the missing link. In *The Latest on the Best: Essays on Evolution and Optimality,* John Dupre, ed. Pp. 277–306. Cambridge: MIT Press.

———. 1989. Evolutionary psychology and the generation of culture, part II. Case study: A computational theory of social exchange. *Ethology and Sociobiology* 10:51–97.

———. 1992. Cognitive adaptations for social exchange. In *The adapted mind: Evolu-*

tionary psychology and the generation of culture, J. H. Barkow, L. Cosmides, and J. Tooby, eds. Pp. 163–228. Oxford: Oxford University Press.

Cronk, Lee. 1991. Human behavioral ecology. *Annual Review of Anthropology* 20:25–53.

Cullen, Ben. 1995. On cultural group selection. *Current Anthropology* 36:819–820.

Daly, Martin, and Margo Wilson. 1988. *Homicide.* New York: Aldine de Gruyter.

———. 1997. Crime and conflict: Homicide in evolutionary psychological perspective. *Crime and Justice: A Review of Research* 22:51–100.

Davies, Paul Sheldon, James H. Fetzer, and Thomas R. Foster. 1995. Logical reasoning and domain specificity: A critique of the social exchange theory of reasoning. *Biology and Philosophy* 10:1–37.

Dawkins, Richard. 1976. *The Selfish Gene.* Oxford: Oxford University Press.

———. 1993. Viruses of the mind. *Free Inquiry* (Summer):34–41.

Durham, William H. 1976. The adaptive significance of cultural behavior. *Human Ecology* 4:89–121.

———. 1979. Toward a coevolutionary theory of human biology and culture. In *Evolutionary Biology and Human Social Behavior,* N. Chagnon and W. Irons, eds. Pp. 39–59. North Scituate, Massachusetts: Duxbury Press.

———. 1990. Advances in evolutionary culture theory. *Annual Review of Anthropology* 19:187–210.

———. 1991. *Coevolution: Genes, Culture, and Human Diversity.* Stanford: Stanford University Press.

———. 1992. Applications of evolutionary culture theory. *Annual Review of Anthropology* 21:331–355.

Ellison, Peter T. 1994. Advances in human reproductive ecology. *Annual Review of Anthropology* 23:255–275.

Flinn, Mark. 1997. Culture and the evolution of social learning. *Evolution and Human Behavior* 18:23–67.

Foley, Rob A. 1996. The adaptive legacy of human evolution: A search for the environment of evolutionary adaptedness. *Evolutionary Anthropology* 4:194–203.

Gigerenzer, Gerd, and Klaus Hug. 1992. Domain-specific reasoning: Social contrasts, cheating, and perspective change. *Cognition* 43:127–171.

Grafen, Alan. 1984. Natural selection, kin selection and group selection. In *Behavioural Ecology: An Evolutionary Approach,* J. R. Krebs and N. B. Davies, eds. Pp. 62–84. Sunderland, Massachusetts: Sinauer Associates.

Hames, Raymond B. 1990. Sharing among the Yanomamö, Part I: The effects of risk. In *Risk and Uncertainty in Tribal and Peasant Economies,* E. Cashdan, ed. Pp. 89–106. Boulder: Westview Press.

Hawkes, Kristen. 1990. Why do men hunt? Some benefits for risky strategies. In *Risk and Uncertainty in Tribal and Peasant Economies,* E. Cashdan, ed. Pp. 145–166. Boulder: Westview Press.

———. 1991. Showing off: Tests of an hypothesis about men's foraging goals. *Ethology and Sociobiology* 12:29–54.

———. 1992. Sharing and collective action. In *Evolutionary Ecology and Human Behavior,* E. A. Smith and B. Winterhalder, eds. Pp. 269–300. New York: Aldine de Gruyter.

———. 1993. Why hunter-gatherers work. *Current Anthropology* 34:341–362.

Hill, Kim, and A. Magdalena Hurtado. 1996. *Ache Life History: The Ecology and Demography of a Foraging People.* New York: Aldine de Gruyter.

Irons, William G. 1979. Natural selection, adaptation, and human social behavior. In *Evolutionary Biology and Human Social Behavior,* N. Chagnon and W. Irons, eds. Pp. 4–39. North Scituate, Massachusetts: Duxbury Press.

———. 1990. Let's make our perspective broader rather than narrower: A comment on

Turke's "Which humans behave adaptively, and why does it matter?" and on the so-called DA-DP debate. *Ethology and Sociobiology* 11:361–374.

———. 1998. Adaptively relevant environments versus the Environment of Evolutionary Adaptedness. *Evolutionary Anthropology* 6:194–204.

Kaplan, Hillard, and Kim Hill. 1985. Food sharing among Ache foragers: Tests of explanatory hypotheses. *Current Anthropology* 26:223–246.

Kaplan, Hillard, Kim Hill, and Magdalena Hurtado. 1990. Fitness, foraging and food sharing among the Ache. In *Risk and Uncertainty in Tribal and Peasant Economies,* E. Cashdan, ed. Pp. 107–143. Boulder: Westview Press.

Kaplan, Hillard S., Jane B. Lancaster, John A. Bock, and S. E. Johnson. 1995. Fertility and fitness among Albuquerque men: A competitive labour market theory. In *Human Reproductive Decisions: Biological and Social Perspectives,* R. I. M. Dunbar, ed. Pp. 96–136. London: St. Martin's Press.

Konner, Melvin J. 1982. *The Tangled Wing: Biological Constraints on the Human Spirit.* New York: Harper.

Krebs, John R. 1978. Optimal foraging: Decision rules for predators. In *Behavioural Ecology: An Evolutionary Approach,* J. R. Krebs and N. B. Davies, eds. Pp. 23–63. Sunderland, Massachusetts: Sinauer/Oxford: Blackwell.

Krebs, John R., and Nicholas B. Davies, eds. 1997. *Behavioural Ecology: An Evolutionary Approach,* fourth ed. Oxford: Blackwell.

Lack, David. 1954. The evolution of reproductive rates. In *Evolution as a Process,* J. S. Huxley, A. C. Hardy, and E. B. Ford, eds. Pp. 143–156. London: Allen and Unwin.

Lynch, Aaron. 1996. *Thought Contagion.* New York: Basic Books.

Morgan, Charles J. 1979. Eskimo hunting groups, social kinship, and the possibility of kin selection in humans. *Ethology and Sociobiology* 1:83–86.

O'Brien, Michael J., ed. 1996. *Evolutionary Archaeology: Theory and Application.* Salt Lake City: University of Utah Press.

Orians, Gordon H. 1969. On the evolution of mating systems in birds and mammals. *American Naturalist* 103:589–603.

Palmer, Craig T. 1991. Kin-selection, reciprocal altruism, and information sharing among Maine lobstermen. *Ethology and Sociobiology* 12:221–235.

Peoples, James G. 1982. Individual or group advantage? A reinterpretation of the Maring ritual cycle. *Current Anthropology* 23:291–310.

Pérusse, Daniel. 1993. Cultural and reproductive success in industrial societies: Testing the relationship at the proximate and ultimate levels. *Behavioral and Brain Sciences* 16:267–322.

Pollard, P. 1990. Natural selection for the selection task: Limits to social exchange theory. *Cognition* 36:195–204.

Pulliam, H. Ronald, and Christopher Dunford. 1980. *Programmed to Learn: An Essay on the Evolution of Culture.* New York: Columbia University Press.

Richerson, Peter J., and Robert Boyd. 1989. The role of evolved predispositions in cultural evolution: Or, human sociobiology meets Pascal's wager. *Ethology and Sociobiology* 10:195–220.

———. 1992. Cultural inheritance and evolutionary ecology. In *Evolutionary Ecology and Human Behavior,* E. A. Smith and B. Winterhalder, eds. Pp. 61–92. New York: Aldine de Gruyter.

———. 1998. The evolution of human ultra-sociality. *Ideology, Warfare, and Indoctrinability,* I. Eibl-Eiblsfeldt and F. Salter, eds. Pp. 71–95. London: Berghahn.

———. 1999. Complex societies: The evolutionary dynamics of a crude superorganism. *Human Nature* 10(3):253–289

Rogers, Alan R. 1988. Does biology constrain culture? *American Anthropologist* 4:819–831.

———. 1990. The evolutionary economics of human reproduction. *Ethology and Sociobiology* 11:479–495.

Sahlins, Marshall D., and Elman Service, eds. 1960. *Evolution and Culture.* Ann Arbor: University of Michigan Press.

Sherman, Paul W., and Hudson K. Reeve. 1996. Forward and backward: Alternative approaches to studying human social evolution. In *Evolution and Human Behavior: A Critical Reader,* Laura M. Betzig, ed. Pp. 147–158. Oxford: Oxford University Press.

Smith, Eric Alden. 1983. Anthropological applications of optimal foraging theory: A critical review. *Current Anthropology* 24:625–651.

———. 1985. Inuit foraging groups: Some simple models incorporating conflicts of interest, relatedness, and central-place sharing. *Ethology and Sociobiology* 6:27–47.

———. 1988. Risk and uncertainty in the Aoriginal affluent society: Evolutionary ecology of resource sharing and land tenure. In *Hunters and Gatherers: History, Evolution, and Social Change,* T. Ingold, D. Riches, and J. Woodburn, eds. Pp. 222–252. Oxford: Berg.

———. 1992. Human behavioral ecology, parts I and II. *Evolutionary Anthropology* 1:20–25, 50–55.

Smith, Eric Alden, and Robert Boyd. 1990. Risk and reciprocity: Hunter-gatherer socioecology and the problem of collective action. In *Risk and Uncertainty in Tribal and Peasant Economies,* E. Cashdan, ed. Pp. 167–191. Boulder: Westview Press.

Smith, Eric Alden, and Bruce Winterhalder, eds. 1992. *Evolutionary Ecology and Human Behavior.* New York: Aldine de Gruyter.

Soltis, Joseph, Robert Boyd, and Peter J. Richerson. 1995. Can group-functional behaviors evolve by cultural group selection? An empirical test. *Current Anthropology* 36:473–483.

Symons, Donald. 1979. *The Evolution of Human Sexuality.* Oxford: Oxford University Press.

———. 1987. If we're all Darwinians, what's the fuss about? In *Sociobiology and Psychology: Ideas, Issues and Applications,* Charles Crawford, Martin Smith, and Dennis Krebs, eds. Pp. 121–146. Hillsdale, New Jersey: Erlbaum.

———. 1989. A critique of Darwinian anthropology. *Ethology and Sociobiology* 10:131–144.

———. 1992. On the use and misuse of Darwinism in the study of human behavior. In *The Adapted Mind: Evolutionary Psychology and the Generation of Culture,* J. H. Barkow, L. Cosmides, and J. Tooby, eds. Pp. 137–159. Oxford: Oxford University Press.

Thornhill, Randy, and Nancy Wilmsen Thornhill. 1992. The evolutionary psychology of men's coercive sexuality. *Behavioral and Brain Sciences* 15:363–421.

Tooby, John, and Leda Cosmides. 1989. Evolutionary psychology and the generation of culture, part I: Theoretical considerations. *Ethology and Sociobiology* 10:29–49.

———. 1990. The past explains the present: emotional adaptations and the structure of ancestral environments. *Ethology and Sociobiology* 11:375–424.

———. 1992. The psychological foundation of culture. In *The Adapted Mind: Evolutionary Psychology and the Generation of Culture,* J. H. Barkow, L. Cosmides, and J. Tooby, eds. Pp. 19–136. Oxford: Oxford University Press.

Trivers, Robert L. 1971. The evolution of reciprocal altruism. *Quarterly Review of Biology* 46:35–57.

Turke, Paul W. 1990. Which humans behave adaptively, and why does it matter? *Ethology and Sociobiology* 11:305–339.

Washburn, Sherwood L. 1978. Animal behavior and social anthropology. In *Sociobiology and Human Nature,* M. Gregory, A. Silvers, and D. Sutch, eds. Pp. 53–74. San Francisco: Jossey-Bass.

White, Leslie A. 1959. *The Evolution of Culture.* New York: McGraw-Hill.

Wilson, David Sloan. 1998. Hunting, sharing, and multilevel selection: The tolerated theft model revisited. *Current Anthropology* 39:73–97.

Wilson, Edward O. 1975. *Sociobiology: The New Synthesis.* Cambridge: Harvard University Press.

Winterhalder, Bruce. 1986. Diet choice, risk, and food sharing in a stochastic environment. *Journal of Anthropological Archaeology* 5:369–392.

———. 1990. Open field, common pot: Harvest variability and risk avoidance in agricultural and foraging societies. In *Risk and Uncertainty in Tribal and Peasant Economies,* E. Cashdan, ed. Pp. 67–87. Boulder: Westview Press.

———. 1996. Social foraging and the behavioral ecology of intragroup resource transfers. *Evolutionary Anthropology* 5:46–57.

Winterhalder, Bruce, and Eric Alden Smith. 2000. Analyzing adaptive strategies: Human behavioral ecology at twenty-five. *Evolutionary Anthropology*, in press.

Wood, James. 1994. *Dynamics of Human Reproduction.* New York: Aldine de Gruyter.

PART II

MATING

3

Polygyny, Family Structure, and Child Mortality

A Prospective Study among the Dogon of Mali

BEVERLY I. STRASSMANN

The lyrics of Oumou Sangare, Mali's leading pop-vocalist and feminist, and the witticisms of George Bernard Shaw neatly capture two opposing schools of thought on polygyny. Sangare, the daughter of a third wife, sings about the emotional cost of polygyny for women. Shaw, on the other hand, quipped that: "The maternal instinct leads a woman to prefer a tenth share in a first-rate man to the exclusive possession of a third-rate one." Shaw's view was formalized by the economist Gary Becker (1981), who attempted a mathematical demonstration of the argument that women tend to benefit from polygyny. According to Becker, polygynous men give a smaller fraction of their resources to each wife, but each wife gets more resources than a monogamous man could provide. Becker's approach echoes the polygyny threshold model, originally developed for passerine birds (Verner and Willson 1966; Orians 1969) and subsequently extended to humans (Borgerhoff Mulder 1988, 1990; Josephson 1993). Under the polygyny threshold model, polygyny is driven by female choice of mates who command more resources. However, females might be better off controlling resources themselves, or from a more equitable distribution of resources among males, in which case the emphasis on "female choice" is misleading (Hrdy 1996). Females may exert choice, but only within a restricted array of options.

An alternative to the female-choice model predicts conflicts of interest between members of the two sexes over the optimum mating system (Chisholm and Burbank 1991; Davies 1989; Downhower and Armitage 1971; Hrdy 1996; Irons 1983; Smuts 1995; Smuts and Smuts 1993). This conflict is expected because males may benefit reproductively from concurrent mates, even if the result is lower average fitness for each. Contra Becker, men might attempt to marry two wives even if they offer less than twice as much paternal investment (e.g., resources, time) as monogamous men. Thus, to the extent that male strategies prevail over female strategies in any given society, women who marry polygynously may incur a fitness cost. Females may experience the cost of polygyny through a reduction in fertility or an increase in child mortality.

Demographers have extensively probed the possibility of reduced fertility, but owing to methodological problems, their findings have been inconclusive (e.g. Dorjahn 1958; for review see Wood 1995). The hypothesis that child mortality is higher under polygyny has attracted comparatively little attention, despite its relevance for public health. Both sets of studies are limited by the use of retrospective data and the absence of controls for confounding risk factors (fertility: Pebley and Mbugua 1989; Wood 1994; mortality: Borgerhoff Mulder 1989, 1990; Chisholm and Burbank 1991; Chojnacka 1980; Isaac and Feinberg 1982; Roth and Kurup 1988).

In a study of polygyny and female fitness among the Dogon of Mali, West Africa, I attempted to overcome the methodological problems of previous studies by measuring female fecundability and child mortality prospectively. I measured female fecundability from two years of data on menstrual hut attendance, as corroborated by hormonal profiles (Strassmann and Warner 1998). Significant covariates of fecundability were controlled, including: wife's age, husband's age, marital duration, gravidity, and breast-feeding status. According to both discrete and continuous time survival analyses, there was no association between a woman's marital status and her fecundability (Strassmann and Warner, 1998). I measured child mortality from eight years of data on child survivorship, analyzed by logistic regression (Hosmer and Lemeshow 1989). The results indicated that the odds of death were 7 to 11 times higher under polygyny even in the presence of controls for confounding risk factors (such as age, sex, wealth, and family size) (Strassmann 1997). Here I present two additional logistic regression models that further implicate polygyny as a predictor of mortality.

ETHNOGRAPHIC BACKGROUND

In the fifteenth or sixteenth century, the Dogon established villages in easily defended sites along the Bandiagara Escarpment, a sandstone cliff (260 km long by ca. 500 m high) in Mali, West Africa (Pern 1982). After the French colonial government put an end to raids on Dogon villages by nearby pastoralists, Dogon settlements expanded to include much of the plateau on top of the escarpment as well as the Seno and Gondo plains below. This study took place in Sangui, a plateau-top village with a population of 460 individuals in January 1988, situated at 14° 29′ N, 3° 19′ W. The major subsistence crop in Sangui is millet and other cereals (rice, sorghum, and fonio). Onions are a cash crop that helps make up for deficits in the millet harvest.

The incidence of polygyny varies among villages, but in January 1988, 54% of the married men in Sangui had one wife, 35% had two wives, and 11% had three wives. Dogon polygyny is strictly nonsororal, and related women, such as first cousins, are not allowed to marry into the same patrilineage. Thus the Dogon illustrate the tendency for male kin in patrilineal societies to form powerful coalitions that thwart alliances among female kin (Smuts 1995; Hrdy 1997). First wives have the minor honor of sleeping in the room to the right of the husband's, but are not otherwise in a position of power or privilege. To maintain family harmony, the husband is expected to sleep with his wives on alternate nights. He owes them equal quantities of *yu buburu* (low quality millet) to store in their granaries; the good millet (*yu anran* or male millet) he stores in his own granaries. In dividing the millet, the first wife cuts the pile and the second wife chooses. Parents arrange their son's or daughter's first marriage, but ideally, the new couple does not co-reside until the birth of two children (who will be raised by the wife's parents). Bride-price is absent among the Dogon, but a fiancé shows respect to his parents-in-law by helping in their fields and through small gifts of cash, firewood, cowries, chickens, and grain.

In a strongly male-dominated society, husbands are more likely to be able to subordinate the reproductive interests of their wives in the pursuit of their own reproductive interests. Thus, polygyny is more likely to adversely affect female fitness when females have low status. The inferior status of Dogon women is particularly clear as they get older. An elderly widow is no longer considered useful to her husband's family and must return to her natal village to grow her own food. Elderly men usually enjoy a lighter workload in old age, but according to behavioral scan data, the workload of women does not abate. Across all ages, men spent 29% more time resting than women ($t = 7.71$, df = 127; $p < 0.0001$), and women spent 21% more time working than men ($t = -5.10$, df = 127, $p < 0.0001$) (Strassmann 1996). Women assume the energetic demands of lactation and heavy physical labor but are prohibited from the places where meat is consumed: hangars in the market place and religious shrines.

The indigenous religion is a vehicle through which Dogon males attempt to exert control over female sexuality (Strassmann 1992, 1996). For example, supernatural beliefs regarding menstrual pollution are a tactic for obligating menstruating women to spend the night at a menstrual hut. When a woman obeys the menstrual taboos it is evident that she is no longer in postpartum amenorrhea and that she will soon be ready to conceive. Although all female informants ($N = 113$) disliked the menstrual taboos, hormonal data indicate that menstrual hut visitation was an honest signal of menstruation. By enforcing the taboos, husbands and patrilineages gain precise knowledge of the timing of menstruation, information they consider useful for detecting and preventing cuckoldry (details in Strassmann 1992, 1996). The women of Sangui are also clitoridectomized. Informants had multiple interpretations of clitoridectomy, including the belief that genital surgery promotes paternity certainty through the reduction of sexual pleasure.

The greatest adversity faced by Dogon women is child mortality. The mean number of live births for postreproductive women was 8.6 ± 0.03, but 20% of children died in their first 12 months, and 46% died by age five ($N = 388$) (Strassmann 1992). From a human and primate comparative perspective, this mortality rate is very high (Lancaster and Lancaster 1983). Malaria, measles, and diarrhea caused the most fatalities (Fabre-Test 1985).

METHODS

This study monitored child survivorship longitudinally from 1986 to 1994. The study population included all children ($N = 205$), age ≤ 10 years, who were resident in the village of Sangui between May 1986 and August 1988. Children who were born during this interval were added to the study population. I resided in the village during this initial two-and-a-half-year period and therefore was able to ensure that the census for this period was complete. I recensused the village in 1994, at which time 20 children had left the village and were lost to follow-up. Nine children lived with widowed grandmothers in domestic units that did not include any married adults. I excluded these 29 children and compared the effect of polygyny versus monogamy on mortality among the remaining children ($N =$ 176, 86% of the initial population). The dependent variable was coded 1 for each child who died and 0 for each child who survived to the time of the 1994 census. Since the dependent variable was dichotomous, and data on age at death were unavailable, I analyzed the data using logistic regression. These regressions were carried out in the statistical program SPSS 6.1 (SPSS 1994).

Polygyny, the independent variable of key interest, was defined first by the mother's marital status: first, second, third, or sole wife. This definition excluded from the analysis 46 children whose mothers were widowed, engaged, divorced, or deceased, reducing the sample size to 130. Second, I computed polygyny as the ratio of married women to married men in the child's work-eat group, defined as the people who cultivated the same millet fields and assembled in one compound to eat together. For example, if a work-eat group had two men with two wives and one man with one wife, the polygyny index for that group would be the ratio of 5 women to 3 men, or 1.67. The significance of a work-eat group is twofold: *(a)* members depend on one another economically, and *(b)* they defer to the same family head. Married women cultivated millet alongside the other members of their work-eat group (both male and female) and did not plant their own individual millet fields. Thus, the economic status of women depended on the economic status of their work-eat groups. The sample size for polygyny of the work-eat group was 176 children and the mean (± s.d.) work-eat group size was 15.60 (± 10.64) persons with a range from 3 to 41. Work-eat groups did not correspond to households: if a work-eat group contained several married men, their families slept in different compounds. Co-wives and their children also sometimes had separate compounds. Adolescent boys slept in small compounds with their age mates.

The final models include all variables that improved model fit based on the likelihood ratio test (Hosmer and Lemeshow 1989). To test whether the logit had a quadratic rather than a linear relationship with any of the continuous variables, I added squared terms. If a squared term did not improve model fit based on the likelihood ratio test it was omitted. The values for the independent variables in this analysis were obtained from a combination of direct observation (e.g., child's sex), private interviews (e.g., parent's education), and quantitative measurement (e.g., economic rank). To compare the economic resources (land, grain, onions, and livestock) of all families, the 540 cereal fields and 422 onion fields belonging to the people of Sangui were measured with a compass and meter tape, baskets of grain and onions were counted and weighed, and livestock were tallied by species, maturity (juvenile versus adult), and sex, as described elsewhere (Strassmann and Warner 1998). Year-to-year fluctuations in the wealth of the village from 1986 to 1994 occurred in response to changes in rainfall and market forces but had a negligible impact on the relative wealth of the families, which I expressed as a rank from 1 to 59. After the exclusion of 9 children who lived with widowed grandmothers (see above), no children lived in a family that had a wealth rank below 15.

To compare the standard of living of different work-eat groups, I computed the daily energy requirement of each group from the number of individual members, adjusted for age and sex, using the guidelines of the FAO and WHO (1973). I standardized the wealth of each group by its daily energy requirement. To find out whether children in polygynous families were less well nourished, I used cross-sectional anthropometric data on 77 children age six or younger in 1988. In particular, I compared their observed and expected values for weight/height.

To assess the effect of polygyny on aspects of paternal behavior that were both quantifiable and observable, I compared observations of direct childcare performed by polygynously and monogamously married men. The following behaviors were defined as "direct childcare:" carrying, holding, washing, wiping, feeding, minding (baby-sitting), or otherwise assisting a child. Observations of childcare were obtained via behavioral scan sampling in the agricultural fields and village from December 1987 to May 1988. I divided the number of childcare observations for a given person by the total number of observations for that person, to obtain an approximation of the time that person allocated to direct childcare as opposed to other activities.

RESULTS

Univariate Analyses

As shown in Table 3.1, the chi-square test revealed a nonrandom relationship between mother's marital status and child mortality. More children of first wives died than expected, and fewer children of sole wives died than expected. In a univariate logistic regression, the polygyny index (ratio of married women to married men in a child's work-eat group) was a significant predictor of mortality (odds ratio = 3.14, 95% confidence interval = 1.45–6.78, n = 176). Strikingly, only 3 of 58 children died in the groups with an index of <1.5, while 37 of 118 children died

Table 3.1. Child survivorship (died or lived) by wife type (first, second/third, or sole wife).

Wife Type	*Children*	
	Died	*Lived*
First		
Observed	16	27
Expected	10	33
Second/Third		
Observed	11	32
Expected	10	33
Sole		
Observed	4	40
Expected	11	34

$\chi^2 = 9.57$, df = 2, $p = 0.008$, $n = 130$

in the groups with an index of ≥1.5 ($\chi^2 = 15.18$, df = 1, $p = 0.0001$) (Strassmann 1997).

Multivariate Analyses

In previous multivariate analyses, I coded polygyny as a dichotomous categorical variable, with a work-eat group defined as monogamous if the polygyny index was <1.5, and polygynous if the index was ≥1.5 married women to married men (Strassmann 1997). This approach was based on empirical evidence that the relationship between polygyny and mortality was a step function. After controlling for other predictors of mortality (child's age, child's sex, number of children in family, and economic rank) the odds of death were more than 7 times higher in the polygynous work-eat groups than in the monogamous groups (95% confidence interval = 1.8–29.4, $p = 0.0005$). It should be emphasized that this effect size was based on an empirically derived cutoff point.

Here I employ an alternative approach. Rather than model work-eat group polygyny as a dichotomous variable, I treat it as a continuous variable with values ranging from 1.00 to 3.00. The two best-fitting final models are shown in Table 3.2. They differ from each other in that model 1 includes the number of children (age ≤ 10 years) in the family, whereas model 2 includes the ratio of children (age ≤ 10 years) to married adults. In model 1, the relationship between polygyny and mortality is best modeled as a quadratic function; at $\alpha = 0.05$, polygyny was significant ($p < 0.03$), as was polygyny squared ($p = 0.05$). In this model, the effect of a one- unit increase in the polygyny index was not constant across all values of the index, so the relationship between the predicted probability of death and the polygyny index is best shown graphically (Figure 3.1). In model 2, polygyny

Table 3.2. Predictors of child mortality from 1986 to 1994, with polygyny as a continuous variable (N = 176 children).

	Model 1			*Model 2*		
Predictor	*Coefficient*	*Odds Ratio*	*95% Confidence Interval*	*Coefficient*	*Odds Ratio*	*95% Confidence Interval*
Polygyny index of the work-eat group (1.00–3.00)	8.293**	—	—	1.526†	4.60	1.61–13.11
Polygyny index squared	–2.064*	—	—	—	—	—
Age of child (0–10)	–0.398‡	0.67	0.55–0.81	0.399‡	0.67	0.56–0.81
Sex of child (0 = female, 1 = male)	0.864	2.37	0.96–5.87	0.743	2.10	0.88–5.01
Number of children in family (1–13)	0.235†	1.26	1.08–1.49	—	—	—
Ratio of children to married adults (0.33–2.33)	—	—	—	1.237†	3.44	1.46–8.15
Economic rank (14–59)	–0.087**	0.42	0.2–0.85	–0.0006	0.99	0.68–1.45
Constant	–6.611*	—	—	–4.82†	—	—

* $p \leq 0.05$; ** $p < 0.03$; † $p < 0.005$; ‡ $p < 0.00005$.

Odds ratios are for a one-unit increase in the predictor variable, except the odds ratio for economic rank is for an increase of 10 ranks. In model 1, the relationship between polygyny and mortality is a quadratic function and therefore cannot be represented by just a single odds ratio (see Fig. 3.3).

–2 Log likelihood = 138.0 (model 1) and 143.0 (model 2). Goodness-of-fit statistic: 176.4 (model 1) and 158.8 (model 2). Percentage of outcomes (lived or died) correctly predicted by the model: 81.3% (model 1) and 79.2% (model 2).

squared was not significant so it was preferable to model the relationship between polygyny and the logit as linear. In model 2, as the ratio of married women to married men increased by 1.00, the odds of death increased 4.6-fold ($p < 0.005$). In summary, regardless of whether work-eat group polygyny was modeled as a dichotomous or a continuous variable, the odds of death for Dogon children were significantly lower under monogamy.

Work-eat group polygyny was more predictive of mortality than mother's marital status. For example, after controlling for the other predictors of mortality in model 2, the odds of death were higher for the children of first wives (odds ratio = 3.7, $p = 0.07$, $n = 130$) and for the children of second wives (odds ratio = 1.8, $p = 0.41$, $n = 130$) than for the children of sole wives, but these results were not significant at $\alpha = 0.05$. In this analysis, the sample size was reduced from 176 to 130 because only 130 children had mothers who were married and living in the village. The loss of significance, however, was not merely due to sample size. When work-

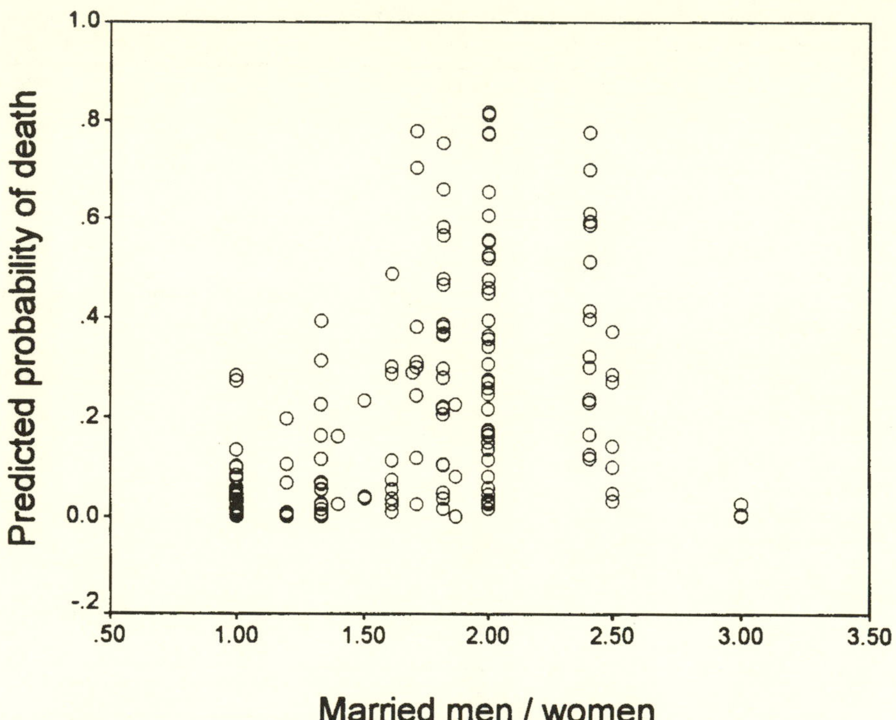

Figure 3.1. The predicted probability of death for each child (n = 176) plotted against the polygyny index of the work-eat group. Unlike a simple plot of the percentage of children who died at each level of the index, these predicted probabilities reflect each child's particular values for all the covariates in model 1. Thus, predictors of mortality other than polygyny are controlled.

eat group polygyny (as a continuous variable) was substituted for mother's marital status in the same sample ($n = 130$), the odds of death were 5.1 times higher under polygyny ($p = 0.006$).

Other variables, beyond mother's marital status, that were not significant predictors of mortality are listed in Table 3.3. For example, after controlling for the variables in Table 3.2, no interactions were significant. According to the likelihood ratio test, Sex × Age was marginally significant when polygyny was modeled as a dichotomous variable (Strassmann 1997), but was nonsignificant when polygyny was modeled as a continuous variable (model 1: $p = 0.07$, model 2: $p = 0.16$).

The wealth rank of the work-eat group was positively correlated with the ratio of married females to married males ($r^2 = 0.28$, $n = 45$, $p = 0.0001$) (Figure 3.2). Work-eat groups in which this ratio was ≥1.5 farmed more land ($p = 0.001$), and produced more grain ($p = 0.009$) and onions ($p = 0.002$) than did families in

Table 3.3. Independent variables that did not predict mortality (p >> 0.05 after controlling for variables in table 3.1; $N = 176$ children).

Father's age
Mother's age
Number of married women in work-eat group
Number of married men in work-eat group
Whether father resident in village
Whether mother resident in village
Father's education[1]
Whether father had worked in city
Polygyny × Sex
Polygyny × Economic rank
Polygyny × Number of children in family
Polygyny × Ratio of children to adults
Economic rank × Number of children in family
Economic rank × Ratio of children to adults

[1]Although some of the fathers had been to primary school for a few years, none of the mothers had any formal schooling.

which this ratio was <1.5 (Strassmann 1997). When work-eat group wealth was standardized by energy requirements, the polygynous groups were still slightly wealthier than the monogamous groups ($r^2 = 0.09$, $n = 45$, $p = 0.03$) (Figure 3.3) because they had more revenue from onions ($p = 0.01$) (Strassmann 1997). On other measures of wealth, polygynous and monogamous families were comparable (Strassmann 1997).

The dependency ratio provides another estimate of the parental resources (e.g., wealth, time) available to children. As this variable increased by one additional child, the odds of death increased by a factor of 2.9 ($p = 0.02$). However, as shown by model 2, mortality was much higher under polygyny even after controlling for the dependency ratio.

The expected weight/height for each girl or boy was obtained from quadratic regressions of weight/height against age. These equations are as follows: weight/height (Dogon girls) = 9.17 + Age(1.53) + Age^2 (0.10) ($r2 = 0.74$, $n = 34$, $p < 0.0001$); and weight/height (Dogon boys) = 9.47 + Age(1.98) + Age^2(–0.16) ($r^2 = 0.71$, $n = 43$, $p < 0.0001$). If the children in the polygynous families were leaner than those in the monogamous families, then they should have tended toward negative residuals (observed weight/height < expected weight/height) while the children in monogamous families should have tended toward positive residuals (observed weight/height > expected weight/height). As shown in Figure 3.4, there was a very weak tendency in the predicted direction that was not quite significant ($r^2 = 0.04$, $n = 74$, $p = 0.07$). Controlling for this weak relationship had no effect on the coefficient for polygyny in the subset of observations ($n = 74$) for which weight-for-height measurements were available.

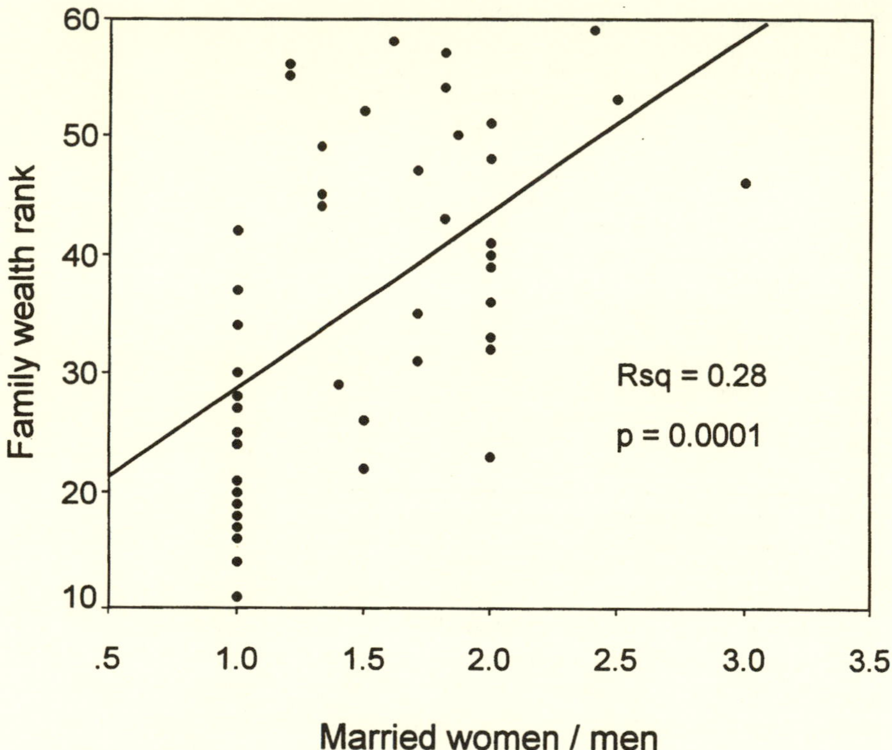

Figure 3.2. Regression of the wealth rank of the work-eat group on the polygyny index (number of married women / number of married men) of the work-eat group ($n = 44$). Groups in which an elderly widow or widower worked alone or with a grandchild are excluded.

The behavioral scan data indicated that the participation of adult males in direct childcare was negligible, regardless of whether a man was monogamously or polygynously married. The difference in the amount of childcare performed by males and females was highly significant ($\chi^2 = 111.7$, df = 1, $p < 0.000001$).

DISCUSSION

A vast, though inconclusive, literature is devoted to the effect of polygyny on fertility, but only a few studies tested the hypothesis that child mortality is higher under polygyny. A limitation of these studies is that they use retrospective data on child survivorship over a woman's reproductive career. Such data may be prone to recall and reporting bias. Another problem is absence of controls for confounding variables: two studies were strictly univariate (Chisholm and Burbank 1991;

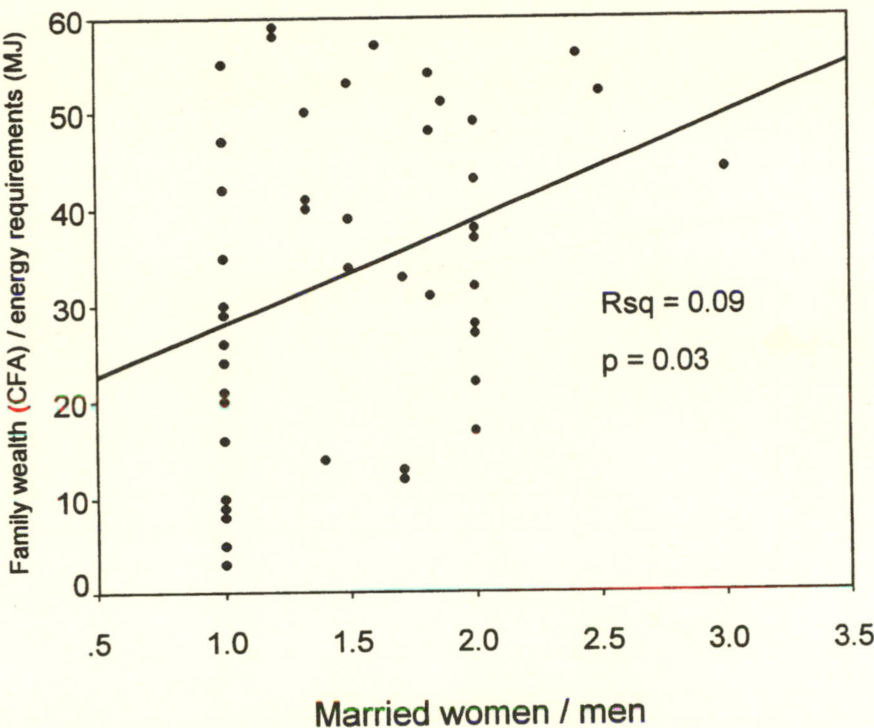

Figure 3.3. Regression of work-eat group wealth (CFA) per work-eat group energy requirements (MJ) on the polygyny index ($n = 45$).

Chojnacka 1980) and two others controlled only for the age of the mother (Isaac and Feinberg 1982; Roth and Kurup 1988). Borgerhoff Mulder (1990) and Chisholm and Burbank (1991) focused on the number of surviving offspring, but in these analyses fertility and mortality are confounded. By contrast with previous studies, the data presented here provide a prospective, longitudinal test of the polygyny-mortality hypothesis. Through logistic regression analysis, other risk factors for mortality were systematically identified and controlled, including age, sex, number of children in the family, ratio of children to married adults, and economic rank.

Before the effect of polygyny on mortality is discussed, it will be helpful to consider these other risk factors. The odds of death decreased by a factor of 0.67 with each additional year of age, and although one might expect the age effect to level off, age-squared was not significant. Consistent with the public health literature, an increase in economic rank was also associated with lower mortality.

The odds of death increased by a factor of 1.26 as family size increased by one additional child (age 0 to 10 years). This result may reflect competition among

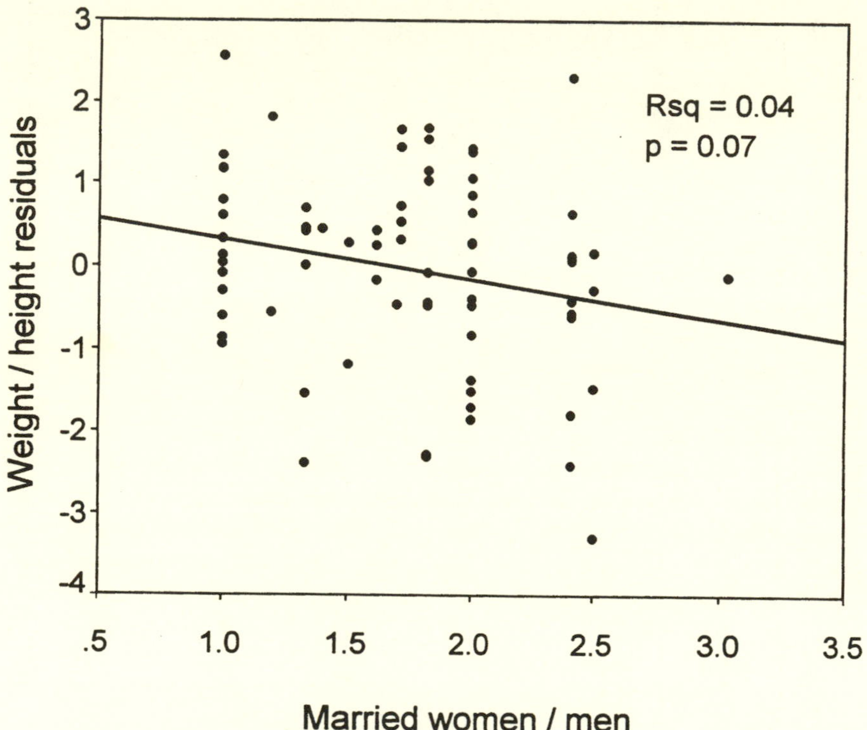

Figure 3.4. Regression of weight for height residuals on the polygyny index of the work-eat group ($n = 74$).

children or increased exposure to infectious diseases such as measles and gastroenteritis (the "daycare effect") (Aaby et al. 1984; Desai 1995). The odds of death increased by a factor of 3.4 as the ratio of children (age ≤ 10 years) to married adults increased by one child. This result could be caused by a decrease in the ratio of net consumers to net producers (Hames 1996). However, resources did not appear to be diluted in the polygynous compared with the monogamous families. Another possibility is that when the ratio of children to adults was higher, each child received less adult supervision.

When polygyny was modeled as a dichotomous variable, the odds of death were 2.5-fold higher for males than for females ($p < 0.05$) (Strassmann 1997). When polygyny was modeled as a continuous variable, the odds of death remained more than twofold higher for males, but this result was not quite significant (model 1: $p = 0.06$, model 2: $p = 0.09$). Nonetheless, the skewed confidence interval for the odds ratio (0.96 to 5.87) (Table 3.2: model 1) suggests that this result is unlikely to be due entirely to chance (see Hosmer and Lemeshow 1989:105).

In the behavioral scans, boys were the recipients of direct childcare significantly more often than girls (correcting for the total number of observations of each sex) ($\chi^2 = 20.9$, df = 1, $p < 0.00001$, $n = 90$ children age ≤ 3 years, $n = 743$ observations). This comparison is restricted to children under 3 years of age because they were the primary targets for direct childcare; they also experienced the greatest level of both overall mortality and sex-biased mortality. The finding that boys received more direct childcare, and ethnographic observations from long-term residence in the village, contradict any suggestion that female-biased parental investment caused boys to have higher mortality.

The Trivers and Willard (1973) effect predicts that wealthy, polygynous families should favor sons more than poor, monogamous families. However, when the children in families above and below the mean wealth rank were analyzed separately, the higher mortality of boys was significant only in the wealthier group (model 1: odds ratio = 3.6, $p < 0.05$, $n = 92$, economic rank > 41). Thus, the higher mortality of boys cannot be explained by the Trivers-Willard hypothesis and remains enigmatic.

After controlling for other risk factors for mortality, the odds of death were significantly higher in polygynous than in monogamous work-eat groups. This was true regardless of whether polygyny was modeled as a dichotomous (see Strassmann 1997) or a continuous (Table 3.2) variable. In the multivariate analyses, mother's marital status was substantially less useful for predicting mortality than the polygyny index for the work-eat group as a whole, a result that underlines the importance of family structure. When members of a patrilineal extended family are economically interdependent, children are affected by the polygyny status of their paternal relatives, not just that of their own parents.

Although these results provide the strongest evidence to date that polygyny is a risk factor for mortality, they leave the underlying mechanism unidentified. Prior to the fieldwork, I expected wealth to be diluted in polygynous compared with monogamous families. The economic and the anthropometric data, however, did not support this hypothesis. Polygynous families were at least as wealthy as monogamous families even after correcting for family size. Weight-for-height residuals declined slightly with the ratio of married women to married men, but even after controlling for this weak effect, polygyny remained highly predictive of mortality. Thus, the relationship between polygyny and mortality in this study appears to be caused by a mechanism other than resource dilution.

The indigenous Dogon explanation is that in their competition to outreproduce each other, co-wives sometimes poisoned each other's children. Boys were said to be more at risk than girls. This belief took expression most forcefully at masked dance rituals in which the men obliged all of the women of the village to assemble for collective chastisement. Future offenders were threatened with death. Malian court cases provide compelling documentation of confessions and convictions for poisoning the offspring of a co-wife. Such cases can be compared with records of child abuse in the United States. Children have about 100 times the risk of death from child abuse if they live with a stepparent rather than with two genetic parents (Daly and Wilson 1988:89), but the baseline rate is still very low. The incidence of poisonings among the Dogon is unknown, but it might be premature to dismiss all such accusations as fictive sorcery. Even if poisonings are rare or absent, fear of mother's co-wife must be a source of stress. Residence with a stepfather and half siblings can affect childhood cortisol levels and lead to immuno-suppression and illness (Flinn and England 1995). Regardless of whether female-female competition results in outright poisoning, immuno-suppression, or simple neglect, the focus on co-wives alone is too narrow. Work-eat group polygyny was a better predictor of survivorship than mother's marital status, implying that if female-female competition results in child mortality, it may not stop with co-wives. Instead it may extend to women married to a set of brothers.

An alternative hypothesis is that polygynous men provide less paternal care to each of their offspring (see Hewlett 1988; Strassmann 1981). Monogamous fathers have fewer children, so each child is a larger component of a father's lifetime reproductive success. Monogamous fathers also tend to be poorer, and are less likely to have future mating opportunities. In their behavior toward their children, they may act as if more is at stake. Polygynous fathers eventually produce a greater number of offspring, so each child represents a smaller fraction of the father's total lifetime reproductive success. Controlling for age, polygynists (aged 24 to 69) had on average two more living offspring for each additional wife ($r^2 = 0.25$, $n = 70$, $p = 0.0001$).

Children whose fathers had more offspring did not have higher odds of death. Thus it does not appear that polygynous men simply spread their investment among a greater number of existing children. Instead they might have diverted resources from paternal effort to mating effort, and gained increased prospects for producing future offspring. If their resources were diverted to somatic effort (buying meat or beer in the marketplace), then polygynous males did not pursue an optimum fitness strategy. Clearly, a great deal more needs to be learned about the allocation of effort on the part of polygynous and monogamous men.

What might polygynous men have withheld from their children that was important for survivorship? Both polygynous and monogamous men left most of the direct childcare to women (see Draper 1989; Hewlett 1991), so it is doubtful that there was a critical deficit in time spent with children. Another possibility is that polygynous men were less willing to pay for costly medical care. Given the prevalence of parasitic and infectious diseases, differential access to medical care could have a dramatic impact on mortality. This hypothesis should be tested after controlling for any differences in morbidity under monogamy and polygyny.

A shortcoming of the paternal care hypothesis is that it does not explain why work-eat group polygyny was a better predictor of child survivorship than parent's marital status. One solution is to broaden the paternal investment hypothesis to include the nepotistic investment of relatives other than fathers. Men in polygynous work-eat groups may have been less inclined to pay for medicines and other treatments for childhood illnesses. The father himself was not necessarily the one who withheld investment. Instead it might have been the child's uncle, particularly if he was the work-eat group boss. The Dogon described the relationship between a boy and his paternal cousins as one of competition and distrust, whereas his relationship with his maternal cousins (with whom he was not in competition for resources) tended to be amicable and relaxed. Conflicts of interest between paternal relatives often became sufficiently intense that the entire work-eat group fissioned along lines of genetic relatedness (see Chagnon 1981). In future research, it would be useful to explore these conflicts of interest further, and to determine how they might influence nepotistic investment in children (see also Castle 1993). This line of inquiry appears promising because, after controlling for the covariates in model 2, the odds of death were 74% lower for children whose father or grandfather was work-eat group boss rather than the child's uncle (odds ratio = 0.26, 95% confidence interval = 0.09–0.77).

Given the high mortality of children in polygynous work-eat groups, it appears likely that, when all else was equal, Dogon women achieved higher fitness under monogamy. To test this proposition, it would be useful to compare the number of surviving grandchildren for women in polygynous and monogamous groups (Josephson 1993). However, although it is easy to make such a comparison, it is difficult to make it well. A woman's marital status at the time she is censused cannot simply be compared to her number of grandchildren because her marital status may have changed. Instead one needs to track marital status and work-eat group polygyny retrospectively over the course of a woman's marital life. Any changes make it difficult to determine the polygyny or marital status relevant to a particular grandchild. One approach is to restrict the sample to women who had been in no more than one marriage. But child mortality can be a cause of divorce, so these women are likely to be those whose children survived. In such a biased sample, it may be difficult to detect any effect of polygyny. Another problem in retrospective studies is the difficulty of controlling for confounding variables such as age, family size, and wealth. To make matters worse, these variables change over time. To date, no retrospective study has fully surmounted these difficulties (see Borgerhoff Mulder 1988, 1996; Josephson 1993).

The problem of time-varying covariates is less severe in a prospective analysis such as this one because changes in the independent variables can be more easily monitored and taken into account. These changes are also likely to be smaller because of the shorter time span involved. Whereas retrospective studies of postmenopausal women span several decades, this study spanned only eight years. Nonetheless, to find out if the changes that did occur might alter my conclusions, I constructed alternative models that used either the value of the variable at the beginning of the study or the value at the end. For example, I compared the ratio of married women to married men at the beginning and end of the study and found that the results were essentially the same. A better approach is to use survival analysis with time-varying covariates, but this method will not work with a dichotomous dependent variable (lived or died). Future studies of child mortality should gather data on age at death so that survival analysis can be employed.

In view of the high mortality of children in polygynous families, why are women willing to become junior co-wives? Prior to the fieldwork, I predicted that women who entered marriage as a second or third wife were of lower mate value. However, contrary to this prediction, the monthly probability of conception was not associated with marital status. Junior co-wives were just as fecundable as senior wives and monogamously married women (Strassmann and Warner 1998). Nor was there a relationship between a woman's marital status and her nutritional status based on standard anthropometric indices such as weight for height and sum of skinfolds (Strassmann, unpublished data). Moreover, contrary to expectation, the decrease in survivorship was greatest for the offspring of first wives, not second or third wives (Figure 3.1). Because of the prospective study design, this result cannot be attributed to a tendency for husbands to marry a second wife if many children by the first wife died. In sum, the hypothesis that women of lower fitness were relegated to polygynous marriages was not supported.

Instead, it appears that many young, well-nourished, fecund women were forced into polygynous situations simply because there were too few monogamous opportunities available. The shortage of monogamous opportunities was caused by the excess of women relative to men on the marriage market. Dogon wives were on average eight years younger than their husbands. This difference in age at marriage, in conjunction with the pyramidal age-structure for the population, ensures that the cohort of women looking for husbands is larger than the cohort of men looking for wives. Many women are thereby forced into polygyny (Chisholm and Burbank 1991; Dorjahn 1959; Pison 1985). The tendencies for men to marry at a later age and to die at a younger age generate a surplus of widows relative to widowers. Among the Dogon, these widows generally remarried even after menopause, which also produces a surplus of women on the marriage market (Pison 1985), regardless of the age-structure of the population. Last, Dogon polygyny is promoted by a female-biased operational sex ratio (Dorjahn 1959). In this study, the skew was caused by higher male mortality and urban migration.

Even girls who succeed at entering monogamous marriages and work-eat groups have no guarantee that monogamy will prevail. The Malian government has acknowledged their predicament by passing a law that requires all men who contract civil marriages to commit themselves, on paper at least, to either monogamy or potential polygyny. Not surprisingly, few men choose to limit their options. If a woman seeks to avoid polygyny, her most effective tactic is divorce, or the threat of divorce. Both men ($n = 71$) and women ($n = 113$) interviewed in Sangui emphasized that divorce was primarily female-initiated (Strassmann 1997). In a sample of 88 divorces, the wife said that she had been the initiator in 95% of divorces, and the four most frequently cited reasons were: (1) husband pursuing wage labor in the city (25%), (2) dislike of husband (18%), (3) dislike of co-wife (10%), and (4) too many children died in that marriage (6%). Forty-one percent of divorces were attributed to miscellaneous other reasons, each of which was less commonly cited than the above. Although women may resist polygyny through divorce, few escape it entirely. In preparation, young girls are taught to sing, "I'm not afraid of my husband's other wife."

SUMMARY

1. This study tested the effect of the polygyny index on child survivorship from 1986 to 1994. The polygyny index was defined as the ratio of married women to married men in the family, and ranged from 1.0 to 3.0. As this ratio increased by one, the odds of death for Dogon children (n = 176) increased approximately 4.6-fold.
2. By contrast with previous analyses, this study employed a prospective design and controlled for other predictors of mortality, including age of the child, sex of the child, number of children in the family, the dependency ratio of the family, and economic status.
3. Mother's marital status (first, second, third, or sole wife) predicted child mortality in univariate analyses. In multivariate analyses, however, only the polygyny index for the family as a whole was critical. This result suggests that when members of a patrilineal extended family depend on one another economically, child survivorship is influenced by the polygyny status of paternal relatives. Family structure, not simply the marital status of parents, needs to be taken into account.
4. Hypotheses regarding the mechanism through which polygyny adversely affects child survivorship need to consider the roles of resource dilution, co-wife competition, paternal investment, and nepotistic investment. The data did not support resource dilution, but it is premature to exclude any of the remaining possibilities.
5. Becker's economic model and the polygyny threshold model view polygyny as the outcome of female choice. However, the eight-year difference in the age of spouses generates a surplus of Dogon females on the marriage market, obliging many wives to accept polygyny. Dogon men who achieve polygyny gain reproductively while their wives lose (at least in the offspring generation), implying that male preference is more likely to be the driving force behind this marriage system.

ACKNOWLEDGMENTS

I especially want to thank the people of Sangui for their friendship and participation; Gadiolou Dolo, Goziolum Dolo, Sylvie Moulin, and Thomas Stevenson for many months of help with the fieldwork; Klena Sanogo for assistance in obtaining research authorization; Sally Slocum, Anagaly Dolo, and U.S. Peace Corps Mali for invaluable logistical support; and Brenda Gillespie and John Warner for statistical advice. I also appreciate the helpful input of Lee Cronk, Kathy Dettwyler, Barry Hewlett, Kim Hill, Sarah Hrdy, and John Mitani. This research was supported by the L. S. B. Leakey Foundation, the University of Michigan, and the National Science Foundation (BNS-8612291).

REFERENCES

Aaby, P, P. J. Bukh, I. M. Lisse, and A. J. Smits. 1984. Overcrowding and intensive exposure as determinants of measles mortality. *American Journal of Epidemiology* 120:49–63.

Becker, G. S. 1981. *A Treatise on the Family*. Cambridge: Harvard University Press.

Borgerhoff Mulder, M. 1988. The relevance of the polygyny threshold model to humans. In *Human Mating Patterns,* C. G. N. Mascie-Taylor and A. J. Boyce, eds. Pp. 209–230. Cambridge: Cambridge University Press.

———. 1989. Marital status and reproductive performance in Kipsigis women: Re-evaluating the polygyny-fertility hypothesis. *Population Studies* 43:285–304.

———. 1990. Kipsigis women's preferences for wealthy men: Evidence for female choice in mammals? *Behavioral Ecology and Sociobiology* 27:255–264.

———. 1996. Marrying a married man: A postscript. In *Human Nature: A Critical Reader,* L. Betzig, ed. Pp. 115–117. Oxford: Oxford University Press.

Castle, S. E. 1993. Intra-household differentials in women's status: Household function and focus as determinants of children's illness management and care in rural Mali. *Health Transition Review* 3:137–157.

Chagnon, N. 1981. Terminological kinship, genealogical relatedness, and village fissioning among the Yanomamö Indians. In *Natural selection and social behavior,* R. Alexander and D. Tinkle, eds. Pp. 490–508. New York: Chiron Press.

Chisholm, J. S., and V. K. Burbank. 1991. Monogamy and polygyny in southeast Arnhem Land: Male coercion and female choice. *Ethology and Sociobiology* 12:291–313.

Chojnacka, H. 1980. Polygyny and the rate of population growth. *Population Studies* 34:91–107.

Daly, M., and M. Wilson. 1988. *Homicide.* New York: Aldine de Gruyter.

Davies, N. B. 1989. Sexual conflict and the polygamy threshold. *Animal Behavior* 38: 226–234.

Desai, S. 1995. When are children from large families disadvantaged? Evidence from cross-national analyses. *Population Studies* 49:195–210.

Dorjahn, V. R. 1958. Fertility, polygyny, and their interrelations in Temne society. *American Anthropologist* 60:838–860.

———. 1959. The factor of polygyny in African demography. In *Continuity and Change in African Cultures,* W. R. Bascom and M. J. Herskovits, eds. Pp. 87–112. Chicago: University of Chicago Press.

Downhower, J. F., and K. B. Armitage. 1971. The yellow-bellied marmot and the evolution of polygamy. *American Naturalist* 105:355–370.

Draper, P. 1989. African marriage systems: Perspectives from evolutionary ecology. *Ethology and Sociobiology* 10:145–169.

Fabre-Test, B. 1985. *Evaluation Sanitaire du Cercle de Bandiagara.* Direction Nationale de l'Hygiene et de l'Assainissement, Ministère de la Santé Publique et des Affaires Sociales, Republic of Mali.

FAO/WHO. 1973. *Energy and Protein Requirements.* Report of a Joint FAO/WHO Ad Hoc Expert Committee. FAO Nutrition Meetings Report Series, No. 22. WHO Technical Report Series, No. 522. Rome: FAO and WHO.

Flinn, M. V., and B. G. England. 1995. Childhood stress and family environment. *Current Anthropology* 36:854–866.

Hames, R. 1996. Costs and benefits of monogamy and polygyny for Yanomamö women. *Ethology and Sociobiology* 17:181–199.

Hewlett, B. S. 1988. Sexual selection and paternal investment among Aka pygmies. In *Human Reproductive Behaviour: A Darwinian Perspective,* L Betzig, M. Borgerhoff Mulder, and P. Turke, eds. Pp. 263–276. Cambridge: Cambridge University Press.

———. 1991. Demography and childcare in preindustrial societies. *Journal of Anthropological Research* 47:1–37.

Hosmer, D. W., and S. Lemeshow. 1989. *Applied Logistic Regression.* New York: John Wiley and Sons.

Hrdy, S. B. 1996. Raising Darwin's consciousness: Female sexuality and the prehominid origins of patriarchy. *Human Nature* 8:1–49.

Irons, W. 1983. Human female reproductive strategies. In *Social Behavior of Female Vertebrates,* S. Wasser, ed. Pp. 169–213. New York: Academic Press.

Isaac, B. L., and W. E. Feinberg. 1982. Marital form and infant survival among the Mende of rural Upper Bambara Chiefdom, Sierra Leone. *Human Biology* 54:627–634.

Josephson, S. C. 1993. Status, reproductive success, and marrying polygynously. *Ethology and Sociobiology* 14:391–396.

Lancaster, J. B., and C. S. Lancaster. 1983. Parental investment: The hominid adaptation. In *How Humans Adapt: A Biocultural Odyssey,* D. Ortner, ed. Pp. 33–65. Washington, D.C.: Smithsonian Institution Press.

Orians, G. H. 1969. On the evolution of mating systems in birds and mammals. *American Naturalist* 103:589–603.

Pebley, A., and W. Mbugua. 1989. Polygyny and fertility in sub-Saharan Africa. In *Reproduction and Social Organization in Sub-Saharan Africa,* R. Lesthaege, ed. Pp 338–364. Berkeley: University of California Press.

Pern, S. 1982. *Masked Dancers of West Africa: The Dogon.* Amsterdam: Time-Life Books.

Pison, G. 1985. La démographie de la polygamie. *La Recherche* 168:894–901.

Roth, E. A., and K. B. Kurup. 1988. Demography and polygyny in a southern Sudanese agro-pastoralist society. *Culture* 8:67–73.

Smuts, B. 1995. The evolutionary origins of patriarchy. *Human Nature* 6:1–32.

Smuts, B. B., and R. W. Smuts. 1993. Male aggression and sexual coercion of females in nonhuman primates and other mammals: Evidence and theoretical implications. *Advances in the Study of Behavior* 22:1–63.

SPSS. 1994. *Advanced Statistics* 6.1. Chicago: SPSS Inc.

Strassmann, B. I. 1981. Sexual selection, paternal care, and concealed ovulation in humans. *Ethology and Sociobiology* 2:31–40.

———. 1992. The function of menstrual taboos among the Dogon: Defense against cuckoldry? *Human Nature* 3:89–131.

———. 1996. Menstrual hut visits by Dogon women: A hormonal test distinguishes deceit from honest signaling. *Behavioral Ecology* 7:304–315.

———. 1997. Polygyny as a risk factor for child mortality among the Dogon. *Current Anthropology* 38:688–695.

Strassmann, B. I., and J. Warner. 1998. Predictors of fecundability and conception waits among the Dogon of Mali. *American Journal of Physical Anthropology* 105:167–184.

Trivers, R. L., and D. E. Willard. 1973. Natural selection of parental ability to vary the sex ratio of offspring. *Science* 179:90–98.

Verner, J., and M. F. Willson. 1966. The influence of habitats on mating systems of North American passerine birds. *Ecology* 47:143–147.

Wood, J. W. 1994. *Dynamics of Human Reproduction: Biology, Biometry, Demography.* New York: Aldine de Gruyter.

4

Paternal Investment and Hunter-Gatherer Divorce Rates

NICHOLAS G. BLURTON JONES, FRANK W. MARLOWE, KRISTEN HAWKES, and JAMES F. O'CONNELL

Ideas about the evolution of human pair bonding[1] have centered around the role of men as provisioners of wife and children. The idea rings true for many of us, but in this chapter we present comparative data from hunting and gathering societies that argues against provisioning by males as a cause of pair bonding. Our results imply that we should look more closely at competition over sexual access as an influence on pair bonding in our species.

Several authors have suggested that hunting was a crucial factor in human evolution because it allowed males to provision females and offspring, increasing the number of offspring a female could bear and keep alive (Lancaster and Lancaster 1983). Males would then trade off effort invested in provisioning mate and offspring (parenting) against effort invested toward fathering a greater number of offspring by a variety of females (mating effort). If provisioning was effective, costs of desertion by males would be great. Males would not desert and the result would be an enduring pair. Much research has been provoked by this scenario, and many predictions were confirmed.

Research on mating systems in simple farming and herding societies (Borgerhoff Mulder 1988; Cronk 1991; Hames 1996) has been primarily concerned with understanding the occurrence of polygamy, monogamy, and polyandry. This literature draws attention to the readiness with which men convert wealth not to healthier children with higher survivorship but to greater numbers of wives. Among researchers on hunting and gathering societies, the economy closest to that envisaged for the "environment of evolutionary adaptedness"—the context in which male provisioning, monogamy, mate preferences, and the nuclear family are supposed to have evolved—the assumption that hunting primarily functions as provisioning by males has been vigorously debated (Hawkes 1993; Hill and Kaplan 1993).

Hawkes (1990, 1991, 1993) argues that hunting is a poor way to provision wife and children. In some ecologies gathering provides more energy per hour of effort than hunting, and in some, hunting and trapping small game gives much lower variance in offspring food intake, even after allowing for the effect of sharing meat from large game (Hawkes et al. 1991). Furthermore, hunters feed other men's children more than their own. Meat from large animals is widely shared, seemingly taking the form of a public good. The hunter is unable to restrict access to his catch, apparently unable to sanction those who take without giving in kind. A request is in order for clearer demonstrations of the route by which fathers or husbands make a difference to child survival and growth (when they do).

We began to analyze Hadza marriage and divorce because it seemed to offer data independent of our data on Hadza hunting and sharing (Hawkes et al. 1991) with which we could test for an influence of paternal provisioning. For instance, if male provisioning was important, and men stayed in a marriage because of the cost to their children from desertion, women with more small children should be less likely to get divorced (because smaller children are likely to be more vulnerable than older children to loss of paternal support). A similar argument would lead one to predict that divorced or widowed women with many small children were less likely to remarry than same-aged women with fewer small children. Buckle and colleagues (1996) presented positive results of such tests on North Americans and Europeans, supporting the paternal investment viewpoint. But thus far we have failed to produce any significant effects in such analyses of Hadza data. Negative findings do not make a convincing report, and further fieldwork is scheduled that will at least make their negativity more credible. Our analysis showed that despite the lack of evidence for an influence of provisioning on divorce and remarriage, Hadza were clearly living as couples. Very few individuals had more than one spouse at a time; many couples stayed together for more than the decade of our fieldwork; and many of these had been reported as married couples by previous fieldworkers. We turned to a comparative analysis.

Woodburn (1968b), emphasizing the ease with which a Hadza marriage is considered ended, reported a high divorce rate. In Blurton Jones et al. (1996) we attributed the supposed difference between Hadza and !Kung divorce rates to the difference between Hadza and !Kung children's contributions to their own food intake. Hadza children provide up to half their own daily requirement from age five onward. !Kung children seem to forage very little (Blurton Jones et al. 1994; Hawkes et al. 1995). We suggested that a father diverting resources from his children might have less effect on the survival of the children among the Hadza than among the !Kung. We reported census data showing that Hadza children's mortality was indeed no greater if their father died or divorced their mother, whereas death of mother had a striking effect. Thus costs of desertion were apparently low and could account for a higher divorce rate. Our analysis gave no attention to the opportunity to remarry, nor to the payoff that might accrue from a change in spouse.

Hurtado and Hill (1992) examined marital stability in the Ache and Hiwi. Although the effect of father upon child survival was much less among Hiwi than among Ache, Hiwi marriages were much more stable than Ache marriages. Hurtado and Hill sought to assess the tradeoff between benefits gained from continued paternal care and benefits from a new marriage. Divorce was assumed to lead to removal of paternal care from the children, at some cost to their survival ("father effect") and thus to diminish their contribution to their father's fitness. But it led, after successful but costly competition with other men, to a new marriage and new children. Hurtado and Hill assess the opportunity for a new marriage and new paternity by their measure "fertility units per male" (FU/m). This measure is obtained by multiplying the number of females age 15–40 by the total fertility rate (TFR), and dividing by the number of males age 20–55. Hurtado and Hill combine father effect, and fertility units per male, into a "parenting/mating index" that compares the effect of father on children's survival with the opportunity for new matings or added paternity. It turned out that although the effect of fathers on Ache children's survival was much higher[2] than the effect of Hiwi fathers, the difference in FU/male overwhelmed this effect. Among the Ache, where marriages are extremely unstable, opportunities for new matings, which FU/male aims to reflect, are much greater than among the Hiwi, and this apparently accounts for the difference.

Three points need to be made about the parenting/mating index. First, fertility units per male is similar to the "operational sex ratio," which has been proposed as a determinant of animal mating systems (Clutton-Brock and Parker 1992; Kvarnemo and Ahnesjo 1996). It indicates the strength of male-male competition for paternity. Second, for desertion to pay off, the prospective fertility of the new mate should exceed the continuing fertility of the current mate. The hidden assumption, that men are leaving less fertile (older?) wives for more fertile (younger?) ones, should be tested (e.g., Lockhard and Adams 1981) and examined for the further implication that men are seeking long-term relationships in which to recoup the gains of the new wife's greater reproductive value.

Third, father effect as measured by Hurtado and Hill is a good measure of father's cost of desertion but not necessarily of the size of male economic contributions. If loss of paternal care by a deserting father is offset by a willing stepfather, or by increased effort by the deserted mother, or by lengthened interbirth interval, desertion will not be associated with much increase in child mortality. But this is just what we need to measure to assess the father's cost of desertion. If care by another compensates for his lack of caregiving, his cost was low. This implies that economic contributions of men could be greater than indicated by this measure.

Comparisons that involve just two data points, like our !Kung-Hadza comparison and Hurtado and Hill's Ache-Hiwi comparison, can be informative but they are also dangerous. Predictions can be proved wrong with a two- case sample, but it is probably too easy for them to come out right. Here we will attempt the comparison with all four populations—Ache, Hiwi, !Kung, and Hadza. Is marriage stability predicted by the effect of loss of father upon children's survival, by his opportunity for new matings, or by the ratio of these two variables?

ETHNOGRAPHIC BACKGROUND

The 700–800 eastern Hadza occupy a 2,500 km^2 area in the Eastern Rift Valley, south and east of Lake Eyasi, in northern Tanzania.[3] The climate of this region is warm and dry. Annual rainfall is in the 300–600 mm range, falling in a six- to seven-month wet season (November–May). Vegetation is primarily mixed savanna woodland; medium/large animals are locally abundant. Ethnographic data on the eastern Hadza are available in the publications of James Woodburn (1968a, 1968b, 1979, 1988).

The language, Hadzane, has been studied by Woodburn and others, and recently by Sands (1995) and Sands and colleagues (1993). Linguists agree only that its connection to any other African language family is very remote indeed. Hadza must have remained culturally distinct from their neighbors (who currently represent the Bantu, Nilotic, and Cushitic language families) for many hundreds of years. At the beginning of this century, it appears that only the Hadza occupied this country (Obst 1912). They apparently lived entirely by hunting and gathering. Local incursions by non-Hadza pastoral and agricultural groups are recorded as early as the 1920s and have continued to the present (McDowell 1981; Woodburn 1988). Archaeological evidence suggests that farmers and pastoralists have been present for several centuries, hunter-gatherers far longer (Mehlman 1988; Mabulla 1996). During the past 50 years, various segments of the Hadza population have been subjected to government- and mission-sponsored settlement schemes designed to encourage them to abandon the foraging life in favor of farming. None of these schemes has been successful, and in every case most of the Hadza involved returned to the bush, usually within a few months. In each instance some Hadza avoided settlement and continued to live as full-time hunter-gatherers.

A summary of the daily cycle gives some feel for life in a Hadza bush camp. Between 7 and 9 A.M. people arise and wait for the cold to wear off; women sharpen and harden their digging sticks (sometimes helped by their children) and muster to go out to forage. Men leave, individually, for an early morning "walk about" (hunt) and move to "the men's place" on the edge of or just outside camp where those in camp spend the day. Small children face the question, "Will mother take me with her or leave me in the care of older brother?" Teenage girls decide whether to go with the women or stay home; teenage boys decide whether to go as "guards" for the women or stay home, often to leave later with a few friends. Between 9 and 11 A.M. the children in camp usually do some foraging. Between 11 A.M. and 1 P.M. they might forage more, or eat and play. The temperature reaches its daily high by 1 P.M. Between 1 and 3 P.M. everyone who is in camp tends to be resting in the shade. Between 3 and 5 P.M. the women come home, and children rush to get a share of the food they brought. Between 5 and 7 P.M. the temperature has fallen to pleasant levels and most people are at home. Children play vigorous games, forage some more, and if there are several teenage girls in camp singing and dancing will begin and last until 9:30 or 10 at night.

Late in the dry season men will organize and prepare themselves for a cold night in a hunting blind at a nearby waterhole or game trail. By 7 P.M. all but the men who left for the night are in their houses and around the fire. People eat an evening meal, and then visit and chat in each other's houses and fireplaces. On moonless nights an epeme dance may be held, in which all participate. Silence, but for coughs, the occasional crying child, once in a while a noisy domestic dispute, closely investigating hyenas, and distant comforting lions, lasts from late evening until next morning. Thus, while a couple shares a house, in which man and wife sleep along with their younger children, eat much of the food that each other acquires (including shares of meat from other men), and eat an evening meal together, their daytime lives are, as Woodburn reported (1968a, 1968b), noticeably separate.

During our observations in the 1980s less than 5% of the food of people on whom we collected behavioral and ecological data came from domesticated sources. The proportion was greater in some parts of Hadza country. During the 1990s hunting became progressively more difficult as interference by outside agencies continued and incursions by other lifestyles increased, and the habitat was degraded. The situation in 1997 indicates imminent submersion of the Hadza into a new lower rung of Tanzanian rural society.

The !Kung of northwestern Botswana and northeastern Namibia, and their lifestyle of the 1950s to 1970s, are now so well known to anthropologist readers as to need little introduction. As among the Hadza, couples share a house in which they sleep along with their younger children. Houses are clustered in small "camps" of from two to a dozen or so houses to which people return daily. Camps are moved frequently in the wet season, much less frequently in the dry season when few water sources are available. Little formality accompanies either marriage or divorce, but our reading of the accounts suggest that parental influences may be greater among the !Kung than among the Hadza.

The Ache of Paraguay are also becoming well known to anthropological readers (Hill and Hurtado 1996 and references therein). Their pre- settlement, full-time forager lifestyle was much more mobile than the life of the other populations discussed here. Small groups moved almost daily through the forest, clearing a new sleeping area each evening. Couples and their children shared a fire, but people lived in much greater proximity at these overnight camps than in a Hadza or !Kung camp. Upon settlement people lived in larger houses and, Hill and Hurtado comment, the previously very high divorce rate declined. While !Kung are known to have practiced occasional infanticide, and Hadza claim never to have heard of such a practice, Ache regularly used to kill one or more children upon the death of their father. Hill and Hurtado describe informants' interpretations of this practice.

The Hiwi of southwestern Venezuela have been studied under more settled conditions than the other three populations, although they still subsist in large part on hunted and gathered wild foods. People are more mobile in the dry season than the wet, leaving the two residential settlements for smaller bush camps for up to four weeks at a time. Hurtado and Hill (1992) note the endurance of Hiwi marriages.

PROCEDURE

The !Kung data reported here are from Howell (1979), with additions from Pennington and Harpending (1988). The Hadza data come from our own fieldwork from 1984 to 1995. In addition to extended stays for behavioral and ecological observation that fuelled many of our papers (e.g., Blurton Jones et al. 1996; Hawkes et al. 1997; Marlowe 1997; O'Connell et al. 1992) we have conducted a series of censuses and anthropometry sessions between 1985 and 1997. In 1992 and 1995, 120 different Hadza women were interviewed about their reproductive histories, with previous census data in hand to provide a check and prompts. These data were combined to give a record of marriages, divorces, remarriages, deaths and widowings, and births and deaths of children. Data from a census conducted by Lars C. Smith in 1977 are also used to identify the longest-lasting marriages.

Father Effect

Survival of Hadza children (less than 5 years old at the start of the census period) across the five-year periods 1985–1990 and 1990–1995 was calculated from the interviews. Table 4.1 shows the number surviving or dying among those whose father died or divorced their mother at any time during the five-year period, and among those whose father stayed with their mother. An earlier analysis of survival until 1991 of children under 5 in the 1985 census also showed no increase in survival when father was present (Blurton Jones et al. 1996).

Comparison among the four populations is not easy. Hurtado and Hill (1992:50) report father effect as offspring survivorship to adulthood with father divided by offspring survivorship without father, yet their table 1 gives a figure for

Table 4.1. Survival of Hadza children under 5 years of age whose fathers died or left their mother. (Mantel-Haenszel chi-square for association between father stay and child survive, controlling for observation period, = 0.001, $p = .975$)

	Child Survived	*Child Died*
1985–1990		
Father stayed	12	14
Father died or left	3	7
1990–1995		
Father stayed	13	9
Father died or left	12	5
Both Periods Summed		
Father stayed	25	23
Father died or left	15	12

Hiwi, which they say is based on survivorship to age five (1992:45). Pennington and Harpending (1988) report deaths as infants, and deaths as children. In demographic usage, infants are 0 to 1 year old, but these authors state that "children" means infancy to adulthood (1988:310). Our data on father effect among Hadza concerns survival through a five-year period by children age 0–5 at the beginning of the period. In most populations mortality declines sharply with age from birth to 1 year, rapidly from 1 to 5 years of age, and thereafter mortality is quite low. Hurtado and Hill's figures 1 and 2 show that the difference between survivorship of children with and without father continues to diverge slightly as the children grow beyond age 5. Thus comparing Ache survival to adulthood (age 15), !Kung survival to 1 or 15, Hiwi survival to 5, and Hadza survival from 0 to 5 and 5 to 10 combined may be less dangerous than at first appears. We discuss the vulnerability of our conclusions in the appendix to this chapter.

Fertility Units per Male

Hurtado and Hill (1992) took the number of females age 15–40, multiplied by the total fertility rate, and divided by the number of men age 20–55. Population age-sex structure for the !Kung from Howell (1979) and for the Hadza from Blurton Jones and coauthors (1992) allows us to compute the numbers of men age 20–55 and women age 15–40 (Table 4.2). In the appendix we show that the impact of altering the age groups included in this measure is slight.

Among the !Kung, the number of females can easily be extracted from Howell's table 12.1. Determining the number of males age 20–55 is not straightforward because Howell's table 12.2 gives 10-year age blocks with unusual starting ages. Inspection of the age pyramids diagrammed in her figure 2.6 suggests that the number within a block can be divided by the number of years to allow us to reconstitute numbers for our age blocks.

Marriage Stability

Hurtado and Hill report two measures of the stability of Ache and Hiwi marriages: (1) number of husbands reported by women of a given age and (2) proba-

Table 4.2. Fertility units per male (calculated as in Hurtado and Hill 1992: table 1).

Population	*Females 15–40 (N)*	*Males 20–55 (N)*	*Proportion of Females/Males*	*Total Fertility Rate*	*Fertility Units per Male*
Ache	122	108	1.129	7.8	8.81
Hiwi	18	25	0.720	5.4	3.89
!Kung	90	114	0.789	4.7	3.71
Hadza	138	134	1.029	6.2	6.385

Ache and Hiwi data from Hurtado and Hill 1992
!Kung female/male data from Howell 1979: tables 12.1 and 12.2
Hadza data from Blurton Jones et al. 1992.

bility of divorce by length of the marriage. Our aim is to examine marriage as the absence of desertion. The cost of desertion is in decreased fitness of offspring. Thus it makes most sense to examine rates of breakdown of marriages that have lasted long enough to produce a child. Consequently we prefer to ignore reported number of spouses, which is heavily influenced by the number of brief liaisons, usually early in adult life. Data on the number of husbands reported by Hadza women are not abundant, nor is their reliability impressive.

The data from the Hadza censuses are not directly comparable with the interview reports for the other populations. The Hadza data allow direct computation of crude annual divorce rates, which are very close to the rate reported by Woodburn (1968b) from his fieldwork in the early 1960s. Crude annual divorce rates are unsatisfactory for comparison across populations because they are strongly influenced by population age-structure. However, some approximations to probability of divorce by age of marriage can be obtained, and compared with figures from the !Kung, Ache, and Hiwi.

In Table 4.3 we show the divorce rate between 1990 and 1995 of Hadza couples who got married between 1985 and 1990 (marriages 0–4 years old), couples who were together in 1985 and still together in 1990 (marriages >5 years old), and couples who were listed in Lars Smith's 1977 census and were still together in 1990 (marriages >13 years old).

RESULTS

Is There a "Father Effect" among Hadza?

Blurton Jones and colleagues (1996) report no significant difference between survival of children whose fathers left after 1985 and those whose fathers were still with the mothers in 1991. There was a striking effect of loss of mother. The data in Table 4.1, for the periods 1985–1990 and 1990–1995, also give no significant indication of an effect of father's death or divorce upon young children's survival. No data on mother's death are shown because these are children whose life histories were obtained by interviewing their mothers in 1992 or 1995.

Is There a Father Effect among the !Kung?

Pennington and Harpending (1988) claim "The importance of male parental care for the survival of !Kung offspring is supported by the observation that infant mortality was significantly higher among offspring of women who had more than one husband." They also report, "At Ngamiland the risk of death of an infant whose mother married more than once (24%) is almost double that of an infant whose mother married only once (13%) . . . $p < .005$" (1988:312). They are thus suggesting a strong effect of fathers upon offspring survival, "almost double," but actually, as measured by Hurtado and Hill, the ratio of survivorship with father to

Table 4.3. Divorce rates of Hadza and !Kung.

	Hadza			
	Divorced 1990–1995	*Stayed Together 1990–1995*	*Probability of Divorce*	*Nearest !Kung Equivalent*
Got married between 1985 and 1990 (marriage 0–4 yrs)	11	17	.393 (11 of 28 marriages)	.373*
Married in 1985 and same spouse in 1990 (married > 5 yrs)	11	26	.297 (11 of 37 marriages)	.078 – .143†
Married in 1977 and same spouse in 1990 (married > 13 yrs)	8	25	.242 (8 of 33 marriages)	.030 – .080‡

* Probability of marriages less than 5 years old surviving the next 5 years. Howell's table 12.6 gives 323 marriages at risk, minus 15 deaths of husbands, for a total sample of 308. There were 115 divorces during the five-year period. 115/308 = .373.

† Probability of marriages that had lasted at least five years surviving the next five years: 150 marriages minus 10 husbands' deaths = 140. With 11 divorces, 11/140 = .078. Or, since the Hadza sample includes marriages that lasted much longer than 5 years, let us add in all subsequent !Kung divorces: with 19 divorces, 19/140 = .143

‡ Probability of divorce for marriages that had lasted 10 years (we bias the !Kung figures upward, to handicap our chance of showing a difference from the Hadza, in preference to choosing a limit of 15 years, which biases in favor of our expected result). 108 marriages minus 9 husbands' deaths = 99. With 3 divorces, 3/99 = .030. Or, adding in all subsequent divorces: 8/99 = .080.

survivorship without father is only a father effect of 1.14. Pennington and Harpending's table 2 allows us to calculate father effect on children as well as infants. Taking postmenopausal Ngamiland women who reported only one marriage we sum the number of offspring that died as infants and as children (57 + 81 = 138), and the number that survived childhood (194), to find 332 births of which 194/332 survived (.5843). For women who reported more than one marriage the figure is .4609. The ratio (father effect) is .5843 / .4609 = 1.27.

The survival of !Kung children to adulthood increases less with the presence of their father than the survival of Ache children increases when their father is present. But the effect of !Kung fathers on child survival is larger than the effect of Hiwi fathers. !Kung fathers' presence increases child survival to 1 year old slightly more than the presence of Hiwi fathers increases child survival to 5, and the effect of !Kung fathers on survival to adulthood is much higher than this. If the Hadza show no effect on survival of father's presence between 5 and 10, it is unlikely to appear between 10 and 15. We thus rank father effect as, highest to lowest effect: Ache > !Kung > Hiwi > Hadza.

Fertility Units per Male

Among the Hadza in our 1985 census there were 138 females age 15–40 and 134 males age 20–55. Hadza total fertility rate (TFR) was estimated at 6.2 (Blurton Jones et al. 1992). FU/male works out as 6.38 for the Hadza, about halfway between the figures calculated for the Hiwi and the Ache.

For the !Kung, Howell's table 12.1 gives 90 females age 15–40. We estimated 114 men age 20–55, for a ratio of .789 females per male. A TFR of 4.7 (Howell 1979) yields 3.71 FU/male. Using the TFR of 5.0 suggested by Blurton Jones (1994) for !Kung women living the forager lifestyle increases FU/male to 3.945, just higher than the figure for the Hiwi and substantially lower than those of the Ache and Hadza. These results are shown in Table 4.2.

Completing the Table: Parenting/Mating Index for the Hadza and !Kung

The !Kung and Hadza figures plus those from Hurtado and Hill's Table 1 are reported in Table 4.4. The fertility units/male (an index of mating opportunities), and the father effect (the factor by which a child's survival to adulthood increases with father's continued presence) are listed in the first two columns. The parenting/mating index is the ratio of these used by Hurtado and Hill to estimate the tradeoff men faced between remaining married and providing a father effect, and leaving to seek another mate.

Predicting Stability of Marriages

We can use the first three columns of Table 4.4 to derive simple predictions about marriage stability in the four populations from different hypotheses about desertion. All the hypotheses share the assumption (quite provisional and questionable) that marriage breakups primarily reflect desertion by males, although we know that sometimes women leave, or expel their husband. But among each of these populations women very seldom desert their offspring when they leave, or throw out, their husband; women usually keep the children with them (sometimes Hadza children stayed with their mother's mother for a while when their mother

Table 4.4. Marital stability and possible predictors. Marital stability is shown both as "divorce rate" and "staying" rate.

Population	*Fertility Units/Male*	*Father Effect*	*Parenting / Mating Index*	*Divorce Rate (1 = highest; 4 = lowest)*	*Marital Stability (1 = most stable; 4 = least stable)*
Ache	8.81	1.62	0.184	1	4
Hiwi	3.89	1.09	0.282	4	1
!Kung	3.71	1.27	0.342	3	2
Hadza	6.38	1.0	0.157	2	3

remarried). If costs of desertion (assessed by father effect) are the best predictor of marriage stability, then Ache men should desert least often, !Kung men a little more, and Hadza and Hiwi men should desert most often. If the parenting/mating index is the best predictor, then the !Kung should have the most stable marriages, followed by Hiwi, then Ache, with Hadza showing the least stability.

Stability of Marriages

As in many populations (see summary in Fisher 1989), Ache, !Kung and Hadza marriages are most at risk in their early years. Howell (1979:figure 12.1) and Hill and Hurtado (1996:figure 7.12) show a rapid decline in probability of divorce during the first 5 years of marriage. Howell's table 12.6 shows that after 5 years, divorce rates level off at between .02 and .07 per year (see Table 4.4). Hill and Hurtado's figure for precontact Ache shows a decline that reaches .05 between 5 and 6 years and decreases to almost zero by the eighth year of a marriage. However, their figure presents the results of a fitted logistic regression model, which might give a distorted impression of the prospects for the few lengthy marriages. Hill (personal communication) finds that Ache marriages that had lasted 5 or more years nonetheless break up at a rate of 19% per year. This annual rate of attrition will result in 65% of a cohort of marriages that have lasted 5 years ending in divorce by the end of the next 5 years.

Table 4.3 shows the divorce rate between 1990 and 1995 of Hadza couples who got married between 1985 and 1990 (marriages 0–4 years old), couples who were together in 1985 and still together in 1990 (marriages >5 years old), and couples who were listed in Lars Smith's 1977 census and were still together in 1990 (marriages >13 years old). Probability of divorce among Hadza marriages seems to be similar to that of the !Kung in the early years but subsequently is much higher.

The rate at which marriages break up after having lasted five years or more allows us to rank the Ache above the Hadza and the Hadza above the !Kung in terms of marital instability. Although we dismissed the use of Hadza accounts of numbers of previous spouses, the researchers on Hiwi and !Kung express confidence in their reports. This measure, the average number of spouses by the end of a woman's child-bearing career, allows us to rank !Kung (2.45 from figures in Howell's table 12.3, 1979:235) above Hiwi (1.7 from Hurtado and Hill 1992). Since the !Kung fall below the Hadza and Ache on the other measure, we rank Hiwi also below Hadza and Ache. Thus from highest divorce rate to lowest: Ache > Hadza > !Kung > Hiwi.

What Is the Best Predictor of Stability of Marriages?

Table 4.4 shows the values for father effect, fertility units per male, and parenting/mating index alongside the ranking of marriage stability. The best candidate for predictor of marriage stability (probability of divorce for marriages that have lasted 5 years) is fertility units per male. Marriages are less stable when there are more fertility units per male. There are several technical reasons for regarding this apparent relationship with caution and we discuss them in the appendix. There is no suggestion of support here for the importance of male parental care, and very weak support for prediction using the parenting/mating index of the tradeoff between care and mating opportunity.

DISCUSSION

We followed Hurtado and Hill 1992 (who in turn followed Maynard-Smith's mate desertion models) in examining (1) the effect of fathers upon offspring survival (parenting, cost of desertion), (2) opportunities for new matings (fertility units per male), and (3) the ratio of these two values, intended to display the relative balance of costs and benefits from desertion. Hurtado and Hill compared Ache and Hiwi and found that their parenting/mating index predicted divorce rate, whereas father effect did not. Here we added the Hadza and !Kung to the sample and showed that neither father effect nor parenting/mating index predicted divorce rate. Divorce rate was predicted by fertility units per male (and by both of its components—total fertility rate and reproductive adult sex ratio).

The view that higher costs of desertion lead to more enduring pair bonds received no support from this comparative analysis. Neither father effect, nor the ratio of father effect to mating opportunity (P/M index) predicted divorce rate. The results are difficult to reconcile with the widely accepted view that paternal provisioning favors pair bonding. This view fails to predict the observed association of higher divorce rates with higher numbers of "fertility units" per male. The measure "fertility units per male" is very close to the measures of "operational sex ratio," which biologists have found to be a good predictor of many features of mating systems (Kvarnemo and Ahnesjo 1996). It is regarded as a good measure of the strength of competition among males. This suggests we might consider monogamy as an outcome of male competition.

This result is surprising to those of us who have long believed in the unique importance of paternal care in the evolution of human pair bonding. We note, however, the many findings in the recent literature that cast doubt on the equally long assumed importance of paternal care in avian pair bonding. We note also that findings such as ours, and those of Hawkes (1990, in press), may open the way to much closer comparison with results of research on other primate breeding systems (Hrdy 1997; Manson 1997; Smuts and Gubernick 1992).

In the appendix we discuss many details of the measurements that could be thought to affect this conclusion. But we see one simple way to overturn our conclusion—adding more populations to the sample and showing that the association disappears. Other simple interpretations of our result are possible. (1) Perhaps ease of discovery of extramarital intercourse varies among these societies and the result reflects variation in ease of discovery, and a constant rate of retribution by aggrieved spouses. (2) Perhaps FU/m reflects the opportunity for men to obtain matings outside marriage, and such matings carry a constant risk of discovery and retribution by wives. Our finding would then reflect merely variation in "temptations and discoveries"! But these interpretations require an explanation for a spouse's retribution.

Alternatives to Paternal Provisioning Theory

If we remove paternal provisioning as an explanation for pair bonding, we create many orphaned observations. Can other theories account for them, and do they generate additional, distinct predictions? What are the alternatives?

Models offered by Hawkes, Rogers, and Charnov (1995) suggest that expenditure on competition, or mate guarding, will be extensive and an even distribution of resources is likely to follow. An even distribution might result in ceaseless "wife swapping," or a more static system, with fewer risks, perhaps especially where lethal weaponry is widely available (see Woodburn 1979). This might be enough to produce some semblance of pair bonding.

Pair bonding as a solution to male contests (not a new idea; e.g., see Symons 1979) draws attention to the social nature of marriage more forcefully than paternal provisioning has done. The knowledge and interest of individuals outside the couple is an obvious feature of marriage. Everyone knows who is married to whom, and tries to keep their information up to date. Are the bystanders' interests part of the mechanism that solves the conflict and maintains monogamy? Could the interests of "bystanders" help account for the persistence of marriage across a variety of economic systems (in which male opportunities to offer resources to females may vary widely)? Why should bystanders care who is married and who is single, and whether a couple is getting divorced? Both paternal provisioning and male competition theories offer quick, but differing, suggestions—who will be burdened with the "orphans" (a problem for their kin), whose mate might be attracted to the newly single people (a problem for all adults of reproductive age, and for kin of offspring at risk of desertion)? Who might be set in renewed contest against whom?

Female Support for a Conventional Solution to Male Contests

Most of us find it difficult to envisage human mating systems without female preferences. Would women have an interest in supporting a conventional solution to male contests over sexual access? Recent literature has commented on the disruption, occasional injury, and loss of time incurred by females as a result of male attempts at mating and competition for sexual access (Clutton-Brock and Parker 1995). Females might gain from mating with the most effective competitors, but this gain is offset by costs in time and accidental injury, and ability to time conceptions optimally. When female time is valuable, the benefit of fewer time-consuming disruptions might exceed the value of mating with the winners of the disruptive competition. Can we link the occurrence of pair bonding among birds and among humans to the high value of female time spent caring for and provisioning offspring? Elsewhere (e.g., Hawkes et al., chapter 11, this volume) we have pointed to the significance of food sharing between females and offspring as differentiating all human foragers from other primates. We linked this to a shift from exploiting resources which are easily exploited by juveniles to exploiting the abundant but hard-to-access roots, tubers, and nuts that human foragers use so much more than other primates. The woman's current infant, and to a greater or lesser extent all her previous offspring (her weaned pre-adult children), depend upon her foraging time. In this sense her foraging time, and her control over this time, may be much more reproductively valuable than that of other primate females. Interference thus becomes much more costly. Perhaps this makes female support of male mate-guarding conventions worthwhile. Our suggestion generates the expectation that women might prefer men who are better able to guard them and keep other men away (either by their ability in contests, or by their reputation and its effect on other men's readiness to concede to them). But these ideas imply that many females settle for lower-quality males than they might have obtained from continued competition. Our speculations call urgently for systematic modeling!

Female Preference for Providers

It has long been argued that females might prefer males who provide resources, and it has long been assumed that females are able to put this preference into effect. Males might then benefit from conforming to female preferences and, for example, compete for females by providing more resources. Does this lead us straight back to the paternal provisioning hypothesis? Would it give the same predictions as traditional assumptions about paternal provisioning? We think not, for two reasons. First, Hawkes's (1990) "showoff" model illustrates that it may pay males not to conform with female preferences for a provisioner where there are modest returns to effort seeking extra matings. Second, provisioning or child care given in competition for sexual access should vary with factors that affect the payoffs from effort to gain and maintain sexual access, such as female fertility, and the intensity of competition among males. Provisioning as paternal investment should vary with vulnerability of offspring and effectiveness of male care, and with male estimates of paternity. While paternal provisioning can account for the differences between stepfathers and biological fathers (Daly and Wilson 1987; and see Marlowe 1997 on Hadza stepfathers), it has difficulty accounting for the care that stepfathers do show. If childcare and/or provisioning is part of the bargain that maintains sexual access to a female, stepfathering is easily accounted for. Giving food or care in exchange for lasting sexual access may imply one kind of bargaining situation (perhaps similar to that described in Hewlett 1992). Giving food or care in proportion to its effect on offspring fitness suggests another, perhaps with more closely shared interests of males and females.

If marriages involve only mutual investment in offspring our options for accounting for the great number of marriages that break up before children are born are limited to guessing how long partners might wait to test fertility. If marriages involve a bargain over sexual access, then the early years of a marriage may involve assessment of various aspects of the bargain and its prospects. We find this suggestion the more likely of the two to provoke investigation.

If marriage does incorporate complicity in a conventional solution to male contest and/or constitutes some kind of bargain, then both partners will be interested in the bargaining position of the other, and in signs that the other will keep the bargain. Can some of the mate preference criteria tapped by widely used questionnaires be seen as indicators of bargain-keeping? If so, we might better understand the similarity between the sexes in the mate preference criteria that some readers find to be the most striking finding in mate preference studies.

CONCLUSION

If we loosen the grip of paternal provisioning on our thinking, we can attend to a wider array of behavior associated with pair bonds or marriage, and to a richer array of ways to account for variation in human mating systems. Anthropologists have long told us that marriage is a social phenomenon (Bell 1997), and psychologists have long told us that marriage is an uneasy bargain (e.g., Schoeninger and Wood 1969). Armed only with paternal provisioning theory we have been quite restricted in our exploration of these (Kerber 1994), and often tempted to dismiss them as describing "trappings of modern civilization" or "socially imposed monogamy" and so forth. Freed from paternal provisioning, and by paying more attention to male competition, we may find it possible to understand, even predict or derive, more of the complexities that anthropologists and psychologists have observed.

SUMMARY

1. We added two more populations (Hadza and !Kung) to the comparison of divorce rates among Ache and Hiwi reported by Hurtado and Hill (1992).

2. Divorce rate is not predicted by father's cost of desertion, nor is it predicted by either of two versions of Hurtado and Hill's parenting/mating index.

3. Instead, in this very limited sample of four hunter-gatherer populations, divorce rate is found to be higher when there are more "fertility units per male," a measure of the strength of competition among males.

4. We suggest that pair bonding be examined again as a solution to male-male competition.

ACKNOWLEDGMENT

We wish to thank the Tanzania Commission on Science and Technology for permission to conduct research in Tanzania. We thank several hundred individual Hadza for their patience and good spirits, and our field assistants Gudo Mahiya and the late Sokolo

Mpanda for their expertise and collegiality. We thank Lars C. Smith for introducing us to the Hadza and allowing us to use data from his 1977 census of the eastern Hadza, David Bygott and Jeannette Hanby for providing a home away from home and vital logistic facilities, Professors C. L. Kamuzora and Audax Mabulla of the University of Dar es Salaam, and numerous citizens of Mbulu and Karatu districts for help and friendship. The research was funded by the National Science Foundation, the Swan Fund, B. Bancroft, the Leakey Foundation (by a grant to Frank Marlowe), the University of Utah, and the University of California Los Angeles.

NOTES

1. We use "pair bonding" to refer to lasting cohabitation of a man and a woman. We attend primarily to ideas about why men stay in such a relationship. We pay little attention to female choice, even though its existence is quite apparent.
2. Although the Ache father effect is apparently primarily due to infanticide following desertion or death of the father, Hill and Hurtado describe Ache informants linking infanticide to the cost of providing for orphans.

APPENDIX: HOW IMPORTANT ARE THE WEAKNESSES IN THE STUDY? DEFINITION OF MARRIAGE

Comparative studies have many problems and this study is no exception. Do "married" and "divorced" mean the same in each population? Would a couple recorded as married in one population be recorded as married by a different ethnographer in a different population? All evidently attend to coresidence, and all seem to imply consensual intercourse, and a social recognition of these two features. In each society there appears to be a view that couples can be recognized by other individuals. There is some variation in what informants say about extramarital sex and jealousy, but strong constancy in reports of violence between men over women. Concepts of "legitimacy" vary. Among the Ache "secondary fathers" are recognized and seem to influence an orphan's survival prospects. Among the Hadza a woman's children by a previous husband quickly become named as "children of" her current husband.

Sampling

While the data on each population result from an immense amount of work by each team of fieldworkers, a sample size of four populations is still dangerously small. Probably other populations could be added to this comparison with limited data analysis by other ethnographers. One problem with this sample warrants a special caution. The Ache figures are very different from the other three. Do these differences have an undue influence on the result, the picture we get from the sample? Are divorce rates among hunters and gatherers really rather invariant, with the exception of the Ache? We cannot answer this question without a larger sample.

Measures of Marital Stability

Hurtado and Hill (1992) used two measures of marital stability, divorce rate and number of husbands reported by postreproductive women. There are problems with using number of husbands as a measure of marriage stability.

1. In 1996 Marlowe asked 17 women how many times they had been married. His impression was that, even more so with his larger sample of men, the older individuals omitted brief partnerships from long ago, which younger individuals seemed inclined to report. His data give no indication of an increase in number of husbands with a woman's age. Fifteen of these women were found in our census records. The record for ten of them showed the same number of spouses as they reported to Marlowe. Of the remaining five, four reported one less spouse than the record showed, and one reported more. These census records cover a period of 10 years, less than half a woman's reproductive career. Hadza women's reports of number of husbands appear to be substantial underestimates of the actual number.
2. A large proportion of Hadza women of postreproductive age remain unmarried after their husband dies or leaves them. If Hadza differ in this from other populations, then number of spouses reported will also be expected to be lower for Hadza women of postreproductive age.
3. Number of husbands includes those acquired by a widow. Thus the figure will be influenced by husband's mortality rates, and since these are associated with age, and with the age gap between husband and wife, it may also vary from one population to another.
4. Number of husbands is probably overweighted by the rate of dissolution early in a marriage. We argued that rate of divorce in marriages that had lasted long enough to produce children was the best test of a "costs of desertion" theory of divorce. Hadza and !Kung divorce rates differed more with respect to marriages that had lasted five years than they did among the "younger" marriages. Marriages tend to be at highest risk in their first to fourth year, and among younger individuals. Howell (1979) attributes some of the divorces among the !Kung to the tendency for women's first marriages to be at a very young age and to much older men. This is apparently not entirely at the girls' choice, and they frequently leave their older husband. We see little sign of social pressure on Hadza girls to marry a particular man (but in 1997 we witnessed two instances of girls being put under pressure to reach a decision between rival suitors "before violence broke out"), and age at first marriage appears to be greater for Hadza women than among the !Kung (although age at first birth seems to be very similar). These factors may account for the apparently lower tendency of Hadza marriages to break up in the first year or two.

If we had used women's interview reports of the number of husbands as our measure of stability we would have clustered the Hiwi (1.7 by end of reproductive career) and Hadza (1.5) very close together, with the !Kung (2.45 husbands reported by women over 45) a little higher, and the Ache (12.1 average of husbands for postreproductive women) as a distant outlier. This ranking suggests higher divorce rates are associated with higher father effect, the opposite of the paternal provisioning prediction.

Father Effect

The effect of fathers on children's survival has been measured in slightly different ways, although the problems of comparison between them are quite limited. Pennington and Harpending's evidence about the effect of !Kung fathers is rather indirect. They compared the infant and child mortality of children borne to women who had lost a husband (usually through death, they report) with that of women who had not lost a husband. Some of the effect may reflect simultaneous strikes by epidemics (killing husband and children but sparing the woman to survive to be interviewed!). Nor do we know whether the infant deaths preceded or followed the paternal deaths, or whether less healthy men get less able wives.

The link between father effect and paternal provisioning is not established for any of these populations. The Ache, with their pattern of food sharing and their high incidence of infanticide, might appear to offer a particularly poor example. However, Hill and Hurtado (1996) offer emic evidence that Ache men resented giving food to "orphans," and that the infanticide represented removal of the fitness loss that would result from feeding a dead man's children.

Father effect might underestimate the economic value of husbands because women must be presumed to allocate resources optimally between care and fertility. Thus when the father leaves, she may delay the next birth, and any shortfall in resources will then have less effect on current offspring than if she had continued bearing new offspring at her previous rate. This does not weaken the usefulness of father effect as a measure of desertion costs, but it does imply that resources she may have obtained from the father could have more effect on her fitness than our measure might be taken to indicate. If females allocate resources under their control between fertility and care, then, if we follow Smith and Fretwell's venerable (1974) model, a male who transfers resources to a female can have no effect on offspring survival, only on their number.

Hill (personal communication) suggested that father effect measured by absolute number of children lost would better reflect costs of desertion. If we make this recalculation, ranking on father effect does not change but parenting/mating index does, in a direction that counters the Hurtado and Hill (1992) finding: Hiwi

Table 4.5. Recalculating father effect as number of offspring lost by desertion.

Population	*Survivorship with Father*	*Survivorship without Father*	*Fertility*	*Father Effect (N of Children)*	*P/M Index*
Ache	.86	.53	7.8	2.57	.29
Hiwi	.57	.52	5.4	0.27	.07
!Kung	.58	.46	4.7	0.58	.16
Hadza	.48	.44	6.2	0.25	.04

(.07) have a lower parenting/mating index than Ache (.29) and should desert more readily, which they do not (Table 4.5).

Fertility Units per Male

Is fertility units per male a good measure of benefit from desertion? It measures the number of units of paternity available per male, and thus opportunity to gain paternity. This should be a good measure of opportunity and probability of returns from pursuing matings outside the marriage. But first, it does not directly measure the reproductive benefit to be gained by giving up the continuing fertility of the current wife for the fertility of a new wife. On average, over a span of, say, five years, these would be the same, unless men only leave their wife for a woman of higher fertility. This could happen on two time scales—he might desert a pregnant or lactating wife for one who is neither (the mirror image of the strategy suggested by Fisher [1989] in which a man is predicted to leave his wife just as she returns to fecundability). He might desert a wife who is nearing the end of her reproductive career for one who is at peak fertility, or has much of her career ahead of her (Lockhard and Adams 1981). Because we are dealing with populations that have broad-based age pyramids, with many more younger people than older, FU/m will tend to correlate with the number of younger females per male, so failure to specifically measure the benefit of new matings may not have greatly distorted the picture.

Second, TFR (total fertility rate) is a component of FU/m. If infant and child mortality rate varied among these populations, mortality might account for some of the variance in TFR and FU/m. Ache infant mortality appears to be lower than the Hiwi, !Kung, or Hadza rates, which are very similar to each other. If Ache infant mortality increased, replacement births would increase and raise TFR and thus Ache FU/m would be raised, and our correlation would remain.

Third, FU/m may be a good measure of the operational sex ratio (OSR) and male-male competition. OSR has often been measured by reproductive "downtime"—how much less of the time are females available for reproduction (fertility units, conceptions, not copulations) than males? For noncontracepting human females, in cultures where babies are suckled for two years or more, and where lactational infertility is found, high TFR must accompany a greater number of opportunities for fertilization. In such populations it seems reasonable to note the parallel between Hurtado and Hill's FU/m and Clutton-Brock and Parker's OSR.

Fourth, FU/m depends on the reproductive age span. We use Hurtado and Hill's span of 15–40 for women, but Hazda women's reproductive career would be better represented as 18–45. For the !Kung should we use the average age at last birth reported by Howell (age 34), or the much higher modified figure obtained by Blurton Jones (1994) for bush-living women who may have avoided the highest incidence of secondary sterility due to disease?

Fifth, the answer to the question of determining reproductive age span is even less obvious for men. If the measure is supposed to reflect competition, should it reflect the ages during which men are actually trying to compete? How do we determine this? Hurtado and Hill comment on age variation in men's ability as hunters, implying that this influences their competitive ability. Should we limit the age range to those producing viable sperm? This measure is difficult to obtain! If we determine it by the ages at which men are married, or at which they still have a prospect of getting married, this seems in danger of getting circular—we end up using the proportion that competed successfully as part of a measure of intensity of competition. We note that the evolution of menopause increased the number of men competing for each woman of reproductive age compared to when the reproductive spans of the two sexes were similar.

Would our results be different if we changed the age ranges? Most of the Hadza men age 55–65 were married. If FU/m is intended to measure the degree of competition for paternity among men "in the market," then perhaps we should include these men. There were 23 men age 55–65 (80% of them married). Adding these to our sample yields 157 men and an FU/m of 5.88. Although this is a substantial reduction, it leaves the ranking unchanged. Hadza FU/m still lies about halfway between the !Kung and Ache rates; this actually makes the relationship between divorce rate and FU/m more nearly linear.

Among the !Kung, Howell reported that men first marry in their late twenties. If we remove men age 20–25 (say 13 of the 25 men estimated to be age 20–29) then we have 90 women, 101 men, and a TFR of 4.7 results in a !Kung FU/m of 4.19. Then the association between FU/m and divorce rank would be perfect.

And finally, why does "fertility units per male" vary so much among these populations? Total fertility rate and reproductive age spans both contribute to this variation, and so does adult sex ratio. Are adult sex ratios in these small populations stable enough to affect reproductive strategies? Hurtado and Hill argue that the Ache and Hiwi figures have a time depth of at least 30 years but offer no explanation for them.

REFERENCES

Bell, D. 1997. Defining marriage and legitimacy. *Current Anthropology* 38:237–254.

Blurton Jones, N. G. 1994. A reply to Dr. Harpending. *American Journal of Physical Anthropology* 93:391–397.

Blurton Jones, N. G., K. Hawkes, and P. Draper. 1994. Foraging returns of !Kung adults and children: Why didn't !Kung children forage? *Journal of Anthropological Research* 50:217–248.

Blurton Jones, N. G., K. Hawkes, and J. F. O'Connell. 1996. The global process, and local ecology: How should we explain differences between the Hadza and the !Kung? In *Cultural Diversity in Twentieth Century Foragers,* Susan Kent, ed. Pp. 159–187. Cambridge: Cambridge University Press.

Blurton Jones, N. G., L. C. Smith, J. F. O'Connell, K. Hawkes, and C. L. Kamuzora. 1992. Demography of the Hadza, an increasing and high density population of savanna foragers. *American Journal of Physical Anthropology* 89:159–181.

Borgerhoff Mulder, M. 1988. The relevance of the polygyny threshold model to humans. In *Mating Patterns,* C. N. Mascie-Taylor and J. Boyce, eds. Pp. 84–102. Cambridge: Cambridge University Press.

Buckle, L., G. G. Gallup, and Z. Road. 1996. Marriage as a reproductive contract: Patterns of marriage, divorce, and remarriage. *Ethology and Sociobiology* 17:363–378.

Clutton-Brock, T. H., and G. A. Parker. 1992. Potential reproductive rates and the operation of sexual selection. *Quarterly Review of Biology* 67:437–456.

———. 1995. Sexual coercion in animal societies. *Animal Behavior* 49:1345–1365.

Cronk, L. 1991. Wealth, status, and reproductive success among the Mukogodo of Kenya. *American Anthropologist* 93:345–360.

Daly, M., and M. Wilson. 1987. Child abuse and other risks of not living with both parents. *Ethology and Sociobiology* 6:197–210.

Fisher, H. 1989. Evolution of human serial pair bonding. *American Journal of Physical Anthropology* 78:331–354.

Hames, R. 1996. Costs and benefits of monogamy and polygyny for Yanomamö women. *Ethology and Sociobiology* 17:181–200.

Hawkes, K. 1990. Why do men hunt? Benefits for risky choices. In *Risk and Uncertainty in Tribal and Peasant Economies,* E. Cashdan, ed. Pp. 145–166. Boulder: Westview Press.

———. 1991. Showing off: Tests of an hypothesis about men's foraging goals. *Ethology and Sociobiology* 12:29–54.

———. 1993. Why hunters work: An ancient version of the problem of public goods. *Current Anthropology* 34:341–361.

———. 2000. Big game hunting and the evolution of egalitarian societies. In *Hierarchies in Action: Cui Bono?* Center for Archaeological Investigations, Occasional Paper No. 27:59–83. Michael W. Diehl, ed. Southern Illinois University.

Hawkes, K., J. F. O'Connell, and N. G. Blurton Jones. 1991. Hunting income patterns among the Hadza: Big game, common goods, foraging goals and the evolution of the human diet. *Philosophical Transactions of the Royal Society of London* B 334:243–251.

———. 1995. Hadza children's foraging: Juvenile dependency, social arrangements, and mobility among hunter-gatherers. *Current Anthropology* 36:688–700

———. 1997. Hadza women's time allocation, offspring provisioning, and the evolution of long post-menopausal lifespans. *Current Anthropology* 38:551–577.

Hawkes, K., A. R. Rogers, and E. L. Charnov. 1995. The male's dilemma: Increased offspring production is more paternity to steal. *Evolutionary Ecology* 9:662–677.

Hewlett, B. S. 1992. Husband-wife reciprocity and the Father-infant relationship among Aka Pygmies. In *Father-Child Relations: Cultural and Biosocial Contexts,* B. S. Hewlett, ed. Pp. 153–176. New York: Aldine de Gruyter.

Hill, K. and A. M. Hurtado. 1996. *Ache Life History: The Ecology and Demography of a Foraging People.* New York: Aldine de Gruyter.

Hill, K. and H. Kaplan. 1993. On why males foragers hunt and share food. *Current Anthropology* 34:701–706.

Howell, N. 1979. *Demography of the Dobe Area !Kung.* New York: Academic Press.

Hrdy, S. 1997. Raising Darwin's consciousness; female sexuality and the prehominid origins of patriarchy. *Human Nature* 8:1–49.

Hurtado, A. M., and K. R. Hill. 1992. Paternal effect on offspring survivorship among Ache and Hiwi hunter-gatherers: Implications for modeling pair-bond stability. In *Father-Child Relations: Cultural and Biosocial Contexts,* B. S. Hewlett, ed. Pp. 31–55. New York: Aldine de Gruyter.

Kerber, K. B. 1994. The marital balance of power and quid pro quo: An evolutionary perspective. *Ethology and Sociobiology* 15:283–298.

Kvarnemo, C., and I. Ahnesjo. 1996. The dynamics of operational sex ratios and competition for mates. *Trends in Ecology and Evolution* 11:404–408.

Lancaster, J. B. 1997. The evolutionary history of human parental investment in relation to population growth and social stratification. In *Feminism and Evolutionary Biology,* P. A. Gowaty, ed. Pp. 466–488. New York: Chapman and Hall.

Lancaster, J. B., and C. S. Lancaster. 1983. Parental investment: The hominid adaptation. In *How Humans Adapt: A Biocultural Odyssey,* D. J. Ortner, ed. Pp. 33–69. Washington, D.C.: Smithsonian Institution Press.

Lee, R. B. 1979. *The !Kung San.* Cambridge: Cambridge University Press.

Lockhard, J., and R. M. Adams. 1981. Human serial polygyny: Observations and demographic evidence? *Ethology and Sociobiology* 2:177–186.

Mabulla, A. Z. P. 1996. Middle and later stone age land-use and lithic technology in the Evasi Basin, Tanzania. Ph.D. dissertation, University of Florida.

Marlowe, F. 1999a. Showoffs or providers?: The parenting effort of Hadza men. *Evolution and Human Behavior* 20 (6):391–404.

———. 1999b. Male care and mating effort among Hadza foragers. *Behavioral Ecology and Sociobiology* 46:57–64.

Manson, J. H. 1997. Primate consortships: A critical review. *Current Anthropology* 38:353–374.

McDowell, W. 1981. A brief history of the Mangola Hadza. Ms. prepared for The Rift Valley Project, Ministry of Information and Culture, Dar es Salaam, Tanzania.

Mehlman, M. 1988. Later Quaternary Archaeological Sequences in Northern Tanzania. Unpublished Ph.D. dissertation, Department of Anthropology, University of Illinois, Champaign-Urbana.

Obst, E. 1912. Von Mkalama ins Land der Wakindiga. *Mitteilungen der Geographischen Geselleschaft in Hamburg* 26:3–45.

O'Connell, J. F., K. Hawkes, and N. G. Blurton Jones. 1992. Patterns in the distribution, site structure and assemblage composition of Hadza kill-butchering sites. *Journal of Archaeological Science* 19:319–345.

Pennington, R., and H. Harpending. 1988. Fitness and fertility among Kalahari !Kung. *American Journal of Physical Anthropology* 77:303–319.

Sands, B. 1995. Evaluating Claims of Distant Linguistic Relationships: The Case of Khoisan. Ph.D. dissertation, University of California, Los Angeles.

Sands, B., I. Maddieson, and P. Ladefoged. 1993. The phonetic structures of Hadza. *UCLA Working Papers in Phonetics* 84:67–88.

Schoeninger, D. W., and W. D. Wood. 1969. Comparison of married and ad hoc mixed-sex dyads negotiating the division of a reward. *Journal of Experimental Social Psychology* 5:483–499.

Smith, C. C., and S. D. Fretwell. 1974. The optimal balance between size and number of offspring. *American Naturalist* 108:499–506.

Smuts, B. B., and D. J. Gubernick. 1992. Male-infant relationships in nonhuman primates: Paternal investment or mating effort? In *Father-Child Relations: Cultural and Biosocial Contexts,* B. S. Hewlett, ed. Pp. 1–30. New York: Aldine de Gruyter.

Symons, D. 1979. *The Evolution of Human Sexuality.* Oxford: Oxford University Press.

Woodburn, J. C. 1968a. An introduction to Hadza ecology. In *Man the Hunter,* R. B. Lee and I. DeVore, eds. Pp. 49–55. Chicago: Aldine.

———. 1968b. Stability and Flexibility in Hadza residential groupings. In *Man the Hunter,* R. B. Lee and I. DeVore, eds. Pp. 103–110. Chicago: Aldine.

———. 1979. Minimal politics: the political organization of the Hadza of north Tanzania. In *Politics and Leadership: A Comparative Perspective,* W. Snack and P. Cohen, eds. Pp. 244–266. Clarendon Press, Oxford.

———. 1988. African hunter-gatherer social organisation: Is it best understood as a product of encapsulation? In *Hunters and Gatherers,* T. Ingold, D. Riches, and J. Woodburn, eds. Vol. 1, pp. 31–64. Oxford: Berg.

5

Fertility, Offspring Quality, and Wealth in Datoga Pastoralists

Testing Evolutionary Models of Intersexual Selection

DANIEL W. SELLEN, MONIQUE BORGERHOFF MULDER, and DANIELA F. SIEFF

One of the greatest challenges for evolutionary anthropology is to account for the wide variation in human marriage and mating practices using Darwinian logic. Early studies of human marriage systems were strongly influenced by Emlen and Oring's (1977) theoretical model linking mating systems and resource distributions. Thus the strong associations of polygyny with marked differences in wealth and power among men (e.g., Betzig 1986; Chagnon and Irons 1979; Irons 1979) were seen as evidence that men commonly use their resource-holding power to monopolize women and render them unavailable to other men (e.g., Flinn and Low 1986). Over the years behavioral ecological models have broadened considerably. Recently, the potential for conflict between the sexes has been emphasized (Gowaty 1995; Smuts and Smuts 1993; Westneat and Sargent 1996). The notion of mating systems has also become problematic since sexual relations may take place beyond the so-called breeding pair. This chapter explores the impact of polygynous marriage on a variety of fitness indices in the Datoga of Tanzania and attempts to delineate some of the dynamics of sexual conflict in their marriage system.

Polygyny has been a topic of enormous interest to sociocultural anthropologists. Comparativists have elucidated many of the conditions in which polygyny obtains, but they have focused almost exclusively on men's strategies. Thus White and Burton (1988) attribute the causes of polygyny worldwide primarily to expansionary fraternal interest groups that capture women and bride-wealth through warfare. Similarly Spencer (1980) views polygyny in Africa as the consequence of men's attempt to differentiate themselves in wealth and power, often through gerontocratic processes. There are problems with such male-biased sociocultural approaches (Borgerhoff Mulder 1992b). Most notably, they do not look at how the dynamics of sexual conflict shed light on marriage systems. This is where an evolutionary model might be helpful.

From a biological perspective, polygyny almost inevitably has fitness advantages for males in any species. From the females' point of view however, its consequences may be quite different. Two sets of theoretical models have been used to explain the extent of polygyny in birds and mammals—one predicated on female choice, the other on male coercion (though both can interact; Searcy and Yasukawa 1989). These models have not been systematically explored in humans. The first assumes that females have at least some autonomy in their mating choices. In situations where males offer critical resources to females, co-mates are likely to suffer the cost of competition over these limited resources. According to the original polygyny threshold model (Verner and Willson 1966), females can compensate for (and thus offset) these costs by selecting as polygynous mates only those males offering more resources than eligible unmated males. The logic follows Fretwell and Lucas's (1970) ideal free distribution model (Vehrencamp and Bradbury 1984). The second family of models assumes that females' mating options are severely limited; in starkest terms, they are coerced by males. Even where there is no direct coercion, however, conflicts of interest between males and females can restrict the latter from fully compensating for the costs of polygyny (Clutton-Brock and Parker 1995). Additional accounts for the evolution and maintenance of polygyny can be proposed by dropping various assumptions of the above models. For example, females might suffer no costs from sharing their mates, or they might accrue advantages from the presence of other females (Altmann et al. 1977).

Tests of evolutionary models have been made only in a handful of human populations, but the findings so far are intriguingly variable. In some cases there is support for a female choice model, as among East African pastoral and agropastoral populations (Borgerhoff Mulder 1992b) and the Yanomamö (Hames 1996), where the costs associated with polygyny are low. In other contexts a male coercion model seems more compelling, for example in some Australian (Chisholm and Burbank 1991) and West African populations (Strassmann 1997) where there are generally high fitness costs to polygynous marriage. In yet other cases it appears that the reproductive costs associated with polygyny are recouped in the second generation, as in Josephson's (1993) study of the Mormons. Elements of co-wife cooperation have also been examined (Chisholm and Burbank 1991; Irons 1983). The outstanding issue now is not to differentiate between the two types of model because coercion by men and judicious choice and strategy by women coexist in most if not all human populations. Rather, it is to identify the strategies of each sex, and in particular to determine the mechanisms whereby marital status affects the various components of fitness (Brabin 1984; Sellen 1995; Strassman 1997).

Thus there remains a need for further empirical tests of the evolutionary significance of human polygyny. Our investigations of the fitness costs of polygyny, and the mechanisms whereby these costs might be mediated, are based on the Datoga, a pastoral Tanzanian population. For several reasons, pertaining primarily to the considerable economic autonomy of women (at least in contrast to many other East African pastoral populations), we hypothesized that polygyny in this population would entail no, or only very limited, costs.

THE STUDY POPULATION

The population studied occupies an area containing a wide variety of arid vegetative communities and terrain (Figure 5.1) in the Eyasi and Yaeda basins. Rainfall averages 300–500 mm per year (Tanaka 1969) and is bimodal, falling in November to December (short rains) and April to June (long rains). There is substantial year-to-year variation in total rainfall. Herds of cattle, sheep, and goats are either used to provide raw materials for household implements and milk, blood, fat, and meat for the diet, or they are sold to generate cash for the purchase of maize, cloth, shoes, women's jewelry, tobacco, honey (for brewing beer), and veterinary medicines. Maize cultivation has been attempted by a few households since at least the 1960s (Tomikawa 1978), but productivity is extremely low today. The Datoga are relatively poor among East African pastoralists (Sellen 1995; Sieff 1995), child mortality rates are high (Borgerhoff Mulder 1992a), and data on morbidity, child growth, and adult body size strongly suggest high rates of infection and undernutrition (Sellen 1999a; Sellen 1999b; Sellen 2000).

Marriage and family formation involves a complex system of cattle exchanges and bride-wealth which, though typical of other East African pastoral groups, gives women considerably more autonomy than appears to be the case elsewhere (see also Klima 1964). First, although all women marry, elopement, desertion, divorce, and remarriage occur rather frequently. For example, just over half of 399 Datoga women questioned reported having chosen their current husbands themselves, and one-third of these women were in second or higher-order marriages (Borgerhoff Mulder 1992a); interestingly, divorce and remarriage do not lower overall reproductive output in this population. Second, though bride-wealth is minimal (a single non-negotiable heifer) a so-called dowry gift *(dug bataid)* of between 1 and 13 cattle is made to the bride by her parents (Klima 1970) (Borgerhoff Mulder 1991). In an area of the world where women's property rights are usually curtailed (Dahl 1987), this is remarkable. Our observations suggest that women retain rights of ownership to these animals; that is, they are not subsumed into the husband's herd. Furthermore, Klima (1964) notes that women with large dowry herds have significant economic power in the household.

All adult women are married, 85% in polygynous unions and 35% as the first-married wife within a polygynous union. There are no recognized rankings of seniority among co-wives, other than the general respect that usually accompanies increasing age, and Datoga tradition states that all wives be treated equally. At any

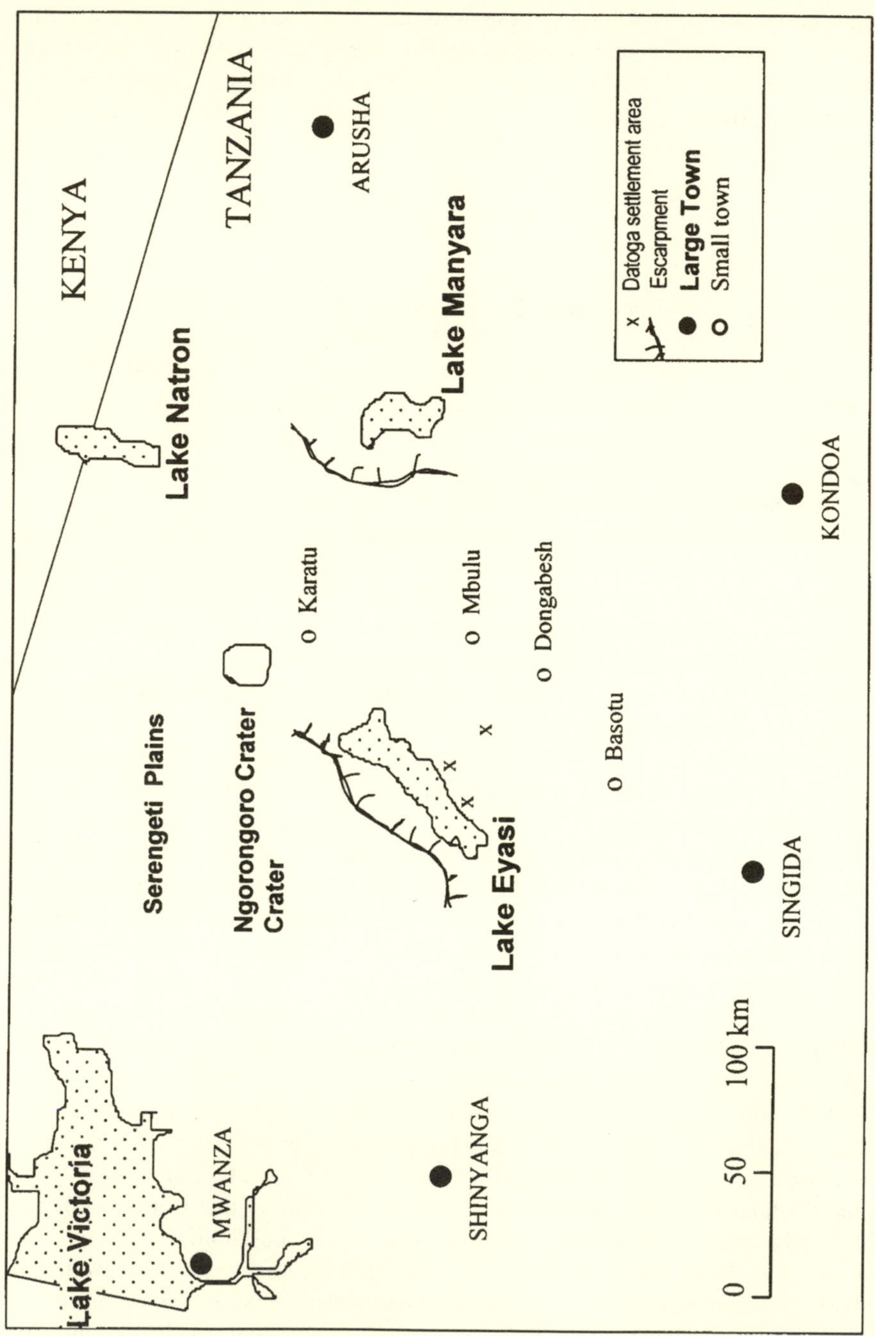

Figure 5.1. Map indicating the location of the communities studied in the Lake Eyasi and Yaeda basins.

given time, 40% of families are polygynous, with individual men marrying up to eight wives. Within polygynous families, a single wife and her living children form the smallest domestic unit (the *ga*). Each wife is expected to provide for the needs of her own children. Her contribution to the health and survival of her children depends on the milk of her own cows (see "Women's Wealth" below), on the amount of maize allocated to her by the husband, on her own labor contributions in secondary food processing, childcare, and on the products of her own work. These tasks include milking and watering livestock, collecting water and fuel wood, grinding the maize (by hand), processing milk products and cooking, and occasionally herding. In addition to caring for their own children, co-wives take turns cooking for their husband and his visitors.

A household consists of one or a group of marital units who share living structures and a common herd; in some cases several independent households occupy a single homestead. The Datoga regard the senior man in each household as the household head, and the household herd is referred to under his name. There may be other adult men in the household who run their livestock in with those of the senior man. These are usually married sons, unmarried brothers, or recently married brothers of the senior man who have not yet set up their own independent households. Even though individual ownership rights (sometimes anticipatory) are recognized, this combined herd is emically referred to as a distinct group of livestock more or less accessible to all household members, all of whom help out with livestock management duties. For analysis, we will refer to this as a household herd. For all practical purposes one can equate any individual man's wealth with his household's wealth. Where several men share a household and do not differentiate their herd, they may be thought of as having similar wealth in livestock.

There is substantial variation among households in their size and livestock holdings. Even though wealthier households contain more and larger families, wealth per capita increases with absolute wealth in livestock across households. Such variability in absolute and relative livestock holdings means that male household members clearly differ in their potential for offering resources to prospective wives. Indeed the level of polygyny achieved by household heads is weakly correlated with current household wealth in livestock. There are also temporal variations in wealth, presenting a problem for analysis, which we address in the discussion.

THE HYPOTHESIS

The available ethnographic evidence suggests a female choice model could account for the practice of polygyny among the Datoga. Fewer constraints apply than in the Kenyan Kipsigis where women's marital choices are essentially made by their parents, where economic autonomy of women has been (until very recently) minimal, and where divorce and remarriage is forbidden (Borgerhoff

Mulder 1990). Directly or indirectly, Datoga co-wives compete for access to the food resources produced in their households. One way for a woman to minimize reproductive costs associated with polygyny might therefore be to enter a polygynous marriage with a rich man, or to leave a poor man should he take additional wives. If such strategies are successful, then all women's marriages should follow an ideal free distribution with respect to fitness outcomes, and empirical tests should reveal few differences among women of different marital status.

The logic of this theoretical reasoning is challenged by field observations of conflicts among some co-wives. These suggest an alternative hypothesis that fitness costs might be observed among at least some women with co-wives. Furthermore, these costs may be experienced unequally with respect to wife rank (the order of marriage to the present husband in relation to other wives) or the number of co-wives in the union. In this paper we look only at the latter, since marital rank provides less information about the arrangements within families.

METHODS

Anthropometric, socioeconomic, and demographic studies were conducted at several semipermanent settlements around Lake Eyasi and in the Yaeda Basin between 1987 and 1996. For this analysis, we triangulated findings from various data sets collected and examined as described below. Statistical analyses were performed using either SAS (SAS Institute 1989) or SPSS (SPSS Inc. 1993) on a personal computer.

The Demographic Study

Reproductive histories were collected from women living at eight semi-permanent settlements between 1987 and 1989 (Borgerhoff Mulder 1992a). The demographic sample consists only of women who were in their first or second marriages. The measures analyzed here are based only on a woman's current marriage, if it had lasted more than one year; this helps to ensure reliability of the data since details were cross-checked with husband and wife. Women were aged either according to their reported birth year, or on the assumption that their first marriage occurred when they were 18 years old, the median age at first marriage. Demographic indicators were calculated from data on 103 women of childbearing age, and 28 who had completed reproduction, defined as either reaching 49 years of age or not having produced a child within the previous five years. The date of birth of each live-born child was established through retrospective demographic interviews and reference to local event calendars. The year and season of death was determined for those who subsequently died.

Marital status was measured as the number of a woman's living and co-resident co-wives. Even within the current marriage a woman's marital status can change, whenever her husband marries or one of her co-wives deserts or dies. Accordingly, for yearly hazards of fertility (data not presented here) and child mortality, an annual measure of marital status was used. For measures averaged across years (e.g., production of surviving offspring) a modal measure of marital status was used, calculated as the most common number of co-wives a wife experienced in her current marriage.

Household wealth was estimated from information collected by structured interview at one or more points between 1987 and 1989. It was measured as the total number of animals in the husband's household herd (see above). Livestock numbers are expressed in Tropical Livestock Units (TLU), a measure by which cattle, sheep, and goats can be tallied in terms of their mutual exchange value. By means of this index households were categorized as being richer (upper tercile), medium (middle tercile), or poorer (lower tercile).

The Growth Study

Longitudinal data on the growth status of all children under 3.5 years of age with no younger siblings were collected at three semipermanent settlements in 1992 as part of a prospective study of growth and diet (Sellen 1998). The initial anthropometric status of the youngest child of 86 mothers from 62 families clustered into 41 households is examined here. Analyses of covariance were performed to test for associations between children's growth status, marital status of the mother, and indicators of household wealth while controlling for the age and sex of children.

The same observer (DWS) took all anthropometric measures following standard procedures (Frisancho 1990; Gibson 1990; Jelliffe and Jelliffe 1989). Year and month of birth of children measured were obtained from interviews with parents or other family members, using standard crosschecking methods (Blurton Jones et al. 1992; Borgerhoff Mulder 1992a; Pennington and Harpending 1993). Informants were asked to place the date of birth of each child on a local calendar of events (Sellen, Sieff, and Borgerhoff Mulder 1993). Measures of recumbent length, weight, age, and sex of each child were used to derive standardized measures of achieved growth by comparison to the appropriate reference sample in the CDC/NCHS/WHO tables (Department of Health Education and Welfare 1977a, 1977b). The relative growth performance of any child at the time of measurement was expressed in terms of deviation from the appropriate reference value: Z-score = (Observed Reference$_{age, sex}$)/s.d. reference. The weight-for-age Z-scores (WAZ) and length-for-age Z-scores (HAZ) for all children for whom a reliable age and height were obtained were calculated using a computer program (CDC 1991).

Marital status of the mother was measured as the number of a woman's living and co-resident co-wives at the time of observation. All of the mothers in this sample were in their first or second marriage and had been married to their current husband for at least a year. An indicator of household wealth was calculated from the size of the domestic herd using structured interviews at 34 of the 41 households

(62 children from 46 families). The domestic herd is that portion of the total herd that is kept at the homestead and is available to the women and children living there. It is distinct from an additional portion of the herd, which, in the case of some households (11 in this sample), was kept at "cattle homes" *(ged dug)* by warrior-class males. Since these animals are not directly available to the household members, they were not included in estimates of household wealth in livestock. Household wealth was measured as TLU and households were categorized into terciles based on the average size of the domestic herd in 1992.

The Study of Women's Wealth

Within households, individual women have some livestock that are strictly their own; they also have different kinds of rights to livestock within their husband's household herd. Data on these internal herd breakdowns (Sieff 1995) are based on 141 women, living in 74 different households (68 women interviewed in 1993; 82 interviewed in 1996). The information from the two surveys was pooled for comparisons across women of different marital status. Two sorts of data are used here. First, the total number of animals in the woman's husband's herd at the time of the interview was determined. By this method, women could again be ranked in terciles according to their husband's household wealth. Second, three categories of livestock are considered as "women's wealth" for the purposes of this study. Based on elaborate indigenous terms we were able to distinguish livestock given to a woman on her marriage by her natal family *(dug bataid),* livestock in her sons' herds *(dug geshaded),* and those livestock allocated for her use by her husband *(dug end).* We adopt this procedure because these are the stock with which a woman provisions herself and her immediate family.

RESULTS

Reproductive Success

We examined the number of offspring successfully raised to their fifth birthday in relation to the modal number of co-wives a woman experienced in her current marriage in the two demographic samples. We use this as an index of reproductive success since most mortality occurs prior to the fifth birthday (Borgerhoff Mulder 1992a). The result was quite unexpected. Among women of childbearing age, those in marriages with a single co-wife showed a lower rate of production of surviving offspring than women with two co-wives (Figure 5.2); all pair-wise comparisons between samples were significant. A similar pattern was observed in the postmenopausal sample, although even when women with two or more co-wives were combined the difference was marginally significant ($F_{2,24} = 3.10$, $p < 0.06$), possibly because of the small sample size.

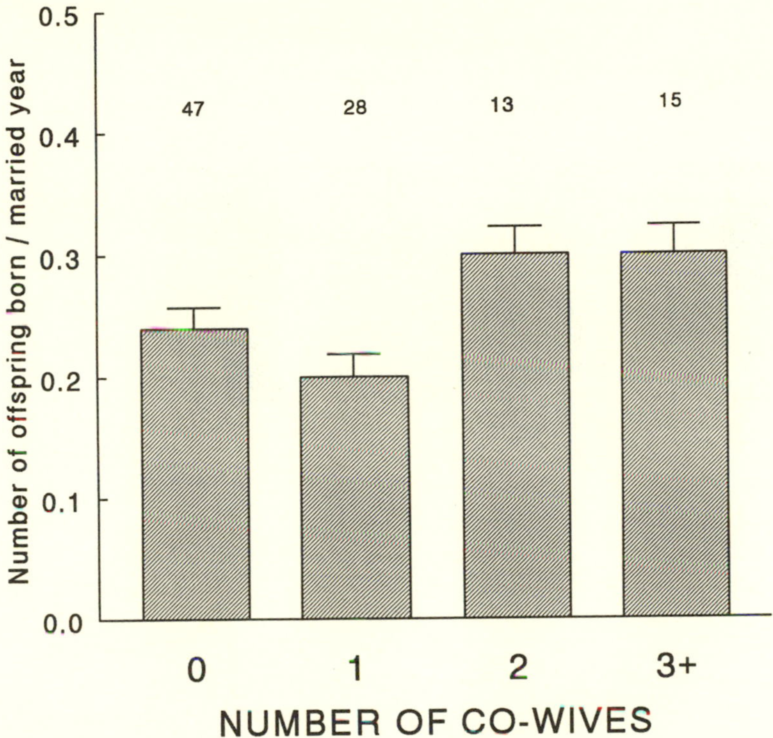

Figure 5.2. Surviving offspring born per married year to currently childbearing women according to modal number of co-wives (n = 103 women). Analysis of variance shows main effects of number of co-wives ($F_{3,98} = 3.86$, $p = 0.012$). Bars represent means and standard errors. Numbers above bars indicate sample sizes.

Child Growth and Mortality

Variation in two outcome measures of growth performance, length for age and weight for age, was examined for associations with the current number of co-wives. This measure of marital status was included as a main effect in an initial general linear model along with sex of the child and birth order (first- or later-born) as dichotomous control variables, age in months as a covariate, and all two-way interactions. Children measured were small for their ages in comparison to international references. Only child's age and number of mother's co-wives were significantly associated with the child's length and weight at the time of first measurement (Figure 5.3). Those children born to women with one current co-wife showed poorer growth than all others did, similar to the pattern for reproductive success. Pair-wise comparisons of these children to those in each other category were not significant.

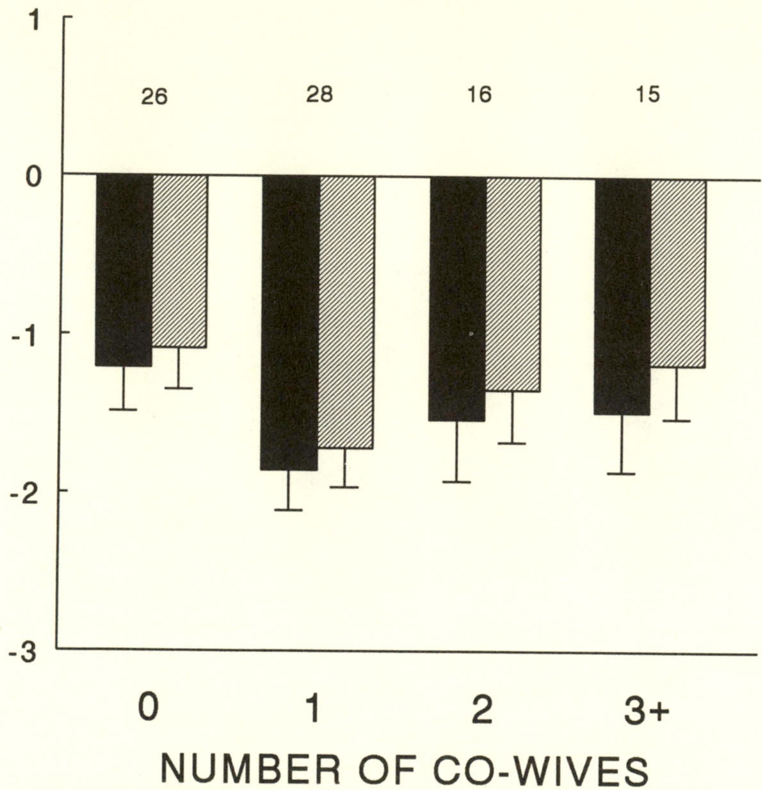

Figure 5.3. Growth status of young children, 0–3.5 years, according to number of co-wives of the mother (n = 86 surviving children). Bars represent estimated residual means and standard errors after adjusting for age and sex of child. Numbers above bars indicate sample sizes. Median lengths and weights of American children would fall on the $y = 0$ reference line. Analysis of covariance shows main effects of number of co-wives (HAZ: $F_{4, 76} = 5.625$, $p = .001$; WAZ: $F_{4, 86} = 4.017$, $p = 0.005$) and child's age at measurement (HAZ: $F_{1, 76} = 5.231$, $p = .025$; WAZ: $F_{1, 85} = 4.787$, $p = .032$), and no significant interaction of these effects.

The risk of a live-born child dying before his or her fifth birthday was examined in relation to the marital status of the mother at the child's birth. Data were combined for menopausal and currently childbearing women. Although the probability of death was highest among children of mothers with a single co-wife (0.31, compared to 0.27 [no co-wives], 0.21 [2 co-wives], and 0.23 [>2 co-wives]), a logistic regression model showed that number of co-wives was not a significant predictor of child mortality. Thus the length and weight deficits of children born to women with a single co-wife found in the prospective growth study are not matched by differences in child mortality in the retrospective demographic study. However, greater mortality among the possibly poorer-growing children of women with a single co-wife is indicated when the sample is stratified by wealth (see below).

Effects of Wealth

There was wide variation in wealth of the households of which the women in our samples were members. For women in the demographic sample, point estimates of household wealth in livestock varied up to 30-fold (sample of 115 households; Borgerhoff Mulder 1992a). Among a subsample (n = 20) of households in which child growth was studied, mean monthly domestic herd size varied 20-fold (Sellen 1995). Similarly Sieff (1995), using a more precise method of livestock enumeration, found that point estimates of total herd size varied 35-fold in a sample of 37 households. Importantly, polygynous unions tend to be more common and larger in wealthier households. One consequence is that a higher proportion of monogamous women in the population are married to poor husbands, while polygynously married women tend to be married to richer husbands. In the sample of women for whom women's wealth (as defined above under "Methods") was recorded, married women in richer households had more livestock than married women in poorer households did (Figure 5.4). Furthermore, in the medium and poorer categories women with more co-wives had fewer livestock of their own. This result suggests that the costs of polygyny may be more marked among women married in poorer households, prompting a reanalysis of the data by wealth of households. Three wealth strata were constructed for each sample to identify interactions between numbers of co-wives and access to livestock resources in the associations with reproductive rates, child growth, and child mortality.

For currently childbearing women the effects of household wealth and modal number of co-wives on the rate of production of surviving offspring were examined (Figure 5.5). Women with a single co-wife produced fewer surviving offspring per married year in the two lower wealth categories, but not in the richest category, and the interaction term was significant (see legend).

Significant effects of the number of co-wives on growth scores were observed only among children in poor households, where low weight was associated with children born to mothers with one co-wife (Figure 5.6). The wealth pattern is interesting. Child growth scores tended to be highest in households of medium wealth or richer households with many co-wives.

Mortality risks prior to the fifth birthday were examined in relation to the marital status of the mother at the time of the birth. Children of married women in poor households were at highest risk (Figure 5.7). Furthermore, although child mortality was elevated among women with a single co-wife in all wealth strata, this effect was only significant when the woman was married to a man in a poor household.

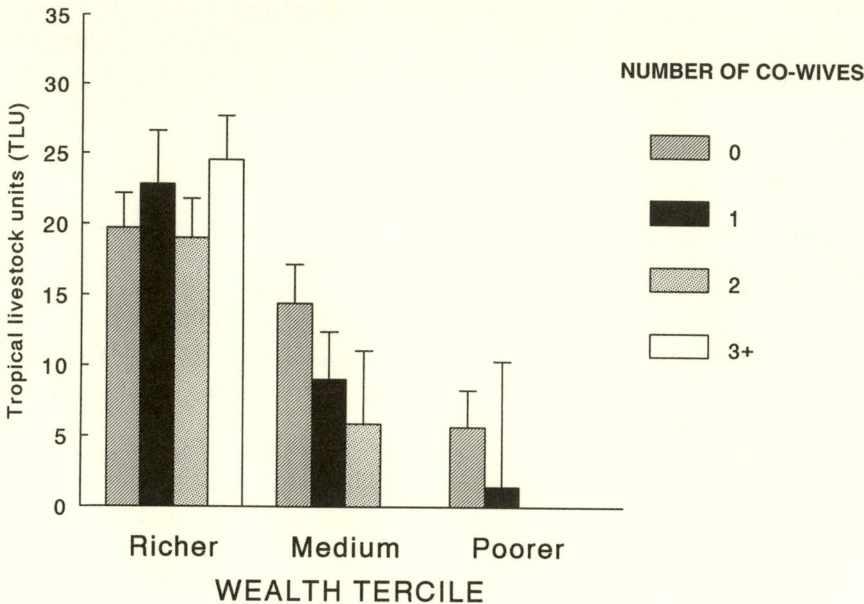

Figure 5.4. Women's wealth in relation to household wealth and number of co-wives (n = 141 women). Bars represent estimated means and standard deviations. Numbers above bars indicate sample sizes. Women are categorized according to the reported size of the household herd at interview (richer tercile, >39 TLU; medium tercile, 14–39 TLU; poorer tercile, <14 TLU). Contrasts in women's wealth by co-wife status are significant only within the medium wealth category ($F_{2, 28} = 3.773$, $p = 0.032$)

DISCUSSION

An Explanation for the Findings

Taken together these data suggest that some but not all women in polygynous marriages suffer fitness costs in terms of both offspring quantity and quality. Women married to men with a single co-wife produce fewer surviving offspring per year spent married than do other women, and their children grow more poorly during the first three years of life. The possible causes of this rather surprising pattern become clearer when we incorporate into the analysis differences in wealth among households. We consistently find that the costs associated with having a single co-wife are more marked among women married to men in poor households. In some analyses (reproductive success) we show clear interaction effects between wealth and marital status, whereas in others (growth and mortality) we show that the co-wife effect is restricted to poorer contexts. We conclude first that some women in the population are unable to make marriage choices that fully mit-

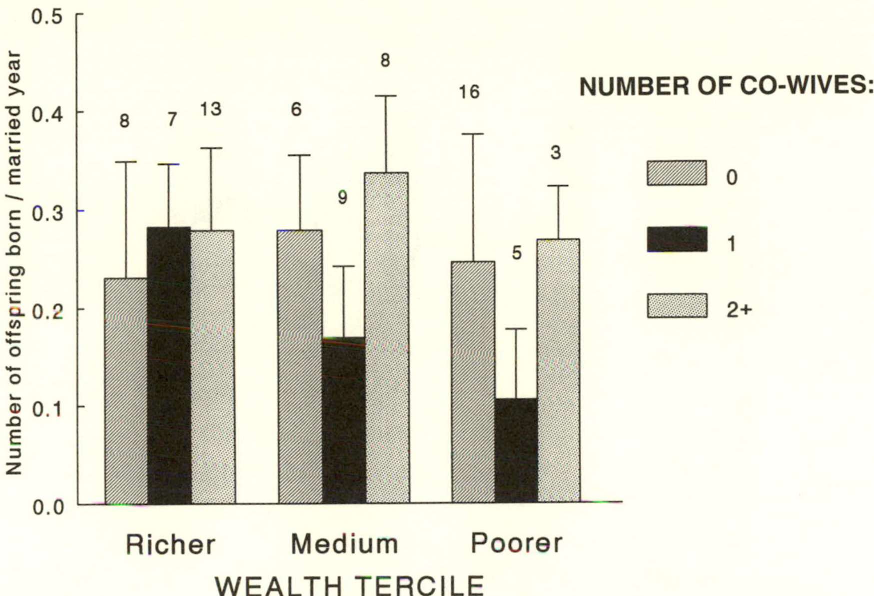

Figure 5.5. Surviving offspring born per married year to currently childbearing women according to modal number of co-wives and household wealth (n = 75 women). Bars represent means and standard errors. Numbers above bars indicate sample sizes. Wealth is measured as the reported size of the household herd at interview (richer tercile, <60 TLU; medium tercile, 21–60 TLU; poorer tercile, <20 TLU). Women with two or more co-wives are combined because of small samples. Analysis of variance shows a main effect of number of co-wives ($F_{2,65} = 6.06$, $p = 0.004$) and an interaction of co-wife and wealth effect ($F_{4,65} = 2.78$, $p = 0.034$). The main effect for wealth is marginally significant across all wealth strata ($0.05 < P < 0.10$). The effect of number of co-wives is not significant in the richer households ($F_{2,25} = 0.85$, NS), is marginally significant in the poorer households ($F_{2,20} = 3.16$, $p = 0.063$), and is significant in the households of medium wealth ($F_{2,19} = 10.50$, $p = 0.008$).

igate the costs of polygyny, and second that these costs are mediated through behavioral and physiological mechanisms that compromise young children's growth and increase child mortality rates.

Why might this be? It is likely that resource stress contributes to the deleterious fitness outcomes for women with a single co-wife. Critical household resources that must be shared among co-wives include *(i)* the principal food sources, livestock and grain; *(ii)* more direct forms of paternal investment, such as the husband's labor and any cash he may have; and *(iii)* gifts from outside the household made directly into the husband's herd. A basic problem of allocation among co-wives exists. Indeed, we can show that a woman really does have limited access to livestock if she is married into a poor household or one of medium wealth (especially

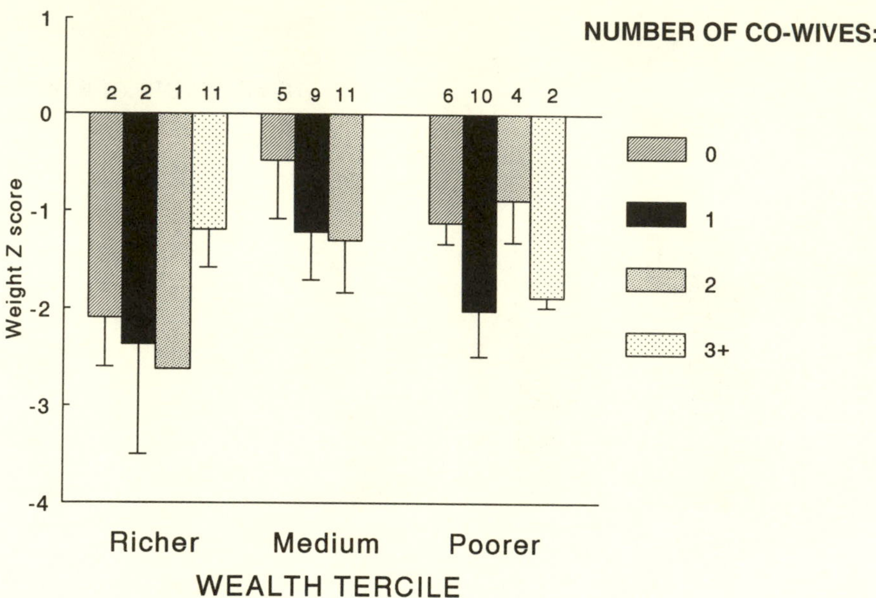

Figure 5.6. Young child growth performance in relation to number of co-wives and size of domestic herd (n = 86 children 0–3.5 years of age). The distribution of heights for age is very similar to the distribution of weights for age, shown here. Bars represent estimated residual means and standard errors after controlling for sex of the child and age at measurement. Numbers above bars indicate sample sizes. Wealth is measured as the average size of the domestic herd during 1992 (richer tercile, >30 TLU; medium tercile, 12–30 TLU; poorer tercile, <12 TLU). Analysis of variance across all wealth strata shows that after controlling for the general decrease in growth scores observed among surviving Datoga children over this age range, the main effect of wealth is significant for WAZ ($F_{3,63} = 3.974$, $p = 0.012$) and marginally significant for HAZ ($F_{3,56} = 2.520$, $p = .069$). The effect of wealth disappears after controlling for co-wife status of the mother at the time of measurement. Overall, the number of co-wives is not a significant main effect for either measure of growth after controlling for household wealth and age of the child; the interaction of wealth and number of co-wives is not significant. No data are available for mothers from households of medium wealth with three or more co-wives. However, the number of co-wives is significantly associated with child weights in the poorer households ($F_{3,17} = 3.648$, $p = 0.025$). Although within each wealth stratum, child growth appears to follow a pattern of decrease and then increase with the number of co-wives in the household, sample sizes are inadequate for drawing a firm conclusion about this.

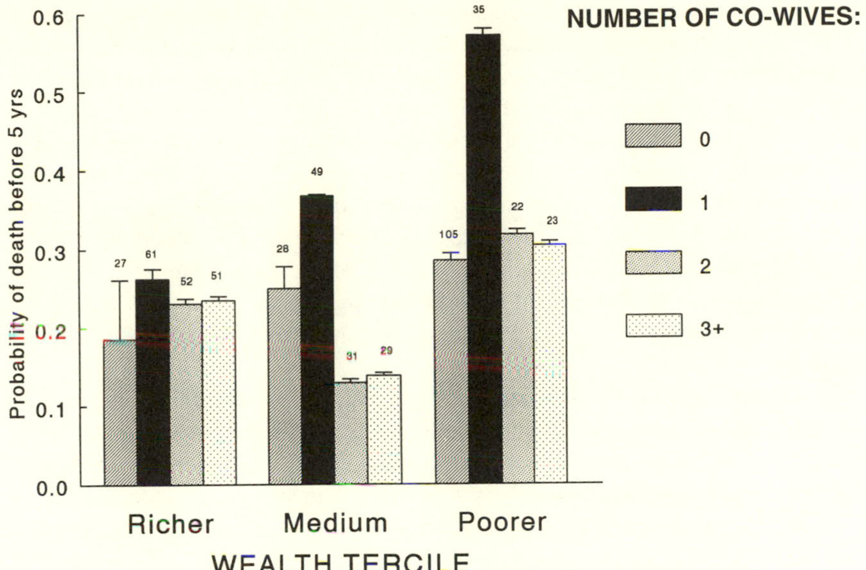

Figure 5.7. Risk of a live-born child dying before his or her fifth birthday according to number of co-wives and household wealth (n = 513 children with wealth data). Bars represent means and standard errors. Numbers above bars indicate sample sizes. Wealth is measured as the reported size of the household herd at interview (richer tercile, >65 TLU); medium tercile, 28–65 TLU; poorer tercile, <28 TLU). Logistic regression, combining women with two or more co-wives, shows a significant effect of number of co-wives (Wald statistic = 13.31, df = 2, P = 0.001) and wealth (Wald statistic = 8.37, df = 2, P = 0.015). Log likelihood values show that the effect of number of co-wives is significant only in the poorer households (2LR = 9.38, df = 3, p = 0.025), though the wealth/co-wife interaction effect is not statistically significant.

if she has co-wives; Figure 5.4). It is therefore plausible that direct access to critical food resources, particularly the milk and meat products of animals classified as "women's wealth," underlies the fitness differentials we identify.

However, the observation that fitness indicators do not decline monotonically with number of co-wives is initially puzzling in light of this explanation, and it forces us to question whether resource stress is indeed the only explanation for the pattern reported here. One alternative explanation we should consider is co-wife cooperation, for which there is considerable indirect evidence in our results. First, with respect to the production of surviving offspring, the fact that women with more than one co-wife prosper even in poor households suggests effective co-wife cooperation under such circumstances. Since there are plenty of opportunities for mutual labor assistance among women in Datoga households, such cooperative strategies may be important in mitigating the risks of child mortality among co-wives married to poor husbands, at least when there are more than two co-wives. Second, when all wealth categories are combined, women with two (and three or more) co-wives have significantly more surviving children than those in other categories, possibly indicative of positive co-wife interactions at all wealth levels.

The second alternative explanation for the high mortality and growth reductions of children born to at least some polygynously married women is disease. Isaac and Feinberg (1982) and Roth and Korup (1988) have proposed that there is increased mortality in such households because of greater exposure to infectious disease. Since this hypothesis (at its simplest) predicts a monotonic increase in mortality with number of co-wives, it is also not well supported among the Datoga.

In summary, among the rich, marital status is largely irrelevant for fitness outcomes. In poorer households monogamously married women prosper, most likely because they do not have to share their husbands' wealth. However, if women married to poor husbands find themselves with more than a single co-wife, they seem to be able to mitigate the costs of resource stress in some way, possibly through cooperation.

Proximate Factors

Polygyny has until recently been thought to affect demographic outcomes more through depressing fertility than affecting mortality. All early work pointed to reduced fertility outcomes (Culwick and Culwick 1939; Dorjahn 1959), a pattern commonly attributed to either the large spousal age differences among polygynously married women and their spouses or to the spread of sexually transmitted diseases among multiple wives. Though not presented here, logistic regressions showed no effects of any measure of marital rank, or spousal age differences, on Datoga women's fertility. As reported, the varying fitness outcome we see results from child mortality. The challenge now is to identify how numbers of co-wives, in conjunction with resource shortages, affect child survival.

At a more proximate level, differential child survival may result from differences in nutrition, susceptibility to infection, and maternal time allocation to childcare and competing tasks reflecting differences in workloads and household food security. Children in many traditional populations and developing nations are likely to grow poorly because mothers are too busy to provide high-quality childcare (especially critical during periods when children have illnesses that cause diarrhea and loss of appetite) or lack the time and ingredients to prepare an adequate weaning diet (Brown et al. 1995; McGuire 1991; McGuire and Popkin 1989). Furthermore, growth faltering among young children is an indicator of increased risk of death (Martorell and Habicht 1986; Pelletier et al. 1995) and increased risk of reduced adult body size and functional capacity in many contexts (Allen 1990; Beaton et al. 1990; Martorell 1985, 1989; Martorell et al. 1994). We suspect that polygyny and poverty, particularly when they act in conjunction with each other as they do in this population, are likely to affect child outcomes through a similar suite of mechanisms (see also Sellen 1995).

Differences in mortality rates among children of mothers of different marital status, though not statistically significant across the sample, are consistent with the differences in observed growth. Most child mortality occurs before age five in this population (previously estimated at about 20% of all births [Borgerhoff Mulder 1992a], but shown to be 26% for this more reliable sample). Some of these deaths stem from underlying causes that may not be under the direct influence of maternal behaviors (e.g., congenital malformations, malaria, and other infections). Nevertheless, an evolutionarily significant proportion is most likely attributable to the interaction between infection and factors such as frequency and duration of breastfeeding, quality of weaning foods, and childcare arrangements (Tomkins and Watson 1989). Earlier work shows that Datoga mothers vary greatly in their breast-feeding and weaning practices (Sellen 1998); in addition, those with poorly growing children tend to breastfeed their infants longer but less frequently (Sellen, unpublished data). Therefore, where there are few household resources and just two co-wives, childcare and feeding may be less adequate, resulting in higher levels of undernutrition and infection among children and increased lactational amenorrhea among mothers (mediated by continued breast-feeding and diminished maternal energy balance).

Potential Problems with the Data and Analysis

Some important methodological limitations to our study should be considered when drawing inferences about Datoga women's marital decisions. Although our three samples overlap, the sampling frame varies, and the data were collected at various times up to six years apart; in addition, slightly different methods were used for measuring marital status and wealth.

With respect to marital status, whereas in the growth study current marital status was used to structure comparisons between women, in the demographic study either the marital status of the woman at the time of the focal child's birth or the modal marital status she experienced in her marriage was used. We justify this approach on the grounds of using the measure most synchronic to the fitness outcome of interest. With respect to household wealth, growth outcomes are related to domestic herds whereas reproductive outcomes are related to total livestock holdings. The rationale for this is that the size of the domestic herd best captures the availability of nutritional resources to mothers immediately preceding the time their young children were weighed and measured, whereas the total livestock holding more likely reflects the resources available to women during their marriage to the current husband. The consequence for the analysis is that the wealth tercile ranges are not the same in each study. Nevertheless, since domestic and total livestock holdings are closely correlated, we maintain that the use of incommensurate terciles to reflect wealth rank is preferable to the use of commensurate but less appropriate indices of resource availability.

Several other problems arise from the practical challenges of studying African pastoral populations in general (Sellen 1996) and from the specific difficulty of incorporating the full complexity of the Datoga socioecological system in our analyses. Ideally, the relationship between poor child growth and increased mortality should be tested for each individual. However, it is difficult to implement follow-ups of sufficient sample size and duration to relate long-term survival to early anthropometry in this type of population. Unstable residence and high rates of household migration complicate longitudinal work and data analysis. Of 124 households (containing the families of 135 men) visited by one of us (DWS) between May 1989 and December 1992, 34 (27%) arrived in the Eyasi area during the study period and 51 (41%) had moved on by the end. A further 14 households (11.3%) moved from, and then returned to, the study area during this period.

Measures of wealth are inevitably complicated in pastoral populations by the temporal stochasticity in herd sizes and the complexity of changes over the household cycle (Borgerhoff Mulder and Sellen 1994). Also, given the high levels of sharing of food and labor within and among households, we remain very unclear about the net associations between absolute wealth in livestock (some measure of the total value of livestock owned by members of a household), relative wealth in livestock (the same measures, but divided by the numbers of persons, or adult-equivalent consumers, in the household), the time and energy expended in work, and actual food intakes of individual household members. Indeed, the relationship between child growth and household wealth may be related to variations between wealth strata in dependency ratios and *relative* household wealth, both of which affect labor organization and thus the ability of mothers to care for children, *within households.* Whereas absolutely richer households often contained a high proportion of unmarried or widowed adults, middle wealth households tended to achieve a balance in the ratio of adult caretakers to young children and livestock per capita that was more favorable to child growth (for more discussion, see Sellen 1995). Moreover, the complex pattern of shared ownership of a household herd blurs the functional distinctions between the wealth of individual men and the wealth of the households of which they are key members. By explicitly recognizing the close linkage of husband's and household's wealth in our analysis, we have modeled women's marital choices as contingent on the broad conditions within potential husband's households.

Finally, tests of the polygyny threshold model should examine women's marital decisions based on the available choices among men at the time they married, as in the study of polygyny among the Kipsigis (Borgerhoff Mulder 1990). This is much harder to do in a population as mobile as the Datoga, where it would be nearly impossible to know what the pool of men or women was for any given marriage.

The Female Choice Model

Given these problems, it is intriguing that such consistent patterns emerge. The observation that fitness costs are relatively low among women with many co-wives is consistent with the polygyny threshold model and may be explained by the fact that these women are in most cases married to wealthy men, or into wealthy households. Even where women are married polygynously to poor men, they manage to offset these costs if they have more than one co-wife with whom to cooperate (see Chisholm and Burbank 1991 for more evidence of women's compensatory strategies). However, insofar as women in poorer households with a single co-wife do suffer severe fitness costs, we can conclude that at least some assumptions of the polygyny threshold model are violated. This would be consistent with Searcy and Yasukawa's (1989) "partial compensation" model. Apparently, some women are not able to "choose" optimal marriages at the time they are eligible. Why might this be?

There are several possible constraints on women's optimal choices. First, there is parental choice. We might expect that women in marriages to which they reportedly had "eloped" without parental consent would be more likely to end up in favorable marital circumstances, but this is not supported by the data; "stolen" marriages show patterns that are not statistically differentiated from those presented here. Similarly women in their first marriages (over which parents may be expected to exert greater control) might be more likely to end up in unfavorable marriages, for example, polygynously married to men in poor households; this again is not supported by the data.

Second, we need to recognize that all marital choices are made with imperfect knowledge. Not only are a husband's future marriages unknown, but the size of his household's herd is highly volatile (see the point about stochasticity, above); it is difficult for a woman to know whether or not that herd will continue to grow or collapse over time. Still, since this uncertainty affects all women equally, it cannot precisely explain the single co-wife effect in the Datoga, though it can explain the absence of a strict polygyny threshold.

Third, there is the issue of broader constraints. Very few women, irrespective of whether or not it is their first marriage, enter the marriage market entirely free from set constraints by kin, clan, and household. Men show considerable concern over their sisters', classificatory sisters', and daughters' marital arrangements and often try to restrict or encourage particular marriages or even extramarital affairs. We have observed many incidents where tensions arise over marital choices and alliances. Conflicts of interest within pastoral households are endemic, and they interfere with any simple optimality analyses (Borgerhoff Mulder and Sellen 1994), including the polygyny threshold model.

Fourth, it is possible that a woman's marital status influences the assistance she gets from her natal home. On the one hand this may compensate some women for the costs of an unfavorable marital outcome. On the other hand, we cannot discount the possibility that withdrawal of assistance from natal kin is actually one of the mechanisms through which the costs are mediated. The data presented here show that junior wives in poorer households have fewer livestock of their own. This is evidence against the natal kin-compensation hypothesis but, in the absence of information about the resources available in the natal home, we cannot evaluate the natal kin-retrenchment hypothesis. Yet another possible dynamic that we have not considered in this analysis is that husbands' allocations *(dug end)* to their wives tend to compensate for low dowry (Sieff 1997). Clearly, stronger interpretations of these patterns of fitness differences may emerge from further clarification of these dynamics.

CONCLUDING REMARKS

We are woefully lacking in comparative data on the fitness consequences of polygyny across a range of African pastoralists, let alone other groups, and it would be premature to draw broad inferences from a handful of cases. Nevertheless the present results suggest that we have identified another polygynous society in which many women do not achieve an ideal free distribution with respect to fitness payoffs through the exercise of marital choices. In some senses the result is surprising. Where coercion predominates (e.g., the harem societies described in Betzig 1986), or where co-wives are ranked in seniority as in Mormons and some West African societies, we expect marked fitness costs. Among the Datoga, by contrast, where women enjoy considerable autonomy with respect to marriage and livestock, we had expected there would be few indications of fitness costs, as predicted by the female choice model. In another sense, however, the Datoga result is not surprising. Datoga polygyny conforms in many ways to Spencer's model (1980), in which polygyny is clearly an outcome of competitive processes among men upon which women have little impact. Clearly the plight of polygynously married women, and the strategies open to them, lie at the heart of intersexual competition.

SUMMARY

1. Anthropologists generally attribute polygynous marriage to competition among men, but human evolutionary ecologists are now interested in the interplay between models predicated on male coercion and female choice.
2. It is very difficult to investigate this dynamic in human populations because of the paucity of data on the fitness consequences of polygyny across different human populations.

3. We used data from three related investigations conducted over a nine-year period to address the mechanisms whereby polygyny is maintained among Eyasi Datoga pastoralists of Tanzania.

4. Given the apparent marital autonomy enjoyed by women in this community, we predicted on the basis of female choice models that we would find few indications of fitness costs among polygynously married women.

5. Contrary to these predictions, the results indicate that Datoga women do not achieve an ideal free distribution with respect to fitness payoffs through the exercise of marital choices. In particular, women with a single co-wife produce fewer surviving offspring, and their children grow more poorly in the first three years of life.

6. The possible causes of this unexpected pattern become clearer when we show that the fitness costs associated with having a single co-wife are most marked among women married to poor men. These costs are shown consistently for several different fitness indicators.

7. Our results suggest mechanisms whereby marital status affects fitness in this population. First, the costs of polygyny are mediated through reduced access to livestock. Second, a variety of behavioral and physiological sequelae of poverty negatively affect young children's growth and survival. Third, co-wife cooperation can mitigate the costs of competition over resource access in some circumstances.

8. We conclude that fitness costs are appreciable for some women in polygynous unions. Although the female choice model can explain some aspects of the persistence of polygyny in the Eyasi Datoga, we now need to investigate further the factors that constrain Datoga women's choices if we are to better understand the marriage system.

REFERENCES

Allen, L. 1990. Functional indicators and outcomes of undernutrition. *Journal of Nutrition* 120:924–932.

Altmann, S. A., S. Wagner, and S. Lenington. 1977. Two models for the evolution of polygyny. *Behavioural Ecology and Sociobiology* 2:397–410.

Beaton, G., A. Kelly, J. Kevany, R. Martorell, and J. Mason. 1990. Appropriate uses of anthropometric indices in children. United Nations Administrative Committee on Coordination Sub-Committee on Nutrition State-of-the-Art Series Nutrition Policy Discussion Paper.

Betzig, L. L. 1986. *Despotism and Differential Reproduction.* New York: Aldine.

Blurton Jones, N., L. Smith, J. O'Connell, K. Hawkes, and C. Kamuzora. 1992. Demography of the Hadza, an increasing and high density population of savanna foragers. *American Journal of Physical Anthropology* 89:159–181.

Borgerhoff Mulder, M. 1990. Kipsigis women prefer wealthy men: Evidence for female choice in humans. *Behavioural Ecology and Sociobiology* 27:255–264.

———. 1991. Datoga pastoralists of Tanzania. *National Geographic Research and Exploration* 72:166–187.

———. 1992a. Demography of pastoralists: Preliminary data on the Datoga of Tanzania. *Human Ecology* 20:383–405.

———. 1992b. Women's strategies in polygynous marriage. *Human Nature* 3:45–70.

Borgerhoff Mulder, M., and D. Sellen. 1994. Pastoralist decision-making: A behavioral ecological perspective. In *African Pastoralist Systems: An Integrated Approach,* E. Fratkin, K. Galvin, and E. Roth, eds. Pp. 205–230. Boulder: Lynne Rienner.

Brabin, L. 1984. Polygyny: An indicator of nutrional stress in African agricultural societies. *Africa* 54:31–45.

Brown, K., H. Creed de Kanashiro, and K. Dewey. 1995. Optimal complementary feeding practices to prevent childhood malnutrition in developing countries. *Food and Nutrition Bulletin* 16:322–339.

CDC. 1991. Epi-Info. Atlanta: Centers for Disease Control and Prevention. Chagnon, N. A., and W. Irons. 1979. *Evolutionary Biology and Human Social Behavior: An Anthropological Perspective.* North Scituate, Massachusetts: Duxbury Press.

Chisholm, J., and V. Burbank. 1991. Monogamy and polygyny in southeast Arnhem Land: Male coercion and female choice. *Ethology and Sociobiology* 12:291–313.

Clutton-Brock, T. H., and G. A. Parker. 1995. Sexual coercion in animal societies. *Animal Behaviour* 49:1345–1365.

Culwick, A. T., and G. M. Culwick. 1939. A study of population in Ulanga, Tanganyka Territory. *Sociological Review* 31:377–379.

Dahl, G. 1987. Women in pastoral production. *Ethnos* 53:246–279.

Department of Health Education and Welfare. 1977a. *NCHS Growth Curves of Children, Birth–18 Years United States.* Vol. 165. Series 11. Washington: DHEW Publication No. (PHS) 78–1650.

———. 1977b. *NCHS Tables of Growth, Birth–18 Years, United States.* Vol. 124. Series 11. Washington.

Dorjahn, V. R. 1959. The factor of polygyny in African demography. In *Continuity and Change in African Cultures,* W. Bascom and M. Herskovits, eds. Pp. 87–112. Chicago: University of Chicago Press.

Emlen, S. T., and L. W. Oring. 1977. Ecology, sexual selection, and the evolution of mating systems. *Science* 197:215–223.

Flinn, M. V., and B. S. Low. 1986. Resource distribution, social competition, and mating patterns in human societies. In *Ecological Aspects of Social Evolution,* D. I. Rubenstein and R. W. Wrangham, eds. Pp. 217–243. Princeton: Princeton University Press.

Frisancho, A. 1990. *Anthropometric Standards for the Assessment of Growth and Nutritional Status.* Ann Arbor: University of Michigan Press.

Fretwell, S. D., and H. L. Lucas. 1970. On territorial behaviour and other factors influencing habitat distribution in birds. *Acta Biotheoretica* 19:16–36.

Gibson, R. 1990. *Principles of Nutritional Assessment.* New York: Oxford University Press.

Gowaty, P.A. 1995. Battles of the sexes and origins of monogamy. In *Partnerships in Birds,* J. Black, ed. Pp. 21–52. Oxford: Oxford University Press.

Hames, R. 1996. The costs and benefits of monogamy and polygyny for Yanomamö women. *Ethology and Sociobiology* 17:1–19.

Irons, W. 1979. Culture and biological success. In *Evolutionary Biology and Human Social Behavior: An Anthropological Perspective,* N. A. Chagnon and W. Irons, eds. Pp.257–272. North Scituate, Massachusetts: Duxbury Press.

———. 1983. Human female reproductive strategies. In *Social Behavior of Female Vertebrates,* S. L. Wasser, ed. Pp. 169–213. New York: Academic Press.

Isaac, B., and W. Feinberg. 1982. Marital form and infant survival among the Mende of rural Upper Bambara Chiefdom, Sierra Leone. *Human Biology* 54:627–634.

Jelliffe, D., and E. Jelliffe. 1989. *Community Nutritional Assessment with Special Reference to Less Technically Developed Countries.* New York: Oxford University Press.

Josephson, S. C. 1993. Status, reproductive success, and marrying polygynously. *Ethology and Sociobiology* 14:391–396.

Klima, G. 1964. Jural relations between the sexes among the Barabaig. *Africa* 34:9–19.

———. 1970. *The Barabaig: East African Cattle Herders*. New York: Holt, Rinehart and Winston.

Martorell, R. 1985. Child growth retardation: A discussion of its causes and its relationship to health. In *Nutritional Adaptation in Man,* K. Baxter and C. Waterlow, eds. Pp. 13–30. London: John Libbey.

———. 1989. Body size, adaptation and function. *Human Organization* 48:15–20.

Martorell, R., and J.-P. Habicht. 1986. Growth in early childhood in developing countries. In *Human Growth: A Comprehensive Treatise.* Vol. 3: Methodology: Ecological, genetic and nutritional effects on growth, second ed., F. Falkner and J. Tanner, eds. Pp. 241–262. New York: Plenum Press.

Martorell, R., L. Kettel Khan, and D. Schroeder. 1994. Reversibility of stunting: Epidemiological findings in children from developing countries. *European Journal of Clinical Nutrition* 48:45–57.

McGuire, J. 1991. Quality vs. quantity of infant diets: Translating research into action. *Food and Nutrition Bulletin* 13:132–134.

McGuire, J., and B. Popkin. 1989. Beating the zero-sum: Women and nutrition in the third world. Part 1. *Food and Nutrition Bulletin* 11:38–63.

Pelletier, D., E. Frongillo, D. Schroeder, and J.-P. Habicht. 1995. The effects of malnutrition on child mortality in developing countries. *Bulletin of the World Health Organisation* 73:443–448.

Pennington, R., and H. Harpending. 1993. *The Structure of an African Pastoralist Community.* Research Monographs on Human Population Biology. Oxford: Clarendon Press.

Roth, E. A., and K. B. Korup. 1988. Demography and polygyny in southern Sudanese agropastoralist society. *Culture* 8:67–73.

SAS Institute. 1989. SAS/PC 6.0. Cary, North Carolina: Statistical Analysis Software, Inc.

Searcy, W., and K. Yakusawa. 1989. Alternative models of territorial polygyny in birds. *American Naturalist* 134:323–343.

Sellen, D. 1995. *The socioecology of young child growth among the Datoga pastoralists of northern Tanzania.* Ph.D. dissertation, University of California at Davis.

———. 1996. Nutritional status of sub-Saharan African pastoralists: A review of the literature. *Nomadic Peoples* 39:107–134.

———. 1998. Infant and young child feeding practices among African pastoralists: The Datoga of Tanzania. *Journal of Biosocial Science,* 30:481–499.

———. 1999a. Polygyny and child growth in a traditional pastoral society: The case of the Datoga of Tanzania. *Human Nature: An Interdisciplinary Biosocial Journal* 10:329–371.

———. 1999b. Growth patterns among semi-nomadic pastoralists (Datoga) of Tanzania. *American Journal of Physical Anthropology* 109:187–209.

———. 2000. Age, sex and anthropometric status of children in an African pastoral community. *Annals of Human Biolgoy* 27:1–21.

Sellen, D., D. Sieff, and M. Borgerhoff Mulder. 1993. *Human Ecology, Subsistence, and Reproduction of Pastoralists in the Lake Eyasi Area of Arusha Region, Tanzania*. Dar es Salaam, Tanzania: Tanzania National Research Council.

Sieff, D. 1995. *The Effects of Resource Availability on the Subsistence Strategies of Datoga Pastoralists of North West Tanzania.* Ph.D. thesis, University of Oxford.

———. 1997. Herding strategies of the Datoga pastoralists of Tanzania: Is household labor a limiting factor? *Human Ecology,* 25:519–544.

Smuts, B. B., and R.W. Smuts. 1993. Male aggression and sexual coercion of females in nonhuman primates and other mammals: Evidence and theoretical implications. *Advances in the Study of Behavior* 22:1–63.

SPSS Inc. 1993. SPSS proprietary software, release 6.0. Chicago: Statistical Package for the Social Sciences, Inc.

Spencer, P. 1980. Polygyny as social differentiation in African society. In *Numerical Techniques in Social Anthropology,* J. C. Mitchell, ed. Pp. 117–60. Philadelphia: Institute for the Study of Human Issues.

Strassmann, B. 1997. Polygyny as a risk factor for child mortality among the Dogon. *Current Anthropology* 38:688–695.

Tanaka, S. 1969. Natural environments of Mangola. *Kyoto University African Studies* 3:27–54.

Tomikawa, M. 1978. Family and daily life: An ethnography of the Datoga pastoralists of Mangola, 1. *Senri Ethological Studies* 1:1–36.

Tomkins, A., and F. Watson. 1989. Malnutrition and infection: A review. In United Nations Administrative Committee on Coordination Sub-Committee on Nutrition State-of-the-Art Series Nutrition Policy Discussion Paper.

Vehrencamp, S., and J. Bradbury. 1984. Mating systems and ecology. In *Behavioral Ecology: An Evolutionary Approach,* second ed., J. Krebs and N. Davies, eds. Pp. 251–278. Sunderland, Massachusetts: Sinauer.

Verner, J., and M. Willson. 1966. The influence of habitats on mating systems of North American passerine birds. *Ecology* 47:143–147.

Westneat, D. F., and R. C. Sargent. 1996. Sex and parenting: The effects of sexual conflict and parentage on parental strategies. *Trends in Ecology and Evolution* 11:87–91.

White, D. R., and M. L. Burton. 1988. Causes of polygyny: Ecology, economy, kinship and warfare. *American Anthropologist* 90:871–887.

6

Manipulating Kinship Rules

A Form of Male Yanomamö Reproductive Competition

NAPOLEON A. CHAGNON

Biologist Richard D. Alexander cogently argued that societal rules and laws interfere with individual reproductive strategies and probably exist in order to thwart them. In his view, "the function of laws is to regulate and render finite the reproductive strivings of individuals and subgroups within societies, in the interest of preserving unity in the larger group" (1979:240). In this paper I discuss the relationship of kinship rules to societal laws and argue that in tribal societies with prescriptive rules of marriage, kinship classification rules are like the societal laws Alexander has in mind, and they serve the same purpose.

The history of cultural anthropology has included a major effort to determine if laws as we know them exist in the preindustrial (tribal) world, and indeed, several of the prominent founders of anthropology were trained in law and pursued this question in their early works (Maine 1861; Morgan, 1851, 1870; see Fried 1967 for a discussion of the legal backgrounds of a number of pioneers in anthropology). Many of the early founders of anthropology were also fascinated with kinship classification systems, a field of study that dominated anthropology for most of its history. Leslie A. White (1957) went so far as to argue that the work of Lewis Henry Morgan on Iroquois kinship marked the official origin of anthropology as we know it, a profession based on field studies of other societies. Note also that Elman R. Service's ultimate book (1985) documented in great detail that the first century of anthropology was dominated by arguments and controversies over what primitive kinship classifications and kinship terms meant.

What is puzzling, however, is that pioneers in the anthropology of law and pioneers in the study of kinship systems viewed primitive law and kinship rules as fundamentally different things. Today, almost all anthropologists agree that most of the social action between individuals in the tribal world is "embedded in" kinship and kinshiplike institutions. As to law and whether or not it exists in these same kinds of societies, Robert Redfield's summary (1964) probably represents a generally held view: whatever is said about primitive law, the most conspicuous thing is that there is not much of it. The view from anthropology is therefore kinship rules are everywhere and universally found, but societal laws as we know them are rarely found in the primitive world. Ergo, kinship rules are not societal rules.

I believe that one of the primary reasons that anthropologists have generally regarded studies of kinship rules as being very different from the study of primitive law is the widely held view that kinship systems and rules of kin classification have little or nothing to do with reproduction and/or the frequent conflicts of interest that result from reproductive striving. A milestone in the anthropology of kinship that could have, but did not, change this view was the 1949 work of Claude Lévi-Strauss, who made the remarkable observation that all of the world's known systems of kinship classification fell into one of two distinct categories. Some of them had what he called prescriptive rules of marriage in which marriageable partners were specified by kinship terms. All other systems fell into a second category in which one's potential marriage partner was not prescribed by kinship classification. The first group had "positive" rules of marriage and led to the development of "elementary" social systems and the second group had "negative rules" and resulted in "complex" social systems like our own.

It should have been obvious to anthropologists thereafter that some kinship classification systems—those that Lévi-Strauss called "elementary systems"—defined marriage and reproductive rights and that in these kinds of systems, kinship rules should be viewed as "rules" or "laws" regulating reproduction and to thwart and avert conflicts of interest that result from reproductive striving. Whereas Lévi-Strauss explicitly argued that these social systems existed to regulate the flow of women, goods, and services between groups of relatives, most social anthropologists focused on how the "flow of women" established systematic elegant "structural systems" based on patterns of "alliances," but materialist cultural anthropologists continued to focus narrowly on competition for and flow of scarce, strategic material goods—land, pigs, hunting territories, etc. Neither group of anthropologists paid serious attention to the implications of prescriptive marriage rules as societal laws existing to regulate conflicts of interest over reproductive rights in women. Indeed, cultural materialists puzzled for years over the "causes" of widespread warfare and other forms of conflict in places like Highland New Guinea and completely missed the fact that much of it might have been over women. It took a Protestant missionary, apparently unaware of or unpersuaded by then- existing anthropological "truths" that fighting and conflicts must always be over material resources, to cast new light on much Dani warfare and, by extension, possible causes of fighting that ethnographers might have ignored in other areas of Highland New Guinea. Over approximately 30 years he simply documented the causes of fights, feuds, brawls, and wars among the Dani: the single most common cause of conflicts was competition for women (Larson 1987; see also Chagnon 1980).

I argue that in elementary systems of kinship where marriage possibilities are specified by kinship categories and classifications, rules of classification are essentially societal laws about male proprietary rights to marriageable females

(Lévi-Strauss 1949). Where female mates are scarce and difficult to obtain, kinship classification and misclassification are conceptual tools used by adult males in the general arena of mate competition. Among the Yanomamö (and other societies with a similar system of classification and rules of marriage), from both the male and female points of view, there is one and only one relative of the opposite sex who is a legitimate potential mate. Men must marry women they classify as *suaböya* and women must marry men they classify *heãroya* (a simple but narrow gloss for both terms being bilateral cross cousin). Marriage and/or sex with someone who is not in these categories is considered to be incest—*yawarei, yawaremou*—and is a violation of the rules. The outrage, anger, and conflict that follows when a man marries a woman who is not his *suaböya* can be intense and sometimes causes villages to fission. The outrage, however, seems to have very little to do with a natural or inherent human "abhorrence" of incest: it has more to do with detecting a cheater who, by marrying a prohibited person, has deprived some other male from the opportunity to marry her. Societal outrage over the "incestuous act" comes mainly from male reproductive competitors and their close kin.[1]

If we view kinship classification in prescriptive marriage systems as a strategic decision-making activity in the arena of mate competition, then a number of comparative questions come to mind. In an earlier paper (Chagnon 1988) I demonstrated that men were systematically misclassifying some female relatives in order to put them into the *suaböya* category and thereby increase their own mating opportunities. I did not directly test the hypothesis that adult men were, in general, more accurate than adult women in classifying their relatives, although I suspected that was true because men were better informants for genealogical information and faster at identifying and classifying all relatives (Chagnon 1988), suggesting that they knew genealogies more accurately than females did and were more familiar with the rules of classification than females were. Adult males also initiated the misclassifications of kin in order to enhance their own marriage possibilities and those of their sons and younger brothers.

This suggests at least two paradoxes. First, if adult males are the perpetrators of misclassifications, how could they also be more accurate than females in classification of kin? Second, Alexander (1979:241ff.) argues that we can use Darwinian theory to predict that young males from households where one parent, particularly the father, is not present should be more likely to break the rules than males from households with both parents present because males with only one parent present may receive less assistance from kin with such problems as obtaining wives. I will directly test the first of these paradoxes and discuss the second one and related topics.

BACKGROUND TO THE STUDY

During my 1985 field research I collected approximately 11,000 kinship responses from 104 Yanomamö informants in three different villages.[2] Informants ranged in age from approximately 5 years to approximately 75 years, 85% falling between 13 and 40 years (Chagnon 1988). Approximately equal numbers of male and female informants were interviewed for each age grouping.

Classification responses were solicited from each informant for every co-resident in the following way: each was shown a color polaroid close-up photograph of every co-resident of the village and asked "What do you call this person?" The person's name was whispered into the informant's ear as the question was asked to make sure the informant also knew verbally who the co-resident alter ego in question was and did not have to rely only on photographic identification. The responses were tape-recorded and later entered into computer files. The responses are described here as "observed" kinship classifications.

My preliminary report (Chagnon 1988) focused primarily on deviations from expected classifications by male informants for female kin. "Expected" was defined in terms of the known rules of Yanomamö kinship classification for genealogically defined relationships between Ego and Alter Ego. For example, was the woman that many informants identified as the mother of a particular person actually classified as "mother" by that person? Genealogical relationships between all co- residents had been established during many previous field trips. The depth of the genealogies ranges from 6 generations for the very young informants to 2 or 3 generations for the older informants.

The general objective of the study was to test hypotheses generated from Darwinian theory. One of the hypotheses was that adult males would reclassify female kin from categories of lesser reproductive utility into categories of greater reproductive utility. This prediction was confirmed: adult males were shown to demonstrate a bias in misclassifying female kin so as to move matrimonially ineligible females from other taxons into the "wife" taxon; in other words, they "created" more wives than any other type of female kin when they misclassified female kin.

Another hypothesis was that since males had a harder time finding mates than females did, and given the mortality patterns of the population, males should be expected to track their kinship and genealogical world more carefully than females. Yanomamö mortality patterns are such that individuals are unlikely to have living, coresident genetic parents by the time they are 20 years old. Since marriages are arranged by parents and older (usually agnatic) kin, finding mates becomes more of a problem for males than for females. Females are usually promised in marriage before reaching puberty, but males are usually about 20 years of age or slightly older and by this age, relatively few of them have living, coresident fathers (Chagnon 1981, 1982, 1988). Males, therefore, must often depend on male kin other than their fathers to help them in this regard. It was hypothesized that males would be more likely to learn genealogies and classifications of kin sooner in life and more thoroughly and accurately than same-age females, since this information would be more crucial to their marital and reproductive possibilities. This hypothesis was not tested directly in my preliminary report (Chagnon 1988), but I did show that males, in general, were *faster* at classifying coresident kin than females were, suggesting that they might know kinship classification and genealogies more thoroughly and accurately than females. I test this hypothesis below.

ANALYSIS OF CLASSIFICATIONS OF FIRST ASCENDING GENERATION KIN

The present paper addresses three points, focusing on male and female classifications of kin in the first ascending generation:

1. Accuracy of classification by adult male and adult female informants.
2. The possibility that accuracy of classification declines as a function of the coefficient of relationship between classifiers and classified.
3. The possibility that cultural factors, such as laterality (which side of the family the kin are on), affect classification accuracy.

Age, Sex, Village Fissioning, and the Distribution of Ego's Coresident Kin by Type

The informants were asked to classify only those kin who then lived in their village, although they had many other kin in other villages as well. I have elsewhere (Chagnon 1981, 1982) described how, over a person's lifetime, kinsmen get separated from each other and why particular kinds of relatives—and how many of them—live together in the same community. Among the Yanomamö, the primary factors are village fissioning and natality/mortality patterns.

Fissioning. As villages grow, they eventually reach a size that cannot be effectively organized by the principles of kinship obligations, descent, marriage reciprocity, and the limited charisma of the political leaders (Chagnon 1997 [1968], 1974). Villages eventually fission, separating kinsmen of various types into two independent villages. In general, social allies remain together and separate from their social competitors.[3] Social allies turn out to be, for men, those adult males who are likely to be wife givers, usually cross cousins of varying degrees of genealogical closeness, while competitors are usually parallel cousins, especially patrilateral parallel cousins (Chagnon 1981, 1982). Thus, an adult man might have dozens of patrilateral parallel cousins, but only a fraction of them would be co-residents. This means that kin of some genealogical categories will be over- or underrepresented; this is especially true for ascending generation kin where the effects of fissioning have led to the diaspora of certain kinds of kin from the vantage of adult classifiers.

Age and Sex Distribution. The age and sex distribution of the Yanomamö population reflects the typical natality and mortality patterns found in the primitive world. The population is "young," there are more males than females in the younger age categories, and the number of older people decreases rapidly by ascending age category (Melancon 1982; Swedlund and Armelagos 1976).

It follows that the number and kinds of coresident kin a person has will be a function, in part, of his or her age. Adults will have few ascending generation kin, many more own-generation kin, and most kin will be in the descending generations. Since this paper focuses on accuracy of classification by adult informants for their *first ascending generation* coresident kin, it therefore focuses on the smallest category of kin the typical adult would have around him or her. The findings here must therefore be taken to be tentative until the entire body of data is analyzed.

Genealogical specifications of the types of kin considered in this paper are kin who fall into the first ascending generation from Ego's perspective. The study is presently restricted, in this generation, to kin no more remote from Ego than first parallel cousins of Ego's parents. A major reason for this has to do with the decline in predictability of Ego's "expected" kin usage for cross cousins of Ego's parents (Chagnon 1974:app. C).

Age of Adult Informants. Informants estimated to be 14 years old or older at the time of the field research are considered to be adults in this paper. There is no hard and fast rule for specifying age at adulthood, and the exact age used is rather arbitrary in even our own culture, where, for some purposes and in some states, a person is an adult at age 18 (voting, drinking), 19 (conscription), or 21. I have chosen 14 years mainly because, by that age, a typical Yanomamö has probably accumulated the major fraction of knowledge he or she will ever have regarding classification rules and genealogical information for coresident kin.[4]

Analytical Methods

Classifications by the informants in all three villages were pooled. Village sizes were 61, 111, and 170 residents in which 46, 26, and 32 informants were interviewed, respectively (Chagnon 1988). Informants age 14 and older amount to approximately 80% of the original 104 informants: those under age 14 are excluded from the analyses except where indicated.

Each informant was compared, by computer search, to every co-resident in his/her village to determine if they were related by one or more genealogical connection. Where the informants were not shown to be related genealogically to co-residents, the particular dyad was eliminated from consideration. Informants were related to approximately 90% of all co-residents, and only these dyads comprise the data set analyzed here. Furthermore, where the informant was related to a co-resident by more than two genealogically known connections, as is often the case in populations as highly "inbred" as this one, just the two closest connections were considered in the analysis.

The kinship term used by each informant for every co-resident was established in the field as described above. This datum is defined here as "observed" kinship usage. The "expected" kinship usage was established by the formal rules of Yanomamö classification (see Chagnon 1974, 1982, 1988). The "expected" classifications are therefore how people "ought" to classify their kin on the basis of their principles of classification. These are basically the "rules" determined by general field inquiries, such as "What should you call a sister of your father? Your mother's brother? Your father's mother?"

Accuracy, therefore, refers to the degree of conformity of the "observed" classification to the "expected" classification.

Each of the genealogically specified positions were assigned discrete "muddles" codes, i.e., genealogical specifications for that position (discussed in detail in Chagnon 1988 and below). The primary reason for keeping track of the two closest genealogical connections in cases where Ego and Alter Ego were related by more than two connections was to distinguish between "full" and "half" relationships. Thus, siblings with the same genetic parents are full siblings but should not be terminologically distinguished in the "rules" of classification from half siblings, i.e., siblings who have the same father but different mothers, or the same mother but different fathers. For example, an informant's male full sibling would be characterized by the "muddles" FS *and* MS, but a male half sibling would be *either* FS *or* MS.[5] The statistics reported here treat each person as single entity; in other words, if two "muddles" connect Ego to Alter Ego, the person is counted just once—as a full rather than a half relative of a specific genealogical position.

Determining whether or not full and half relatives of various categories are classified equally accurately is one of the objectives of this paper and projected similar analyses. While the formal rules of classification do not prescribe different terminological usage for full and half relatives, kin selection theory suggests that closer kin are often treated differently than more distantly related kin—and a full cousin is more closely related to Ego than a half cousin, etc. Moreover, ethnographic studies show that relatives on one side of the family are more important for some purposes than equally closely related relatives on the other side and it is possible that the relative importance of matri- or patrilaterality can be explored quantitatively. Similar questions regarding kin in own versus other descent groups can also be explored in more detail, but are not examined here.

A table (matrix) was generated by the computer summarizing the number of kin the informants had in the first ascending generation, pooling the information for informants less than 14 years of age (juveniles) and for informants 14 years old or older (adults). The number of times these various kin were accurately classified was recorded, and a percentage of accuracy for each kind of relative was calculated.

Findings

Overall Accuracy of Adult Male and Female Informants. Figure 6.1 compares the accuracy of male and female informants. The first pair of bars on the graph ("All") portrays all 104 informants' responses (i.e., includes those less than

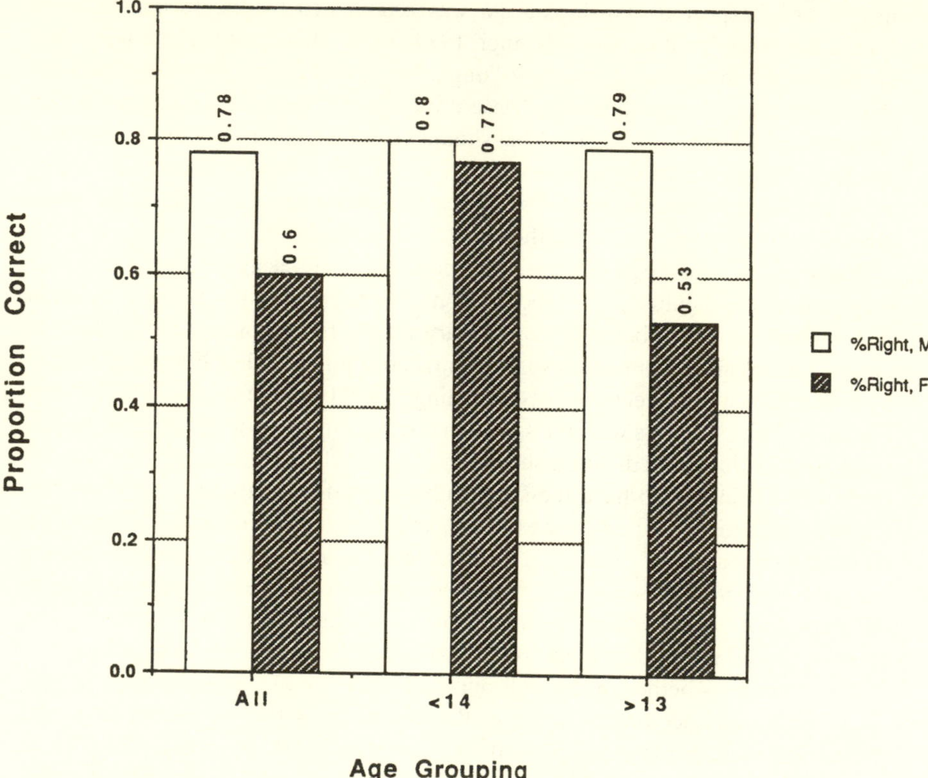

Figure 6.1. Male and female accuracy by age. The difference in accuracy for informants below 14 years of age is not statistically significant ($t = 0.57$, df = 252, $p = 0.2843$) but the difference in accuracy for informants 14 years of age and older is ($t = 8.11$, df = 870, $p = 0.0000$).

14 years old) to provide a general comparison of all male to all female informants for all ages. It shows that male responses in general are more accurate than females' in general.

When the informants are then segregated into juveniles (<14 years) and adult (14 years old or older) categories, the result is that juvenile male and female informants are nearly equally accurate in classifying kin in the first ascending generation, but that adult informants differ in accuracy by sex: males are more accurate than females. Thus, accuracy of kin classification by males appears to improve after they are 14 years of age.

Data regarding accuracy of male classification confirm one of the predictions made in my 1988 paper: males should be more accurate than females. However, they lend only tentative support to another argument—that young boys will be more accurate than young girls because boys must learn genealogies and classification more thoroughly since, in the likely absence of parental kin to help them find mates when they reach age of marriage, they will have to finesse a wider network of kin to help them in this regard whereas girls are universally married off. In other words, while boys probably have to participate more actively than girls in the marriage-arranging activities conducted by older kin on their behalf, and that "participation" probably entails learning who the most likely kin allies would be and "favoring" them socially, conspicuous increases in their greater accuracy appear to develop after they enter the older juvenile and younger adult age categories.

Accuracy by Laterality by Sex of Adult Informant. Figure 6.2 summarizes the data regarding differences in accuracy of adult male and female informants in classifications of kin on the patri- and matrilateral sides of the family. The purpose of

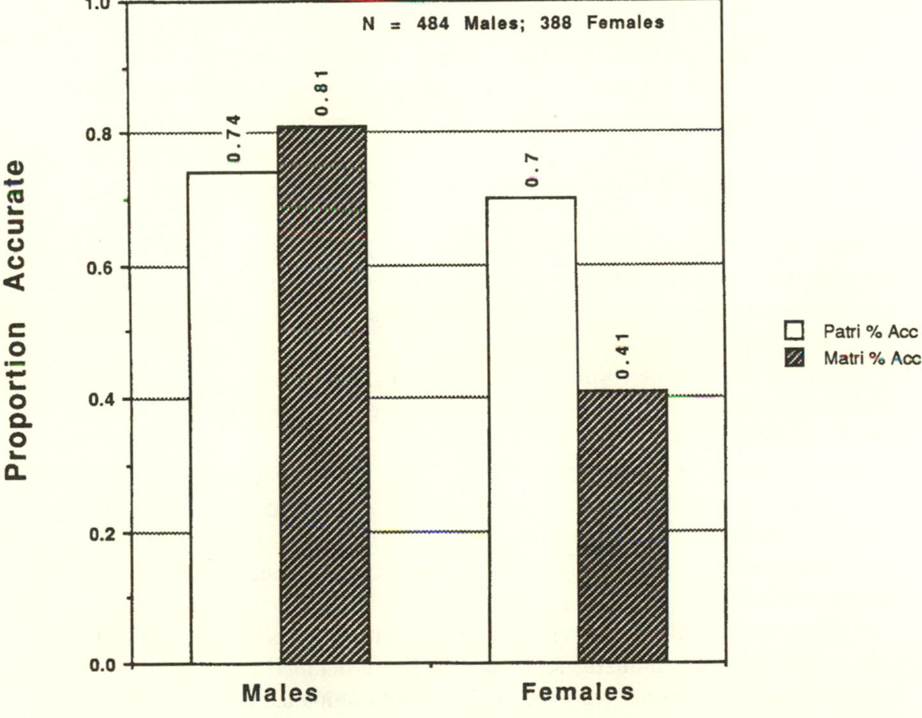

Figure 6.2. Accuracy by laterality and sex of adult informants. While males are significantly more accurate in classifying kin related to them through their mothers ($t = -1.66$, df = 482, $p = 0.0485$), females are significantly more accurate in classifying kin related to them through their fathers ($t = 5.66$, df = 386, $p = 0.0000$).

this analysis is to determine if "cultural factors" like laterality introduce biases in how manipulations of classification occur. For example, people are equally related to parallel cousins on the mother's side and the father's side of the family (assuming paternity certainty is equal), but are they equally likely to misclassify them?

Adult males tend to be more accurate than adult females on *both* sides of the family, but the difference in degree of accuracy is much more marked for kin on the matrilateral side. Thus, the overall greater accuracy of males (Figure 6.1) seems to be accounted for, in the first ascending generation, primarily by a much greater degree of accuracy in classification of matrilateral kin compared to patrilateral kin. This suggests that adult male manipulations of kinship classification are biased toward the patrilateral side; in other words, patrilaterally related females are more likely to be moved out of appropriate taxons than matrilateral kin, but this conclusion is partially contingent on a consideration of the accuracy of classifications in *other* generations—if you misclassify an aunt, for example, you are likely to extend the misclassification to the generation above her.

Figure 6.2 confirms other and more general arguments I have made about "allies" and "competitors" (Chagnon 1981, 1982; Irons 1979). Thus, a male should be expected to manipulate the classifications of females on the side of his family in which more of his mate competitors are found. In the case of the Yanomamö, a man's main competition comes from his patrilateral kin because such kin compete with him for the same pool of potential mates.

Closeness of Relatedness and Accuracy. The coefficients of relatedness between informants and all kin were calculated for every taxon. A comparison was then made using the value of Fg (relatedness calculated from genealogical data) as the independent variable.[6]

Figure 6.3 shows the results in graphic form, indicating that as closeness of relatedness wanes, so also does classification accuracy for males and females of all ages pooled.

This finding is of considerable interest from the perspective of kin selection theory and nepotism. Informants, in general, seem most reluctant to "tamper with" kinship classification for kin who are very closely related, but they appear to be increasingly more willing to do so in proportion to the decline in relatedness to the kin they misclassify.

As was stated earlier in this chapter, the present analysis is only of data for the first ascending generation (Generation +1). More detailed consideration of this finding cannot be pursued until the analyses are completed for each informant's own and first descending generations (Generations 0 and <->1), where the informants have the majority of their relatives. For example, kin who are related by Fg = 0.5000 in the above data can only be genetic parents, and, since most of the informants are adults, there are comparatively few cases of informants having living, coresident genetic parents. When Generations 0 and <-1> are considered, the numbers of kin for the Fg value 0.5000 will expand considerably, since these gen-

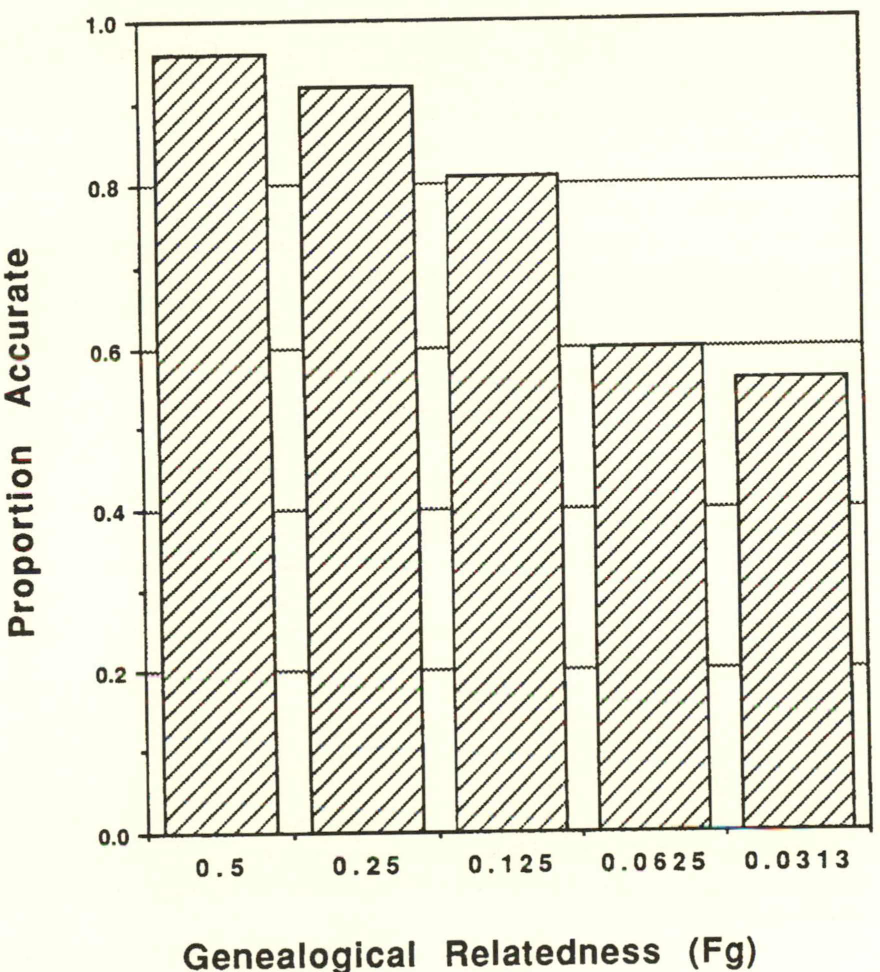

Figure 6.3. Accuracy by genealogical relatedness (Fg) among all informants. Kin terms are more accurately used for close kin than for distant kin (Spearman rank correlation, one-tailed: R = 1.0, M = 5, $p = 0.0080$).

erations will include full siblings and offspring. I do not anticipate that these projected analyses will reverse the findings shown in Figure 6.3.

DISCUSSION

The above data indicate that although adult males seem to initiate misclassifications—break the rules—they also seem to adjust their manipulations by restricting how far (genealogically) out (or away from) the misclassified person they logically extend their "modified" classification of that person. For example, if they misclassify a "niece" as "wife," they usually also extend the misclassification for this person up one generation and call that woman's mother by the term meaning "mother-in-law = wife's mother." But they appear to stop the process at this point whereas their female kin seem to be less likely to do so, resulting in what statistically emerges in this analysis as lower "accuracy" among female classifiers. In the field, this appears to the researcher to be female informants' uncertainty, confusion, and out-loud deliberation of rhetorical questions like " . . . well, let me think. I call his mother 'X' and I call his wife 'Y' and therefore I should call him 'Z,' but because he calls me 'A' I should call him. . . . " Male informants usually give a quick response with little or no hesitation.

A specific example of the greater reluctance of adult males to deviate from "accurate" classifications after a misclassification is the following. In one of the villages (not included in the above analysis) a widely known misclassification of several women (sisters to each other) was initiated by the headman so his sons could marry them, and they did. His sons were willing to adjust their kinship usage for other men who were eligible to marry these same women, but those men refused to reciprocate and would not answer my question "What do you call X?" They avoided a direct answer, even though I repeated my question several times, and kept responding by saying: "He calls me brother-in-law." They should have called each other by "brother" terms as they had done all their lives, but the losers in this manipulation refused to acknowledge the winner's gain publicly and would not reciprocally call him "brother-in-law" but also would not call him "brother" like they used to before the manipulation.

It is interesting to reflect on the differences between patterns of male rule breaking in our own society and in societies like the Yanomamö where marriages are arranged for young men by older men and where important rules in male-male mate competition revolve around kinship classification of women. As Alexander pointed out (1979), law-breaking men in our society tend to be young and tend to come from homes with a nonresident father whose direct role in the reproductive success of his sons is marginal. Almost the opposite is true in societies like the Yanomamö because the most relevant laws and rules are more directly related to reproductive striving: calling a niece "wife" is more directly related to the reproductive success of a young Yanomamö male than is a burglary or a car theft to the reproductive success of a young man in our kind of society. In the Yanomamö case, the first step must be taken by a relatively senior agnate of the young man, like his father, and thus rule breaking is more likely to occur in homes where the father is resident, has seniority and the experience to know how to break rules and deal with the consequences, and thereby is able to assist in the reproductive success of his son(s) through rule breaking. In effect, the sons simply "endorse" the rule breaking initiated by their fathers and older agnates.

There is the more general question of why parents want their children to know and understand the rules as intimately and accurately as possible. If, as Alexander argues, rules generally function to thwart the reproductive strivings of males and foster in-group unity, then knowing the rules accurately makes it easier to break them effectively. Thus, Yanomamö fathers not only break the rules on behalf of their sons' reproductive success, they also encourage them to learn genealogies and the rules of classification as accurately as possible so they can do it for their sons. Knowing the rules makes it easier to demand that others follow them by quickly detecting and protesting the kin misclassifications of others that threaten your own reproductive interests and those of your sons.

These data raise a broader and more intriguing question about sexual selection theory and the extent to which marriage/reproduction in the environment of evolutionary adaptedness (EEA) and in contemporary tribal societies with prescriptive rules of marriage are the result of female choice and female preferences for older men with higher than average amounts of "material" resources . . . or whether differential male reproductive success is measurably affected by male preferences for females with a symmetrical face, clean complexion, or a sexually appealing waist-to-hip ratio. My data show that the vast majority of Yanomamö babies result from arranged unions in which men produce offspring with women they classify as *suaböya,* and much of the male-male competition has to do with getting as many females into this category as possible, regardless of facial symmetry, complexion, or waist-to-hip ratios of the little girls they are legitimately able to marry or those they sometimes reclassify to achieve this end.

This brings us back to some of the possibly yet unexplored implications of Lévi-Strauss's extremely important distinction between elementary systems and complex systems. He emphasized that in systems of prescriptive marriage (elementary systems) individuals had *no* choice in at least the category of potential mates they would marry, but perhaps might have had some choice within that prescribed category (see also Needham 1962; Fox 1979). In nonprescriptive systems of marriage like our own, individuals can exercise a broader range of choice of marriage partners and are not constrained by prescriptive rules. It is theoretically possible that human mate choice emerged and evolved in only those kinds of systems, which currently far outnumber and embrace many times more people than prescriptive systems do. All biologists, anthropologists, and sociobiologists come from these systems, and it is natural that they think in terms of the characteristics of these kinds of systems and theorize about the EEA on the assumption that they were characteristic of marriage patterns there as well. This is both a theoretical and an empirical question—are empirical data from contemporary tribesmen with systems of prescriptive marriage systems a useful guide for thinking about the conditions in the EEA?

Whether the EEA included both kinds of marriage/mating systems is therefore an interesting and new problem because the answer to this question is likely to shed light on the sexual selection questions of male and female mate preferences and mate choice. The simplicity and efficiency of the kind of marriage system the Yanomamö have—prescriptive bilateral cross-cousin marriage, brother-sister exchange, and patrilineal bias in descent group organization—is widespread in the primitive world. There are compelling reasons to argue that it might have been the original—or at least an extremely common—marriage system in the EEA (see Fox 1967 and Service 1962 for similar arguments). All that it would take to get it started would be for two groups to expel one of the sexes when the individuals reached reproductive maturity, take in the expelled individuals from the other group as mates, and for individuals to mate with (marry) individuals of approximately the same age. Chimpanzees and lions do this in the wild. To have what is effectively a prescriptive system of bilateral cross-cousin marriage (like the Yanomamö system and similar systems in aboriginal Australia and elsewhere), all that they need are kin classifications that identify males and females by own group/other group and own generation/other generation, and a simple rule that says males can only mate with other-group/own-generation females. If they could but give words, incoming female chimpanzees would be classified as "*suaböya*" by local group males, whose own sisters would be expelled from their group and eventually mate with the brothers of those females who come into theirs. In a few generations all matings in both groups would be between bilateral cross cousins. The next and final step would be for the two groups to unite into a single community and continue doing the same thing, but within the now dually organized group. In small groups, male freedom to mate with females who were not "other group/own generation" would probably be very destructive to within-group unity, and that is probably why prescriptive rules to thwart this came into existence. Enforcing these kinds of rules would probably become increasingly difficult with increased group size, and perhaps that is why "complex" social systems with greater mate choice came into existence. My suspicion is that it happened after the emergence of elementary systems . . . and possibly could not have emerged in human history before them. If I am correct, then much of what we argue about in terms of human mate preferences appeared in our history either very late in the Paleolithic, or after it.[7]

SUMMARY

1. In societies where marriage possibilities are specified by kinship categories and classifications, rules of kin classification are essentially societal laws about male proprietary rights to marriageable females, and kin classification and misclassification can be used by males as tools in the arena of mate competition.

2. Yanomamö men have been shown to misclassify female relatives by putting them into the only marriageable category, that of a female cross-cousin or *suaböya* (Chagnon 1988).

3. Because males have a harder time finding mates than do females, it is hypothesized that males will learn their kinship system and their genealogies more thoroughly and accurately than females in order to be better able to manipulate them.

4. Although young males are no more accurate in classifying their kin than are young females, adult males are significantly more accurate than adult females in this regard.

5. Adult male informants are more accurate in classifying their matrilateral than their patrilateral kin, suggesting that adult male manipulations of kinship classification are biased toward the patrilateral side. This may be due to the competition among patrilineally related men for the same pool of potential mates.

6. All informants are more accurate in classifying close than distant consanguineal kin. This suggests that Yanomamö informants are more willing to tamper with their kinship classification system with regards to distant kin than with regards to close kin.

7. These data raise questions about the importance to mate selection of various measures of physical attractiveness, such as waist-to-hip ratios and facial asymmetries, in societies with prescriptive marriage rules.

ACKNOWLEDGMENTS

I would like to thank Albert Spaulding posthumously for running statistical tests on the data used to produce Figures 6.1, 6.2, and 6.3. I would also like to thank David R. Abbott, then (1989) an archaeology graduate student at UCSB, for similar tests he subsequently made and which are included in the captions for the figures.

NOTES

1. It would be useful to compare the extent and nature of purported outrage about incest violations in societies that have prescriptive rules of marriage and those that do not. It is possible that in societies with prescriptive marriage rules "outrage" about incest is better interpreted as anger because someone cheated in mate competition.

2. An additional 5,000 to 6,000 responses were collected in the same villages in 1987 but are not included in the present analysis.

3. See Irons 1979 for a discussion of the concepts *social allies* and *social competitors*.

4. Lifetime changes in classification accuracy by age and sex of informant is an interesting question but beyond the objectives of this paper. How a Yanomamö classifies his or her relatives changes over their lifetimes for the reasons discussed in this paper and in Chagnon 1988 and elsewhere.

5. F = Father, M = Mother, S = Son.

6. See Chagnon 1974, 1975 for a discussion and definition of Fg and similar statistics.

7. The data in this paper were extracted from my field notes and computer files in 1989 to explore some of the issues raised by my preliminary paper (Chagnon 1988). I would like to thank Dante De Lucia for extracting these data from my files and running the analyses through KINDEMCOM, a computer program I had developed with many computer experts

between 1970 and 1984. Some of the computer results provided to me by De Lucia were used in a class I taught in 1989 and I had hoped that additional analytical input from the graduate students in that class would have warranted their inclusion as coauthors in some kind of publication, but that did not happen.

REFERENCES

Alexander, Richard D. 1979. *Darwinism and Human Affairs*. Seattle: University of Washington Press.

Chagnon, Napoleon A. 1974. *Studying the Yanomamö*. New York: Holt, Rinehart and Winston.

———. 1975. Genealogy, solidarity, and relatedness: limits to local group size and patterns of fissioning in an expanding population. *Yearbook of Physical Anthropology* 19:95–110.

———. 1980. Highland New Guinea models in the South American Lowlands. In *Studies in Hunting and Fishing in the Neotropics,* Raymond

Hames, ed. Pp. 111–130. Working Papers on South American Indians, No. 2., Bennington College, Vermont.

———. 1981. Terminological kinship, genealogical relatedness and village fissioning among the Yanomamö Indians. In *Natural Selection and Social Behavior: Recent Research and New Theory,* R. D. Alexander and D. W. Tinkle, eds. Pp. 490–508. New York: Chiron Press.

———. 1982. Sociodemographic limits of nepotism in tribal populations: man the rule breaker. In *Current Problems in Sociobiology,* King's College Sociobiology Group, eds. Pp. 291–318. Cambridge: Cambridge University Press.

———. 1988. Male manipulations of kinship classifications of female kin for reproductive advantage. In *Human Reproductive Behaviour: A Darwinian Perspective,* L.

Betzig, M. Borgerhoff Mulder, and P. Turke, eds. Pp. 23–48. Cambridge: Cambridge University Press.

———. 1997. *Yanomamö*. New York: Harcourt, Brace College. (Originally published in 1968)

Fox, Robin. 1967. *Kinship and Marriage*. Baltimore: Penguin Books.

———. 1979. Kinship Categories as Natural Categories. In *Evolutionary Biology and Human Social Behavior: An Anthropological Perspective,* N. A. Chagnon and W. Irons, eds. Pp. 132–144. North Scituate, Massachusetts: Duxbury Press.

Fried, Morton H. 1967. *The Evolution of Political Society: An Essay in Political Anthropology*. New York: Random House.

Irons, William. 1979. Investment and primary social dyads. In *Evolutionary Biology and Human Social Behavior: An Anthropological Perspective,* N. A. Chagnon and W. Irons, eds. Pp. 181–212. North Scituate, Massachusetts: Duxbury Press.

Larson, Gordon F. 1987. *The Structure and Demography of the Cycle of Warfare among the Ilaga Dani of Irian Jaya.* Ph.D. dissertation, University of Michigan, Ann Arbor.

Lévi-Strauss, Claude. 1969 *The Elementary Structures of Kinship,* revised ed., H. H. Gell, J. Richard von Sturmer, and R. Needham, trans. Boston: Beacon Press. (Originally published in 1949)

Maine, Henry Sumner. 1861. *Ancient Law: Its Connection with the Early History of Society and Its Relation to Modern Ideas*. London: Oxford University Press.

Melancon, Thomas. 1982. *Marriage and Reproduction among the Yanomamö Indians.* Ph.D. dissertation, Pennsylvania State University. University Microfilms, Ann Arbor.

Morgan, Lewis Henry. 1954. *The League of the Ho-de-no-sau-nee, or Iroquois*. New Haven: Behavior Science Reprints. (Originally published in 1851)

———. 1870. *Systems of Consanguinity and Affinity of the Human Family*. Washington, D.C.: Smithsonian Institution.

Needham, Rodney. 1962. *Structure and Sentiment*. Chicago: University of Chicago Press.

Redfield, Robert. 1964. Primitive law. *University of Cincinnati Law Review* 33(1):1–22.

Service, Elman R. 1962. *Primitive Social Organization*. New York: Random House.

Swedlund, Alan, and George Armelagos. 1976. *Demographic Anthropology*. Dubuque: Wm. C. Brown.

———. 1985. *A Century of Controversy: Ethnological Issues from 1860 to 1960*. New York: Academic Press.

White, Leslie A. 1957. How Morgan came to write *Systems of Consanguinity and Affinity*. *Papers of the Michigan Academy of Sciences, Arts, and Letters* 42(1956):257–268.

7

Physical Attractiveness, Race, and Somatic Prejudice in Bahia, Brazil

DOUG JONES

INTRODUCTION: SOMATIC PREJUDICE

"Somatic prejudice" may be defined as a form of prejudice in which members of one racial or ethnic group are evaluated more or less favorably than members of another on the basis of their physical appearance. The study of somatic prejudice lies at the intersection of two normally separate areas of inquiry: the psychology of physical attractiveness and the sociology and history of racial and ethnic relations.

There are at least two reasons why somatic prejudice is theoretically important. First, the study of physical attractiveness has lately developed as one of the most active areas of inquiry in the new discipline of "evolutionary psychology." Evolutionary psychology is based on two propositions. (1) Human beings are biologically specialized for certain kinds of information processing, so that some learning tasks come much more easily and automatically than others. (2) The modern theory of evolution by natural selection may be particularly useful in figuring out what form such specialized "programmed learning" is likely to take. Because the theory of sexual selection is an especially successful area of modern evolutionary theory, many evolutionary psychologists have been interested in applying it to understanding standards of physical attractiveness among humans (reviewed in Jones 1996b). Much of the work of evolutionary psychologists regarding standards of attractiveness has ignored the larger social context—and especially the ethnic context—in which judgments of attractiveness operate. However, the study of the ethnic and racial dimension of attractiveness should ultimately allow a revision and expansion of our theories of the psychology of attractiveness.

There is a second reason why the study of somatic prejudice is important: it offers the chance to revise not only our understanding of attractiveness, but also our understanding of racial and ethnic prejudice. Studies of relations between groups frequently note positive or negative responses to the physical appearance of members of different groups (Hoetink 1967; Isaacs 1975:46–70). However, the theories of human nature commonly employed by historians and social scientists make it difficult to get a handle on such somatic prejudice. On the one hand, utilitarian theories of human nature, in which individuals are chiefly concerned with their own material well-being and social position, make it difficult to understand why such importance seems to attach to details of physical appearance. On the other hand, cultural constructionist theories of human nature make it difficult to explain—or even recognize—cross-cultural commonalities in the psychology of attractiveness. The new picture of the psychology of attractiveness coming out of evolutionary psychology may thus make it easier for researchers in ethnic and race relations to give somatic prejudice the attention it deserves.

Finally, it is worth noting that apart from its intellectual interest, somatic prejudice has important practical consequences for the lives of individuals; members of groups subject to negative somatic prejudice are generally keenly aware of this prejudice and its social effects. Greater understanding of the roots of somatic prejudice may make it possible to combat such prejudice and to alleviate some of its consequences.

This paper is concerned with the phenomenon of somatic prejudice, and with the mutual relevance of evolutionary-psychology theories of attractiveness and studies of race and ethnic relations. In the next section I summarize some current theory and evidence regarding the evolutionary psychology of attractiveness, with special emphasis on principles of attractiveness likely to be most relevant to understanding somatic prejudice in modern multiracial societies. In the following section, I focus on the racially stratified society of Bahia, Brazil, summarizing some of the relevant social history, and presenting results of research I have conducted on racial classification, physical attractiveness, and somatic prejudice in Bahia. In the last section I discuss implications for evolutionary psychology and for studies of race and ethnic relations.

VARIANTS AND INVARIANTS IN PHYSICAL ATTRACTIVENESS

Richard Dawkins (1989) coined the phrase "the selfish gene" to distill modern evolutionary biology's view that adaptations are designed to propagate the genes that produce them. The survival and well-being of individuals is evolutionarily relevant only insofar as it has historically contributed to their reproduction, or to the reproduction of kin who share their genes. This gene-centered view of life has been particularly productive in the study of mate choice. The modern theory of mate choice begins with the proposition that because organisms' mate preferences are likely to have been shaped by natural selection, organisms are likely to have adaptations for assessing the "mate value" of potential mates. The mate value of animal A for animal B can be defined as the expected fitness that B would have from mating with A, divided by B's expected fitness from mating at random or from mating with an individual of maximum mate value. (In fact, there might be several different mate values of A for B, depending for example on whether a long- or a short-term mating relationship is considered.) Mate preferences, in other words, can be regarded as the product of adaptations for reproduction (Andersson 1994; Jones 1996a).

A number of investigators have suggested that this approach might apply to humans as well as to other animals, and might apply especially to the phenomenon of physical attractiveness in our species. Social psychological research (Hatfield and Sprecher 1986) demonstrates that physical attractiveness is at least moderately important in social relationships, including dating and marriage, in the United States, while cross-cultural surveys (Buss 1989) and ethnographic and historical evidence (Ford and Beach 1951) show that concern for attractiveness is not limited to modern industrialized and media-saturated societies. From one point of view these findings are merely a confirmation of folk wisdom, but from another they are paradoxical, since it is difficult to see what advantage individuals gain from choosing an attractive sexual or social partner over an unattractive one, or why individuals should have the standards of attractiveness that they do. A "selfish gene" perspective may help to resolve this paradox: the advantage to choosing an attractive mate may be a reproductive advantage, and variations in physical attractiveness may track variations in mate value. More precisely, whether or not perceived attractiveness is correlated with mate value in modern—and evolutionarily "unnatural"—environments, the development of standards of attractiveness in our species is likely to be governed by adaptations which historically functioned to track variations in mate value.

What people find physically attractive today may thus depend on what physical characteristics in the past predicted fecundity, health, ability and willingness to provision offspring, and other components of mate value. However, the past environments and selective pressures that shaped the psychology of mate choice cannot have been absolutely uniform, and evolutionary psychologists must explain how ancestral humans solved the problem of homing in on correlates of mate value across a range of environments. One approach to this problem is to look at physical cues like bilateral symmetry (Grammer and Thornhill 1994), facial neoteny (Jones 1995), and low waist-to-hip ratios (Singh 1993) that have probably been relatively invariant indicators of health, female fecundity, or other components of mate value, and might operate as relatively universal and "hard-wired" criteria of attractiveness. However, many physical characteristics are likely to have been positively correlated with mate value only in some environments, and uncorrelated or negatively correlated in others. Natural selection may favor individuals who can modify their emotional and aesthetic responses to such characteristics in response to environmental cues. The evidence suggests that there is significant variation across time and space in criteria of physical attractiveness in human societies. For example, Singh's (1993) research on the waist-to-hip ratio

(WHR) demonstrates that winners of the Miss America beauty pageant since the 1920s and *Playboy* centerfolds since the 1950s have had consistently low WHRs. But this same research shows that both sets of women have grown thinner over the course of time, both in absolute terms and relative to the average U.S. female. An evolutionary psychologist might expect variation in aesthetic responses to fatness versus leanness, because the selective benefits of having a fat or a lean mate are likely to have varied over the course of evolution with variation in workload and reliability of food supply. But such variation clearly raises a host of questions about how individuals use environmental cues in developing standards of attractiveness.

Biologists studying mate choice in nonhuman animals have devoted increasing attention to the influence of environmental and social cues. Some particularly interesting work integrating sexual selection and ecological variation comes from studies of guppies. Male guppies normally develop orange patches on their sides, and these patches seem to be a product of sexual selection; female guppies commonly prefer males with brighter patches. Why females show this preference is not certain; based on analogies with other species the patches may be honest advertisements of male nutritional status and resistance to infection (Endler and Lyles 1989). Although bright patches may benefit males in sexual competition, they also carry serious costs in some environments: experiments demonstrate that brighter males can suffer higher rates of predation, with the added risk varying enormously across habitats depending on which predator species are present in a given stream (Endler 1980). The result is that bright patches are far from an invariant marker of mate value across guppy populations, because when a female chooses a bright mate in a stream well-stocked with predators, the brightly colored sons that result are especially likely to be eaten before they reach adulthood. Females adapt to this situation in several ways. There are sometimes genetic differences between populations in the intensity of female preferences for bright males (Dugatkin and Godin 1995). However, females are also capable of modifying their preferences based on observations of other females. Dugatkin (1996) shows that a female who sees another female apparently choosing the duller of two males will shift her own preference away from bright males—but only if the differences in brightness are not too great.

The guppy case demonstrates that standards of attractiveness are likely to involve some relatively invariant, species-typical preferences, but those standards may also be adaptively modified to some degree by experience and imitation. A comparable mixture of the invariant and the environmentally contingent is likely to operate among humans. This paper will consider both invariant and variable criteria of physical attractiveness, concentrating especially on three—color, averageness, and status indicators—likely to contribute to somatic prejudice in modern multiracial societies. The remainder of this section will review cross-cultural evidence and theoretical arguments regarding these three, and the next section will consider their role in somatic prejudice in Bahia.

Color

A preference for lighter than average skin, at least among males evaluating females, is reported with very high frequency in the ethnographic literature (van den Berghe and Frost 1986). Investigators working in modern, racially stratified societies often assume that preferences for lighter skin result from the political and social dominance of light-skinned over dark-skinned peoples (Lancaster 1991). However, cross-cultural evidence makes it clear that racial hierarchies, while they may exaggerate skin color preferences, do not create them. Some of the evidence comes from historical records of societies in which darker-skinned people dominated lighter-skinned subjects. In both the ancient Roman and the Islamic worlds the presence of large numbers of light-skinned northern slaves went hand in hand with an idealization of whiteness or lightness as a criterion of female beauty. More evidence comes from relatively unstratified societies that show a consistent pattern of preference for lighter than average skin color in females. This preference occurs across populations with a wide range of skin colors, and it is found even in societies whose standards of attractiveness with regard to fatness and facial proportions are sharply at variance with contemporary Western standards. It is reported by male and female and Western and non-Western ethnographers, and it is manifest both in informants' statements and in cosmetic practices. Evidence regarding female preferences for male skin color is much more mixed.

Why should there be a widespread preference for lighter than average skin color, and why should this preference be more marked in males' evaluations of females than vice versa? Skin color, like the waist-to-hip ratio, seems to be a relatively invariant marker of female mate value. Estrogen production suppresses melanin production, so that females typically lighten with the onset of puberty, gradually darkening in step with declining ovarian function from young adulthood to old age. In light-haired populations hair color too may track changes in female fecundity. Thus an attraction to light-skinned mates may be a genetic adaptation in human males. This attraction, however, is also affected by experience and social cues. Men adapt their preferences to local conditions, so that while men in dark-skinned populations commonly report an attraction to lighter than average females, they also commonly report an aversion to Europeans whose skin color puts them far outside the local normal range of variation. And in some modern societies, social responses to sun-tanning may also modify skin color preferences.

Average Features

When researchers use computer graphic software to produce "composite" facial images by blending a number of individual facial photographs, the resulting composites are judged more attractive than most of the photographs going into them (Langlois and Roggman 1990). Attractiveness, in other words, is partly a matter of having features close to the average. This finding suggests that people mentally combine the faces they see around them to arrive at an image of the average face, and base their standards of attractiveness partly on this image (Symons 1979). Koeslag and Koeslag (1994) argue that "koinophilia"—a preference for modal or average features—is widespread among animals, and is adaptive because individuals distant from the local average often carry a higher genetic load or have suffered from stress during development. Koinophilia will sometimes be overridden by innate or acquired preferences for extreme values of particular traits, but the "default" preference in the absence of such influences seems to be for the average. To the extent that standards of attractiveness are koinophilic, culturally isolated populations are expected to have an ethnocentric standard of beauty, judging the attractiveness of outsiders by their "somatic distance" from the local norm.

Status Markers

While people may come equipped with a relatively "hardwired" attraction to relatively invariant markers of high mate value in the opposite sex, standards of attractiveness also seem to be responsive to social cues. Some of the best evidence for this proposition comes from changes in standards of attractiveness in the wake of Western political, economic, and cultural expansion. A great deal of evidence shows that non-Europeans commonly found European physical features unattractive on first contact, as expected under the koinophilia hypothesis (reviewed in Jones 1996a:122–125). In much of the non-Western world, however, ethnocentric standards of attractiveness have partly given way to Eurocentric standards.

One of the best descriptions of this process comes from Wagatsuma's (1968) essay on standards of attractiveness in Japan. In 1860, just after Japan was opened to the outside world, a group of samurai visited Washington, D.C. Their reactions to American women, recorded in their diaries, reflect both an attraction to light skin and an ethnocentric response to facial proportions and hair color: "The women's skin was white, and they were charming in their gala dresses decorated with gold and silver but their hair was red and their eyes looked like dog eyes, which was quite disheartening," and "Occasionally I saw women with black hair and black eyes. They must have been of some Asian race. Naturally they looked more attractive and beautiful" (1968:136). By the early twentieth century, Japanese standards of attractiveness had begun to change. "The subtle, not fully conscious, trend toward an idealization of Western physical features by the Japanese apparently became of increasing importance by the twenties" (1968:139). The political climate of the 1930s and early 1940s discouraged open expression of such attitudes, but by 1954 the Westernization of standards of attractiveness had gone far enough for novelist Shusaku Endo to have a character observe

> I do not know why and how only the white people's skin became the standard of beauty. I do not know why and how the standard of beauty in sculpture and paintings all stemmed from the white body of the Greeks, and has been so maintained until today. But what I am sure of is that in regard to the body, those like myself and

> Negroes can never forget miserable inferiority feelings in front of people possessing white skin, however vexing it might be to admit it. [Cited in Wagatsuma 1968:140]

Wagatsuma notes that Westernization in Japanese standards of attractiveness is expressed today in artificial waving and curling of hair, hair lightening, the use of surgery to reduce epicanthic folds, and in an idealization of Western looks in popular media.

Further evidence for Westernization in standards of attractiveness around the world is summarized in Jones (1996a:130–132). For the United States, where nonwhites are not only commonly of lower social status but also numerically in the minority, white influence on nonwhite standards of attractiveness is especially evident. Russell et al. (1992) summarize a large body of historical and current evidence for somatic prejudice both against African Americans as a group and among African Americans of varying appearance in *The Color Complex: The Politics of Skin Color among African Americans.*

The widespread Westernization of standards of attractiveness, even in countries where Westerners are not present in large numbers, is evidence of the importance of social cues in formulating standards of attractiveness; more specifically, it is evidence that people may develop an attraction to physical features associated with high status. This phenomenon deserves some discussion from an evolutionary perspective. A number of authors have noted that high social status may be associated with high mate value, because over the course of human evolution high status individuals have probably commanded more of the resources needed to provision offspring. And cross-cultural evidence shows that social status is usually an important component of sexual attractiveness, especially in women's evaluations of men (Buss 1989; Ellis 1992). However it is less clear why physical traits associated with high status, as opposed to high status itself, should be attractive. One possibility is that status may be an indicator of the direction of selection. Suppose that directional selection on physical traits has commonly been at least moderately strong, but varying in direction. For example, suppose that food supplies have commonly varied enough that the optimal body size and level of fatness have differed from one population and time period to another. In this case correlations between social status and body size and fatness might provide evidence regarding the current direction of selection. Using high status individuals as models when choosing a mate may be a mechanism for adapting to local variations in selection pressures.

The evidence suggests that color, averageness, and status markers are all components of attractiveness, and there are plausible—albeit unproven—evolutionary arguments why each of these might have been an indicator of mate value in the evolutionary past. It is more doubtful that they are good indicators of mate value in modern multiracial societies, but emotional responses that were adaptive in the past may persist and produce somatic prejudice in the present.

RACIAL CLASSIFICATION AND SOMATIC PREJUDICE IN BAHIA

In this section I report results of research on race and standards of attractiveness in Bahia, Brazil. In 1989 I travelled to Salvador, the capitol of Bahia, for a pilot study of physical attractiveness. From 1990 to 1991, I conducted more fieldwork at the Federal University of Bahia in Salvador and in a lower-class community on the city's northern outskirts. Finally in 1992 I began a long-term study of criteria and consequences of physical attractiveness in the Bahian coastal village of Arembepe. This research is part of a larger, ongoing investigation of standards of attractiveness across cultures that has also involved work in the United States, Paraguay (among Ache Indians), and Russia. More details on research protocols and results can be found in Jones and Hill (1993) and Jones (1995, 1996a). Kottak (1992) provides both ethnographic and quantitative descriptions of Arembepe. Below I provide some background on race in Brazil and then present research results.

Race in Brazil

From the sixteenth to the nineteenth centuries, approximately four million Africans, more than one-third of the Atlantic slave trade, were transported to Brazil (Thomas 1997:804). The descendants of these slaves today make up the largest population of African descent in the New World. In the Brazilian Northeast people claiming some African descent are a majority of the population—80% in the state of Bahia (Scheper-Hughes 1992:544).

Everywhere in the Americas slavery entailed the establishment of racially stratified societies in which free as well as enslaved blacks experienced political exclusion, economic discrimination, and social stigma, and everywhere in the Americas blacks continue on average to occupy a lower economic and social position than whites. But within this common framework of slavery and racial hierarchy there were and are significant variations between countries, deriving in part from differences between their European founders. The differences in race relations between Anglo-America and Latin America, and more specifically between the United States and Brazil, have long been noted by both travellers and scholars (Degler 1971; Harris 1964). Degler (1971:224) argues that the crucial difference between the two countries lies not so much in the position of slaves and persons of African descent as in the position of persons of mixed race.

> The key that unlocks the puzzle of the differences in race relations in Brazil and the United States is the mulatto escape hatch. Complex and varied as the race relations in the two countries have been and are today, the presence of a separate position for the mulatto in Brazil and its absence in the United States nevertheless define remarkably well the heart of the difference.

The United States for most of its history has followed the "one drop rule" or something close to it in defining blacks: individuals with even very small proportions of known African ancestry were and are counted as black (Davis 1991). By contrast, Brazilians of mixed ancestry commonly are not regarded either by themselves or by other people as black, but rather as white or as racially intermediate. They may escape much of the stigma that attaches to blacks. While race—at least the black/white distinction—is treated as a categorical variable in the United States, it is treated as more of a continuous variable in Brazil. And while the U.S. American system of racial classification mostly emphasizes descent—the child of a black parent is black—the Brazilian system puts more emphasis on appearance—even children of the same parents may belong to different racial categories if their appearances differ sufficiently.

While lower class and minority political mobilization since the 1960s has brought great changes to both the United States and Brazil (Fontaine 1985), racial boundaries still operate differently in the two countries. Friendship, romance, and marriage across "racial" lines (at least as U.S. Americans define race) are more common in Brazil than in the United States. The fuzziness of Brazilian racial categories also affects political life. In the past it precluded solidarity among whites; now it blocks the consolidation of a U.S.-style black nationalist movement, black voting bloc, or affirmative action agenda. Some Brazilian political activists, inspired in part by the U.S. civil rights movement, have encouraged all Brazilians with African ancestry to think of themselves as blacks (*negros*), but most mixed-race Bahians I encountered in the course of my fieldwork put themselves in some intermediate racial category, or identified themselves white.

No very clear line divides whites from blacks in Brazil, but the country is quite racially stratified. Brazilians sometimes call their country Bel-India—half Belgium and half India. Southern Brazil is overwhelmingly white and relatively prosperous; nonwhites (excluding Asians) are concentrated in the poor Northeast. While 44% of the population identified themselves as *pardo* (black or mixed race) in the 1990 census, "[d]ark-skinned persons have rarely if ever reached the highest levels of industry, business, the professions, or the government. . . . Blacks have achieved success only in athletics and entertainment" (Levine 1997:16).

> [In 1990] of Brazilians earning more than five hundred dollars a month, fewer than 10 percent [were] nonwhites. . . . Black Brazilians account for two-thirds of families surviving on fifty dollars a month or less. Even in the capital city of Salvador, Bahia, where 80% of the two million residents are black, the city has never had a black mayor. . . . And Bahian "society" is still controlled by a tiny Euro-Brazilian white elite (Scheper-Hughes 1992:543–544).

Major cities like São Paulo, Rio de Janeiro, and Salvador are strongly segregated by race, with nonwhites being greatly over-represented in the favelas (slum and shanty neighborhoods) and whites over-represented in upper-class neighborhoods. Studies that consider subdivisions among nonwhites generally find that mulattoes have a higher social status than blacks, but are closer to blacks than whites (Fontaine 1985).

Racial Classification

Because Brazilians use a large number of labels to classify racial types, my first step in investigating somatic prejudice in Bahia was a study of Brazilian racial classification. For this study I used a series of facial photographs of Salvadoran females collected in 1989. To collect photographs, I positioned myself in several public places and, at set time intervals, approached the nearest female who seemed to be in her late teens or early twenties and was not visibly working or in a hurry. I asked each woman if I could take her photograph; after taking photographs I asked each subject her age. Owing to variable lighting conditions and problems with developing film, 11 of the photographs were of too poor a quality to be used, leaving 30 for the present study. The women who declined to have their photographs taken may have been of lower than average attractiveness: several gave this as a reason for declining. Given the neighborhoods I worked in, there may have been some bias toward upper-and middle-class subjects, but it is probably fair to say that the photographs span the whole range of physical types common in Bahia.

During 1992 fieldwork in Arembepe, I asked 40 males and 40 females to identify the "race" *(qualidade)* of each of the 30 people in the photographs. Subjects gave a total of 50 racial categories, although just 11 of these accounted for 94% of all categorizations. The categories include labels like *loira* (blond) that are not based on membership in a descent group, which seems to confirm that Bahian racial categories overlap with, and are partly defined by, categories based on appearance. All 50 categories are tabulated in Jones 1996a:138–139.

I have used monotonic Kruskal Multi-Dimensional Scaling (MDS) to investigate how different categories are related to one another. MDS uses data about similarities and dissimilarities between items to construct a multidimensional space in which similar items are placed closer together. To illustrate with a simple example, if people are asked to classify pairs of colors as similar or dissimilar, they will classify red and orange as similar, red and green as dissimilar, and so on. Applying MDS to ratings of similarity between pairs of colors in the spectrum will yield a two-dimensional space in which points corresponding to different colors are arranged around a circle, with purple between red and blue, and so on. That the colors fall in a circle rather than, say, an arc or a few separate clumps tells us something about human color perception.

Applying MDS requires first constructing a similarity matrix in which element $\{i, j\}$ is some measure of the similarity between item i and item j. For the present analysis, the "items" are the different racial categories, and the measure of similarity between racial categories i and j is the Spearman correlation coefficient over all photographs of the number of times the photograph was assigned to category i

and the number it was assigned to *j*. For example, *branca* (white) and *clara* (light) were strongly positively correlated ($r = .91$), because the same photographs most often labeled *branca* were also most often labeled *clara. Branca* and *escura* (dark), on the other hand, were strongly negatively correlated ($r = .74$).

Figure 7.1 presents the results of MDS applied to the similarity matrix of racial categories described above, with each circle corresponding to one category. The most commonly used categories are labeled. Dimension 1 (horizontal) is largely a color axis: terms at the left end of the scale (*negra, escura, morena*) label people as dark or black, while terms at the right (*branca, clara*) label people as light or white. Dimension 2 (vertical) is an axis of African versus non-African features, independent of color: *morena,* at the low end of dimension 2, implies dark color but not necessarily African features, while *sarará,* at the high end, refers specifically to African physiognomy and hair form combined with light skin and hair. Thus the initial results of MDS suggest that Bahian racial classification, beneath a

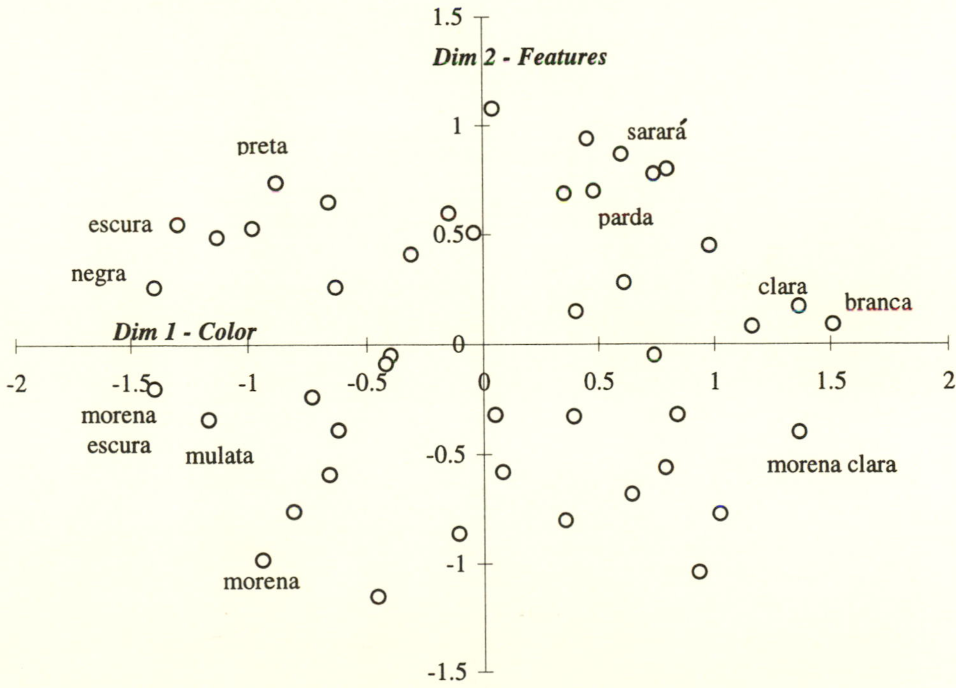

Figure 7.1. Brazilian racial categories and Multi-Dimensional Scaling. Each circle represents one category. The closer points are to one another, the more often the corresponding categories were applied to the same photographs. From left to right, categories refer to dark or light color. From bottom to top, categories refer to non-African or African features. The most frequently used categories are labelled.

bewildering profusion of labels, is largely concerned with labeling individuals first by color and then by African versus non-African features independent of color.

In principle, Brazilian racial terminology could be used to specify objectively and fairly exactly both color and other racial features of individuals. In practice, however, Brazilians' use of this terminology is affected by local ideology and etiquette. This can be demonstrated with another set of results. Each of 30 females in the photographic sample can be assigned a position on dimensions 1 and 2 by averaging her scores on each dimension over all 80 categorizations given her. Figure 7.2 shows the results, with each female represented by a circle.

Several things stand out in this figure. First, all but three of the points in Figure 7.2 fall on the lower half of the scale. While Brazilian racial terminology contains many terms with high positive scores on dimension 2 (referring to African fea-

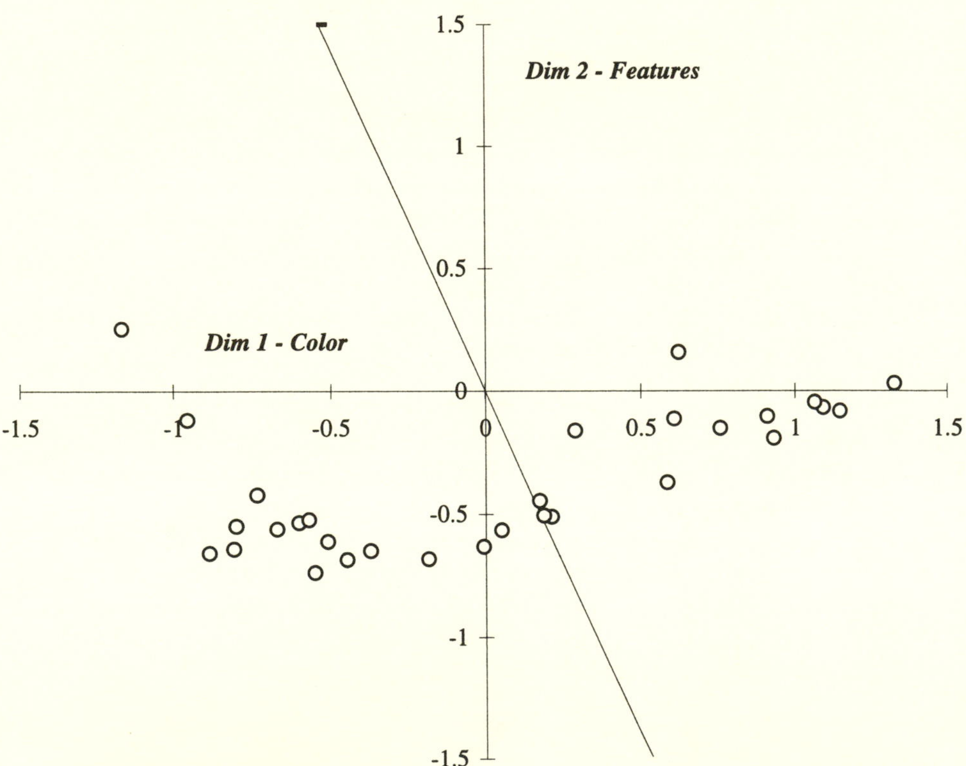

Figure 7.2. Racial classification of photographs of Brazilians. Each circle represents one photograph. Each photograph was assigned a position on Dimensions 1 and 2 by averaging over racial categories given to it. The diagonal line shows the Combined Index given by Equation 1; scores on this index are correlated with ratings of attractiveness.

tures, independent of color), and while many photographic subjects did have pronounced African features, raters tended to stay away from labels clearly indicating these features (including *negra* = Negro/black, 2% of classifications; *preta* = black, 2%; and *sarará,* 2%). Instead, the most commonly used terms were *morena* (brown, 39%) and variants thereof (*morena clara* = light brown, 11%, and *morena escura* = dark brown, 4%), while various terms designating white or light color (*branca* = white, 21%, and *clara* = light, 6%) were also common. *Morena* is a very general word which can be applied to dark-skinned whites, and it seems to operate as a euphemism in a context where African features are not highly esteemed.

Second, and quite oddly, scores on dimension 1 are strongly and significantly correlated with scores on dimension 2 ($r = .57$, $p < .01$). Taken at face value, the direction of the correlation would imply that light-skinned people are more likely than dark-skinned people to have an African physiognomy and hair form. Obviously this is not really the case in Bahia, nor does it seem to be the case among the women in the photographic sample. Rather, raters seem to be employing terminology in such a way as to downplay racial distinctions. Two women in the sample presented such a strong combination of dark skin and African features that they were often labeled *preta* or *negra* (the two points above and just below the x-axis on the left of Figure 7.2). But for the most part classification was dominated by two trends: *branca* and *clara* were often applied not just to whites but to light-skinned blacks, and whites were likely to be labeled *morena.* (Every female in the sample, including several with no discernable African ancestry and not especially dark skin, was classified as some kind of *morena* by more than 10% of raters.) Instead of emphasizing the distinctions between black people and white people, this use of terminology emphasizes the different ways people combine black and white characteristics.

The low average scores on dimension 2 and the positive correlation between scores on dimensions 1 and 2 reflect two frequently noted aspects of Brazilian—and especially Bahian—race relations. Negative stereotypes and social prejudice against blacks are widespread, and there is a corresponding resistance to labeling oneself or others as simply "black" (*preta, negra,* etc.). But there is a tolerant or even somewhat positive attitude to miscegenation, an attitude reflected, for example, in the ideology of *mestiçagem* (racial mixture), which encourages Brazilians to think more about their common identity as *mestiços* than their separate identities as blacks, whites, Indians, or Asians.

Race and Attractiveness

To extend this investigation from racial classification to somatic prejudice, I collected ratings of the attractiveness of the 30 photographs from 25 male and female subjects in Arembepe. Ages of subjects ranged from 19 to 35. When asked about their racial identity, four-fifths chose labels implying dark color or mixed ancestry (*moreno, pardo,* etc), one-fifth called themselves white (*branco*), and none called themselves black (*negro, preto*). Subjects were mostly working class; all described themselves as literate. Pictures were laid out in three-by-three blocks and rated on a scale of one to nine according to a procedure described in Jones (1996a); each rater rated 27 randomly selected pictures. Attractiveness ratings were generated for each photograph by averaging across raters.

Scores on dimensions 1 and 2 are each moderately correlated with ratings of attractiveness (dimension 1: $r = .29$, n.s.; dimension 2: $r = .36, p < .05$). The directions of the correlations suggest somatic prejudice against dark color and African features, but given the correlation between dimension 1 and dimension 2, it is worth considering the two dimensions together. The best predictor of attractiveness in this sample is a combined index given by:

$$\text{Combined Index} = \text{dimension } 1 - 2.8 \times \text{dimension } 2 \tag{1}$$

This index, which is highest for individuals combining light color and non-African features, is strongly and significantly correlated with ratings of physical attractiveness ($r = .68$, $p < .01$). According to equation 1, color (dimension 1) is only 1/2.8 times as important as other racial features (dimension 2). But since standard deviations of scores on dimension 1 are 2.6 times greater than those for dimension 2, the two dimensions are actually about equally important.

The diagonal line in Figure 7.2 represents the Combined Index calculated using equation 1. The scores of each photograph on this index are given by the positions of their projections on this line. Note that the major axis of the cloud of points—running somewhat upward from left to right—is almost at right angles to the line of the Combined Index—running sharply downward from left to right. This means that even though subjects assigning racial labels tended to de-emphasize the black/white distinction (dark skin and African features on the upper left vs. light skin and non-African features on the lower right), the distinction showed up clearly when subjects made judgments of attractiveness. Figure 7.3 shows physical attractiveness ratings as a function of Combined Index scores. Although the two females with negative index scores are outliers, the correlations are virtually the same when recomputed using rank orders ($r = .72, p < .01$) or with the outliers omitted ($r = .69, p < .01$).

The strong correlation between race and attractiveness in this sample seems to reflect a prejudice against pronounced black appearance more than it reflects a prejudice in favor of pronounced white appearance. Suppose we compare attractiveness ratings for three groups: the 10 women with the lowest scores on the Combined Index (group I, average attractiveness rating = 3.5), the 10 women with intermediate scores (group II, average = 5.3), and the 10 women with the highest scores (group III, average = 6.3). Women in the first group, with the strongest combination of African features and dark skin, have significantly lower attractiveness ratings than women in the other two groups (I vs. II, $p = .004$; I vs. III, $p = .0005$, two-tailed unpaired t-tests). But women in the intermediate second group

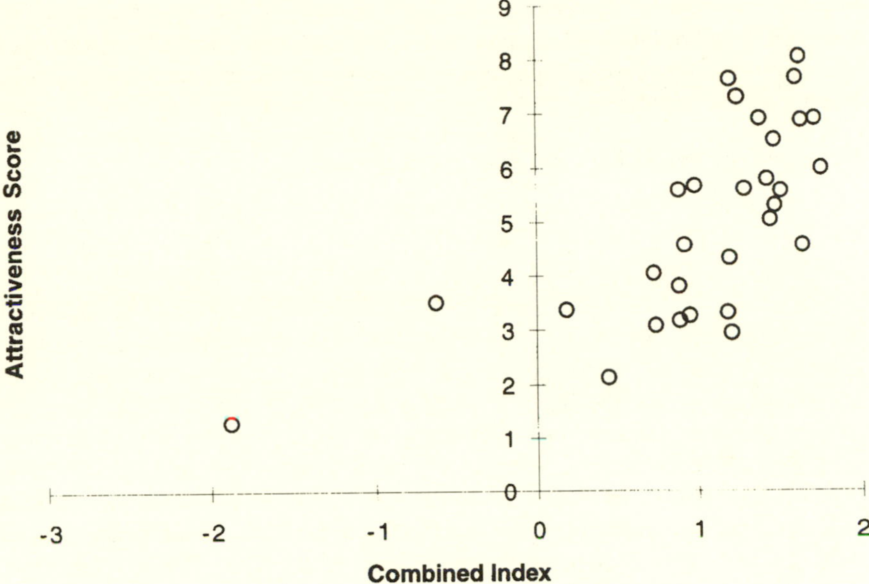

Figure 7.3. Racial classification and ratings of attractiveness. Individuals with high scores on the Combined Index—combining light color and non-African features—generally receive higher attractiveness ratings.

are not rated significantly less attractive than women in the third group, the one with the strongest combination of non-African features and light skin (II vs. III, $p = .16$). There is other evidence suggesting that Bahians do not have a particularly strong attraction to whites relative to people of mixed race. In another study involving photographs of Bahian university students who were mostly whites and light-skinned blacks, U.S. American raters gave higher attractiveness ratings to students with Caucasian physical features like thin lips and narrow noses, but Bahian raters did not (Jones 1996a:142). And in rating photographs of U.S. university students, U.S. but not Bahian raters gave significantly higher ratings to blond women (both groups gave significantly lower ratings to blond men; Jones 1996a:98). While Bahians in this study show strong somatic prejudice against blacks, they are far from perceiving whites as supernormally attractive.

DISCUSSION

The data presented above demonstrate significant somatic prejudice against women with dark color and African features. The effect is a strong one: the difference in average attractiveness ratings between women in the "blackest" tercile and other women is 1.7 standard deviations. Below I consider the relevance of these findings both for evolutionary theories of attractiveness and for studies of racial and ethnic relations. I conclude by considering the prospects for change in Brazil and elsewhere.

Evolutionary Psychology and Somatic Prejudice

At least three general principles of human physical attractiveness—attraction to markers of social status, to "average" features, and to fair color (in females)—may contribute to the somatic prejudice documented in this paper.

Social cues, specifically those afforded by correlations between physical appearance and social status, are probably the most important source of somatic prejudice in the study population. Innate preferences may account to some extent for the attraction to light color, but it is less plausible that they account for negative responses to African facial morphology and hair form. Some evidence suggests that men have an innate attraction to adult females with "neotenous" facial proportions—large eyes in relation to the vertical dimensions of the face, gracile jaws, small noses, and full lips (Jones 1995). But Africans are not systematically more craniofacially neotenous than Europeans (Lahr 1996:248–263); they are more neotenous on some facial characters (nasal projection, lip width), less on others (nose width, lower facial prognathism), and simply different on others (face width, hair form). And while Bahian women, like other women, do not evidence much attraction to neotenous male faces, they do show somatic prejudice against blacks in research involving photographs of a racially mixed sample of U.S. Americans (Jones 1996a:123–125). All this, together with cross-cultural evidence for changing standards of attractiveness in response to Western influence, makes it likely that Bahian somatic prejudice results to a very large degree from an awareness of the low economic and social position of blacks both locally and in the world system. This is an important finding for evolutionary psychology: while the adaptive basis, if any, of status effects on standards of attractiveness is not well-understood, these effects can be powerful, and they need to be taken into account by any theory of attractiveness.

A combination of the "averageness" effect and status effects may account for the apparent nonlinearity in the relationship between race and ratings of attractiveness. If ratings of attractiveness depended only on "averageness," one might expect that individuals at either extreme of the Bahian racial continuum would be rated as less attractive than those in the middle. If ratings of attractiveness depended only on correlates of status, one might expect that attractiveness would vary linearly with race. Instead, both effects seem to be at work, reinforcing one another at the black end of the scale but partly canceling each other out at the white end so that whites are not rated significantly more attractive than those in the middle. However, more research is needed to determine whether a similar nonlinear effect operates in societies without Brazil's "mulatto escape hatch."

Finally, regarding color, two factors—local correlations between color and status, and a near-universal (and perhaps innate) male attraction to women of lighter-than-average color—may each account for some of the negative response to dark color observed in the present study. However, it will take more research to disentangle the relative contributions of these factors. Specifically, if future fieldwork in Bahia shows that color, relative to other features, is less important for male attractiveness than for female attractiveness, this will support the argument that responses to skin color involve more than just its correlation with social status.

Standards of Beauty, Racial Prejudice, and the Prospects for Change

A considerable literature in social psychology now demonstrates the importance of physical appearance and attractiveness in social and especially sexual relationships. This literature, in conjunction with evidence suggesting the importance of somatic prejudice, raises the possibility that prejudice and discrimination based on race may overlap with prejudice and discrimination based on attractiveness. The social consequences of somatic prejudice is a large topic; here I will mention just one direction that research might take.

One of the characteristic institutions of the African diaspora in the New World is the matrifocal family. In Latin America, the Caribbean, and the United States, family life among blacks, more than among whites, involves female-headed households and unstable relationships between men and women. Some scholars (Herskovits and Herskovits 1947) emphasize the African roots of New World matrifocality, arguing that the matrifocal family has arisen because West African traditions of female economic and social independence have survived among New World blacks, while West Africa's unilineal descent groups mostly have not. Others emphasize the legacy of slavery and the attendant disruption of long-term monogamous relations between blacks (Frazier 1939). For the West Indies, Smith argues that the racial hierarchy associated with slavery resulted in the establishment of a "dual marriage system." "Whereas white women did not (with few exceptions) enter non-legal unions, colored women were reputed to prefer concubinage with a white man over marriage with a colored man" (1996:75). Some features of this dual marriage system have persisted to the present (see also Martinez-Alier 1974). More immediate causes of matrifocality may include economic circumstances making it difficult for poor men to support a family (Wilson 1996), and low sex ratios facilitating male mate switching (Guttentag and Secord 1983). While no single factor is likely to account for the matrifocal family, I suggest that somatic prejudice may be part of the story. When ethnic groups differ in physical appearance, standards of attractiveness may affect ethnic relations, and individuals' and groups' social position, including their bargaining power in the mating and marriage market, may depend not just on their economic and political resources but on how closely they attain to the local somatic ideal (Hoetink 1967).

The sexual and reproductive options for women at the bottom of a society's aesthetic hierarchy may not include much possibility of a stable relationship with an acceptable man. This is a topic I plan to investigate in future research; I have begun collecting photographs and life history data for sibling pairs, aiming in part at investigating the social and life history consequences of being the more or less attractive of a set of siblings.

Somatic prejudice, involving as it does a very personal and visceral dimension of a major public problem, is obviously a disturbing topic, but not one that should be approached in a spirit of fatalism. A number of political and cultural groups in Bahia are actively involved in trying to cultivate a more Afrocentric standard of beauty among Bahians as part of a larger program of black consciousness raising (*conscientização*). Such efforts had had little impact on the groups I studied at the time of my fieldwork, but nothing in the results or theory presented in this paper rules out the possibility that they might have more influence in the future. Doing the evolutionary psychology of attractiveness is not only a matter of discovering an invariant, species-typical hierarchy of aesthetic values. It may also involve understanding standards of attractiveness in any given culture as the joint and mutable product of human nature and history.

SUMMARY

1. The evolutionary psychology of physical attractiveness may contribute to understanding "somatic prejudice," in which members of one racial or ethnic group are evaluated more or less favorably than members of another on the basis of their physical appearance. Three well-documented and universal or near-universal components of attractiveness–color, "averageness," and status markers–are likely to be especially relevant to understanding somatic prejudice.

2. Brazil is a racially stratified country in which whites have considerably higher status than blacks, but Brazilians generally treat race as a continuous rather than a categorical variable. An investigation of the complex racial terminology in the state of Bahia in northeastern Brazil shows that (a) Bahian racial classification is largely concerned with labeling individuals first by color, and then by African versus non-African features independently of color, and (b) in accordance with the ideology of *mestiçagem* (mixture), individuals labeling photographs tend to avoid labels clearly indicating African features, and to emphasize the way different individuals combine white and black features, rather than differences between blacks and whites.

3. Although Bahians downplay black/white differences in labeling photographs, these differences play a major role in assessments of attractiveness: photographic subjects with pronounced African color and features are rated substantially less attractive than others (1.7 standard deviations), while subjects with intermediate features are not rated significantly less attractive than those with

pronounced European features. These findings demonstrate that evolutionary psychology must consider the role of social cues in the development of standards of attractiveness.

NOTE

1. Terms referring to Indian or mixed Indian ancestry (*indio, caboclo*) fell at the low end of dimension 2. These terms were used only infrequently, but if my sample had included significant numbers of individuals with marked Indian appearance, they might have added a third dimension to the MDS results.

REFERENCES

Andersson, M. 1994. *Sexual Selection.* Princeton: Princeton University Press.

Barkow, J., L. Cosmides, and J. Tooby, eds. 1992. *The Adapted Mind: Evolutionary Psychology and the Generation of Culture.* New York: Oxford University Press.

Buss, D. M. 1989. Sex differences in human mate preferences: Evolutionary hypotheses tested in 37 cultures. *Behavioral and Brain Sciences* 12:1–49.

Davis, F. J. 1991. *Who Is Black?: One Nation's Definition.* University Park, Pennsylvania: Penn State University Press.

Dawkins, R. 1989. *The Selfish Gene.* New York: Oxford University Press.

Degler, C. 1971. *Neither Black Nor White: Slavery and Race Relations in the United States and Brazil.* Madison, Wisconsin: University of Wisconsin Press.

Dugatkin, L. A. 1996. Interface between culturally based preferences and genetic preferences: Female mate choice in *Poecilia reticulata. Proceedings of the National Academy of Sciences,* USA 93:2770–2773.

Dugatkin, L. A., and J. G. J. Godin. 1995. Variability and repeatability of female mating preferences in the guppy. *Animal Behaviour* 49:1427–1433.

Ellis, B. 1992. The evolution of sexual attraction: Evaluative mechanisms in women. In *the Adapted Mind: Evolutionary Psychology and the Generation of Culture,* J. H. Barkow, L. Cosmides, and J. Tooby, eds. Pp. 267–288. New York: Oxford University Press.

Endler, J. A. 1980. Natural selection on color patterns in *Poecilia reticulata. Evolution* 34:76–91.

Endler, J. A., and A. M. Lyles. 1989. Bright ideas about parasites. *Trends in Ecology and Evolution* 4:246–248.

Fontaine, P., ed. 1985. *Race, Class, and Power in Brazil.* Los Angeles: University of California.

Ford, C. S., and F. Beach. 1951. *Patterns of Sexual Behavior.* New York: Harper.

Frazier, F. 1939. *The Negro Family in the United States.* Chicago: University of Chicago Press.

Grammer, K., and R. Thornhill. 1994. Human *(Homo sapiens)* facial attractiveness and sexual selection: The role of symmetry and averageness. *Journal of Comparative Psychology* 108:233–242.

Guttentag, M., and P. Secord. 1983. *Too Many Women? The Sex Ratio Question.* Beverly Hills: Sage.

Harris, M. 1964. *Patterns of Race in the Americas.* New York: W. W. Norton.

Hatfield, E., and S. Sprecher. 1986. *Mirror, Mirror: The Importance of Looks in Everyday Life.* Albany: State University of New York Press.

Herskovits, M. J., and F. S. Herskovits. 1947. *Trinidad Village.* New York: Alfred A. Knopf.

Hoetink, H. 1967. *The Two Variants in Caribbean Race Relations: A Contribution to the Sociology of Segmented Societies.* London: Oxford University Press.

Isaacs, H. R. 1975. *Idols of the Tribe: Group Identity and Political Change.* New York: Harper and Row.

Jones, D. 1995. Sexual selection, physical attractiveness, and facial neoteny: Cross-cultural evidence and implications. *Current Anthropology* 36:723–748.

———. 1996a. *Physical Attractiveness and the Theory of Sexual Selection: Results from Five Populations.* Ann Arbor: Museum of Anthropology, University of Michigan.

———. 1996b. An evolutionary perspective on physical attractiveness. *Evolutionary Anthropology* 5:97–109.

Jones, D., and K. Hill. 1993. Criteria of physical attractiveness in five populations. *Human Nature* 4:271–296.

Koeslag, J. H., and P. D. Koeslag. 1994. Koinophilia. *Journal of Theoretical Biology* 167:55–65.

Kottak, C. 1992. *Assault on Paradise: Social Change in a Brazilian Village.* New York: McGraw-Hill.

Lahr, M. M. 1996. *The Evolution of Modern Human Diversity: A Study of Cranial Variation.* Cambridge: Cambridge University Press.

Lancaster, R. N. 1991. Skin color, race and racism in Nicaragua. *Ethnology* 30:339–353.

Langlois, J. H., and L. A. Roggman. 1990. Attractive faces are only average. *Psychological Science* 1:115–121.

Levine, R. M. 1997. *Brazilian Legacies.* London: M. E. Sharpe.

Martinez-Alier, V. 1974. *Marriage, Class and Colour in Nineteenth-Century Cuba: A Study of Racial Attitudes and Sexual Values in a Slave Society.* London: Cambridge University Press.

Russell, K., M. Wilson, and R. Hall. 1992. *The Color Complex: The Politics of Skin Color among African-Americans.* New York: Harcourt Brace Jovanovich.

Scheper-Hughes, N. 1992. *Death Without Weeping: The Violence of Everyday Life in Brazil.* Berkeley: University of California Press.

Singh, D. 1993. Adaptive significance of female physical attractiveness: Role of waist-to-hip ratio. *Journal of Personality and Social Psychology* 65:293–307.

Smith, R. T. 1996. *The Matrifocal Family: Power, Pluralism, and Politics.* New York: Routledge.

Symons, D. 1979. *The Evolution of Human Sexuality.* New York: Oxford University Press.

Thomas, H. 1997. *The Slave Trade: The Story of the Atlantic Slave Trade, 1440–1870.* New York: Simon and Schuster.

van den Berghe, P. L., and P. Frost. 1986. Skin color preference, sexual dimorphism and sexual selection: A case of gene-culture coevolution? *Ethnic and Racial Studies* 9:87–113.

Wagatsuma, H. 1968. The social perception of skin color in Japan. In *Color and Race,* J. H. Franklin, ed. Pp. 129–165. Boston: Houghton Mifflin.

Wilson, W. J. 1996. *When Work Disappears: The World of the New Urban Poor.* New York: Knopf.

PART III

PARENTING

8

Parental Investment Strategies among Aka Foragers, Ngandu Farmers, and Euro-American Urban-Industrialists

BARRY S. HEWLETT, MICHAEL E. LAMB,
BIRGIT LEYENDECKER, and AXEL SCHÖLMERICH

In this chapter, we examine characterizations and explanations of parental investment strategies in forager, farmer, and urban-industrial (also called Western, modern, and global-scale) cultures. Observational data on 20 Aka forager families and 21 Ngandu farming families in the Central African Republic and 21 upper-middle-class Euro-American families in Washington, D.C. are utilized to evaluate models developed by evolutionary ecologists and psychological anthropologists to explain differing parental investment strategies in these communities. These groups are not necessarily representative of their respective modes of production and live in quite different ecologies, but they afforded an opportunity to evaluate evolutionary models of parental investment in these different settings. As far as we know, we are the first researchers to use observational methods to compare parental investment strategies in populations with three markedly different modes of production. Systematic behavioral comparisons have been made between foragers and urban-industrialists (e.g., !Kung vs. U.S.: Konner 1976), and between farmers and urban-industrialists (e.g., Gusii vs. U.S.: LeVine et al. 1994; Richman et al. 1988, 1992), but no researchers have directly compared foragers, farmers, and urban-industrialists (urban-industrialists will be referred to as Euro-Americans in the rest of the chapter).

Table 8.1 summarizes "adaptationist" models of parental investment proposed by Draper and Harpending (1982), LeVine (1994), and Blurton Jones (1993). By developing a model focused on the effects of family context on individual reproductive strategies, Draper and Harpending (1982) were among the first to explain differences in parental investment using evolutionary theory. Draper and Harpending were influenced by the Whitings' (1975) cross-cultural research on aloof as opposed to intimate husband-wife relationships. The Whitings proposed that aloof husband-wife relationships (husband and wife eat, sleep, and have leisure activities apart) led to lower paternal involvement and hypermasculine males

Table 8.1. Models of parental reproductive strategies.

	Foragers	*Farmers*	*Urban-Industrialists (middle or high SES)*
Draper and Harpending 1982, 1987; Belsky et al. 1992	"parental effort" societies; high parental investment; father involvement; sensitive, supportive, positively affectionate; responsive to infant demands	"mating effort" societies; low parental investment; low father and high sibling care; harsh, rejecting, insensitive or inconsistent caregiving; less responsive to infant demands	"parental effort" societies; high parental investment; father involvement; sensitive, supportive, positively affectionate; responsive to infant demands
LeVine et al. 1994	does not discuss	"pediatric model"; proximal parental behaviors—quick response to fuss/cry, frequent breast-feeding, always holding; minimal distal-verbal stimulation	"pedagogical model"; distal-verbal parental behaviors—frequent face-to-face interaction, verbally interactive, stimulating
Blurton Jones 1993	"survivorship enhancers"—quick response to requests; protect/keep infant from danger and exposure; nurturant and warm	"production enhancers"—unresponsive to infant demands; sibling care to decrease demands on mother	"ORS enhancers"—begin to teach children cognitive skills important to their RS; frequent face-to-face interaction, stimulation

whereas intimate husband-wife relationships led to greater father involvement and more egalitarian gender relationships. They further suggested that aloof husband-wife relationships existed when warfare made it necessary to socialize hypermasculine warriors. Draper and Harpending placed the aloof versus intimate dimension in an evolutionary life history framework, suggesting that individuals raised in an "intimate" husband-wife context, with low marital stress and contributions to subsistence by both parents, develop a reproductive strategy that emphasizes parental effort (i.e., more time and energy invested in a few children) whereas individuals raised in "aloof" father-absent households develop reproductive strategies that emphasize mating effort, having more children with different spouses, and investing less time and energy in each child.

LeVine (1994), a psychological anthropologist, was also a student of the Whitings and was influenced by their suggestion that "maintenance systems" (e.g., subsistence patterns) explain infant and child care. LeVine proposed that parental goals could be viewed as adaptations to different maintenance systems, and he specifically described agrarian (also called pediatric) and urban industrial (also called pedagogical) parental goals. Agrarian parental goals focus on the survival, health, and physical development of infants because infant mortality levels are high—often only half of the children survive to reproductive age. In order to monitor and respond to health and survival indicators, agrarian parents are expected to keep their infants close (holding or keeping them in proximity), respond quickly to fusses or cries, and feed infants on demand. This contrasts with the urban-industrial parental goals that focused on active engagement, social exchange, stimulation, and proto-conversation with infants. LeVine reasoned that urban parents were concerned with the acquisition of cognitive skills essential for survival when infant mortality is low, children cost more and contribute less, and there is a competitive labor market operating through an academically graded occupation hierarchy.

Blurton Jones (1993) built on recent contributions to life history theory (Clutton-Brock 1991), hypothesizing the existence of three basic parental investment strategies characterized, respectively, by "survivorship," "production," and "offspring reproductive success" (ORS) enhancers. His survivorship-enhancing and production-enhancing patterns were similar to the parental and mating effort patterns described by Draper and Harpending, whereas parents who adopted the ORS-enhancing pattern, like LeVine's prototypical urban-industrial parents, were expected to have very few offspring and to invest heavily in their children's cognitive development to ensure their reproductive success. Blurton Jones associated the survivorship-enhancing strategy with low-fertility hunting and gathering groups such as the !Kung; the production-enhancing strategy with high-fertility agricultural societies; and the ORS-enhancing strategy with high socioeconomic status parents in industrial societies (1993:311), but he also pointed out that forager and farmer parental investment strategies vary dramatically in response to variations in natural and social ecologies.

There are several similarities and clear differences among these models' assumptions and predictions. Most important, from a life history perspective, is the fact that demographic features—fertility, mortality, birth intervals, or population density—are central to each of the models. LeVine used differences in infant mortality to explain differences between the agrarian and industrial parental strategies, whereas Blurton Jones mentioned threats to infant and child survival (e.g., predators) when explaining the survivorship-enhancing strategy. Chisholm's (1996) and Belsky's (1997) refinements of the Draper and Harpending model focused on the extent to which local mortality affected the relative prominence of mating as opposed to parental investment.

The Draper and Harpending and Blurton Jones models suggested that foragers should have lower fertility than farmers because they invest more time and energy in each child; farmers should have more children and invest less in each child. Draper and Harpending linked the tradeoffs in care and number of offspring to father absence or presence whereas Blurton Jones suggested that forager-farmer differences in parental investment were due to differential environmental hazards (e.g., predators); he proposed that forager parents invest more time and energy in each child to ensure "survivorship" in an especially hazardous environment whereas farmers emphasize "production." Both models predict that foragers should be characterized by relatively high investment by both parents; proximal care; and sensitive and responsive parental behavior. Although it is clear that middle-class Euro-American parents have fewer children than parents in "traditional" populations, cross-cultural studies of forager and farmer (horticulturist) mortality and fertility rates reveal few differences on these demographic dimensions (Bentley et al. 1993; Hewlett 1991).

One important difference between the three models lies in their characterization of group differences in parental investment. Most importantly, LeVine described farmers as proximal (e.g., holding or staying close to their infants), responsive, and sensitive to their infants whereas the other two models suggested that farmers provide harsh, rejecting, and insensitive parenting. Draper and Harpending proposed similarities between foragers and Euro-Americans whereas LeVine and Blurton Jones suggested that these groups should differ. Draper and Harpending (1987:225) noted that:

> among parents of Western, industrialized nations there is an apparent return to a system of parent caretaking. Family life is much more like that of the nomadic !Kung, a hunting and gathering people whose parent-child relationships are similar to those of other nomadic peoples. Rates of child mortality are moderate among hunter-gatherers in comparison with those of primitive agriculturists or contemporary underdeveloped countries. Low mortality among foragers has various causes, including low population density and especially long birth spacing. . . .

In this chapter, we evaluate the characterizations of and explanations for parental investment strategies provided by proponents of these three models. The applicability of the models is explored by examining parent-infant interactions in three populations: Aka foragers and Ngandu farmers of the Central African Republic and upper-middle-class Euro-Americans from Washington, D.C. Our evaluation of the models is limited to data gathered when infants in all three groups were 3 to 4 months old. This, of course, limits evaluation of the models because parent-infant strategies and behaviors obviously change over time. On the other hand, we were able to conduct more hours of observation for a specific age and control for the confounding effects of child age and maturity on parent-child interactions. In most anthropological studies, infants of diverse ages are observed for brief periods of time. It is also important to note that the LeVine and Blurton Jones models explicitly dealt with parental investment in infancy whereas the Draper and Harpending model dealt with parental investment more generally. We have extrapolated a parent-infant pattern from their general model.

LIFE HISTORY THEORY

All three models utilize modified versions of life history theory, and the proponents of all models would probably argue that parental behavior evolved because it enhanced the parents' reproductive success. A commonly utilized life history model (Williams 1966) identifies two conceptually distinct categories of effort—somatic and reproductive effort—in which individuals engage in order to be biologically successful. Somatic effort refers to the risks and costs of assuring physical survival—obtaining shelter, ensuring protection from predators and conspecifics, seeking food, keeping healthy, and so forth. Reproductive effort involves ensuring representation of one's genes in subsequent generations, and comprises three broad categories of activities—parental effort (rearing children), mating effort (attracting, keeping, and guarding spouses), and nepotistic effort (helping genetically related individuals besides one's own children). The principle of allocation implicit in life history theory holds that energy utilized for one purpose cannot be used for another, and thus that individuals are frequently forced to make choices or decisions. The two basic tradeoffs in life history theory are the tradeoff between current and future reproduction and the tradeoff between number and fitness of offspring produced (Hill and Hurtado 1996). The first tradeoff focuses on whether individuals pursue small and immediate reproductive gains or wait for a larger reproductive gains in the future, whereas the second focuses on the costs and benefits associated with the quantity as opposed to the quality of offspring.

Charnov's (1993) recent contribution to female mammalian life history theory proposes that adult mortality and life span, along with juvenile growth rate, constrain several important life history variables, including age at maturity, adult weight, fertility, and juvenile mortality (see Hawkes et al., chapter 11, for a more extensive discussion of Charnov's model). Charnov's model predicts that, when adult mortality levels are high and juvenile growth rates are rapid, individuals should invest in current rather than future reproduction. Charnov's model is important in the present context because it draws attention to the effects of adult mortality on parental investment, whereas the three models described above emphasize the effects of juvenile mortality on parental investment.

Because all three of the models summarized in Table 8.1 rely to some extent on life history theory, we evaluate the assumptions of the three models and attempt to place Aka, Ngandu, and Euro-American parental investment in the context of contemporary life history theory. We focus on tradeoffs between parental and mating effort, and examine maternal investment/expenditure of what Clutton-Brock (1991) calls "depreciable" care (i.e., care that affects only one child at a time [e.g., feeding, holding] as opposed to "nondepreciable" care, which affects several children at the same time [e.g., defense of family resources, maintenance of kin networks]).

NATURAL AND SOCIAL ECOLOGIES

Parental investment strategies are influenced by their natural and social ecologies so it is essential to provide a brief overview of the environmental contexts of the three cultures.

The Aka foragers and Ngandu farmers in this study are neighbors in the rural southern regions of the Central African Republic (population density less than one person per square km), where they make a living in the same dense humid tropical forest. Both Aka and Ngandu have relatively high fertility and mortality as most women have more than four live births and juvenile mortality (under age 15) is usually over 35%. Infertility and female reproductive variability is greater among the Ngandu than it is among the Aka. Mid-adulthood mortality is also relatively high by Western standards, with infectious and parasitic diseases being the primary causes of adult death, although maternal mortality in childbirth and accidental deaths (e.g., falling from trees, hunting accidents, snakebite) are also not unusual.

Despite these similarities, the Aka and Ngandu live in very different physical and social settings. The Aka camps comprise 25 to 35 related (by blood or marriage) individuals living in five to eight dome-shaped houses, each just large enough for one 4-foot-long bed. All family members sleep on this bed, and all of the houses in the camp occupy an area about the size of a large living and dining room in the United States. By comparison, Ngandu villages consist of 50 to 400 related (including clan affiliation) individuals. Each house is at least 10 feet away from the next, but there are no walls or fences between houses. Polygyny is more common among the Ngandu than it is among the Aka (about 40% among Ngandu vs. 15% among Aka) and each wife lives with her children in a house or a room in a large house. Intermarriage between Aka and Ngandu is rare.

The Euro-American households we studied were all located in relatively wealthy suburban Washington, D.C. Each house had several bedrooms and a large backyard. Infant mortality in such communities is less than 1%, child mortality less than 5%, the total fertility rate is less than 2, and polygyny does not exist. Mid-adulthood mortality is rare in upper-middle-class communities, and chronic diseases are the primary causes of death in adulthood (e.g., coronary artery disease, cancer).

Aka and Ngandu have frequent social, economic, and religious interactions and see each others' infant caregiving on a regular basis, yet have distinct modes of production, male-female relations, and patterns of infant care. The Aka are net-hunting foragers (also known as hunter-gatherers), move their villages several times a year, have minimal political hierarchy (i.e., chiefs with little/no power over others) and relatively high gender and intergenerational egalitarianism, whereas the Ngandu are slash and burn farmers, are relatively sedentary, have stronger chiefs and marked gender and intergenerational inequality. Upper-middle-class Euro-Americans have the greatest level of political and socioeconomic hierarchy, relatively high gender equality, and low intergenerational egalitarianism.

Aka and Ngandu cultures share more and are in many ways more egalitarian than Euro-American cultures, but Aka sharing and egalitarianism are also substantially greater than among the Ngandu. The Ngandu focus on maintaining egalitarianism and sharing between households; households that accumulate more than others and do not share with neighboring families are prime targets of sorcery, which is believed to cause illness or death. Sharing between households is not as frequent as it is among the Aka (i.e., not daily), and there is marked inequality within Ngandu households, with men and the elderly receiving more than others. The Aka, on the other hand, share with many people in many households on a daily basis, and there is greater gender and age egalitarianism. To foster egalitarianism, Aka also avoid drawing attention to themselves and eschew evaluative rankings, while also respecting individuality and autonomy. Upper-middle-class neolocal families rarely share with others outside the household, but regularly share food and resources with household members (i.e., between husband and wife). Differences among individuals are evaluated on a near daily basis.

The Aka subsistence system involves "immediate returns" in that food is consumed within a few days after capture or collection. By contrast, Ngandu and Euro-American economic systems involve "delayed returns," in that the products of investment are delayed until harvest or payday (Woodburn 1982). This helps to explain the different sharing systems—Aka share more frequently in part because relatively little is invested and food is not stored.

Aka and upper-middle-class Euro-American men and women contribute extensively to subsistence, whereas Ngandu women are the primary providers. Ngandu men clear and burn plantations, while women plant, weed, harvest, and prepare all subsistence food items (manioc, corn, peanuts, plantains, etc.). Unlike the Aka, the Ngandu are actively engaged in a local cash economy and many women are small-scale merchants, selling plantains, peanuts, nuts, mushrooms, and alcohol. Men are responsible for limited coffee production, hunt with trap lines or guns, and may search for gold or diamonds in the local streams. Ngandu women are responsible for home maintenance, laundry, and collecting water and firewood. The workload of Ngandu mothers also appears to be greater than that of the Aka, especially given the extensive sharing and cooperation among the Aka.

Like the !Kung, Aka infants are carried in slings on the left-hand side of the adults' body (Konner 1976, 1977). This leaves the head, arms, and legs free, and allows the infant to nurse on demand. By contrast, Ngandu infants are tied rather snugly on the adults' backs. When the adults are sitting, both Aka and Ngandu careproviders place infants on their laps or between their legs facing outward. When infants are laid down, they are always placed on their backs. Aka infants sleep with their parents and siblings whereas Ngandu infants often sleep with their mothers (or in separate cots, when husbands come to visit). Euro-American infants sleep alone in their own room in a crib.

Upper-middle-class Euro-American infants are placed in a variety of technological devices—infant seats, swings, etc.—generally facing toward the parent. Caregivers are usually home alone with the infant, and there are few adult or juvenile visitors. Euro-American infants have the most caregiving devices (e.g., clothes, diapers, baths, toys); the Ngandu have more caregiving devices than Aka. Some Ngandu parents make small chairs, beds, or mats for the infants to lie on. Ngandu infants also have more clothes than Aka, are often dressed more warmly than adults even in the middle of a hot day, and are washed once or twice a day. By comparison, Aka infants seldom have more than a protective forest cord around their waists and are infrequently given a complete bath. Both Aka and Ngandu caregivers carefully keep insects and debris off their infants.

Although Aka are primarily foragers and Ngandu predominantly farmers, all Aka today farm at least part of the year and most Ngandu, men in particular, spend part of the year in the forest hunting or gathering forest products. Aka fields are far in the forest, and they sometimes build Ngandu-style houses near their fields.

METHODS

Twenty Aka, 21 Ngandu, and 21 Euro-American families with 3- to 4-month-old infants were observed for 3 hours on four different days for a total of 12 hours per infant. Families were asked to follow their everyday activities and try to ignore the presence of the observer. Aka and Ngandu were observed between 6 A.M. and 6 P.M. on all days of the week whereas the Euro-Americans were observed between 8 A.M. and 8 P.M. on weekdays only.

The naturalistic observational procedure and coding system were modified from the scheme originally developed by Belsky et al. (1984). The observer watched for 20 seconds and recorded for 10 seconds. After 45 minutes, the observer took a 15 minute break, and then resumed observation. The beginning and end of each time-sampling unit were signaled through an ear phone from a small tape recorder or electronic timing device. Observers noted on a checklist the occurrence of 11 caregiver and 10 infant behaviors, 6 dyadic behaviors, as well as the location, position, and identity of the careprovider and infant (see the appendix for a list of these codes). Further details about the methods are provided by Hewlett et al. (1998) and Leyendecker et al. (1997).

There are clear limitations to these methods. The Euro-American and Ngandu mothers seldom attended social events in part, we believe, because the observer was present. Ngandu mothers would go to the fields or work around the house but they found it difficult to go to the market or health clinic, in part because these are such social activities and others were so curious about the observations. It is difficult to know precisely how much the adults changed their daily activities to accommodate the observation. Aka generally do not accommodate others very much, so they undertook a greater variety of activities inside and outside their homes and camps.

THE SAMPLE POPULATIONS

Table 8.2 summarizes the demographic features of the three samples. All of the Euro-Americans were first-borns whereas only about 15 percent of the Aka and Ngandu infants were first-borns. About 15% of the Aka and Ngandu fathers had more than one wife. None of the Aka had a formal education or were engaged in a cash economy. All men and women engaged in subsistence activities during the observation period. Most observations took place during the dry season. Most of the Ngandu men and several of the Ngandu women had an elementary education. Men and women engaged in subsistence and market activities, but neither group was employed outside the household. All of the observations took place during the dry season.

All Euro-American parents were college educated and half of them had graduate degrees. Ninety-five percent of these Euro-American mothers were employed full-time before the birth but took leave during the first few months after delivery, and all returned to work by the time the infants reached 12 months of age. Mothers were always in the house during observations, and observations took place primarily during the summer months. All the fathers were employed full-time, and all infants had their own crib in their own room. The mean family income in 1991 was about $80,000 per year. Some may prefer to call this the "yuppie" sample. Because the Euro-American mothers were getting ready to return to paid employ-

Table 8.2. The infants and their families.

	No. of infants	*Males*	*Females*	*1st Born*	*Later Born*	*No. Polygynous Familes*	*Mean Age of Mothers*	*Mean Age of Fathers*
Aka foragers	20	13	7	3	17	3	27	33
Ngandu farmers	21	12	9	3	18	5	26	37
Euro-Americans	21	13	8	21	0	0	31	34

ment, they may have been especially interested in holding and interacting with their infants.

RESULTS

In order to evaluate the models summarized in Table 8.1, the behavioral codes were divided into three categories: proximal behaviors (i.e., caregiver holding or staying close to infant); warmth and responsiveness behaviors; and distal-verbal behaviors (i.e., caregiver-infant looking, vocalization or stimulation). It is important to note that "infant looks at caregiver" included en face, mutual visual, and infant looks at caregiver codes while "caregiver looks at infant" included en face, mutual visual, and caregiver watch/check infant codes. The codes were combined in order to determine the total amount of time caregivers or infants looked at each other. Figures 8.1 to 8.3 and Table 8.3 summarize the behavioral and statistical data for each of the three groups. Figure 8.1 focuses on proximal behaviors and demonstrates marked differences among groups in the frequencies with which infants were held, proximal (defined as within an arm's reach of caregiver), or were alone (i.e., caregiver not in room or not in sight). Aka infants were almost always held and never alone; Ngandu infants were held half as frequently as Aka

Table 8.3. Levels of statistical significance between groups for variables in Figures 1–3.

	Significant Difference Between Groups (Scheffe)		
	Aka-Ngandu	*Aka-EAs*	*Ngandu-EAs*
Proximal Behaviors (Fig. 1)			
Infant held	0.000	0.000	0.000
Caregiver proximal (within 1 meter)	0.000	0.000	NS
Infant alone	0.005	0.000	0.000
Warmth and Sensitivity Behaviors (Fig. 2)			
Caregiver affect toward infant	NS	NS	NS
Caregiver soothes infant	NS	NS	NS
Adult feeds	NS	NS	NS
Infant fuss/cry	0.000	NS	0.016
Distal-Verbal Behaviors (Fig. 3)			
Caregiver stimulates-arouse	NS	0.000	0.000
Caregiver vocalizes to infant	NS	0.000	0.000
Caregiver looks at infant	NS	NS	NS
Infant looks at caregiver	NS	0.001	0.000
Infant smile	NS	0.000	0.000
Infant vocalizes	0.020	0.000	0.000

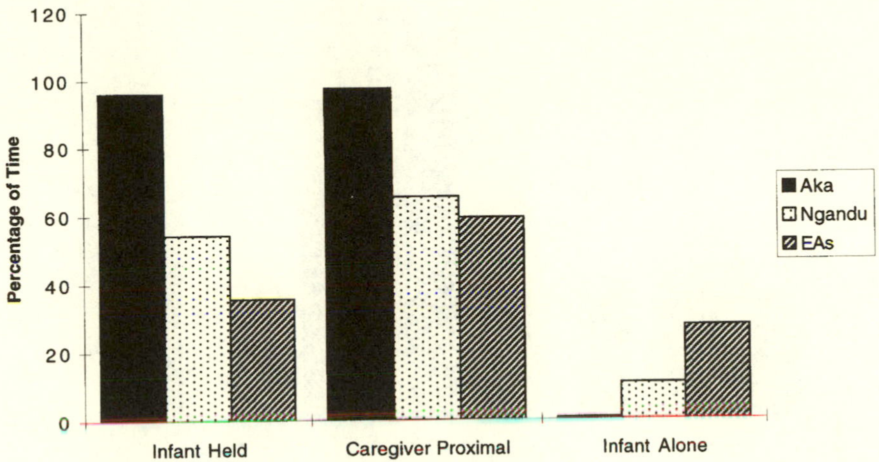

Figure 8.1. Group differences and similarities in proximal behaviors.

but significantly more than Euro-American infants. There were no significant differences between the Ngandu and Euro-American samples with respect to how often the caregivers were within arms' reach of the infants.

Figure 8.2 presents variables linked to the parents' warmth and responsiveness toward their infants. There were no differences among the three groups with respect to the frequencies with which parents showed affect (hugging, kissing), soothed, or fed their infants. There were significant differences in the length of time that infants fussed or cried, however, with Ngandu infants fussing or crying substantially longer than both Aka and Euro-American infants. There were no statistical differences in fussing or crying between the Aka and Euro-American infants, however.

There were no group differences in the total amounts of time infants were fed, but there were dramatic differences in how often mothers fed their infants (all Aka and Ngandu infants were breast-fed; Euro-Americans were breast-fed and bottle-fed). Aka mothers fed their infants significantly more often than did Ngandu and Euro-Americans (Aka 4.02 times per hour, Ngandu 2.01 times per hour, and Euro-Americans 1.61 times per hour).

Figure 8.3 displays group differences and similarities in careprovider and infant distal-verbal behaviors. There were no group differences in the frequencies with which careproviders looked at their infants, but Euro-American adults were much more likely than Aka or Ngandu adults to stimulate (e.g., tickle) and vocalize to their infants. As a result, Euro-American infants were significantly more likely than Aka and Ngandu infants to smile, look at, and vocalize to their careproviders.

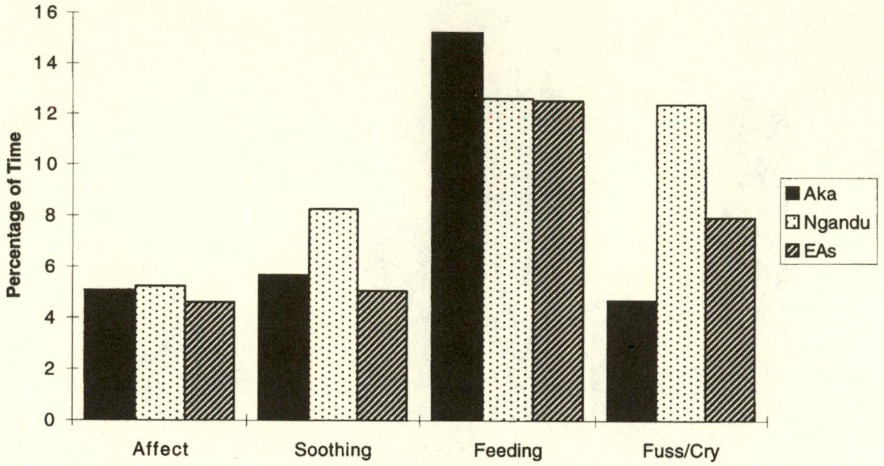

Figure 8.2. Group differences and similarities in warmth and responsiveness.

The amounts of time different caregivers held the infants are presented in Table 8.4. Mothers were the most frequent caregivers in all groups, but alternative caregivers among the Aka and Euro-Americans were more likely to be adults whereas alternative caregivers among the Ngandu were more likely to be juveniles. When we examined the proportion of total holding time, we found that the Aka and Euro-American fathers held their infants proportionately more than Ngandu fathers and that juvenile Ngandu females held the infants proportionally more than juvenile Aka females (no Euro-American juveniles held infants).

INTRACULTURAL VARIABILITY

Thus far, our analysis has focused on between-group differences, but an emphasis on mean differences between groups obscures the enormous intracultural variability on all of these measures. Evolutionary theory encourages researchers to examine within-culture variability because natural selection takes place at the individual level. Table 8.5 explores intracultural variability in the three groups of variables by examining the associations between each variable and maternal workload, which is widely believed to constrain the nature and frequency of maternal care (Blurton Jones 1997; Hurtado and Hill 1990; Nerlove 1974). Aka women worked an average of 28% of the time (range 2–63%) whereas Ngandu women worked an average of 39% of the time (range 1–64%). The difference was not statistically significant. At the time of the observations, none of the Euro-

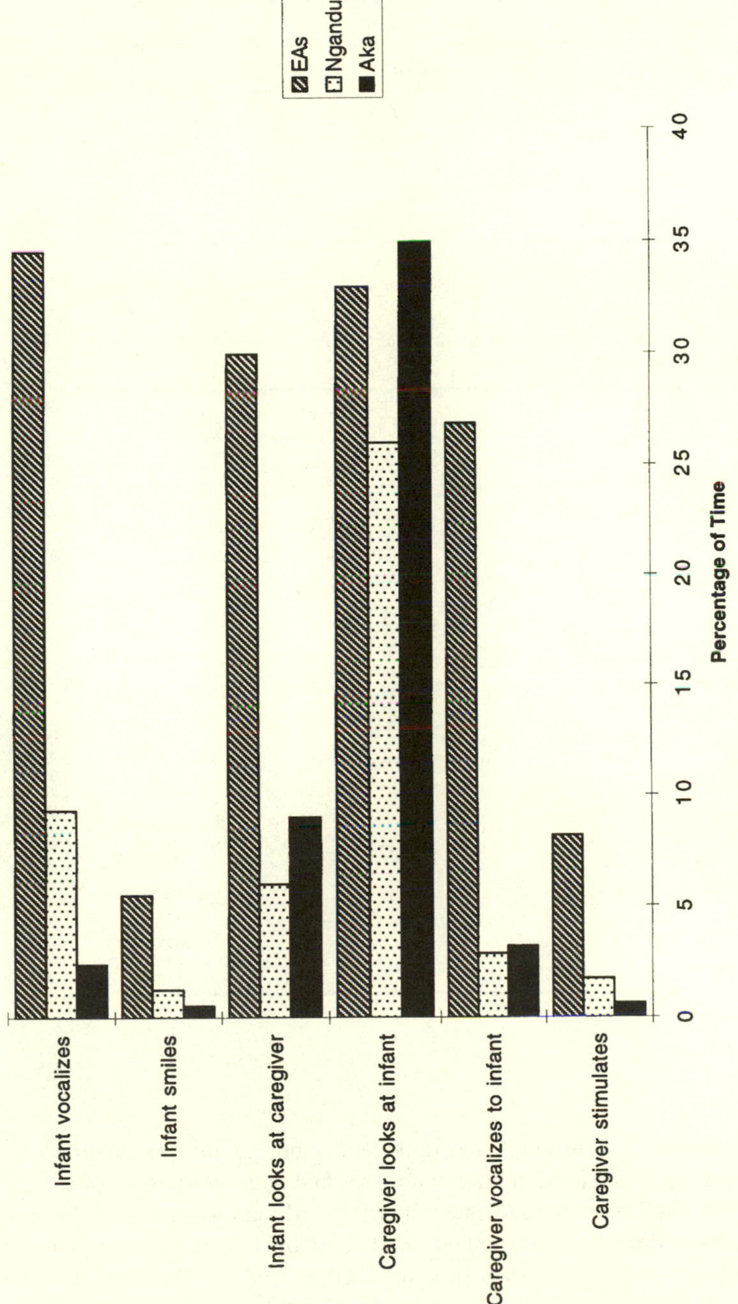

Figure 8.3. Group differences and similarities in distal-verbal interactions.

Table 8.4. Percentage of time different caregivers held infant during daylight hours.

	CAREGIVERS		
	Mother	*Other Adults*	*Other Juveniles*
Aka	72	17	5
Ngandu	37	5	10
Euro-Americans	29	4	0

Table 8.5. Correlation between each variable and mother's work for two ethnic groups.

	Correlation Coefficient (r)	
	Aka	*Ngandu*
Proximal Behaviors (Fig. 1)		
Infant held	.31	.69**
Caregiver proximal (within 1 meter)	.12	.34
Infant alone	.10	.19
Warmth and Responsiveness Behaviors (Fig. 2)		
Caregiver affect toward infant	.14	.04
Caregiver soothes infant	.56**	.32
Total time infant feeds	.17	.01
Frequency per hour infant feeds	.32	.59**
Infant fuss/cry	.35	.37
Distal-Verbal Behaviors (Fig. 3)		
Caregiver stimulates-arouse	.25	.40
Caregiver vocalizes to infant	.19	.14
Caregiver looks at infant	.16	.23
Infant looks at caregiver	.38	.47*
Infant smile	.17	.48*
Infant vocalizes	.38	.11

**$p < .01$
*$p < .05$

American mothers were employed outside the home, and the amount of time devoted to food acquisition, food preparation, and housework was not assessed.

Table 8.5 and Figure 8.4 indicate maternal workload was most likely to affect the amount of time Ngandu mothers held their infants and the frequency with which they fed (but not the total time devoted to feeding) their infants: Ngandu mothers who worked more held and fed their infants less frequently. Maternal workload did not affect the amount of time Aka mothers held their infants or the

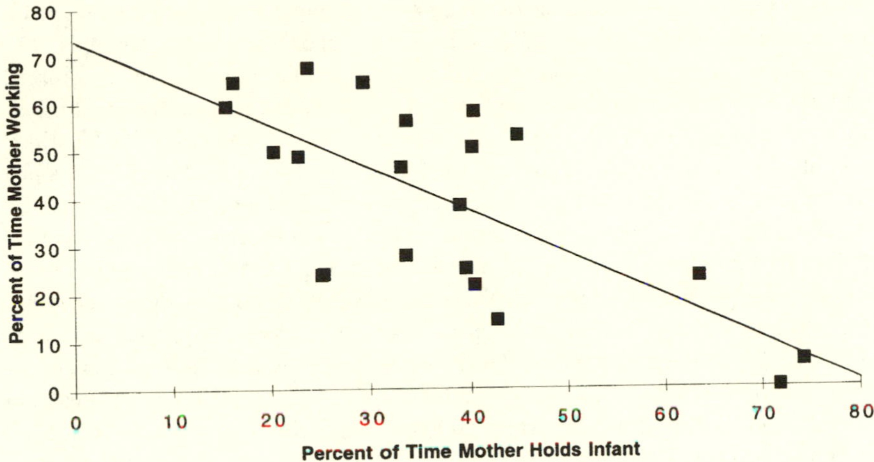

Figure 8.4. Relationship between Ngandu amount of time mothers work and mothers hold their infants.

frequencies with which they fed their infants even though they held and fed their infants almost twice as frequently as Ngandu mothers. Aka mothers who worked more spent more time soothing their infants, in part because of a slight increase in infant fussing and crying associated with increased maternal work. The link between maternal workload and infant fussing and crying was not statistically significant when each ethnic group was considered separately, but when the two were combined there was a significant association between maternal workload and infant fussing or crying ($r = .49$, $p = .001$).

DISCUSSION

How well do the three models of parental investment predict behavior among foragers, farmers, and urban industrialists?

The data raise serious questions about LeVine's depiction of "indulgent" (i.e., frequent holding and feeding, rapid response to fuss/cry) agrarian parental strategies. Infants among the agrarian Ngandu fussed and cried substantially more than the Euro-American infants, they were fed almost as frequently (bouts per hour) as Euro-American infants, and there were no differences between Euro-American and Ngandu infants in the amounts of time that infants were near their caregivers. Euro-American infants were not held as often and they were more likely than Ngandu infants to be alone. Such findings instead support Draper and Harpending's and

Blurton Jones' characterizations of the agrarian parental investment strategy, with parents emphasizing "production" and minimal responses to infant demands.

Analyses of the warmth and responsiveness variables likewise provided mixed support for the three models. To the extent that they are less responsive to their infants' fussing and crying, Ngandu parents manifest a "production" or "mating" parental investment strategy, but they show affection to and feed their infants just as frequently as Aka and Euro-American parents. Meanwhile, analyses of the distal-verbal measures tended to support LeVine's and Blurton Jones' predictions regarding Euro-American parental investment strategies, although one has to be careful interpreting these results. Theorists have assumed that these behaviors (i.e., face-to-face and verbal exchange) reflect Euro-American parents' concerns about cognitive development and ORS. Some interview data support this (Richman et al. 1992), but it is also important to examine differences in the physical and social contexts. The Euro-American mothers were often home alone with their infants. The only persons with whom they could interact were their infants, and the infants were often placed in infant seats facing their mothers. On the other hand, Aka and Ngandu caregivers can readily converse with many others, and their infants are placed on their lap facing outward while careproviders are sitting and talking to others. Aka and Ngandu infants are thus exposed to as much language as Euro-American infants are, although it is less likely to be directed to them. In addition, by the time their infants are 9 to 10 months old, Ngandu caregivers provide their infants with much more verbal and distal stimulation than Aka caregivers, who remain very close to their infants (Hewlett et al. 1998). Existing models also imply that little communication and stimulation takes place while infants are being held, which is not necessarily the case (McKenna et al. 1991).

It is important to note that infants in all three groups received equal amounts of affection from caregivers, however. Farmers may not be very responsive to fussing and crying, foragers may not stimulate their infants very much, and Euro-Americans may not hold their infants often, but infants in all groups receive similar amounts of affection and soothing from caregivers.

In sum, although there are some similarities between forager and urban-industrial investment strategies (e.g., husband-wife provisioning and cooperation), the forager patterns evident in this study were more similar to those of the neighboring farmers than those of the Euro-Americans. Aka and Ngandu groups both have high mortality and fertility rates and are relatively more proximal (e.g., holding, time infant alone) and less verbal and distal than the Euro-Americans, although the Aka and Ngandu themselves have no problem categorizing each other as "parenting effort" and "mating effort" societies, respectively. The Ngandu perceive the Aka as more indulgent with their children (Ngandu say the Aka always hold and spoil their children and do not train children to respect and obey their parents) and the Aka perceive the Ngandu as sexual animals who want to have sex several times each night and with multiple partners. The different behavioral propensities do not lead to the predicted differences in greater fertility or mortality, however.

Explanations for Differences among Parental Investment Strategies

Each of the three models identifies key factors that explain cross-cultural variability in parental investment. LeVine utilizes infant mortality to explain differences between agrarian and urban industrial populations, but our data suggest a more complex picture. Euro-American parent-infant interactions were more visual and distal, but it is not clear whether this reflected their greater interest in cognitive development or their physical and social circumstances (i.e., home alone with infant). Contrary to LeVine's prediction, Ngandu careproviders were also less responsive to infant fussing.

The key factors for Draper and Harpending are the husband-wife relationship and father saliency/involvement during a sensitive period in childhood. Individuals (or cultures) with close husband-wife relationships and involved fathers are expected to develop a parenting effort strategy and then to focus on raising a few "quality" children, whereas individuals without involved fathers are expected to develop a mating effort strategy and to focus on "quantity." Again, the data paint a more complex picture. Aka and Euro-American parents have close and more cooperative husband-wife relationships, with more involved fathers than among the Ngandu. Aka and Euro-American careproviders were more sensitive to their infants' fussing and crying, as the hypothesis predicts, but the Aka were clearly more similar to the Ngandu in terms of the "quantity" of children they have and the Ngandu were much more likely to hold their infants than were the Euro-Americans.

Draper (1988) also suggested that foragers tend to view subsistence resources as limited because they must rely on few alternative adult careproviders, whereas farmers can call upon many juvenile caregivers. She hypothesizes that forager children have fewer sources of sustenance and that this in turn leads them to believe that resources are limited and so lowers their fertility. As predicted, we found that, among the Aka, alternative caregivers were more likely to be adults whereas they were more likely to be juveniles among sedentary farmers. Contrary to Draper's prediction, however, we found that foragers had a trusting and confident view of the environment that was associated with especially (by Western standards) sensitive and responsive infant and childcare patterns. Farmers may have a more limited view of environmental resources because infant and childhood experiences are not as predictable and secure.

Blurton Jones (1993) focused on environmental hazards, including predation, to explain why foragers are more likely than farmers to hold their infants and why Hadza and !Kung foragers have different investment strategies. The "survivorship" label is somewhat misleading in the present study because it gives the impression that the forager environment is necessarily more dangerous than the farming environment. We do not have systematic data to evaluate this hypothesis, but we are unaware of any Aka or Ngandu infant deaths from predation. If predation is a primary concern, why would Aka caregivers place infants on the ground in order to chase and tackle animals while hunting? Although frequent holding has been described as a hazard prevention strategy among foragers (Kaplan and Dove 1987), it may be a result of the regular carrying needed to transport infants when moving camp, visiting relatives, hunting, and gathering as well as the adults' relative unfamiliarity with the places they take their infants and the emotional attachment parents develop because they hold their infants so frequently (Hewlett et al. 1998).

None of the parental investment models incorporates "culture" as an independent variable. This study suggests that cultural mechanisms (Boyd and Richerson 1985; Hewlett and Cavalli Sforza 1988) may, in part, help to explain some of the parental investment differences. For instance, the Aka and Ngandu live in the tropical rainforest, have similar mortality and fertility patterns, and see each other's parenting patterns on a regular basis. Neither parenting style seems to increase/decrease infant survival. Cultural processes pattern part of the individual's rearing environment, and it is possible these parental investment models, especially those of Chisholm and Belsky which focus on local mortality and family stress, may explain differences within rather than between cultures.

Finally, it is important to point out that most of the characterizations of white middle-class urban industrial parent-child relations were based upon studies conducted in the 1970s or earlier when holding and attending to a fussing/crying infant were not seen as important by most parents. Parenting ideologies have changed, and our data suggest that upper-middle-class parents are holding and responding to fusses and cries substantially more frequently than in previous Euro-American studies.

Life History Theory

Table 8.6 estimates the key variables in Charnov's theory for the three ethnic groups and summarizes the corresponding features of the parent-infant interactions we observed. Charnov has proposed that, across species, adult mortality and juvenile growth rates pattern the remaining life history variables, and we thus undertook a speculative cross-cultural analysis inspired by his model.

First, it is necessary to describe how we arrived at the qualitative measures (e.g., low, medium and high) reflected in Table 8.6. Adult mortality is higher in the Aka and Ngandu than it is among the Euro-American, but we lack reliable information about age at death in these populations to specify differences between Aka and Ngandu adult mortality more precisely. Bailey (1991) has shown that children among the Efe (another African forager "pygmy" population similar to Aka) grow more slowly than children among the neighboring farmers and Euro-Americans.

Table 8.6. Summary of behavioral results and life history variables among the three ethnic groups.

	Aka Foragers	*Ngandu Farmers*	*Washington DC Urban Industrialists*
Life History Variables			
Adult mortality	High	High	Low
Juvenile growth	Very slow	Slow	Rapid
Age at maturity	Late	Early	Very early
Adult weight	Low	Medium	High
Fertility	High	High	Low
Child mortality	High	High	Low
Parent-Infant Interactions			
Proximity	Very proximal	Proximal	Distal
Responsiveness	Very responsive	Not very responsive	Responsive
Verbal Interaction	Not very verbally interactive	Verbally interactive	Very verbally interactive
Nonmaternal (alternative) caregivers	Adults and juveniles	Juveniles	Adults

The age of sexual maturity has been determined for the Aka (15 years) and upper-class Euro-Americans (12 years), but not for the Ngandu. Field observations indicate that the age of first birth is earlier among Ngandu females than it is among the Aka. Mean adult female weight is about 42 kg among the Aka, 54 kg among the Ngandu, and 61 kg among middle-class white Americans (Hewlett 1992). We have already discussed fertility and child morality differences in the three groups. While many of the variables are estimates, they provide a starting point for discussing the applicability of Charnov's model.

Charnov's model predicts that, if adult mortality levels are high and juvenile growth rates rapid, individuals should invest in current rather than future reproduction. The data provide mixed support for this hypothesis. On the one hand, the predicted relationship between adult mortality and current versus future reproduction is supported by the fact that the Aka and Ngandu have relatively high adult mortality rates and invest in current reproduction (i.e., many children) whereas upper-middle-class Euro-Americans have low adult mortality rates and focus on future reproduction. On the other hand, the Aka and Ngandu have slower juvenile growth rates than U.S. children from upper-middle-class backgrounds. This may, in part, reflect the relatively unusual (by cross-cultural standards) nature of highly stratified urban industrial societies, in which there is relatively easy access to food, which leads to rapid juvenile growth, and sexual maturity does not coincide with the social and cognitive maturity necessary to survive and reproduce (e.g., formal education to acquire skills necessary to obtain high salary) as it typically does in small-scale cultures.

How does Charnov's model help to understand the parent-infant interactions described in this study? First, the model is useful for understanding infant care in the three ethnic groups because it underscores the importance of adult mortality and other variables when explaining parental investment, thereby helping to contextualize the tradeoffs between parenting and mating efforts. Second, Charnov's model underscores the importance of environmental context, since much of the variability in observed life history variables and parental investment patterns can be explained by exposure to different physical and social environments. The Aka physical and social environment promotes especially high levels of all types of sharing (food, caregiving, domestic tasks, hunting, etc.) because the people living together are often genetically related or have regular and intimate knowledge of other camp members (necessary for intense reciprocal altruism), and food is consumed within a few days. Ngandu sharing is less frequent and extensive than among the Aka, in part because living conditions are less intimate, subsistence involves delayed returns, neighbors are less familiar with one another than among the Aka, and parents, especially mothers, are under greater pressure to provide food and care ("depreciable" forms of investment) for their infants. This increased stress may help to explain why Ngandu caregivers are less responsive to their infants. Euro-Americans have the lowest levels of sharing, which places enormous stress/expectations on the husband-wife relationship.

SUMMARY

Although we have been somewhat critical of existing parental investment models, we want to underscore the significance of these contributions to life history theory. In addition to being provocative and heuristically valuable, they introduce the consideration of reproductive interests to child development theory, place reproductive interests in a life-course perspective, and encourage cross-cultural anthropologists to examine variability within cultures.

Our results suggest the following conclusions:

1. In a context of high infant mortality, Ngandu farmers are not as responsive to their infants as LeVine's model would suggest. The data instead support Draper and Harpending's and Blurton Jones' characterizations of farmer parent-infant interactions. The farmers' parenting style does not necessarily lead to the predicted pattern of greater "production" (higher fertility) than that found among foragers.
2. Contrary to the Draper and Harpending model, there are substantial differences between forager and urban-industrial parental investment strategies. Blurton Jones's description of "ORS enhancers" in urban industrial societies is a useful extension of their model.

3. Euro-Americans are more interactive and engage in more distal-verbal interaction with infants, in part because of the different physical and social settings and infant technologies.

4. Maternal workload among the Ngandu influences the frequency of infant holding and breast-feeding bouts per hour. Maternal work does not influence these factors among the Aka, in part because infants are held in all contexts and because sharing is so frequent.

5. Life history theory is a useful tool for interpreting parental investment strategies.

ACKNOWLEDGMENTS

The authors are grateful to the Aka, Ngandu, and Euro-American families for graciously allowing impersonal behavioral observations by strange anthropologists and psychologists. We would also like to thank the several people who assisted in data collection and analysis: Patricia Evans, Hope Hallock, Nan Hannon, Nancy Kimmerly, Christina Larson, Laura Scaramella, and Donald Shannon. We acknowledge and thank the government of the Central African Republic for authorizing the research. We also would like to thank Eric Charnov and an anonymous reviewer for their comments on early drafts of this paper. The research was supported by the National Institute of Child Health and Human Development and the Swan Fund.

REFERENCES

Bailey, R. C. 1991. The comparative growth of Efe pygmies and African farmers from birth to age five years. *Annals of Human Biology* 18:113–120.

Belsky, J. 1997. Attachment, mating and parenting: An evolutionary interpretation. *Human Nature* 8:361–381.

Belsky, J., M. Rovine, and D. G. Taylor. 1984. The Pennsylvania Infant and Family Development Project, Part III. The origins of individual differences in infant-mother attachment: Maternal and infant contributions. *Child Development* 55:718–728.

Belsky, J., L. Steinberg, and P. Draper. 1991. Childhood experience, interpersonal development, and reproductive strategy: An evolutionary theory of socialization. *Child Development* 62:647–670.

Bentley, G. R., T. Goldberg, and G. Jasienska. 1993. The fertility of agricultural and non-agricultural traditional societies. *Population Studies* 47:269–281.

Blurton Jones, N. 1993. The lives of hunter-gatherer children: Effects of parental behavior and parental reproductive strategy. In *Juvenile Primates,* M. E. Pereira and L. A. Fairbanks, eds. Pp. 309–326. New York: Oxford University Press.

———. 1997. Too good to be true? Is there really a trade-off between number and care of offspring in human reproduction. In *Human Nature,* L. Betzig, ed. Pp. 83–86. New York: Aldine de Gruyter.

Boyd, R., and P. J. Richerson. 1985. *Culture and the Evolutionary Process*. Chicago: University of Chicago Press.

Charnov, E. L. 1993. *Life History Invariants.* Oxford: Oxford University Press.

Chisholm, J. 1996. The evolutionary ecology of attachment organization. *Human Nature* 7:1–38.

Clutton-Brock, T. H. 1991. *The Evolution of Parental Care.* Princeton, NJ: Princeton University Press.

Draper, P. 1988. African marriage systems. *Ethology and Sociobiology* 10:145–169.

Draper, P., and H. Harpending. 1982. Father absence and reproductive strategy: An evolutionary perspective. *Journal of Anthropological Research* 38:255–273.

———. 1987. Parent investment and the child's environment. In *Parenting across the Life Span,* J. Lancaster et al., eds. Pp. 207–235. New York: Aldine de Gruyter.

Hawkes, K., J. F. O'Connell, and N. G. Blurton Jones. 1995. Hadza children's foraging: Juvenile dependency, social arrangements, and mobility among hunter-gatherers. *Current Anthropology* 36:688–700.

Hewlett, B. S. 1991. Demography and childcare in preindustrial societies. *Journal of Anthropological Research* 47:1–37.

———. 1992. Husband-wife reciprocity and the father-infant relationship among Aka pygmies. In *Father-Child Relations: Cultural and Biosocial Contexts,* B. S. Hewlett, ed. Pp. 153–175. New York: Aldine de Gruyter.

Hewlett, B. S., and L. L. cavalli Sforza. 1986. Cultural transmission among Aka pygmies. *American Anthropologist* 88:922–934.

Hewlett, B. S., M. E. Lamb, D. Shannon, B. Leyendecker, and A. Schölmerich. 1998. Culture and early infancy among Central African foragers and farmers. *Developmental Psychology* 34:653–661.

Hill, K., and A. M. Hurtado. 1996. *Ache Life History.* New York: Aldine de Gruyter.

Hurtado, A. M., and K. Hill. 1990. Seasonality in foragers: A study of variation in the diet, work effort, fertility and the sexual division of labor among the Hiwi of Venezuela. *Journal of Anthropological Research* 46:293–345.

Kaplan, H., and H. Dove. 1987. Infant development among the Ache of Paraguay. *Developmental Psychology* 23:190–198.

Konner, M. J. 1976. Maternal care, infant behavior and development among the !Kung. In *Kalahari Hunter-gatherers,* R. B. Lee and I. DeVore, eds. Pp. 218–245. Cambridge: Harvard University Press.

———. 1977. Infancy among Kalahari Desert San. In *Culture and Infancy: Variations in the Human Experience,* P. H. Leiderman, S. T. Tulkin, and A. Rosenfeld, eds. Pp. 287–328. New York: Academic Press.

Lancaster, J., and C. S. Lancaster. 1987. The watershed: Change in parental-investment and family-formation strategies in the course of human evolution. In *Parenting Across the Life Span,* J. B. Lancaster, J. Altmann, A. S. Rossi, and L. R. Sherrod, eds. Pp. 187–206. New York: Aldine de Gruyter.

LeVine, R. A. 1989. Human parental care: Universal goals, cultural strategies, individual behavior. In *Parental Behavior in Diverse Societies,* R. A. LeVine, P. M. Miller, and M. M. West, eds. Pp. 3–12. San Francisco: Jossey Bass.

LeVine, R. A., S. Dixson, S. LeVine, A. Richman, P. H. Leiderman, C. H. Keefer, and T. B. Brazelton. 1994. *Child Care and Culture: Lessons from Africa.* Cambridge: Cambridge University Press.

Leyendecker, B., M. E. Lamb, A. Schölmerich, and D. Miranda Fricke. 1997. Contexts as moderators of observed interaction: A study of Costa Rican mothers and infants from differing socio-economic backgrounds. *International Journal of Behavioral Development* 21:15–34.

McKenna, J. J., S. Mosko, C. Dungy and J. McAninch. 1991. Sleep and arousal patterns of co-sleeping human mother/infant pairs: A preliminary physiological study with impli-

cations for the study of Sudden Infant Death Syndrome (SIDS). *American Journal of Physical Anthropology* 83:331–347.
Nerlove, S. B. 1974. Women's workload and infant feeding practices: A relationship with demographic implications. *Ethnology* 13:207–214.
Richman, A. L., R. A. LeVine, R. Staple New, G. A. Howrigan, B. Welles-Nystrom, and S. E. LeVine. 1988. Maternal behavior to infants in five cultures. In *Parental Behavior in Diverse Societies,* R. A. LeVine, P. M. Miller, and M. Maxwell West, eds. Pp. 81–98. San Francisco: Jossey-Bass.
Richman, A. L., P. M. Miller, and R. A. LeVine. 1992. Cultural and educational variations in maternal responsiveness. *Developmental Psychology* 28:614–621.
Whiting, B. B., and J. W. M. Whiting. 1975. *Children of Six Cultures.* Cambridge: Harvard University Press.
Williams, G. C. 1966. Natural selection, the costs of reproduction, and a refinement of Lack's principle. *American Naturalist* 10:687–690.
Woodburn, J. 1982. Egalitarian societies. *Man* (n.s.) 17:431–451.

APPENDIX: LIST OF CODES USED FOR THE OBSERVATION OF CAREGIVER-INFANT INTERACTION AT 3 MONTHS

Dyadic Behaviors

En face
Mutual visual
Proximity within arm length
Caregiving
Feeding
Holding

Caregiver Behaviors

C attention is focused on infant
C checks on infant (brief glances)
C stimulates/arouses
C physical soothe
C non-physical soothe
C physical affect
C non-physical affect
C vocalizes to infant
M leisure
M work (except EA sample)
C talks to others

Infant Behaviors

I asleep
I drowsy
I fussing
I crying
I vocalizes
I smiles
I looks at C
I responds to caregiver stimulation
I distracts self with objects (incl. own body)

Other Behaviors

Location (lap, bed, arms, sling)
Room (in house, outside house, forest, plantation)
Caregiver (mother, father, elderly female, adult female, juvenile female, elderly male, adult male, juvenile male) (except EA sample)

9

Parenting Other Men's Children
Costs, Benefits, and Consequences

JANE B. LANCASTER and HILLARD S. KAPLAN

A basic issue in the life history of the human male is his patterned allocation of resources available for reproduction. He is faced with two fundamental tradeoffs (Low 1978; Sterns 1992; Trivers 1972). The first is between investment in himself (somatic effort or future reproductive effort) or in producing offspring (present reproductive effort), and the second is a tradeoff within reproductive effort between investment in mating opportunities and parental investment in offspring already produced (Clutton-Brock 1991). Mating effort promotes higher numbers of offspring and parental investment promotes higher quality of offspring.

For higher primate species, investment in self (somatic effort) mostly involves good nutrition, which promotes healthy immune function, stable growth, and large completed body size in combination with the acquisition of social networks and resource acquisition skills (Charnov 1993; Charnov and Berrigan 1993; Kaplan 1996). For humans, however, we speak more formally of the concept of embodied capital, that is, the stock of attributes embodied in an individual that can be converted, either directly or, more commonly, in combination with other forms of capital, into fitness-enhancing commodities (Becker 1991, 1993; Kaplan 1994; Kaplan et al. 1995). Embodied capital includes investment in body mass and complexity, skills and knowledge, and social capital. Parental investment in the embodied and social capital of offspring can affect their survival, future income, and social status. The latter two, in turn, form the budget for each offspring's investment in its own and the next generation's reproduction.

Among humans the combination of determinant growth (that is, growth which does not continue indefinitely) and the particular pattern of intergenerational support in which parental and senior generations are committed to feed juveniles tends to concentrate the acquisition of embodied capital into the juvenile and early adult years (Borgerhoff Mulder 1992; Kaplan 1994, 1996; Lancaster and Lancaster 1987). This leads to a life history strategy in which resources that early on are exclusively invested in somatic growth eventually become largely diverted into reproduction. The timing of this shift from somatic growth to finding mates and producing offspring varies according to environmental conditions that determine how rapidly embodied capital can be acquired and how much is sufficient to the tasks of reproduction in the local context. Our interest here is to analyze the fertility and parental investment patterns of men living in a contemporary city in the United States (Albuquerque) to see how well these two tradeoffs describe issues faced by contemporary men in a world with a monetized economy, competitive labor markets, and very low fertility based on birth control.

Following Lazarus (1990) we propose that a fundamental tradeoff faced by these contemporary men can be directly linked to the conflict between investing resources in finding mates who will bear children and investing in children already produced. Since the number of children that a man can produce may be increased by having more than one mate (because of the inevitable limitations placed on each woman by her reproductive biology), men who desert and do not help to raise their own children have the opportunity to produce more offspring with other women. We have taken "ceasing to live with a child" as a measure we can use to capture the withdrawal of male parental resources both in terms of time and money during a child's development. Of course, we recognize that many men are conscientious about investing time and financial resources in their children even after divorce; however, marital breakup does lead to a reduction in the total time a man spends with his genetic offspring (Cooksey and Fondell 1996). Furthermore, the longitudinal study by Bloom, Conrad, and Miller (1996) of men in the United States has shown that men who fail to pay court-ordered child support are more likely to remarry and have more children than men who comply with their child support orders. "Ceasing to live with a child" cannot lead to future investment in more children if the man does so because of his own death. Therefore, our measure is about the withdrawal or reduction of male parental investment because of desertion or divorce. It is generally recognized that desertion, divorce, and remarriage as practiced by a man can both extend the length of his reproductive period, if he marries progressively younger women, and promote his total fertility. In effect, it is a form of polygyny, or serial monogamy, which raises male fertility in the same way as polygyny in more traditional human societies (Lockard and Adams 1981; Mackey 1980).

Figure 9.1 presents a causal pathway that describes the tradeoff that men face between quality and quantity of offspring when they make a decision to remain or to cease to live with a child before it is fully grown. Divorce or desertion has two main effects on a man's children: it may raise a man's completed fertility (quantity) through the formation of additional mateships and the likelihood of producing more children. In turn, it should reduce the total amount invested in each child because of the diversion of resources to mating effort and the probable increase in the total number of children having to share the same limited pot of father's resources (Weiss and Willis 1985).

Such division will reduce the quality of each child as measured by educational and economic outcomes. Hence, the predicted effects of divorce/desertion or ceas-

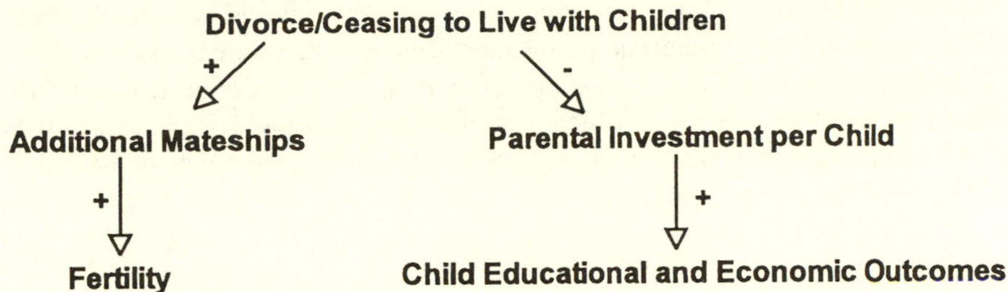

Figure 9.l. Ceasing to live with children as a tradeoff between quantity and quality of offspring.

ing to live with a child are both positive and negative. There is really only one major tradeoff: both the length and intensity of parenting affect child quality, and reductions in investment lower child quality but also have the potential to raise a man's fertility through investment in more mateships.

METHODS: THE ALBUQUERQUE MEN DATA SET

Between 1990 and 1993 Kaplan and Lancaster's Albuquerque Men project completed 7,107 short (4-page) and 1,325 long (96-page) structured interviews with a representative, random sample of men in Albuquerque recruited at the New Mexico Motor Vehicles Division (MVD) (Anderson, Kaplan, and Lancaster, n.d.; Kaplan et al. 1995, 1998). All men who appeared to be over 18 years of age were considered eligible for the initial contact. On the basis of information obtained in the short interview, eligible participants were invited to participate in the long interview. The criteria for eligibility were: (1) having come to the MVD for the purpose of a driver's license origination, renewal, or for a photo ID, and (2) being over 25 for the short interview and over 30 for the long.

The Albuquerque Men data set was designed to test theories of fertility, mating, and parental investment using a representative sample of men living in a modern society with a competitive, skills-based labor market. The short interview sampled a man's current condition. The long interview was a history of employment/training, reproductive relationships, and children produced and parented. A fuller description of the interviews can be found in Kaplan and Lancaster (chapter 14, this volume). The first set of results presented here come from the analysis of the short interview, which was given to 3,762 Anglos, 2,789 Hispanics, and 556 others. Our interview requested information on three generations, the man himself, his parents, and the children he produced and/or parented. For the last analyses presented in this chapter on a man's investment in children's education, we used data from the long interview, which was given to 1,325 men. We analyzed data from 615 of these men about their investments in 1,246 children who had received a year or more of higher education.

RESULTS

Men Who Ceased to Live with Their Own Offspring

Men differ in their quality and their ability to invest in mates and offspring (Lancaster and Kaplan 1992). As a result, the impact of tradeoffs between mating effort and parental investment differ for different men, with some men paying higher costs, and others paying lower costs for ceasing to live with a child. One of the most significant reasons why costs should vary between men is variability in their own embodied capital. In other words, the less a man has to offer, the less the cost to the child of withdrawing his presence and financial support. We predict that the following set of three conditions will have strong effects on the values of these tradeoffs. All are measures of embodied capital: (1) a man's education, (2) a man's income, and (3) the age at which the man first started reproduction. In this case an early age of first reproduction means less investment in his own embodied capital by diverting resources from own education and training to acquisition of mates and production of offspring.

We have chosen to look separately at data resulting on separation from a child before age 6 (early childhood), between ages 6 and 16 (school age), and men who stay with their children over the age of 16, presented by child's birth cohort. We also restricted our analyses to the two ethnicities, Anglo and Hispanic, for which we had a large enough sample to control for socioeconomic status and birth cohort. Hispanic refers to all men who identified themselves as Hispanic regardless of race and Anglo (an ethnic classification peculiar to the Southwest) to non-Hispanic men who classify themselves as white and generally speak English in the home. Most Hispanics in our sample are native New Mexicans tracing their family history to the early settlement of the Southwest. The break down of our sample into these ethnic divisions is appropriate to the Southwest and helps us to analyze the impact of socioeconomic status and birth cohort on behavioral differences often assigned to ethnicity and religion.

Father's ethnicity and child's birth cohort. Figure 9.2 presents the effects of the father's ethnicity on the probability of his ceasing to live with a child before the age of 16, presented as a function of the child's birth cohort (the data on sample size, standard deviations and standard errors for Figures 1–6 and Figures 9–10

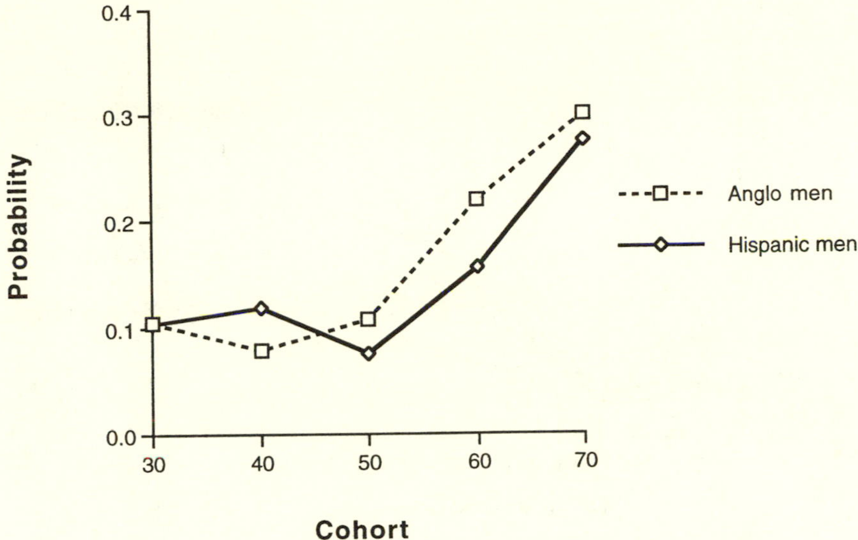

Figure 9.2. Effects of father's ethnicity on the probability of ceasing to live with a child before it reaches age 16.

are given in the appendix). Ethnicity had remarkably little effect although Anglo men showed a slightly greater tendency to cease living with a child after 1950. The most striking result presented in this figure is not in differences between ethnicities but in the general upward trend in ceasing to live with children in each birth cohort since 1950 beginning with a low of 8% in 1950 and rising to 29% in 1980. This striking rise in frequency of father-child separation was found in both Anglo and Hispanic men.

Father's education. Figure 9.3 presents the effects of the father's education on the probability of ceasing to live with his child before the age of 6. It shows the changing likelihood of ceasing to live with a child under the age of six as a function of the child's year of birth and the man's education. A very small percentage of children (about 5%) born before 1960 ceased to live with their father before age 6, regardless of parental education. However, as father/preschool child separation becomes increasingly likely through time, the effects of education become readily apparent. For the cohort of children born in the 1980s, the probability of separating from the father before the age of six increases to about 25% for children whose father has less than a high school diploma, 18% for those whose father has a high school diploma, 12% for children of men with a bachelor's degree, compared to only 8% for children of men with a post-graduate degrees. We could not look at the outcomes for older children in this latest birth cohort because few were over age 6.

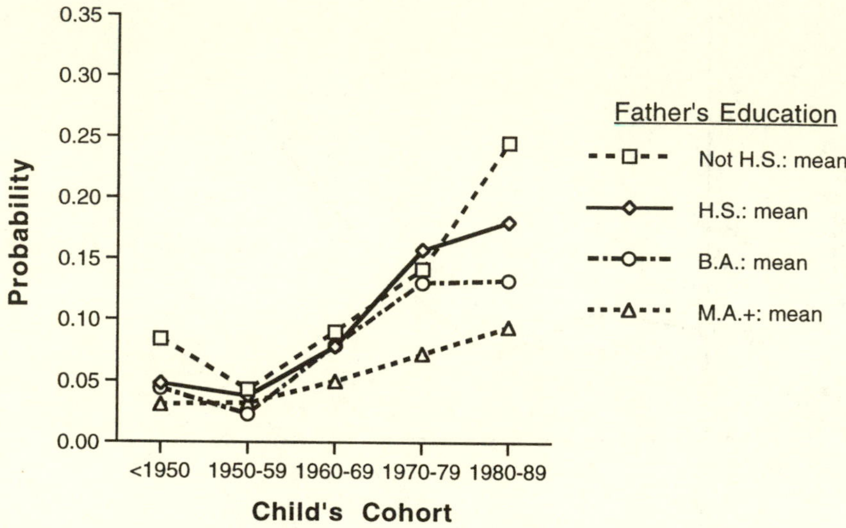

Figure 9.3. Effects of father's education on the probability of ceasing to live with a child before it reaches age 6.

It may be relevant that the rate of return on embodied capital (education) had a abrupt upward shift when the U.S. labor market restructured during the mid-fifties to the mid-sixties away from semi-skilled and manufacturing employment toward industries requiring specialized and technical training (Herrnstein and Murray 1994; Jorgenson and Fraumeni 1989; Murphy and Welsh 1989). We might expect then that the similarity of behavior of the fathers of the pre-1960 child cohorts regardless of differences in education may reflect similar rates of return on education during that era. As the returns on education in producing male adult income increased, the cost (in terms of child quality) to fathers of ceasing to live with their offspring becomes increasingly differentiated between those with little education and those with more.

Father's income. Figures 9.4a and b present the effects of the father's income on the probability of ceasing to live with his child before it reaches age 6 and age 16. The lowest income quartile is the most different from the others. This means that the effect of father's income on probability of divorce or desertion is not evenly distributed by similar increments through the income quartiles but is strongest at the bottom of the economic scale. In the latest children's birth cohort (1970–79) 43% of fathers ceased to live with a child before it reaches the age of 16. For separation before age 6 the lowest income quartile has a rate nearly double that of the other three quartiles for the 1980–89 birth cohort.

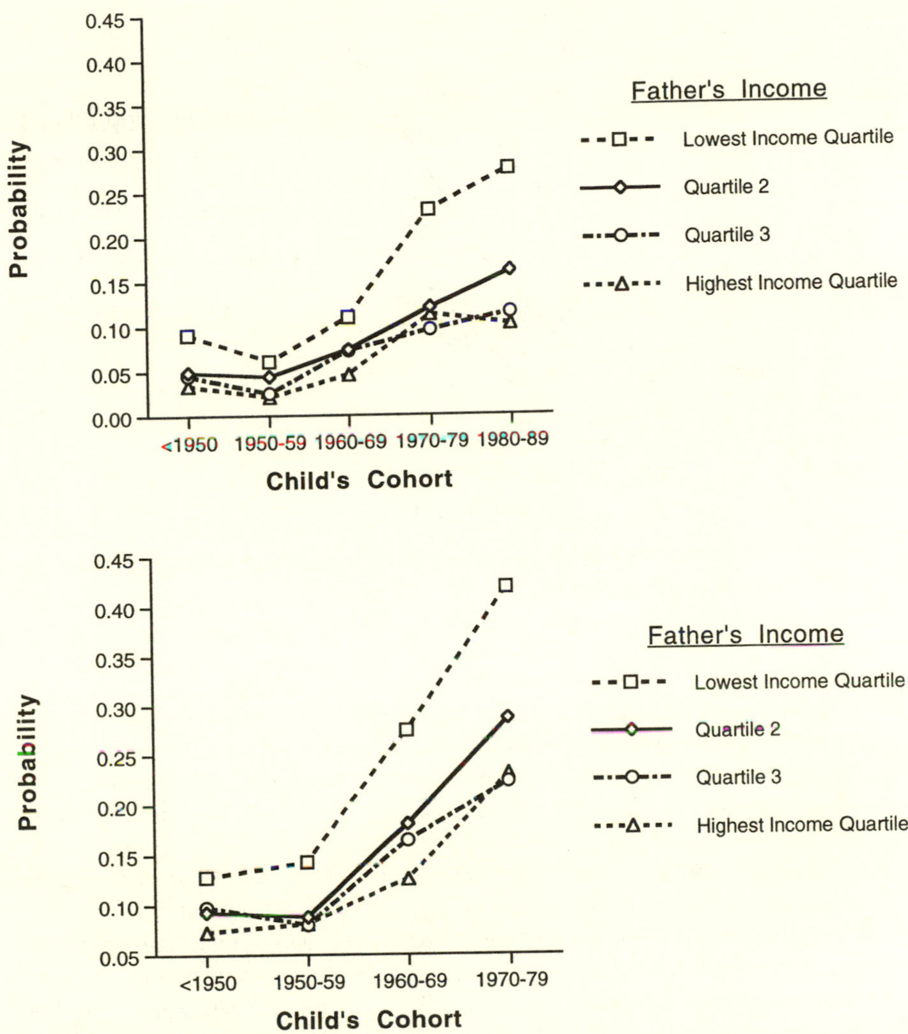

Figure 9.4a–b. Effects of father's income on the probability of ceasing to live with a child before the age of (a) 6 and (b) 16.

Father's age at first reproduction. Figure 9.5 presents the effects of father's age at first reproduction on the probability of his ceasing to live with a child before it reaches the age of 16. This is a separate life history measure of the father's embodied capital because it is a marker of the timing of the shift from somatic to reproductive investment in his life course, whereas education and income are measures

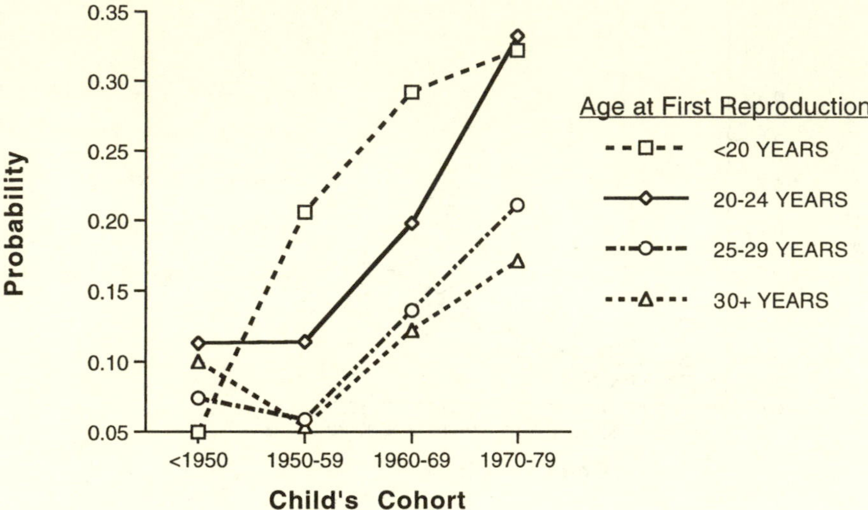

Figure 9.5. Effects of father's age at first reproduction on the probability of ceasing to live with a child before the age of 16.

of the amount of embodied capital he has acquired. Reproduction early in the life course does in fact raise the probability of ceasing to live with a child in both early childhood (<6 years) and during the school-age years (6–16 years) (Brian and Willis 1995; Kaplan and Lancaster, unpublished analyses). The cutoff point for such effects appears to be for fathers aged 25 and over at first reproduction.

There has been significant historical change in the median age of first reproduction for men in this century. Among Anglos in the Albuquerque data set, age at first reproduction was late early in the century, dropped to a minumum among men born in the 1930s, and then began to increase. Median ages of first reproduction for Anglos are: 30.7 (born before 1920), 27.7 (born 1920–29), 25.8 (born 1930–39), 28.2 (born 1940–49), and 31.7 (born 1950–59), respectively. Median ages of first reproduction for Hispanics are: 28.5 (born before 1920), 25.8 (born 1920–29), 25.0 (born 1930–39), 24.4 (born 1940–49), and 25.9 (born 1950–59), respectively. Since 1940, then, differences between Anglos and Hispanics in mean age of first reproduction has increased considerably. There is no national data set available for comparison. Median age of first reproduction is determined for mothers but not for fathers in national surveys. However, the temporal changes we found in male age at first reproduction mirror trends for median age of first marriage in national data sets. Nationally median age of first marriage for men was 22.8 years in 1950, 24.7 in 1980, and 26.3 in 1990 (U.S. Bureau of the Census 1992).

In summary, the four sets of analyses we have presented on the impact of father's ethnicity, education, income, and age of first reproduction, all by birth cohort, point to embodied capital as a critical predictor of a man's likelihood of not fully raising one or more of his children. The prediction that men with less embodied capital (as measured by education, income, and age of first reproduction) may have less to lose from their desertion in terms of reducing child quality and hence, may be more willing to do so is supported.

The Effects of Not Fully Raising Own Offspring on a Man's Fertility

Our path model presented in Figure 9.1 proposed that the diversion of resources from raising children after divorce or desertion would enable men to invest in future mating opportunities and so enhance their completed fertility. Figure 9.6a compares the fertility of Anglo men who did not live with at least one of their children to age 6 with those who lived with all of their children to age 6. Figure 9.6b shows similar results when we compared the fertility of those men who did not live with at least one of their children to age 16 with those who lived with all of their children to that age. Ceasing to live with at least one child has the predicted effect of raising mean male fertility as much as one half a child for cohorts in which the man was born before 1950, providing the man deserted before the child reaches the age of 6. Fertility benefits to deserting children between the ages of 6 and 16 were reduced to approximately one quarter.

The predicted effect is not evident in the younger cohort, that of men born since 1950. The effect is also not evident among Hispanics, except for men born before 1930 (data not shown). However, this is not a clear outcome because many of these men may not have completed their fertility, particularly those who are reproducing in a series of mateships, because reproduction through changing mates may have some cost in startup time between relationships. These younger males born between 1950 and 1960 were only 30–40 years old when they were interviewed, whereas our older cohorts were over 40 and more likely to have completed fertility.

Men Who Raise Other Men's Offspring

Whereas some men in all human societies do not fully raise their offspring, there are always some men who are willing to raise other men's offspring. In the nineteenth century in the United States most women with dependent children who were available for remarriage were widows (Vinovskis 1990, citing Uhlenberg 1980). As late as the beginning of the twentieth century the proportion of children who had one or both deceased parents before reaching the age of 15 was 24%. Today among single mothers only 6.7% are single as a result of their partners' death (Vinovskis 1990), and unrelated men enter mother-child households more often because of single parenthood or divorce. Allocation of male investment from

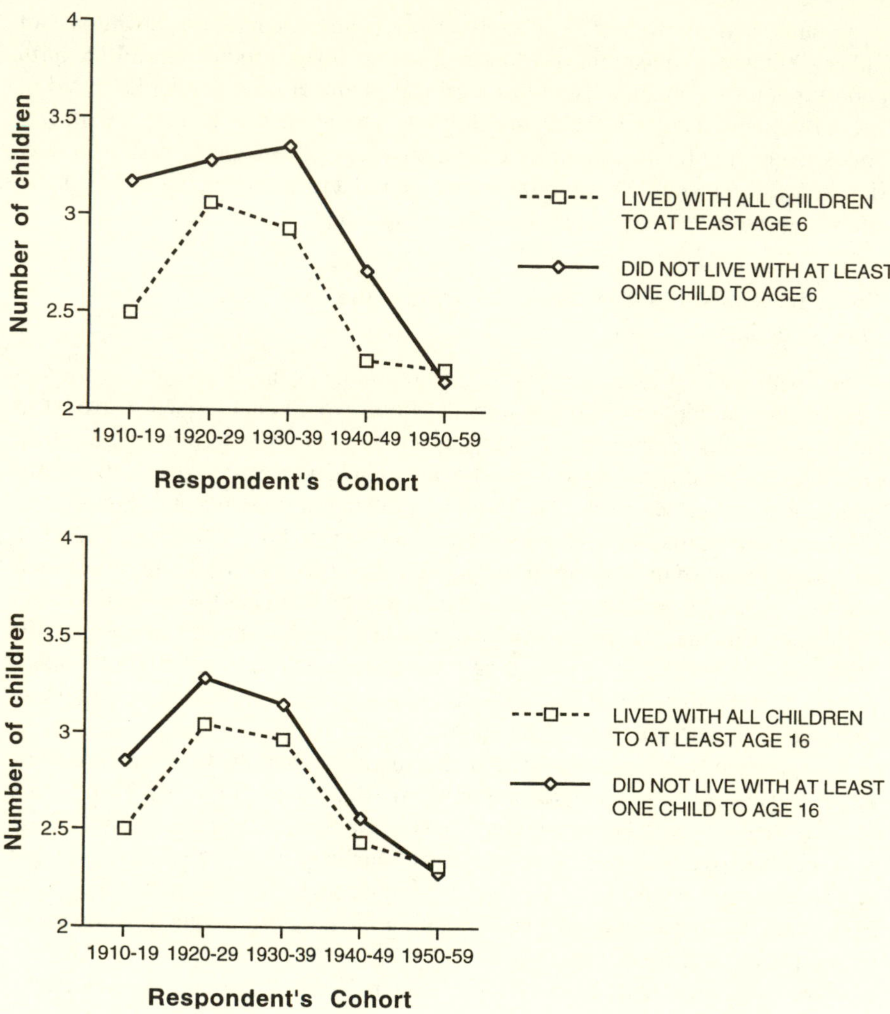

Figure 9.6a–b. Fertility effects of Anglo men not living with at least one child to age (a) 6 and (b) 16.

self and/or own children to other men's children raises intriguing questions about the characteristics of these men (Daly and Wilson 1994, 1996).

Among humans the division between mating effort and parental effort is not so cleanly struck as life history theory might seem to imply. The reason for this is that human females are characterized by a reproductive strategy (the feeding of juveniles) that commits them to the dependency of multiple young of different ages and needs (Lancaster 1997). For this reason male support for a previously born child can be classified as male parental investment for the genetic father, but it also serves as a form of courtship behavior (mating effort) for either the genetic father or an unrelated male because it raises the probability for either type of man of fathering the next child a woman bears. Such behavior has been reported for nonhuman primates by Smuts and Gubernick (1991) in which young and low-status males who favor and protect infants of other males raise their own probability of mating with the mother when she weans and is ready to conceive again. Similarly in "lonely hearts" advertisements in the United States men who list the fewest resources (no mention of professional career or home ownership) are much more likely to express a willingness to raise other men's children ("Kids OK") (Waynforth and Dunbar 1995).

To begin our analysis using the combined sample of 7,107 men of all ethnicities, we asked all men who had helped rear a child for at least one year what their relationship was to the child to whom they allocated that parental effort. The results are presented in Figure 9.7. Some men had never helped raise a child, either their own or another male's (16.6%), at the time of the interview. Most of the men in our sample had raised only their own children (62.8%), and an additional 16.6% had raised their own and the children of other men as well. This category of others' offspring raised in combination with own offspring included both kin (3.6%) and nonkin (12.3%). Only 4.7% raised only other men's children. Together a total of 20.6% of men in the sample helped to raise some children not their own. Generally, then, men parent their own children, nearly two-thirds in our sample, but an additional 20.6% parent other men's children as well. Only a small minority had reared only other men's children.

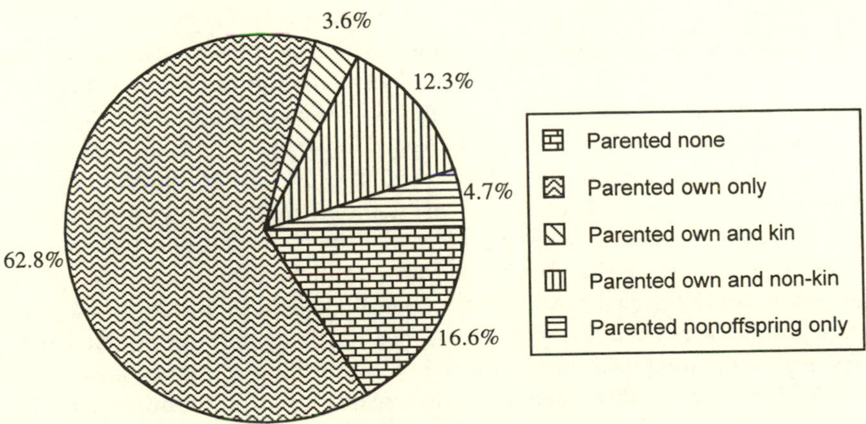

Figure 9.7. Allocation of male parenting effort for all ages of men.

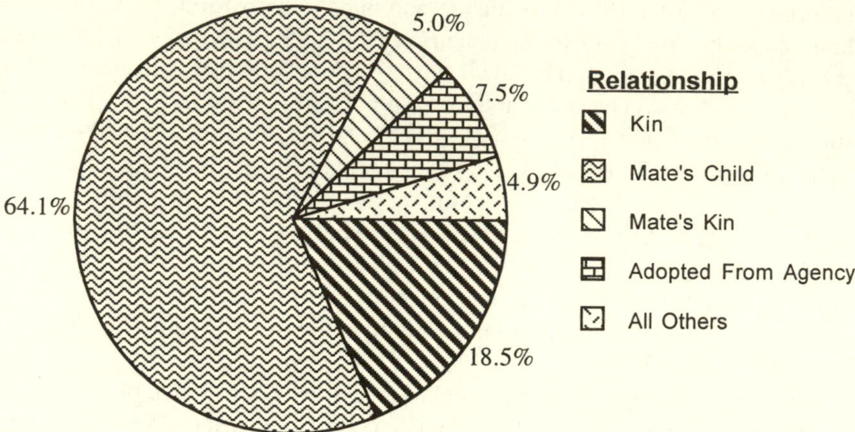

Figure 9.8. Relationship to others' offspring parented by males of all ages and ethnicities.

A closer look at the 20.6% of our men who had raised at least one child not his own for at least a year revealed a variety of relationships between the man and that child. Figure 9.8 presents the relationship of the male to the 2,613 offspring of other men raised by men of all ages in the sample. The vast majority of such relationships in this sample can be attributed to mating effort. In other words 69.1% of the children were related to a man through his current mate, either as her child from a previous relationship (64.1%) or as her dependent kin (5%). As we will show below, this form of parenting comes with sexual access to a woman who has previously reproduced or has dependent relatives, and should sexual access end, investment is dramatically curtailed. A further 18.5% of the children were kin to the man, such as grandchildren or nieces and nephews. This behavior can be classified as kin selection because these children are carriers of the man's genes just as his own children are. The remaining 15% of the offspring children were either adopted from an agency (9%) or the children of friends or neighbors (6%) who tended to be older and only temporarily placed in the man's home.

Our data thus support the hypothesis that, although men do sometimes parent other men's children, this behavior is likely to further the men's own genetic interests. In the modern United States this behavior is by far the most likely to be associated with getting access to a mate who had previously reproduced or had dependent kin of her own. A less frequent but still significant pattern was the parenting of own kin other than offspring. Generally, then, most men in our sample who parented, raised their own children, at least partially. The parenting of other men's children can be interpreted as either mating effort or kin investment. The altruistic parenting of unrelated stranger children is a relatively infrequent event but deserves further attention.

Outcomes for Children of Not Being Fully Raised by Both Parents

Our original pathway in Figure 9.1 predicted a cost to children in not being fully raised by their genetic fathers. We were able to test these effects using three outcome measures: marital stability, education acquired, and adult income of the not fully parented child. We see strong negative effects for all three. As in earlier analyses we separated the effects of early from later desertion/divorce in terms of when it occurred in both the man's and his child's life. Although these analyses are based on the respondents ceasing to live with both parents before a particular age, the vast majority of such cases involved the absence of the father, especially so for the preschool years and before the 1990s when fathers were rarely the custodial parent after divorce.

Figures 9.9a and b present the effect of the age at which the respondent father no longer lived with both parents (before the age of 6, between 6–16, or over 16 years) on the probability of ceasing to live with his own child before the age of 6 (Figure 9.9a) or between the ages of 6 and 16 (Figure 9.9b). The results show that by far the strongest effect is found in the likelihood that a man who stopped living with both parents when he was between the ages of 6 and 16 will separate from his own child before it reaches the age of 6. We also note strong cohort effects: whereas before 1960 how long a man lived with both parents had little effect on his own marital stability, after 1960 the impact on men separated from both parents between the age of 6 and 16 nearly doubles, but only in regards to separating from preschool children.

It may seem counter-intuitive that a man's separation from a parent during his school-age years has the strongest effect on his ceasing to live with one of his own children before the age of 6, and that the effects of being separated from a parent during early childhood and of remaining with both parents until 16 or older are virtually the same. Draper and Harpending (1982, 1988) and Belsky, Steinberg, and Draper (1991) present a hypothesis which suggests that during the early years of development both sons and daughters form expectations about family formation strategies based on modeling their parents' behavior. These expectations include relations with the opposite sex and with children based on the perception of how necessary a stable partner is to rearing children as well as how critical an emotional and sexual commitment in marriage is. If our data can be interpreted as supporting this hypothesis, it suggests that the preschool years of life are not important but that a critical learning experience might occur only during the school-age years (Figures 9.9a and b) and that this effect is only expressed in the likelihood of ceasing to live with own child before it reaches the age of 6.

Alternately, this effect of age to which the man was raised by both parents could be mediated through the effects on a man's education and income (an embodied capital effect). Espenshade (1984) has estimated that the cost of raising a child in our society increases as a child matures and nearly doubles in total if

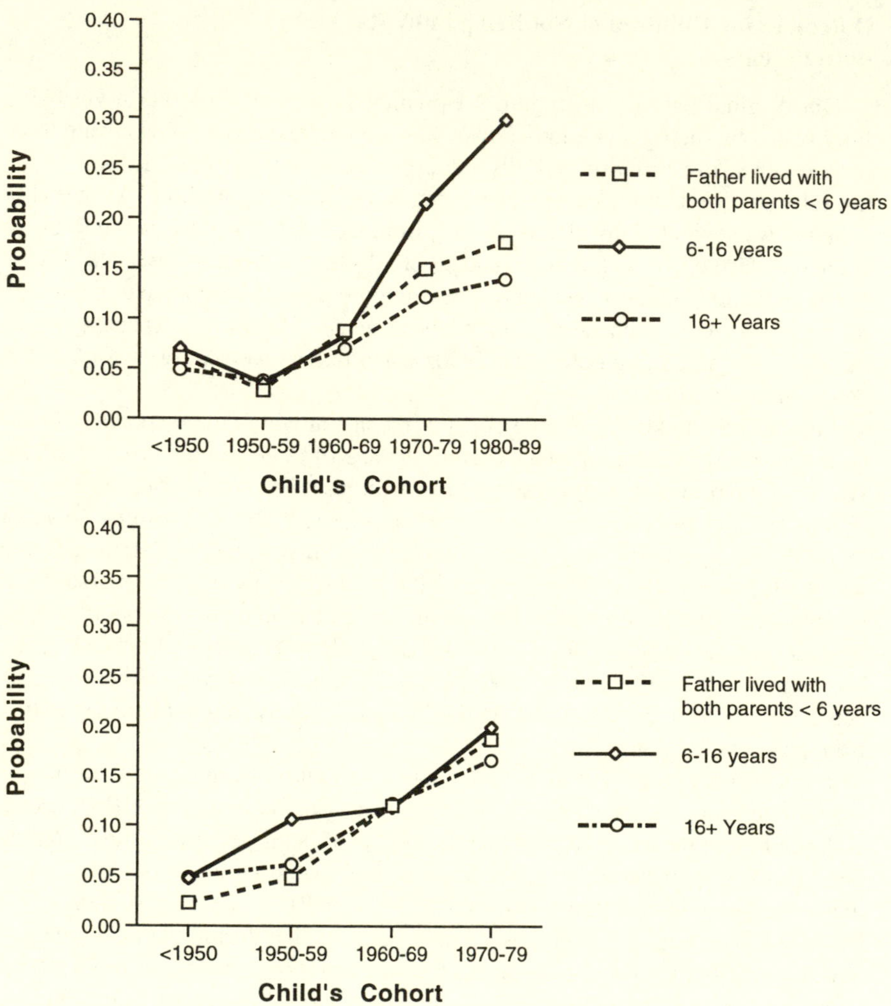

Figure 9.9a–b. Effects of the age to which respondent lived with both parents on the probability of his ceasing to live with a child (a) before the age of 6 and (b) between the ages of 6 and 16.

parents provide support for higher education. Monetary investment in a child should, therefore, become even more important as the child matures so that investment after age 16 may be particularly critical in its impact on a child's adult level of embodied capital. Calculations of lifetime earnings show that workers who do not finish high school can expect to earn $0.6 million whereas holders of professional degrees will earn $3.0 million in spite of their shorter employment careers (Population Reference Bureau 1994).

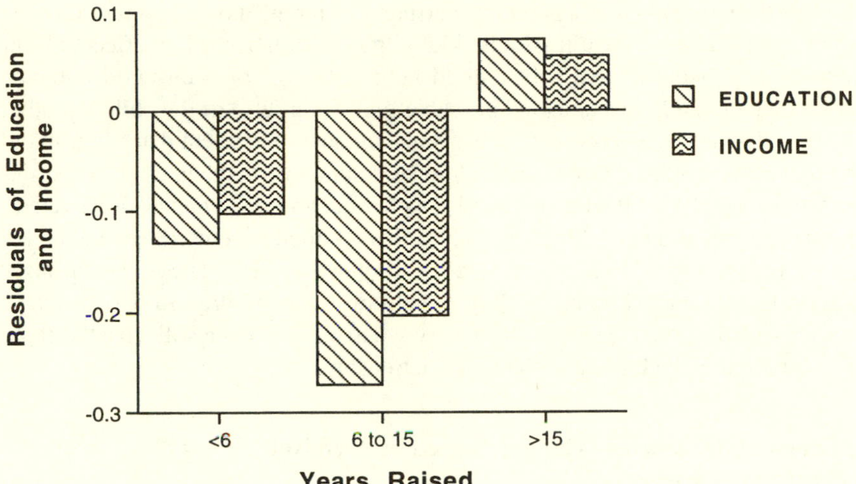

Figure 9.10. Effects of age to which men lived with both parents on their education and income.

We first regressed education and income on respondent's age and ethnicity. Figure 9.10 presents the effects of years raised by both parents on the residuals of completed education and current income. As predicted, we found a negative effect of a child having had a parent cease to live with him before age 16 on both his education and adult income. The effect was stronger on education than income. This parallels the strong effect reported above on the probability of ceasing to live with own child; that is, the negative effect is strongest for men who ceased to live with both parents during their school-age years compared with those who ceased to live with a parent during their early childhood.

It is interesting that the negative impact of not being fully raised until the age of 16 is stronger on education than on adult income. At this point we do not know what mediates this effect. Education may be a better proxy for the total value of lifetime earnings than current wages (Kaplan 1994). It might also be that the impact of father loss is strongest during the year it occurs and hence children's educational progress is disturbed and never made up. Children whose fathers leave during the preschool years have time to adjust to their loss before entering school.

This leaves the question as to why being separated from father during the preschool years has such a minimal impact since such a child is also deprived of his father's support during both school-age and later years. One possible answer is that fathers who leave early are more readily replaced by stepfathers who buffer the economic consequences of separation from the genetic father. Remarriage of a young woman without children is more likely than for a woman encumbered with children from her first relationship (Buckle, Gallup, and Rodd 1996). However, remarriage after divorce is only marginally affected by the number of children the mother had by a previous marriage; by far the most important variable is her age (Mackey 1980). It is quite likely that the relatively low effects of our measure of ceasing to live with a child before the age of 6 on child outcome reflects the probable low age (and probable high fecundity) of the child's mother and the relatively good prospects of her replacing lost investment in the household through her remarriage. For example, Mackey found that in the late seventies, single women aged 14–29 with children by a previous marriage had a 57.2% rate of remarriage. Women aged 30–39 had a 30.9% likelihood of remarriage, and by the age of 40–49 (end of fertility) the rate had dropped to 11%. These data strongly suggest that the men who are willing to help raise the children from a woman's previous relationship (see Figure 9.5) do so when these women still have the capability of producing children in the new relationship.

Outcomes for Children Who Are Raised by Men Not Their Genetic Fathers

As presented above, children who are raised by men not their genetic fathers are most likely to be children of his current mate. As such, this is a form of mating effort. We have two outcome measures that tell us something about men's willingness to invest in children not their own and the complex relationships between genetic relatedness to the child and the presence of the child's mother in the household. These results come from analysis of our long interview, which was given to a subsample of 1,325 men of which 642 men raised 1,246 children who went on to receive at least a year of higher education, about half of whom received some male parental support (Anderson, Kaplan, and Lancaster, 1999; Kaplan and Lancaster, this volume). Table 14.6 (in Kaplan and Lancaster, this volume) presents a logistic regression model of the probability of a man providing financial support for a child's higher education. The effects of genetic relatedness and the respondent's relationship to the child's mother are interesting. Children are divided into four groups. Children who live in intact families (the genetic offspring of the respondent and whose mother is still living with the respondent) are the baseline. Not surprisingly, they receive the most monetary investment.

The next highest level of investment is given to (a) a genetic offspring whose mother is separated from the respondent and (b) to an unrelated child whose mother is living with the respondent; they both receive over $2,000 less investment than the child of an intact family. The very least investment is given to a child who is not the genetic offspring of the respondent and whose mother no longer lives with him, a decrease of $4,600 below the baseline.

This reduction in investment is costly to a child who is raised by a man who is or was living with his mother or whose father no longer lives with his mother. Table 14.7 (in Kaplan and Lancaster, this volume) presents the least squares regression of the number of years of education obtained by children aged 23 and older raised by the respondent. Again, using intact families as the baseline, we find strong effects of both genetic paternity and the respondent's current relationship to the child's mother. A child who is not genetically related to the respondent but whose mother was living with the man when the child was 18 achieves about .75 years less education than a respondent's genetic offspring whose mother was living with him at 18 years of age. Genetic offspring of the respondents whose mothers ceased to live with the respondent before the child turned 18 achieve about 1.3 years less education, whereas a child who is not a genetic offspring and whose mother ceased to live with the respondent before the child turned 18 achieved 2.6 years less education. In this case the child of a woman who is living with the man does better than his own genetic offspring whose mother did not live with him at age 18.

Taken together, these results suggest that although investment made by a man in his current mate's child from a previous relationship is not as great as he might make if he and the woman were both genetic parents of the child, it is nevertheless significant and not very different from what he might do for his own child after divorce. However, the power of a woman to extract investment for her child from a man unrelated to the child but with whom she was once but is no longer living is greatly diminished. Male parental investment as mating effort clearly depends on the continued presence of his mate.

SUMMARY

1. Between 1990 and 1993 Kaplan and Lancaster's Albuquerque Men project completed approximately 7,100 short and 1,250 long structured interviews with a representative, random sample of men in Albuquerque recruited at the New Mexico Motor Vehicles Division (Kaplan et al. 1995a, b). The short interview sampled a man's current condition: mostly demographic information on three related generations, the man himself, his parents, and the children he produced and/or raised himself. The long interview was a history of employment/training, reproductive relationships, and children produced and raised. Most of the results presented here come from the analysis of the short interview given to 3,762 Anglos and 2,789 Hispanics. Our analyses of men's investment in children's education came from the long interview, which contained much more specific information about investment in each child at specific ages.

2. Men who do not fully parent are more likely to have low amounts of embodied capital as measured by their income, education, and early age of first reproduction and hence inflict lower costs on their offspring for ceasing to live with them than do men with high amounts of embodied capital.

3. The outcome of ceasing to live with a child before it reaches age 16 is a slight elevation in the father's fertility (child quantity) up through the Baby Boom years but not for the succeeding Post-boom cohort. However, this result may be an

artifact of the fact that many of these men may not yet have ceased producing children.

4. Men who raise other men's offspring are more likely to raise a child who belongs to his current mate (mating effort) or his own relative (kin investment). Only 15% of men who raised offspring of other males raised a stranger child or children of friends or neighbors.

5. Outcomes for children who are not raised by both parents show negative effects on both adult education and income of the child and increased likelihood of the child not forming stable reproductive relationships as an adult. The effect of ceasing to live with a father is strongest when it occurs during the school-age years. This is true for both its effects on the probability of ceasing to live with own children and on future educational and economic outcomes of children whose fathers ceased to live with them before adulthood.

6. Outcomes for stepchildren who are raised by men other than their father are reduced investment compared with children who live with their genetic fathers. However, they do experience nearly equal investment both before the age of 18 and for college education as that of a man's genetic child whose mother does not live with him. However, if the child's mother and stepfather separate, his investment in his stepchild plummets.

7. In sum, there is clear evidence that genetic paternity is relevant to male parental investment. Men invest less in children from their previous mates' unions. While expenditures on young children are not affected by genetic paternity (see Kaplan and Lancaster, this volume), both time investment and support during the college years is greater for genetic offspring than for a mate's child. In addition, full investment in a mate's child is contingent on a continuing relationship with that partner. Men cease to invest in a child after they stop living with the child's mother, unless the child is also the genetic offspring of the man, and even then, support is reduced significantly. The effect of those reduced investments is also seen in child outcomes, with children who are raised by men other than their genetic father or who are not fully raised by their father achieving lower educational outcomes (even after parental income and education are controlled for).

ACKNOWLEDGMENTS

Support for the research project, male fertility and parenting in New Mexico, began with two seed grants from the University of New Mexico Biomedical Research Grants, 1988 and 1989, and one from the University of New Mexico Research Allocations Committee, 1988. Further seed money as well as interim funding came from the William T. Grant Foundation (#89130589 and #91130501). The major support for the project came from the National Science Foundation 1990–1993 (#BNS-9011723 and #DBS-911552). Both National Science Foundation grants included Research Experience for Undergraduates supplements. Support for management of the data base and analysis came from the William T. Grant Foundation (#95166395). Other analyses are based upon work supported under a National Science Foundation Graduate Research Fellowship granted to Kermyt G. Anderson.

The authors would like to thank Phil Szydlowski and Joanna Scheib for helpful comments on drafts of this paper as well as the many undergraduate and graduate students at the University of New Mexico who worked on the Albuquerque Men project in interviewing, coding, data entry, office management, and data management and analysis. They would also like to thank Ted Bergstrom, Erik Charnov, Phil Ganderton, Steve Gangestad, Kristen Hawkes, Kim Hill, Nick Blurton Jones, David Lam, and Robert Willis for stimulating discussions about the theory of fertility and Kishore Gawande for discussions on economic models.

REFERENCES CITED

Anderson, K. G., H. Kaplan, and J. Lancaster. n.d. Paying for children's college costs: Mating and paternal tradeoffs among Albuquerque men. Copies available from the authors at the Department of Anthropology, University of New Mexico, Albuquerque.

———. 1999. Parental care by genetic and stepfathers I: Reports from Albuquerque men. *Evolution and Human Behavior* 20(6):405–432.

Becker, G. S. 1991. *A Treatise on the Family,* enlarged ed. Cambridge: Harvard University Press.

———. 1993. *Human Capital,* third ed. Chicago: University of Chicago Press.

Belsky, J., L. Steinberg, and P. Draper. 1991. Childhood experience, interpersonal development, and reproductive strategy: An evolutionary theory of socialization. *Child Development* 62:647–670.

Bloom, D. E., C. Conrad, and C. Miller. 1996. *Child Support and Fathers' Remarriage and Fertility.* National Bureau of Economics Research, Working Paper 5781.

Borgerhoff Mulder, M. 1992. Reproductive decisions. In *Evolutionary Ecology and Human Behavior,* E. A. Smith and B. Winterhalder, eds. Pp. 339–374. New York: Aldine de Gruyter.

Brien, M. J., and R. J. Willis. 1996. The costs and consequences of early fatherhood: The impact on young men, young women, and their children. In Rebecca Maynard, *Kids Having Kids: Economic Costs and Social Consequences of Teen Pregnancy.* Washington, DC: Urban Institute Press.

Buckle, L., G. G. Gallup, Jr., and Z. A. Rodd. 1996. Marriage as a reproductive contract: Patterns of marriage, divorce, and remarriage. *Ethology and Sociobiology* 17:363–377.

Charnov, E. L. 1993. *Life History Invariants: Some Explorations of Symmetry in Evolutionary Ecology.* Oxford: Oxford University Press.

Charvov, E. L., and D. Berrigan. 1993. Why do female primates have such long life spans and so few babies? *or* life in the slow lane. *Evolutionary Anthropology* 1:191–193.

Clutton-Brock, T. H. 1991. *The Evolution of Parental Care.* Princeton: Princeton University Press.

Cooksey, E. C., and Fondell, M. M. 1996. Spending time with his kids: Effects of family structure on fathers' and children's lives. *Journal of Marriage and the Family* 58:693–707.

Daly, M., and M. Wilson. 1994. Stepparenthood and the evolved psychology of discriminative parental solicitude. In *Infanticide and Parental Care,* S. Parmigiani and F. vom Saal, eds. Pp. 121–134. Chur, Switzerland: Harwood Science.

———. 1996. Violence against stepchildren. *Current Directions in Psychological Science* 5:77–81.

Draper, P., and H. Harpending. 1982. Father absence and reproductive strategy: An evolutionary perspective. *Journal of Anthropological Research* 38:255–273.

———. 1988. A sociobiological perspective on the development of human reproductive strategies. In *Sociobiological Perspectives on Human Development,* K. MacDonald, ed. Pp. 340–373. New York: Springer-Verlag.

Espenshade, T. J. 1984. *Investing in Children: New Estimates of Parental Expenditures.* Washington, D.C.: The Urban Institute.

Herrnstein, R. J., and C. Murray. 1994. *The Bell Curve.* New York: The Free Press.

Jorgenson, D. W., and B. Fraumeni. 1989. Investment in education. *Educational Researcher* 18:35–44.

Kaplan, H. 1994. Evolutionary and wealth flows theories of fertility: Empirical tests and new models. *Population and Development Review* 20:753–791.

———. 1996. A theory of fertility and parental investment in traditional and modern human societies. *Yearbook of Physical Anthropology* 39:91–135.

Kaplan, H., J. B. Lancaster, and K. G. Anderson. 1997. Human parental investment and fertility: The life histories of men in Albuquerque. In *Men in Families: When Do They Get Involved? What Difference Does It Make?* A. Booth and N. Crouter, eds. Pp. 55–110. New York: Lawrence Erlbaum.

Kaplan, H., J. B. Lancaster, J. A. Bock, and S. E. Johnson. 1995a. Does observed fertility maximize fitness among New Mexican men? A test of an optimality model and a new theory of parental investment in the embodied capital of offspring. *Human Nature* 6:325–360.

———. 1995b. Fertility and fitness among Albuquerque Men: A competitive labor market theory. In R. I. M. Dunbar, *Human Reproductive Decisions.* London: St. Martin's Press. Pp. 96–136.

Lancaster, J. B. 1997. The evolutionary history of human parental investment in relation to population growth and social stratification. In *Feminism and Evolutionary Biology,* P. A. Gowaty, ed. Pp. 466–488. New York: Chapman and Hall.

Lancaster, J. B., and H. Kaplan. 1992. Human mating and family formation strategies: The effects of variability among males in quality and the allocation of male effort and parental investment. In *Topics in Primatology,* Vol. 1, T. Nishida, W. C. McGrew, P. Marler, M. Pickford, and F. B. M. de Waal, eds. Pp. 21–33. Tokyo: University of Tokyo Press.

Lancaster, J. B., and C. S. Lancaster. 1987. The watershed: Change in parental-investment and family-formation strategies in the course of human evolution. In *Parenting across the Life Span: Biosocial Dimensions,* J. B. Lancaster, J. Altmann, A. S. Rossi, and L. R. Sherrod, eds. Pp. 187–205. New York: Aldine de Gruyter.

Lazarus, J. 1990. The logic of mate desertion. *Animal Behavior* 39:672–684.

Lockard, J. S., and R. M. Adams. 1981. Human serial polygyny: Demographic, reproductive, marital, and divorce data. *Ethology and Sociobiology* 2:177–186.

Low, B. S. 1978. Environmental uncertainty and the parental strategies of marsupials and placentals. *American Naturalist* 112:197–213.

Mackey, W. C. 1980. A sociobiological perspective on divorce patterns of men in the United States. *Journal of Anthropological Research* 36:419–428.

Murphy, K., and Welsh, F. 1989. Wage premiums for college graduates: Recent growth and possible explanations. *Educational Researcher* 18:17–27.

Population Reference Bureau. 1994. Speaking graphically: Education still drives income. *Population Today* 22:6.

Smuts, B. B., and D. J. Gubernick. 1991. Male-infant relationships in nonhuman primates: Paternal investment or mating effort? In *Father-Child Relations: Cultural and Biosocial Contexts,* B. S. Hewlett, ed. Pp. 1–30. New York: Aldine de Gruyter.

Sterns, S. C. 1992. *The Evolution of Life Histories.* Oxford: Oxford University Press.

Trivers, R. L. 1972. Parental investment and sexual selection. In *Sexual Selection and the Descent of Man, 1871–1971,* B. Campbell, ed. Pp. 136–179. Chicago: Aldine.

U. S. Bureau of the Census. 1992. Marital status and living arrangements: March 1991. *Current Population Reports* P-20, no. 461.
Vinovskis, M. A. 1990. Death and family life in the past. *Human Nature* 1:109–122.
Waynforth, D., and R. I. M. Dunbar. 1995. Conditional mate choice strategies in humans: Evidence from lonely hearts advertisements. *Behaviour* 132:755–779.
Weiss, Y., and R. J. Willis. 1985. Children as collective goods and divorce settlements. *Journal of Labor Economics* 3:268–292.

APPENDIX

Data for Figure 2

	Anglo			*Hispanic*		
Cohort	*N*	*S.D.*	*S.E.*	*N*	*S.D.*	*S.E.*
1930	200	0.31	0.02	86	0.31	0.03
1940	719	0.27	0.01	318	0.33	0.02
1950	1297	0.31	0.01	829	0.27	0.01
1960	1577	0.41	0.01	1614	0.36	0.01
1970	929	0.46	0.02	1193	0.45	0.01

Data for Figure 3

	No High School			*High School*			*B.A.*			*M.A. or Greater*		
Cohort	*N*	*SD*	*S.E.*	*N*	*SD*	*S.E.*	*N*	*SD*	*S.E.*	*N*	*SD*	*S.E.*
1930	103	0.22	0.02	140	0.23	0.02	26	0.27	0.05	19	0.32	0.07
1940	232	0.30	0.02	486	0.21	0.01	177	0.20	0.01	142	0.14	0.01
1950	394	0.20	0.01	956	0.19	0.01	429	0.15	0.01	347	0.18	0.01
1960	498	0.29	0.01	1599	0.27	0.01	592	0.27	0.01	502	0.22	0.01
1970	382	0.35	0.02	2014	0.36	0.01	591	0.34	0.01	511	0.26	0.01
1980	208	0.43	0.03	1116	0.38	0.01	371	0.34	0.02	320	0.29	0.02

Data for Figure 4a

	Lowest Income Quartile			*Quartile 2*			*Quartile 3*			*Highest Income Quartile*		
Cohort	*N*	*SD*	*S.E.*	*N*	*SD*	*S.E.*	*N*	*SD*	*S.E.*	*N*	*SD*	*S.E.*
1930	72	0.26	0.03	56	0.23	0.03	59	0.22	0.03	42	0.26	0.04
1940	226	0.30	0.02	212	0.21	0.01	228	0.21	0.01	190	0.16	0.01
1950	413	0.24	0.01	457	0.21	0.01	514	0.16	0.01	483	0.14	0.01
1960	665	0.31	0.01	744	0.26	0.01	757	0.26	0.01	762	0.21	0.01
1970	748	0.42	0.02	844	0.33	0.01	875	0.30	0.01	772	0.32	0.01
1980	428	0.45	0.02	453	0.37	0.02	504	0.32	0.01	508	0.30	0.01

Data for Figure 4b

	Lowest Income Quartile			*Quartile 2*			*Quartile 3*			*Highest Income Quartile*		
Cohort	*N*	*SD*	*S.E.*	*N*	*SD*	*S.E.*	*N*	*SD*	*S.E.*	*N*	*SD*	*S.E.*
1930	70	0.34	0.04	56	0.29	0.04	59	0.28	0.04	42	0.38	0.06
1940	226	0.34	0.02	212	0.29	0.02	228	0.30	0.02	190	0.22	0.02
1950	413	0.35	0.02	457	0.28	0.01	514	0.27	0.01	483	0.27	0.01
1960	665	0.45	0.02	744	0.39	0.01	757	0.37	0.01	762	0.33	0.01
1970	439	0.49	0.02	523	0.45	0.02	524	0.42	0.02	463	0.42	0.02

Data for Figure 5. Age at First Reproduction

	< 20 years			*20–24 years*			*25–29 years*			*30+ years*		
Cohort	*N*	*SD*	*S.E.*	*N*	*SD*	*S.E.*	*N*	*SD*	*S.E.*	*N*	*SD*	*S.E.*
1930	35	0.17	0.03	178	0.34	0.03	55	0.23	0.03	18	0.38	0.09
1940	64	0.24	0.03	406	0.31	0.02	335	0.27	0.01	232	0.29	0.02
1950	160	0.41	0.03	1030	0.32	0.01	526	0.24	0.01	410	0.23	0.01
1960	346	0.46	0.02	1834	0.40	0.01	707	0.34	0.01	304	0.33	0.02
1970	245	0.47	0.03	1167	0.47	0.01	464	0.41	0.02	246	0.38	0.02

Data for Figure 6a

	Lived with all to age 6			*Did not live with one to age 6*		
Cohort	*N*	*SD*	*S.E.*	*N*	*SD*	*S.E.*
1910	400	1.26	0.06	30	1.66	0.30
1920	316	1.51	0.08	18	2.05	0.48
1930	402	1.41	0.07	65	1.78	0.22
1940	607	1.01	0.04	157	1.53	0.12
1950	388	0.96	0.05	144	1.26	0.11

Data for Figure 6b

	Lived with all to age 16			*Did not live w/ one to age 16*		
Cohort	*N*	*SD*	*S.E.*	*N*	*SD*	*S.E.*
1910	375	1.26	0.07	54	1.52	0.21
1920	291	1.51	0.09	43	1.75	0.27
1930	347	1.44	0.08	110	1.56	0.15
1940	375	1.10	0.06	232	1.32	0.09
1950	60	1.36	0.18	57	1.52	0.20

Data for Figure 9a. Length of time father lived with both parents

	Until <6 years old			*6–16 years*			*16+ years*		
Cohort	*N*	*SD*	*S.E.*	*N*	*SD*	*S.E.*	*N*	*SD*	*S.E.*
1930	57	0.19	0.02	46	0.36	0.05	185	0.20	0.01
1940	220	0.25	0.02	139	0.20	0.02	678	0.22	0.01
1950	569	0.17	0.01	254	0.19	0.01	1303	0.19	0.01
1960	761	0.28	0.01	350	0.28	0.01	2080	0.26	0.01
1970	845	0.36	0.01	358	0.41	0.02	2295	0.33	0.01
1980	458	0.38	0.02	204	0.46	0.03	1353	0.35	0.01

Data for Figure 9b. Length of time man lived with parents

	<6 yrs			*6–16 yrs*			*16+ yrs*		
Cohort	*N*	*SD*	*S.E.*	*N*	*SD*	*S.E.*	*N*	*SD*	*S.E.*
1930	55	0.19	0.03	39	0.22	0.04	175	0.22	0.02
1940	205	0.14	0.01	133	0.21	0.02	644	0.21	0.01
1950	553	0.21	0.01	245	0.31	0.02	1254	0.24	0.01
1960	694	0.33	0.01	321	0.32	0.02	1934	0.33	0.01
1970	444	0.39	0.02	176	0.40	0.03	1214	0.37	0.01

Data for Figure10

	Education			*Income*		
Years Lived	*N*	*SD*	*S.E.*	*N*	*SD*	*S.E.*
<6	1062	1.17	0.04	1062	4.75	0.15
6 to 15	602	1.23	0.05	602	2.50	0.10
>15	4199	1.18	0.02	4199	3.54	0.05

10

Female-biased Parental Investment and Growth Performance among the Mukogodo

LEE CRONK

One of the boldest predictions about behavior to come out of evolutionary biology is the idea that in certain circumstances parents should be expected to bias their investment in favor of one sex of offspring or the other. Previous work among the Mukogodo of Kenya (Cronk 1989b, 1990b, 1991b, 1993) has provided tentative support for this prediction in one human society, where parents appear to be biasing their investment in favor of daughters, who tend to have better marital and reproductive prospects than sons. This chapter reports on new research among the Mukogodo that both confirms and elaborates upon the earlier findings.

THEORETICAL BACKGROUND

Sex biases in parental investment and the closely related topic of sex ratio evolution have been important topics in evolutionary biological theory since Fisher (1934) explained why parents in a population should, on average, invest equally in sons and daughters. Fisher's reasoning was as simple as it was powerful. Because every individual in a sexually reproducing, diploid species gets half its nuclear genetic material from its mother and half from its father, selection should favor parents who invest equally in daughters and sons because a single unit of investment in an individual of one sex will have the same effect on a parent's fitness as a unit invested in the other sex.

Later theoreticians explored circumstances in which selection might favor individual parents who bias their investment in favor of one sex or another. Hamilton (1967), for example, examined circumstances in which siblings of one sex compete with one another for mates. In such situations, the competition makes individuals of the competitive sex more costly to produce from the point of view of the parents than individuals of the other sex, and so selection should favor parents who produce more of the other sex. Subsequently, others explored situations in which one sex of offspring is more expensive than the other because it competes with parents or siblings for resources (local resource competition; see Clark 1978), situations in which one sex of offspring is cheaper than the other because it provides resources that benefit parents or siblings (local resource enhancement; see Gowaty and Lennartz 1985), and situations in which one sex of offspring is cheaper because it enhances the mating success of parents or siblings (local mate enhancement; see Sieff 1990).

Those models are all essentially refinements of Fisher's principle in that they predict that overall parental investment in sons and daughters, including not only investments that parents can control but also those they cannot, will be equal (Cronk 1991b; see also Hoogland 1981). Robert Trivers and Dan Willard (1973) broke from this pattern by proposing that in some circumstances natural selection should favor parents within a population whose overall investment is truly biased in favor of one sex of offspring. Specifically, they hypothesized that where the reproductive prospects of sons and daughters differ in ways that can in some way be predicted from the situation of the parents, selection should favor parents who invest more heavily in the offspring with the better prospects. Among polygynous mammal species, for example, the variance in reproductive success is typically greater among males than among females, and so the conditions in which individuals are reared may have a greater impact on male than on female reproductive success. If an individual's rank, physical condition, or access to resources is affected by his or her parents' condition, then parents in good condition should favor sons because a very successful son will be more successful than a very successful daughter. Parents in poor condition, on the other hand, should favor daughters because an unsuccessful daughter will still be more successful than an unsuccessful son.

Though the Trivers-Willard hypothesis was greeted with skepticism (e.g., Williams 1979), eventually the effects it predicts were observed in a variety of nonhuman species (see Clutton-Brock and Iason 1986; Gray 1985; Hrdy 1987, 1988). *Evolutionary Biology and Human Social Behavior: An Anthropological Perspective* (Chagnon and Irons, eds. 1979) included some of the earliest tests of the model with data from human societies. Chagnon, Flinn, and Melancon (1979) tested the hypothesis among the Yanomamö, predicting that headmen and men who belong to larger lineages would have more male than female offspring. Their reasoning was that headmen are prestigious and respected individuals who have, on average, more than twice as many offspring as other men (Chagnon 1979) and that men in large lineages are at an advantage compared with men in smaller lineages because they have larger numbers of allies. Neither prediction was supported by the data. Chagnon and colleagues suggested that the failure of the model may be due to a lack of fit between the conditions that must be present for it to apply and the circumstances of the Yanomamö. Specifically, in that particular population there may be very little correlation between the size of a man's lineage or his individual status in the community and the reproductive prospects of his offspring.

In that same volume, Mildred Dickemann presented data on male-biased parental investment from three historical societies that do seem to have the preconditions required by the Trivers-Willard model. Among the elites of feudal north India, imperial China, and medieval Europe, high-status males generally had better reproductive prospects than their sisters, and parents appear to have biased investment in favor of sons. The details of the male bias vary from case to case. In north India during the late seventeenth and early eighteenth centuries, for example, members of the ruling Jhareja subcaste reportedly killed almost all female infants. Female infanticide was also common among other high-status groups in that region while being rare or absent among lower-status groups. These two studies helped demonstrate the strength and promise of the new Darwinian paradigm in at least three ways. First, they showed the ability of the paradigm to direct researchers' attention to topics, such as sex biases in parental investment, that had previously received little attention from anthropologists. Second, they demonstrated the power of the new approach to help make sense of previously unexplained observations, such as the Indian infanticide data. Third, they demonstrated the determination of those working in this new field to adhere closely to the standards of scientific method, including Popperian falsificationism. This helped to set the stage for the study described in this chapter.

THE MUKOGODO

The Mukogodo are a low-status, impoverished group of Maasai-speaking pastoralists in north-central Kenya. Until early in the twentieth century, they were a relatively isolated group of hunter-gatherers and beekeepers. They lived in small rockshelters in the Mukogodo Hills, spoke a unique Eastern Cushitic language called Yaaku, and married among themselves, paying beehives as bride-wealth. As a result of population growth and population movements caused by British colonial policies, during the first few decades of the twentieth century the Mukogodo came into increasing contact with a variety of Maasai-speaking pastoralist groups, including not only large and famous groups like the Samburu and the Maasai themselves, but also smaller groups like the Digirri, Ilng'wesi, and Mumonyot. Intermarriage with Maasai-speakers, which always involved livestock rather than beehive bride-wealth payments, led to a situation in which Mukogodo males had to obtain livestock in order to get married. Subsequently, the Mukogodo rapidly lost their old way of life, including their old language, and adopted the language, culture, and subsistence patterns of their new Maasai-speaking neighbors (Cronk 1989a).

The Mukogodo transition to pastoralism transformed them from a group of relatively independent hunter-gatherers to the bottom stratum of a regional hierarchy of wealth, status, and marital success (Cronk 1990a). The transition was so recent that typical Mukogodo herd sizes are still far behind those of neighboring groups.

Maasai-speakers look down on the Mukogodo and refer to them by the derogatory term *il-torrobo* because of their recent history as hunter-gatherers, a way of life considered suitable only for wild animals, and because until recently they spoke a language other than Maasai (see Galaty 1979 for details on the concept of *il-torrobo*). As a result of their poverty and low status, polygyny rates are lower and men's ages at first marriage are higher among the Mukogodo than among neighboring groups. However, the difficulties that Mukogodo men have in obtaining wives are not experienced by Mukogodo women, all of whom get married, often to men from wealthier neighboring groups.

FEMALE-BIASED PARENTAL INVESTMENT

The difference in the reproductive prospects of Mukogodo males and females sets the stage for a test of the Trivers-Willard hypothesis, which would predict that Mukogodo parents should favor daughters over sons. Between 1985 and 1987 I conducted fieldwork among the Mukogodo and collected data relevant to this prediction. The first hint that there might be female-biased parental investment came from their childhood (ages 0–4) sex ratio, which in 1986 was equivalent to 67 boys for every 100 girls. Although good data on the sex ratio at birth was impossible to come by owing to Mukogodo women's reticence to discuss child deaths, there seemed little reason to believe that the bias was due to any sort of physiological mechanism affecting the survivorship of male sperm or fetuses, and other data sources suggested that the sex ratio bias was due to unusually high male childhood mortality produced by greater parental solicitude toward daughters. For example, some data suggest that Mukogodo daughters may have been nursed longer than sons ($p < 0.10$; see Cronk 1989b, 1991b). Data from a local dispensary and a clinic run by Roman Catholic missionaries showed a statistically significant tendency for Mukogodo parents to take their daughters for medical care more often than their sons. This tendency did not appear among parents from neighboring Maasai-speaking groups. Those groups have been marrying each other and the Mukogodo since early in this century and are culturally almost indistinguishable from one another, making it highly unlikely that this is due to any cultural difference among the groups in, say, beliefs about childcare or about boys' and girls' needs for medical treatment.

All of these data support the predictions of the Trivers-Willard model: Mukogodo parents appeared to be favoring the sex with the best reproductive prospects. This does not, by itself, rule out other possible explanations. For example, it may be that Mukogodo parents favor daughters over sons not (or not only) because of their superior reproductive prospects, but rather (or also) because of the bridewealth payments they attract. If this were true, then men with more daughters from their first marriages should have more wives subsequently than men with few or no daughters from their first marriages, and men with more sisters should have more wives than men with few or no sisters, because of the ability of men to use the bride-wealth attracted by their daughters and sisters to obtain more wives for themselves. Neither prediction is supported by the data. In a sample of 220 Mukogodo men, there is a low (Pearson's coefficient = 0.111) and statistically insignificant (p [one-tailed] = 0.1) relationship between numbers of daughters from their first marriages who survived to age 15 and their total numbers of wives. In fact, the mean number of wives for men with one or more daughters from their first marriages who survived to age 15 (1.320) is actually lower than the mean number of wives for men with no such daughters (1.333), though the difference is not statistically significant ($p > 0.25$). Similarly, only a very slight (Pearson's coefficient = 0.095) and statistically insignificant ($p = 0.084$) negative relationship was found between men's numbers of wives and their numbers of full sisters surviving to age 15 ($N = 330$). The lack of a relationship among these variables probably reflects the difficulty of Mukogodo poverty. Mukogodo men lend and borrow a great deal of livestock, and it may be the case that most Mukogodo men who receive livestock as bride-wealth must tend to their debts rather than use the windfall to obtain additional wives for themselves or their sons.

CAREGIVER BEHAVIOR AND CHILDREN'S GROWTH PERFORMANCE

The 1986 research established that there was reason to believe that the Mukogodo were favoring their daughters over their sons and that this behavior fit the predictions of the Trivers-Willard model. However, the limited measures of parental behavior and the lack of details about the effects of biased parental investment on the children themselves raised new questions. Accordingly, I returned to the Mukogodo from May through August of 1993 to explore the details of everyday childcare and their effects on boys' and girls' growth performance, health, and, ultimately, survivorship. To assess patterns of parental investment, I collected several different types of data, including systematic observations of the behaviors of caregivers and children, mothers' reports on their children's morbidity, and usage statistics for two local clinics. To assess children's growth performance, I collected basic anthropometric data, including recumbent length, weight, and head circumference.

The Sample and Its Characteristics

Upon arrival I surveyed all of the Mukogodo settlements within reasonable walking and driving distance of my home base at Kuri-Kuri Primary School, located about three kilometers outside the Mukogodo Division headquarters town of Don Dol. Parents were able to provide exact birth dates, which are often recorded on immunization record cards by the staffs of local clinics, for almost all of the youngest children in the area. For children with unknown birth dates, I used tooth eruption patterns to help estimate ages (Townsend and Hammel 1990). I also collected tooth eruption data for the children with recorded birth dates, and the close fit between age estimates based on tooth eruptions and those based on recorded birth dates was reassuring. Children under 30 months old were the intended focus of the study for two reasons, one practical and the other theoretical. On a practical level, tooth eruption patterns become unreliable as indicators of age after about 30 months. On a theoretical level, I wanted to concentrate my attention on the youngest children because they are the most dependent upon parental care and hence potentially the most vulnerable to variations in its quality and quantity. However, in order to achieve the desired sample size, two children slightly outside this age group, a girl aged 32 months and a boy aged 31 months, needed to be included as well. Good birth date information was available for both of those children. The twenty boys in the study ranged from five months to 31 months old, with a mean age of 17.5 months. The twenty girls ranged from one month to 32 months old, with a mean age of 11.35 months.

The Focal Follow Data

Using methods pioneered mainly by ethologists (e.g., Altmann 1974) and later adapted by human behavioral ecologists and anthropologists (Borgerhoff Mulder and Caro 1985; Gross 1984; Hames 1992), I conducted systematic behavioral observations, called "focal follows," on all forty children in the sample. At two separate randomly chosen times between 6:30 A.M. and 6:30 P.M., I arrived unannounced at the home of each child and conducted an hour of observations. The identity of each caregiver, caregiver behaviors, and the behaviors of the child were all checked off on prepared sheets every fifteen seconds, as indicated by a watch alarm that I muffled with a heavy cloth and carried in my shirt pocket. I recorded such caregiver behaviors as an estimate of the number of meters between the caregiver and the child, whether the caregiver was holding the child in his or her arms or in a sling, any touching of the child, any vocalizations directed toward the child, and other behaviors such as dressing, washing, and feeding. I recorded such child behaviors as position (lying, sitting, standing, etc.), vocalizations, crying, feeding, nursing, and sleeping. At the end of each hour of observations, I compensated the main caregiver in charge, usually the child's mother, with a small cash payment.

From the original observations I have derived three simple and straightforward indicators of caregiver solicitude: the mean distance between the caregiver and the child, the proportion of time the caregiver was observed holding the child, and the proportion of time the child was observed to be nursing. Of course, these are not meant to be seen as independent or completely separate measures of solicitude: a nursing child is usually being held, and a child who is either nursing or being held has a caregiver-child distance of zero. The means for all of these indicators are biased in favor of females (Table 10.1). This by itself is not surprising given that the females are younger, on average, than the males, and, of course, a few months

Table 10.1. Means for a variety of measures of caregiver solicitude, based on two hours of focal follow observations of each child.

	Distance[a]				
	All caregivers	*Mothers*[b] *only*	*Non-mothers*	*Child-holding*[c]	*Nursing*[d]
Boys	1.153	1.139	1.373	32.3%	4.3%
Girls	0.379	0.319	0.637	58.7%	11.0%
All children	0.766	0.780	0.989	45.5%	7.6%

a Mean caregiver-child distance estimate, in meters.
b Non-nursing observations only
c Mean percent of time children were held by caregivers
d Mean percent of time children were nursed.

Table 10.2. Regression coefficients for a variety of measures of caregiver solicitude.

Dependent variable	*Constant*	*Regression coefficient for age in months*	*Regression coefficient for sex (0 = male, 1 = female)*
Mean caregiver-child distance	0.633	0.030	–0.592
p (one-tailed)	0.012	0.014	0.004
Mean proportion of time	0.606	–0.016	0.165
children were held	0	0.002	0.03
p (one-tailed)			
Mean proportion of time	0.144	–0.006	0.032
children were nursed	0	0	0.07
p (one-tailed)			
Proportion of time children were	0.651	–0.008	–0.100
cared for by their mothers	0	0.154	0.098
p (one-tailed)			

can make a big difference in the amount of time a child is held or nursed. However, even when age is statistically factored out, a female bias in caregiver solicitude remains. Table 10.2 shows the beta coefficients yielded by regressions of the three indicators of solicitude against the children's ages in months and their sexes, coded as a dummy variable. Another way to approach this is to calculate the correlation between sex and the three indicators of solicitude while controlling for age. Such partial correlation coefficients are obtained by regressing both sex and the three indicators of solicitude against age, saving the residuals, and then calculating the correlations between the residuals for sex and each of the indicators of solicitude. The partial correlation coefficients between sex and mean caregiver-child distance, proportion of time the child was held, and the proportion of time the child was nursed are –0.417, 0.303, and 0.240, respectively. In sum, even controlling for age, the females in the sample tended to be closer to their caregivers and tended to be held and nursed more often than the males in the sample. The focal follows also provide a window onto a possible sex bias in nursing behavior. Part of the reason why the average proportion of time spent nursing is lower for boys than for girls is that while only the oldest female in the sample was never observed to nurse, seven males, one as young as 13 months, were never observed to nurse.

The focal follows also provide information about who takes care of Mukogodo infants and toddlers. Primary caregiver observations are fairly evenly divided between mothers (49%) and other individuals, most often the focal child's sister (16%). Surprisingly, mothers cared for the boys in the sample slightly more than the girls. However, a regression of the proportion of time each child was observed to be cared for primarily by his or her mother against age and sex yields small and nonsignificant regression coefficients (see Table 10.2), and the partial correlation between sex and the proportion of time each child was cared for by his or her mother is low (–0.167). Interestingly, the sex difference in mean child-caregiver distance is present for both mothers and others (Table 10.1). Setting aside instances of nursing, which bias the caregiver-child distance figures in favor of mothers over other caregivers, mothers still tend to stay closer to the focal children than do other caregivers (Table 10.1), but only slightly. The absence of any large difference between the quality of care given by mothers and that of other caregivers matches the findings of Borgerhoff Mulder and Milton (1985) among the Kipsigis of western Kenya, where other caregivers actually tended to keep closer to infants than did mothers. In sum, there does not appear to be much of a difference in the care given by mothers and others, and so the proportion of time a child is cared for by his or her mother does not seem to be a very good indicator of solicitude. Therefore, the lack of any significant correlation between this variable and sex is not surprising.

Morbidity and Medical Care Reports

After I conducted an hour of focal follow observations on a child, I then asked the child's mother, if she was present, whether the child had been ill the day before and what, if any, treatment was given. The girls' mothers were available to answer this question after all focal follows. They reported that their daughters had been ill on the previous day 19 (47.5%) times. Fourteen of those times (74% of 19) they were taken for treatment to the clinics run by the local Roman Catholic mission or the local government. Five of those times (26% of 19) they were given no treatment. The boys' mothers were available to answer this question at 37 of the 40 focal follows of boys. They reported that their sons had been ill on the previous day 22 times (59% of 37). Seventeen of those times (77% of 22) they were given treatment either at one of the local clinics (14 times) or with purchased, over-the-counter medicines (3 times). Five of those times (36% of 22) they were given no treatment. None of these differences is statistically significant.

Clinic and Dispensary Visits

Data for 1992, the last complete year before the field season, were collected for several different categories of clinic and dispensary use. Mukogodo children were identified by their surnames. Table 10.3 shows data for visits by children ages 0–4 from the Don Dol Roman Catholic dispensary. The Mukogodo figures are for the entire year, while the non-Mukogodo figures are for a random sample of 25 days from throughout the year. As in 1986, there is a male bias for the non-Mukogodo and a slight female bias for the Mukogodo, but the bias is no longer statistically significant ($\chi^2 = 1.904, p > .05$; cf. Cronk 1989b). Table 10.4 shows the same sort

Table 10.3. Visits by children ages 0–4 to the Don Dol Roman Catholic dispensary, 1992, by ethnic group, sex and type of visit.

	Mukogodo[a]				*Non-Mukogodo*[b]			
	Males		*Females*		*Males*		*Females*	
	New Visit	*Repeat Visit*	*New Visit*	*Repeat Visit*	*New Visit*	*Repeat Visit*	*New Visit*	*Repeat Visit*
n	51	48	63	41	76	36	66	31
N	99 (49%)		104 (51%)		112 (53%)		97 (47%)	

a. All patients treated during 1992 ages 0–4 with recognizably Mukogodo surnames.
b. Based on a random sample of 25 days from throughout 1992.

Table 10.4. Visits by children ages 0–4 to the Don Dol government clinic, 1992, by ethnic group, sex and type of visit.

	Mukogodo[a]				*Non-Mukogodo*[b]			
	Males		*Females*		*Males*		*Females*	
	New Visit	*Repeat Visit*	*New Visit*	*Repeat Visit*	*New Visit*	*Repeat Visit*	*New Visit*	*Repeat Visit*
n	71	39	67	38	57	9	34	14
N	110 (51%)		105 (49%)		66 (58%)		48 (42%)	

a. All patients treated during 1992 ages 0–4 with recognizably Mukogodo surnames.
b. Based on a random sample of 25 days from throughout 1992.

of data, collected in the same way, from the local government-run clinic, showing a slight male bias in clinic use among the Mukogodo and a very strong male bias among non-Mukogodo. The male bias in government clinic use among the non-Mukogodo is so strong that the Mukogodo figures are actually significantly female-biased (or at least less male-biased) in comparison ($\chi^2 = 4.00, p < .05$). In sum, although the female bias in clinic and dispensary use among the Mukogodo does not appear to have been as strong in 1992 as in 1986, Mukogodo parents do not appear to have anything like the strong male bias shown by their neighbors.

Anthropometry

Following standard procedures (Frisancho 1990; Gibson 1990; Jelliffe and Jelliffe 1989), I collected a variety of standard anthropometric data. Here I will report on height (measured as recumbent length), weight, and head circumferences. The height and weight data were analyzed with the help of EpiInfo (CDC 1991), a computer program developed by the Centers for Disease Control that provides weight-for-age (WAZ), height-for-age (HAZ), and weight-for-height (WHZ) *z*-scores by comparing children's measurements to a standard body of reference data published by the National Center for Health Statistics (Department of Health, Education, and Welfare 1977a, 1977b). Those data are not assumed to represent ideal growth patterns; rather, they provide a benchmark against which we can compare the growth performance of children of different ages and sexes. Figure 10.1 shows the means for boys and girls for all three measures of growth performance. By all three measures, the girls appear to be doing better than the boys. The differences for WAZ ($t = 2.394, p < .025$) and WHZ ($t = 2.161, p < .05$) are statistically significant, though the difference for HAZ ($t = 1.611, p > .05$) is not.

The head circumferences were compared with a body of reference data from the United States (Roche et al. 1987). The reference data are available for children at birth, at one month, at three months, and then at three-month increments up to twelve months, and at six-month increments after that. The sample children were compared to the data for the increment they had most recently passed. The results are inconclusive. The mean *z*-score for head circumferences is slightly greater for males than for females (0.135 vs. –0.727), but the difference is not statistically significant (p [one-tailed] $> .05$).

DISCUSSION

My earlier work on sex-biased parental investment among the Mukogodo was a good example of chance favoring a prepared mind. When I originally began my research among them, I had no intention of looking at parental behavior and no hint that Mukogodo parents might favor one sex over the other. Fortunately, evo-

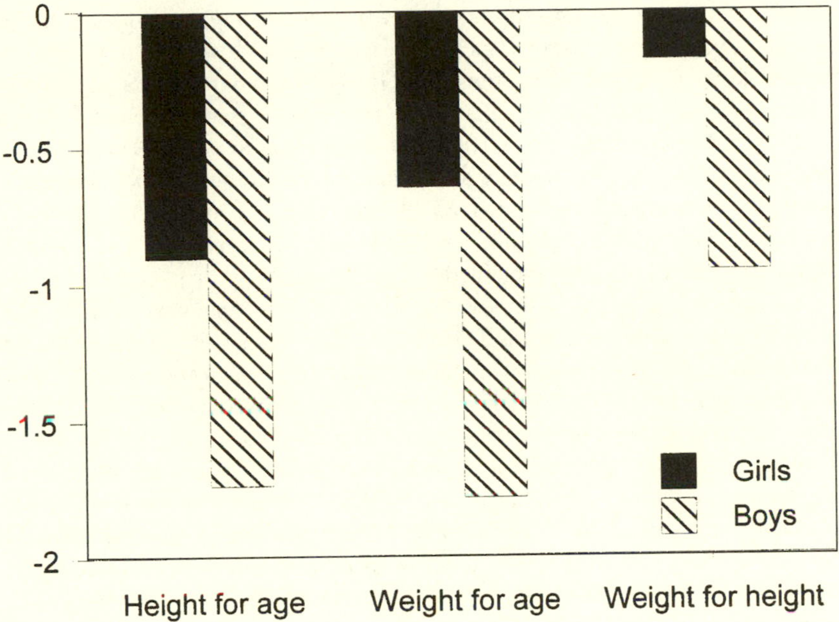

Figure 10.1. Mean height-for-age (HAZ), weight-for-age (WAZ), and weight-for-height (WHZ) *z*-scores for boys and girls in the sample.

lutionary theories of sex ratios and parental investment had been parts of my education going back to my first undergraduate course in biological anthropology, and I immediately sat up and took notice when my first rough age-sex pyramid scribbled in my field notebook revealed such a strong female bias in the childhood sex ratio. The data that I subsequently gathered almost as an afterthought on dispensary and clinic use was enough to convince many people that the Mukogodo appeared to fit the predictions of the Trivers-Willard hypothesis.

The data collected in 1993 both corroborate and elaborate upon those from 1986. Mukogodo parents and other caregivers not only are more likely to provide girls than boys with medical treatment, they also hold and nurse daughters more and maintain less distance between themselves and girls than between themselves and boys. Possibly as a result of these biases in caregiver behaviors, Mukogodo girls appear to have significantly better growth performance than Mukogodo boys. Recent research in other societies suggests that such a female bias among lower-status groups may be relatively widespread. Bereczkei and Dunbar (1997) have shown that Hungarian Gypsy parents tend to invest more heavily in daughters than sons compared with other Hungarians, as indicated by the sex ratio at birth, duration of breast-feeding, length of education, and the likelihood that a birth of a girl or boy is followed by an abortion. In keeping with the predictions of the Trivers-Willard hypothesis, Gypsy parents have more grandoffspring through their daughters than through their sons, owing chiefly to a tendency toward hypergyny from that low-status group to higher-status non-Gypsy Hungarians. In a study of contemporary Americans, Gaulin and Robbins (1991) found that women with annual household incomes of less than $10,000 or without an adult male present were more likely to breast-feed their daughters than their sons, and women without an adult male present tended to breast-feed their daughters an average of 5.5 months longer than their sons (see Cronk 1991b for more examples of female-biased parental investment possibly explained by the Trivers-Willard and other models).

This study also helps to address some of the criticisms that have been directed at the earlier one. For example, Sieff (1990:32) suggests that "it is conceivable that [Mukogodo] daughters were discriminated against in terms of food allocation and consequently became ill more often," leading their parents to take them to the local clinics more often. Neither the focal follow data on nursing frequencies nor the anthropometric data support the idea that Mukogodo boys are fed more generously than girls. Sieff (1990:32) also criticizes the fact that "the data on reproductive success of men versus women come from reproductive histories of adults while the evidence of investment favoring daughters comes from current children," but it is hard to imagine how it could be otherwise. Although natural selection would surely favor an ability among parents to be prescient about the reproductive prospects of their offspring were such an ability to arise, both phylogenetic constraints and, ultimately, the physical laws of our universe conspire to make this virtually impossible. All that Mukogodo parents and we researchers have to go on when gauging their offspring's reproductive potential is the way things are now. Thus, what Sieff identifies as a weakness of the study is actually one of its strengths.

Fix (1990:36) has a different problem with the earlier study: "what has evolved? Mukogodo parents of females might have more grandchildren than those with male offspring, but a hereditary bias for producing females could not increase through natural selection because there is no consistency across generations." As Sieff (1990:44) has explained, Fix assumes that the female bias is an obligate trait, while the bulk of research on sex-biased parental investment among both humans and nonhumans suggests that it is, in fact, a facultative trait. Even some insects have been shown to have the ability to facultatively alter the sex ratio of their offspring depending on local circumstances (e.g., Werren 1980). Given that the ability to adaptively adjust parental investment patterns has also been demonstrated among a variety of nonhuman primates and other mammals (see Clutton-Brock and Iason 1986), it is probably also a very ancient trait, shared not only by our entire species but also by a large clade of organisms of which humans are just a small part. The current situation among the Mukogodo may be helping to maintain this trait in our species, but I know of no one who has ever argued that the female bias observed there is either an obligate trait or isolated to the Mukogodo population.

Another criticism of this type of research is that sex ratios are population parameters, not phenotypes, and hence not subject to natural selection. Unless selection is in fact acting on sex ratios at the level of the population, an idea considered unlikely by most evolutionary biologists since the publication of Williams's (1966) critique of group selectionism, then this criticism is absolutely correct. This is why all of my work on the Mukogodo has been phrased in terms of sex-biased parental investment, not the female-biased Mukogodo childhood sex ratio, which is only a symptom of the underlying behavioral phenomenon postulated to be a product of selection. There is also another sense in which the female-biased childhood sex ratio cannot be said to be either "adaptive" or "an adaptation." As far as can be determined, the sex ratio at birth among the Mukogodo is the same as most human populations, in other words, slightly male biased. Hence the female bias in the childhood sex ratio is most likely the result of an excessive number of deaths among male infants. Dead baby boys are not adaptive for Mukogodo parents, and I have no evidence at all that Mukogodo parents engage in deliberate infanticide. The deaths of their sons are one of the costs of their behavior, not a benefit. If Mukogodo parents could somehow keep their daughters as healthy as they do while also keeping more of their sons alive, surely they would do so. Their situation simply does not allow them that luxury.

Methodologically, this study helps to demonstrate the value of quantitative methods in the assessment of parental behavior and its effects. Casual observations and subjective impressions are no substitute for the systematic recording of behavior and careful physical measurements. My own subjective impressions when I conducted this fieldwork, for example, were that I would find no significant differences between the growth performances of Mukogodo boys and girls and that no significant differences in caregiver solicitude toward boys and girls would be discerned in the focal follow data. I was wrong on both counts. It is simply too easy for a casual observer, even one who is doing all of the anthropometric measurements and recording all of the caregiver behaviors, to fail to notice subtle differences between different children and caregivers.

Future studies of parental behavior will surely make further refinements in methodology. On a theoretical level, what is most needed now in this field is some clarification of the psychological mechanisms involved in sex-biased parental behavior. Specifically, it remains unclear what sorts of environmental cues parents are picking up on when they favor sons or daughters. One possibility is that they are looking at their condition, including their socioeconomic status, in a very general way, without any specific attention to the marital or reproductive prospects of their sons and daughters. Another possibility is that it is not the parents' overall condition that matters but simply their expectations about their sons' and daughters' reproductive prospects. The study of the Mukogodo does not help to clarify this because both possibilities could explain the behavior of Mukogodo parents: We have no way of telling whether Mukogodo parents are reacting to their overall socioeconomic status or to the relative marital and reproductive prospects of their daughters and sons. What are needed instead are studies in societies where socioeconomic status and the relative marital and reproductive prospects of daughters and sons have become disentangled. If, for instance, socioeconomic status is not a good predictor of the relative marital and reproductive prospects of sons and daughters in a particular society, but low-status parents still favor daughters and high-status ones still favor sons, this would suggest that it is socioeconomic pure and simple, rather than some estimation of the reproductive prospects of sons and daughters, that is the essential cue. None of the existing studies of sex-biased parental investment directly addresses this issue, but Gaulin and Robbins's (1991) study of poor American women suggests that low socioeconomic status alone may be enough to lead women to favor daughters over sons.

As I have advocated elsewhere (Cronk 1995, 1999) future research should also explore the role of culture in the production of parental behavior. The relationship between culture and behavior in general can be difficult to understand, and confusion about the meaning of the term "culture" does not help. Unfortunately, many common definitions of the term culture actually include the category of behavior, making it impossible to tease them apart so that culture can be used in a meaningful way to help explain behavior. Following the lead of some cognitive, symbolic, and hermeneutic anthropologists (see Keesing 1974), many advocates of an evolutionary approach to behavior have begun to advocate limiting the term "culture" to ideational elements (e.g., Barkow 1989; Cronk 1995, 1999; Durham 1992). The definition that I use is simple and limited: culture is simply a shorthand for *socially transmitted information.*

One window onto the culture of parenting is parents' stated sex preferences for children. Table 10.5 shows the responses Mukogodo women gave in 1986 and 1993 to a question about their desired family size and composition. The 1986 data were collected by Beth Leech during female reproductive history interviews with 121 Mukogodo women; the 1993 data were collected by Scola Ene Matunge during female reproductive history interviews with the mothers of the 40 children in

Table 10.5. Stated offspring sex preferences of Mukogodo women.

Preference	*1986*	*1993*
More boys	14 (12%)	10 (25%)
More girls	9 (7%)	2 (5%)
Even	44 (36%)	12 (30%)
No preference	54 (45%)	16 (40%)
Total	121	40

the sample. In both cases, most mothers have no sex preference, but those who do express a preference are more likely to say that they prefer sons than daughters. Furthermore, the two mothers who expressed a preference for daughters in 1993 may in fact have been expressing nothing of the kind. One of them was simply elaborating on the fact that she wanted no more children beyond the two daughters and one boy she already had, while the other was actually hoping that her next child would be both a boy and her last child, which would have given her more daughters than sons. These kinds of mismatches between parents' stated sex preferences for offspring and their behavior toward them may be quite common. In an earlier review of the literature on female-biased parental investment, stated preferences and behavior toward children did not match in either of the other societies (Ifaluk and Herero) for which both stated sex preferences of parents and data on parental care are available (Cronk 1991b; see Betzig and Turke 1986 and Burrows and Spiro 1957 for information on Ifaluk; see Pennington and Harpending 1993 for information on the Herero).

The stated male bias of Mukogodo parents may be surprising given the evidence about their actual behavior, but it is not surprising given the culture and beliefs of the Mukogodo and other Maasai-speakers. Maasai culture is very male-biased, and parents in Maasai-speaking groups routinely and openly express a preference for sons (see Jacobs 1973:403; Llewellyn-Davies 1981:339; Spencer 1965:211). The statements of preference for sons may be best understood not as genuine attempts to convey their own behavioral tendencies but rather as attempts to conform to the norms of Maasai-speakers and to send the message that the Mukogodo should be considered legitimate "Maasai" rather than *il-torrobo.* In short, the value of those statements may have more to do with manipulation of the impressions of others than with communication of information (see Cronk 1994a, 1994b, 1995; Dawkins and Krebs 1978; Krebs and Dawkins 1984 for more on this view of communication).

Additionally, intermarriage between the Mukogodo and neighboring groups is quite common, so many of the Mukogodo mothers included in these studies were raised among non-Mukogodo groups. This both makes their stated preferences more understandable and reduces the likelihood that the Mukogodo will ever develop a female-biased culture of parenting that matches their actual behavior. Furthermore, although many anthropologists and other social scientists may be tempted by the notion that evolutionary biology may have a role to play in the explanation of human universals but that explanations of behavioral variations among human societies must be only in terms of culture, this is a good example of the fact that behavioral variations can occur among human societies in the absence of cultural variation. Despite the fact that the Mukogodo and other Maasai-speaking pastoralists share a stated, culturally encoded bias in favor of sons, their actual behavior towards sons and daughters varies according to their particular situation. Given that such behavioral variations are routinely found among nonhuman species that do not have any significant amounts of culture, this really should not be surprising. If culture does have any role in the production of Mukogodo parental behavior, it may simply be in mitigating what otherwise would be an even stronger preference for daughters, as suggested by, for example, the data from the government-run clinic (Table 10.4).

SUMMARY

1. Previous research among the Mukogodo, a group of Maasai-speaking pastoralists in Kenya, has indicated that Mukogodo parents bias their investment in favor of daughters and that Mukogodo women have better marital and reproductive prospects than Mukogodo men.

2. Mukogodo favoritism toward daughters fits the prediction of the Trivers-Willard hypothesis that parents should bias investment in favor of the sex with the best reproductive prospects.

3. Data collected in 1993 confirm and elaborate upon the earlier findings. Mukogodo parents and other caregivers remain closer to girls than to boys, hold girls more than boys, and nurse girls more than boys. As in 1986, Mukogodo parents show a female bias when compared with parents from neighboring groups in their use of local medical facilities. The growth performance of Mukogodo girls is superior to that of Mukogodo boys, with significant differences in mean weight-for-age and weight-for-height *z*-scores.

4. The stated sex preferences of Mukogodo mothers are biased in favor of males, not females. This matches a male bias found in the cultures of all Maasai-speaking peoples and suggests that the female bias in Mukogodo parental behavior has little to do with culture. A comparison of the Mukogodo and other Maasai-speakers also provides a good example of behavioral diversity in the absence of cultural diversity.

ACKNOWLEDGMENTS

I would like to thank David Carlson, Kathy Dettwyler, Lore Guilmartin, Urs and Esther Herren, Paul Jamison, Becky Jobling, Beth Leech, Toshora Ole Lentolla, Peter Seem Ole Matunge, Scola Ene Matunge, Daniel Ole Matunge, Anna Lee Presley, Reniel Rodriguez Ramos, and Daniel Sellen for their help with this project. I especially appreciate the cooperation given to me by the Mukogodo, particularly the children in my sample and their mothers. I am also indebted to the Don Dol Roman Catholic Mission and the Kenyan government's clinic in Don Dol for access to their records. My 1986 fieldwork among the Mukogodo was made possible by funding from the National Science Foundation, the Population Council, and the Institute for Humane Studies. My 1993 fieldwork was funded by a Fulbright Grant and Texas A&M University. Of course, I retain responsibility for any errors or shortcomings in this chapter.

REFERENCES

Altmann, J. 1974. Observational study of behavior: Sampling methods. *Behavior* 48:1–41.

Barkow, Jerome H. 1989. *Darwin, Sex and Status: Biological Approaches to Mind and Culture.* Toronto: University of Toronto Press.

Bereczkei, Tamas, and R. I. M. Dunbar. 1997. Female-biased reproductive strategies in a Hungarian Gypsy population. *Proceedings of the Royal Society of London,* Series B 264:17–22.

Betzig, Laura. L., and Paul W. Turke. 1986. Parental investment by sex on Ifaluk. *Ethology and Sociobiology* 7:29–37.

Borgerhoff Mulder, Monique, and T. Caro. 1985. The use of quantitative observational techniques in anthropology. *Current Anthropology* 25:323–335.

Borgerhoff Mulder, Monique, and M. Milton. 1985. Factors affecting infant care among the Kipsigis. *Journal of Anthropological Research* 41:231–262.

Burrows, E. G., and M. E. Spiro. 1957. *An Atoll Culture: Ethnography of Ifaluk in the Central Carolines.* Westport, Connecticut: Greenwood Press.

Centers for Disease Control and Prevention (CDC). 1991. Epi Info. Atlanta: Centers for Disease Control and Prevention.

Chagnon, Napoleon A. 1979. Is reproductive success equal in egalitarian societies? In *Evolutionary Biology and Human Social Behavior: An Anthropological Perspective,* Napoleon A. Chagnon and William Irons, eds. Pp. 374–401. North Scituate, Massachusetts: Duxbury Press.

Chagnon, Napoleon A., and William Irons, eds. 1979. *Evolutionary Biology and Human Social Behavior: An Anthropological Perspective.* North Scituate, Massachusetts: Duxbury Press.

Chagnon, Napoleon A., Mark V. Flinn, and Thomas F. Melancon. 1979. Sex-ratio variation among the Yanomamö Indians. In *Evolutionary Biology and Human Social Behavior: An Anthropological Perspective,* Napoleon A. Chagnon and William Irons, eds. Pp. 290–320. North Scituate, Massachusetts: Duxbury Press.

Clark, A. B. 1978. Sex ratio and local resource competition in a prosimian primate. *Science* 201:163–165.

Clutton-Brock, T. H., and G. R. Iason. 1986. Sex ratio variation in mammals. *Quarterly Review of Biology* 61:339–374.

Cronk, Lee. 1989a. From hunters to herders: Subsistence change as a reproductive strategy among the Mukogodo. *Current Anthropology* 30:224–234.

———. 1989b. Low socioeconomic status and female-biased parental investment: the Mukogodo example. *American Anthropologist* 91:414–429.

———. 1990a. Stratification, bride-wealth, and marriage patterns among the Mukogodo and their neighbors, Laikipia District, Kenya. *Research in Economic Anthropology* 12:89–109.

———. 1990b. Comment on "Explaining biased sex ratios in human populations" by Daniela Sieff. *Current Anthropology* 31:35–36.

———. 1991a. Intention vs. behaviour in parental sex preferences among the Mukogodo of Kenya. *Journal of Biosocial Science* 23:229–240.

———. 1991b. Preferential parental investment in daughters over sons. *Human Nature* 2:387–417.

———. 1993. Parental favoritism toward daughters. *American Scientist* 81:272–279.

———. 1994a. Evolutionary theories of morality and the manipulative use of signals. *Zygon: Journal of Religion and Science* 29:81–101.

———. 1994b. The use of moralistic statements in social manipulation: A reply to Roy A. Rappaport. *Zygon: Journal of Religion and Science* 29:351–355.

———. 1995. Is there a role for culture in human behavioral ecology? *Ethology and Sociobiology* 16(3):181–205.

———. 1995. *That Complex Whole: Culture and the Evolution of Human Behavior*. Boulder, Colorado: Westview.

Dawkins, Richard, and John R. Krebs. 1978. Animal signals: Information or manipulation? In *Behavioural Ecology: An Evolutionary Approach,* first ed., John R. Krebs and N. B. Davies, eds. Pp. 282–309. Oxford: Blackwell Scientific.

Department of Health, Education and Welfare (HEW). 1977a. *NCHS growth curves of children, birth–18 years, United States.* Vol. 165. Series 11. Washington, D.C.: HEW, Public Health Service.

———. 1977b. *NCHS tables of growth, birth–18 years, United States.* Vol. 124. Series 11. Washington, D.C.: HEW, Public Health Service.

Dickemann, Mildred. 1979. Female infanticide, reproductive strategies, and social stratification: A preliminary model. In *Evolutionary Biology and Human Social Behavior: An Anthropological Perspective,* Napoleon A. Chagnon and William Irons, eds. Pp. 321–367. North Scituate, Massachusetts: Duxbury Press.

Durham, William H. 1992. *Coevolution: Genes, Culture, and Human Diversity.* Stanford: Stanford University Press.

Fisher, R. A. 1934. *The Genetical Theory of Natural Selection.* Oxford: Clarendon.

Fix, Alan G. 1990. Comment on "Explaining biased sex ratios in human populations" by Daniela Sieff. *Current Anthropology* 31:36–37.

Frisancho, A. Roberto. 1990. *Anthropometric Standards for the Assessment of Growth and Nutritional Status.* Ann Arbor: University of Michigan Press.

Galaty, John G. 1979. Pollution and pastoral anti-praxis: The issue of Maasai inequality. *American Ethnologist* 6:803–816.

Gaulin, S. J. C., and C. J. Robbins. 1991. Trivers-Willard effect in contemporary North American society. *American Journal of Physical Anthropology* 85:61–69.

Gibson, R. 1990. *Principles of Nutritional Assessment.* New York: Oxford University Press.

Gowaty, P. A., and M. R. Lennartz. 1985. Sex ratios of nestling and fledging red-cockaded woodpeckers *(Picoides borealis)* favor males. *American Naturalist* 126:347–353.

Gray, J. Patrick. 1985. *Primate Sociobiology.* New Haven: HRAF Press.

Gross, D. 1984. Time allocation: A tool for the study of cultural behavior. *Annual Review of Anthropology* 13:519–558.

Hames, Raymond. 1992. Time allocation. In *Evolutionary Ecology and Human Behavior,* Eric Alden Smith and Bruce Winterhalder, eds. Pp. 203–235. New York: Aldine de Gruyter.

Hamilton, William D. 1967. Extraordinary sex ratios. *Science* 156:477–488.

Hoogland, J. L. 1981. Sex ratio and local resource competition. *American Naturalist* 117:796–797.

Hrdy, S. B. 1987. Sex-biased parental investment among primates and other mammals: A critical evaluation of the Trivers-Willard hypothesis. In *Child Abuse and Neglect: Biosocial Dimensions,* R. J. Gelles and J. B. Lancaster, eds. Pp. 97–147. New York: Aldine de Gruyter.

———. 1988. Daughters or sons? *Natural History* 97(4):63–83.

Jacobs, A. 1973. The pastoral Maasai of Kenya and Tanzania. In *Cultural Source Materials for Population Planning in East Africa,* Vol. 3: Beliefs and Practices, A. Molnos ed. Nairobi: East African Publishing House.

Jelliffe, D., and E. Jelliffe. 1989. *Community Nutritional Assessment with Special Reference to Less Technically Developed Countries.* New York: Oxford University Press.

Keesing, Roger. 1974. Theories of culture. *Annual Review of Anthropology* 3:73–97.

Krebs, John R., and Richard Dawkins. 1984. Animal signals: Mind reading and manipulation. In *Behavioral Ecology: An Evolutionary Approach,* second ed., John R. Krebs and N. B. Davies, eds. Pp. 380–402. Oxford: Blackwell Scientific.

Llewellyn-Davies, M. 1981. Women, warriors, and patriarchs. In *Sexual Meanings: The Cultural Construction of Gender and Sexuality,* S. B. Ortner and H. Whitehead, eds. Pp. 330–358. Cambridge: Cambridge University Press.

Pennington, Renee, and Henry Harpending. 1993. *The Structure of an African Pastoralist Community: Demography, History, and Ecology of the Ngamiland Herero.* Oxford: Clarendon.

Roche, Alex F., Debabrata Mukherjee, Shumei Gui, and William H. Moore. 1987. Head circumference reference date: Birth to 18 years. *Pediatrics* 79(5):706–712.

Sieff, Daniela F. 1990. Explaining biased sex ratios in human populations: A critique of recent studies. *Current Anthropology* 31:25–48.

Spencer, P. 1965. *The Samburu.* London: Routledge and Kegan Paul.

Townsend, Nicholas, and E. A. Hammel. 1990. Age estimation from the number of teeth erupted in young children: An aid to demographic surveys. *Demography* 27(1):165–174.

Trivers, Robert L., and D. E. Willard. 1973. Natural selection of parental ability to vary the sex ratio of offspring. *Science* 179:90–92.

Werren, J. H. 1980. *Studies in the Evolution of Sex Ratios.* Ph.D. dissertation, University of Utah, Salt Lake City.

Williams, G. C. 1966. *Adaptation and Natural Selection.* Princeton: Princeton University Press

———. 1979. The question of adaptive sex ratios in outcrossed vertebrates. *Proceedings of the Royal Society of London,* Series B 205:567–580.

11

Why Do the Yomut Raise More Sons than Daughters?

WILLIAM IRONS

The Trivers-Willard hypothesis specifies conditions under which parents can be expected to invest more in offspring of one sex than the other (Trivers and Willard 1973). Stable systems of social stratification in human populations appear to satisfy these conditions. The Yomut occupy a high position in a hypergynous hierarchy of descent and ethnic groups and appear to raise more sons than daughters as a consequence. This chapter uses data from the Yomut to test the Trivers-Willard hypothesis. Survey data gathered in 1973–1974 and ethnographic data gathered in 1965–1967, 1970, and 1973–1974 are combined for this purpose.

THE TRIVERS-WILLARD HYPOTHESIS

In a polygynous breeding system, there is a greater variance in reproductive success among males than among females. This means that being above the population mean has somewhat different consequences for males than for females. If we look at the portion of the population that is above the population mean in reproductive success, we will see that, within this group, males are on average more successful than females. They fall on average higher above the mean. This is simply a restatement of the proposition that males have a higher variance in reproductive success. The situation in the portion of the population below the mean is a mirror image of this. Females below the mean are, on average, closer to the mean and therefore more successful than males. The original form of the Trivers-Willard hypothesis states that when the condition of offspring is predictable from the condition of a mother, natural selection should favor a facultative ability to invest more in the sex with the greater probability of a high reproductive success. In a polygynous population, this means that mothers should invest more in sons when maternal condition predicts high success and more in daughters when low success is predicted.

Various forms of social stratification in human populations may create conditions fitting the Trivers-Willard model. For this to be the case, however, the system of stratification must be stable across generations so that the social rank of the offspring can be predicted from that of the parents. Systems of ethnic and descent group stratification associated with polygyny and hypergyny would seem to represent one type of human social system that meets these conditions. Hypergyny refers to a tendency for women to marry men of higher status than the women's natal group, or social rules allowing or encouraging such marriages.

A social system of this sort enhances the pool of potential mates for men of the highest-ranking group. They have all the women of their own group and a number of women from lower groups as potential wives. In effect, they draw wives from the entire population. The system has the opposite effect on women in the highest group. They can only marry men of their own group and must compete with women from lower groups for access to these men. The situation is reversed in the lowest ranking group. Men of the lowest ranking group will have as potential mates only those women of their own group who do not marry up. Women at the bottom have the entire population as potential mates. For groups that are not at the top or the bottom of the hierarchy, the same trends in mating opportunities occur but in lesser degree. Men of groups near but not at the top experience a smaller enhancement of their mating pool, and those near but not at the bottom experience a smaller restriction of their mating pool. The situation is reversed for women.

The Trivers-Willard hypothesis logically predicts that, in a situation of this sort, parents at the top of the hierarchy will bias their parental investment toward sons. The original hypothesis was phrased in terms of mothers only, but in human populations where both sexes invest significantly in rearing offspring, the prediction logically should apply to both sexes. This will occur, however, only if sufficiently similar conditions have occurred frequently enough in past human populations to cause the evolution of an ability to facultatively adjust the sex ratio in response to predictable differences in the reproductive opportunities of males and females. A study of the sort presented here is a test of whether or not human beings have such an adaptation. Tests of this sort in many different human populations will be necessary to resolve this issue.

Thus the hypergynous-hierarchy version of the Trivers-Willard model predicts that the following conditions will occur together: (1) a social system with stable stratification in conjunction with polygyny and hypergyny, (2) greater average reproductive success for men than women in high-ranking groups, and the reverse in low-ranking groups, (3) biases of parental investment toward sons in the high-ranking groups, and the reverse in low-ranking groups. In terms of causation, the first condition, a stable ranking, causes the second condition, higher success for males at the top and females at the bottom. The second condition then causes the third condition as an adaptive facultative response by parents to the differences in reproductive success by sex. However, for purposes of testing with synchronic data the prediction evaluated here is simply that the three conditions will occur together. A clear falsification of Trivers-Willard would occur if conditions 1 and 2 existed but not condition 3. This would indicate the absence of the ability to make an adaptive facultative response to a situation in which one sex is predictably more successful than the other. The presumption would then be that such an adaptation did not evolve. An adaptation of this sort could only evolve if, in the environment of human evolution, parents could frequently use their own social status to predict the reproductive opportunities of sons versus daughters.

THE YOMUT DATA

The Yomut Turkmen are one of several large Turkmen descent groups occupying a contiguous area in Central Asian Turkestan. This area includes the current Republic of Turkmenistan (formerly the Turkmen Soviet Socialist Republic) and some immediately adjacent areas of neighboring countries. The data examined here were gathered among the Yomut living in the part of Iran known as the Gorgan Plain. This region is immediately south of the Republic of Turkmenistan and east of the Caspian Sea. The ethnography and recent history of the Yomut of the Gorgan Plain have been described elsewhere (Irons 1975).

The demographic data used were gathered in northern Iran in 1973–1974 by myself, my wife Marjorie Rogasner, and Daniel Bates (Anthropology, Hunter College, CUNY). The data were gathered from a random stratified sample of households from the Qojuk and Igdar descent groups in the vicinity of the city of Gonbad-e Kavus. The sample was stratified in such a way as to represent the wealthy and poor segments of Yomut society equally. The Qojuk and Igdar are two of a number of territorial subgroups of the Yomut. The Qojuk are a largely agricultural group and the Igdar are largely pastoral. (See Irons 1975 for details concerning these specific Yomut descent groups.) The data were gathered in the Turkmen language using a questionnaire written in Turkmen. The interviews were conducted by the researchers named above and by trained and closely supervised Turkmen interviewers.

The questionnaires largely focused on demographic and economic data. These data include the reproductive and marital histories of all members of sample households, the household's current wealth in land and livestock, and the household's patrimony of land and livestock at the time of its founding. Data on daughters married out of the household and on sons who had separated to form independent households were also recorded.

Age data, which are crucial to demographic analysis, were relatively easy to gather. The majority of adult Yomut, at the time of the survey, were not literate. However, they do know their ages. The Yomut keep track of their ages and of other events in the past with the aid of the cycle of twelve animal years brought to this region from the Far East by the Mongols in the thirteenth century. Every individual knows the animal year of his or her birth and this makes it possible to pinpoint the year of his or her birth. Most of the actual survey was conducted in the Year of the Leopard *(bars yil)*, and any individual born in this year had to be either less than one, twelve, twenty-four, thirty-six, and so on. (The Turkmen Year of the Leopard corresponds to the Year of the Tiger in the more familiar Chinese version of the twelve-year cycle. There are other differences between the Turkmen and Chinese versions of the twelve-year cycle, but these differences do not affect the usefulness of the system as an aid to reckoning age.) Combining this information with a glance at the person in question makes determining age easy. Actually the Yomut themselves are adept at moving from knowledge of a person's animal year to his or her age, and most Yomut can state their age when asked. Some individuals respond by stating their animal year and then calculating their numerical age. A few individuals need the help of bystanders to go from animal year to numerical age. On various occasions it is important for the Yomut to know their ages for religious purposes; for example, when one is old enough to be obligated to fast in Ramadan and say prayers five times a day. When one is 63 years of age, the prophet Mohammed's age at death, one must celebrate by hosting a feast for the local community. This sort of religious obligation presumably serves as part of the motivation for keeping track of the year of one's birth.

The qualitative ethnographic data used here were gathered by Irons in thirty months of field research among the Yomut. This includes sixteen months of field research from December of 1965 to November of 1967, two months in the summer of 1970, and twelve months from August of 1973 to August of 1974. The latter field session in 1973–1974 included both the survey mentioned above and additional collection of qualitative ethnographic data.

DESCENT AND ETHNIC GROUP STRATIFICATION AMONG THE TURKMEN

The Yomut are near the top of a system of descent and ethnic stratification that entails strict hypergyny. Members of higher-ranking descent groups can take wives from lower-ranking groups but will marry their women only to members of their own or higher-ranking groups. (Most marriages among the Yomut are arranged by the parents of the bride and groom.) Most marriages are within the same descent and ethnic groups, as is preferred by all the groups involved. However, some marriages are hypergynous and thus women to some degree flow up the social strata at marriage. Ethnic and descent identity is inherited from the father, so the children of women who marry up are members of their father's group. The highest-ranking group is the Teke Turkmen, the next highest is the Yomut Turkmen, the next is the Goklan Turkmen, followed by the Ewlad Turkmen (these groups trace descent from the first four Khalifs), and then by local non-Turkmen ethnic groups. Among the non-Turkmen, those who speak a Turkic dialect are preferred to those whose language (Persian or Baluchi) is foreign.

From the closing of the border with the Soviet Union in 1932 until the time of the survey, the Yomut had no contact with the main body of Teke and so for all practical purposes the Yomut were at the very top of the local hypergynous system of ethnic groups. In the survey sample, 8% of the wives of Yomut men were from lower-ranking groups. The men in the sample are married to 969 Yomut women and 82 non-Yomut women. The survey included questions about daughters and sisters married out of the sample households, and these questions found zero cases of Yomut women marrying non-Yomut men. There is one village of Teke living among the Yomut. These are people who fled the Soviet Union during the 1930s when the Soviets collectivized livestock. However, the survey revealed no cases of Yomut women marrying any Teke men.

Thus the Yomut were effectively at the top of a hypergynous system of ethnic stratification. The result of this hypergyny is to increase the number of potential mates available to Yomut men. As Moslems, Yomut men are allowed four wives, but local customs limit the extent to which they can acquire multiple wives. Bridewealth is high and is usually 2.5 times as high for a married man seeking a second wife as for a young man seeking his first wife. Usually only wealthy men take second wives while their first wife is still living and usually then only after their first wife is approaching the end of her fertile years. Thus polygyny occurs primarily among older, wealthy men. Seven percent of the men in the 1973–1974 sample who were 40 years old or older had two wives at the time of the survey. None had three wives simultaneously. Thus polygyny is limited, but not rare. Some men become polygynists when a brother dies and a leviratic marriage is arranged. These men are not necessarily wealthy, and they usually marry widows who have already produced a number of children. The consequences for reproductive success are, thus, less than when a wealthy man marries a young virgin. Wealthy men who take a second wife later in life usually take a young virgin of lower social status.

REPRODUCTIVE SUCCESS OF YOMUT MEN AND WOMEN

There are several standard demographic measures of reproductive success that can be used to determine whether one sex has a higher average reproductive success than the other. One such measure is the total fertility rate (TFR). This is the number of children that a woman (or man) will bear if she lives to the end of her reproductive years and follows the population's average schedule of age-specific fertility rates (Howell 1979:122–124, Pressat 1972:188–189). The 1973–1974 Yomut data yield the total fertility rates shown in Table 11.1. The rate for men is considerably higher than the rate for women, which could be taken as confirmation of the Trivers-Willard model. However, there are some serious problems with using this measure to compare males and females. The reproductive lifespans of Yomut men and women are very different. The average age at reproduction for Yomut women is 30.1 and the average age at reproduction for men is 39.6. Other

Table 11.1 Standard Demographic Measures of Yomut Reproductive Rates

Demographic Parameter	*Male*	*Female*
Total Fertility Rate (TFR)	10.6	7.74
Modified Net Reproductive Rate†	6.84	5.97

†Net reproductive rate is usually the number of daughters born to women or the number of sons born to men. Here the parameter is the number of children of both sexes born to both women and men.

things being equal, earlier reproduction is favored by natural selection, and the earlier reproduction of women might be taken as outweighing the disadvantage of a lower TFR. Another difficulty lies in the fact that the TFR is the number of children born to an individual who completes her or his reproductive lifespan. Yomut women do this when they reach age 50. Men do this when they reach age 75. This observation makes meaningful comparison of the two measures difficult. Also the male TFR is a somewhat unrealistic measure given the fact that life expectancy is well below 75 for Yomut men in the time period covered by the survey. Estimates of life expectancy for males in the time period covered by the survey are in the range of 42 to 45.[1]

Another conventional demographic measure that can be used to estimate the difference in reproductive success of Yomut men and women is the net reproductive rate developed by Lotka and Fisher. This parameter combines the fertility and mortality rates. It is usually measured by applying the mortality and fertility schedules characteristic of the population to a hypothetical cohort of 100 or 1,000 (or more) individuals born. Starting with this cohort at birth, the number of individuals that will survive through each age interval of the reproductive life span is calculated using the mortality schedule. The number of births they will have during each interval is then calculated from the fertility schedule (Howell 1979:214–215, 273–274; Pressat 1972:350–355). The births this hypothetical cohort produces over a lifetime divided by the size of the cohort at birth is the net reproductive rate. The usual way to calculate the net reproductive rate is to estimate daughters born to women and sons born to men. This seems like a bad idea for purposes of comparing the relative reproductive success of men and women in a population that does not have a sex ratio of 100 at birth. Therefore, I have used a modified version of the net reproductive rate that includes all children for both men and women. This modified net reproductive rate seems more realistic, but there is still a problem surrounding the fact that the average ages at birth (the generation length) for Yomut men and women are quite different.

In view of these difficulties in comparing the relative reproductive success of Yomut men and women, I believe the best measure is a simple (but inelegant) empirical one. I have calculated the average number of living children for all men and women in the sample who are age 45 or older. The results are in Table 11.2.

Table 11.2. Reproductive Success of Yomut Men and Women 45 or Older

	Sample Size	*Ave. Nr. Living Children*	*Variance*
Men	267	5.122	8.072
Women	216	3.868	7.088

t = 37.1 df = 579 $p < .001$

These results probably underestimate the differences, between the sexes, in reproductive success. Few women in the over-45 category will reproduce in the future, but many men over 45 will. The number of children born per woman after age 45 in this population is about .25 children. On the other hand, the number of living children of a 45-year-old woman will decline as she ages because some of her children will die. In contrast, the number of living children for men 45 or over will change both because of births and deaths. The average number of births a man will have if he lives from 45 to 75 is 4.3. His chance of surviving from age 45 to his seventy-fifth birthday is .38, and therefore we can estimate that, after reaching age 45, Yomut men will have 1.6 more children on average. (The chance of a woman over 45 surviving long enough to have a child is less of an issue since most women who do have a child after turning 45 do so soon after their forty-fifth birthday.) Of course the estimate of 1.6 more children after age 45 for men and of .25 for women apply only to those at the very beginning of this interval. Nevertheless, I think these data make the point that the number of living children for men over 45 is more of an underestimate than the comparable figure for women. The empirical figure for the number of living children is a little more than one child higher for Yomut men than for Yomut women, and the difference is statistically significant. The fact that the number for men is more of an underestimate than the figure for women makes it safe, in my opinion, to accept this result. Thus the data fit the Trivers-Willard model.

EVIDENCE FOR GREATER INVESTMENT IN SONS

The above evidence indicates that the combined forces of stable descent and ethnic stratification, hypergyny, and polygyny cause Yomut men to have more children on average than Yomut women. As noted, the Trivers-Willard hypothesis predicts that under these conditions parents should facultatively adjust their parental investment so as to favor sons. There are three bodies of evidence that can be used to test this prediction: qualitative ethnographic data, sex ratio data, and survivorship data.

Qualitative Ethnographic Data

The qualitative ethnographic data are the hardest to interpret, but nevertheless they do support the prediction of greater investment in males. The Yomut have a stated preference for sons and express this preference in many ways (Irons 1975). When a son is born it is customary to celebrate. An animal is sacrificed and neighbors invited to feast. After the birth of a son, a member of the local community gives the Moslem call to prayer. This announces to the entire community that a son has been born. No such call is given for a daughter and no celebration is held.

When a child dies, neighbors come to offer condolences, and it is customary to say to the bereaved, “May God give you another son!” This is said whether the deceased child was a boy or a girl. When a girl is born, especially if a series of births has produced girls, it is common practice to give the girl a name expressing a wish for a son. Names such as “Boy Needed” (Oghul Gerek) or “Last Daughter” (Songi Qiz) are common for girls. In general, concern for the health and well-being of sons tends to exceed that for daughters.

If asked whether they prefer sons or daughters, Yomut invariably state a preference for sons. However, the preference seems stronger among men than women. As Cronk demonstrates (Chapter 10, this volume), such publicly proclaimed preferences can be misleading. However, the data presented below support the view that in the case of the Yomut, the stated preference and actual behavior are in line. The main message the Mukogodo seem to be sending by saying they prefer sons is that they are true Maasai and that like other Maasai they prefer sons. This may be a case of trying to claim a higher ethnic status than many of their neighbors will grant them. The Yomut have no such reason to try to elevate themselves in the local system of ethnographic stratification.

Yomut Sex Ratios

A typical situation in human populations is that more boys are born, but they have a higher death rate than girls so that fewer survive to maturity. This means that as a cohort of newborns ages their sex ratio declines and eventually there is an excess of females (Alexander 1987:54–55; Fisher 1930:158–160; Teitelbaum 1972; Trivers 1972). Fisher explained how this situation can correspond to equal parental investment in male and female offspring. More males are born than females, but more males die before reaching the age at which parental investment is completed. Thus the average expenditure of effort in rearing a newborn boy is less than that for a newborn girl. More boys, but less investment per boy, can equate with equal investment in children of each sex, which is what Fisher predicted.

As can be seen in Table 11.3, the Yomut do not exhibit this pattern of an excess of males at birth, but a sex ratio that declines in older age categories and eventually arrives at an excess of females. The Yomut have a male-biased sex ratio in the older age categories as well. According to data gathered in a demographic survey in 1973–1974, this population has a sex ratio at birth of 112.2 males for every 100 females. (Sex ratios are conventionally described as the number of males per 100 females.) The sex ratio of the living population as a whole, according to these same survey data, is 111.7 males for every 100 females. Table 11.3 presents the age-sex composition of the Yomut sample population. A statistical test to show that the sex ratio of newborns and the sex ratio of the total living population are not significantly different seems unnecessary given the size of the two samples and the close values of the two sex ratios. The numbers in Table 11.3 include only Yomut individuals. Married-in non-Yomut women are not included. Since we are looking for evidence that the Yomut raise more sons than daughters, the sex ratio of the population without married-in non-Yomut women is most relevant.

Many theoreticians reason that in a polygynous population males evolved to be more competitive than females and as a consequence have a higher death rate at every age (Alexander 1987:54–55; Trivers 1972). The assumption is that males are inherently more vulnerable and, with equal nurturance by parents, males will have a higher death rate. The greater vulnerability of males is built into their developmental and physiological processes. This appears to be a widespread cross-species pattern in polygynous species, and the human species clearly appears to have a history of polygynous breeding (Alexander 1974; Foley and Lee 1989; Wrangham 1987). If we accept this view, then the sex ratios of the Yomut are evidence of differential nurturance. It appears from these data that Yomut parents are more solicitous of the needs of sons than of daughters.

Note that if Yomut men did not marry women from outside the Yomut population, the average reproductive success of men would be lower than that of women by virtue of the fact that there are more of them. The total number of children produced in the next generation divided by the number of parents available in the preceding generation of such a closed population would yield the average number of children produced. Since there are more men, the number of children per man would have to be lower. As Fisher (1930) observed long ago, when the sex ratio is unequal, the more numerous sex has diminished reproductive opportunities. However, hypergyny, in effect, makes Yomut males the less numerous sex in their pool of potential mates.

Survivorship Data

The 1973–1974 data contain a record of everyone who died in a sample household during the five years preceding the survey. This is a relatively small body of data since it covers only five years. Also since the population structure is sharply

Table 11.3 Age-Sex Structure of Yomut Sample Population

Age Interval	*Men*	*Women*	*Sex Ratio*
0–29	1567	1436	109.1
30–59	503	432	116.4
60+	91	67	135.8
Total Population	2161	1935	111.7

pyramidal, there are few individuals and few deaths in the older age categories. The reproductive history data also contain a record of the survivorship of all offspring born to living women in the sample, and to deceased wives of living men in the sample. This body of data is much larger because it covers a longer time period (roughly the 35 years preceding) and because the Yomut are a high-fertility population. I draw on both bodies of data to see whether survivorship data support the prediction that the Yomut invest more in sons.

There are no data on nutritional status or focal follow data of the sort that has proven valuable in addressing the issue of per individual investment in sons or daughters in other societies (see Cronk, Chapter 10). Therefore the data on the question of per son versus per daughter investment are limited. Nevertheless, the survivorship data that do exist provide a test of the prediction of greater investment in sons.

Table 11.4 summarizes the evidence on survivorship from these two bodies of data.[2] The data on survivorship for the first 20 years of life are derived from the reproductive history data. Those for ages 20–44 are derived from the death register. As can be seen, the usual pattern of males having higher death rates at all ages does not hold for the Yomut. On the other hand, a simple reversal of this pattern also does not hold. From birth to age four, 72.5% of males and 75.4% of females survive. Here the more common pattern of higher male death rates is found. However, for the fifteen-year interval following the first five years of life, there is no statistically significant difference in male and female death rates. There is only a statistically insignificant trend in the direction of lower mortality for males. From age 20 to an individual's forty-fifth birthday, the situation changes dramatically and 97% of men survive, but only 88% of women. However, this later period is probably not related to parental investment.

In my opinion, the most straightforward interpretation of these data is that Yomut parents are, overall, more nurturing toward their sons than toward their daughters. The extra nurturance toward sons is not enough to counteract the developmental and physiological propensity of males to exhibit higher death rates. In the first five years of life (ages 0 through 4) males have a slightly higher death rate than females. From the fifth to the twentieth birthday, male and female mortality rates are the same. I take the equal mortality rates in the age interval 5–19 as evidence of greater nurturance of males. This is corroborated by the qualitative ethnographic data. The conclusion would be stronger with focal follows and nutritional

Table 11.4 Survivorship Data: Percentage Surviving Various Intervals

Age Interval	*Male*	*Female*	*z-score*	*p-value*
0–4	72.5%	75.4%	1.18	.04
5–19	94%	93%	1.0	.16
20–44	97%	88%	2.02	.02

status data. However, the evidence available does support the prediction of greater investment in males.

A more skeptical interpretation of these data might hold that the Yomut treat sons and daughters equally for the first twenty years of life. Actually this interpretation flies in the face of strong qualitative data. Nevertheless some skeptics are inclined to reject all qualitative data. If this more skeptical interpretation were accepted, the Yomut would still have to be seen as investing more in sons than daughters because the number of sons reared is larger than the number of daughters reared.

I assume in interpreting these data that the period of parental investment corresponds to the first twenty years of life. One could argue that the first fifteen years would correspond more closely to the period. However, the death rates for males and females still do not show a statistically significant difference for the interval 5–14. The conclusion would have to be the same.

As in most human populations, there is no clear-cut point at which parental investment ceases (Irons 1975). Most children begin to contribute significant labor to their household at about age 15 (Irons 1980:455). Most women do not leave their natal household to take residence in their husbands' patrilateral extended family until about age 18. The typical pattern is for young women to marry at about age 15, but not to take up residence with their husbands until around age 18. Then during the first year of coresidence with their husbands, they return frequently to their natal households for periods of a week or two. This first year of coresidence with their husbands is called the year of comings and goings (*gidip gelyen yil*). Also, a woman takes a dowry of variable value with her to her husband's household. The dowry is usually, but not always, of little value compared with the bride-wealth that the husband's family pays the bride's family to contract the marriage. Deciding when in this process parental investment in daughters ceases is difficult.

Males follow a different pattern. The age at which they marry is more variable, with wealthier men marrying younger. Often they do not marry till after their twentieth birthday, and when they do marry, their parents pay a large bride-wealth (almost always several times larger than the dowry) to contract the marriage. Following this they stay in their parents' household for a number of years (sometimes two decades or more) and contribute economically to the household through their labor. However, eventually they separate from their parents and form independent households, at which point they take a portion of their parents' wealth with them as patrimony. Thus, in their early adult years their relationship with their parents involves a flow of benefits in both directions, and finding a point where parental investment ceases is difficult. It is possible that the flow of benefits during this period is equal in both directions, but that the flow is greater from parents to son (and daughters) for the first 15 years of life. Data analyzed in an earlier paper (Irons 1980:453–456) support this interpretation. Given this, the period of parental investment could be seen as ending at age 15. As noted above, whether one uses age 15 or age 20 does not change the picture in terms of male-female differences in death rates during the period of parental investment.

Despite these difficulties of interpretation, the most skeptical interpretation of the data supports the conclusion that the Yomut invest more in the rearing of sons.

SUMMARY

1. The Trivers-Willard hypothesis predicts that human parents will invest more in the rearing of sons when the following conditions are met: they are part of a population that is at the top of a hypergynous hierarchy of descent and ethnic groups, and their sons have the opportunity to marry polygynously. The Yomut meet these conditions, and therefore they are expected to invest more in the rearing of sons.

2. The evidence available for testing this prediction consists of (*a*) qualitative ethnographic data on the relative value the Yomut place on sons and daughters, (*b*) data on sex ratios at various ages, and (*c*) data on the mortality and survivorship of sons and daughters. The survivorship data do not present a simple pattern, but the most reasonable interpretation of these data is that the Yomut invest more in the rearing of sons. The ethnographic data and the sex-ratio data support the theoretical predictions in a simple, direct way. Overall, the evidence supports the prediction that Yomut parents will invest more in the rearing of sons. In terms of numbers, they very clearly raise more sons than daughters.

3. Taken as a whole the data presented in this chapter support the Trivers-Willard hypothesis. The evidence supports the view that the Yomut rear more sons than daughters because of an evolved ability to facultatively adjust the sex ratio in the manner suggested by that hypothesis. Yomut men enjoy a higher reproductive success on average than Yomut women, and Yomut parents take advantage of this fact by raising more sons than daughters.

ACKNOWLEDGMENTS

I owe a debt of gratitude to Mildred Dickemann for first developing and testing the Trivers-Willard model for stratified hypergynous human populations. Her classic paper (Dickemann 1979) was published in the Chagnon and Irons (1979) volume which the current volume commemorates. The collection, coding, and analysis of the data reported here was supported by the National Science Foundation Program in Cultural Anthropology, the Ford Foundation Program in Population Research, and the H. F. Guggenheim Foundation. The sampling procedures used in Iran were designed by Alan Ross of the Johns Hopkins University School of Public Health, Department of Population Dynamics. In 1976–1977, Clifford Clogg, then in the sociology department at Pennsylvania State University, served as a statistical consultant, and the tests of statistical significance used for demographic rates were developed by him. Analyses of the 1973–1974 survey data have appeared in earlier publications (Irons 1979, 1980, 1986, 1994). I am indebted to Lee Cronk and John Hartung for helpful comments on early drafts of this paper. I alone am responsible for its flaws and limitations.

NOTES

1. These life expectancy estimates were made by taking the empirical survivorship data for the first twenty years of life and looking for the model life table in Coale and Demeny 1966 with the best fit. The tables yielding best fit were South 11 and 12. These model tables give life expectancies for men of 42 years (South 11) and 47 years (South 12). Note the revised tables in Coale and Demeny 1983 are essentially the same in terms of life expectancy estimates. They differ only in the second or third decimal place. All of the other estimates of Yomut demographic parameters in this chapter are derived empirically from the 1973–74 survey data without use of Cole and Demeny's models or any other model data. See Irons (1980) for a fuller explanation of the 1973–74 data.

2. The data from the reproductive histories used here are the same as those used in Irons 1979 and 1980. The algorithm for calculating z-scores and p-values is explained in Irons 1980 and was developed by Clifford Clogg.

REFERENCES

Alexander, Richard D. 1974. The evolution of social behavior. *Annual Review of Ecology and Systematics* 5:325–383.

———. 1987. *The Biology of Moral Systems.* New York: Aldine de Gruyter.

Chagnon, Napoleon A., and William Irons, eds. 1979. *Evolutionary Biology and Human Social Behavior: An Anthropological Perspective.* North Scituate, Massachusetts: Duxbury Press.

Coale, A. J. and P. Demeny. 1966. *Regional Model Life Tables and Stable Populations.* Princeton: Princeton University Press.

———. 1983. *Regional Model Life Tables and Stable Populations,* second ed. New York: Academic Press.

Dickemann, Mildred. 1979. Female infanticide, reproductive strategies, and social stratification: A preliminary model. In *Evolutionary Biology and Human Social Behavior: An Anthropological Perspective,* N. A. Chagnon and W. Irons, eds. Pp. 321–367. North Scituate, Massachusetts: Duxbury Press.

Fisher, Ronald A. 1930. *The Genetical Theory of Natural Selection.* Oxford: Clarendon Press.

Foley, R. A., and P. C. Lee. 1989. Finite social space, evolutionary pathways, and reconstructing hominid behavior. *Science* 243:901–906.

Howell, Nancy. 1979. *Demography of the Dobe !Kung.* New York: Academic Press.

Irons, William. 1975. *The Yomut Turkmen: A Study of Social Organization among a Central Asian Turkic Speaking Population.* Anthropological Paper 58. Museum of Anthropology, University of Michigan, Ann Arbor.

———. 1979. Cultural and biological success. In *Evolutionary Biology and Human Social Behavior: An Anthropological Perspective,* N. A. Chagnon and W. Irons, eds. Pp. 284–302. North Scituate, Massachusetts: Duxbury Press.

———. 1980. Is Yomut social behavior adaptive? In *Sociobiology: Beyond Nature/Nurture,* G. W. Barlow and J. Silverberg, eds. Pp. 417–473. Boulder: Westview Press.

———. 1986. Yomut family organization and inclusive fitness. In *Proceedings of the International Meetings on Variability and Behavioral Evolution.* Pp. 227–236. Rome: Accademia Nazionale dei Linei.

———. 1994. Why are the Yomut not more stratified? In *Pastoralists at the Periphery: Herders in a Capitalist World,* Claudia Chang and Harold A. Koster, eds. Pp 275–296. Tucson: The University of Arizona Press.

Pressat, Roland. 1972. *Demographic Analysis: Methods, Results, Applications.* Judah Matras, trans. New York: Aldine.

Teitelbaum, Michael. 1972. Factors associated with sex ratio in human population. In *The Structure of Human Populations,* G. A. Harrison and A. J. Boyce eds. Pp. 90–109. Oxford: Clarendon Press.

Trivers, Robert L. 1972. Parental investment and sexual selection. In *Sexual Selection and the Descent of Man,* B. Campbell, ed. Pp. 136–179. Chicago: Aldine.

Trivers, Robert L., and Dan E. Willard. 1973. Natural selection of parental ability to vary the sex ratio of offspring. *Science* 179:90–92.

Wrangham, R. 1987. The significance of African apes for reconstructing human social evolution. In *The Evolution of Human Behavior: Primate Models,* W. Kinsey, ed. Pp. 51–71. Albany: SUNY University Press.

12

The Grandmother Hypothesis and Human Evolution

KRISTEN HAWKES, JAMES F. O'CONNELL,
NICHOLAS G. BLURTON JONES, HELEN ALVAREZ,
and ERIC L. CHARNOV

Humans differ from other primates in feeding their offspring long after weaning, and in their extended postmenopausal lifespans. Recent research among contemporary hunter-gatherers suggests that these characteristics are evolutionarily related and tied to the use of low-variance, high-yield resources, such as deeply buried tubers (Hawkes, O'Connell, and Blurton Jones 1989, 1997). Where such foods are available, senior women can provision their daughters' weaned offspring, thereby enhancing the children's survivorship and allowing their daughters to produce more children sooner. The resulting fitness increase for grandmothers favors extended postmenopausal lifespans.

This hypothesis has been tested with comparative data on several life history variables by using recent theoretical and empirical work which links the other life history variables with lifespans across a wide range of animal taxa (Charnov 1991, 1993; Charnov and Berrigan 1991, 1993). If human lifespans are extended because of grandmothering, and life histories are assembled as proposed on the basis of this work, then other features of human life histories (including age at maturity and birth rate) should differ in predictable ways from those of other primates, especially the pongids. Analyses completed so far show that they do (Alvarez, 1999; Hawkes, O'Connell, Blurton Jones, Alvarez, and Charnov 1998; O'Connell et al. 1999).

The grandmother argument challenges a fundamental hypothesis about human evolution, namely that our long childhoods are due to the development of the nuclear family, which evolved when husbands/fathers hunted to support their wives and offspring. Here we summarize the grandmother hypothesis and the life history patterns it may explain, note that it joins other challenges to the hunting hypothesis, and develop alternative predictions about human evolution based on the idea that mother-child food sharing and the grandmothering it permits are among our most important behavioral characteristics.

THE ARGUMENT

Grandmothering and Maternal Tradeoffs

Recognition of the evolutionary importance of grandmothers was stimulated by research among the Hadza, a small population of traditional hunter-gatherers living in the Eastern Rift Valley, northern Tanzania (Blurton Jones et al. 1992; Kohl-Larson 1958; Obst 1912; Woodburn 1968). During several periods of fieldwork beginning in the mid-1980s, detailed quantitative data were collected on Hadza demography, settlement patterns, time allocation, foraging, and food sharing (Blurton Jones et al. 1996, and references therein). Among other things, this work documented the unanticipated industry of senior women (Hawkes et al. 1989), the surprisingly active foraging of children (Blurton Jones et al. 1989), and the effect of children's foraging capabilities on mothers' foraging tactics (Blurton Jones et al. 1994; Hawkes, O'Connell, and Blurton Jones 1995). While women were found to organize their foraging in ways that took advantage of resources children could exploit efficiently, they were also seen to target foods that youngsters could not handle for themselves. They could afford to take these foods only because returns were high enough to cover their children's nutritional needs as well as their own. These same high rates were also earned by postmenopausal women (Hawkes et al. 1989). The help the older women provided by feeding their grandchildren was especially important when child-bearing women cut down their foraging with the arrival of a newborn, indicating a "division of labor" between mothers and grandmothers in the production of surviving youngsters (Hawkes, O'Connell, and Blurton Jones 1997).

Grandmothers and Long Postmenopausal Lifespans

This division of labor suggested a solution to the riddle of menopause in humans. In other apes, maximum lifespan is generally estimated at no more than about 50 years (Harvey and Clutton-Brock 1985). As this threshold is approached, all aspects of physiology, including fertility, decline in tandem. In humans, however, the pattern is quite different: maximum lifespan is nearly 100 years, but fertility in women universally ends in about half that time, well in advance of other aspects of physiological frailty (Pavelka and Fedigan 1991). The question is how natural selection came to favor this distinctly human "postreproductive" component of life history.

Many have assumed that the answer lies in Williams's (1957) suggestion that early termination of fertility would likely evolve when extended maternal care became crucial to offspring survival. Aging mothers who stopped bearing additional offspring and devoted their reproductive effort to insuring the survival of children already born would leave more descendants than those who continued to bear new offspring unlikely to survive mother's death.

This stopping-early hypothesis continues to stimulate useful work (Hill and Hurtado 1991, 1996; Peccei 1995; Rogers 1993; Turke 1997), but there are good reasons to be skeptical about it. Other primates among whom extended maternal care is vital fail to show the predicted "early" end to fertility. In chimpanzees, for example, available data indicate low survival probabilities for late-borns (Goodall 1986, 1989), yet a substantial fraction of aging females still continue to produce them (Caro et al. 1995). In humans maternal death has large effects on the survival of young offspring (Hill and Hurtado 1991) but life expectancy at last birth is decades longer than those critical years. Among the reasons for questioning the stopping-early hypothesis, the most compelling is that human reproduction does not end early in comparison with other apes. Our reproductive spans are at least as long as those of chimpanzees. The striking difference between us and the other great apes lies in our long average lifespans *after* menopause. Schultz's (1969) often reprinted figure makes the point (Figure 12.1) (see also Hill and Hurtado 1991; Kaplan 1997). This feature, not menopause itself, is the derived human trait.

Long average adult lifespans depend on low average adult mortalities. Adult mortality rates are directly linked to patterns of senescence, those age-related declines in performance readily observed as years advance. Evolutionary explanations for senescence depend on the fact that the force of selection declines with age (Medawar 1952). Because the risks of mortality accumulate over time, there are always fewer individuals in older cohorts for selection to affect. Deleterious mutations expressed before maturity may not be passed on at all; those acting after maturity are removed more slowly. Consequently deleterious effects on adaptive performance accumulate at later ages either because of mutation-selection balance or inter-temporal tradeoffs in reproductive effort (reviewed in Partridge and Barton 1993). Mutation-selection balance is reached when the force of selection is no greater than the mutation rate. Thus deleterious mutations are removed no faster than they arise. Inter-temporal tradeoffs occur because the same genes that have positive effects on fitness at one time in an organism's life history can have negative effects at another. The net result depends on the tradeoff between these opposing effects, and (other things equal) earlier effects weigh heavily. So genes that have positive effects at younger ages may be favored, even though they have negative effects later in life. Those that have positive effects late in life will be disfavored if they have negative early effects. Senescence results from this antagonistic pleiotropy (Williams 1957).

Grandmothering could slow aging by either process. It would strengthen selection against late-acting deleterious mutations by increasing the fitness of longer-lived females through the increased reproductive success of their daughters. It would also change the tradeoffs between opposing effects expressed at different ages. Slower senescence generally comes at the cost of reduced fertility at younger ages (Kirkwood and Rose 1991) as more effort allocated to somatic maintenance leaves less for current reproduction. If ape lifespans are in equilibrium in terms of this tradeoff, then they age early by human standards because mutations that improve adaptive performance at later ages are selected against due to reductions they impose on fertility earlier in life. Regular mother-child food sharing could

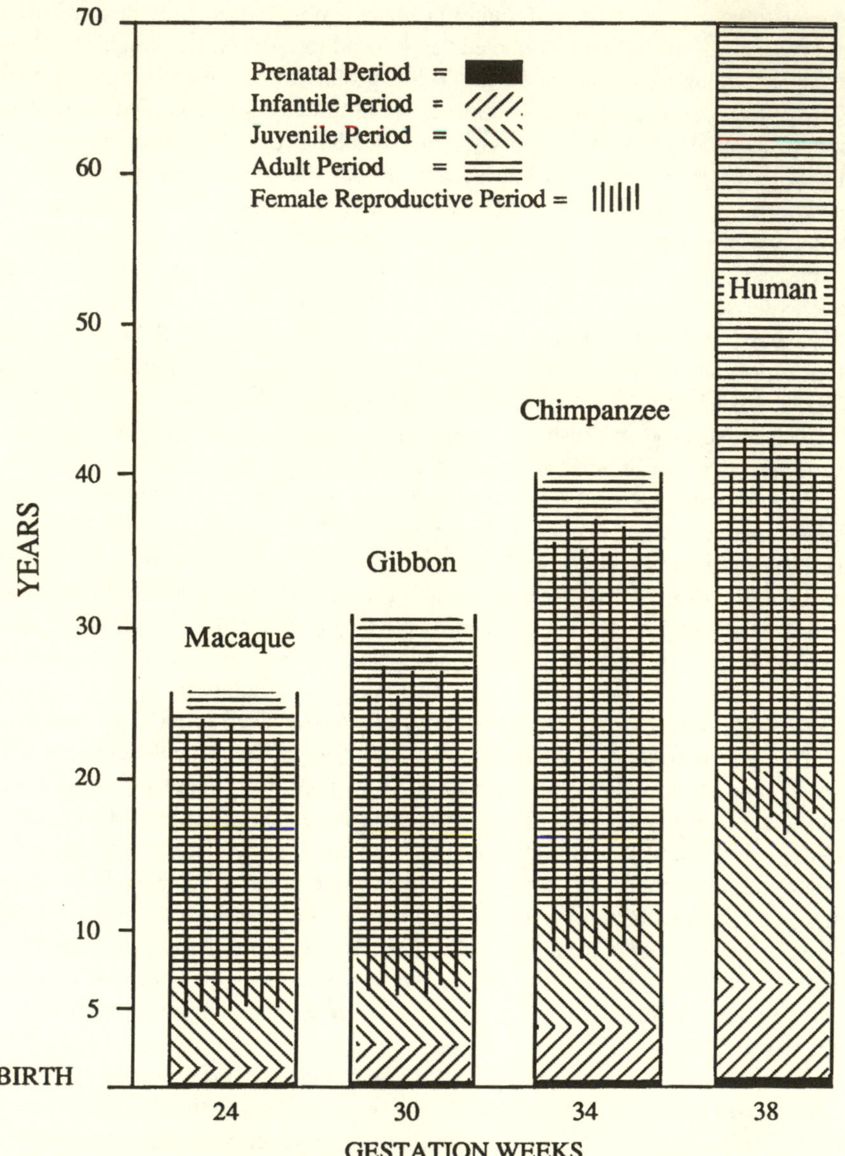

Figure 12.1. Schultz's representation of the length of life history stages in different primate species (redrawn from Schultz 1969).

perturb that equilibrium by increasing the fitness payoffs for late vigor as able senior women earned fitness by feeding grandchildren. Increased somatic effort that slowed aging would allow less allocation to reproduction at younger ages, but the contributions of senior females would increase the reproductive success of childbearers more than enough to offset the reduced expenditure on current reproduction by the childbearers themselves. Continued childbearing, on the other hand, which would conflict with grandmothering, would interfere with this compensation and so be no more favored than in other ape species. According to this model, senescence in all aspects of physiology *except fertility* would be slowed as a result of grandmothering.

Dimensionless Life History Patterns

Recent work in life history theory provides a basis for further development and testing of this argument. Charnov (1991, 1993; Charnov and Berrigan 1991) has shown that life history patterns in large classes of organisms can be characterized by dimensionless invariants, numbers that capture relationships among certain life history variables because they remain constant across large transformations in the variables themselves. To explain these patterns, Charnov assumes stationary populations and so constrains the relationship among three demographic averages: the average rate of offspring production over the adult life span, the average length of adult lifespan, and the probability of offspring survival to maturity. Average adult lifespan sets tradeoffs that determine other life history variables. If grandmothering results in greater longevity, and the tradeoffs in Charnov's mammal model apply, then other aspects of human life history should be affected accordingly.

The mammal model assumes that production can be allocated to growing either oneself or one's offspring. Growth is thus divided into two periods: (1) conception to independence (weaning), where growth is set by mother's production (a function of her size); and (2) independence to maturity (α), where growth is a function of an individual's own body size. At maturity, production previously allocated to growth is redirected to babies. Growth rates are a function of body mass (W), a characteristic production coefficient (A), and an allometric exponent (c). Individual growth rates take the form: $dW/dt = AW^c$, where production energy at time t for an individual of body mass W equals the production coefficient times body mass to the c power.

This model accounts for the correlations long recognized among life history variables and body size (Peters 1983) by tracing them to similarities in the production function. The model also accounts for correlations among life history variables when the effect of body size is removed. Primates, for example, have slow life histories compared with other mammals of similar size (Harvey et al. 1989). Charnov's model draws attention to the low primate A, averaging less than half that of other mammals. Primates thus grow more slowly and have less production (for a given size) to put into babies. So they are relatively small at a given age of maturity with low fecundity for size (Charnov and Berrigan 1993).

Charnov assumes that, given adult lifespan, selection sets the duration of independent growth (α) according to the tradeoff between (1) the benefits of growing longer, and so having more production to put into offspring; and (2) beginning to reproduce sooner, and so having a greater chance to reproduce before dying. He captures key features of the mortality schedule by assuming an early burst of high mortality that incorporates any density-dependent effects. Mortality then drops to a constant adult level before age of first reproduction. Since the instantaneous adult mortality rate (M) (the inverse of the average adult lifespan) sets the time available to use the gains of growing longer, it determines the optimal age at maturity. As adult lifespan increases (adult mortality rate falls), selection favors delayed maturity to reap the gains of larger size. Thus, both α and M vary widely but inversely. Their product (αM) is approximately invariant.

There is another constraint in this model. The size at which babies are weaned is a function of adult body size. For a sample of mammals (and for primates separately), the ratio of size at independence (weaning) to adult size ($W_0/W_\alpha = \delta$) is approximately constant (Charnov 1993). Since δ scales almost isometrically with body size while production scales up with the growth allometry (a power of about 0.75 [Reiss 1989]), the size of weanlings increases faster with maternal size than does the production mother can put into them. Thus, annual fecundity, the number of daughters produced per year (b), goes down as age at maturity (α) goes up. Larger mothers produce larger but fewer babies, making αb another approximate invariant.

These assembly rules for mammalian life histories seem quite robust. The general fit of empirical patterns to the model predictions (since confirmed on other, larger data sets [Knobel and van Jaarsveld 1997; Purvis and Harvey 1995]) suggests that it points to real tradeoffs that shape mammalian life histories. Several extensions of the basic model (Charnov 1993; Kozlowski and Weiner 1997) are discussed elsewhere but do not play a role in the comparisons made here. The invariants reveal natural scaling rules: some life history variables are adjusted to others. Fecundity depends on age at maturity; age at maturity is adjusted to adult lifespan. If ancestral human lifespans increased due to grandmothering, then that hypothesis combined with Charnov's mammal model predicts distinctive effects on age at maturity, time or size at weaning, and fertility.

Age at Maturity, Interbirth Intervals, Weaning Weights, and Fecundity

In the dimensionless model, αM is approximately invariant because longer lifespans favor more advanced age at maturity. If fitness gains from growing longer continue to accumulate after menopause, then α should be adjusted to the complete adult life span, not just to the fertile component. Again Schultz's graphic

(Figure 12.1) displays the contrast. Maturity in humans is delayed relative to other apes (Table 12.1). The delay is commensurate with our longer average adult life-spans (1/M). Consequently, αM remains approximately invariant across the hominoids. (Alvarez 1999 considers a larger sample of primate species.)

The grandmother hypothesis further implies that childbearing women will produce babies faster than otherwise expected because of grandmothers' contribution to that production. Human interbirth intervals (IBI) are shorter than those of other great apes (Table 12.1)—one thing *wrong* in Schultz's classic comparison (Figure 12.1). In principle, grandmothers might contribute to this pattern in either, or both,

Table 12.1. Average Values for Selected Life History Variables

	Average Adult Lifespan[1] *(1/M)*	*Age at Maturity*[2]	*Age at Weaning*[3]	α[4]	αM	*Ratio of Weight at Weaning/ Adult Weight*[5] δ	*Daughters/ Year*[6] *b*	αb
Orangutans	17.9	14.3	6.0	8.3	.46	.28	.063	0.52
Gorillas	13.9	9.3	3.0	6.3	.45	.21	.126	0.79
Chimpanzees	17.9	13.0	4.8	8.2	.46	.27	.087	0.70
Humans	32.9	17.0	2.8	14.5	.44	.21	.142	2.05

Notes

1. The method described in Charnov 1993:194 (caption to figure 5.6) is used to estimate average adult lifespan (1/M) from maximum observed lifespans (T_{max}): $1/M = 0.4T_{max} - 0.1$. Values for orangutans: Leighton et al. 1995; gorillas: Stewart et al. 1988; chimpanzees: Nishida et al. 1990. The human value is estimated from Howell's (1979) oldest observed !Kung individual (aged 88) and Hill and Hurtado's (1996) oldest observed (forest-living) Ache individual (aged 77).
2. Age at first birth minus gestation. Orangutans: Leighton et al. 1995; gorillas: Stewart et al. 1988; chimpanzees: the mean of the means from Wallis (1997) for Gombe, Nishida et al. 1990 for Mahale, and Sugiyama 1994 for Bossou; humans: the mean of the mode for !Kung in Howell 1979 and Ache in Hill and Hurtado 1996.
3. Orangutans: Galdikas and Wood 1990; gorillas: Stewart et al. 1988; chimpanzees: the mean of the estimate from Goodall 1986 for Gombe and from Nishida et al. 1990 for Mahale; humans: the mean of the median for !Kung in Howell 1979 and Ache in Hill and Hurtado 1996.
4. Defined as the period of independent growth, from weaning to maturity.
5. Data from Lee et al. (1990) for the great apes. Maternal size for orangutans is estimated to be 40 kg; gorillas, 93 kg; chimpanzees, 40 kg. In that data set, δ for humans is 0.16 with maternal size at 55kg (the upper end of the range for modern foragers who are generally smaller that either contemporary nonforagers or pre-Mesolithic moderns). We use the mean of the !Kung (Howell 1979) (who are at the lower end of the size range for modern foragers) and the Ache (Hill and Hurtado 1996) (who are at the upper end) to represent humans.
6. Great ape data from Galdikas and Wood (1990), who reappraise birth spacing in all species in the same way. We use medians calculated therein (for closed intervals) plus two months to approximate the mean interval; then divide by 2 to get the rate in daughters. Galdikas and Wood use the Gainj, a population of horticulturalists in highland Papua New Guinea, to represent humans, for which $b = 0.132$. We use the mean of the !Kung (Howell 1979) and the Ache (Hill and Hurtado 1996).

of two ways: (1) by feeding lactating mothers and their still-nursing infants, thereby adding to the production that goes into babies, who then grow to independence faster; (2) by substituting shared food for mother's milk, thereby allowing mothers to wean their infants before they reach independence.

The second option is suggested by the Hadza patterns: grandmothers provision weaned grandchildren directly (Hawkes, O'Connell, and Blurton Jones 1997). If this practice were common in an ancestral human population, then it could have allowed mothers to wean infants early and at lower body weights (Hawkes, O'Connell, Blurton Jones, Alvarez, and Charnov 1998). Weaning would then mark a shift to grandmother's support, not feeding independence. If so, then δ (the ratio of weaning weight to adult weight) should be low for humans relative to its values among other apes.

As expected on the basis of the grandmother hypothesis, human δ is lower than that for chimpanzees and orangutans. However, it is not lower than that for gorillas. Here we note two of the possible reasons for this failure of our expectation. First, the relatively low δ for gorillas could be a reflection of the body size trend across the primates. Although the dimensionless model takes δ to be approximately constant, the ratio actually varies slightly, and negatively, with maternal size in both primates and other mammals (Charnov 1993; Purvis and Harvey 1995; cf. Knobel and van Jaarsveld 1997). The average δ for the primate order is around 0.33 (Charnov 1993:fig. 5.4). All great apes have δ values lower than the primate mean (Table 12.1). The sample of apes is too small and too skewed by body size itself to allow a meaningful test of systematic effects of maternal size on δ; but, given the trend of decreasing δ with body size across the order, we might expect a grandmotherless ape of human size to wean at a greater relative size than do the much larger gorillas.

A second possibility is that the human δ value reported in Table 12.1 (0.21), derived from a sample of two modern foraging populations, may be too high. Lee et al. (1990) report much greater variation in adult than weanling weights in humans. Ethnographically known foragers are small by pre-Mesolithic human standards. The human maternal and weaning weights provided by Lee and colleagues come from a sample not restricted to foragers. The larger adult size might be more representative of Paleolithic moderns. It gives a δ of 0.16, well below that for any of the great apes.

Other comparisons of primate weaning patterns are pertinent here. More than a decade ago, Lefebvre (1985) developed, tested, and rejected an early-weaning hypothesis. He suggested that food sharing might be an alternative that allowed mothers to save the metabolic costs of lactation as well as the cost of delayed fertility imposed by lactational amenorrhea. In his sample, however, weaning age was no earlier for the two species of primates (chimpanzees and golden-lion tamarins) where parent-offspring food sharing is reported to be more frequent than for other nonhuman primates. He also noted that human weaning age did not differ from the general primate pattern when regressed on adult weight, gestation length, and age at maturity.

Lefebvre's focus was on weaning age, while δ pertains to size. In Charnov's mammal model, size varies with time, but rate of growth to weaning depends on the production function and so on both the coefficient A and the allometric exponent c. Since A is even lower for humans than for other primates (Hill and Hurtado 1996), we require more time to reach a given size, or to grow offspring to a given size, than do other species in the order. A human mother nursing her baby for the same amount of time (Lefebvre's measure) as the average nonhuman primate of similar size "grows" it less. The addition of grandmother's production could accelerate infant growth (faster than expected, given our A), or acceleration could be combined with some reduction in weaning size as grandmother takes over production (see analysis across a larger sample in Alvarez 1999).

The relatively high fertility of humans is actually much greater than suggested by direct comparison of IBIs with other hominoids. Across all mammals, including primates, fecundity (b) scales negatively with age at maturity. αb is approximately invariant. But if later maturity in humans is due to grandmothering, then grandmother's contribution to production should have important countervailing effects that increase b. The αb value for humans is more than double those of the other large-bodied apes (Table 12.1). As the grandmother hypothesis predicts, αb should be high because it incorporates the production of both mothers and grandmothers. The baby production of the entire life span is concentrated in the childbearing years.

Combined with Charnov's mammal model, the grandmother hypothesis predicts several distinctive features of human life history, including long lifespans after menopause, late age at maturity, short interbirth intervals, and high fertility. Other hypotheses have been offered to account for each of these individually (Hill 1993; Smith and Tompkins 1995), but grandmothering may explain all of them simultaneously.

IMPLICATIONS

The grandmother hypothesis suggests a different model of human evolution than the conventional one that makes men's big game hunting and provisioning of mates and offspring the keystone human adaptation. Wide reliance on the hunting model continues in spite of accumulating reasons to reject it. Here we summarize its principle features and review critical shortcomings; then we outline an alternative argument about evolutionary transitions based on the grandmother hypothesis and identify some possible archaeological tests.

The Hunting Hypothesis: Review and Critique

According to the hunting hypothesis, ancestral males took up hunting to provide for their mates and children (Washburn and Lancaster 1968). Provisioning fathers made nuclear families basic social units; the sexual division of labor permitted greater investment in children over longer periods of time (Lancaster and Lancaster 1983). This increased investment was favored because it allowed the development of improved cognitive and social skills and more social learning. Enhanced capacities for cooperation increased the advantages for males allied with kin to ensure the support and protection of their families. Uniquely human patterns of group composition and social behavior emerged as a result.

The appeal of this model lies in its capacity to incorporate widely held ideas about human sociality and cognition, account for contrasts between human behavior and that of other primates, and draw support from the archaeological and hominid fossil records. Nonhuman primate males do not provision offspring; persistent, exclusive consort relationships are all but absent in communities with multiple males. By contrast, among all ethnographically known human foragers, men hunt, women gather, and nuclear families are evident social and reproductive units. The support of hunting fathers is presumed to fund longer juvenile dependence, which allows the elaborated learning and cognitive complexity that results in the broad geographical dispersal, expanded tool kits, and distinctive social traditions typical of humans. The putative material signature of this pattern, the association of stone tools with the bones of large animals at central places, dates to the beginning of the archaeological record, and coincides broadly with the origin of genus *Homo* itself (Klein 1999). For many, this makes men's hunting and meat sharing the fundamental framework around which all other aspects of human evolution were subsequently organized (Isaac 1978).

This picture is so compelling that disputes within paleoanthropology over the past few decades have centered not on its basic features, but on when the characteristics it embodies first emerged. Initial arguments linked male provisioning with bipedalism, hunting, and the use of stone tools, and dated all of them to the beginning of the Pleistocene (Isaac 1978). This formulation was undercut by the demonstration that bipedality preceded clear evidence of either hunting or stone tool use by millions of years (Johanson and White 1979). Subsequent arguments placed the onset of male provisioning at one or another of several different points in the record, including the early Pliocene (Lovejoy 1981), based primarily on the date for bipedality; the Plio-Pleistocene boundary (Bunn and Kroll 1986), based on possible evidence for the transport of large animal body parts to central places; and the mid-Upper Pleistocene (Binford 1985; Soffer 1992), based on a different interpretation of the animal body part data and other archaeological evidence read to indicate the presence of nuclear family households. Where the date assigned is late, patterns in human or hominid social organization and food acquisition that prevailed earlier, and were sufficiently distinct from those of other primates to account for the formation of the archaeological record, remain essentially unimagined (O'Connell 1995).

The resilience of the hunting model is especially impressive in light of the weaknesses recently revealed in the proposed link between hunting and paternal provisioning. Chimpanzees have been shown to hunt much more frequently and successfully than previously supposed (Boesch and Boesch 1989; Stanford 1996, 1999; Wrangham and Bergman-Riss 1990). As with humans, hunting is a male specialty and the meat obtained is widely shared; yet chimps lack nuclear families, paternal provisioning, a sexual division of labor, and extended childhoods. The proposition that these are the evolutionary products of male hunting and meat sharing is accordingly undercut.

The assumption that human males hunt to provision their families has also been challenged. Recent work among tropical hunter-gatherers shows that "encounter" hunting (sensu Binford 1980) is a risky business, even with relatively sophisticated projectile weapons. Among the Hadza, for example, where average rates of meat consumption are high, individual hunters fail to kill or scavenge large game on 97% of all hunting days (Hawkes et al. 1991). When a hunter is successful, the meat is widely shared, most going to individuals outside his nuclear family rather than to his own wife and children. Other strategies that would provision families more reliably with meat (small game hunting and trapping) are consistently ignored. Hunters would supply even more calories to their households by plant food collecting (Hawkes 1993). Similar patterns are observed among other low-latitude hunting populations where hunting supplies a collective good from which all benefit, regardless of their relationship with the hunter (Hawkes 1990). It is women's foraging, not men's hunting, that differentially affects an individual family's nutritional welfare.

Questions can also be raised about another key element of the hunting hypothesis: the notion that longer childhoods are favored because they expand human technological and social capacities and skills. While it is now widely appreciated that humans are not the only tool-using animals, our dependence on technology has long been assumed to result from feedback between hunting and the extended childhoods for learning locally efficient tactics of resource acquisition that hunting fathers support. But recent studies of modern hunter-gatherers indicate wide variation in the ages at which children begin to forage, even in broadly similar ecological circumstances (Blurton Jones et al. 1989, 1994). There is no indication that it takes long years of practice to acquire human foraging skills (Blurton Jones et al. 1997).

The hunting hypothesis also includes the proposition that social learning was uniquely favored in humans when local groups of hunters cooperated to support and protect their mates and dependent offspring (e.g., Alexander 1990). Arguments about the selection pressures that social life places on the evolution of intelligence (e.g., Humphrey 1976) have drawn attention to the sophisticated capacities for social manipulation that characterize primates generally (Byrne and Whiten 1988). Both competition for resources and the advantages of alliances (Harcourt and de Waal 1992) usually increase with group living, so the differences in social intelligence between humans and other hominoids, to say nothing of differences among species of nonhuman primates or social mammals generally, require additional explanation.

A comparative picture that includes nonprimate and nonmammalian taxa does not support the supposition that long juvenile periods require increased parental investment, or that delayed maturity generally results in greater brain size when the effects of body size are controlled (Austad and Fischer, 1992; Charnov 1993; Harvey et al. 1979). Species with small brains may also have late ages of maturity for their size. Our long juvenile periods *may* have evolved for uniquely human reasons. But that can only be established if more general explanations fail.

Finally, the inference that coalitions of male kin form the usual core of human and more generally hominid foraging communities is also open to question. Paired with the fact that male philopatry is the common pattern among chimpanzees, the patrilocality of hunter-gatherers stimulated the hypothesis that female natal dispersal has characterized all descendants of our common ancestor (Foley and Lee 1989; Rodseth et al. 1991; Wrangham 1987). The idea that modern human hunters are typically patrilocal dates at least to the early part of this century (Kelly 1995). It was briefly overturned in the wake of *Man the Hunter* (Lee and DeVore 1968), because the best studied cases discussed there were not patrilocal. Subsequently, the older view was resurrected by Ember's (1978) tabulation of a larger sample of cases showing patrilocality to be the most common residential arrangement. The variation shown in these data is substantial: patrilocality is actually less frequent among non-equestrian, non-fishing-dependent hunters than in the societies in Murdock's (1967) *Ethnographic Atlas* sample as a whole (56% vs. 71%).

Although humans might be expected to display more variation in social organization with local ecology than any nonhuman primate species, the other descendants of our common ancestor with *Pan* vary much more than the widely repeated generalizations suggest. Among bonobos, where females form larger, more cohesive groups than do common chimpanzees, males do not display the territorial kin-based coalitions seen in the latter (Wrangham and Petersen 1996). Patterns of natal dispersal among chimpanzees vary within and between study sites. Five of the eleven resident female adults in the habituated population at Gombe did not emigrate at maturity (Pusey et al. 1997). Fifi, an especially famous illustration, staying with her mother Flo, has logged the highest reproductive success ever recorded for a free-living chimpanzee (Goodall 1986; Pusey et al. 1997). At Tai, dispersal patterns are not yet documented, but the recent report that more than half the infants were not sired by resident males (Gagneux et al. 1997) raises fundamental questions about male territorial alliances and suggests the possibility of low rates of female dispersal there as well. In the small chimpanzee population at Bossou, Guinea, male migration (often assumed to be ruled out in this species because stranger males would be killed by residents elsewhere) has been more frequent than female (Sugiyama and Koman 1979). A visit by stranger males at this site generated great excitement, but no aggression from the resident males. In captivity, male chimpanzees show remarkable interest and facility in constructing and manipulating alliances with unrelated stranger males (de Waal 1982), patterns consistent with an evolutionary history in which those capacities were often useful.

The Grandmother Hypothesis: A Comprehensive Alternative

These various challenges notwithstanding, the hunting hypothesis continues to form the core of most arguments about human evolution, largely, in our view, because of the absence of an alternative. The grandmother hypothesis provides one. Three directions can be nominated for future work.

Local Group Composition. The grandmother hypothesis focuses attention on mother-child food sharing and the fitness payoffs available to coresident mothers and daughters that arise when resources that young juveniles cannot handle efficiently become important in the diet. As daughters grow, they acquire the strength and skill needed to help feed their younger siblings. When they mature, the assistance of aging mothers continues to enhance the benefits of proximity. From this perspective, long postmenopausal lifespans, late age at maturity, and high fertility suggest an ancestral pattern of co-residence among related females.

The ethnographic record shows that among foragers the tendency toward matrilocality increases with women's relative contribution to subsistence and (separately) with increased dependence on gathering (Ember 1975). The grandmother hypothesis should stimulate increased attention to the activities of older women and explicit examination of the spatial proximity of mothers and daughters. Even in cases classified unequivocally as patrilocal, female kin may often be co-residents and senior women contribute to the domestic workload of their daughters (e.g., Denham 1974; O'Connell, unpublished Alyawara data).

Grandmothers can certainly enhance their fitness by aiding sons, but evidence of grandmothering effects on human life histories points more strongly to mothers helping daughters. Mothers and daughters face similar tradeoffs, whereas sons must invest in mating competition (Hawkes, Rogers, and Charnov 1995). A food-sharing mother might attract females to her son's group, but this would not assure her son paternity of those females' offspring. His fitness would depend on his success in competing with other males. Winners of that competition would enjoy higher reproductive success whether or not their mothers contributed to the fertility of their mates. Even if a grandmother could identify her son's offspring and single out grandchildren to feed, her potential fitness gains through increased fertility of "daughters-in-law" would be devalued by the uncertain paternity of subsequent children more quickly born to the mothers of those grandchildren.

Molecular studies may provide evidence about ancestral social organizations. Sex-biased patterns of dispersal can have characteristic effects on the relative variation of mitochondrial and nuclear genes in descendant populations. The grandmother hypothesis provides a rationale for the modeling needed to identify critical tests. According to one suggestive appraisal, patterns of variation in "small aboriginal populations indicate that their genetic structure and levels of female dispersal are similar to those in macaque populations," where males but not females usually disperse (Melnick and Hoelzer 1993:8). Further development of this approach is clearly in order.

Extended Juvenile Periods and Social Learning. Primates generally have long juvenile periods compared with mammals of the same adult body size (Harvey et al. 1989). If maturity is delayed when adult mortalities are low as explained in Charnov's mammal model, then primate social intelligence could result as the "waiting time" is allocated to serve the juvenile's fitness. Drawing the causal arrow from late maturity to learning (Janson and van Schaik 1993), instead of the other way around, may help explain the differences in cognitive elaboration between primates and other mammals (who, on average, have shorter juvenile periods for their body sizes, and face less within group competition), and also the differences among primate species, especially between humans and other apes.

Evolutionary Scenarios. In principle, we expect grandmothering to have been favored under ecological conditions that promoted use of resources that yield high return rates to adults but that youngsters cannot handle efficiently on their own. Taking a lead from the Hadza case, such resources might have included (though need not have been limited to) tubers that require substantial upper body strength and endurance to collect, and various forms of treatment (especially roasting) to eliminate toxins and improve palatability and nutrient yield (see also Coursey 1973; Stahl 1984). Though tubers with these qualities are commonly exploited by ethnographically known hunter-gatherers worldwide, they are generally unimportant, if not entirely absent, in the diets of most other primates (Whiten and Widdowson 1992). They may have entered human or hominid diets initially either as a function of technological innovations that improved handling efficiency (e.g., adoption of digging sticks, development of controlled use of fire) or as a result of declines in the availability of less expensive resources previously favored. Such declines may have been caused by changes in climate, especially increased aridity and seasonality, and would in themselves have favored technological changes that improved efficiency in the exploitation of resources previously ignored (Hawkes and O'Connell 1992).

As these new resources were adopted and the offspring provisioning they allowed became established, contingent adjustments in life history and ecology should have followed accordingly. Relatively small size at weaning, delayed maturity, and reduced rates of senescence in all aspects of physiology except fertility should have been among the results. Shorter IBI and relaxed density-dependent effects on juvenile mortality (Charnov 1991, 1993; Hill and Hurtado 1996) may have stimulated sharp increases in local population densities. Use of tubers in particular may have permitted use of highly seasonal (especially arid) habitats previously unexploited because of the inability of juveniles to feed themselves there efficiently.

Currently available data strongly suggest that australopithecines and the earliest representatives of genus *Homo* had life histories comparable to those of modern pongids (Smith and Tompkins 1995). Subsequent adjustments in the direction of the modern human pattern, coincident with at least some of the proposed ecological and technological correlates, are evident at least three points in the prehistoric record:

1. The initial appearance of *Homo erectus* (more narrowly, *ergaster*) about 1.8 million years ago (Feibel et al. 1989) is associated with the acceleration of a long-term global climatic trend toward cooler, drier, more seasonal conditions and the expansion of savanna habitats (deMenocal 1995). *H. erectus* displays evidence for delayed maturity relative to earlier hominids (Walker and Leakey 1993; Clegg and Aiello 1999), significant expansion of geographical range (Swisher et al. 1994), and (highly controversial) evidence for the use of fire (Gowlett et al. 1981). The possibility that grandmothering explains the evolution of *Homo erectus* is explored in detail in O'Connell et al (1999).
2. Early archaic *Homo sapiens* (up to 600,000 years ago; Clark et al. 1994) appears in the wake of a further shift toward cool, dry climates and is more widely distributed than previous forms, notably in cool temperate habitats in various parts of Eurasia (Roebrucks et al. 1992). Controlled use of fire is more clearly indicated, at least among later populations (James 1989). Maturity may be delayed longer than in *erectus* (Tompkins 1996), although recent work suggests that age at maturity in *erectus* may have been in the modern range (Clegg and Aiello 1999).
3. The dispersal of anatomically modern *Homo sapiens* (about 50,000 years ago) begins shortly after the sudden onset of the last glaciation. Not long ago some paleoanthropologists hypothesized that fully modern life histories appeared only with our species (Trinkhaus and Tompkins 1990), which enjoys unprecedented success in the exploitation of arid habitats, especially at high latitudes (Klein 1995).

Further research is clearly required to determine the point at which modern human life histories and the adaptive advantages they provide first became established. The complexity of the record suggests diversity among hominids that has no modern counterpart. There is no reason to suppose that life history patterns must take either the modern human form or that of modern great apes. If the grandmotherless great ape pattern is one equilibrium, and the modern human pattern is another, what might set—and what perturb—additional equilibrium points? Answers to this question may offer leverage for explaining the diversity among hominids. [Recent reappraisal of the record (Wood and Collard 1999a,b) holds out hope of simplifying some of the diversity.]

Male Strategies. In focusing attention on links among female foraging strategies and features of female life history, the grandmother hypothesis may seem to be silent on males. But changes in the foraging strategies of women should have significant effects on the tradeoffs faced by men. For example, differences in the size of female groups, a variable directly related to feeding competition, have important consequences for male strategies in other apes (Wrangham et al. 1996).

Feeding competition among females should decline if extractive requirements, rather than resource density, limit return rates. If mothers and daughters also benefit from sharing food, larger and more cohesive groups should be common. The changes in female group size, foraging range, and the habitat expansion predicted to occur in association with grandmothering should therefore alter the competitive arena for males.

One effect that the grandmother hypothesis could have on the investigation of male strategies is indirect. Since male provisioning is not required to account for our late maturity and high fecundity, this gives additional weight to the ethnographic observations that hunters are not supporting their families (Hawkes 1990, 1993; Hawkes et al. 1991). Wider appreciation that paternal provisioning is not ubiquitous among foragers should invite alternative explanations for the long-term pairing of husbands and wives characteristic of humans. Mating patterns vary among the great apes, but all display clear male hierarchies in which high-ranking males succeed in claiming disproportionate mating access to fertile females (Furuichi and Ihobe 1994; van Schaik and van Hoof 1996; Watts 1996). In contrast, human foraging societies are often "egalitarian" (Boehm 1993; Fried 1967), and most adult men successfully claim mating priority for a particular wife. Because of assumptions about the central role of paternal provisioning, mating competition has been deemed less important among human males (cf. Chagnon 1979). More attention paid to it should generate novel hypotheses about both the origins and maintenance of marriage (Hawkes 2000; Blurton Jones et al., Chapter 4, this volume).

Given that most adults do marry, the life history patterns associated with grandmothering have an additional implication. With long postmenopausal lifespans, the age profile of fertility no longer coincides with aging in most aspects of female adaptive performance. General health and competence become poor fecundity cues. Male preference for young partners, which sharply distinguishes men (Jones 1996) from chimpanzees (Morin 1993), could be favored as a consequence.

Combined with a dimensionless approach to life histories, the grandmother hypothesis shows that several distinctive human characteristics may be systematic variations on a general primate pattern. Novel ancillary predictions about behavioral patterns in the modern world, as well as in the past, follow. The development of theoretically warranted hypotheses quite different from those currently favored should contribute to our understanding of human evolution, whatever the outcome of further tests.

SUMMARY

1. Humans are unique among the great apes for the importance of mother-child food sharing and long postmenopausal lifespans. We elaborate a grandmother hypothesis that identifies an evolutionary link between these features. Combined with a model of mammalian life histories, the hypothesis explains our

long lifespans with mid-life menopause, and also the late age at maturity, and high fertility that distinguish humans from the other apes.

2. Without food sharing, mothers accompanied by young juveniles are tied to resources that youngsters can handle effectively for themselves. Sharing releases mothers to exploit resources that give high return rates to adults but not young children. The same high return resources allow other adults to help mothers feed dependent toddlers. Grandmothers who provide such help increase their own genetic success because their daughters can have more babies sooner. This division of labor between older women and their younger kin would strengthen selection against senescence in all aspects of physiology except fertility.

3. Some predictions of the grandmother hypothesis are tested by comparing human life history averages to those of the other great apes using Charnov's model of life history invariants. Life history traits vary widely with body size, but they remain correlated with each other even when body size is removed. Charnov's model explains the invariant relationship between key pairs of life history traits across transformations of body size and phylogeny. In his model adult mortalities (M) (the inverse of average adult lifespans) determine the optimal age at maturity (α) and rate of births (b). If long human lifespans are a consequence of grandmothering, and Charnov's model is approximately correct, then our age of maturity should be adjusted to the entire lifespan, not just the period from maturity to menopause; and our fertility rates should reflect the contribution of both mothers and grandmothers. Comparisons with the other hominoids show that human αM and αb values are consistent with this reasoning. The results show that grandmothering can explain a cascade of adjustments long attributed to other causes.

4. The grandmother hypothesis challenges the popular model in which men's hunting to provision wives and offspring is key to the evolution of distinctively human patterns of social organization and child development. Although the hunting hypothesis has been criticized from many directions, scenarios of human evolution continue to use it routinely in the absence of a comprehensive alternative. The grandmother hypothesis, with the life history adjustments it can explain, is such an alternative. We briefly consider implications for a range of ideas about the human past.

ACKNOWLEDGMENT

We thank Ursula Hanly for redrafting the figure from Schultz 1969.

REFERENCES

Alexander, R. D. 1990. *How Did Humans Evolve? Reflections on the Uniquely Unique Species.* University of Michigan Museum of Zoology, Special Publication No. 1. Ann Arbor.

Alvarez, H. 1999. The grandmother hypothesis and primate life histories. Ms., Department of Anthropology, University of Utah, Salt Lake City (submitted for publication).

Austad, S. N., and K. E. Fischer. 1992. Primate longevity: Its place in the mammalian scheme. *American Journal of Primatology* 28:251–261.

Binford, L. 1980. Willow smoke and dogs' tails: Hunter-gatherer settlement systems and archaeological formation processes. *American Antiquity* 45:4–20.

———. 1985. Human ancestors: Changing views of their behavior. *Journal of Anthropological Archaeology* 4:292–327.

Blurton Jones, N. G., K. Hawkes, and P. Draper. 1994. Foraging returns of !Kung adults and children: Why didn't !Kung children forage? *Journal of Anthropological Research* 50:217–248.

Blurton Jones, N. G., K. Hawkes, and J. F. O'Connell. 1989. Studying costs of children in two foraging societies: Implications for schedules of reproduction. In *Comparative Socioecology of Mammals and Man,* V. Standon and R. Foley, eds. Pp. 365–390. London: Blackwell.

———. 1996. The global process and local ecology: How should we explain differences between the Hadza and the !Kung? In *Cultural Diversity among Twentieth Century Foragers: An African Perspective,* S. Kent, ed. Pp. 159–187. Cambridge: Cambridge University Press.

———. 1997. Why do Hadza children forage? In *Uniting Psychology and Biology: Integrative Perspectives on Human Development,* N. Segal, G. E. Weisfeld, and C. C. Weisfeld, eds. Pp. 279–313. Washington, D.C.: American Psychological Association.

Blurton Jones, N. G., L. C. Smith, J. F. O'Connell, K. Hawkes, and C. Kamazura. 1992. Demography of the Hadza, an increasing and high density population of savanna foragers. *American Journal of Physical Anthropology* 89:159–181.

Boehm, C. 1993. Egalitarian society and reverse dominance hierarchy. *Current Anthropology* 34:227–254.

Boesch, C., and H. Boesch. 1989. Hunting behavior of wild chimpanzees in the Tai National Park. *American Journal of Physical Anthropology* 78:547–573.

Bunn, H. T., and E. Kroll. 1986. Systematic butchery by Plio-Pleistocene hominids at Olduvai Gorge. *Current Anthropology* 27:257–272.

Byrne, R. and A. Whiten, eds. 1988. *Machiavellian Intelligence: Social Expertise and the Evolution of Intellect in Monkeys, Apes, and Humans.* Oxford: Clarendon Press.

Caro, T. M., D. W. Sellen, A. Parish, R. Frank, D. M. Brown, E. Voland, and M. Borgerhoff Mulder. 1995. Termination of reproduction in nonhuman and human female primates. *International Journal of Primatology* 16:205–220.

Chagnon, N. 1979. Is reproductive success equal in egalitarian societies? In *Evolutionary Biology and Human Social Behavior: An Anthropological Perspective,* N. Chagnon and W. Irons, eds. Pp. 374–401. North Scituate, Massachusetts: Duxbury Press.

Charnov, E. L. 1991. Evolution of life history variation in female mammals. *Proceedings of the National Academy of Sciences* (USA) 88:1134–1137.

———. 1993. *Life History Invariants: Some Explanations of Symmetry in Evolutionary Ecology.* Oxford: Oxford University Press. Charnov, E. L., and D. Berrigan. 1991. Dimensionless numbers and the assembly rules for life histories. *Philosophical Transactions of the Royal Society* (London), Series B 33:241–248.

———. 1993. Why do female primates have such long lifespans and so few babies? or Life in the slow lane. *Evolutionary Anthropology* 1:191–194.

Clark, J. D., B. Asfaw, G. Assefa, J. W. K. Harris, H. Kurashina, R. C. Walter, T. D. White, and M. A. J. Williams. 1994. Paleoanthropological discoveries in the Middle Awash Valley, Ethiopia. *Nature* 307:423–428.

Clegg, M. and L. Aiello. 1999. A comparison of the Nanokotoma *Homo Erectus* with juveniles from a modern human population. *American Journal of Physical Anthropology* 110(1):81–93.

Coursey, D. G. 1973. Hominid evolution and hypogeous plant foods. *Man* 8:634–635.

deMenocal, P. B. 1995. Plio-Pleistocene African climate. *Science* 270:53–59.

de Waal, F. 1982. *Chimpanzee Politics: Power and Sex among the Apes.* New York: Harper and Row.

Denham, W. W. 1974. Infant transport among the Alyawara tribe, central Australia. *Oceania* 44:253–277.

Ember, C. 1975. Residential variation among hunter-gatherers. *Behavioral Science Research* 3:199–227.

———. 1978. Myths about hunter-gatherers. *Ethnology* 4:439–448.

Feibel, C. S., F. H. Brown, and I. MacDougal. 1989. Stratigraphic context of fossil hominids from the Omo Group deposits: Northern Turkana Basin, Kenya and Ethiopia. *American Journal of Physical Anthropology* 78:595–622.

Foley, R., and P. Lee. 1989. Finite social space, evolutionary pathways, and reconstructing hominid behavior. *Science* 243:901–906.

Fried, M. H. 1967. *The Evolution of Political Society.* New York: Random House.

Furuichi, T., and H. Ihobe. 1994. Variation in male relationships in bonobos and chimpanzees. *Behaviour* 130:211–228.

Gaganeux, P., D. S. Woodruff, and C. Boesch. 1997. Furtive mating in female chimpanzees. *Nature* 387:358–359.

Galdikis, B., and J. Wood. 1990. Birth spacing patterns in humans and apes. *American Journal of Physical Anthropology* 63:185–191.

Goodall, J. 1986. *The Chimpanzees of Gombe: Patterns of Behavior.* Cambridge: Harvard University Press.

———. 1989. Gombe: Highlights and current research. In *Understanding Chimpanzees,* P. Heltne and L. Marquardt, eds. Pp. 2–21. Cambridge: Harvard University Press.

Gowlett, J. A. J., J. W. K. Harris, D. Walton, and B. A. Wood. 1981. Early archaeological sites, hominid remains, and traces of fire at Chesowanja, Kenya. *Nature* 294:125–129.

Harcourt, A. H., and F. B. M. de Waal, eds. 1992. *Coalitions and Alliances in Humans and Other Animals.* Oxford: Oxford Scientific.

Harvey, P. H., and T. Clutton-Brock. 1985. Life history variation in primates. *Evolution* 39:559–581.

Harvey, P. H., D. E. L. Promislow, and A. F. Read. 1989. Causes and correlates of life history differences among mammals. In *Comparative Socioecology of Mammals and Man,* V. Standen and R. Foley, eds. Pp. 305–318. London: Blackwell.

Hawkes, K. 1990.Why do men hunt? Some benefits for risky strategies. In *Risk and Uncertainty,* E. Cashdan, ed. Pp. 145–166. Boulder: Westview Press.

———. 1991. Showing off: Tests of an hypothesis about men's foraging goals. *Ethology and Sociobiology* 12:29–54.

———. 1993. Why hunter-gatherers work: An ancient version of the problem of public goods. *Current Anthropology* 34:341–361.

———. 2000. Big game hunting and the evolution of egalitarian societies. In *Hierarchies in Action: Cui Bono?* M. Deihl, ed. Center for Archaeological Investigations, Occasional Paper No. 27, pp. 59–83. Southern Illinois University.

Hawkes, K., and J. F. O'Connell. 1992. On optimal foraging models and subsistence transitions. *Current Anthropology* 33:63–66.

Hawkes, K., J. F. O'Connell, and N. G. Blurton Jones. 1989. Hardworking Hadza grandmothers. In *Comparative Socioecology of Mammals and Man,* V. Standen and R. Foley, eds. Pp. 341–366. London: Blackwell.

———. 1991. Hunting income patterns among the Hadza: Big game, common goods, foraging goals, and the evolution of the human diet. *Philosophical Transactions of the Royal Society,* Series B 334:243–251.

———. 1995. Hadza children's foraging: Juvenile dependency, social arrangements and mobility among hunter-gatherers. *Current Anthropology* 36:688–700.

———. 1997. Hadza women's time allocation, offspring production, and the evolution of long postmenopausal life spans. *Current Anthropology* 38:551–577.

Hawkes, K., A. R. Rogers, and E. L. Charnov. 1995. The male's dilemma: Increased offspring production is more paternity to steal. *Evolutionary Ecology* 9:1–16.

Hawkes, K., J. F. O'Connell, N. G. Blurton Jones, H. Alvarez, and E. L. Charnov. 1998. Grandmothering, menopause, and the evolution of human life histories. *Proceedings of the National Academy of Sciences* 95 (3):1336–1339.

Hill, K. 1993. Life history theory and evolutionary anthropology. *Evolutionary Anthropology* 2:78–88.

Hill, K., and A. M. Hurtado. 1991.The evolution of reproductive senescence and menopause in human females: An evaluation of the grandmother hypothesis. *Human Nature* 2:313–350.

———. 1996. *Ache Life History: The Ecology and Demography of a Foraging People.* New York: Aldine de Gruyter. Howell, N. 1979. *Demography of the Dobe !Kung.* New York: Academic Press.

Huang W., R. Ciochon, Y. Gu, R. Larick, Q. Fang, H. Schwarcz, C. Yonge, J. De Vos, and W. Rink. 1995. Early *Homo* and associated artifacts from Asia. *Nature* 378:275–278.

Humphrey, N. K. 1976. The social function of intellect. In *Growing Points in Ethology,* P. G. Bateson and R. A. Hinde, eds. Pp. 303–317. Cambridge: Cambridge University Press.

Isaac, G. Ll. 1978. The food sharing behavior of protohuman hominids. *Scientific American* 238(4):90–108.

James, S. 1989. Hominid use of fire in the Lower and Middle Pleistocene: A review of the evidence. *Current Anthropology* 30:1–26.

Janson, C. H., and C. P. van Schaik. 1993. Ecological risk aversion in juvenile primates. In *Juvenile Primates: Life History, Development and Behavior,* M. E. Periera and L. A. Fairbanks, eds. Pp. 57–76. Oxford: Oxford University Press.

Johanson, D., and T. D. White. 1979. A systematic asessement of early African hominids. *Science* 203:321–330.

Jones, D. 1996. An evolutionary perspective on physical attractiveness. *Evolutionary Anthropology* 5:97–109.

Kaplan, H. 1997. The evolution of the human life course. In *Between Zeus and the Salmon,* K. W. Wachter and C. E. Finch, eds. Pp. 175-211. Washington, DC: National Academy Press.

Kelly, R. L. 1995. *The Foraging Spectrum: Diversity in Hunter-Gatherer Lifeways.* Washington, D.C.: Smithsonian Institution.

Kirkwood, T. L. L., and M. R. Rose. 1991. Evolution of senescence: Late survival sacrificed for reproduction. *Philosophical Transactions of the Royal Society,* Series B 332:15–34.

Klein, R. G. 1995. Anatomy, behavior, and modern human origins. *Journal of World Prehistory* 9:167–198.

———. 1999. *The Human Career: Human Biological and Cultural Origins* (2nd ed.) Chicago: University of Chicago Press.

Knobel, D. L., and A. S. van Jaarsveld. 1997. Mammalian life-history evolution: An evaluation of Charnov's model. Ms., Department of Zoology and Entomology, University of Pretoria.

Kohl-Larson, L. 1958. *Wildbeuter in Ost-Afrika: Die Tindiga, ein Jager-und Sammlervolk.* Berlin: Dietrich Reimer.

Kozlowski, J., and J. Weiner. 1997. Interspecific allometries are by-products of body size optimization. *American Naturalist* 149:352–380.

Lancaster, J., and C. Lancaster. 1983. Parental investment: the hominid adaptation. In *How Humans Adapt,* D. Ortner, ed. Pp. 33–69. Washington, D.C.: Smithsonian Institution Press.

Lee, R. B., and I. DeVore, eds. 1968. *Man the Hunter.* Chicago: Aldine.

Lee, P. C., P. Majluf, and I. J. Gordon. 1990. Growth, weaning and maternal investment from a comparative perspective. *Journal of Zoology* 225:99–114.

Lefebvre, L. 1985. Parent-offspring food sharing: A statistical test of the early weaning hypotheis. *Journal of Human Evolution* 14(3):255–261.

Leighton, M., U. S. Seal, K. Soemarna, Ajisasmito, M. Wijaya, T. Mitra Setia, G. Shapiro, L. Perkins, K. Traylor-Holzer, and R. Tilson. 1995. Orangutan life history and VORTEX analysis. In *The Neglected Ape,* R. D. Nadler, B. F. M. Galdikas, L. K. Heeran, and N. Rosen, eds. Pp. 97–107. New York: Plenum Press.

Lovejoy, C. O. 1981. The origin of man. *Science* 211:341–350.

Medawar, P. B. 1952. *An Unsolved Problem of Biology.* London: H. K. Lewis.

Melnick, D. and G. Hoelzer. 1993. What is MtDNA good for in the study of primate evolution? *Evolutionary Anthropology* 2:2–10. Morin, P. A. 1993. Reproductive strategies in chimpanzees. *Yearbook of Physical Anthropology* 36:179–212.

Murdock, G. P. 1967. *Ethnographic Atlas.* Pittsburgh: University of Pittsburgh Press.

Nishida, T., H. Takasaki, and Y. Takahata. 1990. Demography and reproductive profiles. In *The Chimpanzees of the Mahale Mountains: Sexual and Life History Strategies,* T. Nishida, ed. Pp. 63–97. Tokyo: University of Tokyo Press.

Obst, E. 1912. Von Mkalama ins Land der Wakindiga. *Mitteilungen der Geographischen Gessellschaft in Hamburg* 26:2–27.

O'Connell, J. F. 1995. Ethnoarchaeology needs a general theory of behavior. *Journal of Archaeological Research* 3:205–255.

O'Connell, J. F., K. Hawkes, N. Blurton Jones. 1999. Grandmothering and the Evolution of *Homo erectus. Journal of Human Evolution* 36:461–485.

Partridge, L., and N. H. Barton. 1993. Optimality, mutation and the evolution of aging. *Nature* 362:305–311.

Pavelka, M. S. M., and L. M. Fedigan. 1991. Menopause: A comparative life history perspective. *Yearbook of Physical Anthropology* 34:13–38.

Peccei, J. S. 1995. The origin and evolution of menopause: The altriciality-lifespan hypothesis. *Ethology and Sociobiology* 16:425–449.

Peters, R. H. 1983. *The Ecological Implications of Body Size.* Cambridge: Cambridge University Press.

Purvis, A., and P. H. Harvey. 1995. Mammalian life-history evolution: A comparative test of Charnov's model. *Journal of Zoology* 237:259–283.

Pusey, A., J. Williams, and J. Goodall. 1997. The influence of dominance rank on the reproductive success of female chimpanzees. *Science* 277:828–831.

Reiss, M. J. 1989. *The Allometry of Growth and Reproduction.* Cambridge: Cambridge University Press.

Rodseth, L., R. W. Wrangham, A. M. Harrigan, and B. B. Smuts. 1991. The human community as primate society. *Current Anthropology* 32:221–254.

Roebroeks, W., N. Conard, and T. van Klofshoten. 1992. Dense forests, cold steppes, and the Palaeolithic settlement of Europe. *Current Anthropology* 33:551–586.

Rogers, A. R. 1993. Why menopause? *Evolutionary Ecology* 7:406–420.

Schultz, A. H. 1969. *The Life of Primates.* New York: Universe Books.

Smith, H., and R. L. Tompkins. 1995. Toward a life history of the Hominidae. *Annual Reviews in Anthropolology* 24:257–279.

Soffer, O. 1992. Social transformations at the Middle to Upper Paleolithic transition: The implications of the European record. In *Continuity or Replacement? Controversies in* Homo sapiens *Evolution,* G. Brauer and F. H. Smith, eds. Pp. 247–259. Rotterdam: Balkema.

Stahl, A. B. 1984. Hominid dietary selection before fire. *Current Anthropology* 25:151–168.

Stanford, C. 1996. The hunting ecology of wild chimpanzees: Implications for the evolutionary ecology of Pliocene hominids. *American Anthropologist* 98:96–113.

———. 1999. *The Hunting Apes.* Princeton; Princeton University Press.

Stewart, K. J., A. H. Harcourt, and D. P. Watts. 1988. Determinants of fertility in wild gorillas and other primates. In *Natural Human Fertility: Social and Biological Determinants,* P. Diggory, M. Potts, and S. Teper, eds. Pp. 22–38. Hampshire: MacMillian Press.

Sugiyama, Y. 1994. Age specific birth rate and lifetime reproductive success of chimpanzees at Bossou, Guinea. *American Journal of Primatology* 32:311–318.

Sugiyama, Y., and J. Koman. 1979. Social structure and dynamics of wild chimpanzees at Bossou, Guinea. *Primates* 20:323–339.

Swisher, C. C., G. H. Curtis, T. Jacob, A. Getty, A. Suprijo, Widiasmoro. 1994. Age of the earliest known hominids in Java. *Science* 263:1118–1121.

Tompkins, R. L. 1996. Relative dental development of Upper Pleistocene hominids compared to human population variation. *American Journal of Physical Anthropology* 99:103–116.

Trinkhaus, E., and R. L. Tompkins. 1990. The Neandertal life cycle: The possibility, probability, and perceptibility of contrasts with recent humans. In *Primate Life History and Evolution,* C. J. DeRousseau, ed. Pp. 153–180. Monographs in Primatology, Vol. 14. New York: Wiley-Liss.

Turke, P. W. 1997. Hypothesis: Menopause discourages infanticide and encourages continued investment by agnates. *Evolution and Human Behavior* 18:3–13.

van Schaik, C. P., and J. A. R. M van Hoof. 1996. Toward an understanding of the orangutan's social system. In *Great Ape Societies,* W. McGrew, L. Marchant, and T. Nishida, eds. Pp. 3–16. Cambridge: Cambridge University Press.

Walker, A., and R. Leakey. 1993. *The Nariokotome* Homo erectus *Skeleton.* Cambridge: Harvard University Press.

Wallis, J. 1997. A survey of reproductive parameters in free-ranging chimpanzees of Gombe national park. *Journal of Reproduction and Fertility* 109:297–307.

Washburn, S. L., and C. S. Lancaster. 1968. The evolution of hunting. In *Man the Hunter,* R. B. Lee and I. DeVore, eds. Pp. 293–303. Chicago: Aldine.

Watts, D. P. 1996. Comparative socio-ecology of gorillas. In *Great Ape Societies,* W. McGrew, L. Marchant, and T. Nishida, eds. Pp. 16–28. Cambridge: Cambridge University Press.

Whiten, A., and E. M. Widdowson. 1992. *Foraging Strategies and the Natural Diet of Monkeys, Apes, and Humans.* Oxford: Clarendon Press.

Williams, G. C. 1957. Pleiotropy, natural selection, and the evolution of senescence. *Evolution* 11:398–411.

Wood, B. and M. Collard 1999a. The human genus. *Science* 284:65–71.

———. 1999b. The changing face of genus *Homo. Evolutionary Anthropology* 8(6):195–207.

Woodburn, J. 1968. An introduction to Hadza ecology. In *Man the Hunter,* R. Lee and I. DeVore, eds. Pp. 49–55. Chicago: Aldine.

Wrangham, R. W. 1987. The significance of African apes for reconstructing human social evolution. In *The Evolution of Human Behavior: Primate Models,* W. G. Kinzey, ed. Pp. 51–71. Albany: State University of New York Press.

Wrangham, R. W. and E. v. Z. Bergmann-Riss. 1990. Rates of predation on mammals by Gombe chimpanzees, 1972–1975. *Primates* 31:157–170.

Wrangham, R. W., and D. Peterson. 1996. *Demonic Males: Apes and the Origins of Human Violence.* New York: Houghton Mifflin.

Wrangham, R. W., C. A. Chapman, A. P. Clarke-Arcadi, and G. Isabirye-Basuta. 1996. Social ecology of Kanyawara chimpanzees: Implications or understanding the costs of great ape groups. In *Great Ape Societies,* W. C. McGrew, L. F. Marchant, and T. Nishida, eds. Pp. 45–57. Cambridge: Cambridge University Press.

PART IV

THE DEMOGRAPHIC TRANSITION

13

An Adaptive Model of Human Reproductive Rate Where Wealth Is Inherited

Why People Have Small Families

RUTH MACE

Humans, like most large mammals, invest a great deal in each offspring. Competition for parental investment can be fierce through the long period of childhood. In societies with high fertility, there is evidence that the lengths of both the preceding and subsequent birth intervals influence the risks of mortality and morbidity of babies and young children (e.g., Alam 1995; Bohler and Bergstrom 1995; Madise and Diamond 1995). There is also evidence that older children compete for food (e.g., LeGrand and Phillips 1996; Ronsmans 1995). At maturity, siblings may compete for their parents' heritable resources. There is considerable evidence that wealth is positively correlated with reproductive success in traditional societies. When key resources like land or livestock are individually owned, resources inherited by children from their parents can be an important determinant of their future reproductive success (e.g., Low 1991; Mace 1996a). Thus evolutionary models of parental investment should help us to understand patterns of wealth inheritance. Parents would be expected to allocate resources among their children in such a way as to maximize their own long-term reproductive success. Crucially, wealth has the capacity to generate more wealth.

In societies where inherited resources are crucial, children with no prospect of any inheritance may contribute little or nothing to their parents' long-term fitness. The cost of feeding those children may even reduce the potential reproductive success of their siblings by reducing the wealth of the household. Thus decisions about how many children to have and how many resources to give each of them at the end of the parents' reproductive lives will be related, and both are likely to depend on the wealth of the parents. All these features are characteristic of a traditional, camel-herding community—the Gabbra. In this community, as in other pastoralist communities, wealth has been shown to correlate with reproductive success (Mace 1996a). The area the Gabbra inhabit in the north of Kenya is too arid for farming, so this group provides an example of a system where wealth can be quantified through one single measure (the size of the herd) and thus the relationship between wealth and reproductive success can be investigated relatively easily. The model I present here is based on the Gabbra system (which is described in more detail below), but is general enough to apply to almost any system where inherited wealth is an important component of future wealth and future reproductive success.

A large proportion of the research in human demography over the past few decades has focused on the demographic transition. This is the term used for a phenomenon observed throughout the world, when, in societies formerly characterized by high fertility and high mortality, an increase in living standards and a decrease in mortality risks are generally associated with a decline in fertility. Most societies in the developed world underwent a demographic transition in the nineteenth century or earlier; those in the developing world entered into it more recently, with Africa only just beginning the trend now. Most human populations are actually still growing rapidly, but the rate of growth is now declining virtually everywhere. A single socioeconomic correlate of the onset of demographic transition has remained the elusive goal of demographers (Cleland 1995). Evolutionary anthropologists have, however, taken a broader, cost-benefit approach to understanding determinants of family size. On the face of it, the observation of smaller families in the presence of enhanced resources represents a serious challenge to evolutionary theory; although a number of mechanisms by which some quantity/quality tradeoff might be occurring have long been familiar to evolutionary ecologists, going back to Lack (1968).

I shall describe a decision-making model that is adaptive in that it optimizes reproductive success. I shall use the model to investigate the influence of a number of parameters on optimal fertility and inheritance strategies, to see which are likely to produce outcomes similar to those observed in societies undergoing fertility decline. I investigate mortality risk, risk in the environment (which I model by reducing the risk of drought), and the economic costs of raising children (such as their food requirements). These are three variables generally assumed to be associated with the demographic transition. Development agencies (such as governments and NGOs) normally concentrate on the first two of these, in an effort to increase people's standard of living. The last is often a consequence of an increased standard of living. That such economic changes lead to demographic change, albeit not in consistent ways, is certainly well documented, although a theoretical framework for predicting that change has been largely lacking.

A THEORETICAL FRAMEWORK FOR PREDICTING REPRODUCTIVE DECISIONS

Here I shall use a stochastic dynamic model to analyze which combinations of fertility and wealth inheritance strategies maximize the expected number of grandchildren. Dynamic optimality models can be used to find behavioral decisions that maximize fitness over a given time period (Houston et al. 1988; Mangel and Clark 1988). Anderies (1996), Beauchamp (1994), and Mace (1996b) have all used dynamic optimality models to analyze family size in humans over a single generation. Beauchamp (1994) and Anderies (1996) use lifetime reproductive success as the currency to be maximized, not taking into account any effect the level of parental investment in each child might have on their future reproductive success once they have survived childhood. In previous work (Mace 1996b), I used married children as the currency to be maximized and explored how varying the minimum investment necessary to marry off a child will influence optimal fertility in Gabbra pastoralists. The results of a simulation of a population following the optimal decision rules arrived at for the Gabbra system, assumed to have started with the average herd size reported for the cohort that has now completed its fertility, are shown in Figure 13.1. The model is broadly successful at predicting family sizes that are close to those seen in the Gabbra. There is an over-representation of families with no or one child. Evolutionary models do not generally favor deciding to have no children, or so few that random childhood mortality leaves a person

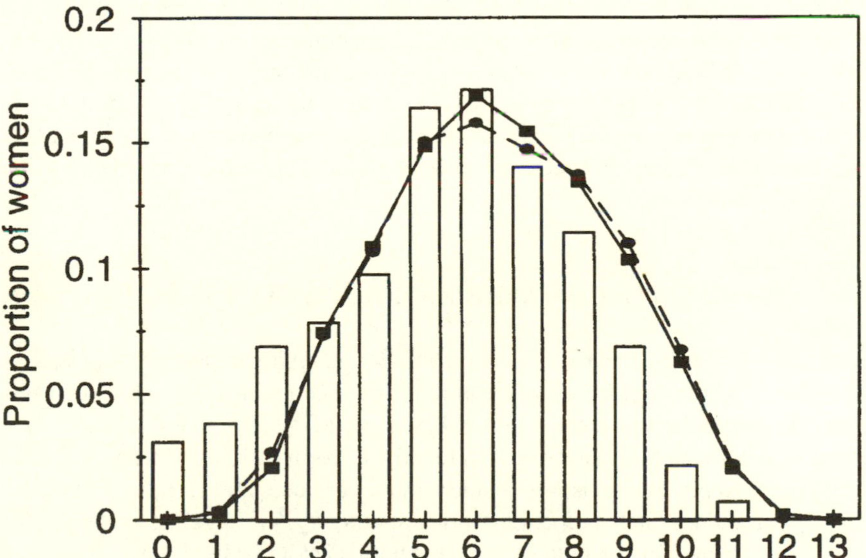

Figure 13.1. The observed distribution of completed family size of Gabbra women over 45 years of age in 1993 (bars, $n = 421$), and the predicted distribution based on women following the decision rules derived in Mace (1996b) assuming families started with initial herd sizes of 10 camels (the mean reported for that cohort); solid and dotted lines are the predicted distributions given two different estimates of mortality; see Mace and Sear 1997b).

with one or none. But it is unlikely that these small families are the result of decisions in this case; they are more likely to be due to involuntary infertility (which is not included in the model). Most women completed their fertility with about six living children (thus on average three living sons), as the model predicted they should.

I have demonstrated (Mace 1996b) that the costs of marriage are predicted to have a strong influence on optimal family size. In that model I entered marriage costs as a given, but in fact parental investment in children at marriage also represents a decision by the parents. If we want to understand why family sizes might change as the environment changes, then it is important to allow the allocation of wealth among children to change. In the model described in this chapter, I use a dynamic optimality model to find decisions that maximize number of grandchildren, given an optimal allocation of family wealth between children. The key variable of optimal investment in each child through inheritance (or marriage gifts, which are effectively similar) is derived from the model rather than assumed.

The fertility decisions I will investigate here are made many times within one generation. I measure the reproductive value of children as the number of grandchildren they are expected to produce, given the wealth allocated to them at the beginning of their reproductive lives. The strategy that maximizes grandchildren is not necessarily identical to the strategy that maximizes very long-term fitness in every case, although it will roughly approximate that strategy for most purposes (e.g., Fisher 1958). I use stochastic dynamic programming to find the combination of the optimal allocation of wealth to children and the reproductive decisions that maximize the reproductive value of the whole family, given the optimal allocation of wealth between siblings.

A TRADITIONAL AFRICAN SUBSISTENCE SYSTEM

The model I present here is based on a traditional African pastoralist system—that of the Gabbra—which shares features in common with many other such systems. In particular, livestock are the key units of wealth. They provide food directly, through milk and meat, and indirectly, through cash raised from their sale. They can also provide transport, leather, and other necessities. They are used for social transactions such as for bride-price and dowry. The food and other yields from a herd relate directly to the size of that herd. Pastoralist herds have often been likened to investment accounts: when pastoralists are given other opportunities to earn money, they frequently put that money straight into increasing herd size. Wealth will rise and fall when the herd grows or shrinks as a result of births and deaths from consumption, sales, or wasted mortality (such as in drought). These features of the system characterize many other systems based on the individual ownership of resources; in particular, it encapsulates the processes whereby those with a great deal of wealth will find it easier to maintain and increase their wealth, whereas those with very low levels of wealth are at greater risk of destitution.

This particular model is based on a group of camel-keeping pastoralists. Camels provide milk, even in harsh conditions, and transport. They are rarely bought or sold, but are inherited or given as bride-price. Goats are also kept, for meat, milk, sale, and dowry. The Gabbra inhabit an arid area, which is remote from government services even today. They are subject to frequent but unpredictable droughts (the most recent were in 1984, 1992, and 1997, all of which caused livestock mortality and, but for the provision of food aid from the government of Kenya and the international community, could have led to human starvation). These pastoralists are among the most nomadic in Africa, moving according to the availability of grazing.

The Gabbra social system is patrilineal and patrilocal. When a man marries, his family must pay a fixed bride-price to the family of the bride, but the greater expense is that he must provide a herd of livestock (almost always given by or inherited from his father) with which to support his new family. Polygyny is limited (88% of women were the only living wife of their husbands). Virtually all women marry between the ages of 15 and 25. Most men marry between the ages of 25 and 45. The singulate mean age of marriage (which is calculated from the proportion of people married in each age group and therefore does not rely on their reporting of past events) is 21 in women and 33 in men. The mean age of reproduction is 28 in women and 40 in men. Women do not reproduce before marriage; nor do they remarry if widowed, but they may continue to bear children that the Gabbra consider to be the legitimate children of their dead husbands. Men allocate wealth among their sons as they please, or, if they fail to do so, on his father's death the eldest son inherits the herd. Daughters virtually never inherit camels but may receive a small dowry from their parents on marriage, normally in goats.

In most societies, the gifts given to sons on marriage or as inheritance are much more valuable than those given to daughters: more than half of the societies in the *Ethnographic Atlas* (Murdock 1967) show male-biased inheritance, and none exhibit female-biased inheritance. Reproductive success is much more strongly related to wealth in males than in females in the Gabbra (Mace 1996a), as in many other cultures, and thus male-biased parental investment would be expected on evolutionary grounds (Hartung 1982; Trivers 1972; Trivers and Willard 1973). The bride-price Gabbra receive for daughters is generally more than the dowry they take with them at marriage; daughters may be roughly "cost-neutral" to their parents (Mace 1996a). In societies such as the Gabbra, reproductive decisions appear to be based more on number of sons rather than number of children. I have shown that the number of sons in a family has a much greater influence than number of daughters on the birth interval to the next child (Mace and Sear 1997), the probability that a son will be fostered out to another family (Mace and Sear 1997a,

1997b), and the probability that a man will take a second wife when his first wife reaches menopause (Mace 1996b). All these results indicate that it is sons that comprise the major cost consideration in Gabbra reproductive decision making. Thus the optimal family may be defined by number of sons, as number of daughters is not particularly important to the decisions considered here.

ASSUMPTIONS IN THE MODEL

The model of reproductive decision making in a subsistence system is based on a herd of livestock with dynamics described in Table 13.1, and a human population with the demographic parameters described in Table 13.2. Mortality risks were estimated in Mace and Sear (1996, 1998). But in respects other than precise parameter values, the model is general enough to apply to a range of subsistence systems based on individually owned resources.

This model is used to investigate the decisions of parents in a monogamous marriage. Male and female reproductive decisions would not be expected to differ under monogamy, so the decision-making unit is referred to as the household. Given that daughters do not inherit wealth, the model considers only sons. This simplification means that marriage decisions (which determine the reproductive success of daughters) do not have to be considered in the model. When parents decide to have another baby, that baby is assumed to have a 50% chance of being male. The parameter values used to determine the cost of raising a son are double

Table 13-1. Parameter values used to describe herd dynamics in the baseline case.

Annual probability of drought	0.2
Variables per female stock unit:*	
p(birth) - *p*(death) in non-drought year	0.11
p(birth) - *p*(death) in drought year	–0.14
Food yield when living (i.e., milk)	10 units/year
Food yield if sold/slaughtered	20 units
Variables for human food requirements:	
Food requirements (fr) of an adult ($15 years)	15 units/year
Food requirements (fr) of a child (<15 years)	1 unit/year for each year of age
Household food requirement (children + two parents)	fr(ch,t) + 30
Maximum herd size	45

*One stock unit is approximately equal to one female camel, although reproductive potential has been enhanced to account for the fact that, for each camel owned, the Gabbra will also own a number of faster-reproducing sheep and goats (which are not included explicitly in the model to simplify calculations).

Table 13-2. Parameter values used to describe human demographic parameters in the baseline case.

Probability of adult death	0.005 per year
Probability of child death (<4 years)	0.05 per year
Probability of child death (age 4–15)	0.008 per year
Reproductive lifespan of an adult	30 years
Economic lifespan of a household	40 years
Minimum interbirth interval	2 years
Risk of maternal mortality (death in childbirth)	0.005 per birth

those assumed to be the cost of raising one child (as used in Mace 1996b), on the assumption that for each son, a family will also have, on average, one daughter. Thus reproductive and inheritance decisions are based on number of living sons in the family, which empirical evidence suggests is the case for the Gabbra (Mace 1996b; Mace and Sear 1997).

Decisions will depend on the state of the household, which is described by three variables: wealth (w) and number of living sons (ch), and t, the number of time steps of reproductive life that have passed (t is measured in two-year steps). Households have a finite reproductive life of 30 years, or whenever the mother dies if sooner, and a finite economic life of 40 years. Reproductive decisions about whether or not to have a baby are made every two years throughout the reproductive life of the mother. Decisions about how to allocate wealth are made at the end of the parents' life, which is taken as 10 years after the end of their reproductive life—in other words, 40 years after marriage. Thus the generation time in the model is 40 years (which is the mean generation time of males in Gabbra society) and generations do not overlap. The separation in the timing of the decisions to have babies and the decisions about how much wealth to give each son does reflect the human condition. Children take many years to raise, over which time some children may die, parents risk death, and household wealth may rise or fall. Thus parents have to make decisions about when to have another baby based on their current circumstances combined with their knowledge of the environment in which they live, and the value of heritable wealth to their sons' future reproductive success. While the time at which each decision is made may be separated by up to 40 years, the rules of wealth inheritance that the parents plan to follow will influence their reproductive decisions throughout their life.

Stochastic dynamic programming is used to find the optimal strategy set of fertility and inheritance rules for maximizing number of grandchildren. The equations used to determine the optimal policy in a range of different environments are described in the box (taken from Mace 1998).

To model the reproductive decisions of when to have a baby (b) and how many children should receive an inheritance (i), several quantities need to be defined. Consider a household in state w, ch. Then

$p(w, w')$ is the probability that a herd of size w will be a herd of size w' after two years, based on a binomial probability of each female animal giving birth to another surviving female, and a binomial probability that each animal will die. Details of parameters which influence this probability are given in Table 13.1.

$p(ch, ch)$ is the probability that a household with ch sons, will have ch' sons after two years, after having experienced the risk of child mortality ($ch' < ch$). The parameters determining the risk of mortality are shown in Table 13.2.

b is the decision to have another baby ($b = 1$) or not ($b = 0$).

$b = 0$ if $t > 15$ (which is 30 or more years of marriage).

$ps(b)$ is the probability that the mother survives two years, given decision b.

$R(w, ch, T)$ is the reproductive value of a family of ch sons with w units of wealth allocated optimally between them, at the end of the parents' household's life ($T = 20$, which is 40 years after marriage). $R(w, ch, t)$ is the expected reproductive value of a family in state w, ch when t is the number of time steps of reproductive life that have passed. $R(w, 0, 0)$ is therefore the expected reproductive value of newlywed parents with wealth w, at the beginning of their reproductive lives, $R(w, ch, T)$ is estimated for the first iteration of the model (to values between 0 and 1), but thereafter can be calculated by

$$R(w, ch, T) = \max_i R(w/i, 0, 0) \cdot i \qquad (1)$$

where i is the number of sons between which the household wealth will be divided in order to maximize grandchildren, where i is less than or equal to ch. $R(w, ch, t)$ is the reproductive value of a household at time t in state w, ch given that they always make the optimal decision b, and it can be calculated from $R(w, ch, t + 1)$ by

$$R(w, ch, t) = \max_b \Sigma_{w'ch'}(p(w, w') \cdot (p(ch, ch') \cdot (ps(b) \cdot R$$
$$(w' - fr(ch, t), ch' = b, t + 1) + (1 - ps(b)) \cdot R(w' - fr(ch, t), ch', T) \qquad (2)$$

where the summation is over all possible values of w' and ch' and $fr(ch, t)$ is the food requirements of a family of ch sons aged t (see Table 13.2 for parameters that influence $fr(ch, t)$). If w falls to zero at any time, the household is considered destitute, and fitness (R) is 0.

Initially, $R(w, ch, T)$ is simply estimated (to values where $R(\max_w, \max_{ch} = 1$ and $R(0, ch, T) = 0$ and $R(w, 0, T) = 0$). $R(w, ch, T - 1)$ can then be calculated from equation (2), as can $R(w, ch, T - 2)$ and thus, by backward iteration, after 20 time steps $R(w, 0, 0)$ is calculated and the optimal scheduling of births over the whole reproductive lifespan is also known. When $t = 0$, $R(w, ch, T)$ for the next iteration is recalculated by equation 1, which gives the optimal value of i over all combinations of w and ch. $R(w, ch, T)$ is then normalized (by dividing all values by $R(\max_w, \max_{ch}, T)$ and the process is repeated. After a small number of iterations, $R(w, ch, t)$ and the optimal values of i and b for each value of w and ch converge This is the optimal strategy set of fertility and inheritance rules for maximizing grandparental fitness (from Mace 1998).

The model is used to predict both the decision rules that parents should follow to maximize their grandparental reproductive success (whether or not they should have a baby and the number of sons between which they should divide their wealth) for each state of wealth and current family size that they may find themselves in. These rules can be used to find the population outcomes of a group of people following those decision rules. The population outcomes are determined by running a simulation of a population following the optimal decision rules, subject to the same environment for which that decision rule is optimal. That environment includes, of course, the stochasticity inherent in the system, which has been taken into account in determining the optimal decision rules. The starting conditions for the simulation were estimated for the first iteration. Thereafter, the distribution of herd sizes at household formation gained by inheritance from parents, generated by the model, is used as the starting state of the population. After a small number of iterations, a stable distribution of initial herd sizes is reached.

RESULTS

Reproductive Decision Making in a Range of Environments

The model is used to explore how we would expect reproductive decisions, and hence population outcomes, to be influenced by environmental circumstances. I explore these changes by comparing outcomes with a baseline case. The baseline case is that of the Gabbra cohort shown in Figure 13.1, who live in the system just described, characterized by the parameter values which are given in Tables 13.1 and 13.2. I have shown elsewhere (Mace 1998) that both the predicted range of completed family sizes and the average allocation of wealth that each new family inherited are broadly in line with that observed in the Gabbra. The aim here is to see which variables would cause these patterns to change. It is in this sense that modeling can be most useful. In the real world, opportunities rarely arise whereby individual variables are altered in a controlled way, such that the effects of such actions can be observed. A modeling framework such as this one allows us to explore which environmental changes might be expected to influence reproductive decisions, and what the response and impact on the population might be.

Figures 13.2–13.5 show optimal decision rules or stable state population distributions for four different environments: the baseline case, a high costs case (where it assumed that the cost of raising a child is double that of the baseline), a low drought probability case (where it is assumed droughts only occur half as often, raising the mean and reducing the variance in the productivity and growth rate of the herd), and a low mortality case (where all extrinsic mortality risks are an order of magnitude lower than the baseline case).

Figure 13.2 shows the optimal fertility strategy in each of these four cases. The fertility strategy shown is the optimal strategy for a couple that has been married for 20 years, who could thus have between 0 and 10 children, and have another 10

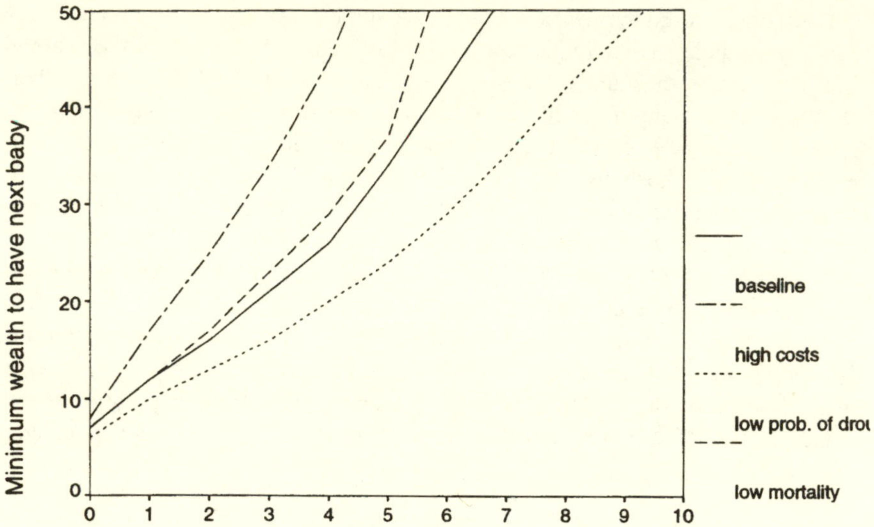

Figure 13.2. The optimal decision rule of the minimum wealth needed to have another baby, based on the number of living sons you already have, shown for four different environments: the baseline case (line), high costs of children (dashed and dotted line), low probability of drought (dotted line), and low mortality risk (dashed line).

years of reproductive life remaining. The line indicates the optimal number of sons for that level of wealth. Parents in households in the area above the line, who have more children than the optimum for their level of wealth, would reduce their expected grandparental fitness if they had another baby. If a child died or the herd size increased, they might move into a region where they were below the line again, and thus they should have another baby. Thus decision making is dynamic, changing with current circumstances. Parents are predicted to quickly "replace" dead children.

In all cases shown in Figure 13.2, wealth would be expected to be positively correlated with reproductive success. This correlation has been shown in numerous traditional societies, including the Gabbra (Mace 1996a). The wealth at which it is optimal to have the first child is not especially sensitive to environmental conditions, but thereafter the environmental parameters altered here do have effects, in some cases marked effects, on the minimum wealth at which to have subsequent children.

Figure 13.3 shows the stable distribution of completed family sizes (living sons) that would result for women who survived their entire reproductive lives, in each of the four environments. Most families are predicted to have many fewer than the maximum possible number of sons, in any of the environments modeled.

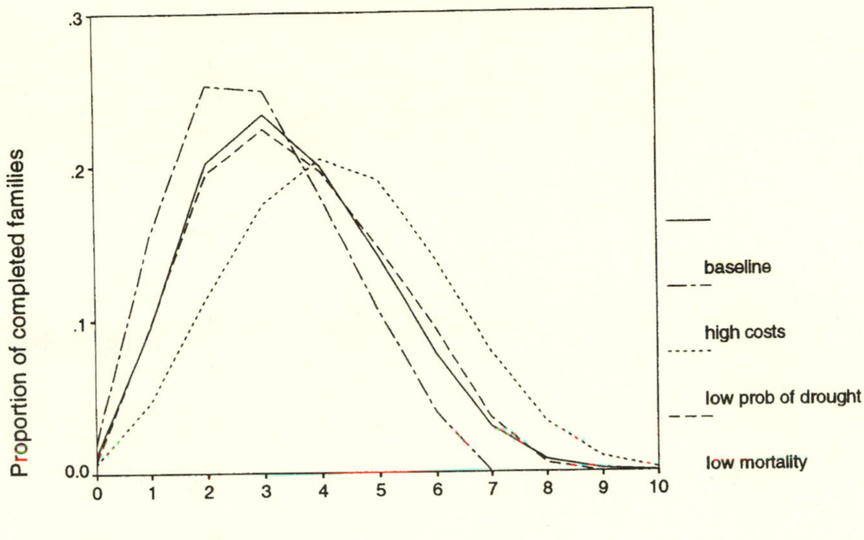

Figure 13.3. Predicted stable-state distribution of completed family sizes for households after 40 years of marriage, for different environments: the baseline case (line), high costs of children (dashed and dotted line), low probability of drought (dotted line), and low mortality risk (dashed line).

Figure 13.4 shows the decision rule for the optimal inheritance of wealth between sons at the end of the parents' economic lives. In all cases, the maximum number of sons to be given an inheritance depends strongly on parental wealth. The wealthier the parents, the more sons they will give herds to. The lines are not curved, indicating that the size of the inherited herds would not increase with parental wealth unless the number of sons living at that time was below the maximum to given an inheritance. If the number of sons they have is above that maximum, then no parental fitness advantage is gained by giving the "extra sons" any inheritance. Primogeniture, in this case, appears to be a response to poverty rather than wealth. I have shown elsewhere that, in the Gabbra, the more elder brothers a man has, the more he is disadvantaged with respect to inherited wealth, his age at marriage, and his reproductive success (Mace 1996a).

Figure 13.5 shows the stable distribution of initial herd sizes (i.e., those herds inherited by sons starting their own households) predicted in each of the four environments. As is evident from Figure 13.4, very few individuals are predicted to be given very large herds, as the division of resources between many sons (if they have them) is a better reproductive strategy for wealthy families.

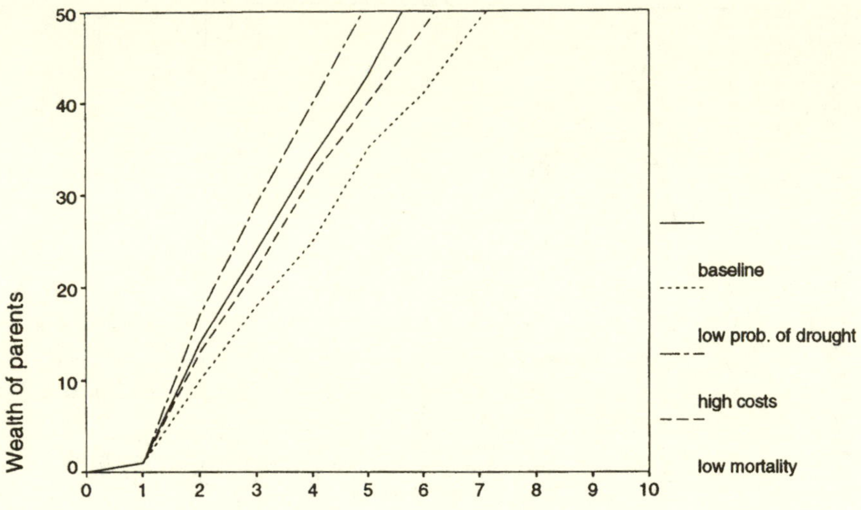

Figure 13.4. The predicted maximum number of sons among whom the household herd should be divided, given the level of parental wealth, for four different environments: the baseline case (line), high costs of children (dashed and dotted line), low probability of drought (dotted line), and low mortality risk (dashed line).

Which Effects Are Most Likely to Cause a Demographic Transition?

Reducing the Risk of Drought. It is clear that simply improving the productivity and reliability of the subsistence base is not predicted to lead to any of the effects generally considered to be a demographic transition; in fact the opposite occurs. The minimum wealth at which it is optimal to have another baby is significantly reduced, for all family sizes, and thus fertility above the level seen in the baseline case is predicted. Completed family sizes are significantly larger, and the inheritance given to each of those children is slightly smaller, such that the distribution of household wealth with which each new generation starts married life is slightly toward the poorer end of the spectrum than in the baseline case. When living conditions are easier, parents can afford more children and do not need to be so generous to each child in order to maximize their grandparental reproductive success.

Reducing the Risk of Mortality. A reduction in mortality is probably considered one of the most important correlates of fertility decline, although it can either precede or follow it (Cleland 1995). The case I model here investigates the lower-

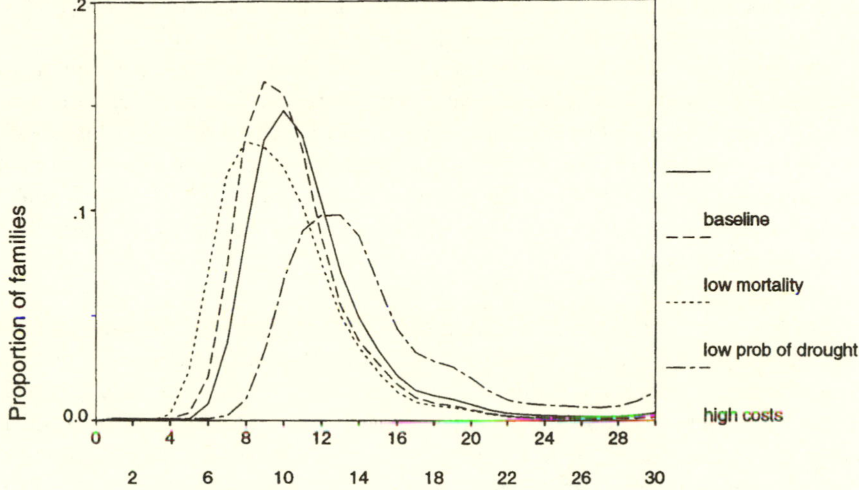

Figure 13.5. The predicted stable-state distribution of the wealth of new families at household formation, which is the amount received in inheritance from parents, shown for four environments: the baseline case (line), high costs of children (dashed and dotted line), low probability of drought (dotted line), and low mortality risk (dashed line).

ing of mortality by an order of magnitude, which is the difference, in many cases, between the developed and developing world; it is also a level of difference that can nearly be achieved in developing countries when effective medical services are provided in an area that previously had none (e.g., Pison et al. 1993; Weaver and Beckerleg 1993). The model predicts that reducing mortality will definitely decrease number of births, as decisions are dependent on number of living children. Dead children are replaced by more births whenever possible. Numerous demographic studies have shown this to occur.

What is of interest here, however, is that the effect of a substantial decline in mortality on other aspects of reproductive and inheritance strategies is relatively small. Having children that die does waste time and resources, leading to slightly lower wealth and fewer new families each generation. The minimum wealth at which it is optimal to have another baby is higher in the low-mortality environment, especially for parents with large families. This compensates, almost perfectly, for those children that would be expected to be lost in the baseline case, such that the stable distributions of completed family sizes are very similar in the baseline and low-mortality environments. The maximum number of sons to be given an inheritance, for a given level of wealth, is slightly higher in the low-mortality scenario—each son needs slightly less if he will not be wasting resources on raising children that do not survive. But the difference is not great. This model does assume that most mortality is concentrated among very young children, and the impact of higher mortality might be greater if it occurred throughout childhood; however in most societies it is the infants who are at the greatest risk of death.

Demographers have focused on changes in fertility (i.e., rates of giving birth) not least because they are relatively easy to measure. But it is living children that really matter. Lowering mortality does lower fertility, but, according to this model, it is not expected to lower family size substantially or increase the level of parental investment in each child. These are probably the two most characteristic features of post-transition families, so we cannot look to reduced mortality alone to explain demographic transitions.

High Cost of Children. Doubling the costs of children causes a marked change in both fertility and inheritance strategies. The minimum wealth at which to have another baby is much higher than in the baseline case. This leads to much smaller completed families, most with only two sons. That the costs of children are expected to influence reproductive rate is a common theme of examinations of reproductive rate in economics and anthropology (albeit with varying theoretical justifications). The framework presented here is clearly based on reproductive success, and it allows the extent of the effect to be predicted precisely if the relevant parameter values are known.

The number of sons to be given an inheritance, for each level of wealth, is lower than the baseline case, and each son is given a larger inheritance. This leads to more couples starting out their married life with larger inherited herd sizes. The average family in the stable population is wealthier.

These are all features of post-transition societies. An increase in costs of children could be associated with sending children to school, either because school costs money or because their labor is lost to the household economy when they are at school. Education is frequently cited as a correlate of low fertility, although most demographers concentrate on the educational status of the mother rather than the costs of educating her children, which this model suggests might be more explanatory of her fertility. Why parents feel the need to educate children is beyond the scope of this model, although it does seem unlikely that uneducated children would be successful (either economically or in competition for mates) in societies where all the other children were educated.

CONCLUSION AND DISCUSSION

Increasing parental investment in children is the key to decreases in fertility. When inherited wealth makes an important contribution to fitness and the costs of successfully raising children are high, small families are favored. Further, the model suggests that these conditions will be associated with a wealthier population in general. The model described here is not explicitly based on a society in a developed country, but these are factors that might change as a less-developed society becomes more developed. All parents like to raise children at least to a standard of living approaching their own, and parents in modern societies frequently refer to the cost of education and similar costs as deterrents of large completed family size. In developed societies, girls are generally as costly as boys, and biased inheritance with respect to sex or birth order is not popular (Judge and Hrdy 1992). In some cases it is not even legal; for example, primogeniture was outlawed in nineteenth-century France, causing a marked decline in fertility at that time (Johansson 1987). If it is assumed that all children, rather than just sons, are costly and benefit from inheritance, then models such as those described here could clearly predict very small family sizes as optimal.

It could be argued that the presence of government-funded support systems may have ameliorated or even removed the costs of large families in some modern societies. One would not necessarily expect our decision rules to keep pace with recent social and political changes of this nature and reach an optimum, although there is plenty of evidence that economic change can have a near-instant effect on birth rates: fertility in East Germany dropped dramatically after unification with West Germany in 1989, when many state benefits relating to children were removed (Conrad et al. 1996). Hoem (1993) documents an increase in the fertility of Swedish women in the 1980s in response to increasingly generous maternity benefits. Thus our reproductive decisions are constantly influenced by our environment, even in modern, industrial societies.

Why Do Richer People Have Smaller Families?

All the cases modeled here do, however, predict a positive correlation between wealth and fertility (as do other evolutionary models such as that in Rogers 1995); yet such a correlation has not been widely demonstrated in post-transition societies. Frequently, area-level or country-level statistics are used to explore comparative relationships. Such comparisons frequently lead to the conclusion that wealth is negatively related to reproductive success. Some have used this to argue that evolutionary models are not appropriate models of contemporary human reproductive behavior (Vining 1986). Yet, where this relationship has been investigated in clearly defined, homogeneous populations, such as is frequently the case in anthropological studies, the opposite is found.

What is shown here is that, when costs of children are high, levels of inheritance will also be high, and the average wealth of families will be high. Thus, if costs of children vary between groups, then the average wealth of those groups is also likely to vary. An important conclusion of this finding is that reproductive decisions concerning parental investment have to be investigated with respect to a very clearly defined group, if they are to be understood in ecological terms. While none of the models presented here predicts anything but a positive relationship between wealth and reproductive success within a homogeneous group, they do show that if a society actually comprised several different groups, each of which are following different decision rules, then this correlation between wealth and fertility may break down. If different people have different fertility policies, perhaps because they have different risks of mortality or different costs of raising children, or different perceptions of these risks and costs (which is not true of an unstratified society such as the Gabbra, but is true of most modern, conglomerate societies containing peoples of many different origins), then it is likely that those in a higher income bracket might be following a decision rule leading to a smaller family than another family with a lower level of wealth, because they are following a different policy. When looking at the correlation between wealth and fertility across society as a whole, fertility and wealth may appear to be decoupled or even negatively correlated, because the richest families would have the smallest number of children.

Does Parental Investment Increase Children's Reproductive Potential in Modern Societies?

A fully evolutionary model of high parental investment does require that increased parental investment is rewarded by increasing the reproductive potential of those children. Education is the most obvious and expensive form of parental investment in modern societies, but it is generally considered to have a negative influence on fertility. However, as I stated above, it would be most informative to look within very homogeneous groups to see whether the education individuals received increased their fertility relative to others in that group. Part of the difficulty in addressing this problem is that there are few studies of modern populations in developed countries that concentrate on strictly homogeneous groups. One rare example is that of Hubback (1957), who charts the reproductive success of English women graduates from Britain's best universities in the mid-twentieth century, clearly a highly educated and socially and financially privileged group. Those who went to Oxford and Cambridge were a particularly select group, as only a very small minority of colleges in these universities admitted women up until less than twenty years ago. I have reproduced some of Hubback's findings in Table 13.3. Family wealth correlated positively with reproductive success. So, incidentally, did the class of degree that these women obtained: those attaining the highest marks in exams had the most children. It is not possible to dissociate wealth from educational achievement in these figures. But it is interesting to note that those features traditionally associated with fertility decline were clearly associated with enhanced fertility within this homogeneous group.

Kaplan and his colleagues (1995) found that ethnicity and birth cohort were much stronger determinants of fertility than was wealth in a large sample of New Mexican men (also see Chapters 9 and 14, this volume). Children of parents from large families had lower levels of educational achievement and lower incomes as adults, so some features of the reduced level of parental investment had the potential to influence future generations of offspring. Hispanics, originally from Mex-

Table 13-3. Correlates of family size among women who graduated from English universities between 1930 and 1950 (adapted from Hubback 1957)

A. Fertility and income.
Upper figure: family with less than ,1,000 per year
Lower figure: family with more than ,1,000 per year (in italics)

	Duration of marriage (years)			
Age at marriage	*5–6*	*7–9*	*10–14*	*15–25*
< 25	1.4	2.1	2.4	2.6
	2.5	*1.9*	*2.7*	*2.8*
25–29	1.4	2.5	1.9	2.0
	1.9	*2.3*	*2.3*	*2.9*
30–34	0.6	1.1	1.8	
	1.7	*1.9*	*1.8*	

B. Fertility and academic achievement. Class of degree indicates the standard of marks received in final exams, first class being the highest level of achievement and pass being the lowest. Competition for places at Oxford and Cambridge was more intense than for other universities, especially for women.

Degree (class)	*Oxford and Cambridge*	*n*	*Other Universities*	*n*
First	2.32	72	2.02	53
Second	2.27	366	1.64	241
Third and Fourth	2.15	104	1.37	41
Pass	2.0	19	1.57	181

ico, had higher fertility than Anglos, and Kaplan and colleagues argue that some are reducing their fertility over time in order to take advantage of better educational opportunities, which are followed by opportunities to earn higher incomes. However, those with the most children also had the highest number of grandchildren; thus, in this case, there is no evidence that a decision to limit fertility for educational or other benefits is evolutionarily adaptive in the long run.

What Are the Implications for Development Projects?

A reduction in the size of families is frequently an explicit aim of development agencies (whether governments or NGOs). This is usually addressed by providing advice on family planning, and making modern contraceptives available. I myself have used this approach when working for an NGO with the Gabbra. Rural Gabbra women were interested in hearing about contraception, but not because they felt any pressing need for it. Infertility was far more likely to be raised as an issue that could benefit from medical intervention. Faced with my own data and my theoretical perspective on it, I should have realized sooner that most of these women, who were living a traditional lifestyle that may not have changed greatly since the adoption of pastoralism, were probably having roughly the number of children they wanted to have.

It is changes in economic and environmental circumstances that are more likely to trigger an interest in small families. Development projects are, inadvertently, frequently concentrating on some areas that are likely to move things in the direction of larger, not smaller, families. Improving the productivity and reliability of the subsistence base is generally the main objective of most integrated rural development projects. Other things being equal, that is likely to push fertility up. This can be counterproductive, even causing an overall decline in the average wealth of households. Reducing mortality is the obvious aim of any project with a public health component. That is likely to reduce fertility (number of births), but this model predicts it will have little effect on the number of living children in a family.

This model suggests that increasing the cost of children to parents is the factor that is likely to reduce family size and, where resources are heritable, will also improve the general wealth of the population, as parents leave each child a larger inheritance. Increasing the costs of children is unlikely ever to be the explicit aim of a development project. Nor is there any real reason why it should be. Increasing the cost of raising children increases hardship, and the population becomes wealthier partly because poor families fall out of the system. Innovations that reduce the drudgery of life, such as improving water supplies, probably reduce the cost of children and thus would be predicted to push fertility up. However, educational uptake is frequently an aim of governments and NGOs. Governments pass as much of this cost as possible onto parents. If parents know that a good education is likely to produce good returns, they will take it more seriously, and consider having fewer, but better-educated, children. If mortality is reduced, then investing in children at a younger age will also be more likely to occur.

While it is tempting to exclude modern societies from evolutionary analyses, I believe that evolutionary models have great potential to explain our decision making in this area. It is an open question as to how much of our behavior in modern environments is adaptive, but an understanding of how our decision making on these matters is likely to be guided must be useful. Most social scientists have been slow to appreciate that evolutionary theory has anything to offer their fields of enquiry. Yet increasingly, evolutionary models making testable predictions about human behavior have been found to be useful and successful. Evolutionary demography is one such field.

SUMMARY

1. In most human societies, the inheritance of wealth is an important part of parental investment. Patterns of wealth inheritance and other reproductive decisions, including family size, would be expected to influence each other. Here I present an adaptive model of human reproductive decision making under condi-

tions in which there is inheritance of wealth, using a state-dependent dynamic model. Two decisions made by parents are considered: when to have another baby, and thus the pattern of reproduction through life, and how to allocate resources between children at the end of the parents' life. Optimal decision rules are those that maximize the number of grandchildren.

2. Decisions are assumed to depend on the state of the parents, which is described at any time by two variables: number of living sons and wealth. The dynamics of the model are based on a traditional African pastoralist system, but it is general enough to approximate to any means of subsistence where an increase in the amount of wealth owned increases the capacity for future production of resources. Over a range of environmental conditions, a range of levels of fertility are optimal; however, reproduction is always predicted to be below the maximum possible rate.

3. Most traditional societies are now undergoing a transition to lower fertility, known as the demographic transition. The model is used to examine the possible effect of different variables to see which, if any, produce changes in the population similar to those observed during demographic transitions: the effects of reducing mortality, reducing the unpredictability of the environment, and increasing the costs of raising children on fertility and wealth inheritance strategies are explored.

4. Reducing mortality has very little effect on completed family size or on the wealth children inherit. It has little effect on the average wealth of the population.

5. Reducing the risk of drought (increasing the productivity and reliability of the subsistence base) increases family size without increasing average household wealth. In fact, the model suggests the overall effect on the population could be counterproductive, with average household wealth declining slightly.

6. Increasing the costs of raising children decreases optimal fertility and increases the inheritance left to each child at each level of wealth, and has the potential to reduce fertility to very low levels. The average wealth of households increases. Only increasing parental investment captures the essential features of demographic transitions.

7. The results illustrate that reproductive decisions have to be examined in homogeneous groups if they are to be understood in ecological terms. Within homogeneous groups, a positive relationship between wealth and reproductive success is predicted. But across a heterogeneous group (such as, for example, country-level data) the model explains why those with the greatest wealth might also have the smallest families.

ACKNOWLEDGMENTS

This research was funded by a University Research Fellowship from The Royal Society of London and a grant from the European Commission. A version of this paper was presented at the 1996 American Anthropological Association meeting in San Francisco.

REFERENCES

Alam, M. 1995. Birth-spacing and infant and early childhood mortality in a high fertility area of Bangladesh: Age-dependent and interactive effects. *Journal of Biosocial Science* 27:393–404.

Anderies, J. M. 1996. An adaptive model for predicting !Kung reproductive performance: a stochastic dynamic programming approach. *Ethology and Sociobiology* 17:221–246.

Beauchamp, G. 1994. The functional analysis of human fertility decisions. *Ethology and Sociobiology* 15:31–53.

Bohler, E., and S. Bergstrom. 1995. Subsequent pregnancy affects morbidity of previous child. *Journal of Biosocial Sciences* 27:431–442.

Cleland, J. 1995. Obstacles to fertility decline in developing countries. In *Human Reproductive Decisions,* R. Dunbar, ed. Pp. 207–229. London: Macmillan.

Conrad, C., M. Lechner, and W. Werner. 1996. East German fertility after unification: Crisis or adaptation? *Population Development Review* 22:331–358.

Fisher, R. A. 1958. The genetical theory of natural selection. 2nd rev. ed. New York: Dover.

Hartung, J. 1982. Polygyny and the inheritance of wealth. *Current Anthropology* 23:1–12.

Hoem, J. 1993. Public policy as the fuel of fertility—effects of a policy reform on the pace of childbearing in Sweden in the 1980s. *Acta Sociologica* 36:19–31.

Houston, A. I., C. W. Clark, J. McNamara, and M. Mangel. 1988. Dynamic models in behavioural and evolutionary ecology. *Nature* 332:29–34.

Hubback, J. 1957. *Wives Who Went to College.* London: Heinnemann.

Johansson, S. 1987. Status anxiety and demographic contraction of privileged populations. *Population Development Review* 13:439–470.

Judge, D. S., and S. B. Hrdy. 1992. Allocation of accumulated resources among close kin—inheritance in Sacramento, California, 1980–1984. *Ethology and Sociobiology* 15:495–522.

Kaplan, H., J. Lancaster, J. A. Bock, and S. E. Johnson. 1995. Does observed fertility maximize fitness among New Mexican men? A test of an optimality model and a new theory of parental investment in the embodied capital of offspring. *Human Nature* 6:325–360.

Lack, D. 1968 *Ecological Adaptations for Breeding in Birds*. London: Methuen.

Legrand, T., and J. F. Phillips. 1996. The effect of fertility reductions on infant and child mortality: Evidence from Matlab in Rural Bangladesh. *Population Studies* 50:51–68.

Low, B. 1991. Reproductive life in 19th century Sweden: An evolutionary perspective on demographic phenomena. *Ethology and Sociobiology* 12:411–448.

Mace, R. 1996a. Biased parental investment and reproductive success in Gabbra pastoralists. *Behavioral Ecology and Sociobiology* 38:75–81.

———. 1996b. When to have another baby: A dynamic model of reproductive decision–making and evidence from Gabbra pastoralists. *Ethology and Sociobiology* 17:263–274.

———. 1998. The co-evolution of human fertility and wealth inheritance strategies. *Philosophical Transactions of the Royal Society* (London), Series B 353, 389–397.

Mace, R., and R. Sear. 1996. Maternal mortality in a Kenyan pastoralist population. *International. Journal of Gynecology and Obstetrics* 54:137–141.

———. 1997a. Birth interval and the sex of children in a traditional African population: An evolutionary analysis. *Journal of Biosocial Sciences* 29:499–507.

———. 1997b. Reproductive decision-making in the face of demographic risks in Gabbra pastoralists. *Nomadic Peoples,* 1:151–163.

Madise, N. J., and I. Diamond. 1995. Determinants of infant mortality in Malawi: An analysis to control for death clustering within families. *Journal of Biosocial Sciences* 27:95–106.

Mangel, M., and C. W. Clark. 1988. *Dynamic Modelling in Behavioral Ecology*. Princeton: Princeton University Press.

Murdock, G. P. 1967. *Ethnographic Atlas*. Pittsburgh: University of Pittsburgh Press.

Pison, G., J. F. Trape, M. Lefebvre, and C. Enel. 1993. Rapid decline in child mortality in a rural area of Senegal. *International Journal of Epidemiology* 22:72–80.

Rogers, A. 1995. For love or money: The evolution of reproductive and material motivations. In *Human Reproductive Decisions,* R. Dunbar, ed. Pp. 76–95. London: Macmillan.

Ronsmans, C. 1995. Patterns of clustering of child mortality in rural area of Senegal. *Population Studies* 49:443–461. Trivers, R. 1972. Parental investment and sexual selection. In *Sexual Selection and the Descent of Man,* B. Campbell, ed. Pp. 136–179. Chicago: Aldine.

Trivers, R. L., and D. E. Willard. 1973. Natural selection of parental ability to vary the sex ratio of offspring. *Science* 179:90–92.

Vining, D. R. 1986. Social versus reproductive success—the central theoretical problem of human sociobiology. *Behavioral and Brain Sciences* 9:167–260.

Weaver, L. T., and S. Beckerleg. 1993. Is health a sustainable state? A village study in The Gambia. *Lancet* 341:1327–1331.

14

The Evolutionary Economics and Psychology of the Demographic Transition to Low Fertility

HILLARD S. KAPLAN and JANE B. LANCASTER

There is mounting evidence that people in modern state societies in the developed world do not maximize fitness through their fertility decisions (e.g., Irons 1995; Kaplan, Lancaster, Bock, and Johnson 1995; Vining 1986). Observed fertility behavior deviates from the predictions of fitness maximization in two ways. First, and most important, observed fertility is lower than would be predicted based on models of fitness maximization. For example, we showed that among men in Albuquerque, New Mexico, number of third-generation descendants (i.e., grandchildren) is highest among those who produced the most (i.e.,>12) children, yet the observed modal fertility is 2 (Kaplan et al. 1995). Higher parental fertility in modern developed societies is associated with lower achieved educational and economic status of offspring (see Blake 1989 and Downey 1995 for reviews), but the lower earning capacity of children from large families does not decrease their fertility and so there is no apparent fitness reduction associated with lowered parental investment per child.

The second way in which modern behavior deviates from the predictions of simple budget constraint models of quantity-quality tradeoffs is that higher-earning adults produce no more children than their lesser-earning counterparts, even in well-controlled studies. Whereas available data on preindustrial societies consistently exhibit a positive relationship between resources or power and reproductive success (Barkow 1989; Betzig 1986; Boone 1986; Borgerhoff Mulder 1987; Cronk 1991a; Flinn 1986; Hughes 1986; Irons 1995; Kaplan and Hill 1985; Low 1990; Mealey 1985; Turke and Betzig 1985; Voland 1990), studies of post-demographic transition societies either find no relationship (Kaplan, et al., 1995) or a negative one (Lam 1986; Pérusse 1993; Retherford 1993; but see Simons 1974 for data suggesting a positive correlation among wealth and fertility within socioeconomic groups).[1]

An adequate theory of the reduction in fertility in modern states (referred to as "the demographic transition") must accomplish two things. First, it must specify what changes led to a reduction of fertility and the observed relationship between wealth and fitness. Second, it must account for why those changes produced the observed responses within a larger theory of the determinants of fertility in general. From an evolutionary perspective, it is necessary to specify the critical differences between pre- and post-demographic transition societies and to show why the suite of proximate mechanisms that evolved to regulate fertility and parental investment in the past might produce the fertility and parental investment behavior observed in modern, postindustrial societies.

This paper presents the results of an in-depth study of fertility and parental investment among a representative sample of men from Albuquerque, New Mexico. Our goal is to develop and test a general theory of human fertility and parental investment, with a specific focus on explaining recent historical trends in family behavior within developed nations. We present a theoretical framework that unifies life history theory, developed in biology, with human capital and household allocation theories, developed in economics. We then offer a specific theory of modern fertility reduction based upon the emergence of skills-based competitive labor markets. This theory generates a set of empirical predictions that are tested with data derived from the sample of Albuquerque men. The empirical analysis focuses on age at first reproduction, completed fertility, the formation and dissolution of marital and quasi-marital relationships, investment in children, and child outcomes. The analysis examines both historical trends and variation among men within cohorts and time periods.

LIFE HISTORY THEORY AND THE ECONOMICS OF THE FAMILY

Biological and economic theories of life histories and fertility decisions developed independently, yet they share some formal properties and substantive conclusions. They both assume that individuals act to optimize the allocation of limited resources through the life course so as to maximize some currency. Biological models assume that *fitness,* defined in terms of quantity of descendants or the instantaneous growth rate of genes, is the ultimate currency that individuals are designed to maximize. Economic models assume that *utility* or satisfaction is the ultimate currency.

With respect to fertility decisions, both biological and economic approaches treat the problem in terms of a tradeoff between quantity and quality of offspring. This tradeoff is presumed to result from the facts that parents have limited resources to invest in offspring and that each additional offspring necessarily reduces average investment per offspring. Most biological models operationalize this tradeoff as number versus survival of offspring (e.g., Lack 1954, 1968; Lloyd 1987; McGinley and Charnov 1988; Rogers and Blurton Jones 1992; Smith and Fretwell 1974). Natural selection is expected to shape investment per offspring and offspring number so as to maximize the number of surviving offspring.[2]

In economic models (e.g., Becker 1991; Becker and Lewis 1973; Becker and Tomes 1986; de Tray 1973; Willis 1973), parents are thought to derive satisfaction from both child quality and child quantity, and to chose the combination of offspring number and offspring quality that maximizes the satisfaction derived from children and other forms of consumption.[3] In economic models quality is implicitly considered to be an index of the human capital embodied in children. *Human capital* may be defined as a stock of attributes embodied in an individual, such as skills and education, that affect the value of time allocated to labor, and hence affect both earnings and the utility of time spent outside the labor market.

These two approaches can be usefully unified to build on the strengths of each. A major strength of biological models is the causal closure provided by the theory of natural selection and the use of fitness as the currency to be maximized. The theory of evolution by natural selection specifies the causal processes by which the characteristics of organisms change and a justification for why organisms should be designed to maximize fitness. In contrast, the economic assumption that people maximize utility is not derived from a known causal process, but rather is maintained as a working heuristic because it seems to characterize human behavior. Thus, economic models are less specific about the nature of interpersonal utility functions. However, the theory of human capital in economics is much more developed than the corresponding theory of investment in somatic effort in biology.

Figure 14.1 unifies biological and economic approaches with life history decisions by extending the economic concept of human capital to organisms in general (with the term *embodied capital*) and by utilizing biological fitness as the ultimate currency. Ontogeny (the process of development) can be seen as a process in which individuals and their parents invest in a stock of embodied capital. In a physical sense, embodied capital is organized somatic tissue. In a functional sense, embodied capital includes strength, immune competence, coordination, skill, and knowledge, all of which affect the profitability of allocating time and other resources to alternative activities such as resource acquisition, defense from predators and parasites, mating competition, parenting, and social dominance. Since the stock of embodied capital tends to depreciate with time because of physical entropic forces and direct assaults by parasites, predators, and conspecifics, allocations to maintenance such as feeding, cell repair, and vigilance can also be seen as investments in embodied capital. Individuals may invest not only in capital embodied in their own soma, but in the capital embodied in offspring, other relatives, and other individuals with whom they interact.

Figure 14.1 begins with *lifetime income.* Income is defined here in the general sense of the total value of time allocated to alternative activities, such as resource acquisition, childcare, rest, etc. At each age, an individual's income will be a function of her embodied capital. Income can be invested directly in reproductive effort, or in embodied capital. Embodied capital, in turn, can be divided into stocks affecting the ability to acquire the resources for reproduction and stocks affecting the probability of survival.

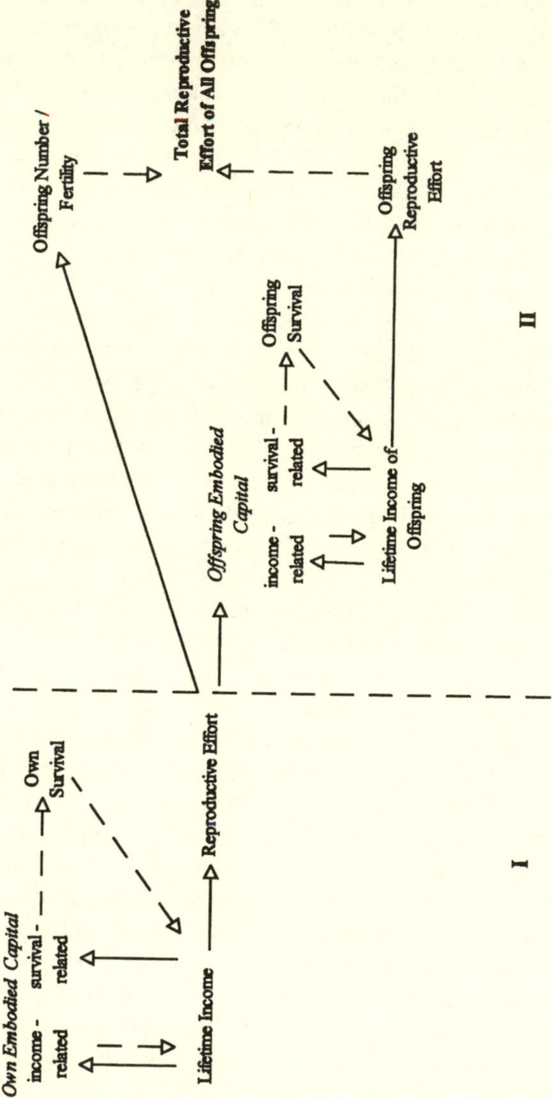

Figure 14.1. Decision model for life history of investments.

The solid arrows depict investment options. The dotted arrows depict the impacts of investments. Investments in income-related capital, such as growth, physical coordination, skills, and knowledge, affect lifetime income through the value or productivity of time in the future. Investments in survival-related capital, such as immune function, predator defense, and tissue repair, affect lifetime income through increasing the expected lifespan of earnings. From an evolutionary point of view, however, income must ultimately be invested in reproduction, since an organism that does not reproduce leaves no descendants. Thus, the first problem acted upon by natural selection is to maximize lifetime allocations to reproduction by optimally allocating income among investments in future income, survival, and reproduction at each age.

The second part of the figure shows the relationships between investments and outcomes for two generations. Here, both the parent and the offspring can invest in the offspring's survival- and income-related capital. For parents, the optimal allocation between fertility and investments in embodied capital of offspring should maximize the total lifetime allocations by offspring to their own reproduction (summed over all offspring). This requires consideration not only of the effects of parental investment on offspring survival, but also on the adult income of offspring as well. If individuals in each generation allocate investments in their own and their offspring's embodied capital optimally, then the "dynastic" or multigenerational fitness of the lineage is maximized.

In this model life histories vary because relationships between investments and outcomes vary ecologically. There is ecological variability in the benefits from investing in income-related capital. The relationships between body size and productivity depend on feeding niche. The value of knowledge, skill, and information-processing ability depends on the type of foods exploited, and more generally on the economy. This is illustrated in Figure 14.2. In panel 2A, two relationships between time invested in development and adult food production are illustrated, representing two different ecologies. In one ecology there is a relatively low payoff to investment in development, and in the other, the payoff is higher. In both ecologies there are increasing returns to investment at low levels of investment (i.e., the slope of the line increases). However, at some point the rate of return begins to diminish with additional time invested in development (i.e., the slope of the line decreases). The principal difference between the two ecologies is that *diminishing returns on investment* occur at a higher level of investment in the high-payoff environment. This difference could be due to the importance of skill or strength in resource production, since skill acquisition and growth require time. In general, the optimum will occur when returns on investment diminish because extra time in development begins to yield a smaller increase in adult income. Thus, the optimum amount of time (T*) to invest in development is lower for the low-skill environment than for the high-skill environment.

Panel 2B illustrates ecological variability in investment in mortality reduction. Depending on local ecology each major class of mortality (predation, disease,

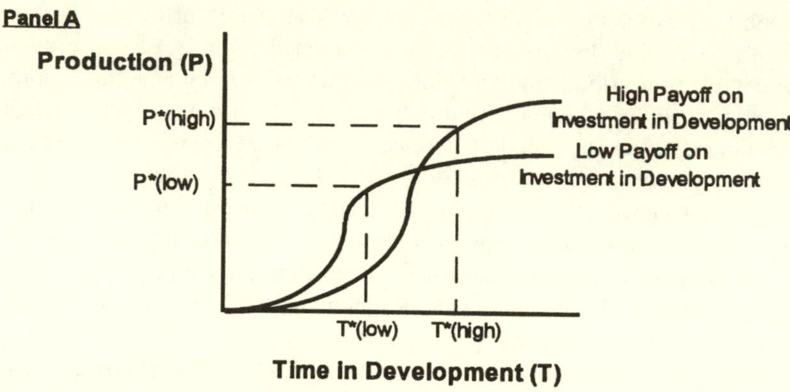

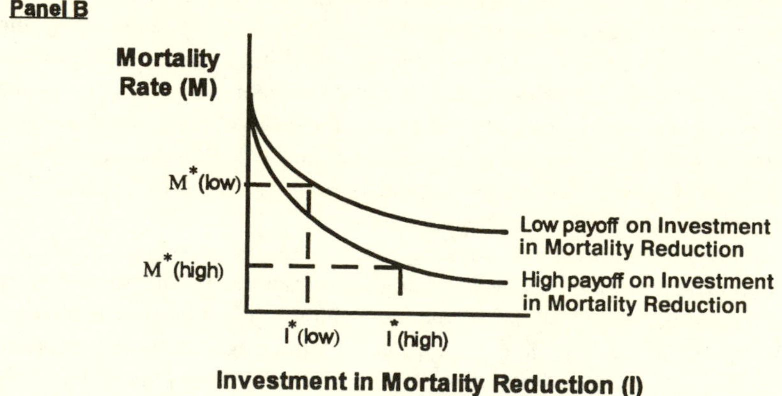

Figure 14.2. Ecological variability in payoffs on investments in development and mortality reduction.

intraspecific violence, accidents, starvation) will exhibit a different relationship between the probability of dying and preventative investments made by the organism. Again, two ecologically variant relationships between investments and mortality are depicted. Returns on investments in lowering mortality diminish earlier in the low-payoff than in the high-payoff environment. For example, Austad and Fischer (1991, 1992, 1993) show that the value of tissue repair in order to slow down the rate of aging depends on the ability to escape predation. Primates and bats, which can leave the ground, suffer lower rates of predation than terrestrial mammals of similar body size. They also age more slowly and therefore live longer. Similarly, mammals living on islands with few predators age more slowly than their conspecifics living in continental environments. Thus, diminishing returns to investment in survival occur at higher levels of investment in low-predation environments.

FERTILITY AND PARENTAL INVESTMENT IN TRADITIONAL HUMAN SOCIETIES: AN ECOLOGICAL MODEL

One of the hallmarks of humanity has been the colonization of most of the world's terrestrial and coastal habitats. The life history theory developed above suggests that natural selection would favor sensitivity to environmental variability in returns on investment and the evolution of proximate mechanisms that detect diminishing returns on investment in survival and future income. One of the most important problems in understanding contemporary demographic processes is that the proximate physiological and psychological mechanisms underlying fertility, parental investment, and family formation evolved primarily in the context of a hunting and gathering lifestyle. All but the most recent 10,000 years of evolution in the hominid line occurred among foraging populations. Since most people now live in environments radically different from our ancestral environment, we require an understanding of how our evolved physiology and psychology responds to modern environments. Our goal for this section is to analyze the demands of the hunting and gathering lifeway as they vary across ecologies and to specify the kinds of proximate mechanisms that are likely to have evolved in the past in order to understand how people will react to modern environments.

Compared with those of other primates and mammals, human life histories have three distinctive characteristics: (1) an exceptionally long lifespan with older nonreproductive individuals supporting their offspring's reproduction, (2) an extended period of juvenile nutritional dependence coupled with the provisioning of young of different ages, and (3) marriage and the involvement of men in the care and provisioning of children (Kaplan 1997; Lancaster and Lancaster 1987). Since all hunting and gathering groups for which we have substantial information exhibit these three characteristics, it is likely that some fundamental features of the traditional human lifeway account for their evolution. Kaplan (1996, 1997) has proposed that those three features of the human life course are interrelated outcomes of a feeding strategy emphasizing nutrient-dense, difficult-to-acquire foods. The logic underlying this proposal is that effective adult foraging requires an extended training period during which production at young ages is sacrificed for increased productivity later in life. The returns on investment in training depend on adult survival rates, favoring increased investment in mortality reduction. An extended postreproductive, yet still productive, period supports both earlier onset of reproduction by next-generation individuals and the ability to provision multiple dependent young at different stages of development (see Kaplan, Hill, Lancaster, and Hurtado, in press, for empirical tests of this theory). This life history pattern implies the existence of two critical phases of human parental investment. The first phase is infancy, in which children are fed through lactation and require intensive care. The second phase is childhood and adolescence, in which children require less direct supervision and are provisioned with solid foods (see Kaplan 1994 and Kaplan et al. 2000 for data showing that this second period can extend into the late teen years in traditional hunting and gathering groups and forager-horticulturalists).

Since humans generally nurse only one infant at a time, the intensity and length of infant investment is a critical decision variable determining fertility. With respect to infant survival, there are two critical forms of parental investment: breast milk and direct care. It is useful to think of infancy in terms of a gradual transition from complete dependence on breast milk to complete dependence on other foods. The provision of breast milk increases during the first few months of life as the baby grows, and then supplemental foods are introduced at about four to six months of age, constituting an increasing proportion of food in the child's diet as its caloric needs increasingly exceed the energy its mother can provide with breast milk (Oftedal 1984; Vitzthum 1994; Whitehead and Paul 1981). Ecological factors affect the relationship between the rate of these transitions and offspring survival (Lee et al. 1991). The digestibility of available foods is one such factor. The level of maturation of the child's digestive system along with the kinds of foods available will determine the optimal age for introducing new foods and the optimal proportion of milk to other foods in the child's diet at each age (Sheard and Walker 1988). Disease organisms are another factor. The density and intensity of diseases that infect individuals through ingestion should be related to length of the breast-feeding period for two reasons. First, breast milk increases the child's immunocompetence (Hanson 1982; Howie et al. 1990). Second, babies that are sickly require the high-quality nutrition provided by breast milk (Sheard and Walker 1988). On the other hand, the relative importance of diseases that are unaffected by diet should be positively correlated with the speed of weaning, since breast milk will account for less of the variance in survival (Borgerhoff Mulder 1992; Harpending et al. 1990; Pennington and Harpending 1988).

In addition, because infancy and early childhood are also the periods during which offspring require the most direct care, maternal food production, and hence her budget for reproduction, should be affected by ecological factors affecting the relationship between direct care and survival. The availability of safe spaces for children, which should be negatively associated with mobility, and the dangers in the environment should both affect the age-specific benefits of direct maternal care. For example, Kaplan and Dove (unpublished data) found that Ache mothers spend much more time in tactile contact with infants and young children when on mobile foraging trips (about 90% of all observations of children under 4 years of age) than at the settlement where safe spaces are cleared for children, even after time spent walking and carrying children is excluded from the analysis.

Parental investment during childhood and adolescence depends on the age-specific productivity of children, which in turn is also likely to depend on ecological factors. The dangers associated with acquisition of different food types should affect whether and how much children forage. This issue has received extensive treatment in a series of papers contrasting the foraging behavior of !Kung and Hadza children (see for example Blurton Jones, Hawkes, and O'Connell, in press;

Hawkes, O'Connell, and Blurton Jones 1997, and references cited therein). The costs and benefits of children's food production differ for !Kung and Hadza foragers. In the !Kung environment, foraging is dangerous for children because it is easy to get lost and food resources are far from water holes where camps are located. In the Hadza environment, topographic relief makes it harder to get lost and fruits are often abundant near camps. This favors greater protection of children and more provisioning by parents among the !Kung than among the Hadza.

In addition, as discussed above, the suite of resources available and the impacts of skill and strength on foraging return rates should determine both children's time allocation to productive labor and the total amount they produce (cf. Bock 1995; Draper and Harpending 1987; Hawkes et al. 1995). Children also face a potential tradeoff between early productivity and later adult production. This tradeoff is clearly evident in the development of hunting skills. Although boys spend a great deal of time hunting during the teen years in many hunting and gathering societies (see Blurton Jones et al. 1999 and Kaplan 1997 for data and discussions), they have very low hunting success until their mid-twenties. Thus, parents face decisions about how long and how much to provision children and adolescents on the basis of features of the environment that affect the productivity of unskilled and smaller individuals, the dangers associated with food production, and the impacts of nonproductive practice/learning on later adult productivity. It is the shape of the relationship between investments and outcomes that determines the optimal amount to invest. When returns on an extra unit of investment in offspring income or survival produce a smaller fitness improvement than a comparable investment in fertility, it no longer pays to invest more in the offspring, even if the investment is beneficial. A slightly longer nursing period, a slightly lower work requirement for children, and slightly more food given to children than are actually observed probably would increase their survival or adult income. However, natural selection appears to have favored people who possess psychological mechanisms that detect diminishing returns and to adjust investment accordingly (Borgerhoff Mulder 1992; Harpending et al. 1990; Pennington and Harpending 1988).

The length and intensity of parental investment during these two phases affect the number of children that people can afford to raise. Thus, there must be some mechanisms by which these parental investment decisions translate into number of children born. This translation process appears to be performed by physiological mechanisms in women. Although the exact details of the process still remain to be identified, it is clear that breast-feeding affects female fecundity by decreasing the likelihood of ovulation, and perhaps implantation (Ellison 1990; Ellison et al. 1993; Jones and Palloni 1994; McNeilly et al. 1985). The impacts of provisioning on fertility also appear to be mediated through the effects of women's net energy balance (energy consumed less energy expended) on the likelihood of ovulation and implantation (Ellison et al. 1993; Huffman et al. 1987; Hurtado and Hill 1990; Prentice and Whitehead 1987). Women's net energy balance should decrease as more food is given to children and as women work more to produce the food consumed by a family. These two main constraints on reproduction, the length of the infancy period and the net energy balance among women, may vary in their importance in different ecological contexts. When food is abundant, the main constraint on fertility may be the health impacts of weaning. This would likely correspond to periods of maximum population growth rates (cf. Hill and Hurtado 1996: chap. 14). When population density is high relative to the productivity of the environment, the net energy flow to women may be most important.

To summarize, the proposal here is that selection acts on the coordinated outcome of mechanisms that regulate both parental investment and fertility. Investment may be regulated by psychological mechanisms that direct attention to fundamental relationships between investments and outcomes and that detect diminishing returns to investment. Actual decisions will be the product of those mechanisms and some reliance on cultural norms that benefit from accumulated experience. The regulation of fertility may be controlled primarily by physiological mechanisms responsive to breast-feeding regimes and net energy balance. This is not to say that people in traditional societies do not think about fertility. The inability to produce a child is one of the most common reasons given for divorce by people in traditional societies (Rosenblatt et al. 1973). Short birth spacing is also recognized as a problem. For example, the Ache have a term for too short of a birth space, and this can sometimes lead to infanticide.

The critical constraints on fertility and parental investment appear to be the time needed to give intensive care to infants and very young children, and the energy to feed parents and multiple children of varying ages. The physiological mechanisms tracking breast-feeding and energy balance have evolved to respond to those constraints. In environments where the critical constraints on fertility and parental investment include extrasomatic resources, such as land, cattle, or money, it is unclear whether we should expect adaptive responses, given this suite of evolved proximate mechanisms. Since parental investment in modern societies does entail many kinds of goods and services other than food and direct care, there is reason to suspect that nonadaptive responses are likely.

PARENTAL INVESTMENT AND LOW FERTILITY IN INDUSTRIAL SOCIETIES: THE COMPETITIVE-LABOR-MARKET MODEL

The next step in the analysis is to determine which aspects of modernization, in interaction with those evolved psychological and physiological mechanisms, led people to lower their fertility. In brief, our theory is that *skills-based competitive labor markets* increased the payoffs to parental investment. When wages are earned in skills-based labor markets in conjunction with lower child and adult mortality rates, parents do not detect diminishing returns on investment in children until they reach very high levels. This leads to a desired investment per child that does not permit more than two or three children. There is a conflict between the fertility schedule that our physiological response system would produce and consciously desired fertility. This has stimulated the demand for effective birth control technology.

In order to understand the payoffs on parental investment in modern societies, it is necessary to understand the processes by which wages are determined (see Willis 1987 for a review). Given modern technologies of production, profit-maximizing firms will combine labor and capital in an optimal mix to minimize the costs of producing the goods and services they sell. The value of labor in the production of goods, however, depends on the skills and knowledge embodied in workers. In general, workers with greater education and skills are more valuable (i.e., add more to production for every hour on the job) than less skilled, less educated workers. At the same time, acquiring skills and education is a costly process, because it takes time (e.g., for every year spent in full-time schooling, there is a year of lost earnings) and often requires resource investments (e.g., in the form of tuition). Therefore, there would be little incentive to acquire skills unless skilled workers were paid more than unskilled workers.

From the perspective of the firm, it must decide how many workers of each level of skill to hire. Diminishing returns are important here as well. For example, imagine a firm that already has ten managers whose education allows them to increase production through efficient planning. Adding the eleventh manager might not increase production as much as adding the tenth manager did. If managers are paid twice as much as assembly line workers, at some point adding two assembly line workers will increase production more than adding another manager. Thus, firms are expected to *demand* an optimal mix of workers of different levels of skill. The amount of each type they demand will depend on the type of good or service they produce, on the technologies of production (because they affect the values of workers with different levels of skill), and on the wages that must be paid to workers of different skill levels.

From the perspective of a worker who will *supply* labor to some firm, he or she must decide how much to invest in skill and education. This will depend on both the cost of skill attainment and the increase in wages earned from an extra unit of skill. Becker's (1975) seminal analysis showed that at the optimum, an individual will invest in human capital until the point where an extra unit of investment increases lifetime wages (in real buying power after taking the interest rate into account) by less than the cost of that investment (measured both in terms of lost wages during the training period and direct costs of schooling).

The final result is that wages and the number of workers hired at every level of skill are determined by the interaction of demand for workers of different levels of human capital by all the firms in the economy and the supply of human capital by individuals who are attempting to maximize net lifetime earnings. The resulting equilibrium occurs when supply is equal to demand; at equilibrium, the differences between wages paid for jobs requiring different levels of embodied capital are equal to the costs of obtaining the capital, measured in terms of real lifetime income.[4]

As in the case of traditional human societies, much of this investment in embodied capital is financed by parents. The number of children that parents can afford to raise will be determined by the amount they invest in each child and by their own income (measured in terms of both time investments and resources). Thus, in principle, parents face a choice between producing fewer higher-earning offspring and more lower-earning offspring. If all parents were equal, the theory of human capital investment would predict that they would be indifferent to alternative combinations of child quantity and quality. Those who produced more children would have fewer grandchildren per child (because of their children's lower earnings) and those who produced fewer children would have more grandchildren per child, with the net result being equal numbers of grandchildren, on average. As mentioned in the introduction, this is not the case empirically. Most people have few children, and there is either no or a negative relationship between parental income and fertility. One possible explanation of this finding is that higher-earning parents invest more in children than lesser-earning parents, producing higher-earning children in turn. Higher-earning parents will themselves tend to have higher levels of embodied capital. If parents with more embodied capital can produce embodied capital in their children more efficiently (i.e., at less cost), then they may reach diminishing returns on investments at a higher level of investment than lower-earning parents with less embodied capital (see Becker et al. 1990 for a similar suggestion).

First, consider inputs of parents' time. There is significant evidence that the nature of parent-child interaction varies with the educational level of parents (Hart and Risley 1995; Hoff-Ginsberg and Tardif 1995). For example, Hart and Risley (1995) report that by the age of three, children hear six million words if their mothers are professionals, three million words if their mothers are "working class," and only only one million words if their mothers are on welfare. By the time children enter the public education system there are clear differences among them in school-related skills, and those differences are related to socioeconomic status. This is illustrated in Figure 14.3A. The dotted curve depicts the relationship between parental time inputs and the child's embodied capital at school entry for lower-earning parents with less embodied capital; the solid curve represents the same function for higher-earning parents. Returns diminish more rapidly for the former than for the latter. Therefore, parents with more embodied capital may actually spend more time with children if the impact of their time is greater at each level than that of the time of parents with less capital [T*(H) vs. T*(L)].

Second, the rate at which a child learns may depend on the knowledge and skills she already possesses. Much of the education offered in schools is based upon the premise that knowledge is cumulative (Cromer 1993). Basic skills are acquired first, and those skills are used as a foundation for the acquisition of the next set of skills. This would imply that the impact of the child's time inputs would depend upon skills already in place. The impacts of inputs, such as child's time,

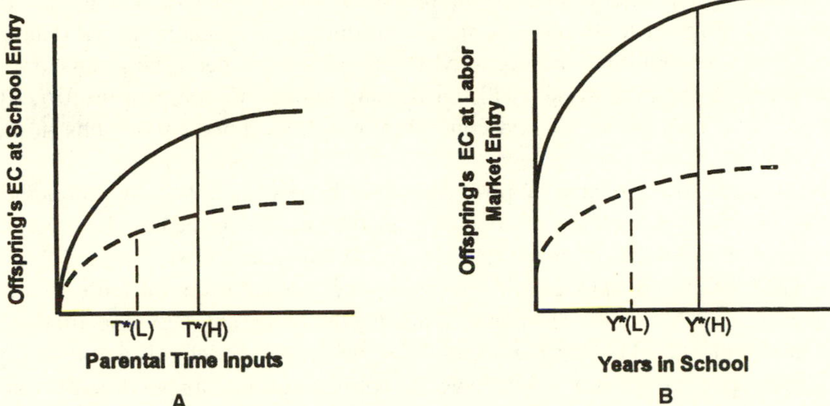

Figure 14.3. Impacts of investment in children's embodied capital as a function of parental embodied capital.

parents' time, others' time (e.g., teachers), and resources, will be greater as the recipient's (i.e., the child's) stock of embodied capital increases. This is important because it means that at each age, optimum investment in the child will be a positive function of the skills the child already possesses, and that variance in investment will increase with age. Thus, skilled parents should invest more, and parents should also invest more in children who are receiving inputs from higher-quality schools. This is illustrated in Figure 14.3B. With each additional year spent in school, the embodied capital of children from different backgrounds becomes progressively greater. Again, this may mean that optimal years of schooling (i.e., to the point at which an extra year of schooling lowers lifetime income) for children whose parents have less embodied capital will be lower than those whose parents have more [Y*(L) vs. Y*(H)].

If this is true, it has important implications for the supply of and demand for embodied capital in the labor force. Now, the optimal level of investment in children may vary with income. Given the empirical finding that parental income is unrelated to fertility, this would suggest that optimal investments in children increase linearly with income.

This within-population heterogeneity in the costs of embodying capital in children means that diminishing returns on parental investment are not determined by the environment as they would be in primary production economies, but are frequency dependent. First, consider the jobs requiring the highest skill levels. Those jobs would be filled by individuals with the lowest costs of skill acquisition in decreasing rank order until the point is reached when the next cheapest worker is more expensive than the product she produces. Since firms would not be willing to pay more than she produces, the wage would not justify the extra investment in education. Her parents would therefore invest less in her than would be necessary to obtain the highest-level jobs, and she would find employment in the next tier of skill. That tier would then be occupied by individuals in decreasing rank order until the next cheapest worker will not be paid enough to compensate for skill embodiment. This process would continue through the lowest-level jobs in the economy.

Next, consider the related proposition that technological change in production will be positively related to the stock of embodied capital at the population level (Becker et al. 1990). If higher levels of general education of the population are associated with more rapid technical progress, the demand for more skilled workers will increase as more investment is made in education. Through time, then, the demand for new levels of skill will grow. For the simple model, this would imply that skilled parents not only would have the option of producing children of equal or less skill, but will have the opportunity to reinvest the dividend from their own educational investments in even higher levels of skill for their children. As long as technology is constantly growing and generating demand for new levels of skill, sustained fertility reduction over many generations is possible.

Although the continual intergenerational reinvestment of dividends from investments in embodied capital seems hard to sustain indefinitely, it does seem consistent with the past century of technological growth and increasing investment in education (see, for example, Denison 1985; Lesthaeghe and Wilson 1986; Lindert 1986). In fact, there may be some "excess" return from education, especially at high levels, if there is a significant lag between increases in demand for skilled labor and corresponding increases in supply. Since the embodiment of skills takes time, some lags between demand and supply are likely. This would lead to higher rates of return on investments than would be expected at equilibrium. Such "excess" returns could drive fertility to a minimum level.

So far, we have considered only fertility *reduction* and not the quantitative level of fertility. We have also neglected the integer constraints on fertility and have treated fertility as if it were continuous (but it is not possible to have, for example, 2.3 children). However, minimum fertility greater than zero is one. If there were excess returns on investments in embodied capital, one might expect most people to have one child. Yet evidence suggests most people consider an only child to be undesirable and have a target fertility of two or three. There is also evidence that singleton children do not differ in education and achievement from children raised in two-child families (Blake 1989). Yet families with more than two children do show reductions in educational and income achievement (Blake 1989; Kaplan et al. 1995). This suggests decreases in family size below two children do not increase the total capital embodied by children.

This lack of effect may be due to several factors. Some of the costs of investment in embodied capital may be fixed (see Becker 1991 for an analytical treatment of fixed and variable costs). The choice of neighborhood to live in and the taxes paid for social services, including public education, are obvious examples of fixed costs.

Thus as fixed costs become an increasingly large proportion of total costs, the reduction from two to one child may have less of an impact on the resources parents have to invest in children. Also, men in focus-group discussions in Albuquerque expressed the opinion that interactions with siblings were an important contribution to development, and that mutual assistance among siblings was helpful in attaining life goals. Regardless of the reasons for this lack of impact, there seems little positive incentive to reduce fertility below two. Moreover, since number of children is not continuous, a reduction of fertility below two requires a 50% change in fertility. This fact, coupled with the risk associated with the possible loss of an only child, creates a large disincentive. *Therefore, the two child family may be the result of two competing effects: (1) technological growth, with an increasing premium paid for skills and education driving fertility to a minimum; and (2) high risk and lack of benefits associated with a reduction to one child.*

EMPIRICAL PREDICTIONS DERIVED FROM THE MODEL

To summarize, we propose that two characteristics of modern economies might be sufficient to account for a period of sustained fertility reduction and for a corresponding lack of variation in fertility across income levels. The first characteristic is the direct link between costs of investment and wage rates owing to the forces of supply and demand for labor in competitive economies. The second is the increasing emphasis on cumulative knowledge, skills, and technologies in the production of resources. These two characteristics may together produce the historically novel situation in which (1) investments in offspring income do not reach diminishing returns until very high levels, and (2) embodied capital of parents is positively associated with returns on investment in embodied capital of children, with diminishing returns at the individual level set by the frequency-dependent costs of skill embodiment across the population.

These propositions generate a series of predictions with respect to fertility, parental investment, and child outcomes. Patterns of fertility should reflect investments in embodied capital and efficiency in the production thereof. First, the observed relationship between income and fertility (i.e., no effect) should be the result of two opposing causal processes. Increased resources should be associated with higher fertility, but increased efficiency in the production of human capital should decrease fertility. However, since education and training affect both income and efficiency in the production of human capital in the same direction, the two opposing effects cancel each other out. Second, two kinds of fertility effects of embodied capital should be discernible. One effect is due to investments in one's own embodied capital. Men who invest more in their own training and education are expected to delay fertility. Another effect is due to increased investment in offspring embodied capital. When income is held constant, more-educated men are expected to stop reproducing at lower parities. Third, education has become increasingly important in determining economic outcomes during the course of this century (Burck 1976; Herrnstein and Murray 1994:93; Newcomer 1955; Vinovskis 1994), so we should find a pattern of increasing importance of education in determining fertility.

A similar series of predictions can be generated with respect to parental investment. First, within economic strata, more-educated parents should invest more time and resources in each child as well as having lower fertility. This should be especially true of investments in the child's education. Second, parental education should be negatively related to the probability of ceasing to live with an offspring, since the negative effect of lowered parental investment will be greater for children of more educated parents. Third, more academically able children should receive higher levels of investment (especially, school-related investment) than less able children, even within families, because there are higher returns to investment in their human capital (see Becker and Tomes 1976 for a similar argument). Fourth, levels of investment at different stages of the child's development should be positively correlated with one another, contingent on the child's progress. The quantity and quality of early investments should positively affect early educational performance that should, in turn, positively affect later investments. The loss of parental investment from dissolution of the marital relationship should also have a negative impact on child outcomes.

METHODS

As discussed in Chapter 9, the research design for the Albuquerque Men sample consisted of two complementary interviews, a short interview administered to a large, representative sample and a longer interview administered to a subset of those men. Between July 1990 and July 1993, 7,107 short interviews and 1,325 long interviews were conducted.

The Interviews

The short interview was designed to obtain the following information on the respondent: place and year of birth, ethnicity, education, religion, income, current mate's income, years in Albuquerque, number of years lived with each biological parent, number of half and full siblings, the fertility and age of siblings, number and age of biological children, years lived with biological children, number of spouses and women with whom he had children, and the number of step and foster children he parented. Information on the respondent's parents' place and year of birth, education, ethnicity, income, and standard of living were also collected. The long interview collected the following information:

1. Basic demographic information about the respondent's father, his paternal grandfather, his mother, and if his biological parents did not raise him, his primary male and female caretakers.

2. The financial investments made in the respondent by the previous generation, including support for advanced training or education, starting a business, buying a first home, a wedding or establishing a nest egg, and living expenses after marriage.
3. The respondent's employment and income history.
4. Parental investment in each of the respondent's full and half siblings, including how the estates of his father and mother were divided, support given to the parental household by the respondent and his siblings, and the use of physical force on the sibship by parents or primary caretakers.
5. The man's sexual unions, marital relationships, and any relationship that produced a pregnancy, including basic demographic data on the woman, her income and employment history, his attitude about her working, her personality and physical characteristics, conflict over fertility and financial decisions, additional sexual partners of each and their impact on the relationship, causes of any breakups of relationships, techniques of conflict resolution, the use of physical force, information about the relationship after it broke up.
6. A history including outcomes of all pregnancies that the respondent believes or suspects, or someone claimed, he fathered.
7. The parenting of children, both genetic and nongenetic, including information on investment given to each child in elementary and high school; the child's qualities; the way in which he/she was parented; the child's behavioral characteristics; reproductive history; achievements after age 18 (with a special series of questions if the man did not live with the child until age 18 as to why they were separated and what investment the man made in the child); financial investments in all children after the age of 18; money spent on each child during the previous year; the use of physical force or punishment on any of the children parented; and support given by any of these children to the respondent's household.
8. Life course strategies, including data on reproductive or family composition preferences; reasons for not having more children; reasons for not reproducing at all; financial strategies; attitudes about women, relationships, and commitment; engagement in behaviors used by men to get women to have sex with them; total numbers of sexual partners during stages of the life course; and risk-taking behaviors that affect morbidity and mortality.

The Sample

The total short interview sample of 7,107 men comprised 2,789 Hispanics, 3,762 Anglos, and 556 others who were interviewed between July 1990 and July 1993.[5] The long interview sample consisted of 401 Hispanics, 858 Anglos, and 66 others. In New Mexico, the term "Hispanic" is preferred over "Latino" because most people consider themselves native New Mexicans, tracing their family history of residence in this area as far back as living memory extends. In our sample, very few Hispanics were of Mexican origin, and even fewer were from other Latin countries. "Anglo" (an ethnic classification peculiar to the Southwest) refers to non-Hispanic men who classify themselves as white.

Potential respondents for the short interview were solicited at the Bernalillo County Motor Vehicle Division (MVD) that served all of Albuquerque. All men who appeared to be over 18 years of age were considered eligible for initial screening and were approached as they received a driver's license photo. If they agreed to the short interview, which took about seven minutes to administer, it was immediately conducted in a private area. On the basis of the answers to the short interview questions, eligibility for inclusion in the long interview sample was determined. The criteria for eligibility were (1) being age 25 or over and (2) having come to the MVD for the purpose of license origination, renewal, or for a photo ID. The purposes of the study then were explained to eligible men in more detail and they were offered the opportunity to participate in the long interview, for which they received a $30 payment. An appointment was then made to conduct the long interview in either a mobile office vehicle, an office at the University of New Mexico, or at their homes.

Sampling men who are renewing or obtaining driver's licenses and photo IDs at the MVD provides a highly representative sample of the male population in Albuquerque. It is the largest city in New Mexico with a population in 1990 of 480,577 (U.S. Department of Commerce 1992), approximately 32% of the state's population lives in greater Albuquerque. More than 95% of all New Mexican males over age 20 have a current driver's license (U.S. Department of Transportation 1993), compared with an estimated 93.5% telephone availability for the Albuquerque area (U.S. Department of Commerce 1992). In addition, individuals who do not drive use the MVD to obtain valid photo IDs. Drivers' licenses and IDs must each be renewed every four years. By sampling only men who are waiting for license and ID photos, men who visit the MVD more frequently (those who do not have checking accounts and cannot register vehicles by mail, those who frequently pay fines, those who frequently sell and purchase vehicles, etc.) are not over-represented in the sample. Groups who are likely to be absent or under-represented among the licensed drivers include the elderly, disabled, institutionalized, transient, extremely poor, and criminal. These groups are also likely to be under-represented or uncooperative in most other sampling frames as well.

Evaluation of Sample Bias

The methods employed in this study provided several avenues for evaluating potential biases in the composition of the sample. After the first 850 interviews were collected, we compared the demographic characteristics of the sample we obtained with data from other sources such as the census. We arrayed the age and ethnic distributions of our sample against those of licensed drivers and the census population data for males. There were no significant differences in any of these comparisons. In fact, the ethnic breakdown of the sample obtained at the MVD is almost identical to that obtained from the 1990 Census (U.S. Department of Commerce 1991, 1992).

We also examined refusals. About 78% of all men approached agreed to the short interview. One factor that predicted refusals is whether the potential respondent was alone or accompanied at the MVD; accompanied men refused 28% of the time whereas men who were alone refused only 18% of the time. No other biases such as age or time of day were detected. Refusals decreased steadily through time because of improved interviewer training.

Following this phase of unbiased sampling, we increased the proportional representation of Hispanics and others by not interviewing Anglos on about 20% of sample days. In this way, we obtained a sample that was 53% Anglo, 39% Hispanics, and 8% other ethnicities.

Refusals to participate in the long interview have also been analyzed. Early indications suggested that Hispanics were more likely to refuse. We conducted an experiment to determine whether Hispanic short interviewers were more effective with Hispanic respondents in obtaining agreement to participate in the long interview. Our analysis showed that 64% of Hispanic respondents agreed to conduct the long interview when the interviewer was also Hispanic but only 27% agreed when the interviewer was Anglo. Hispanic and Anglo interviewers were almost equally successful with Anglo respondents, achieving 53% and 58% acceptance rates, respectively. On the basis of these results, we increased the percentage of Hispanic interviewers to 75%. With the exception of education, which was positively associated with probability of acceptance, men's income, number of children, and other background variables did not associate with probability of acceptance.

RESULTS

Fertility

Although the lifetime data show no net effects of income on completed fertility (Kaplan et al. 1995, 1998), the relationship between fertility and income is, in fact, complex and bidirectional. Education is a major pathway to higher income, and education clearly depresses fertility at young ages. Table 14.1 summarizes the results of a set of logistic regression analyses designed to determine the impacts of education and income on the probability of having a child during a year at risk, using data from the short interview sample. All years from age of 15 to age 49 are in the risk set. One regression analysis was conducted for each age class and ethnicity. Income at the time of the interview was controlled for in each analysis. Although it would have been preferable to control for income during each year at risk, only the long interview data allow for that analysis (presented below in Table 14.4). In these analyses, we also controlled for period (i.e., whether the year at risk

Table 14.1. Effect of each additional year of education and each additional thousand dollars of income on male fertility by age class and ethnicity

Age Class	*N*	*Education Parameter*	*Education Odds Ratio*	*Partial p*	*Income Parameter*	*Income Odds Ratio*	*Partial p*
All							
15–19	29,873	–0.19	0.83	0.0001	0.008	1.008	0.007
20–24	29,868	–0.12	0.89	0.0001	0.005	1.005	0.0001
25–29	29,812	–0.05	0.96	0.0001	0.006	1.006	0.0001
30–34	26,704	–0.00	1.00	0.5120	0.004	1.005	0.0001
35–39	21,627	0.03	1.03	0.0014	0.000	1.000	0.73
40–44	16,474	–0.01	0.99	0.6947	–0.003	0.997	0.16
45–49	12,028	0.03	1.03	0.2792	–0.006	0.994	0.13
Anglo							
15–19	17,378	–0.24	0.79	0.0001	0.005	1.005	0.30
20–24	17,373	–0.15	0.86	0.0001	0.005	1.005	0.002
25–29	17,347	–0.03	0.97	0.0003	0.007	1.007	0.0001
30–34	15,960	0.01	1.01	0.2228	0.005	1.005	0.0001
35–39	13,435	0.05	1.06	0.0001	0.00	1.00	0.81
40–44	10,602	0.03	1.03	0.1902	–0.001	0.999	0.63
45–49	8,028	0.08	1.08	0.0289	–0.002	0.998	0.70
Hispanic							
15–19	12,495	–0.17	0.85	0.0001	0.01	1.01	0.015
20–24	12,495	–0.10	0.90	0.0001	0.004	1.004	0.025
25–29	12,465	–0.06	0.94	0.0001	0.005	1.005	0.003
30–34	10,744	–0.02	0.98	0.0489	0.004	1.004	0.038
35–39	8,192	0.00	1.00	0.8054	0.003	1.003	0.27
40–44	5,872	–0.03	0.98	0.2155	–0.009	0.991	0.079
45–49	4,000	–0.00	1.00	0.9366	–0.023	0.977	0.023

occurred before, during, or after the baby boom), and for ethnicity, in the analyses dealing with "all" men.

The column labeled N is the sample size in risk years for the specific five-year age class. The education and income parameters are the maximum likelihood estimators of the impact of an additional year of education and an additional thousand dollars of income, respectively, on the log odds of a birth occurring. The odds ratio can be interpreted as approximating the relative risk resulting from a unit change in the independent variable when event probabilities are close to zero. Odds ratios of one indicate no effect on the probability of the event occurring (in this case, on the probability of having a child in a year at risk), because the relative risk is the same; odds ratios of less than one mean that an increase in the independent variable decreases the likelihood of the event occurring, and odds ratios greater than one reflect an increase in the likelihood. For example, in the first row of Table 14.1, the education odds ratio of .83 means that the relative risk of giving birth between ages 15 and 19 decreases by 17% for each additional year of education. However, care must be used in interpreting odds-ratios. First, the odds ratio becomes increasingly different from relative risk as the probability of the event increases, and it is not a very good estimator of relative risks for probabilities above 0.1. Second, the odds ratio depends upon the units chosen for measurement. In Table 14.1, income is measured in thousand dollar units so that the odds ratio refers to the effect of a $1,000 change in income, whereas education is measured in units of one year. The column labeled *partial p* refers to the probability that the education and income parameters are actually zero for the population as a whole (i.e., there is no effect), given the estimated value of the sample statistic and after controlling for the effects of the other independent variables. For example, in the first three age classes, there is less than a one in ten thousand chance that education is really not associated with the probability of giving birth, given the data in our sample.

The results show that for both Anglos and Hispanics education has a strong negative effect on reproduction during the late teens and even through the twenties. It gets gradually weaker with age and, in fact, is mildly positive among Anglos in the 35–39 and 45–49 age classes, suggesting differential scheduling of births. In these analyses, income at the time of the interview either has a small positive effect or no effect on fertility, after education is controlled. The effect of income is generally positive at the ages when the effect of education is negative, suggesting that finances are a constraint on early reproduction.

The impact of education on reproduction has increased through time. Table 14.2 presents the results of logistic models in which the log odds of a birth occurring in a year at risk prior to the age of 30 are regressed on education by decade of birth and ethnicity. For both Anglos and Hispanics, the negative effect of education increases dramatically for men born after 1940. Again, we find that, in general, the positive effect of income is greater for later cohorts among whom the negative effect of education is greater.[6]

There are also period-parity interactions in fertility. Table 14.3 shows the results of logistic models in which the probability of a birth is regressed on period by parity. The baseline period is all years of risk between 1946 and 1962. The pre-boom period (before 1946) and the post-boom period (after 1962) are then compared with the boom period. For both Anglos and Hispanics, the probability of *first* reproduction (i.e., at parity zero) is about half as high during the pre-boom period (see the odds ratio column). This reflects the much later ages at first reproduction during the depression and war years. For the post-boom period, Anglos delay reproduction relative to the boom period (odds ratio = .85), but Hispanics initiate reproduction sooner (odds ratio = 1.13). The progression from one child to two children also occurs more rapidly during the boom period for both Anglos and Hispanics, but the pre- and post-boom periods are not significantly different. The higher parity progressions show a very different trend. There is no significant difference between the boom and preceding periods in the progressions from two or more children to the next higher parity; however, after the baby boom, men are less than half as likely to progress from two or more children to the next higher parity.

Table 14.2. Effect of each additional year of education and each additional thousand dollars of income on fertility for men under 30, by decade of birth

Decade of Birth	*N*	*Education Parameter*	*Education Odds Ratio*	*Partial p*	*Income Parameter*	*Income Odds Ratio*	*Partial p*
All							
< 1920	8,085	–.05	0.96	0.0033	–.01	0.995	.04
1920–1929	7,410	–0.03	0.97	0.0244	0.00	1.00	0.40
1930–1939	11,910	–0.05	0.95	0.0106	0.003	1.004	0.01
1940–1949	24,675	–0.10	0.91	0.0001	0.006	1.006	0.0001
1950–1959	30,765	–0.12	0.89	0.0001	0.007	1.007	0.0001
1960+	6,705	–0.10	0.90	0.0001	0.005	1.005	0.17
Anglos							
< 1920	6,585	–0.05	0.95	0.0148	–0.002	0.998	0.50
1920–1929	5,100	–0.02	0.98	0.1828	0.004	0.977	0.18
1930–1939	7,350	–0.05	0.95	0.0001	0.001	1.001	0.44
1940–1949	14,400	–0.11	0.90	0.0001	0.006	1.006	0.0002
1950–1959	15,960	–0.14	0.87	0.0001	0.012	1.012	0.0001
1960+	2,700	–0.15	0.86	0.0005	0.009	1.009	0.16
Hispanics							
< 1920	1,500	–0.02	0.98	0.5796	–0.022	0.978	0.001
1920–1929	2,310	–0.03	0.97	0.1782	–0.006	0.994	0.18
1930–1939	4,560	–0.05	0.95	0.0003	0.010	1.010	0.0003
1940–1949	10,275	–0.09	0.91	0.0001	0.007	1.008	0.0007
1950–1959	14,805	–0.10	0.91	0.0001	0.002	1.002	0.28
1960+	4,005	–0.09	0.92	0.0001	0.003	1.003	0.53

Table 14.4 examines marital and cohabiting fertility with the smaller, but more detailed, long interview sample. It displays the results of a logistic model of the predictors of the probability of a first birth. With respect to ethnicity, it shows that Anglos are only 93% as likely to reproduce in a given year than are Hispanics. The period effects on marital/cohabiting fertility reveal the different causal processes at work in determining total fertility for the different periods. The pre-boom period is the baseline. The probability of a birth is about 62% higher during the boom period, and only half as high during the post-boom period relative to the pre-boom baseline. For Anglos, total fertility rates are almost the same for cohorts reproducing prior to the baby boom as for those reproducing after the baby boom (Kaplan et al. 1995), whereas marital fertility is much higher prior to the baby boom. This shows that the low completed fertility prior to the baby boom is due primarily to delay in marriage and higher overall rates of non-reproduction, whereas the low completed fertility after the baby boom is due to decreased marital fertility. To examine the parity effects, a parity of zero is used as the baseline. Since all years from age of 15 to age 49 define the risk set, the lowest probability of reproduction occurs before the first birth. After the first birth, men are almost

Table 14.3. Effect of period on male fertility, by previous parity*

	Anglo					*Hispanic*					*All*				
Parity	*N*	*Period*	*Period Parameter*	*Odds Ratio*	*Partial p*	*N*	*Period*	*Period Parameter*	*Odds Ratio*	*Partial p*	*N*	*Period*	*Period Parameter*	*Odds Ratio*	*Partial p*
0	56,652	Pre	–0.73	0.48	0.0001	31,662	Pre	–.95	0.39	0.0001	88,314	Pre	–0.80	0.45	0.0001
		Post	–0.16	0.85	0.0005		Post	0.12	1.14	.03		Post	–.02	0.98	0.50
1	13,565	Pre	–0.43	0.65	0.0001	9,476	Pre	–0.47	0.62	0.02	23,014	Pre	–0.50	0.61	0.0001
		Post	–.54	0.58	0.0001		Post	–0.47	0.63	0.0001		Post	–.45	0.64	0.0001
2	15,995	Pre	–.10	0.90	0.57	10,809	Pre	0.01	1.01	0.97	26,804	Pre	–0.11	0.9	0.45
		Post	–0.78	0.46	0.0001		Post	–1.00	0.37	0.0001		Post	–0.71	0.49	0.0001
3	8,277	Pre	–0.06	.94	0.85	7,248	Pre	0.56	1.75	0.08	15,525	Pre	0.20	1.22	0.39
		Post	–1.06	0.35	0.0001		Post	–1.23	0.29	0.0001		Post	–1.04	0.35	0.0001
4 or	5,634	Pre	0.04	1.04	0.96	7,068	Pre	–0.00	1.00	1.00	12,702	Pre	0.12	1.13	0.68
More		Post	–.80	0.45	0.0001		Post	–1.15	0.32	0.0001		Post	–0.97	0.38	0.0001

*The baby boom period, 1946–1962, are the reference years at risk (i.e. odds ratio=1.00). All parameter estimates, odds ratios, and *p*–values compare years at risk during the pre– and post–boom periods to the reference years. Separate analyses were conducted for each parity progression (parity 0 is for years at risk before the respondent began reproducing, parity 1 is for years at risk between the birth of the first child and the birth of the second child, etc.).

Table 14.4. Logistic regression model for the probability of birth for married and cohabiting couples (N = 10,210, $\chi^2 = 1661.1$, $p < 0.0001$)

Variable	*df*	*Parameter Estimate*	*s.e.*	*Standardized Parameter Estimate*	*Wald* χ^2	*Partial* *p*	*Odds Ratio*
Intercept	1	–4.65	0.81	—	33.24	0.0001	0.01
Anglo	1	–0.08	0.02	–0.07	12.70	0.0004	0.93
During Boom	1	0.49	0.17	0.10	7.68	0.0056	1.62
Post Boom	1	–0.59	0.17	–0.13	12.48	0.0004	0.55
Parity of 1	1	1.08	0.09	0.24	130.41	0.0001	2.94
Parity of 2	1	0.23	0.12	0.05	3.75	0.0528	1.25
Parity of 3	1	0.20	0.17	0.04	1.49	0.2224	1.22
Parity of 4	1	0.95	0.19	0.14	25.57	0.0001	2.59
1st year followng a birth	1	–5.45	0.71	–0.87	58.64	0.0001	0.004
2nd year following a birth	1	–4.51	0.59	–0.63	59.97	0.0001	0.01
Her education (yrs)	1	–0.05	0.02	–0.08	11.44	0.0007	0.95
His education (yrs)	1	0.01	0.01	0.02	0.40	0.5277	1.01
No. of her kids from prev. relationships	1	–0.17	0.08	–0.08	4.94	0.0262	0.84
No. of his kids from prev. relationships	1	–0.07	0.08	–0.03	0.93	0.3343	0.93
Income (in thousands of 1990 dollars)	1	0.015	0.00	0.06	7.15	0.0075	1.015
Her age	1	0.43	0.06	1.87	54.25	0.0001	1.54
Her age (squared)	1	–0.01	0.00	–2.93	96.63	0.0001	0.99

(After Kaplan et al. 1998)

three times as likely to have a second child in a given year. The progressions to higher parities, while higher than the probability of first birth, are much lower than the progression probability from first to second birth. Birth spacing effects are evident as well. The baseline is no child under the age of two. Not surprisingly, if there is a child of one year or younger, the probability of the next birth is only .4% as likely. If the child is between one and two years of age, a birth is 1% as likely.

The data also show that the characteristics of a man's mate are highly determinate of fertility rates. The effects of a man's education on fertility appear to operate solely through his mate's education (the Pearson correlation between the two is .6). When both a man and his mate's education are in the regression model, the woman's education has a strong negative effect on fertility (the odds ratio is .95 for each additional year of education), but the man's education is not significant. In addition, if his mate has children from a previous marriage, they are also less likely to reproduce (see below). If a man has children from a previous relationship, on the other hand, there is no significant decrease in the likelihood of having a child. Since the long interview sample contains data on income earned during each year of a man's life, we can also assess the impact of income on fertility. A man's income in a given year is positively associated with the probability of having a child. This reduces the negative effect of education on fertility.

These data on male fertility indicate that both the onset of reproduction and parity progressions have changed through the course of the century. Age at first reproduction is high for men born early in the century, decreases for men born in 1920–1939, and then increases for men born after 1940. The effect on fertility of investment in the man's own human capital, as measured by years of education, is greatest before the age of thirty. This reflects its greater impact on the onset of fertility than on parity progressions after the first child. However, the impact of investment in one's own human capital on the onset of fertility appears to have changed through time. For men born during the early part of the century, years of education have little effect on age at first reproduction. The delaying effect of education on fertility has increased through time.

One interpretation of these results is that the Great Depression of the 1930s and the World Wars delayed fertility for all men. During the postwar baby boom, low-cost loans for affordable housing and the GI bill allowed men to reproduce at earlier ages, even though investment in education was increasing. Following the baby boom, the onset of fertility is again delayed for everybody, but especially for men investing more in human capital. This may reflect increasing costs of education as well as increasing importance of education in the determination of wages (Burck 1976; Herrnstein and Murray 1994:93; Newcomer 1955; Vinovskis 1994).

The onset of reproduction is probably determined by many factors. In addition to investment in human capital, men must obtain a partner and acquire the resources necessary for reproduction. This is probably why there is a significant delay between completion of schooling and median age of first reproduction (between four and ten years, depending upon ethnicity, cohort, and educational level attained; Kaplan et al., 1998:Table 5). Examination of fertility onset among men without a high school education suggests that those other factors were more important during the early part of this century. Perhaps the earlier onset of reproduction among less educated men in recent cohorts is due to the fact that acquiring the resources for reproduction is less of a constraint now that there are social welfare supports for poor families. It is also possible that educated men are now engaging in more postgraduate on-the-job training. In both national samples (U.S. Department of Commerce 1985) and the Albuquerque sample, men with higher education exhibit greater increases in wages with increasing employment experience than do men with fewer years of education. This may also account for an increasing delay in the onset of fertility with education. Finally, because the educational attainments of spouses are becoming increasingly correlated (Mare 1991) and because women's education is increasingly associated with delayed reproduction (Bianchi and Spain 1996), some of these time trends among men may reflect changes in education, work, and reproduction among women.

There has also been major historical change in the higher parity progressions. For Anglos, the hazard of progressing from one parity to the next is greater during the baby boom than either prior to or after that period. Different causal processes appear to be underlying the low completed fertility prior to and after the baby boom. The principal cause of low fertility prior to the boom is the low hazard of progression from zero children to the first child. Following the boom, the low fertility is also due to the low hazard of progressing from two to more children. Perhaps this change reflects an increasing trend towards investing in the human capital of children and increasing costs of educating them. Men today are much more likely to stop reproducing at the second or third child. Many men who participated in focus group discussions conducted as part of the Albuquerque Men project reported that they consciously decide to stop reproducing at low parities so that they could both invest more time in their children and provide them with funding for education.

The analysis of the long interview data on marital fertility suggests that once a union is established, it is the man's partner's level of education, rather than his education, that significantly lowers marital fertility. One way men may opt into a parental investment strategy is through the selection of a partner. Men marrying educated women may be selecting a low-fertility, high-investment strategy. It is also interesting that after controlling for partner's education, male income positively affects fertility. This result runs counter to conventional wisdom.

Investment

Parental investment in children is multidimensional and difficult to measure. Men can spend time with their children, take an active interest in their development, spend money on them directly, and attempt to influence their well-being through the choice of a partner, residential location, and school system. Here we examine time investments and monetary expenditures, and in Chapter 9 (Lancaster and Kaplan, this volume) we treat divorce and separation from children.

Table 14.5 presents the analysis of men's time investments in children during their elementary school years. The dependent variable is an index of time involvement, derived from summing time spent alone with the child between the ages of 5 and 12 (in five levels, for ranges of average number of hours per week) and involvement in the child's education (low = 1, mid = 3, and high = 5). Hispanic men report higher time involvement with children than Anglos. Neither sex nor income appears to have any effect, although there is a nonsignificant trend towards slightly more involvement with boys. Men report much lower time involvement with children who are not their biological offspring. Similarly, the number of siblings within two years of the focal child is negatively associated with time involve-

Table 14.5. Least squares regression model of men's time investment in elementary-school-aged children (N = 1,173, F = 18.91, $p < 0.001$, $R^2 = 0.115$)

Variable	*df*	*Parameter Estimate*	*s.e.*	*Standardized Estimate*	*T for H0: Parameter=0*	*Prob > ITI*
Intercept	1	–30.55	9.77	0.00	–3.06	0.0022
Anglo	1	–0.70	0.14	–0.15	–4.96	0.0001
Child Sex	1	–0.18	0.12	–0.04	–1.55	0.1219
Income when child was 5*	1	–0.00	0.00	–0.02	–0.60	0.5469
Unrelated child	1	–0.58	0.16	–0.10	–3.69	0.0002
No. of siblings 2 yrs older or younger	1	–0.39	0.09	–0.13	–4.60	0.0001
Child's year of birth	1	0.018	0.01	0.11	3.63	0.0003
His education (years)	1	0.07	0.02	0.11	3.53	0.0004
His assessment of child's intelligence	1	0.46	0.07	0.18	6.33	0.0001

*In thousands of 1990 dollars

ment, suggesting a dilution effect. Men's time involvement has increased during this century, as the child's year of birth is positively associated with investment. Both the respondent's education and his assessment of the child's scholastic intelligence are positively related to time involvement. Only 11.5% of the variance in the dependent variable, however, is accounted for by the independent variables in the model.

Table 14.6 examines financial support by the respondent for offspring's higher education. The cause-and-effect relationship between educational attainment and support for education is difficult to disentangle. If a child decides not to attend college, it is not possible to provide support for college; however, it is also possible that a lack of support is the cause of nonattendance. For this reason, we restrict our analysis to only those children of the respondent who attended college, about half of whom received some support. A logistic regression analysis was conducted. Hispanics are less likely to provide support. Number of siblings (i.e., the child's number of living siblings when he/she reached age 18) is negatively associated with support, and the effect is strong. The respondent's income is also associated with the probability of support, although his mate's is not. The education of both mother and father are significant with small effect sizes, as is the father's prior time involvement with the child (i.e., when she/he was in elementary school; see definition above).

Again, we find strong effects of biological paternity. Men invest less in children from previous unions of their mate. Both time investment and support during the college years is greater for genetic offspring than for a mate's child. In addition, the investment in a mate's child is contingent on a continuing relationship with

Table 14.6. Logistic regression model of the probability of a man providing financial support for an offspring's higher education (N = 387, $\chi^2 = 84.2$, $p < 0.0001$)

Variable	*Parameter Estimate*	*s.e.*	*Z*	*Partial p*	*Odds Ratio*
Intercept	–5.09	1.45	–3.50	0.0005	0.01
Offspring's year of birth	0.05	0.03	1.87	0.0615	1.05
Man's year of birth	–0.03	0.02	–1.36	0.1739	0.97
Sex	0.18	0.25	0.73	0.4648	1.20
Anglo	0.62	0.33	1.86	0.0628	1.85
Total number of siblings when offspring was 18	–0.33	0.07	–4.39	0.0000	0.72
Man's income* when offspring was 18	0.01	0.00	2.88	0.0039	1.01
Wife's income* when offspring was 18	–0.01	0.01	–1.39	0.1638	0.99
Man's education (years)	0.10	0.05	2.03	0.0426	1.10
Mother's education (years)	0.11	0.06	1.80	0.0714	1.11
Man's time involvement with offspring when offspring was young	0.15	0.07	2.13	0.0333	1.16
Unrelated offspring, man lived with the mother when child was 18	–0.99	0.50	–1.97	0.0492	0.37
Genetic offspring, man not living with the mother when child was 18	–1.35	0.40	–3.36	0.0008	0.26
Unrelated offspring, man not living with the mother when child was 18	–3.34	0.94	–3.56	0.0004	0.04

*in thousands of 1990 dollars
(After Kaplan et al. 1998)

that partner. Men cease to invest in a child after they stop living with the child's mother, unless the child is also the biological offspring of the man, and even then, support is reduced significantly (see Weiss and Willis 1985 for a theoretical treatment of this effect, and Anderson, Kaplan, and Lancaster, 1999, for a detailed presentation and discussion of these results).

The predictions of the competitive-labor-market model, discussed above, were supported by the analysis of the data on investment in children and on child outcomes. Consistent with the idea that human capital of parents is positively associated with rates of return on investment in offspring human capital, men's education is associated with higher levels of investment in children, including time involvement and monetary investments. Also, as predicted by the model, men's time involvement with children is positively associated with their assessment of the child's scholastic intelligence, although the direction of causality may be unclear. A third prediction of the model is that investments in children are positively correlated over the child's life course. This prediction is supported by the fact that financial support for college is positively correlated with the man's earlier time involvement with the child during elementary school years. The negative impact of fertility on parental investment is reflected in both time spent with young children and financial support for higher education. This indicates that there is a dilution effect of number of siblings on the investment that children receive. There is no effect of income on time involvement, but it does predict monetary expenditures.

Outcomes

In a previous paper (Kaplan et al. 1995), we reported that the respondents' education and income were negatively associated with numbers of siblings, and positively associated with fathers' income and number of years that they lived with their fathers prior to age 18. Those analyses were based on the short interview data set. Here, we examine outcomes for the respondents' children using the long interview data set. An Ordinary Least Squares regression analysis of the children's years of education is presented in Table 14.7. Only individuals older than 22 years of age are included in the analysis. The child's sex, year of birth, and number of siblings apparently have no effect, once the other predictors are controlled for (even though in uncontrolled analyses, individuals with more siblings have lower educational attainment). Anglos have about 0.6 more years of education, on average. The

Table 14.7. Least squares regression model of the number of years of education obtained by respondents' children age 23 and older (N = 559, F = 16.30, $p < 0.0001$, adjusted $R^2 = 0.263$)

Variable	*Parameter Estimate*	*s.e.*	*Z*	*Partial p*
Constant	11.46	1.06	10.86	0.0001
Sex	0.01	0.19	0.04	0.97
Offspring's year of birth	–0.01	0.02	–0.28	0.78
Man's year of birth	–0.02	0.02	–1.27	0.20
Total number of siblings when offspring was 18	–0.05	0.05	–0.99	0.32
Anglo	0.64	0.26	2.50	0.013
Man's income* when offspring was 18	0.01	0.00	2.62	0.009
Wife's income* when offspring was 18	0.00	0.01	–0.26	0.80
Man's education (years)	0.07	0.03	2.12	0.03
Mother's education (years)	0.21	0.04	5.42	0.0001
Man's time involvement with offspring when offspring was young	0.11	0.05	2.05	0.04
Unrelated offspring, man lived with the mother when child was 18	–0.74	0.36	–2.07	0.04
Genetic offspring, man not living with the mother when child was 18	–1.28	0.30	–4.33	0.0001
Unrelated offspring, man not living with the mother when child was 18	–2.65	0.59	–4.52	0.0001

*(in thousands of 1990 dollars)

respondent's income when the child was 18 is positively associated with educational attainment, although his mate's income is not. Both the respondent's and the child's mother's years of education are positively associated with the child's education, although mother's effect is greater. The respondent's time involvement has an additional positive effect (a separate analysis, not shown, indicates that this effect of time involvement operates through elementary and secondary school). Children who are not genetically related to the respondent but whose mothers were living with the respondent when they were 18 years of age achieve about 0.7 years less education than genetic offspring with both parents living together when they were 18 years of age. Offspring whose mothers ceased to live with the respondent before the child turned 18 achieve about 1.3 fewer years of education, whereas children who are not genetic offspring and whose mothers ceased to live with the respondent before the child turned 18 achieved 2.6 years less education.

The data on outcomes suggest that those investments do increase the educational achievement of children. Interestingly, even after the effects of investments are taken into account, there is still a residual effect of both mother's and father's education on children's educational achievement. This result is consistent with the idea that the rate of return on investments in human capital of offspring increases with the level of parental human capital. However, it is also possible that the effect is due to genetically mediated parent-offspring correlations in academic ability or motivation. Another possibility is that educated parents instill more positive attitudes towards education and greater expectations of educational achievement in their children. The effects of paternity and the man's relationship to the child's mother are also seen in child outcomes, with children who are raised by men other than their biological father or who are not fully raised by their father achieving lower educational outcomes (even after parental income and education are controlled for).

DISCUSSION AND CONCLUSIONS

In this analysis of modern fertility behavior we followed a four-step process. The first step is to develop a general theory of the action of natural selection on the behavior of interest (in this case, fertility and parental investment). To that end, we unified economic and life history theories of fertility and parental investment to develop an overall framework for analysis (see Kaplan 1996, 1997, and Kaplan et al. 2000 for a more complete discussion of the theory). The second step is to apply the theory to the ecology of evolving hominids, with specific reference to what is known about extant hunter-gatherers. Of course, care must be taken in this step because extant hunter-gatherers only represent a small and probably biased sample of the variability exhibited by evolving *Homo sapiens*. The third step is to specify the kinds of psychological and physiological proximate mechanisms that evolved to produce adaptive responses to the ecological conditions of the past. The fourth step is to develop models of how those proximate mechanisms would respond to modern, socioecological conditions and to individual and socioeconomic variation in those conditions. Successful accomplishment of this process is quite difficult because each step is vulnerable to mistaken assumptions. However, we feel that this analytical procedure takes advantage of the knowledge derived from optimality analysis in biology and economics, evolutionary psychology, and the study of cultural evolution. Taken together our results provide substantial indirect support for the embodied capital approach to fertility and parental investment, and for the specific model of investment in embodied capital in skills-based labor markets. However, the support is based largely on qualitative predictions, each of which is potentially consistent with some other theoretical model. An adequate assessment of the model will require more rigorous tests of quantitative predictions.

Two major difficulties must be overcome. First, the model's theoretical constructs are very difficult to measure. Years of education is only a proxy for embodied capital. Measuring the embodied capital of both parents and children is especially challenging, given that it is multidimensional and heterogeneous. Similarly, parental investment is only poorly approximated by our recall-based measures of expenditures of time and money. The effect sizes we obtained are probably smaller than the true sizes because random measurement error always dilutes actual associations. The statistical models could show stronger effects than the true associations if either the measurement error were biased (e.g., if more educated men tended to recall higher investments than they really gave and/or less educated men tended to recall lower ones) or the model was mis-specified and important variables were omitted. In order to determine the quantitative relationship between parental embodied capital and the rate of return on investments in children's embodied capital, a prospective study that overcomes those measurement problems will be necessary.

Selection bias produces another difficulty. Educational achievement, fertility, parental investment and mate selection are endogenous choices. Men are not randomly assigned to educational achievement levels, parities, etc. As a result, it is difficult to assess the impacts of those characteristics on child outcomes. For example, the association between parental education and the child's education could be due in part to unobserved characteristics that affected the parent's choices about how many years of education to pursue as well as to the effect of education, per se. Since the theory presented here implies an intricate causal pathway relating endogenous choices to one another and, ultimately, to child outcomes, the problem of selection bias must be solved so an accurate quantitative assessment of those relationships can be obtained.

There are also alternative and complementary explanations that require consideration. A great deal of scholarly attention has been focused on women and fertility. Many economic models emphasize the opportunity costs of women's time. As women have entered the labor force in increasing numbers and as women's wages have risen, the time costs of caring for children have increased. Other anthropological and sociological models have postulated that women's education and economic autonomy reduce female fertility because children are no longer the only avenue by which women can gain power, and because they are less subject to men's fertility desires. In fact, our data show that a man's mate's characteristics do affect fertility. The increasing effectiveness of birth control technologies is probably also relevant (Barkow and Burley 1980; Easterlin et al. 1980; Potts 1997) because cost-effective birth control lowers unwanted fertility. Cultural transmission of fertility values is also receiving increased attention (Boyd and Richersen 1985; Cleland 1985; Cleland and Wilson 1987; Zei and Cavalli-Sforza 1977). Changing kin networks and the decreased involvement of extended kin in child rearing have been postulated as a cause of the shift to fewer, higher-quality children (Turke 1989). Clearly, future research must focus on testing alternative models within the same study to determine if some alternatives can be excluded and if a complete explanation requires the amalgamation of several models.

In fact, the life history model presented in the second section of this chapter, together with the proximate model of fertility determinants among traditional societies in the third section, suggests another, more general, explanation. Adults not only face a tradeoff between quantity and quality of children, but also between investment in their own embodied capital and reproduction (see Figure 14.1). For most organisms, including humans living under traditional conditions, food energy is the primary source of adult investment in embodied capital, which is then allocated to alternative physiological functions. In modern society, people face a tremendous array of consumption goods, such as housing, clothing, electronic equipment, and vehicles. The medium of exchange for obtaining those goods is money. Money is highly fungible in that it can be translated into any one of those goods. As diminishing returns from consumption of one good are reached, money can be allocated to other goods. Given all the goods that are available, there is always some good of which little has been consumed and for which returns on purchasing some amount of it are still high. The same can be said for investment in offspring's embodied capital, which appears to include investments not only in schooling but in goods associated with social training and social status, such as hobbies and sports, clothing, and toys, much of these investments being commitments to favorable placements of children in the mating market. Our best guess at this time is that the low fertility exhibited in modern societies reflects both the payoffs on investments in offspring income and a perceived lack of diminishing returns from other forms of consumption. Understanding the role of status competition during human evolutionary history may prove particularly illuminating in explaining the pattern of high consumption and low fertility.

The existence of extrasomatic wealth may be the critical condition to which our evolved proximate mechanisms do not respond so as to maximize fitness. By implication, post-demographic transition settings are not the only ones in which deviations from fitness maximization are likely to be observed. When there is heritable wealth, such as cattle or land, the breast-feeding/energy-balance system may generate higher fertility than parents desire in terms of their own wealth and wealth they wish to pass on to their children. Adjustments to this situation may primarily involve differential inheritance, such as primogeniture and illegitimacy, but may also include late age of marriage (Coale and Treadway 1986) or even celibacy (Boone 1986), and lowered rates of polygyny by wealthy men (Luttbeg, Borgerhoff Mulder, and Mangel, this volume). Thus, perhaps we should not be surprised to find deviations from fitness maximization as soon as there are forms of extrasomatic wealth. The extremely low fertility in modern societies may reflect the extreme importance of extrasomatic wealth and the multiple ways in which it can be used.

SUMMARY

1. Modern fertility behavior deviates from fitness maximization in two ways: (1) fertility is much lower than the level that would maximize descendants in future generations, and (2) increases in wealth are not associated with increases in number of children produced.

2. To understand the causes of those deviations, we employed a four-step process in theory building: (1) develop a general theory of the action of natural selection on fertility and parental investment; (2) apply the theory to the ecology of evolving hominids, with specific reference to what is known about extant hunter-gatherers; (3) specify the kinds of psychological and physiological proximate mechanisms that evolved to produce adaptive responses to the ecological conditions of the past; (4) develop models of how those proximate mechanisms would respond to modern socio-ecological conditions and variability among them.

3. We combined life history theory and economic models of human capital investment into a general model of investments in one's own embodied capital, reproduction, and offspring's embodied capital. In a physical sense, embodied capital is organized somatic tissue. In a functional sense, embodied capital includes strength, immune competence, coordination, skill, and knowledge, all of which affect the profitability of allocating time and other resources to alternative activities such as resource acquisition, defense from predators and parasites, mating competition, parenting, and social dominance. The two most important forms of embodied capital investment are those that affect survival and those that affect income. Natural selection is expected to act on embodied capital investment to maximize reproduction effort over the life course and to allocate reproductive effort optimally between quantity and quality of children.

4. Among hunter-gatherers, the critical constraints on fertility and parental investment appear to be the time needed to give intensive care to infants and very young children, and the energy to feed parents and multiple children of varying ages. The level of those investments may be regulated by psychological mecha-

nisms that direct attention to ecologically variable relationships between investments and outcomes and that detect diminishing returns on investment. Most proximally, however, fertility appears to be regulated by physiological mechanisms responsive to breast-feeding regimes and net energy balance.

5. In modern society, investments in one's own and one's offspring's embodied capital includes resources other than food energy. The low fertility in modern societies may be due to the importance of skill in competitive labor markets, which directly link wages to the costs of obtaining skills. The fact that fertility is not correlated with wealth may be due to an increased payoff from investment in children's education by wealthier parents because of their higher levels of education and their ability to impart those skills to children.

6. We tested predictions derived from this model with data collected from men in Albuquerque, New Mexico. Consistent with the theory, we found (1) education has become an increasingly important determinant of age at first reproduction and fertility during this century; (2) holding education constant, increases in income is generally correlated with increased fertility; (3) educated parents invest more in children than less-educated parents, in terms of both time and monetary expenditures; (4) the child's scholastic abilities and earlier parental investments are associated with the likelihood of providing support for higher education; (5) the level of parental investment children receive is positively associated with their educational attainments.

7. Future research must test the predictions of this model alongside other competing and complementary explanations of modern fertility behavior.

The extremely low fertility exhibited in modern society may result not only from the costs of investing in children but because of the large array of consumption goods available and the existence of money as a medium of exchange. Deviations from fitness maximization may exist not only in modern societies evidencing extremely low fertility, but in any society in which there are extrasomatic forms of wealth.

ACKNOWLEDGMENTS

Support for the research project on male fertility and parenting in New Mexico began with two seed grants from the University of New Mexico Biomedical Research Grants (1988 and 1989), and one from the University of New Mexico Research Allocations Committee (1988). Further seed money as well as interim funding came from the William T. Grant Foundation (89130589 and 91130501). Major support for the project came from the National Science Foundation (1990–1993, BNS-9011723 and DBS-911552). Both NSF grants included Research Experience for Undergraduates supplements. Some of these analyses are based upon work supported by an NSF Graduate Research Fellowship granted to Kermyt G. Anderson.

The authors would like to thank Lee Cronk and an anonymous reviewer for helpful comments on drafts of this paper as well as the many undergraduate and graduate students at the University of New Mexico who worked on the Albuquerque Men project in interviewing, coding, data entry, office management, and data management and analysis. We would also like to thank Ted Bergstrom, Monique Borgerhoff Mulder, Erik Charnov, Phil Ganderton, Steve Gangestad, Kristen Hawkes, Kim Hill, Nick Blurton Jones, David Lam, and Robert Willis for stimulating discussions about the theory of fertility, and Kishore Gawande for discussions on economic models.

NOTES

1. Studies of traditional small-scale societies suggest that fertility may be optimized to maximize the production of descendants over the long run (e.g., Blurton Jones and Sibly 1978 and Blurton Jones 1986 for the !Kung in Botswana, but see Hill and Hurtado 1996 for disconfirmation among the Ache). The abrupt change in the association between wealth and fertility that occurs at the same time fertility is historically reduced (Retherford 1993) requires explanation.
2. Trivers (1974) points out that parental and offspring fitness interests conflict to some extent, because parental fitness will be maximized by a lower level of offspring survival than would maximize offspring fitness.
3. Later models (e.g., Becker 1991; Becker and Barro 1988; Becker et al. 1990) treat fertility decisions explicitly in terms of an intergenerational utility function. The individual's optimization problem is to maximize satisfaction derived from both his or her own consumption and the consumption of descendants.
4. Compensation for additional embodied capital can come in the form of benefits, working conditions, and prestige, as well as wages.
5. Individuals were offered the opportunity to conduct the interview in Spanish, but all of our potential interviewees felt comfortable with an English interview.
6. The nonsignificant p-value for the 1960 cohort is probably due to the smaller sample size, given that the parameter estimate is similar to the 1940 and 1950 cohorts with bigger sample sizes.

REFERENCES

Anderson, K. G., H. K. Kaplan, and J. B. Lancaster. 1999. Parental care by genetic and stepfathers II: Reports by Albuquerque Men. *Evolution and Human Behavior* 20(6): 405–32.

Austad, S. N., and K. E. Fischer. 1991. Mammalian aging, metabolism, and ecology: Evidence from the bats and marsupials. *Journal of Gerontology* 46(2):47–53.

———. 1992. Primate longevity: its place in the mammalian scheme. *American Journal of Primatology* 28:251–261.

———. 1993. Retarded senescence in an insular population of Virginia opposums (*Didelphis virginiana*). *Journal of Zoology* (London) 229:695–708.

Barkow, J. 1989. *Darwin, Sex, and Status.* Toronto: Toronto University Press.

Barkow, J., and N. Burley. 1980. Human fertility, evolutionary biology, and the Demographic Transition. *Ethology and Sociobiology* 1:163–180.

Becker, G. S. 1975. *Human Capital,* 2nd ed. New York: Columbia University Press.

———. 1991. *A Treatise on the Family,* 2nd ed. Cambridge: Harvard University Press.

Becker, G. S., and R. J. Barro. 1988. A reformulation of the economic theory of fertility. *Quarterly Journal of Economics* 103:1–25.

Becker, G. S. and H. G. Lewis. 1973. Interaction between quantity and quality of children. In *Economics of the Family: Marriage, Children, and Human Capital,* T. W. Schultz, ed. Pp. 81–90. Chicago: University of Chicago Press.

Becker, G. S., and N. Tomes. 1976. Child endowments and the quantity and quality of children. *Journal of Political Economy* 84:s143–S163.

———. 1986. Human capital and the rise and fall of families. *Journal of Labor Economics* 4:s1–S39.

Becker, G. S., K. M. Murphy, and R. Tamura. 1990. Human capital, fertility and economic growth. *Journal of Political Economy* 98:s12–s37.

Betzig, L. L. 1986. *Despotism and Differential Reproduction: A Darwinian View of History.* Hawthorne, New York: Aldine.

Bianchi, S. M., and D. Spain. 1996. *Balancing Act: Motherhood, Marriage, and Employment among American Women.* New York: Russell Sage.

Blake, J. 1989. *Family Size and Achievement.* Los Angeles: University of California Press.

Blurton Jones, N. G. 1986 Bushman birth spacing: A test for optimal interbirth intervals. *Ethology and Sociobiology* 7:91–105.

———. 1987. Bushman birth spacing: a direct test of simple predictions. *Ethology and Sociobiology* 8:183–203.

———. 1993. The lives of hunter-gatherer children: Effects of parental behavior and parental reproductive strategy. In *Juvenile Primates,* M. E. Pereira and L. A. Fairbanks, eds. Pp. 309–326. Oxford: Oxford University Press.

Blurton Jones, N. G., and R. M. Sibly. 1978. Testing adaptiveness of culturally determined behavior: Do Bushman women maximize their reproductive success by spacing births widely and foraging seldom? In *Human Behavior and Adaptation,* N. G. Blurton Jones and V. Reynolds, eds. Pp. 135–157. London: Taylor and Francis.

Blurton Jones, N. G., K. Hawkes, and J. O'Connell. 1989. Modeling and measuring the costs of children in two foraging societies. In *Comparative Socioecology: The Behavioral Ecology of Humans and Other Mammals,* V. Standen and R. Foley, eds. Pp. 367–390. Oxford: Blackwell.

———.1997. Why do Hadza children forage? In *Unity Psychology and Biology: Integrative Perspectives on Human Development.* N. L. Segal, G. E. Weisfeld, and C. C. Weisfeld, eds. Pp. 279–313. Washington, DC: American Psychological Society.

Blurton Jones, N. G., K. Hawkes, and P. Draper. 1994a. Foraging returns of !Kung adults and children: Why didn't !Kung children forage? *Journal of Anthropological Research* 50:217–248.

———. 1994b. Differences between Hadza and !Kung children's work: Affluence or practical reason? In *Key Issues in Hunter-Gatherer Research,* E. S. Burch Jr. and L. J. Ellanna, eds. Pp. 189–215. Oxford: Berg.

Blurton Jones, N. G., K. Hawkes, and J. F. O'Connell. 1999. Some current ideas about the evolution of human life history. In *Comparative Primate Socioecology,* P. C. Lee, ed. Pp. 140–66. Cambridge, UK: Cambridge University Press.

Bock, J. 1995. *The Determinants of Variation in Children's Activities in a Southern African Community.* Ph.D. dissertation, Department of Anthropology, University of New Mexico, Albuquerque.

Boone, J. 1986. Parental investment and elite family structure in preindustrial states: A case study of late medieval-early modern Portuguese genealogies. American Anthropologist 88:859–878.

Borgerhoff Mulder, M. 1987. On cultural and reproductive success: Kipsigis evidence. *American Anthropologist* 89:617–634.

———. 1988. Reproductive consequences of sex-biased inheritance for the Kipsigis. In *Comparative Socioecology of Mammals and Man,* V. Standen and R. Foley, eds. Pp. 405–427. London: Blackwell.

———. 1992. Reproductive decisions. In *Evolutionary Ecology and Human Behavior,* E. A. Smith and B. Winterhalder, eds. Pp. 339–374. Hawthorne, New York: Aldine de Gruyter.

Boyd, R., and P. Richerson. 1985. *Culture and the Evolutionary Process.* Chicago: University of Chicago Press.

Burck, C. G. 1976. A group profile of the Fortune 500 chief executives. *Fortune* (May), 173–177.

Chagnon, N. 1988. Life histories, blood revenge, and warfare in a tribal population. *Science* 239:985–992.

Cleland, J. 1985. Marital fertility decline in developing countries: Theories and evidence. In *Reproductive Change in Developing Countries: Insights from the World Fertility Survey,* J. Cleland and J. Hobcraft, eds. Pp. 223–252. Oxford: Oxford University Press.

Cleland, J., and C. Wilson. 1987. Demand theories of fertility transition: An iconoclastic view. *Population Studies* 41:5–30.

Cromer, A. 1993. *Uncommon Sense: The Heretical Nature of Science.* New York: Oxford.

Cronk, L. 1991a. Human behavioral ecology. *Annual Reviews in Anthropology* 20:25–53.

———. 1991b. Wealth, status and reproductive success among the Mukogodo. *American Anthropologist* 93:345–360.

Coale, A. J., and R. Treadway. 1986. A summary of the changing distribution of overall fertility, marital fertility and the proportion married in the provinces of Europe. In *The Decline of Fertility in Europe,* A. J. Coale and S. C. Watkins, eds. Pp. 31–181. Princeton: Princeton University Press.

Denison, E. F. 1985. *Trends in American Growth, 1929–1982.* Washington, D.C.: Brookings Institute.

de Tray, D. N. 1973. Child quality and the demand for children. *Journal of Political Economy* 81:s7s–95.

Downey, D. B. 1995. When bigger is not better: Family size, parental resources, and children's educational performance. *American Sociological Review* 60:746–761.

Draper, P., and H. Harpending. 1987. Parental investment and the child's environment. In *Parenting across the Lifespan: Biosocial Dimensions,* J. Lancaster, J. Altmann, A. Rossi, and L. Sherrod, eds. Pp. 207–235. New York: Aldine.

Easterlin, R. A., R. Pollack, and M. L. Wachter. 1980. Toward a more general economic model of fertility preferences. In *Population and Economic Change in Developing Countries,* R. A. Easterlin, ed. Pp. 81–135. Chicago: Chicago University Press.

Ellison, P. T. 1990. Human ovarian function and reproductive ecology: New hypotheses. *American Anthropologist* 92:933–952.

Ellison, P. T, C. Panter-Brick, S. F. Lipson, and M. T. O'Rourke. 1993. The ecological context of human ovarian function. *Human Reproduction* 8:2248–2258.

Flinn, M. 1986. Correlates of reproductive success in a Caribbean village. *Ethology and Sociobiology* 9:1–29.

Hanson, L. A. 1982. The mammary gland as an immunological organ. *Immunology Today* 3:168–172.

Harpending, H. C., P. Draper, and R. Pennington. 1990. Cultural evolution, parental care, and mortality. In *Health and Disease in Traditional Societies,* A. Swedlund and G. Armelegos, eds. Pp. 241–255. South Hadley, Massachusetts: Bergin and Garvey.

Hart, B., and T. Risley. 1995. *Meaningful Differences in the Everyday Experience of Young American Children.* Baltimore: Brookes.

Hawkes, K., J. O'Connell, and N. Blurton Jones. 1991. Hunting income patterns among the Hadza: Big game, common goods, foraging goals and the evolution of the human diet. In *Foraging Strategies and Natural Diet of Monkeys, Apes and Humans,* A. Whiten and E. Widdownson, eds. Pp. 243–251. Proceedings of the Royal Society of London 334. Oxford: Clarendon Press.

———. 1995. Hadza children's foraging: Juvenile dependency, social arrangements and mobility among hunter-gatherers. *Current Anthropology* 36:688–700.

———. 1997. Hadza women's time allocation, offspring provisioning, and the evolution of long post-menopausal lifespans. *Current Anthropology* 38:551–557.

Herrnstein, R. J., and C. Murray. 1994. *The Bell Curve: Intelligence and Class Structure in American Life.* New York: Free Press.

Hill, K., and A. M. Hurtado. 1996. *Ache Life History: The Ecology and Demography of a Foraging People.* Hawthorne, New York: Aldine de Gruyter.

Hoff-Ginsberg, E., and T. Tardif. 1995. Socioeconomic status and parenting. In *The Handbook of Parenting,* vol. 2, M. Bornstein, ed. Pp. 161–188. Hillsdale, New Jersey: Erlbaum.

Howie, P. W., J. S. Forsyth, S. A. Ogston, A. Clark, and C. du V. Florey. 1990. Protective effect of breast feeding against infection. *British Medical Journal* 300:11–16.

Hughes, A. 1986. Reproductive success and occupational class in eighteenth-century Lancashire, England. *Social Biology* 33:109–115.

Huffman, S. L., K. Ford, H. A. Allen, and P. Streble. 1987. Nutrition and fertility in Bangladesh: Breastfeeding and post partum amenorrhoea. *Population Studies* 41:447–462.

Hurtado, A. M. and K. Hill. 1990. Seasonality in a foraging society: Variation in diet, work effort, fertility and the sexual division of labor among the Hiwi of Venezuela. *Journal of Anthropological Research* 46:293–345.

Irons, W. 1979. Cultural and biological success. In *Evolutionary Biology and Human Social Behavior,* N. Chagnon and W. Irons, eds. Pp. 257–272. North Scituate, Massachusetts: Duxbury.

———. 1983. Human female reproductive strategies. In *Social Behavior of Female Vertebrates,* S. K. Wasser, ed. Pp. 169–213. New York: Academic Press.

———. 1990. Let's make our perspectives broader rather than narrower: A comment on Turke's "Which humans behave adaptively, and why does it matter?" and on the so-called Da-Dp debate. *Ethology and Sociobiology* 11:361–375.

———. 1993. Monogamy, contraception, and the cultural and reproductive success hypothesis. *Behavior and Brain Sciences* 16:295–296.

———. 1995. Cultural and reproductive success in traditional societies. Unpublished ms. Department of Anthropology, Northwestern University, Evanston.

Jones, R., and A. Palloni. 1994. Investigating the determinants of post-partum amenorrhea using a multistate hazards approach. *Annals of the New York Academy of Sciences* 709:227–230.

Kaplan, H. 1996. A theory of fertility and parental investment in traditional and modern societies. *Yearbook of Physical Anthropology* 39:91–135.

———. 1997. The evolution of the human life course. In *Between Zeus and Salmon: The Biodemography of Longevity,* K. Wachter and C. Finch, eds. Pp. 175–211. Washington, D.C.: National Academy of Sciences.

Kaplan, H. K., and K. Hill. 1985. Hunting ability and reproductive success among male Ache foragers. *Current Anthropology* 26:131–133.

Kaplan, H., J. B. Lancaster, J. Bock, and S. Johnson. 1995. Does observed fertility maximize fitness among New Mexican men? A test of an optimality model and a new theory of parental investment in the embodied capital of offspring. *Human Nature* 6:325–360.

Kaplan, H., J. B. Lancaster, and K. G. Anderson. 1998. Human parental investment and fertility: The life histories of men in Albuquerque, NM. In *Men in Families: When Do They Get Involved? What Difference Does it Make?* A. Booth and N. Crouter, eds. Pp. 55–110. Mahwah, New Jersey: Lawrence Erlbaum.

Kaplan, H., K. Hill, J. Lancaster, and A. M. Hurtado. 2000. A theory of human life history evolution: Diet, intelligence, and longevity. *Evolutionary Anthropology* 9(5):1–30.

Lack, D. 1954. *The Natural Regulation of Animal Numbers.* Oxford: Oxford University Press.

———. 1968. *Ecological Adaptations for Breeding in Birds.* London: Methuen.

Lam, D. 1986. The dynamics of population growth, differential fertility, and inequality. *American Economic Review* 76:1103–1116.

Lancaster, J. B. 1997. The evolutionary history of human parental investment in relation to population growth and social stratification. In *Feminism and Evolutionary Biology,* P. A. Gowaty, ed. Pp. 466–488. New York: Chapman and Hall.

Lancaster, J. B., and C. S. Lancaster. 1987. The watershed: Change in parental-investment and family-formation strategies in the course of human evolution. In *Parenting across the Life Span: Biosocial Dimensions,* J. B. Lancaster, J. Altmann, A. S. Rossi, and L. R. Sherrod, eds. Pp. 187–205. Hawthorne, New York: Aldine de Gruyter.

Lee, P. C., P. Majluf, and I. J. Gordon. 1991. Growth, weaning and maternal investment from a comparative perspective. *Journal of Zoology* (London) 225:99–114.

Lesthaeghe, R., and C. Wilson. 1986. *Modes of production, secularization, and the pace of fertility decline in western Europe, 1870–1930.* In The Decline of Fertility in Europe, A. J. Coale and S. C. Watkins, eds. Pp. 261–292. Princeton: Princeton University Press.

Lindert, P. H. 1986. Unequal English wealth since 1670. *Journal of Political Economy* 94:1127–1162.

Lloyd, D. C. 1987. Selection of offspring size at independence and other size-versus-number strategies. *American Naturalist* 129:800–817.

Low, B. 1990. Occupational status, landownership, and reproductive behavior in 19th-century Sweden: Tuna Parish. *American Anthropologist* 92:457–468.

Mare, R. D. 1991. Five decades of educational assortative mating. *American Sociological Review* 56:15–32.

McGinley, M. A., and E. L. Charnov. 1988. Multiple resources and the optimal balance between size and number of offspring. *Evolutionary Ecology* 2:77–84.

McNeilly, A. S., A. Glasier, and P. W. Howie. 1985. Endocrine control of lactational infertility. In *Maternal Nutrition and Lactational Infertility,* J. Dobbing, ed. Pp. 1–16. New York: Raven Press.

Mealey, L. 1985. The relationship between social status and biological success: a case study of the mormon religious hierarchy. *Ethology and Sociobiology* 11:83–95.

Newcomer, M. 1955. *The Big Business Executive: The Factors That Made Him, 1990–1950.* New York: Columbia University Press.

Oftedal, O. T. 1984. Milk composition, milk yield and energy output at peak lactation: A comparative review. *Symposium of the Zoological Society of London* 51:33–85.

Pennington, R., and H. Harpending. 1988. Fitness and fertility among the Kalahari !Kung. *American Journal of Physical Anthropology* 77:303–319.

Pérusse, D. 1993. Cultural and reproductive success in industrial societies: Testing the relationship at the proximate and ultimate levels (with comments). *Brain and Behavioral Sciences* 16:267–323.

Potts, M. 1997. Sex and the birth rate: Human biology, demographic change, and access to fertility-regulation methods. *Population and Development Review* 23:1–39.

Prentice, A. M., and R. G. Whitehead. 1987. The energetics of human reproduction. *Symposium of the Zoological Society of London* 57:275–304.

Retherford, R. D. 1993. Demographic transition and the evolution of intelligence: Theory and evidence. Unpublished ms. Program on Population, East-West Center, Honolulu, Hawaii.

Rogers, A. R., and N. G. Blurton Jones. 1992. Allocation of parental care. Unpublished manuscript. Ms. Department of Anthropology, University of Utah, Salt Lake City.

Rosenblatt, P. C., P. Peterson, J. Portner, M. Cleveland, A. Mykkanen, R. Foster, G. Holm, B. Joel, H. Reisch, C. Kreuscher, and R. Phillips. 1973. A cross-cultural study of responses to childlessness. *Behavior Science* Notes 8:221–231.

Sheard, N. F., and W. A. Walker. 1988. The role of breast milk in the development of the gastrointestinal tract. *Nutrition Review* 46:1–8.

Simons, J. L. 1974. *The Effects of Income on Fertility.* Chapel Hill, North Carolina: Carolina Populations Center.

Smith C. C., and S. D. Fretwell. 1974. The optimal balance between size and number of offspring. *American Naturalist* 108:499–506.

Trivers, R. L. 1974. Parent-offspring conflict. *American Zoologist* 14:249–264.

Turke, P. W. 1989. Evolution and the demand for children. *Population and Development Review* 15:61–90.

Turke, P., and L. Betzig. 1985. Those who can do: Wealth, status and reproductive success on Ifaluk. Ethology and Sociobiology 6:79–87.

U.S. Department of Commerce, Bureau of the Census. 1985. Money income of households, families and persons in the United States, 1985. Current Population Reports. Series P-60, No. 156, Table 35. Washington, D.C.: U.S. Government Printing Office.

———. 1991. Census of Population and Housing, 1990: Summary tape files 1 and 3 on CD-ROM (New Mexico). Washington, D.C.: Bureau of the Census.

———. 1992. 1990 Census of Population: general population characteristics (New Mexico). CP-1-33, Table 54, Pg. 82. Washington, D.C.: U.S. Government Printing Office.

U.S. Department of Transportation, Federal Highway Administration. 1993. Highway Statistics 1987. (TD2.22:991) Washington, D.C.: U.S. Government Printing Office.

Vining, D. R., Jr. 1986. Social versus reproductive success: The central theoretical problem of human sociobiology. *The Behavioral and Brain Sciences* 9:167–216.

Vinovskis, M. A. 1994. Education and the economic transformation of nineteenth century America. In *Age and Structural Lag: Society's Failure to Provide Meaningful Opportunities in Work, Family, and Leisure.* M. W. Riley, R. L. Kahn, and A. Foner, eds. Pp. 171–196. New York: Wiley and Sons.

Vitzthum, V. 1994. Comparative study of breastfeeding structure and its relation to human reproductive ecology. *Yearbook of Physical Anthropology* 37:307–349.

Voland, E. 1990. Differential reproductive success within the Krummhörn population (Germany, 18th and 19th centuries). *Behavioral Ecology and Sociobiology* 26:65–72.

Weiss, Y., and R. Willis. 1985. Children as collective goods and divorce settlements. *Journal of Labor Economics* 3:268–292.

Whitehead, R. G., and A. Paul. 1981. Infant growth and human milk requirements: A first approach. *Lancet* 2:161–163.

Willis, R. J. 1973. A new approach to the economic theory of fertility behavior. *Journal of Political Economy* 81:s14–s64.

———. 1987. Wage determinants: A survey and reinterpretation of human capital earnings functions. In *Handbook of Labor Economics,* O. Ashenfelter and R. Layard, eds. Pp. 525–602. Amsterdam: North Holland.

Zei, G., and L. L. Cavalli-Sforza. 1977. Education and birth control. *Genus* 33:15–42.

15

Sex, Wealth, and Fertility

Old Rules, New Environments

BOBBI S. LOW

It is easy to imagine that our evolutionary past is remote, unconnected to our lives today, and of interest only when we think of traditional societies or ancient history. Yet our evolved tendencies interact with today's novel environments—today's cities, no less than yesterday's rain forests and savannas, *are* our environments. Both physical and social aspects of our current environments can be evolutionarily novel, largely the result of our own actions, yet they still interact with our evolved tendencies. What does this mean about the old established relationships between resources and fertility?

In non-human mammals, the positive relationship between resources or dominance and fertility is well established and relatively simple. Although the particular mechanisms vary with phylogeny and ecology and there are interesting subtleties, the resulting pattern is extremely strong. Males who get control of unusually large or rich resources have more offspring than other males; females who fail to acquire some threshold amount, like unsuccessful males, fail to reproduce at all. In some species females, like males, show a high resources-high fertility pattern, but in most mammals, the effect of resources is most obvious when resources limit females' fertility.

In human evolutionary pasts, at least as reflected by the demography of traditional societies, the same pattern seems clear for men. Even in monogamous, late-marrying societies in the demographic transition (below), resource acquisition aided fertility. In most past environments, those who strived for resources and succeeded were those who left children.

In the evolutionary history of all living things including humans, "more" has always been reproductively more profitable: either more babies, or better provisioned—and thus more consumptive—babies. This distinction is crucial: for many species in competitive or densely populated environments, the most successful reproductive tactic in many environments is not to make the maximum number of offspring, but to make fewer, better-invested offspring (MacArthur and

Wilson 1967; in humans, see e.g., Low et al. 1992, Low 1993, Boone and Kessler 1999).

Here I want to examine what we know about relationships between resources and (1) completed lifetime fertility, and (2) timing of fertility (age-specific fertility) for men and for women under different circumstances. As we have applied evolutionary theory to human behavior, the complexity and diversity of our empirical findings have returned, correctly, to deepen and enrich our theory. Yet, as I think will become clear, we have a long way to go before we understand fully the complexities in the resources-reproduction relationships of men and women, across time and societies. I suggest that we seldom have gathered the appropriate data, and that even when the appropriate data exist, they have seldom been analyzed in ways that makes them relevant to these questions. Here, I hope to provide an analytic outline for our questions; the empirical papers in this volume begin to address parts of our confusion usefully.

WEALTH, STATUS, AND FERTILITY

Patterns for Men versus Women

The relationships between resource control and fertility in traditional societies differ for men and women, just as in other, non-human, mammals; they differ in ways we cannot ignore if we wish to ask questions about wealth, fertility, and consumption today. In quite varied societies, wealth or status and reproductive success are positively correlated for men; in diverse traditional societies, status and wealth correlate with male reproductive success (e.g., reviews by Low 1993, 1996, 2000). In contrast, women, like other female mammals, are most affected by resources at the "low end" of variation: malnutrition leads to infertility. The best-nourished, wealthiest woman in any society is not able, as are the wealthiest men, to have orders of magnitude more children than the poorest mother; so women have seldom profited by striving for resources and status in the same way and to the same degree as men.

When people have manipulated the resource-fertility relationship through cultural practices, these normal relationships have sometimes been subverted (e.g., Hrdy 1992, 1999). Perhaps most interesting are those rare societies in which daughters can return significant benefits to the family through status gains: those in which hypergyny occurs, and daughters in poor groups can marry up, while sons cannot. Daughter favoritism shows up in these hypergynous societies, because women, but not men, can "marry up" (Dickemann (1979); often in such societies, daughters are treated favorably in the lower classes, while daughters of higher-status, wealthier families are sent into religious celibacy, or killed as infants. Among the Mukogodo (Cronk 1993, this volume), daughters are favored over sons in a variety of ways (for example, they are breastfed longer), for they can marry outside the Mukogodo, among men of richer groups, while Mukogodo men cannot marry out and up. It is relatively easier for a Mukogodo woman to marry inter-ethnically than for a Mukogodo man, because the bride-wealth required for a Mukogodo woman is relatively low, whereas a Mukogodo man has difficulty getting the livestock for bride-wealth to marry a higher-status, non-Mukogodo, woman.

Resources affect life history variables that influence birth timing and total fertility, such as age at marriage and probability of remarriage. Here again, the patterns of the two sexes differ. In many societies, widows remarry far less frequently than do widowers, with no obvious demographic or economic explanation. Further, women remarry at earlier ages than men, and women's probability of remarriage declines with age. Classical demographers have found such patterns puzzling, for women's economic value, like men's, does not decline with age. But biologically, these patterns make sense: women's reproductive value (RV; Fisher 1958) does decline, with certainty, after the late teens and early twenties. Not surprisingly, when men remarry, they tend to marry young women, of high reproductive value. Again, this means that wealth affects remarriage rates for men, but not women. The sex difference in remarriage rates undoubtedly contributes to the greater fertility of men's second marriages, compared to women's, even in societies with late ages at first marriage and socially imposed monogamy. The patterns are quite strong: widows remarry far less frequently than widowers; widows with dependent children remarry at an even lower rate; and widows commonly do not remarry at all when they are older. In contemporary society, too, these patterns persist (see Low 2000 for references).

The complexity of these interactions—sex, reproductive impact of resources, cultural constraints—means we must be cautious: household data, if male and female information are not separated, and relatedness is unspecified, are inappropriate to answer questions about wealth and fertility.

Resources, Abortion, and Infanticide

Much abortion appears relatively straightforward in an evolutionary perspective: most likely to abort are mothers who are unwell and unlikely to be successful in the current pregnancy, mothers who have no support system, and mothers who are newly paired with a male not the father. Further, under such conditions abortion is more likely among mothers with high reproductive value—women who have further chances to carry a successful pregnancy to term when conditions are more favorable (see contemporary data, Hill and Low 1991; and reviews by Hrdy 1999 and Low 2000).

In humans as in other species, most infanticide is undertaken by non-relatives, but parental infanticide does occur. Infanticide patterns are similar to those of abortion: infanticide is more likely when the current infant is ill, deformed, or otherwise unlikely to thrive; and when the mother has little chance of rearing this child successfully, but has high reproductive value, and thus good future chances.

Both abortion and infanticide patterns suggest that resource scarcity may lead to termination of parental investment when that investment is unlikely to produce a successful, reproductive adult offspring (see Hrdy 1999).

Celibacy

Celibacy, too, probably responds to resource conditions. In birds and non-human mammals, "celibacy" is typically represented by offspring who delay or forego independent reproduction in periods of resource constraint; they stay and assist parents in raising other offspring (e.g., Emlen 1995, 1997); typically these are older siblings helping parents raise younger siblings. During the European demographic transition(s), high proportions of both men and women failed to marry in countries such as England (Wrigley and Schofield 1982), Sweden (Low and Clarke 1992) and Ireland (Strassmann and Clarke 1998); patterns reflected resource constrictions and resulting price fluctuations.

A related pattern of celibacy may be uniquely human: that of later-born, typically male, children entering celibate life in powerful institutions (e.g., the Catholic Church). Are there resource correlations? Both historical and contemporary empirical data are relevant. Throughout the Middle Ages, later-born sons of large families were often consigned to the priesthood (celibate) or the military (non-celibate) (e.g., Boone 1986, 1988). In both cases, younger sons were removed from sibling competition for limited familial resources, and positioned to return resources through political rise in a powerful institution, if clever enough.

In the case of the Church, such a son's reproduction was typically foregone, and it is possible that such arrangements did not usually return lineage advantages. Recent work (Goody 1983; Rice 1990; Sipe 1990; Sweeney 1992) suggests that institutional, rather than familial, political and economic advantages have influenced the Church's historical attempts to impose chastity. Contemporary empirical data also suggest that interactions of resource availability and family dynamics drive much of what we see. In the United States, ordinations and seminary enrollments have declined as family sizes have fallen, and have done so precipitously since 1967 (Plotvin and Muncada 1990). The most cited reason for leaving is mandatory celibacy, and of those who leave, 90% marry. Re-analysis of the data from Plotvin and Muncada suggest that harsher economic conditions correlate with increased numbers of men choosing religious celibacy (Figure 15.1). Family size also matters: larger families are more likely to have a son who becomes a seminarian, and even today, seminarians tend to be later-born sons from large families (Low 2000: 174–175). The interaction of family income and family size is complicated in Plotvin and Muncada's sample, for the seminarians entered across a long time period. For men under 30, there was a birth order–income effect: seminarians were poor men, late-born in large families ($n = 382$, d.f. = 7,374, F = 2.9, $p = 0.0062$). For those 30 and over when entering the seminary, there was no influence of income and family size ($n = 208$, d.f. = 7,200, F = 0.6, $p = 0.75$). The cultural meme of reli-

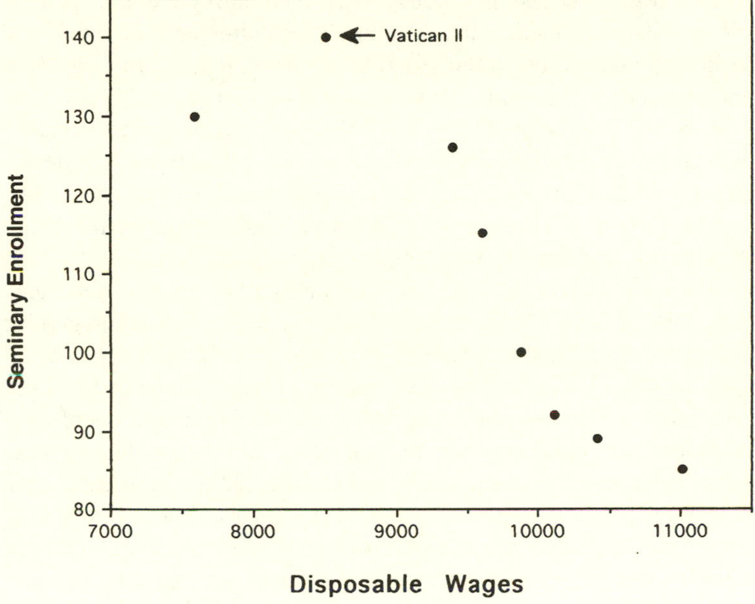

Figure 15.1. In the United States as disposable income (1980 dollars, standardized) increased, enrollment in Catholic seminaries decreased.

giosity also influences these decisions, of course (father's and mother's degree of religious participation and encouragement seem to matter); still, both mothers ($n = 644$, d.f. = 6, $X^2 = 19.7$, $p = 0.0031$) and fathers ($n = 644$, d.f. = 6, $X^2 = 18.8$, $p = 0.0045$) were more likely to encourage, and less likely to discourage, sons in large families to enter celibate priesthood. Using logistic regression, 30% of the variation in parental encouragement was explained by number of children alone ($n = 644$, d.f. = 1, $p = 0.0018$), independent of other factors.

Wealth and Lifetime Fertility in the Demographic Transition

During the nineteenth century in Europe and North America, a major shift occurred, from reliance on agricultural work and small-scale cottage industries to reliance on major industrial enterprises. Concurrently, fertility fell significantly (e.g., Coale and Watkins 1986; Coleman and Schofield 1986). A reasonable hypothesis, the focus of demographic work for thirty years, was that in some (largely unspecified) way, industrialization was at least a proximate cause of fertility decline. The results have been disappointing to many demographers (e.g., Schofield and Coleman 1986), and new data from the developing world also suggest that "industrialization" was a theoretical red herring.

There is reason to suspect that the same rules applied during the demographic transition as in traditional societies: that resource levels affected both men's and women's fertility. There are hints of this pattern even in aggregate data (e.g., marriage rates and fertility rates rose and fell with crop and grain prices; Wrigley and Schofield 1981, Low and Clarke 1992, 1993), although it is difficult to analyze aggregate data to answer the resource-fertility question. Analyses of lineage, rather than aggregate, data strongly suggest that marriage decisions, and fertility, of both men and women were influenced by resource availability during the demographic transition (e.g., Low and Clarke 1992).

In nineteenth-century Sweden, for example, multiparish comparisons (e.g., Low and Clarke 1992; Clarke and Low 1992) found that through the demographic transition (which was local and reversible in Sweden), whenever and wherever variation existed in wealth, wealth mattered to family formation and fertility. Controlling for variation in resource type, geography, and temporal patterns of marriage, wealth influenced both men's and women's lives during the demographic transition (data from 1824–1896; e.g., Low and Clarke 1992). Children of both sexes born to poorer parents were more likely than richer children to emigrate before reaching maturity. Poorer men, and women whose fathers were poorer, were less likely to marry in the parish than others, largely as a result of differential migration. Wealthier men tended to marry younger women than others, and to have more children. The ability to marry was the biggest predictor of fertility. Of all adults of both sexes who remained in their home parish and thus generated complete lifetime records, richer individuals had greater lifetime fertility, and more children alive at age ten, than others.

The clarity of the trends does not mean that the issues are simple; in fact, unless one were looking for the wealth-fertility relationship, one might miss it. For example, the fertility of individuals in Generation Two was influenced by father's wealth status, cohort, and own (men's) or husband's (women's) wealth status. The most reproductively successful individuals in Generation Two were sons and daughters of poorer men, who nonetheless became wealthy (men) or married wealthy men (women) (Figure 15.2a). The effects varied by decade of marriage or reaching adulthood; wealthy men had more children than others except in the period 1851–1870 (Figure 15.2b). It would be easy to focus on the complexity and miss the overall pattern, as we may be doing with contemporary data. The Swedish data, which allow us to see the main patterns, as well as the complexity and variation in outcomes of different analyses, highlight the importance of choosing appropriate data, and appropriate levels of analysis, to answer questions about wealth and fertility.

Wealth and Age-Specific Fertility in the Demographic Transition

Not only total lifetime fertility, but the pattern of age-specific fertility is important. As Fisher (1958) pointed out, in the simplest case, earlier fertility results in

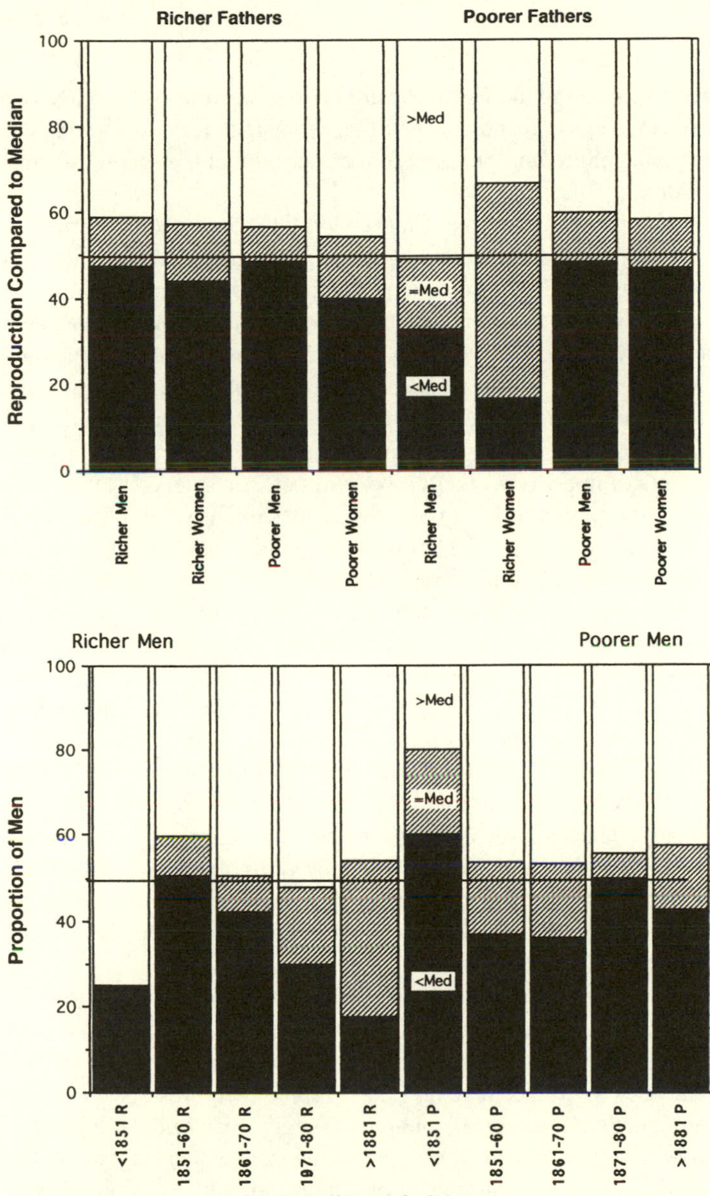

Figure 15.2. In large societies, the intermediate measures of fertility can reflect complexities. (a) In nineteenth-century Sweden, father's wealth/occupation status and own-or-husband's status interacted to affect lifetime fertility for both men and women. Individuals born to poorer fathers who nonetheless grew up to be wealthy had the highest lifetime fertility (see also Low 1994: Figure 2). (b) Men's lifetime fertility showed a cohort effect. "Decade" refers to the 10-year period in which a man reached age 23, or married, for the first time. Wealth and fertility were positively related before 1851 and after 1870. From 1851–1870, poorer men had a reproductive advantage. Despite this complexity, wealthy men had a reproductive advantage overall (Low 1990, 1994, 2000).

greater *m,* the genotypic rate of increase. Consider two women who each have two children, one woman at ages 16 and 18, the other woman at ages 36 and 38. The first woman has grandchildren in the same 5-year period that the second woman is having her children.

In the Swedish sample (e.g., Low and Clarke 1992), the age-specific fertility of richer women rose slightly sooner, and reached a higher peak, than that of poorer women (Low 2000: Figure 8.3). During this period in Sweden, family wealth was men's wealth (no women in the sample were recorded as having independent occupations), and the influence of wealth on women's fertility simply mirrored that of men's. Most fertility (93–98%) occurred within marriage; thus, delayed marriage reflected delayed (and typically lower total) fertility. Historical data from other Scandinavian countries during this period suggest that people themselves considered daughters of upper class men to be "women" (marriageable) at about 18 or 19; while poorer men courting poorer women frequently explicitly stated that they wanted an older woman, with her own household goods, and already able to organize and run a household (e.g., Drake 1969).

There is evidence that resources affected age-specific fertility independent of marriage age. Age-specific fertility peaks shortly after marriage in most societies (certainly those without effective contraceptive technology); this skewed distribution of births probably represents parental attempts to limit further births later in a marriage. The Swedish sample is relevant here. In the parish of Locknevi, which experienced severe resource constriction, marriage was relatively early (20–25), but age-specific fertility peaked later (ages 35–40) than in any other parish. This pattern was contemporaneous with land shifts and out-migration that independently reflect resource constraints. In the parish of Gullholmen, a small island reliant largely on uncertain fishing income, delayed fertility was also apparent, but in this parish, marriage itself was delayed (peaking at 25–30), and fertility, though late, was not delayed after marriage.

The Swedish comparative data highlight a problem: different measures are appropriate to answer different resource-fertility questions—and most data are not collected to answer questions in a way parallel to our analyses of other species. Some insights emerged when the standard demographic measures Total Fertility Rate and Net Reproductive Rate were compared in the Swedish sample to individual measures (more comparable to the non-human data from which theory and predictions arose): NBC, number of biological children born; and RS_{10}, number of children reaching independence and likely to leave the household; and those measures restricted to within-marriage births (Low and Clarke 1991). Using TFR, Nedertorneå (a northern parish with harsh climate and limited agriculture) had clearly higher fertility than all other parishes. However, if we ask about surviving children, either (1) Nedertorneå, Tuna (agriculture, mining in mid-Sweden), and Locknevi parishes were similar, while Gullholmen lagged behind (NBC: all children), or (2) Gullholmen women had more surviving offspring than women in other parishes (RS_{10mar}: children of married women). We need to be careful in matching data to questions.

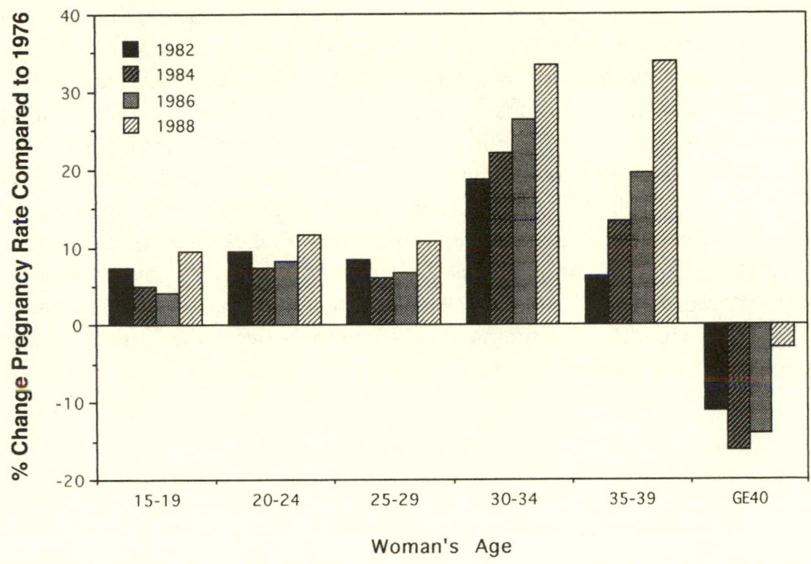

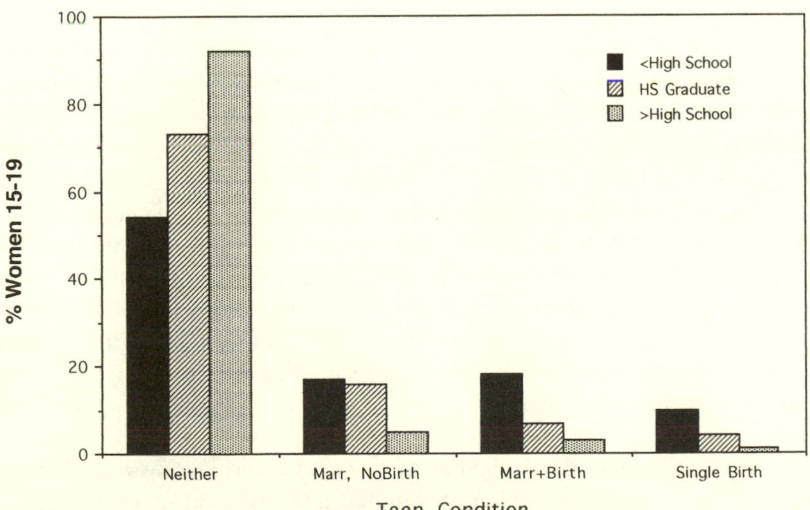

Figure 15.3. (a) U.S. women's age-specific fertility shifted between 1976 and 1988: fertility of ages 30–39 increased dramatically, early fertility increased proportionately less, and fertility after 40 declined (data from Luker 1996). (b) These shifts are probably class- or education-specific, with the fertility increases for older women coming largely from well-educated professionals, and the increases for younger women arising from less-educated women. Birth rates for women 15–19 peaked from 1950–1965 (73.3–91/1000), and while teenage births rates are lower now (51.9/1000 in 1990), these births are largely to women with less than a high-school education (see Luker 1996).

Rather than "the" demographic transition with a singular cause, there is good reason to expect ecologically influenced fertility trends with local, reversible, patterns. Certainly in Sweden, that was true (Lockridge 1983, Low and Clarke 1992). The primary components of population change—fertility, mortality, and migration—respond to ecological conditions at the individual family level in ways that are predictable and familiar to students of non-human populations. At least through the demographic transitions, certain predictable ecological rules underlie patterns of fertility, mortality, and migration, although these may be constrained by a variety of cultural complexities and interactions. For example, as noted above, men's reproductive patterns vary in concert with resource control to a much greater extent than women's patterns; this difference between the sexes is greatest when resources are abundant.

Wealth, Women's Age-Specific Fertility, and Women's Life Paths Today

Analyzing fertility relationships today is complicated for a number of reasons. First, because so many conditions are recent and thus evolutionarily novel, there is a possibility that whatever patterns we see will be emergent phenomena, influenced by forces once—but no longer—related to selective pressures. Second, societies are large, containing quite diverse subcultures whose members may face different pressures. Third, "wealth" and "status" today can mean a multitude of things, and many of these co-vary—so it can be difficult to be certain relationships we think we see are not simply co-variants of the important factors. Because of all these difficulties, many studies have used inappropriate data.

Consider the question of optimum age at first birth. Although much literature focuses on "why do poor women have early fertility?" from an evolutionary perspective, that is a trivial question, easily answered (above): *ceteris paribus,* once the tradeoff in "investment in growth versus reproduction" has been satisfied (Roff 1992, Stearns 1992) earlier fertility means greater lineage increase for any woman. The more interesting question is: "What tradeoffs lead to the sort of delayed fertility we see among women in developed nations today?" The strongest correlates of delayed fertility, in both developed and developing nations, are women's participation in the workforce and women's education (e.g., Kasarda et al. 1986).

Women face harsher tradeoffs than do men when we consider resource-garnering activities versus the production of children and dispersal of investment to them. In post-demographic transition societies, in which it appears that successful children cost more per capita in parental investment, women might actually profit reproductively, in some circumstances, by spending more effort bringing in resources, compared to filling traditional roles of child production. Low fertility and costly children result. The investment level required to produce successful offspring may vary with environment, and specifically with the threshold level of investment required for a child's success—a correlate of the competition offspring face, and in this sense, precisely analogous to the proper use of MacArthur and Wilson's (1967) concept of r- and K-selection (see Boone and Kessler 1999; reviews by Low et al. 1992; Low 1993, 1994). But are there circumstances in which relatively wealthy women who have late and low fertility have greater net lineage increase? We have no data.

What tradeoffs do work and schooling represent for women? Time and opportunity costs? Wealth versus fertility? Evolutionary anthropologists (e.g., Kaplan 1996, Kaplan and Lancaster, this volume), have analyzed the effects of cohort, wealth, and markets on human fertility, but generally, perhaps because of the widespread inappropriate treatment of r- and K-selection in the biological literature, appear to have remained within an economic framework, and not to have made the connection between human patterns and the "low fertility-high investment" patterns in other species first suggested by MacArthur and Wilson (see also Stearns 1992; Roff 1992; Hill 1993; Low 1998).

If poorer parents cannot substantially enhance their children's success, then we might expect large families, concentration of resources in one or a few children, with others leaving early (behavioral ecologists would call this an "alternate strategies" situation). Couples at the high end of the socioeconomic "ladder" might do better by investing more per child to make them competitive with their peers (e.g., education, clothing, status acquisitions; cf. Emlen 1997). And if there are periodic resource shortages and wealthier families have first claim to limited resources (Boone and Kessler 1999), then even if low-fertility/high-investment strategies show no advantage in easy times, they may confer a longer-term advantage (see also Low, Simon, and Anderson 2000).

There may be multiple and complex reasons for earlier versus later fertility. To understand the relationships (if any) of these patterns to evolved patterns, requires that (1) we can rely on the data being accurate; and (2) we can tease apart covariants. Consider the question of welfare payments and fertility. For non-white women in the United States, it appears that the AFDC program increases the likelihood of having a first child (e.g., Taşiran 1995: Table 30), but has no effect on probability of second and subsequent births. In fact, contrary to widespread beliefs about the fertility of welfare mothers, today in the United States poor women have low total fertility. Women on welfare in Wisconsin had 29.4% fewer children than women across the United States, and 32.8% fewer children than women in Wisconsin (Rank 1989); such women tended to be unmarried, Black, and less educated than others.

Poor women's fertility in the United States, although low, tends to be early, which may be adaptive for these women (Geronimus 1996a, b, Geronimus et al. 1997), over and above the simple biological advantage of early reproduction. As they age, poor urban Black women suffer "excess mortality" (Geronimus et al. 1996), and a variety of sub-lethal health problems that make it not only more difficult to conceive, but to raise, children (Geronimus et al., 1997). High mortality among Black males means that the probability of having a male partner declines with a woman's age. Even female assistance networks decline. In the poor Black populations studied (Harlem, central Detroit, Watts), teenage mothers have about a 75% chance that their mother will be alive and able to help when their child is 5 years old; for women who postpone childbearing until age 20, that figure is 40%. Not surprisingly, Geronimus et al. (1997) suggest that early childbearing may mitigate the threat to family economies and caretaking systems (and reproductive success) imposed by the heavy mortality and disease burdens borne by women in these populations. Daly and Wilson (1997) have similar findings: in Chicago neighborhoods, alike except for life expectancy at birth, age at first birth is positively correlated with life expectancy. And Lancaster (1986) made similar suggestions for traditional societies. These data fit the predictions from life history theory remarkably well: the most important variable in setting the timing of fertility is adult mortality (in other species we are usually unable to detect sub-lethal problems).

Early fertility is also associated with low educational achievement. From 1982 to 1988 in the United States, late fertility, among women 30–39, has increased dramatically (mostly arising from births to well-educated professional women; Figure 15.3a). While there are fewer births to teenage women today than in 1950-1965 (Luker 1996; App. 1), these births are largely to women with less than a high-school education (Figure 15.3b).

Resource control (e.g., "wealth" in humans) affects fertility. But what is "wealth"? Men's earnings? Women's? To explore the relationships between resources and women's fertility, we need appropriate and repeatable measures of wealth, information on women's own wealth, separate from husband's or household wealth, and individual (rather than aggregate) data on age-specific fertility. To examine whether wealthy lineages follow different strategies from poor lineages, we need all these individual data across generations. To date, the best study I have found that sorts out co-variants (though not across generations) is Taşiran (1995); the results suggest that some major evolved patterns remain, but that considerable complexity exists in transitory (and probably non-selective) economic and fertility preferences.

Taşiran compares empirical studies and models for Sweden (pre-1935 to 1965 cohorts), and white and non-white U.S. women (pre-1945 to 1966 cohorts), using macro-, micro-, and integrated data (see also Low, Simon, and Anderson 2000). In all three groups, a woman's years of education influence her birth patterns. For non-white U.S. women, 5–9 years of education makes having a first child less likely; 10 or more years makes having a first child more likely. For white U.S. women, significant negative effects of education exist for first and second births. For Swedish women the effects are significant for first and third child (5–9 years; an additional effect is seen on first child for 10+ years of education).

Women's work has always appeared to present women with a fertility tradeoff harsher than men's, but is it money, or time? Taşiran's analysis shows how the tradeoffs work for these populations: when women's work experience is controlled for, women's wages have several positive effects on fertility (first births for Swedish and non-white U.S. women; second births for white U.S. women). This is in sharp contrast to earlier work, which confounded the time costs and the monetary gains of women's work.

Some differences appear to be simple cultural preferences; others seem to reflect cultural costs and benefits of having a child. The effect of "cohort" is significant, reflecting the fact that both economic conditions and cultural preferences may vary over time. In Sweden, whether a woman was married or cohabiting (versus alone) has no effect on her likelihood of having one or more children; social services for parental benefits had a positive influence only on probability of having a third child. A man's wages increased the likelihood of having a first and second child. In Taşiran's study, in the United States a man's income had a negative relationship to a woman's probability of having a first, second, or third child. We have no information (e.g., lineage persistence) to help us understand whether this is a strategy shift (higher per capita investment per child, fewer children), a reproductively costly cultural preference, or remaining co-variation (with woman's age, since "husband" includes second husbands).

What is important is that education and work had time and opportunity costs for women, while income had a positive impact on fertility—but it is very difficult to separate the three. Thus, in many analyses, prescriptions of women's work and women's education to lower fertility may be ineffective, depending on their relationships with women's incomes.

WEALTH, LIFETIME FERTILITY, AND CONSUMPTION TODAY

Finding Appropriate Data

The data from both developed and developing nations today are quite mixed, and it is difficult to be certain the data have been collected in an appropriate manner and at an appropriate level to test the questions raised here about wealth and fertility. Thus, we currently see complexity, and it is tempting to think that there is no clear pattern. But is that true? Taşiran found a cohort effect; of course, cohorts differed in nineteenth-century Sweden as well, yet (when sought) an overall resource-fertility relationship was clear. Is there also an overall effect today? It is difficult to tell from Taşiran's study, which was designed to answer other questions.

There are real-world reasons to specify our questions clearly. Consider Birdsall's (1980) study on population growth in developing nations. She found a slight negative trend between Gross National Product (GNP) per capita and the Total Fertility Rate (TRF) in developing countries (all of which have higher TFRs than Europe and North America). Such data are widely used, for example by policy makers, to argue that high income correlates with lower fertility. But the resource ecology of developed and developing countries is vastly different and, just as in other species, we expect quite different fertility patterns when resource richness and predictability vary, and when levels of competition differ. The resource-fertility question can only be reasonably asked about individuals within the same population.

In fact, Birdsall's within-society comparisons show a linear positive relationship between wealth and fertility in India, and a curvilinear relationship in the other three countries she examined. In no case did the wealthiest quintile have fewer children than the poorest. The required investment may limit the number of children a couple can afford. Within subgroups, however, those with more than sufficient resources may be able to support additional children and still have all be adequately invested. The possible implications of these patterns are of interest, especially in terms of population policies around the world.

Here is a further problem. Within-society comparisons can use individual, household, or aggregate data. In general, for western developed nations, aggregate data (e.g., Pérusse 1993) show no or a slight negative relationship between income and fertility. But this may be an artifact of aggregate data. National aggregate national census data for the nineteenth century in Sweden appear to show a slight negative relationship between status and fertility, but the individual-based data show considerable impact of resource on fertility (e.g., Low 1990, Low and Clarke 1992).

Aggregate data are usually inappropriate to ask the "lifetime fertility" question. Sometimes census data can be examined in fruitful ways for our questions: for example, Daly and Wilson (1983:334) examined fertility by age in married U.S. women in the 1970 census. They found that while lifetime fertility showed no pattern with wealth, the fertility of women married to wealthy men was earlier than that of other women (and this means that richer women had a higher genotypic rate of increase [Fisher 1958] than other women). Studies that actually measure lifetime success are, by necessity, typically rather narrowly focused. Further, many studies attempting to solve this problem are themselves methodologically flawed. Two difficulties are most common: either fertility itself is not measured (e.g., Vining 1986), or fertility is measured—but those who never marry are excluded from the analysis!

Measuring "resources" is, of course, a difficult task. Kaplan and Lancaster (this volume) have an excellent example of how a particular resource (costly training for jobs in sophisticated labor markets) functions in just the way MacArthur and Wilson predicted (see also Kaplan et al. 1995; Kaplan 1996). Careful modeling approaches (e.g., Mace, this volume) can help. For example, Mace measures the reproductive value of children as the expected number of grandchildren arising from them—something that would take enormous time to measure empirically.

Evolutionary anthropologists are asking questions new to demographers, questions that require age-specific fertility and mortality data compiled in the ways behavioral ecologists do. Knowing birth rates and age-specific mortality is still a long way from understanding lineage increase rates (e.g., Mace, this volume).

ANALYTIC POSSIBILITIES

In sum, the analytic possibilities for wealth and fertility relationships today, versus in our evolutionary past, are limited. For men and for women, total lifetime fertility may be positively, negatively, or not related to resource control. Measuring these relationships requires within-population data and measures of variance, as well as independent data for men versus women—more than most studies have managed. Finally, we need measures over multiple generations.

We need individual lifetime and lineage information, not the aggregate statistics that are most commonly available, for two reasons (cf. Mace, this volume). First, aggregate data tell us nothing about variation. For example, if fertility is 1.8 children per couple in much of western Europe, and 2.1 in the United States, is that a "real," significant difference? There is no way to tell. Aggregate data for different occupational groups within countries have varied patterns—but without knowing the variance within groups, and whether wealth in each group is normally distributed or skewed, we can not make any inference.

Second, aggregate data typically under-sample a very important group in any population: the poor and the homeless, who are typically both very poor and with low fertility. Statistically the biggest predictor of variance is the size of the zero-success class (Conover 1980). For example, U.S. census data are taken from households. Suppose poorer households have more children in them than wealthier households. Does that mean wealth and fertility are inversely related in the United States today? By no means. Relationships are not given, and income is not apportioned to individuals, so there is no way to know father's earnings (predicted to increase fertility if it is the main income; see Low 1994, Low and Clarke 1992, Hawkes 1996) versus mother's work effort, with its complex effects. Further, the poorest of the poor have both very low fertility and very low income—and do not appear in census data. If much of the unsampled population comprises the homeless, the statistical analysis is compromised. Unless we ask about them as well, we have no reliable information about the overall pattern of wealth and fertility in the United States.

Sex differences in wealth-fertility relationships need further exploration. In societies for which data exist, both traditional and modern, there appears to be a conflict for women between behaviors that acquire resources and those necessary for effective parental effort. Women, whether they must gather food for themselves and their children, or become educated to a high level to earn salaries in the marketplace, experience more conflict than men between resource-garnering and fertility, since more of women's effort is directed to parental, not mating, effort (above). And when women are single parents, or provide the bulk of resources in a market economy, this conflict will be exacerbated. When monetary resources become central to children's success, women's shift from traditional maternal investment patterns to market employment has complex, usually negative, impact on fertility. This may show up as a correlation with industrialization, but the apparent link to industrialization may simply be an example of a general phenomenon: technological advances may require more education or training (e.g., Knodel et al. 1990; Kaplan and Lancaster, this volume) and thus more investment to produce each competitive child. Such education or training is seldom free; thus, we might expect fertility declines to start among the rich, who have the most to invest in competitiveness.

In western industrialized nations today, in which women are a large part of the labor force (with the conflicts noted), and in which divorce is prevalent, the wealth-fertility pattern for women is probably not linear (Taşiran 1995; Rank 1989; Kasarda et al. 1986; Low 1993). Other dynamics (e.g., the per-capita investment in children) clearly differ for wealthy professional women and poor single mothers, but both spend more time working compared to women in families (mostly middle-income) in which the man provides all income.

When resources become constricted, reproductive responses are likely to be uneven within families. In a resource-constriction period, we might find very unequal investment in children within a family, with heightened investment in older (closer to successful reproduction) sons, whose success in most societies is more dependent on resources than daughters (Low 1993). In the Swedish case, for example, land was overwhelmingly given to the oldest adult son, despite legal "equal inheritance"; and land-owning men had more children than their landless brothers (Low 1990). Indeed, even the aggregate data from developing nations now showing fertility transitions are highly variable—this would be a fertile area for study using the paradigms of evolutionary and behavioral ecology.

When we get the appropriate detail and level of information, the possibilities for any society are limited:

1. Wealth and fertility are still positively, and linearly, related in the society under consideration, and we simply did not understand the relationships because we measured the wrong things. If this is true, when we look inside societies (even with data as crude as Birdsall's), we are likely to find that within societies, wealthier people not only have more children, but may well invest (and thus consume) more per child than poorer people.
2. In societies with wealth disparity, in which women contribute considerable resources to the household (especially through market enterprises), the relationship between wealth and fertility is likely to be non-linear, but with the poorest individuals having the lowest fertility. Contraceptive use is likely to be the mechanism for achieving "desired" fertility. This condition is comparable to (1), but with an important difference: the wealthiest families have shifted to a "super-investment" strategy that may limit their fertility to equal, or even fall below, middle-rank families (above), and more of the household income is probably provided by women's work. When the wealthiest families are thus limited, peak fertility will occur in middle-

wealth families, in which per-capita investment per child is relatively lower than among the wealthiest.

However, any calculation of "genes identical by descent (IBD) times wealth per gene IBD" will still be positive: the wealthiest segment of the population will still control the greatest proportion of available resources.

3. Wealth and fertility are negatively related. When this is true, it may arise from family limitation to get better-endowed children (r- and K-selection, above) when the family has insufficient resources to raise per capita endowment without decreasing number of offspring. Low fertility may arise when children must have more—more education, more resources, and better jobs—to marry successfully. Even in this case, we should not be surprised if men with relatively more resources within each stratum of society have more children than men with fewer resources (e.g., Hughes 1988, Low and Clarke 1993).

   This is a complicated business. "Absolute resources controlled" may be less important than the perceived wealth trajectory (e.g., migrants from a relatively poorer to a relatively richer area may have fertility above native-born individuals of the rich area) or perceived comparative wealth. Several suggest that couples assess their income relative both to their parents' income in the previous generation and to others in their social-economic group, and make deliberate decisions about family size in response to their judgment of available resources; when deliberately chosen family sizes are considered, there is a correlation between income and family size. When accidental pregnancies are considered, the picture becomes less clear. Here is another fertile area for inquiry: how do perceptions of wealth, wealth trajectory, and the value of children, interact to affect fertility?

4. Wealth and fertility show no relationship, because wealth no longer has any impact on fertility. Our novel environment may have muddled past correlates, but people still seek the proximate ex-correlates of fertility. For example, men may simply seek wealth and status for their own sakes, and higher fertility no longer accompanies them. And perhaps women still show some preferences for successful men, but the novelty of birth control means that women's preferences no longer mean more children for successful men. Consider Pérusse's findings (1993, 1994): among a sample of Canadian men, wealthier men had no more children than other men (women used contraception), although they did have greater sexual access.

When we see a linear positive relationship between wealth and fertility (1 above), we suspect no change in the functional relationships of old. A non-linear, roughly bell-shaped curve (2) leads us to suspect class or wealth differences in investment pattern superimposed on the standard functional relationships, as families compete in different environments. Negative (3) or no (4) relationships could arise either because people are inappropriately (non-adaptively) responding to once-valid proximate cues that are today no longer appropriate; or because there are tradeoffs between numbers of children and their probable success due to parental investment.

This is a tricky and subtle business, and most currently available data, gathered to answer other questions, are inadequate. We can use (with appropriate care about assumptions) models to help flesh out our questions, but again, we need more finely honed empirical data. Though it is obvious that the problem is complex, the patterns among women's education, women's work, and fertility suggest that real tradeoffs may exist. We will need longitudinal data (e.g., number of grandchildren) before we can tell.

Does it matter what functional relationships are true? If, as most ecologists think, we face resource and population crunches in the near future, strategies that arise from understanding which of these are true, and why, have better chances of success than simple polemic. And some of the main polemic arguments, I suspect, will be really unsuccessful.

AN EVOLUTIONARY BOTTOM LINE

Reducing Both Fertility and Consumption Is Novel

The problems of wealth, health, and fertility for men and women are not just of academic interest to a few evolutionary anthropologists and behavioral ecologists. I suggest that these questions, and these data, are important in a highly applied context—the global issues often called "population and environment"—as well as for their own intellectual merit. Both the number of people alive and the consumption per person today are higher than at any time in the past. Population patterns—birth, reproduction, and death patterns—are the sum of what individual men and women do: they mate and marry, have children, and die, consuming resources along the way. When, at the Rio Conference in 1992 and again in 1996, the "Northern" (developed) and "Southern" (developing) nations squared off, these were the central issues of conflict, with little progress and no resolution. At the heart of the debate lay conflicts over resources and fertility multiplied up from individual to population levels.

Today, the ecology of reproduction is vastly different for men and women in developing, versus developed, nations, and their appropriate reproductive strategies are likely to differ—yet we are only beginning to ask the evolutionarily appropriate questions. The papers in this volume represent an important step. Yet policy is being made or proposed without the knowledge we need. Understanding both the evolved patterns, and the proximate cues that drive our behavior, might help us devise more useful approaches to population-environment issues.

We have made little progress analyzing modern populations in this light. Lowering fertility does not enhance sustainability if fertility declines are accompanied by consumption increases—as has been the case in past demographic transitions, and as appears to be the case in most developing-nation transitions today. Fertility decline today is promoted by many successful family-planning programs around the world with clear messages that having fewer children means wealthier families. Wealthier families consume more resources, and if one asks about the interplay of population and consumption, fewer-but-more-consumptive families do not lead to decreased or stabilized resource consumption.

Effective solutions begin with understanding why and how we evolved to use resources, and how individual costs and benefits influence our resource exploitation patterns. If self-interest is unlikely to disappear, perhaps we can, through understanding how and why it evolved, learn to use it in solving environmental problems. We need better approaches to understanding the relationships among resource consumption, fertility, and sustainability.

SUMMARY

1. In other species, and in the evolutionary past of humans, resource acquisition has correlated positively with fertility, especially for males.

2. The apparent loss of this relationship is puzzling, and may not be real. Most studies suggesting no, or a negative relationship, between resources and reproductive success is seriously flawed, using inappropriate data.

3. The status of analysis is reviewed, and the analytic possibilities are explored.

REFERENCES

Birdsall, N. 1980. Population growth and poverty in the developing world. *Population Bulletin* 35(5):3–46.

Boone, J. L. III. 1986. Parental investment and elite family structure in preindustrial states: A case sudy oflate medieval-early modern Portuguese genealogies. *American Anthropologist* 88:859–878.

———. 1988. Parental investment, social subordination, and population processes among the 15th and 16th century Portuguese nobility. In *Human Reproductive Behaviour: A Darwinian Perspective,* L. Betzig, M. Borgerhoff Mulder, and P. Turke, eds. Pp. 201–220. Cambridge: Cambridge University Press.

Boone, J. L., and K. L. Kessler. 1999. More status or more children? Social status, fertility reduction, and long-term fitness. *Evolution and Human Behavior* 20:257–277.

Clarke, A. L. 1993. Women, resources, and dispersal in 19th century Sweden. *Human Nature* 4:109–135.

Clarke, A. L., and Bobbi S. Low. 1992. Resources and reproductive patterns: The role of migration. *Animal Behavior* 44:677–693.

Coale, A. J., and S. C. Watkins. 1986. *The Decline of Fertility in Europe.* Princeton: Princeton University Press.

Coleman, D., and R. Schofield (eds.). 1986. The State of Population Theory: Forward from Malthus. Basil Blackwell: London.

Conover, W. J. 1980. *Practical Non-parametric Statistics.* 2nd ed. Wiley, New York.

Cronk, L. 1993. Parental favoritism toward daughters. *American Scientist* 81:272–279.

Daly, M., and M. Wilson. 1983. *Sex, Evolution, and Behavior.* 2nd ed. Belmont, California: Wadsworth.

———. 1997. Life expectancy, economic inequality, homicide, and reproductive timing in Chicago neighborhoods. *British Journal of Medicine* 314: 1271–1274.

Dickemann, M. 1979. Female infanticide, reproductive strategies, and social stratification: a preliminary model. In Evolutionary Biology and Human Social Behavior: An Anthropological Perspective, N. Chagnon and W. Irons, eds. Pp. 321–367. North Scituate, Massachusetts: Duxbury Press.

Drake, M. 1969. *Population and Society in Norway.* Cambridge: Cambridge University Press.

Emlen, S. 1995. An evolutionary theory of the family. *Proceedings from the National Academy of Science USA* 92:8092–8099.

———. 1997. Predicting family dynamics in social vertebrates. In *Behavioural Ecology: An Evolutionary Approach.* 4th ed. J. R. Krebs and N. B. Davies, eds. Pp. 228–253. London : Blackwell Scientific.

Fisher, R. A. 1958. *The Genetical Theory of Natural Selection.* 2nd revised ed. New York: Dover.

Geronimus, A. T. 1996a. Black/white differences in the relationship of maternal age to birthweight: A population-based test of the Weathering Hypothesis. *Social Science and Medicine* 42(4):589–597.

———. 1996b. What teen mothers know. *Human Nature* 7(4):323–352.

Geronimus, A. T., J. Bound, and T. A. Waidmann. 1997. Health inequality, family caretaking systems, and population variation in fertility-timing. Paper presented at 1997 Annual meeting of the Population Association of America, Washington, D. C.

Geronimus, A. T., J. Bound, T. A. Waidmann, M. M. Hillemeier, and P. B. Burns. 1996. Excess mortality among Blacks and Whites in the United States. *New England Journal of Medicine* 335:1552–1558.

Goody, J. 1983. *The Development of the Family and Marriage in Europe.* Cambridge: Cambridge University Press.

Hawkes, K. 1996. The evolutionary basis of sex variations in the use of natural resources: Human examples. *Population and Environment* 18:161–173.

Hill, E., and B. Low. 1991. Contemporary abortion patterns: A life-history approach. *Ethology and Sociobiology* 13:35–48.

Hill, K. 1993. Life history theory and evolutionary anthropology. *Evolutionary Anthropology* 2:78–88.

Hughes, A. 1988. *Evolution and Human Kinship.* Oxford: Oxford University Press.

Hrdy, S. B. 1992. Fitness tradeoffs in the history and evolution of delegated mothering with special reference to wet-nursing abandonment and infanticide. *Ethology and Sociobiology* 13:409–442.

———. 1999. *Mother Nature: A History of Mothers, Infants, and Natural Selection.* New York: Pantheon Books.

Kaplan, H. 1996. A theory of fertility and parental investment in traditional and modern human societies. *Yearbook of Physical Anthropology* 39:91–135.

Kaplan, H. S., J. Lancaster, S. E. Johnson, and J. A. Bock. 1995. Does observed fertility maximize fitness among New Mexican men? *Human Nature* 6(4):325–360.

Kasarda, J. D., J. Billy, and K. West. 1986. *Status Enhancement and Fertility: Reproductive Responses to Social Mobility and Educational Opportunity.* New York: Academic Press.

Knodel J., N. Havanon, and W. Sittitrai. 1990. Family size and the education of children in the context of rapid fertility decline. *Population and Development Review* 16(1): 31–62.

Lancaster, J. 1986. Human adolescence and reproduction: An evolutionary perspective. In *School-Age Pregnancy and Parenthood,* J. B. Lancaster and B. A. Hamburg, eds. Pp. 17–38. New York: Aldine de Gruyter.

Lockridge, K. A. 1983. *The Fertility Transition in Sweden: A Preliminary Look at Smaller Geographic Units, 1855–1890.* Swedish Demographic Database, Umeå University Report #3:1–135.

Low, B. 1990. Occupational status, landownership and reproductive behavior in nineteenth-century Sweden: Tuna Parish. *American Anthropologist* 92:457–468.

———. 1993. Ecological demography: A synthetic focus in evolutionary anthropology. *Evolutionary Anthropology* 1(5):177–187.

———. 1994. Men in the demographic transition. *Human Nature* 5(3):223–253.

———. 1996. Men, women and sustainability. *Population and Environment* 18(2): 111–141.

———. 1998. The evolution of human life histories. In *The Handbook of Evolutionary Psychology: Ideas, Issues and Applications,* C. Crawford and D. Krebs (eds.). Pp. 131–161. Mahwah, NJ: Lawrence Elrbaum.

———. 2000. *Why Sex Matters: A Darwinian Look at Human Behavior.* Princeton: Princeton university Press.

Low, B., and A. L. Clarke. 1991. Occupational status, land ownership,migration, and fanily patterns in 19th-century Sweden. *Journal of Family History* 16:117–138.

Low, B., and A. L. Clarke. 1992. Resources and the life course: Patterns through the demographic transition. *Ethology and Sociobiology* 13:463–494.

———. 1993. Historical perspectives on population and environment: Data from 19th century Sweden. In *Population-Environment Dynamics: Ideas and Observations,* G. Ness, W. Drake, and S. Brechin, eds. Pp. 195–224. Ann Arbor: University of Michigan Press.

Low, B., A. L. Clarke, and K. Lockridge. 1992. Toward an ecological demography. *Population Development Review* 18:1–31.

Low, B., C. P. Simon, and K. G. Anderson. 2000. An evolutionary ecological perspective on demographic transitions: Modeling multiple currencies. In press, *American Journal of Human Biology.*

Luker, K. 1996. *Dubious Conception: The Politics of Teenage Pregnancy.* Cambridge: Harvard University Press.

MacArthur, R. H., and E. O. Wilson. 1967. *The Theory of Island Biogeography.* Princeton: Princeton University Press.

Pérusse, D. 1993. Cultural and reproductive success in industrial societies: Testing the relationship at the proximate and ultimate levels. *Behavioral Brain Sciences* 16:267–322 (including commentary and response).

———. 1994. Mate choice in modern societies: Testing evolutionary hypotheses with behavioral data. *Human Nature* 5(3):255–278.

Plotvin, R. H., and F. L. Muncada. 1990. *Seminary Outcomes: Perseverance and Withdrawal.* Washington, D.C.: Institute of Social and Behavioral Research.

Rank, M. A. 1989. Fertility among women on welfare: Incidence and determinants. *American Sociological Review* 54:296–304.

Rice, D. 1990. *Shattered Vows: Priests Who Leave.* New York: Triumph Books.

Roff, D. 1992. *The Evolution of Life Histories: Theory and Analysis.* New York: Chapman and Hall.

Schofield R. S., and D. Coleman. 1986. Introduction: The state of population theory. In *The State of Population Theory: Forward from Malthus,* D. Coleman and R. Schofield, eds. Pp. 1–13. London: Basil Blackwell.

Sipe, A. W. R. 1990. A Secret World: Sexuality and the Search for Celibacy. New York: Brunner Mazel.

Stearns, S. 1992. *The Evolution of Life Histories.* Oxford: Oxford University Press.
Strassman , B., and A. L. Clarke. 1998. Ecological constraints on marriage in rural Ireland. *Evolution and Human Behavior* 19:33–55.
Sweeney, T. A. 1992. *Church Divided: The Vatican versus American Catholics.* New York: Prometheus Books.
Taşiran, A. C. 1995. *Fertility Dynamics: Spacing and Timing of Births in Sweden and the United States.* Amsterdam: Elsevier.
Vining, D. R. 1986. Social versus reproductive success: The central theoretical problem of human sociobiology. *Behavioral and Brain Sciences* 9:167–187.
Wrigley, E. A., and R. Schofield. 1981. *The Population History of England 1541–1871.* Cambridge: Harvard University Press.

16

To Marry Again or Not
A Dynamic Model for Demographic Transition

BARNEY LUTTBEG, MONIQUE BORGERHOFF MULDER,
and MARC MANGEL

This chapter reports the results of an empirical investigation of a question concerning motivation—do men maximize children, or the amount of wealth they can give their children? Although the method described here can be used to determine what is being maximized in any behavioral domain, we pursue this particular issue because of its implications for understanding demographic transition.

Behavioral ecologists are challenged by the fact that people voluntarily reproduce at lower levels than would apparently maximize their lifetime reproduction. The "demographic transition" refers to the precipitous decline in fertility that started in many European countries in the nineteenth century (e.g., Coale and Watkins 1986) and now characterizes much of the developing world (e.g., Robinson 1992). This fertility shift often occurs in conjunction with improvements in child survival, but its magnitude is greater than would be expected if fertility levels were merely compensating for increased child survival. Furthermore fertility reductions usually occur despite general increases in availability of resources. Sociologists use the marked drop in fertility that accompanies modernization, together with the evidence of negative or indeterminate relationships between income and fertility in industrial societies (Mueller and Short 1983), to question the legitimacy of evolutionary approaches to the study of humans (e.g., Vining 1986). In response, evolutionary social scientists propose hypotheses that might explain why parents with access to plentiful resources would choose low fertility rates. There are three principal hypotheses.

1. In highly competitive environments parents optimize fitness by producing a few children with high levels of investment rather than many with less investment per capita. This hypothesis draws on the quantity/quality tradeoffs organisms face in their allocation of reproductive effort, as recognized in all evolutionary (Kaplan 1996) and some economic (Becker and Lewis 1973) models. According to this hypothesis, low fertility would be favored

in environments in which high levels of parental investment are both critical to the success of the offspring (e.g., Kaplan et al. 1995) and costly to the parent (Turke 1989). This notion was first introduced by Lack (1947) for the study of clutch size in birds. It concurs in some respects with original accounts of how the European demographic transition was a response to socioeconomic changes affecting child costs (e.g., Notestein 1953). Demographers have evaluated this hypothesis by examining the timing of transitions in relation to relevant socioeconomic indicators, which has produced mixed results (Lesthaeghe and Wilson 1986). Behavioral ecologists have developed more direct tests, particularly multigenerational empirical studies and modeling.

2. Lowered fertility rates are a consequence of Darwinian but nongenetic mechanisms of inheritance, by means of which traits associated with certain influential individuals are preferentially imitated by others in the population. Boyd and Richerson (1985) propose that small family sizes might be transmitted through such a process. In an attempt to copy successful individuals in a population, imitators adopt all the traits of the model, irrespective of whether or not these contribute to the model's success. This process, which Boyd and Richerson call "indirect bias," opens up the possibility for the spread of potentially maladaptive traits, by means of Darwinian but nongenetic mechanisms.
3. Lowered fertility is a maladaptive outcome of novel social, technological, and environmental changes that have been so rapid that adaptive responses are not (yet) elicited. An obvious example in this context is birth control technology. Pérusse (1993) shows that the wealthier section of his Canadian sample of men achieve higher copulation rates than do their less wealthy counterparts, but do not achieve higher fertility because of the intervention of birth control. According to this hypothesis, then, low fertility is simply maladaptive.

We turn now to the status of and evidence for each of these hypotheses. Applying optimality models to the function of intermediate-sized families (hypothesis 1) has proved less fruitful than originally hoped. Two empirical studies (Kaplan et al. 1995; Mueller n.d.) looked at whether numbers of grandchildren were greatest among parents who produced intermediate numbers of offspring. Both failed to support the hypothesis. Others have used models to explore how specific assumptions about the relationship between parental effort and offspring success can generate situations in which small family sizes reflect an optimal tradeoff between offspring quantity and quality (e.g., Anderies 1996; Beauchamp 1994; Rogers 1990). As yet, they have failed to identify environments in which the classic features of the demographic transition arise at equilibrium. For example, in the most realistic version of his model, Rogers (1995) is unable to find either an environment in which fertility decreases with wealth (but see "Discussion"), or one in which wealth maximization ensures a higher fitness payoff than simply maximizing number of first generation descendants. Beauchamp (1994; Figure 4) finds that smaller family sizes are favored in competitive but not in noncompetitive environments; in both environments, however, high income groups still out-reproduce low income groups (consistent with Rogers 1995).

The cultural inheritance hypothesis is intriguing. It may well account for the rapid spread of fertility-limiting behavior through populations, and it is intricately linked to the notion now popular among demographers and social scientists that changes in *ideas* (rather than changes in the economy) cause fertility transitions (Bongaart and Watkins 1996). But it raises some questions too. First, why do the influential, trendsetting individuals choose lower fertility in the first place? Granted there will be tradeoffs between seeking socioeconomic status and reproducing early and often. But quite why reproduction is sacrificed to such extremes still needs to be explained, or at least raises questions about how such status-seeking becomes equilibrated in a population where there may be countervailing selection for high fertility, sending us back to hypothesis 1. Second, cultural inheritance theorists build their models on a very different set of assumptions concerning the mechanisms of evolutionary processes than do behavioral ecologists. Such abandoning of the basic organic evolutionary model may still be premature, although the potential importance of such mechanisms is pointed to in newer work, outlined below.

The maladaptationist approach (hypothesis 3), when specifically linked to the existence of birth control technology, fails to provide a satisfactory explanation for demographic transition. The European transition started before the availability of modern birth control technology (Livi-Bacci 1986); furthermore in many parts of contemporary Africa the transition does not occur despite availability of free contraceptives (Jones, et al. 1997). More generally, however, maladaptationist accounts cannot substitute for explanatory theories unless they specify precisely what has changed in the environment, why these changes lead to lowered fertility, and what kinds of evolved mechanisms might underlie this response (see Kaplan et al. 1995).

The present paper adopts a different approach from any of the above. It sets to one side the question (central to hypothesis 1) of whether individuals select fertility levels that maximize the production of grandoffspring. Rather, it turns to an empirical investigation of the simpler but perhaps more fundamental question of whether individuals (men in this case) maximize the numbers of their children or the amount of wealth they can give their children. We work from the premise that understanding reproductive behavioral processes (and the motivational factors that underlie them) is central to explaining the changing relationships between wealth and fertility.

To expose motivations behind reproductive decisions we employ in a novel way a modeling procedure central to behavioral ecology. Dynamic state variable models (Mangel and Clark 1988; Mangel and Ludwig 1992) are used to connect physiological or ecological states, measures of fitness, and behavior of individuals. Conventionally, the fitness currency is specified on the basis of the organism's natural history. On the assumption that natural selection has shaped a decision-making process to maximize this fitness currency, the model is used to explore how variations in an organism's social and material environment shape optimal decisions. We take an alternative approach. We use real world observations of Kipsigis men to determine what fitness currency best accounts for their behavior. We construct alternative models using fitness functions variously weighted toward material versus reproductive motivations, and then test which fitness function best matches the pattern of marriages observed in the real data.

We focus on the marital decisions of men in a rural Kenyan Kipsigis population. There are several reasons why the study of Kipsigis men is particularly rewarding with respect to elucidating reproductive motivation. First, rural Kenya began its fertility transition only in the late 1980s (Robinson 1992). By focusing on men who married between 1941 and 1983, we therefore use data from a pre-fertility transition population (for consistency of reproductive behavior over time, see Borgerhoff Mulder 1987a). Second, many Kipsigis men marry more than one wife, such that there is high variance in men's reproductive success. Though polygynous marriage has little effect on population growth rates, it has a major impact on an individual man's reproductive success. Analyzing the decision whether or not to marry polygynously therefore offers considerable scope for the study of factors motivating men's reproduction. Third, thoroughly verified and cross-checked demographic and marital data (both retrospective and prospective) are available (e.g., Borgerhoff Mulder 1987a, 1987b, 1995).

KIPSIGIS ETHNOGRAPHY

Economy

Kipsigis are Kalenjin Nilotic Kenyans, who have lived for several centuries in what is now southwestern Kenya. Traditionally they were herders, but they have always cultivated millet and semi-domesticated cultivars to supplement a milk-and-meat-based diet. The Abosi population (Borgerhoff Mulder 1990) adopted the practice of individual ownership of land in the 1930s, and thereafter began growing maize for both subsistence and cash purposes. Livestock (cattle, sheep, and goats) remain central to the economy, as sources of milk, meat, and capital.

Since the 1930s, the basic livelihood has been quite stable. Men are the foremost decision-makers for the farm, and the sole owners of land and livestock. Women obtain use rights to land only through their husbands, although they spend much more time in agricultural work than do men (Borgerhoff Mulder et al., 1997). A few acres of land (usually a substantial proportion of the family plot) are put into maize production each year, and the rest is left fallow for livestock grazing. Men usually cultivate a small plot (a half acre or so), whereas women cultivate more, depending on the numbers of their children, their energy, and the size of the plot. A single maize harvest is raised each year, and any surplus over the estimated annual needs of the household is usually sold, in recent years, to a national marketing board. If a man's wife's (or wives') stores become depleted, he must find maize (the staple diet of every family) elsewhere, usually through purchases from local traders or at markets. Women supplement maize production with small gardens of beans and vegetables. Other food items (oil, salt, tea, and occasionally sugar) are bought from local trading posts.

Livestock are grazed primarily on the farm, although unproductive areas (such as steep hillsides) are available as commons. Herds of cattle are heavily skewed toward females (through the sale or slaughter of steers) to enhance milk production, which is used both for domestic consumption and for cash sales to a national marketing board and private customers. Small stock are kept in low numbers, primarily for meat consumption. Livestock are used for bride-wealth payments, as well as for meeting various expenses including supplementary food items, utensils, hoes, pesticides, clothing, medical treatment, and education.

Both maize and livestock production are risky for Kipsigis. Rainfall is adequate for both activities (1,265 mm per year), but is annually variable. Since Abosi lies in the driest part of the Kipsigis range, it frequently suffers years of poor maize yields and minimal milk production. Other factors contributing to an unpredictable food supply are labor shortages, agricultural pests, cattle diseases, and raids. If a man is sick in December, the fields do not get prepared and planted. If women are unhealthy anytime between January and June, their fields turn to weed. Similarly, children who are ill can keep their mothers at home, or busy traveling to distant dispensaries and traditional curers. While community labor pools ameliorate domestic problems, cooperation needs to be reciprocated or it ceases. Indeed, food deficits in households observed in 1982, 1983, and 1991 were commonly caused by labor shortages at critical times. In addition, pest infestations, both in the fields (in years of heavy rain) or in the grain stores, can decimate a crop. Livestock disease further threatens every herd, and is prevalent in the area because of the great expense of veterinary medicines, and cattle raiding still occasionally occurs.

Marriage

Women almost invariably marry soon after puberty, but men's age at marriage is much more variable, with the median ranging from 21 to 25 years between the 1950s and the 1980s. At marriage a man receives a share of his father's livestock and land, and there he settles with his new wife, in a state of semi-independence from his father. Legally these capital resources are not viewed as his until his father's death (or incapacity), yet in practice this share of land and livestock constitutes the final inheritance that a son receives from his father. For the purposes of this paper, a man's reproductive and economic career starts at his marriage. All marriages require a substantial bride-wealth payment to the bride's parents, the amount of which has been quite stable over the period between 1952 and 1991 (Borgerhoff Mulder 1995). A man's first bride-wealth payment is made by his father. Subsequent marriage payments for additional wives are his own responsibility. Men marry multiple wives for many reasons, primarily to obtain women's labor and reproductive services: a man with many wives is admired for numbers of children and for the economic power that derives from a large household. Divorce is not permitted, although some women temporarily withdraw sexual and economic services by running away.

Previous analyses show that the Kipsigis marriage system resembles resource defense polygyny in many respects (Borgerhoff Mulder 1990). Wealthy men can afford multiple bride-wealth payments, thereby gaining multiple wives. Reproductive costs associated with polygynous marriage for women are not high, suggesting that poor men are generally unable to either coerce or attract additional wives.

Raising Children to Independence

Children are produced at a fast rate in Kipsigis society, where cows' milk and solid foods are introduced at 3–4 months, breast-feeding rarely extends beyond 2.5 years, and lactating women frequently conceive. Mortality in the first five years of life is high; the average postmenopausal woman produced 9 live births, with between 5 and 8 of those children (depending on the cohort) surviving to 5 years of age. Children are viewed as an economic and social asset, and national family planning initiatives have had little impact in this and many other rural communities. No woman in the original 1982–1983 demographic study (N = 1,257) reported using western contraceptive methods, and only 1 (N = 120) in the 1991 survey.

Staple foods for children (maize, milk, vegetables, and occasionally meat) are produced on the farm and supplemented by shop-bought items as noted above. Very rudimentary primary health care is available (for cash) at several nearby dispensaries. Two hospitals, both mission-run and expensive, lie within 50 miles of Abosi; credit is permitted in some cases. All of these services are used by the majority of families, often in conjunction with visits to traditional healers, whose services are also not free. Child mortality, and indeed maternal health, bears a close relationship to family wealth (Borgerhoff Mulder 1987b).

Primary school is officially free, although there are various forms of mandatory fundraising. Secondary schooling can be expensive. Only a small number of children, usually sons, progress to secondary school (Borgerhoff Mulder 1998a).

At independence, sons' bride-wealth payments and marriage ceremony costs must be covered. Conversely, daughters bring in a bride-wealth, and their marriage expenses are paid by the groom's family. Daughters inherit no significant property whatsoever. Once married, sons inherit a share of their father's land and livestock, although this property is not considered legally theirs till the father's death, and can be used by the father should he so wish. Sons who do not marry almost inevitably leave home.

EMPIRICAL METHODS AND RESULTS

Field Methods

Detailed reproductive, marital, and economic histories were compiled for 98 men in 1982–1983 and were checked and updated for 88 of these individuals in 1991. Thus 88 men with combined prospective and retrospective data are the subject of the present paper. We have coded for each man the acreage of his plot, the size of his herd, and the number of his wives and children at the end of each seven-year period after his marriage; livestock and land are combined to measure each man's "capital" or wealth. The present paper combines data from three cohorts (Chuma, Sawe, and Korongoro); future analyses will explore variations between these cohorts in the dynamics of polygyny, capital, and investment.

Empirical Results

As in all other published analyses on Kipsigis there is a positive correlation between wealth and polygyny, indicative of a "polygyny threshold" (Borgerhoff Mulder 1990). The relationship between initial (or inherited) capital and number of wives after 21 years of married life is shown in Figure 16.1. Furthermore, richer men take a second wife sooner than do poorer men (data not shown). These results tell us nothing new about the Kipsigis social and economic system, but they do show that this sample is comparable to others drawn from the population, and they provide patterns against which the output of the simulation models can be compared.

A DYNAMIC STATE VARIABLE MODEL FOR MARRIAGE BEHAVIOR

Model and Parameters

In this section we describe a model specifying how food, wealth, and children are produced in the environment and society of Abosi. This model is used to determine optimal marital decisions for each of a man's first 21 years of married life. Optimal marital decisions are modeled as a function of a man's current state (wives, children, and wealth).

We use a dynamic state variable model (Mangel and Clark 1988; Mangel and Ludwig 1992) to detect the motivation behind the marriage behavior of individual

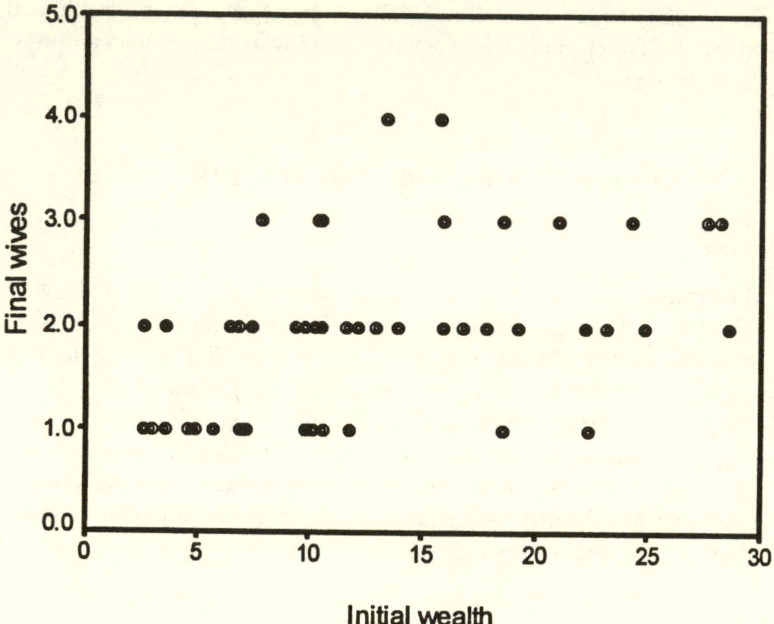

Figure 16.1. Empirical results. The number of wives at the end of the 21-year sampling interval (y) increased with initial value of livestock and land (x), yielding a regression equation of $y = 1.37 + 0.05(x)$, with $r^2 = 0.17$.

men. This type of model proposes that behavior is dependent on the states of individuals. In our model, a man's states are

- W(t) = value of livestock (in thousand Kenyan Shillings, tKS, at their 1960 monetary value) a man has at the start of year *t*
- C(t) = number of wives he has at the start of year *t*
- K(t) = number of children he has at the start of year *t*
- L = amount of land (in acres) he possesses; this value does not vary

These state variables are constrained as follows: $1 \leq C(t) \leq c_{max}$, $w_{min} \leq W(t) \leq w_{max}$, and $0 \leq K(t) \leq k_{max}$, where c_{max} is the maximum number of wives allowed in the model, w_{min} and w_{max} are the minimum and maximum number of livestock allowed, and k_{max} is the maximum number of children allowed.

The limits we placed on the variables are based on empirical data (1982–1983 values; Table 16.1). Although men have married as many as 12 wives, it is unusual for a man to have more than 4 wives, so we set $c_{max} = 4$. Similarly, 24 children is the maximum allowed in the model, although in unusual cases men may have as many as 50 children. The parameters w_{min} and w_{max} for livestock wealth are taken

Table 1. Variables and Parameters in the Model

Symbol	*Interpretation*	*Value*	*Note*
t	Year, with T (= 21) being the terminal year	Varies	
L	Amount of land owned	Fixed	[a]
W(t)	Livestock wealth at the start of year t	Varies	[b]
w_{max}	Maximum possible livestock wealth	50 tKS	[b]
w_{min}	Minimum possible livestock wealth	1 tKS	
ω_T	Total wealth, land and livestock	Varies	
ω_c	Total wealth per child	Varies	
w_{crit}	Critical wealth for raising children so that they contribute to fitness	3	[c]
C(t)	Number of wives, start of year t	Varies	
c_{max}	Maximum number of wives	4	[d]
$cost_w$	Cost of marrying a wife	4.6 tKS	[e]
L_w	Amount of land a wife can farm	1.5 acres	[f]
L_g	Amount of land not being farmed, and being used for grazing cattle		
α	Value of food produced per acre	.93 tKS/acre	[g]
F_p	Parental food requirements per year	.2 tKS	[h]
F_k	Child food requirements per year	.132 tKS	[h]
F_b	Price paid to buy food	1.5 tKS	[i]
F_s	Price received to sell food	1 tKS	[i]
K(t)	Number of children, start of year t	Varies	
k_{max}	Maximum number of children	24	[j]
k_a	Average yearly production of children, per wife	0.27	[k]
$cost_k$	Cost of maintaining children per year	.4 tKS	[l]
$cost_e$	Cost of educating children	1 tKS	[m]
$cost_s$	Cost of sick children	2 tKS	[n]

[a] For simplicity land was held fixed in the model. Productive land (suitable for grazing or cultivation) ranges between 1 and 22.5 acres (tKS value 1.1 – 24.8). Unpublished analyses show the results of this paper are unaffected by whether the model output is compared with the full empirical data set (n = 88) or only those who did not buy or sell land (n = 61).

[b] Livestock holdings range in tKS value between 0.1 and 18.2. Summing livestock and land values, capital varies from 1.8 to 40.2. The model allows w_{max} to reach 50 tKS, to compensate for the fixed land constraint.

[c] Both child mortality (Borgerhoff Mulder 1987b) and wife's temporary desertion rates are high among women married to men with little land.

[d] Two men married 12 wives, but >4 wives is unusual.

[e] Mean for this sample.

[f] See the section on Kipsigis economy.

[g] Based on cattle market exchange rates, retrospective interviews, and group discussions.

[h] Food intake estimates based on observational data and parents' estimates.

[i] Market fluctuations reflecting supply, demand, and government policy.

[j] Some men have >50 children, but >24 children is unusual.

[k] Mean number of offspring surviving to five years for women in this sample is 6.8, over a median reproductive lifespan of 25 years.

[l] These include store-purchased food, such as tea, oil, salt, and sugar, as well as clothing, soap, primary school materials, etc., and are set at 0.32 tKS per year per child. The cost of minor illnesses is set at 0.08 tKS.

[m] Government schools cost about .7 tKS per annum, whereas mission or private schools can exceed 3 tKS. Since most children attending secondary school use government institutions, the average is set at 1 tKS.

[n] Costs vary widely (across hospitals and healers), but 2 tKS was a commonly cited payment for major illnesses of offspring.

from the empirical data; the lower limit is set by social factors extraneous to the model—specifically the customary support that poor or unlucky individuals gain through cattle loaning and grants of assistance (Peristiany 1939).

The Terminal Payoff

We envision that the men behave in a manner to maximize a long-term payoff that is obtained at time T (e.g., after 21 years of marriage to his first wife). T is used to represent terminal time period and t is used to represent earlier time periods. The payoff is a combination of the number of children and the wealth (land plus value of livestock) a man has at time T. We denote this payoff as F(w,c,k,L,T), where W(T) = w, C(T) = c, K(T) = k, and L is the (fixed) amount of land that a man owns. We evaluate the terminal payoff as follows. The total wealth (in tKS) a man has at time T is

$$\omega_T = w + 1.1L \tag{1}$$

where the term 1.1 accounts for the value in tKS of an acre of land. Wealth per child is

$$\omega_c = \omega_T / k \tag{2}$$

We assume that if a man's wealth per child is less than a critical value, w_{crit} (3 tKS), his terminal payoff is 0. We base this assumption on the fact that child mortality increases dramatically among women married to men with little land (Borgerhoff Mulder 1987b), and also on qualitative observations that a wife is much more likely to run away from her husband if he is very poor. Thus, when $\omega_c < w_{crit}$, men attain no fitness.

We use a terminal fitness function (Mangel and Clark 1988; Mangel and Ludwig 1992) that captures the conflict between a man maximizing accumulated wealth and maximizing children. To do this, we use a weighting parameter γ, which ranges between 0 and 1, and which balances these two conflicting goals. In particular, the terminal fitness function is

$$F(w,c,k,L,T) = (1-\gamma)k + 0.1\gamma k(\omega_c - w_{crit}) \tag{3}$$

when $\omega_c > w_{crit}$. In this expression, the coefficient 0.1 is chosen so that the two terms on the right hand side of equation 3 are approximately equal at intermediate values of the weighting parameter γ and wealth.

This fitness function represents the conflicting motivation to maximize children or maximize wealth per child to various degrees. For example, if $\gamma = 0$, then F(w,c,k,L,T) = k, and one would assert that the men are "maximizing children." If $\gamma = 1$, then F(w,c,k,L,T) = $0.1k(\omega_c - w_{crit})$, and one would assert that men are "maximizing wealth per child." Values of γ between 0 and 1 produce fitness functions in which both number of children and wealth per child are important (Figure 16.2).

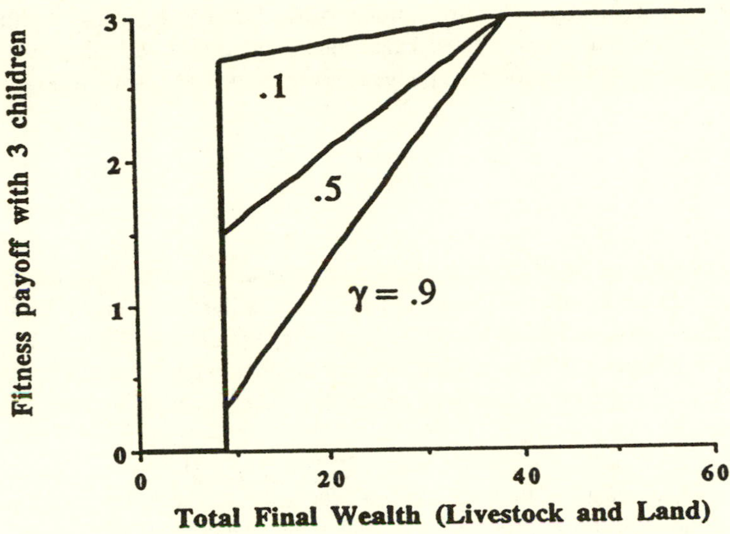

Figure 16.2. The terminal payoff to a man with three children as a function of the total value of livestock and land, for three values of the weighting parameter γ. Smaller values of the weight parameter mean that more emphasis is given to children vs. wealth; hence the slope of the terminal payoff function is shallower. When the weighting parameter is larger, wealth is more important—hence the larger slope. Beyond the level of critical wealth, maximum fitness per child is reached when wealth per child equals 13 (39 for 3 children).

Finally, we assume that if a man's wealth per child is 10 tKS or greater than the critical value, $\omega_c > 13$, his contribution to his child's success saturates. Thus, when $\omega_c > 13$, then $F(w,c,k,L,T) = k$, and the terminal payoff is his number of children.

The Dynamics of Wealth, Wives, and Children

Food, wealth, and children are produced in the following way. Each man possesses a fixed amount of land, L, of which he farms 0.5 acres and each wife can farm L_w acres. Thus the total land that the wives farm is either $L - 0.5$, when land is limited, or cL_w, when land is unlimited; we denote this is by $\min(cL_w, L - 0.5)$. Assuming that the food produced is valued at .93 tKS per acre (based on cattle market exchange rates and retrospective interviews and averaged across years), the total value of food produced by a man and his wives is

$$v_{food} = .93[.5 + \min(cL_w, L - 0.5)] \text{ tKS} \quad (4)$$

The excess land that a man may possess, which is not being farmed, is used for grazing cattle. The land available for grazing, L_g, is either 0, when all of his land is being used for farming, or $L - cL_w - 0.5$. We used an empirically derived regression linking livestock productivity to the amount of land available for grazing (a nonlinear function reflecting the fact that labor constraints limit livestock yields, and particularly milk yields) to compute the yearly value (in tKS) of land used for grazing

$$v_{grz} = \begin{cases} .5\,L_g & \text{if } L_g < 6 \\ 3 + .3(L_g - 6) & \text{if } 6 \le L_g \le 12 \\ 4.8 + .1(L_g - 12) & \text{if } L_g > 12 \end{cases} \tag{5}$$

For simplicity, we have linked livestock productivity to the amount of land available for grazing. This is reasonable, given the strong correlations between land and livestock in all Kipsigis cohorts. The relationship in equation 5 is nonlinear because (*a*) families cannot milk more than a certain number of cows each day and (*b*) men with large farms tend to have land on rocky hillsides, which are not productive for livestock.

We assume that the values in equations 4 and 5 apply in "good years." There are two kinds of "bad years." The first, which occurs 10% of the time, is a total crop failure, so that v_{food} and v_{grz} are 0. The second, which occurs 25% of the time, is a 50% crop failure, so the values in equations 4 and 5 are reduced by 50%.

The food produced by a man and his wives is used to feed the family, and any excess food is sold. We assume that the food requirement for a child, F_k, is .132 (tKS) per year and for an adult, F_p, .2 (tKS) per year; these estimates are based on both observational data and the widely held belief among Kipsigis that one acre of maize (.93 tKS) is sufficient to feed a family of six (husband, wife, and four children) for a year and that children eat about two-thirds as much as an adult. Thus, the value of food (in tKS) required to feed the family is

$$v_{req} = .2(c + 1) + .132k \tag{6}$$

If the total value of food produced exceeds the value of food required, the excess is sold at a price, F_s, of 1 tKS. If less food is produced than is required, we assume that food must be purchased at a price, F_b, of 1.5 tKS for each 1 tKS required. Maize (or maize-flour) purchased a few months before the next harvest can cost more than twice as much as it costs at the time of harvest; hence the scarcity factor of 1.5 is a gross estimate of the additional cost of running out of food.

If a man chooses to acquire a new wife in a given year, then

$$C(t + 1) = C(t) + 1 \tag{7}$$

subject to the constraint that C(t+1) cannot exceed c_{max}. He also pays a cost, $cost_w$, of 4.6 tKS, which was the mean bride-wealth for marriages in the sample.

We assume that the number of children born to a man is a product of his number of wives, with each wife producing a child roughly every four years, k_a being 0.27 children per year, determined from the mean number of surviving offspring in the sample (6.8 children over a median reproductive span of 25 years). If a man currently has C(t) wives and K(t) children, then the number of children next year is

$$K(t + 1) = K(t) + .27C(t) \tag{8}$$

Fractional values of children are removed but are included in the next year's calculation of number of new children.

Children involve three additional costs, other than food requirements. First, there are basic maintenance costs, $cost_k$. These include store-purchased food, such as tea, oil, salt, and sugar, as well as clothing, soap, primary school materials, etc. We set these costs at 0.32 tKS per year per child, on the basis of costs in 1982–1983. In addition, children have minor illnesses, which incur a 0.08 tKS annual cost for the treatment. Thus, the cost of maintaining children, $cost_k$, is 0.40 tKS per year per child. Second, there is the cost of secondary education, $cost_e$, which includes fees and occasional maintenance away from home. Until recently only a few sons (usually aged 12–18) attended secondary school, at an annual cost of 1 tKS. Assuming an even sex ratio and an even age distribution, a man with k children incurs a total cost of k/6 tKS for educating his children. The third cost is that of a major illness or accident, $cost_s$. We assume that children become sick independent of each other and that each child has a 10% chance of incurring a major sickness or accident, costing 2 tKS in treatment.

Choosing Whether to Marry Additional Wives

The model spans 21 years, to match the empirical data. Each year a man decides whether or not to take an additional wife. Marriage entails economic and reproductive consequences. The husband must pay a bride-wealth, reducing his wealth. His additional wife farms some land, if it is not already completely farmed, which may generate food and wealth. She produces children who incur costs. Whether the economic costs of marrying an additional wife outweigh the reproductive benefits depend on the man's current state, and whether the terminal fitness function favors the maximization of children or wealth per child. In the appendix we present details of how the costs and benefits of taking an additional wife are determined and compared.

A Forward Iteration to Predict Behavior and Compare with Observations

To compare the marital decisions produced by the model with the actual decisions of men in the empirical database, we simulated the behavior of these men using the values of land and livestock they possessed at the beginning of their adult lives and the optimal rules generated from equation 17 (see appendix). Because of the various stochastic events in the model, we constructed thirty independent replicates of each man. All simulated men started with one wife and no children.

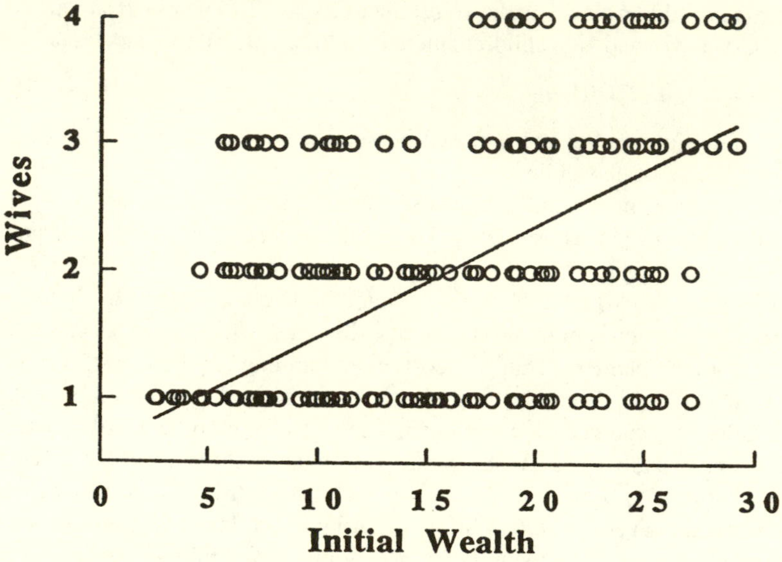

Figure 16.3. Model output. The model predicts that men with more wealth marry more wives. This is analogous to a "polygyny threshold." The regression equation for the model output is $y = 0.617 + 0.08(x)$, $r^2 = 0.5556$.

The Model Predicts Empirical Findings

Consistent with the empirical evidence the model predicts a positive relationship between a man's initial wealth and the number of his wives (Figure 16.3), when an intermediate value of γ is used, 0.7. Also consistent with empirical findings, the model predicts that men with more initial wealth marry a second wife quicker than men with less initial wealth (model output not shown). We now use the model to explore the scatter in the real data by examining the effect of γ on the accuracy of the model's predictions.

The Value of γ Affects Marriage Behavior

The effect of the weighting parameter can be seen in the marriage behavior of model men. As γ is varied, the frequency distribution of wives changes (Figure 16.4). As γ increases, the average number of wives decreases and fewer men are polygynous. Thus there is a "polygyny threshold" in the weighting parameter γ as well as in the initial capital. This prediction parallels that of Beauchamp (1994; see also Mace, this volume). Beauchamp's use of concave and convex functions to determine how parental expenditure affects offspring quality is somewhat similar to our use of the gamma weighting parameter. He found that, for a given wealth category, parents have fewer children in competitive environments (where most of

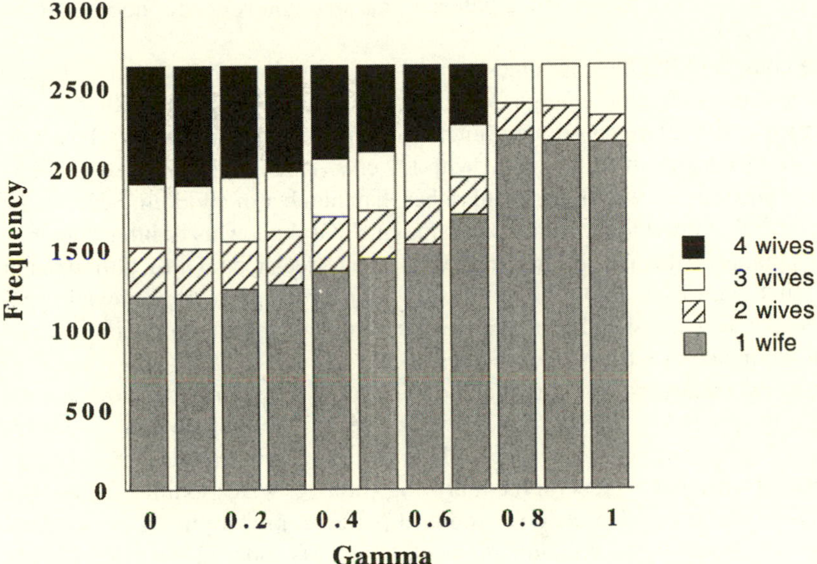

Figure 16.4. The marriage behavior of simulated men varies with the weighting parameter. The frequency distribution shows that when γ is large more men have only one wife and no men have four wives.

the impact of parental effort on offspring success occurs in the higher range of allocation) than in benign environments (where most of the impact on offspring success resulting from parental effort occurs in the lower range of allocation). Similarly our model shows that where men want to preserve resources over their reproductive career (i.e., where gamma is weighted toward 1), they less often marry a second wife.

Observed Marriage Behavior Allows Inference about γ

We compare the behavior of men using fitness functions with different γ weightings with their actual behavior to infer which value of γ best matches the actual "motivations" of Kipsigis men. For each man in the data set the number of wives at period 7, 14, and 21, which we denote by $C_{j,7}$, $C_{j,14}$, and $C_{j,21}$, is recorded. Some of these data are missing due to sample truncation. Similarly, the number of wives of the kth simulated man, $C_{jk}(7|\gamma)$, $C_{jk}(14|\gamma)$, and $C_{jk}(21|\gamma)$, who had the same initial conditions as the jth man in the data set, depends on the value of the weighting parameter used in the fitness function. A simple way to compare the empirical data and the simulation data is the sum of squared deviations of number of wives at years 7, 14, and 21, which depends on the weighting parameter:

$$SSQ(\gamma) = \Sigma_{jk}\{\ [C_{j,7} - C_{jk}(7|\gamma)]^2 + [C_{j,14} - C_{jk}(14|\gamma)]^2 + [C_{j,21} - C_{jk}(21|\gamma)]^2\} \quad (9)$$

This is a measure of the variance between the predictions of the model and the empirical data.

We computed SSQ(γ) for values of γ between and including 0 and 1 (Figure 16.5). A number of points emerge from this computation. First, men with high values of γ (0.7 to 0.9) in their fitness functions behave more similarily to the actual behavior of Kipsigis men than men with lower γ. Thus, it appears that Kipsigis men are maximizing wealth per child rather than number of children. Second, the values of γ that provide the minimum value of SSQ(γ) allow us to infer how men are weighting wealth and children in their marriage decisions. Third, although not shown in Figure 16.5, SSQ(γ) is completely flat over the range of γ shown in year 7. It is only in years 14 and 21 that differences emerge, indicating the importance of long-term and/or retrospective studies.

Sensitivity analyses (not presented here) on a subsample of men show that the error of the predicted relative to the observed results (sum of squares) is always lower at high γ than low γ. The shape of the distribution in Figure 16.5 is largely unchanged when parameters for the following variables were modified: amount of land wife can farm, value of food produced per acre, probability of a total food production failure, costs of maintaining children, costs and probability of a major illness, and level at which inherited wealth maximizes a child's fitness.

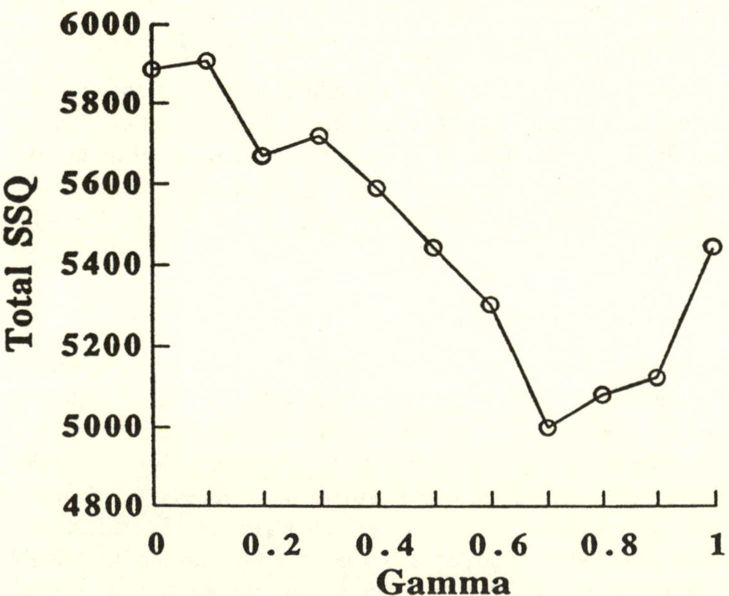

Figure 16.5. The total sum of squares SSQ(γ) computed by comparing the predicted and observed marriage behavior of men. Higher levels of γ produce reproductive decisions that more closely match the actual behavior of the men. The actual values of γ used are shown by circles and the line is interpolated for ease of viewing.

DISCUSSION

For two reasons our results should be taken more as an illustration of the inferences that can be drawn from the method, rather than a conclusion about the precise value of the weighting parameter that the men are using. First, we have not conducted a full sensitivity analysis of the model; second, data from different cohorts have been combined. Regarding this latter point, we stress that our results are not a consequence of using partially censored data since at year 7 the behavior of real men is explained equally well (or poorly) by models predicated on different gamma values; in other words, SSQ(γ) is completely flat (see above). The results, preliminary as they are, nevertheless raise several issues for discussion.

Kipsigis Men's Concern with Wealth

In one sense the finding that Kipsigis men are concerned with the accumulation of wealth over their lifespan is easy to explain. Kipsigis practice patrilineal inheritance of the family estate—primarily of livestock and land. A father's land and livestock are divided among his sons only at his death (until then they have only rights of use). For this reason we did not incorporate a "cost of fledging" in the dynamic state model. In addition, a father needs to preserve resources for the bride-wealth payments of his sons (should they outnumber his daughters). As such Kipsigis men's strategies are likely to be motivated by materialistic concerns. The principal finding of this paper is therefore not surprising. Further, it is in line with conventional qualitative arguments, that pastoralists try to keep their fertility "in balance" with resources (Stenning 1959), and that agriculturalists adopt family-building strategies aimed at providing heirs with adequate estates (Goody 1976; Skinner 1997). Note that while this finding is loosely consistent with the quantity/quality tradeoff hypothesis it offers no information on long-term fitness consequences. The present study is new insofar as it provides quantitative support for material motivations that reduce men's fertility (in this context it says nothing about women's motivations, whose fertility preferences often diverge significantly from those of men).

Before turning to the broader theoretical implications of this study for demographic transition, we need some further discussion of the gamma function (γ). Having γ in the fitness function allows us to vary the effect of a man's wealth on the success of his offspring. More specifically, as γ increases, a man's wealth has a greater impact on the success of his offspring, and the slope of that impact increases (Figure 16.2). The base model used for these analyses specifies that the effects of inherited wealth on sons saturate at 13 tKS (10tKS above the 3 tKS threshold, below which reproduction is unsuccessful), which, assuming a 50:50 sex ratio, is equivalent to capital goods of 26 tKS. Two considerations give us confidence in the appropriateness of this function. First, the empirical data show very few cases where men inherit capital goods of greater value than 26 tKS—in fact the range of inheritances closely matches those of men in the empirical data base;

thus our parameter is empirically valid. Second, sensitivity analyses show that varying the saturating level between 5 tKS and 15 tKS above the threshold has no substantial effect on the pattern shown in Figure 16.5. This gamma function therefore allows us to differentiate strategies aimed at the maximization of reasonable amounts of wealth per child (for the Kipsigis cohorts studied) from strategies geared to the maximization of fertility per se. To test hypotheses about how the costs of children affect fertility (discussed below), we need to vary the costs of children (c_m, c_e, g1) incurred prior to their father's death, as well as the value at which inherited wealth saturates. To test whether individuals select fertility levels that maximize the production of grandoffspring (no studies to date have shown that intermediate fertility levels are optimal; see above), empirical analyses of second-generation effects are required.

In short, the results of this initial paper speak more directly to the issue of reproductive motivation than fitness optimization. We suggest that the method can usefully be applied across a range of different types of human societies (see below).

Implications for Explanations of Demographic Transition

Two key features of the demographic transition were identified above: across societies there is an overall decline in completed fertility despite favorable material conditions (wealth), and within societies there is an erosion of positive correlations between wealth and fertility. What light do the present findings shed on these puzzling phenomena?

With regard to the first, Rogers (1990,1995) tried to determine the precise conditions (social, environmental, or institutional) under which material motivations might be selected over pure reproductive motivations. He used simulation models to see whether in an environment in which wealth is heritable there are circumstances in which long-term fitness is better predicted by an individual's wealth than by the number of his/her children. If such environments exist (and were common in our history) there would be some evolutionary explanation for the apparent predominance of material over reproductive motivations in post–demographic transition societies. Unfortunately, in the most recent and appropriate simulation work, reproductive and material motivations are indistinguishable (Rogers 1995: fig. 5.7).

In this context the present empirically based study becomes interesting. Among Kipsigis men there is a positive correlation between wealth and number of children (here shown only as number of wives, but see Borgerhoff Mulder 1987a). In fact, the Kipsigis case (an example of a highly pronatal community) is commonly cited as evidence that men are concerned with maximizing their fitness. Yet we can now see from the present work that materialist motivations may indeed be implicated, even where wealth-fertility correlations are strong, especially in competitive environments. More generally, as Symons (1987) cautioned, inferring evolved psychological mechanisms from correlational findings is fraught with complexity (see also Irons 1979).

To the extent that materialist motivation is common in other pre-transition populations, it becomes less difficult to explain the demographic transition. Parents in post-transition societies are merely at one end of a continuum with respect to their need for investing material resources (and/or time) into the competitive chances of offspring. Thus studies of pre–demographic transition societies can shed light on the underlying processes entailed in demographic change, a position demographers increasingly appreciate (e.g., Wilson and Airey 1999). Indeed Kaplan and colleagues argue for a general (pre– and post–demographic transition) human psychology designed to maximize the sum of incomes of all descendants produced (Kaplan et al. 1995:131) and Kaplan (1996) points to how investment in human capital in competitive market economies might underlie fertility reductions.

The present study provides empirical evidence for this position by showing that materialist motivations have been around for a long time (certainly since humans began accumulating resources to be transmitted to their offspring), even where tight correlations between wealth and reproductive success have made us think otherwise. How these motivations played out in historical societies, for example, how they differ between societies with different kinds of heritable capital (such as land and livestock based economies), nevertheless remains a major puzzle. We might hypothesize that the proximate cues that hunter-gatherer parents use to determine optimal levels of investment can account for fertility variations (e.g., Kaplan 1996), but we still need to understand how these proximal cues get translated into wealth conservation in land-limited, pastoral, and other kinds of societies. Only then can we grasp how such proximate mechanisms might generate the deviations from fertility-maximizing behavior that we see in post-transition societies. Anthropology is well placed to offer a window onto this diversity (e.g., Low 1994), in combination with theory developed in economics and evolutionary biology.

Finally, we take a brief look at why wealth and fertility become disassociated, the second enigma posed by demographic transition. Why would the wealthy ever produce fewer children than the poor? Here several studies are closing in on an explanation (Borgerhoff Mulder 1998b). Kaplan (1996) argues that what drives wealthy parents to have fewer children than poorer parents is the fact that the time, resources, or skills wealthy parents transmit to their offspring are intrinsically more valuable than those transmitted by parents of lesser means, in part because of the cumulative nature of learning. Under such circumstances the opportunity costs of producing an additional child among the rich are greater than they are among the poor, driving negative or curvilinear relationships between parental wealth and fertility. Mace (this volume) models a similar nonlinear process, whereby different strata in society optimize fitness with different fertility—specifically, the wealthy do so with a lower fertility than the poor. Similarly Rogers, who was until recently unable to simulate an environment in which optimal fertility decreases with wealth (Rogers 1995), now reports that in environments in which inheritance greatly boosts an individual's ability to earn income (each dollar inherited generates on average 2 dollars of earned wealth) wealthy parents at equilibrium produce fewer children than poorer parents (Alan Rogers, University of Utah, unpublished results). New Kipsigis evidence (unpublished data), showing that in recent cohorts men who inherit more capital (land and livestock) become wealthy at a faster rate than those who inherit less capital (because of increased market access in recent years), suggests that such potentially nonlinear responses to investing wealth in children are emerging among Kipsigis, and may precipitate fertility transition. Once low fertility arises among the richest families, it can spread to other social classes even if the appropriate conditions do not exist, by the processes of indirect bias posited in cultural evolution models (Boyd and Richerson 1985). In short, a hybrid theory of demographic transition built on evolutionary psychology, behavioral ecology, and cultural inheritance theory may be materializing (Borgerhoff Mulder 1998b).

SUMMARY

1. The evolutionary rationale for the demographic transition remains elusive, since to date empirical analyses have failed to identify fitness benefits contingent on fertility reduction.
2. We use dynamic state variable models to predict reproductive behavior, specifically a man's decision to take another wife.
3. We build a model of the conditions for production and reproduction in a typical pre–demographic transition agropastoral society. While the parameters are based on a specific group (Kenyan Kipsigis), the model is general enough to apply to many agricultural/pastoral communities.
4. We assume that an individual's lifetime fitness is a combination of accumulated wealth and total reproduction. Weighting these in different ways, we use simulations to determine the optimal marital decisions contingent on what combination of children or wealth per child is being maximized.
5. A comparison of the simulation output with empirical data shows that a decision rule weighted toward "wealth maximization" (a combined function of maximizing children and wealth per child) best predicts the marital careers of men.
6. The concern for wealth accumulation among Kipsigis men is not surprising given their capital-based economy, but the finding is notable for other reasons. First, it provides quantitative support for strong material motivations in a society where wealth-fertility correlations are high. Second, it demonstrates material motivations in a case commonly cited as providing evidence for reproductive motivation.

7. We propose this as a useful method in the study of worldwide fertility variation and decline, insofar as it can identify motivational structures underlying reproductive decision-making and can be used to test these structures against clearly stated alternatives.

ACKNOWLEDGMENT

Kipsigis research was funded by the National Geographic Society and the University of California at Davis (MBM). The work of BTL and MM was partially supported by NSF grants (to MM) and by the Center for Population Biology, University of California at Davis. We thank Sarah Hrdy, Debra Judge, Hilly Kaplan, Eric Smith, Mary Towner, and Bruce Winterhalder for comments and discussion.

APPENDIX

CALCULATION OF COSTS AND BENEFITS OF ADDITIONAL MARRIAGES

For years prior to the terminal payoff, we define F(w,c,k,L,t) as the maximum expected terminal payoff, given that W(t) = w, C(t) = c, K(t) = k, and land is L. The expectation is calculated over the deterministic and stochastic changes in wealth that occur between t and T. The maximum expected value is determined by choosing the marriage profile to maximize the expected terminal payoff.

We can describe the expected fitness and thereby predict the conditions under which a man will acquire a new wife. Imagine a man whose livestock currently has value w, who has c wives and k children.

In a good year, which occurs with a probability 0.65, if the total value of food produced by the man and his wives exceeds their needs, and s of his children become sick with a major illness, livestock value next year will be

$$w'(w,c,k,L,s) = w + (v_{food} - v_{req}) + v_{grz} - k\ cost_k - (k/6)\ cost_e - s\ cost_s \quad (10)$$

On the other hand, if the value of food produced is less than the food requirements, the livestock value next year will be

$$w'(w,c,k,L,s) = w + 1.5(v_{food} - v_{req}) + v_{grz} - k\ cost_k - (k/6)\ cost_e - s\ cost_s \quad (11)$$

In years in which there is a 50% crop failure, reasoning similar to that shown in equations 10 and 11 apply, except that the value of food produced and the value of grazing are reduced by 50%. Thus, the analogues of these equations are

$$w''(w,c,k,L,s) = w + (.5v_{food} - v_{req}) + .5v_{grz} - k\ cost_k - (k/6)\ cost_e - s\ cost_s \quad (12)$$

or

$$w''(w,c,k,L,s) = w + 1.5(.5v_{food} - v_{req}) + .5v_{grz} - k\ cost_k - (k/6)\ cost_e - s\ cost_s \quad (13)$$

Finally, in years in which there is a complete crop failure, the value of livestock next year will be

$$w'''(w,c,k,L,s) = w - 1.5v_{req} - k\ cost_k - k/6\ cost_e - s\ cost_s \quad (14)$$

Equations 10–14 are conditioned on the number of sick children.

We can now compute the fitness value ($V_{no\ marry}$) of a man who chooses to not acquire a wife this year by averaging over the number of sick children and the chance of crop failure:

$$\begin{aligned} V_{no\ marry}(w,c,k,L,t) = E_s\{&.65F[w'(w,c,k,L,s), c, k + .27c, L, t + 1] \\ &+ .25F[w''(w,c,k,L,s), c, k + .27c, L, t + 1] \\ &+ .1F[w.'''(w,c,k,L,s), c, k + .27c, L, t + 1]\} \end{aligned} \quad (15)$$

In this equation, E_s denotes the expectation over the number of sick children (binomial with parameters k and 0.1).

Alternatively, a man who chooses to acquire a wife pays a cost (4.6 tKS, the mean bride-wealth for marriages in the sample), which is subtracted from his wealth. We assume that this occurs before crop failure is known and before it is known how many children will be sick in this year. Thus, the cost of the wife is subtracted from each term in equation 15, and the fitness value of marrying a wife is

$$\begin{aligned} V_{marry}(w,c,k,L,t) = E_s\{&.65F[w'(w,c,k,L,s) - 4.6, c, k + .27c, L, t + 1] \\ &+ .25F[w''(w,c,k,L,s) - 4.6, c, k + .27c, L, t + 1] \\ &+ .1F[w'''(w,c,k,L,s) - 4.6, c, k + .27c, L, t + 1]\} \end{aligned} \quad (16)$$

The optimal pattern of marriage is that which maximizes the expected payoff, hence

$$F(w,c,k,L,t) = \max[V_{no\ marry}(w,c,k,L,t), V_{marry}(w,c,k,L,t)] \quad (17)$$

Equation 17 is solved backward, starting at t = T – 1, and generates the expected payoff for every combination of time and states. It also generates the optimal behavior (to take a wife or not) for every time and state (Figure 16.5). When solving it, we used linear interpolation on wealth and number of children to deal with non-integer values of the state variables (Mangel and Clark 1988).

REFERENCES

Anderies, J. M. 1996. An adaptive model for predicting !Kung reproductive performance: A stochastic dynamic programming approach. *Ethology and Sociobiology* 17:221–246.

Beauchamp, G. 1994. The functional analysis of human fertility decisions. *Ethology and Sociobiology* 15:31–53.

Becker, G. S., and H. G. Lewis. 1973. Interaction between quantity and quality of children. In *Economics of the Family: Marriage, Children, and Human Capital.* T. W. Shultz, ed. Pp. 81–90. Chicago: Chicago University Press.

Borgerhoff Mulder, M. 1987a. On cultural and reproductive success: Kipsigis evidence. *American Anthropologist* 89:617–634.

———. 1987b. Resources and reproductive success in women, with an example from the Kipsigis. Journal of Zoology 213:489–505.

———. 1990. Kipsigis women's preferences for wealthy men: Evidence for female choice in mammals. *Behavioral Ecology and Sociobiology* 27:255–264.

———. 1995. Bridewealth and its correlates: Quantifying changes over time. *Current Anthropology* 36:573–603.

———. 1998a. Brothers and Sisters: Biased investment among the Kipsigis of Kenya. *Human Nature* 9:119–162

———. 1998b. The demographic transition: Are we any closer to an evolutionary explanation? *Trends in Ecology and Evolution* 13(7):266–270.

Borgerhoff Mulder, M., Kerr, A. and M. D. Moore. 1997. Time allocation among the Kipsigis of Kenya. Volume XIV Cross Cultural Studies in Time Allocation. Connecticut: Human Relations Area Files, Inc.

Bongaarts, J. and S. C. Watkins. 1996. Social interactions and contemporary fertility transitions. *Population and Development Review* 22(4):639–682.

Boyd, R, and P. J. Richerson. 1985. *Culture and the Evolutionary Process.* Chicago: University of Chicago Press.

Coale, A. J., and S. C. Watkins, eds. 1986. *The Decline of Fertility in Europe.* Princeton: Princeton University Press.

Goody, J. 1976. *Production and Reproduction.* Cambridge: Cambridge University Press.

Irons, W. 1979. Culture and biological success. In *Evolutionary Biology and Human Social Behavior: An Anthropological Perspective*, N. A. Chagnon and W. Irons, eds. Pp. 257–272. North Scituate, Massachussetts: Duxbury.

Jones, Gavin W., R. M. Douglas, J. C. Caldwell, and R. M. D'Souza. 1997. *The continuing demographic transition.* New York: Clarendon Press; Oxford University Press.

Kaplan, H. S., J. B. Lancaster, J. A. Bock, and S. E. Johnson. 1995. Fertility and fitness among Albuquerque men: A competitive labour market theory. In *Human Reproductive Decisions,* R. I. M. Dunbar, pp. 96–136. London: St Martin's Press.

Lack, D. 1947. The significance of clutch size. *Ibis* 89:302–352.

Lesthaeghe, R., and C. Wilson. 1986. Modes of production, secularization, and the pace of fertility decline in Western Europe, 1870–1930. In *The Decline of Fertility in Europe,* A. J. Coale and S. C. Watkins, eds. Pp. 261–292. Princeton: Princeton University Press.

Livi-Bacci, M. 1986. Social-group forerunners of fertility control in Europe. In *The Decline of Fertility in Europe,* A. J. Coale and S. C. Watkins, eds. Pp. 182–200. Princeton: Princeton University Press.

Low, B. S. 1994. Men in demographic transition. *Human Nature* 5:223–254.

Mangel, M., and C. W. Clark. 1988. *Dynamic Modeling in Behavioral Ecology.* Princeton: Princeton University Press.

Mangel, M., and D. Ludwig. 1992. Definition and evaluation of the fitness of behavioral and developmental programs. *Annual Review of Ecology and Systematics* 23:507–536.

Mueller, E and K. Short. 1983. Effects of income and wealth on the demand for children. In *Supply and Demand for Children,* R. A Bulatao and R. D. Lee, eds. Pp. 590–642. Determinants of Fertility in Developing Countries, Vol. 1. New York: Academic Press.

Mueller, U. n.d. *What is Evolutionary Competition About? Average, Maximal, and Optimal Fecundity.* Mannheim, Germany: Centre for Survey Research and Methodology.

Notestein, F, W. 1953. Economic problems of population change. In *Proceedings of the Eighth International Conference of Agricultural Economists*, pp. 13–31. London: Oxford University Press.

Peristiany, J. G. 1939. *The Social Institutions of the Kipsigis*. London: Routledge and Kegan Paul.

Pérusse, D. 1993. Cultural and reproductive success in industrial societies: Testing relationship at the proximate and ultimate levels. *Behavioral and Brain Sciences* 16:267–322.

Robinson, W. C. 1992. Kenya enters the fertility transition. *Population Studies* 46:445–457.

Rogers, A. R. 1990. The evolutionary economics of human reproduction. *Ethology and Sociobiology* 11:479–495.

———. 1995. For love or money: The evolution of reproductive and material motivations. In Human Reproductive Decisions, R. I. M. Dunbar, ed. Pp. 76–95. London: St Martin's Press.

Skinner, G. W. 1997. Family Systems and Demographic Processes. In *Anthropological Demography: Toward a New Synthesis,* D. I. Kertzer and T. E. Fricke, eds. Pp. 53-95. Chicago: University of Chicago Press.

Stenning, D. J. 1959. *Savannah Nomads.* Oxford: Oxford University Press.

Symons, D. 1987. If we are all Darwinians, what's the fuss about? In *Sociobiology and Psychology,* B. Crawford, M. F. Smith, and D. L. Krebs, eds. Pp. 121–146. Hillsdale, New Jersey: Lawrence Erlbaum Associates.

Turke, P. 1989. Evolution and the demand for children. *Population and Development Review* 15:61–90.

Vining, D. R. 1986. Social versus reproductive success—the central theoretical problem of human sociobiology. *Behavioral and Brain Sciences* 9:167–260.

Wilson, C., and P. Airey. 1999. How can a homeostatic perspective enhance demographic transition theory? *Population Studies 53(2):117–128.*

PART V

SOCIALITY

17

Effects of Illness and Injury on Foraging among the Yora and Shiwiar

Pathology Risk as Adaptive Problem

LAWRENCE S. SUGIYAMA and RICHARD CHACON

He who has experienced it knows how cruel a companion sorrow is to the man who has no beloved protectors.

"The Wanderer" (Anglo Saxon poem)

INTRODUCTION

Current foraging models concerned with "risk analysis" focus on the ways in which the risk of temporal or spatial resource shortages (i.e., *foraging risk*) influences human subsistence behavior (e.g., Cashdan, 1985; Kaplan and Hill 1985a; Hames 1990). The impact of *pathology risk* on adaptations affecting social behavior has received less attention (see, however, Baksh and Johnson 1990; Cashdan 1990; Dettwyler 1991; Kaplan and Hill 1985a; Low 1988; Sugiyama 1996; Trinkaus 1983). Studies that do investigate pathology in foraging populations concentrate primarily on causes of mortality (e.g., Baksh and Johnson 1990; Hill and Hurtado 1996). Yet while both sublethal pathology and mortality risk exert selection pressure for adaptations designed to reduce the risk of their untimely occurrence, a focus on sublethal pathology draws our attention to the selection pressure on, and the design of, adaptations that ameliorate the negative effects of those pathologies that inevitably do occur.

The obvious fitness benefits of avoiding pathological conditions lead one to expect adaptations motivating measured caution in the presence of cues reliably linked with dangerous stimuli over the course of hominid evolution, as well as adaptations dedicated to identifying such cues. A rich body of research supports this hypothesis, indicating the existence of a suite of mechanisms dedicated to the problems of injury and illness. Some examples are: cross-cultural human antipathy toward potentially dangerous or noxious stimuli and/or their cues (e.g., snakes, predators, vermin, heights, vomit, puss, feces, and secondary plant toxins [Marks 1987; Profet 1992; Rozin and Fallon 1987; Rozin et al. 1986]); pronounced fear of strangers during specific stages of childhood (Bowlby 1969); cognitive algorithms dedicated to reasoning about precautions and threats (Fiddick 1999; Rutherford et al. 1996); increased levels of polygynous mating associated with environments of increased pathogen risk (Low 1988); modifying the environment to reduce risk of snakebites (Baksh and Johnson 1990); and anxiety and depression, which have been analyzed as emotional adaptations designed to cope with both social and other sources of threat (Hagen 1999). All of these are strong indicators that humans have adaptations designed to reduce pathology risk. Still other potential risk-aversion adaptations have yet to be fully investigated, such as aversion to animals exhibiting other cues of toxicity or threat (e.g., bright coloring, loud buzzing or hissing, pincers or barbs, direct eye contact, bared teeth).

Obviously these mechanisms are not foolproof: Pathology occurs with considerable frequency across extant, recent prehistoric and earlier *Homo* populations (e.g., Bailey 1991; Baksh and Johnson 1990; Berger and Trinkaus 1995; Chagnon 1997; Hill and Hurtado 1996; Lambert 1993; Low 1988; Sugiyama, 1999; Trinkaus 1983; Truswell and Hansen 1976; Walker 1989). When it occurs, it poses a number of adaptive problems for its victim. Here we report the effects of physical pathology on the foraging productivity of the Yora and Shiwiar of Eastern Amazonia, explore the adaptive problems for human social relations posed by pathology risk, and outline how adaptations designed to elicit behavior to mitigate these problems may operate.

STUDY POPULATIONS

The Yora

The Yora are a hunter/horticulturalist group of Panoan-speaking people who live in the Amazonian lowlands of southeastern Peru near the Mishagua and Manu rivers. The Yora remained relatively isolated until their first peaceful contacts with outsiders in 1984. Within two years, approximately half the population died from introduced diseases (Hill and Kaplan 1989). By the time of this study in the summer of 1990 the population was rebounding and none of the pathology reported herein can be attributed to postcontact epidemics (Sugiyama and Chacon 1993). At that time the Yora were living in three locations: 66 full-time residents lived in the study village of Putaya, 37 persons lived in Cashpajali (as of 1986), and a third group lived in the mission town of Sepahua.

Methods The authors used three methods to obtain quantitative data on Yora consumption patterns and subsistence activities during a 59-day observation period: scan sampling, focal person follows, and departure/return records. During the study period the population of Putaya varied between 56 and 71 people. Two to six instantaneous scan samples were run on each of 29 days, yielding a total of 100 scans and 6,448 individual behavioral observations (Sugiyama and Chacon 1993; Walker et al. 1998). Data on time allocated to subsistence activities and the relative frequency with which different foods were observed being eaten are based on these observations. Additional data were collected by recording the time that foragers left and returned to the village, the tools taken, and the type and weight of food acquired. The authors also accompanied the Yora on a number of foraging trips (focal person follows). These techniques were used to gather data on hunting and fishing returns for all village residents for 42 consecutive days. Foraging returns are based on this period. Significant illnesses and injuries and their effects on foraging were noted, as were minor injuries brought to the authors' attention throughout their stay in the village.

Yora Foraging Initial reports suggested that the Yora relied almost entirely on hunting and gathering for their livelihood (Hill and Kaplan 1989). In 1990, however, horticultural products were a major part of their diet (53% of observed consumption) and 50.9% of subsistence activities were devoted to horticulture. None of the Yora cultigens we observed are particularly rich sources of protein. The main garden staple was sweet manioc; both boiled manioc and manioc beer were part of almost every meal and together comprised 21.6% of observed consumption. Plantains were also an important food and accounted for 9.7% of the foods consumed. Other cultigens consumed were sugar cane, jicama, maize, and sweet potatoes (Sugiyama and Chacon 1993; Walker et al. 1998).

Hunting and fishing provide the bulk of Yora dietary protein. Before contact, men hunted with bow and arrow, either stalking their prey or using hunting blinds. Since first contact, dogs have become prized hunting aids. Of the subsistence activity observed in Putaya, 14.3% was devoted to hunting, and game accounted for 16.5% of observed consumption. The primary prey in the Yora diet were collared peccary (*Tayassu tajacu*), paca (*Agouti paca*), capybara (*Hydrochaeris hydrochaeris*), coati (*Nasua nasua*), agouti (*Dasyprocta sp.*), various primates, tamandua (*Tamandua tradactyla*), and acouchy (*Myoprocta sp.*). A small number of birds and squirrels (*Sciurus sp.*) were acquired as well. Large game was butchered at or near the kill site, and much of it packaged for distribution before returning to the village. Almost all the soft tissue of game animals was eaten, including the tough hide of peccary.

A variety of fish were taken with bow and arrow, cast net, or hook and line, accounting for 22.6% of observed consumption. Among the commonly caught fish were *zungaro, carachama, sabado, bocachico,* and freshwater stingray. The Yora also eat small quantities of turtle and lizard eggs. Although honey was not eaten during the study period, informants report that it is taken at other times of the year, along with seasonally available wild fruits and nuts. Papayas, chickens, and lemons are recently introduced foods not eaten before contact (Sugiyama and Chacon 1993; Walker et al. 1998).

Because meat is distributed throughout the village, it is usually consumed within a day of the kill, and storage of meat or fish is rare. Although distribution is not equal among households, secondary sharing of meat ensures that all households receive a portion of medium and large game, and even small game is shared widely between households. Fish from overnight fishing trips are also widely shared.

The Shiwiar

The Shiwiar are a Jivaroan people who live in the southern Oriente (tropical forest) of Ecuador and northeastern Peru. The Shiwiar, often considered a subgroup of the Achuar, number approximately 2,000 individuals occupying the Corrientes River drainage and its tributaries. Although the term Shiwiar also refers to a specific set of politically aligned villages in Ecuador, here we are using the broader cultural/historical usage. Unnavigable rivers form a barrier to colonial incursion into Shiwiar territory from Ecuador. Border conflict with Peru has limited contacts between Ecuadorian Shiwiar and colonists in the southeast since the 1940s. Prior to the 1970s, when Shiwiar began accepting missionary contact, they lived in scattered households linked by marriage ties and the influence of powerful individuals (Descola 1988). Since missionary contact, Shiwiar have made dirt airstrips around which houses now form loose clusters. Although missionary light aircraft provides some access to medical and other facilities outside Shiwiar territory, subsistence is still based on foraging and horticulture. The data presented here were gathered in the community of Alto Corrientes (population 67) during separate field trips by the authors in 1993 and 1994. Additional information from this area was collected by Sugiyama in 1993 from the Achuar/Quichua village of Conambo (population 181), and from 1994–1995 in the Shiwiar village of Kurintza (population 87).

Methods Focal person follows and departure/return records were used to record all returns from 133 hunts in Alto Corrientes over the course of 89 days during two field seasons. Injury and illnesses that occurred during one of these periods were recorded, as were previous injuries and illnesses that could be documented based either on physical evidence or on the corroborated recollection of informants (Sugiyama 1999).

Shiwiar Foraging Hunting and fishing provide the bulk of Shiwiar dietary protein (Descola 1988). Blowguns, muzzle-loading shotguns, and dogs are used in hunting. Animals such as agouti (*Dasyprocta sp.*) are also killed by hand when cornered in a log or burrow. The terrestrial game taken by Shiwiar is similar to that taken by Yora, the most important being collared peccary (*Tayassu tajacu*), tapir (*Tapirus terrestris*), paca (*Agouti paca*), agouti (*Dasyprocta sp.*), acouchy

(*Myoprocta sp.*), deer (*Mazama americana*), and armadillo (*Dasypus sp.*). Although Shiwiar use dogs to pursue animals such as collared peccary (*Tayassu tajacu*), agouti (*Dasyprocta sp.*), and paca (*Agouti paca*), they hunt without dogs relatively more often than do the Yora (Sugiyama 1998). This, combined with a mixed strategy of blowgun and shotgun use, yields a greater percentage of primates (primarily wooley, [*Lagothrix lagothricha*], howler [*Alouatta sp.*], and capuchin [*Cebus, sp.*] monkeys), birds, and small game (e.g., squirrels [*Sciurus sp.*]) in the Shiwiar than in the Yora diet (Sugiyama 1998).

Fishing is done either with hooks and line or with fish poisons, baskets, spears, and by hand. In the rainy season the bulk of fish are taken by hooks and line. During the transition to the dry season, emphasis on fishing gradually increases as the rivers become shallow and fishing with one of two cultivated poisons, *timiu* (*barbasco*) or *masu,* becomes increasingly efficient. These dry-season fish poisonings are often village-wide events and can produce a large surplus. Fish and meat not eaten on the day of capture are regularly preserved by smoking them over a fire (Descola 1988; Sugiyama 1998). Average daily per capita protein consumption from fish is not included in the present analysis because complete records of fishing returns were impossible to gather. Nevertheless, game accounts for the majority of protein consumed during the rainy season (when foraging data presented here were collected).

Descola (1988) notes that almost no meat was shared between Achuar households during the 1970s. Even in current, more concentrated Shiwiar communities, smaller game is usually not shared beyond the hunter's household. Medium-size and larger game is shared, but even tapir, the largest game animal taken, is only shared amongst a subset of households in some villages. Several factors may limit meat sharing among the Shiwiar. Smoking meat over the fire provides a storage system that reduces day-to-day variance in its availability, thus reducing one benefit of sharing (Cashdan 1985). Similarly, strategic use of blowguns, hunting dogs, and shotguns means that unsuccessful hunting trips are relatively infrequent, further reducing the risk of temporary shortfalls and the benefit of foraging risk reduction via sharing (Kaplan and Hill 1985; Winterhalder 1990). While Shiwiar failed to acquire any game on only 27% of 133 hunts, Yora failed to acquire any game on 45% of 47 hunts ($p < .013$). Shiwiar do experience high absolute variance in hunting returns between trips—sometimes they return with nothing, other times with a squirrel, and still other times with a 115 kg tapir. Nevertheless, in comparison with the Yora, Shiwiar hunters experience relatively few days when they go hunting and return with no game whatsoever, and smoking the game can effectively preserve it for several weeks.

PATHOLOGY RISK AMONG YORA AND SHIWIAR

Yora and Shiwiar engage in many types of behavior found among hunter-gatherers known ethnographically and archaeologically: they live in small kin-based communities in which some foods are shared; they rely on hunting and fishing for most of their dietary fat and protein; they have little easy access to Western medicine; and they depend on relatively simple technology for their livelihood. In these and other ways their living conditions mirror important general features of the environments in which hominids evolved. The hazards of such a life are manifold and come from a variety of sources:

- Lacerations, scrapes, and puncture wounds are common and pose the threat of disability due to serious infections (Baksh and Johnson 1990; Bailey 1991; Sugiyama 1996, 1999).
- Fractures resulting from accidental falls or falling timber cause periods of foraging inactivity and can cause infection that may lead to the loss of limbs (Baksh and Johnson 1990; Chagnon, personal communication; Sugiyama 1996).
- Injuries inflicted by prey are a hazard for hunters. Among the Ache, for example, coati are typically killed by hand and bites are common (Hill & Hurtado 1996). During our study period, one Yora man was bitten on the hand by a coati and another was bitten in the leg by a *paca agouti.*
- Venomous fauna are ubiquitous. Snake bites can cause tissue necrosis leading to long-term disability, loss of limbs, and death (Baksh and Johnson 1990; Chagnon 1997; Hill and Hurtado 1996; Sugiyama 1999). In a survey of injury and illness among the Shiwiar, 13 of 24 adults surveyed reported being bitten by a venomous snake at least once. One man reported six months of disability from a snakebite that became infected with gangrene; another man's foot was permanently disfigured (Sugiyama 1999). Yora report that fresh-water stingrays may inflict injuries that prevent foraging for up to a week. The venom from scorpions, wasps, spiders, and caterpillars can also be disabling for shorter periods. Some insects lay their eggs beneath the skin, which, along with insect bites in general, carries the risk of serious and sometimes lethal infections (e.g. Chagnon 1997; Hill and Hurtado 1996; Sugiyama 1996, 1999).
- Yora report injuries and deaths at the hands of Machiguenga enemies. Shiwiar are wounded in feuds by means of gunshot, lance, and booby traps; while fighting they sustain injuries ranging from minor contusions to broken bones (Sugiyama 1999). In club fights, Yanomamö, Machiguenga, and Ache suffer split scalps, fractured skulls, and concussions (Baksh and Johnson 1990; Chagnon 1979b; Hill and Hurtado 1996). Archaeological evidence shows that interpersonal violence was the source of sublethal trauma in prehistoric foraging societies as well (e.g., Lambert 1993; Walker 1989).
- A variety of pathogens and illnesses (e.g., giardia, amoebas, malaria, chickenpox, stroke, tuberculosis, arthritis) can render individuals incapable of foraging for periods ranging from days to years (Sugiyama 1999).

Significant Injuries During the Study Period

Two infections stemming from minor injuries had appreciable effects on foraging during our Yora fieldwork. One man suffered a puncture wound on the medial aspect of his elbow that became infected some weeks prior to the study period. The infection spread throughout his arm and he did no hunting or fishing for the entire 59-day study period, although a year earlier he was one of the most active hunters in the village (Kim Fowler, Summer Institute of Linguistics, personal communication, 1990). For the analysis below we used the conservative figure of 36 days (the time between our arrival and the man's first attempt at garden work) to calculate foraging days he lost due to injury. However, it is clear that he refrained from foraging for a longer period. Without antibiotics provided by a visiting missionary he might have lost the arm or died, consequences not unknown in this and similar societies.[1]

Another man suffered a puncture wound at the base of his thumb that became infected eight days before we left the village and prevented him from hunting for at least that length of time. We do not know for how much longer he was debilitated by the infection. Undoubtedly, more cuts, puncture wounds, and insect bites occurred than were observed—injuries too common to have been brought to our attention that nevertheless carry significant risk of infection (Baksh and Johnson 1990; Chagnon 1997; Hill and Hurtado 1996; Sugiyama 1999).

Although this analysis concentrates on foraging activities—predominantly but not exclusively male activities among the Yora and Shiwiar—females are, obviously, not immune to sickness and injury. For example, one Yora woman severed her Achilles tendon with a machete prior to the authors' arrival. Although the wound healed, the tendon remained severed and she had a severe limp. She must have been incapacitated for an extended time after she injured herself. When a woman incurs a debilitating injury, someone must make up for her lost productivity or family subsistence will suffer, particularly if she is disabled for a prolonged period. A child's illness may also adversely impact family subsistence. During a whooping cough epidemic among the Shiwiar witnessed by Sugiyama, one woman had to provide constant care for her infant and could do no gardening or foraging for over three weeks. Her husband took over the gardening and the care of their other children during this period, which he claimed prevented him from going hunting.[2]

Costs of Injury to Yora Foraging

Repeated periods of injury or illness can have adverse consequences for growth, life-span, cognitive function, and fertility. Periods of poor maternal health may also have negative effects on unborn or nursing offspring (e.g., Allen 1984; Buzina et al. 1989; Wing and Brown 1980). Such cumulative effects are difficult to assess given the data at hand. Below we consider only the relatively short-term problem of pathology effects on subsistence from foraging. Because long-term negative effects are associated with periods of physical pathology, however, we expect selection to have favored traits that not only enhance ability to survive such periods, but to do so with as little long-term fitness cost as possible.

Within a wide range of values, lowered nutritional intake—particularly of dietary protein and/or fat—entails definite fitness costs. Nutritional decrements have been associated with stunted growth; increased morbidity and mortality; shorter reproductive lifespan; delay of menarche and onset of puberty; fewer offspring; a lower proportion of live births; lower infant survival and body weight; and increased juvenile mortality in a variety of primates (including humans) and other mammals (e.g., Allen 1984; Altmann 1991; Frisch and McArthur 1974; Green et al. 1986; Hill and Hurtado 1996; Kohrs et al. 1976; Manocha and Long 1977; Prentice et al. 1987; Riley et al. 1993; Schwartz et al. 1988). Although we use here the United States Recommended Dietary Allowance (USRDA) of protein as a convenient benchmark for comparison, it should not be taken as an absolute criterion above or below which nutritional variance is insignificant.

An estimate of the cost of injuries in terms of lost foraging returns was calculated in the following manner. The number of days in the observation period that each independent hunter was present and not injured was divided by the number of times he went hunting. The mean of the resulting values for all independent hunters yielded the average period between hunts for these individuals. The number of days potentially lost to foraging include only those periods for which the duration of an injury or illness was longer than the average period between hunts, or for which a foraging trip was aborted due to injury. This figure was divided by the average period between hunts to arrive at an estimate of foraging days lost to injury. This estimate was multiplied by the average returns per hunt in the village (i.e., total returns in the village divided by total number of hunts observed during the study period) to get an estimate of lost hunting returns. The same calculations were then made for fishing. Visits between villages caused village size to vary throughout the study period; these fluctuations were taken into account and visitors were included as both foragers and consumers for the analysis.[3] One man foraged infrequently and complained repeatedly of pain that limited his movement, but because the cause of the discomfort and its effect upon foraging could not be definitively established, we did not count the time he did not forage as pathology-related. He was however, included among active hunters.[4] Young men who fished independently and consistently but did not hunt independently or consistently were calculated in fishing but not in hunting data.

Men who hunted independently were clearly prevented from foraging due to injuries on at least 47 man-days, which represents approximately 10.6% of all man-days observed for independent hunters. On average, individual hunters hunted once every 5.27 days with average returns of 7.65 kg per hunt. The average time between hunts for individual hunters ranged between 2.6 and 7 days. On average, those central to fishing productivity went fishing once every 4.85 days with average returns of 3.35 kg per trip. An estimated total of 8.92 hunts and 9.69 fishing trips were foregone due to pathologies that we can confidently determine, but again this is a conservative estimate.

Figure 17.1 presents average per capita Yora protein consumption from meat and fish.[5] The horizontal axis indicates the USRDA of protein for people of the Yora's stature (45g). Bar 1 presents observed average per capita protein consumption during the study period. Even though injuries interfered with some foraging, protein consumption during this time remained above the USRDA (48.14 g). Bar

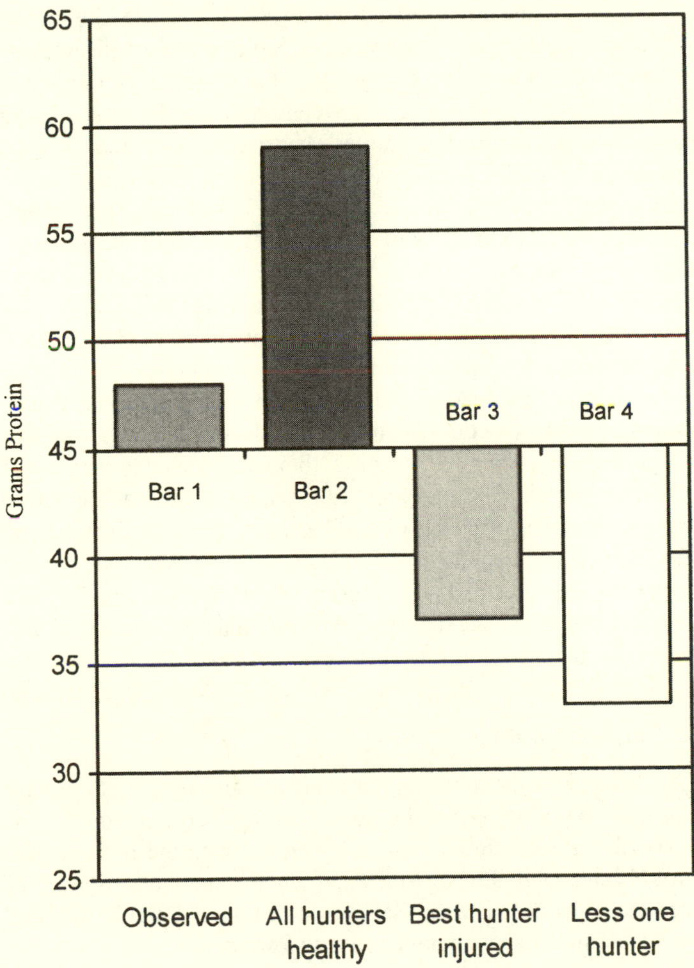

Figure 17.1. Yora daily per capita protein comsumption from game and fish.

2 presents estimated per capita protein consumption had there been no injuries during the study period (58.55 g) to give an idea of the cost of observed injuries—that is, an estimate of what returns would have been had no hunters been injured and were there no change in average rate of foraging. Thus, we estimate an 18% reduction in average per capita protein consumption due to pathologies based on the assumption that observed injuries affected a statistically average hunter.

However, hunting frequency and returns vary across hunters. Kaplan and Hill (1985a) suggest that members of Ache foraging bands might extend greater than average solicitude to the best hunters (and their dependents) when they are injured because group members are loath to lose this important source of meat. If injury prevented the best Yora hunter from foraging, average time between successful hunts in the village would go from an estimated .77 days to 2.8 days. More importantly, without the best hunter, estimated average per capita protein consumption would drop 37%, from 58.55 g to 36.77 g (Bar 3) —that is, from well above to below the USRDA of protein for people of this weight and stature. Other group members certainly do benefit from the best hunter's subsistence contributions and will suffer nutritional declines if he is injured.

If injured, the best hunter and his dependents will also suffer these declines. One way to buffer this risk may be to maintain a sufficient number of sharing partners to provide aid during times of disability. Analysis shows that, indeed, protein intake diminishes a further 7% if the village has even one less hunter of average abilities (and his dependents) while the best hunter is injured (Bar 4, 32.71 g).[6]

One could ask whether the pattern of pathology effects on subsistence described above is an idiosyncratic feature of a short period of time in Yora history or is widespread among similar societies. A study of the Shiwiar documenting significant lifetime injuries and illnesses suggests the latter conclusion: minor injuries are ubiquitous and significant injury and illness are not uncommon within this population (Sugiyama, 1999). Reports of similar injury and disability among other groups further support this hypothesis (e.g., Baily 1991; Baksh and Johnson 1990; Hill and Hurtado 1996; Truswell and Hansen 1976). In the following section, we examine Shiwiar foraging data to see whether effects of pathology on Shiwiar subsistence exhibit a pattern similar to that found among the Yora.

Costs of Injury to Shiwiar Hunting

Figure 17.2 (Bar 2) presents data on Shiwiar average daily per capita protein intake from game from two periods (42 and 47 days, respectively) in which hunting returns were recorded for contiguous days. We then asked the hypothetical question, What would happen if the Shiwiar experienced the same number of injuries experienced by the Yora over a similar period of time?[7] Calculations and estimates were conducted in the same manner as with Yora data.

Figure 17.2 indicates that when all hunters are active, returns from game alone are well over minimum requirements for a population of this stature (Bar 2, 56 g).

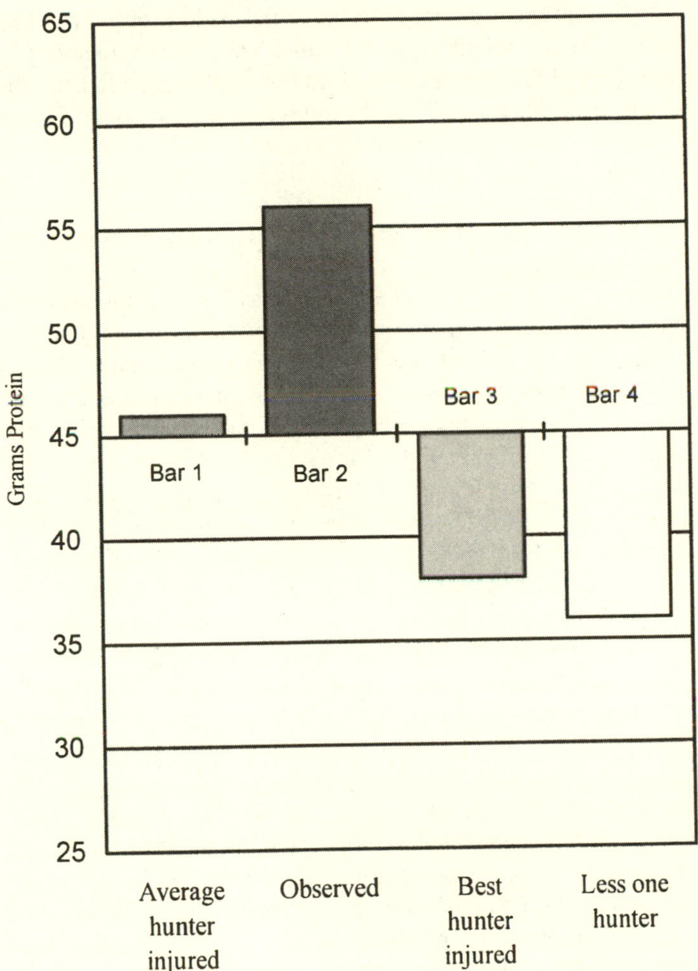

Figure 17.2. Shiwiar daily per capita protein consumption from game.

Injuries to a hunter of average ability would reduce estimated protein consumption from meat alone by 18%, to just over USRDA minimum requirements (Bar 1, 46 g). If the best hunter were to be injured, however, hunting returns would drop 32%, to below minimum requirements (Bar 3, 38 g). And if a hunter of average ability were to leave the group (taking his family with him) while the best hunter were injured, there would be a further nutritional decrement of 4% (Bar 4, 36 g).

For at least one other Amazonian group, then, a similar pattern obtains to that found among the Yora.[8] As one might expect in a group with less foraging risk, more food storage, less food sharing, and a tradition of scattered settlement, the effect of losing a village member appears to be slightly less detrimental for the Shiwiar than for the Yora.

THE ADAPTIVE PROBLEM POSED BY PATHOLOGY RISK

For a given individual, disability due to pathology may last much longer than periods of "bad luck" in foraging. Among the Yora, one hunter did not hunt for eight weeks, more than a month of which was unambiguously due to injury. Baksh and Johnson (1990) estimate that up to 10% of male Machiguenga lose from one to four weeks each year due to cuts from *cana brava* (a plant resembling bamboo with thorns at the joints) alone. Compared with day-to-day variance in hunting success, the effects of pathology on foraging returns can be quite large. Kaplan et al. (1990) estimate that without food sharing a foraging Ache family (in which 67% of calories consumed are from game) would fail to acquire 50% of their necessary calories three weeks in a row due to bad luck only once in 17 years. In the absence of injury, illness, or natural disaster (e.g., catastrophic climatic fluctuations), then, five weeks of unsuccessful hunting will be rare and 3–6 months of unsuccessful hunting (as seen in the Shiwiar cases of snakebite) will be virtually unknown. Further, unlike seasonal variation and some types of spatial variation in resources, illness and injury are, for a given individual and within a wide range of parameters, temporally unpredictable. More importantly, unlike those who are experiencing a temporary slump in foraging returns, those who are severely ill or injured are physically unable to defend themselves and their interests.

One of the critical adaptive problems pathology risk presents, then, is the insurance of an adequate source of support and protection should disability occur. Two complementary explanations have been advanced to explain the evolution of "altruism"-that is, adaptations motivating individuals to provide fitness benefits to others at a fitness cost to themselves: kin selection and reciprocal altruism. A consideration of these explanations highlights the problems that adaptations designed to buffer pathology risk must effectively solve.

Kin Selection

Kin selection theory posits that adaptations designed to provide fitness benefits to others at a cost to their bearers could evolve when the cost to the "altruist" is less than the benefit to the recipient discounted by the probability that they share genes in common (Hamilton 1964). In ancestral populations, however, such factors as migration, high mortality rates, abduction of females, and residence patterns associated with mating would have led to situations in which some individuals lived among people to whom (in comparison to the average degree of relatedness between the other group members) they were only distantly related (e.g., Chagnon 1975, 1979a, 1979b). Over the course of human evolution this circumstance would have been a recurrent problem for some individuals. A trait that, on average, buffers pathology risk for individuals who lack close, coresident consanguineal kin should therefore spread relative to one that buffers pathology only for those who do not lack such kin.

Further complicating matters, the probability that aid to an injured relative will yield inclusive fitness benefits to their provider is increasingly diminished in relation to the likelihood that the injured individual will not recover. This, in turn, increases the relative potential gain from investing in others instead of the injured party. As death of the injured individual becomes increasingly certain, withdrawal and reallocation of aid may become the prudent choice for the potential benefactor, as both evolutionary logic and ethnographic evidence bear out (e.g., Freuchen 1961; Hill and Hurtado 1996; Tooby and Cosmides 1996).

Reciprocal altruism

Reciprocal altruism theory posits that traits designed to provide benefits to others at a fitness cost to their bearers can evolve when there is sufficient probability that compensatory benefits will be recieved (Trivers 1971). Trivers (1971) suggests that the potential benefit from extending aid increases as the need of the recipient increases, because expected compensation for providing the aid will be higher. Herein lies the problem posed by pathology risk: as the need of the injured party increases past critical levels, the probability that the disabled person will live to provide compensatory benefits to the altruist diminishes, and with it the potential benefit of extending aid to him or her.

Further, the ability to recognize and punish cheaters (i.e., exchange partners who do not reciprocate) or exclude them from future exchanges is a necessary feature for the evolution of adaptations arising via the pathway of reciprocal altruism (Axelrod and Hamilton 1981; Cosmides and Tooby 1992; Trivers 1971). Yet disabled individuals lack the physical formidability necessary to compel past exchange partners to reciprocate, and detection of cheaters at the time of injury is of no value to the injured party if he or she dies. Moreover, individuals who are sensitive to current probable payoffs have incentive to renege on exchange commitments to a disabled exchange partner when they are most in need: there is no profit to be gained by investing in someone who cannot reciprocate now and is unlikely to be able to do so in the future (Tooby and Cosmides 1996). Withholding aid further decreases the likelihood that the injured party will recover, making him or her an even worse investment. Although an individual who refused to recompense his disabled exchange partner might face negative repercussions should the injured party recover (i.e., reprisals, loss of reputation, loss of other exchange partners), what constitutes adequate aid in these circumstance can not be well specified: an individual could simply proffer nominal aid—sufficient to damper possible future reprisals but insufficient to sustain the disabled party until he or she recovers. Adaptations arising from reciprocal altruism, particularly the subset based on contingent social exchange, therefore appear to be problematic solutions to the problem of pathology risk. In a world where only the logic of kin selection and reciprocal altruism operate, there comes a point at which abandonment of a sick or injured individual becomes the adaptive choice for potential benefactors. Traits motivating individuals to behave in a way that shifts this critical decision point, causing potential benefactors to provide aid at relatively greater levels of pathology, should be selected for as long as such aid effectively resulted in survival in a critical proportion of cases.

Pathology risk thus poses three major adaptive problems in the human social arena: (1) how to subvert the short-term cost-benefit psychology of potential aid sources such that they are more rather than less likely to invest, even though, all else equal, the current probable payoff of doing so is low relative to other potential uses of the investment; (2) how to stimulate this investment at a time when one lacks the ability to defend one's own interests; and (3) how to do so in a way that circumvents the temporally unpredictable nature of pathological events.

Despite these obstacles, individuals do receive care adequate to survive extended periods of disabling pathology, a phenomenon that arose at least by the time of *Homo Neandertalensis* (Trinkaus 1983; Dettwyler 1991).[9] We suggest that a suite of adaptations evolved to solve these problems.

The Best Hunter Solves the Pathology Risk Problem

Our data suggest that when an average Yora or Shiwiar hunter suffers significant injury, a buffer exists such that, although there is a notable nutritional decline, protein consumption remains adequate. If the best Yora hunter is injured, however, nutritional declines are dramatic and a high-quality source of nutrition is jeopardized. This effect is similar but less pronounced among the Shiwiar. If the best hunter becomes temporarily disabled and group size is low, then the best hunter and his family (as well as other band members with whom he shares meat) will suffer additional nutritional decrement. During such times, the best hunter may benefit from living amongst larger groups of people even though sharing with them may be costly during times when he and his fellow foragers are healthy (see, e.g, Blurton Jones 1984, 1987; Hawkes 1990, 1991; Kaplan and Hill 1985a, 1985b). If the requisite aid can be dispersed amongst a larger group, then the per capita cost of providing the aid is also reduced. Because periods of incapacitation due to disability regularly last much longer than slumps in foraging due to day-to-day variation in returns, estimations of optimal group size or sharing networks based on the latter may well underestimate the degree of risk that must be buffered by these groups, thereby resulting in observations of larger group sizes than predicted by these models (for a review of other such factors see Sugiyama 1996).

These findings suggest that the risk of relatively infrequent periods of long-lasting disability and debilitation is likely to have constituted a selection pressure affecting individual decision-making psychology about the desired size of social groups and social networks. Specifically, pathology risk may select for adaptations motivating their bearers to live in social groups both large enough and motivated enough to provide aid effectively in times of need. The apparent link between depression and lack of sufficient social support seen in modern contexts may be a manifestation of one part of this psychological complex (Hagen 1995). The critical question remains unanswered, however: How are *potential* sources of aid motivated to become *reliable* sources of aid when one suffers severe physical pathology?

As noted above, Kaplan and Hill (1985a) have suggested that among the Ache, good hunters may receive preferential treatment when they are sick or injured because other band members benefit from maintaining access to the meat these hunters provide. Because pathology risk is temporally unpredictable, for good hunters to garner this solicitude they would have to provide meat to others consistently, or risk becoming incapacitated at a time when interest in their continued presence in the band has waned. Indeed, good hunters may not only share game with more individuals than would otherwise be optimal, but may consistently provide more meat to others than they receive in return (e.g., Blurton Jones 1984, 1987; Hawkes 1990; Kaplan and Hill 1985a, 1985b, 1990; Sugiyama 1996). If lack of aid could spell death to the injured party (as seen among other primates) and increased morbidity and mortality risk for any dependents (Chagnon 1997; Hill and Hurtado 1996), and if widespread meat sharing buffers this risk, then adaptations designed to produce consistent widespread sharing may be, within wide parameters, largely impervious to the day-to-day costs of doing so, even if they never yield these benefits during the lifetime of any given individual providing them.

Consistent asymmetric provisioning of meat also provides a strong cue to recipients that, should the hunter become ill or injured, the flow of such benefits will resume if and when he recovers. In other words, because the benefits provided are uncoupled from the psychological framework of social exchange by being made available in the absence of associated cues that reciprocity is expected or desired, then others may treat receipt of the benefits as a consistent byproduct of living with the good hunter, for which they pay no direct costs. Those who acquire such benefits should therefore be highly motivated to retain access to them.

For the hypothesized system to work, not only must the absolute value of the best hunter's contributions be sufficiently high that the loss of these benefits constitutes a significant fitness cost to the recipients, but the cost of acquiring the same benefits elsewhere must also be sufficiently high. As Tooby and Cosmides (1996) point out, one feature of an optimal circumstance is reached when there are no readily available alternative sources for replacing the benefits—that is, when they are irreplaceable. When this is the case, the fitness of the group members receiving the benefits is inextricably tied to the ability of the provider to deliver them, and they should therefore be willing to pay high short-term costs to retain access to the source of these benefits. Just how a system that bypasses the pathways of kin selection and reciprocal altruism could evolve has been discussed in detail by Tooby and Cosmides (1996). With regard to the data at hand, however, it is sufficient to note that among the Yora, injury to the best hunters does have a comparatively large adverse subsistence impact. To replace the benefits provided by the best hunter would entail large time and energy costs associated with resettlement, intervillage politics, or increased foraging by other band members. Among the Shiwiar, the relative benefits provided by the best hunter appear to be fewer, and the apparent costs of losing the best hunter may be further buffered by returns from fishing, particularly in the dry season. In this case aid to injured individuals may be provided by fewer individuals, or predicated upon an individual's conferral of other important benefits to others (see below).

An apparent problem with the preceding analysis is that it leaves open a common goods problem: even though individual social group members may have an intense interest in retaining access to a highly productive hunter, if one individual is willing to pay the costs necessary to effect recovery, then others might profitably refrain from doing so. If all use this reasoning, then no one will provide aid and the injured person will die. While this may be one reason why extended aid to injured conspecifics is rare in the animal world, we think humans solve the problem in the following way. When consistent asymmetric provisioning yields benefits that are difficult to replace, the individual providing them increases others' interest in his or her continued ability to provide these benefits above what they would otherwise be (due, for example, to kin selection). Depending on their own abilities, social networks, and degree of relatedness to the hunter, some of the best hunter's potential benefactors will benefit more by his provisioning than others, and will have more to lose if he dies. Because individuals with the most interest in the best hunter's survival are not themselves injured, they can apply pressure to others to provide aid, thereby shifting the cost-benefit balance of others for doing so. As Tooby and Cosmides (1988) illustrate in an analysis of enforcement problems inherent in the evolution of coalitional aggression, if backed by sufficient credible threat, those who stand to gain most may even get others to incur all the costs of collective action, as well as any costs of enforcement. Humans appear to have cognitive adaptations specifically designed to reason about threats and can compute second-order effects of behavior such as triangular awareness (Brown 1991; Rutherford et al. 1996). All else equal, differential targeting of benefits to those most able to influence the behavior of others may be expected.

Irreplaceable Benefits and Social Niche Differentiation

Although this discussion arises from a consideration of the effects of pathology on hunters and their contributions to others' fitness, the same adaptive logic should hold for individuals who consistently provide other costly-to-replace benefits to their social group. While there may not be as many positions of status in egalitarian bands as there are people to fill them, there certainly are other social roles besides being a good hunter that provide difficult-to-replace benefits, and we therefore expect a proliferation of social niche differentiation as circumstances allow. These roles are not fixed but, rather, dependent on opportunity and circumstance. In fact, when differences between the hunting returns of the best and other hunters are low, when returns from foraging uniformly exceed needs by large margins, when game is shared because it has begun to have diminishing marginal returns for the hunter and his family—i.e., when sharing appears to be due to "tolerated theft" (Blurton Jones 1984)—or when food storage techniques allow individuals to survive long periods of disability without subsistence aid, then being a more successful hunter may not provide irreplaceable benefits or yield higher-than-average solicitude (although subsets of the social group may be highly dependent on a given hunter and therefore motivated to aid him).

Clearly, then, an adaptation specifying that each individual attempt to become the best hunter in his or her group will not solve the pathology risk problem. The solution is dependent upon the evolution of a number of adaptations, including mechanisms that (1) evaluate the abilities of their bearers, (2) identify the important needs of others (or have knowledge of recurrent needs), (3) compare their bearers' ability to provide those needs with the abilities of others, (4) identify the needs that their bearers are most qualified to provide and are not well provided by others, and then (5) cultivate abilities in this area such that they confer needed benefits in a manner that (6) convincingly signals to others that provision of the benefit is a consistent product of living with their provider. Such a system requires the evolution of complementary adaptations designed to recognize important benefits, identify individuals who consistently provide these benefits at no apparent cost to the recipient, and motivate behavior that preserves access to these benefits (for example, by extending aid to individuals who provide uniquely valuable benefits—see Tooby and Cosmides 1996 for psychological mechanisms that appear to operate in this fashion).

Further, because the functional payoff for a behavioral pathway expected to confer unique benefits may never be needed, or may be needed only rarely, there exists a degree of uncertainty that a given niche will indeed provide the benefits, to others and eventually to self, that it is ultimately designed to deliver. For solution, this problem requires a complementary, contingent set of mechanisms: one activated in the specialist condition, designed to assess an interim system of reliable cues confirming that a given behavioral path is indeed providing uniquely valuable benefits, and another activated in the beneficiary condition, designed to provide such signals to uniquely valuable individuals.[10] One signal of the degree to which an individual fills a beneficial social niche for which we might find anthropological evidence is the prestige accorded to the individual who fills it, or the esteem in which he or she is held. Significantly, in a cross-cultural analysis of two social niches that convey special benefits to others (oratory skill and specialized craft production), prestige does indeed appear to be associated with unique ability (Sugiyama and Scalise, Sugiyama 1997).

Shiwiar society provides a case in point, exhibiting both the cultivation of social niche differentiation and the benefits that derive from it. For example, *juunt* (elders or, literally, big men), are the central figures around which settlement, politics, and warfare are organized. Their qualities of leadership, bravery, and strategic decision-making make them important individuals throughout society, particularly to men allied with them (Descola 1988; Hendricks 1993; Patton, this volume). Another important role in Shiwiar society is that of the shaman. The most powerful shamans are also *juunt,* and while feared and hated by their enemies, they are respected and essential parts of their alliance groups and they spend long years in training and practice to attain this role. Notably, a critical benefit they provide is directly related to pathology risk: the curing of sick and injured people. When they cannot or will not fulfill this role, their value is nullified and interest in their continued well-being largely evaporates (Sugiyama, unpublished recordings of a Shiwiar political meeting). When they are successful and aid their social allies without hesitation, their lives and interests are well guarded. For instance, a locally powerful shaman in an alliance of seven Shiwiar villages promised, at what is considered a potentially life-threatening cost to himself, to focus his activities on curing and to forego retaliatory attacks against other shamans (which were interpreted as having unintended negative repercussions for some members of the alliance). He has since been provided an armed escort to protect him from ambush whenever he leaves the vicinity of his village. As of 1998 this security service had been in effect for three years. Conversely, another local shaman who was less generous with his services felt compelled to leave his village of residence in haste when it was made clear that he would receive no support if raiders came to kill him.

Other Shiwiar men are well known for the exceptional quality of the blowguns they make, and they derive trade and positive social connections from this specialized skill. Since accepting contact with missionaries, the roles of local health promoter and preacher have been cultivated by individuals with certain skills. Finally, some people are valuable not for any particular skill but, rather, because they are recognized as being particularly likely to aid their fellows during communal work parties, to share what game they have, or to support their fellows in conflicts (Sugiyama 1996). One might think of this service as something akin to the loyal deputy—not skilled in a particular craft, but eminently dependable and willing to contribute to the interests of others in their social group.

If an individual's success at filling a uniquely valuable role is contingent on there being no one else to readily fill it, attempts by more than one individual to cultivate an occupied niche may be expected to provoke resentment, resistance, even conflict (Tooby and Cosmides 1996). The behavior observed in the study populations suggests that this is indeed the case. Shamans, for example, wage spiritual warfare against each other in battles for status that are a chronic feature of

Jivaroan life. Such competition is not limited to the role of shaman, however. In the Achuar/Quichua village of Conambo, for example, intense social tension developed when an opportunity to train as the village health promoter arose. Two people had the requisite skills to take the course, and conflict arose over who should be selected. The fact that one person was Quichua and the other Achuar made matters worse because village residents saw the issue in terms of their own vested interests, which broke down largely along ethnic lines: the Quichua thought an Achuar promoter would bias distribution of aid toward the Achuar, while the Achuar thought a Quichua promoter would bias the distribution of benefits toward the Quichua.[11]

Conclusions

Whatever the faults of the foregoing analysis, we believe we have identified an important intersection of subsistence and social phenomena: (1) group sizes may be larger than what foraging theory predicts; (2) the best hunters often hunt far more than it "pays" in any of the short-term "currencies" that have previously been examined; (3) debilitating illness and injury are a ubiquitous feature of life among hunting peoples, including the populations studied; (4) subsistence costs of injury and illness, and the fitness costs they entail, are substantial; (5) when the contribution of the best hunter is subtracted from the net take of the groups studied (as it would be whenever he is injured), per capita protein intake drops below the minimum USRDA; and (6) when group size includes one less hunter and his dependents, protein intake drops further. The injury data presented here suggest that temporary disability has been a sufficiently frequent and formidable problem to cause the selection of psychological adaptations dedicated to its solution, and that a suite of these adaptations will be dedicated to solving the problems for social relations that pathology risk entails. The universal striving among people of all ranks to acquire a distinct, acknowledged, and irreplaceable social role may have its roots in the continuous risk that illness and injury posed throughout the lives of our foraging ancestors. Among the Yora, excellence at hunting coupled with consistent widespread sharing of game coincide with the pattern of behavior expected to buffer that risk.

SUMMARY

1. Both severe or repeated pathology and lower protein and fat intake are associated with a variety of indicators of lowered fitness. Potentially severe pathologies are ubiquitous in extant, recent prehistoric, and early *Homo*foraging populations. The nutritional costs of pathologies observed for the Yora and estimated for the Shiwiar are substantial.

2. Pathology risk formed a substantial adaptive problem. One part of this problem was how to ensure high levels of aid in times of disability. Traits that motivated their bearers to behave in ways that solved this problem are expected to have conferred significant fitness benefits upon their bearers. However, as the probability that a sick or injured person will die increases, so too does the probability that any investment in him or her will be lost, making that individual an increasingly bad investment for potential benefactors.

3. This problem may be solved to the extent that individuals provide honest signals that (1) increase the perceived probability that by providing aid potential benefactors will reap future fitness benefits; (2) increase the expected probable size of those future fitness benefits well in excess of any costs of providing extended aid; and (3) reduce the expected cost that each potential benefactor must incur to reap those benefits.

4. Debilitating pathology occurs in a temporally unpredictable manner. Behavior generated by adaptations designed to elicit aid during periods of disability must therefore be engaged in consistently, even when disability aid is not currently needed.

5. Recipients of valuable benefits should be interested in retaining access to them, particularly when they cannot be obtained from another source. An individual can thus increase the aid he/she garners when ill/injured by consistently providing valuable and costly-to-replace benefits to others when able to do so.

6. Behavior of the best hunters among the study groups appears consistent with the criteria for solving the pathology risk problem outlined above:

(a) The fitness benefits provided to others by the best hunters in the study populations, particularly among the Yora, are large and by their very magnitude difficult to replace.
(b) Consistent asymmetric provisioning by the best hunters provides a powerful cue or "honest signal" to recipients that provisioning will continue if and when the provider recovers.
(c) If the groups studied were to have one less hunter and his family while the best hunter was injured, per capita protein intake would further decline. Living in larger groups than might be otherwise desirable reduces the per capita cost of providing adequate aid to a disabled group member.

Conversely this suggests that increased sources of aid when injured may be one benefit that good hunters reap from living and sharing with more people than otherwise optimal.

7. There are other social niches that deliver difficult-to-replace benefits to others besides being an exceptional hunter and sharing meat widely. We therefore expect a proliferation of social niche differentiation where circumstances allow, with prestige or esteem being accorded those who fill such roles, and conflict or tension arising when two or more individuals attempt to fill the same niche. Ethno-

graphic evidence from the Shiwiar and cross-cultural data on status, oratory skill and craft specialization is consistent with these predictions.

ACKNOWLEDGMENTS

We thank Rob Boyd, Nicholas Blurton Jones, Napoleon Chagnon, Leda Cosmides, Larry Fiddick, Debra Guatelli-Steinberg, Ed Hagen, Kim Hill, Magdalena Hurtado, Mike Jochim, Hillard Kaplan, Rob Kurzban, Jane Lancaster, Melissa Rutherford, Don Symons, John Tooby and Phil Walker for valuable information, insights, and/or criticisms regarding issues addressed in this paper. While many of their insights require fuller exploration elsewhere, this paper has nonetheless benefited from them. Of course all lapses in logic, clarity, or content are our own. Leda Cosmides and John Tooby not only provided irreplaceable advice, but encouragement to pursue this line of inquiry and support to conduct some of the research. Hillard Kaplan provided valuable information that made fieldwork among the Yora possible; Napoleon Chagnon provided both inspiration and technical advice. Lee Cronk was patient and provided valuable comments on a draft of this paper. Michelle Scalise Sugiyama read repeated drafts of this paper and provided irreplaceable editorial advice. This research was funded in part by awards from the Andrew Isbell Memorial Fund, University of California Social Sciences Humanities Research Grants (two), University of California Graduate Research Mentorship Program, University of California Dissertation Year Fellowship, USIA Fulbright Fellowship for Research Abroad, and Wenner Gren Foundation for Anthropological Research Small Grant to Sugiyama, and a University of California Social Sciences Humanities Research Grant to Chacon. Additional support was provided by the Center for Evolutionary Psychology through an NSF President's Young Investigator Award and a McDonnell Foundation Grant to John Tooby. Finally, we thank all the Yora and Shiwiar who worked with us and graciously allowed us to live with them.

NOTES

1. For example, in 1991 the authors met a Yanomamö man in the small village of Mokarita-teri whose arm rotted off after a tree fell on him and crushed it.
2. The predominant pattern of sexual division of labor in foraging societies (i.e., women providing the bulk of gathered vegetable foods while men provide the majority of game) may mean that over the course of human evolution there were, on average, differences in how many people were needed to replace the nutrients lost when a man instead of a woman was injured; the necessary age of those individuals; the relative time it took them to replace those nutrients and was therefore lost to other pursuits; and so on. Selection pressure from pathology risk may therefore have had slightly different effects upon male and female psychology, or may on average lead to different behavioral outcomes. Further research is needed to investigate these possibilities.
3. The number of consumer days over the study period was calculated by counting children 11 years old and under as half-consumers, and those over 11 as full consumers.
4. This makes our estimates of pathology effects on foraging more conservative.
5. Protein composition of fish and game was estimated based on the average amount of protein per kg of meat for similar species derived from food composition tables for South America (WHO 1968).

6. This assumes that the hunter has no sons in their late teens who would leave with him. Young men of this age may contribute substantially to protein intake by fishing. If young men of this age left with their father, average daily protein consumption of those left in the village would further decline.

7. Another way of conceptualizing this thought experiment is to frame it thusly: What was the likely effect of a known injury (for instance a snakebite that became infected with gangrene) on foraging activity and returns within the village during the time of the injury?

8. Although Shiwiar protein consumption was higher than reported here because returns from fishing could not be included, within the range of protein consumption observed in this and related Achuar groups, increases in intake from high-quality protein sources are expected to be of dietary benefit (Descola 1988; Kim Hill, personal communication).

9. Such care does not, however, appear to feature largely in the social life of non-human primates, suggesting that they lack the opportunity to provide such aid, the cognitive adaptations necessary to solve the problems outlined above, or the requisite preadaptations needed for those adaptations to evolve.

10. Tooby and Cosmides (1996) discuss the nature of "friendship" in this context.

11. Another example comes from Chagnon's (1975) discussion of Yanomamö village fissioning. The largest Yanomamö patrilineages are able to maintain cohesion necessary to keep together the largest villages. Tellingly, the exception to this occurs when two men from the largest lineage both have the requisite abilities to be the headman, whereupon cohesion cannot be maintained and the village is likely to fission (Chagnon 1975).

REFERENCES

Altmann, S. A. 1991. Diets of yearling female primates predict lifetime fitness. *Proceedings of the National Academy of Science USA* 88:420–423.

Axelrod, R. T. and W. D. Hamilton. 1981. The evolution of cooperation. *Science,* 211:1390–1396.

Bailey, R. C. 1991. *The Behavioral Ecology of Efe Pygmy Men in the Ituri Forest, Zaire.* Ann Arbor: Museum of Anthropology, University of Michigan.

Baksh, M., and A. Johnson. 1990. Insurance policies among the Machiguenga: An ethnographic analysis of risk management in a non-western society. In *Risk and Uncertainty in Tribal and Peasant Economies,* E. Cashdan, ed. Pp.193–228. Boulder: Westview.

Berger, T. D. and Trinkaus, E. 1995. Patterns of trauma among the Neanderthals. *Journal of Archaeological Science* 22:841–852.

Blurton Jones, N. 1984. A selfish origin for human food sharing: Tolerated theft. *Ethology and Sociobiology* 5:1–3.

Blurton Jones, N. 1987. Tolerated theft, suggestions about the ecology and evolution of sharing, hoarding and scrounging. *Social Science Information* 26: 31–54.

Bowlby, J. 1969. *Attachment: Attachment and Loss,* vol. 1. New York: Basic Books.

Brown, D. E. 1991. *Human Universals.* New York: McGraw-Hill.

Buzina, R., C. J. Bates, J. van der Beek, G. Brubacher, R. K. Chandra, L. Hallberg, J. Hesseker, W. Mertz, K. Pietrzik, E. Pollitt, A. Pradilla, K. Subticanec, H. H. Sandstead, W. Schalch, G. B. Spurr, and J. Westenhofer. 1989. Workshop on functional significance of mild-to-moderate malnutrition. *American Journal of Clinical Nutrition* 50:172–76.

Cashdan, E. 1985. Coping with risk: Reciprocity among the Basarwa of Northern Botswana. *Man* 20:454–474.

Cashdan, E., ed. 1990. *Risk and Uncertainty in Tribal and Peasant Economies.* Boulder: Westview Press.

Chagnon, N. A. 1975. Genealogy, Solidarity and Relatedness: Limits to local group size and patterns of fissioning in an expanding population. *Yearbook of Physical Anthropology* 19:95–110.

Chagnon, N. A. 1979a. Mate competition, favoring close kin, and village fissioning among the Yanomamö Indians. In *Evolutionary Biology and Human Social Behavior: An Anthropological Perspective,* N. A. Chagnon and W. Irons, eds. Pp. 86–131. North Scituate, Massachusetts: Duxbury Press.

Chagnon, N. A. 1979b. Kin Selection and Conflict: An Analysis of a Yanomamö Ax Fight. In *Evolutionary Biology and Human Social Behavior: An Anthropological Perspective,* N. A. Chagnon and W. Irons, eds. Pp. 522–526. North Scituate, Massachusetts: Duxbury Press.

Chagnon, N. A. 1997. *Yanomamö,* fifth ed. Fort Worth: Harcourt Brace.

Cosmides, L. and J. Tooby. 1992. Cognitive Adaptations for Social Exchange. In *The Adapted Mind: Evolutionary Psychology and the Generation of Culture,* J. Barkow, L. Cosmides and J. Tooby, eds. Pp. 161–228. New York: Oxford University

Descola, P. 1988. *La Selva Culta: Simbolismo y Praxis en la Ecologia de los Achuar,* 1a ed. Quito, Ecuador: Ediciones Abya-Yala.

Dettwyler, K. 1991. Can paleopathology provide evidence for compassion. *American Journal of Physical Anthropology* 84:375–384.

Fiddick, L. 1999. The deal and the danger: An evolutionary analysis of deontic reasoning. Ph.D. dissertation, Ann Arbor, University of Michigan.

Freuchen, P. 1961. *Book of the Eskimos.* Greenwich, CT: Fawcet.

Frisch, R. E. and McArthur, J. W. 1974. Menstrual cycles: Fatness as a determinant of minimum weight necessary for their maintenance and onset. *Science* 185:949–951.

Green, B. B., J. S. Weiss, J. R. Daling. 1986. Risk for ovulatory infertility in relation to body weight. *Fertility and Sterility* 50:721–726.

Hagen, E. H. 1995. Delusional and somatoform disorders as possible examples of intraspecific Batesian mimicry in humans. Paper presented at the Human Behavior and Evolution Conference, June, 1995, Santa Barbara, California.

Hagen, E. H. 1999. The functions of postpartum depression. *Evolution and Human Behavior* 20:325–259.

Hames, R. B. 1990. Sharing among the Yanomamö: Part I, The effects of risk. In *Risk and Uncertainty in Tribal and Peasant Economies,* E. Cashdan, ed. Pp. 89–106. Boulder: Westview Press.

Hamilton, W. D. 1964. The genetical evolution of social behavior. Parts 1 and 2. *Journal of Theoretical Biology* 7:1–52.

Hawkes, K. 1990. Why do men hunt? Benefits for risky choices. In *Risk and Uncertainty in Tribal and Peasant Economies,* E. Cashdan, ed. Pp.145–166. Boulder: Westview Press.

Hawkes, K. 1991. Showing off—Tests of an hypothesis about men's foraging goals. *Ethology and Sociobiology* 12:29–54.

Hendricks, J. W. 1993. *To Drink of Death: The Narrative of a Shuar Warrior.* Tucson: University of Arizona Press.

Hill, K., and A. M. Hurtado. 1996. *Ache Life History: The Ecology and Demography of a Foraging People.* New York: Aldine de Gruyter.

Hill, K., and H. Kaplan. 1989. Population and dry-season subsistence strategies of the recently contacted Yora of Peru. *National Geographic Research* 5:317–334.

Kaplan, H., and K. Hill. 1985a. Food sharing among Ache foragers: Tests of explanatory hypotheses. *Current Anthropology* 26:223–245.

Kaplan, H., and K. Hill 1985b. Hunting ability and reproductive success among male Ache foragers. *Current Anthropology* 26:131–133.

Kaplan, H., K. Hill, and A. M. Hurtado 1990. Risk, foraging and food sharing among the Ache. In *Risk and Uncertainty in Tribal and Peasant Economies,* E. Cashdan, ed. Pp.107–144. Boulder: Westview Press.

Kohrs, M. B., A. E. Harper, and G. R. Kerr. 1976. Effects of a low-protein diet during pregnancy of the rhesus monkey: 1. Reproductive efficiency. *American Journal of Clinical Nutrition* 29:136–145.

Lambert, P. 1993. Health in prehistoric populations of the Santa Barbara Channel Islands. *American Antiquity* 58(3):504–522.

Low, B. (1988). Pathogen stress and polygyny in humans. In *Human Reproductive Behavior: A Darwinian Perspective,* L. Betzig, M. Borgerhoff Mulder and P. Turke, eds. Pp. 115–121.Cambridge: Cambridge University Press.

Manocha, S. L., and J. Long. 1977. Experimental protein malnutrition during gestation and breeding performance of squirrel monkeys. *Primates* 18:923–930.

Marks, I. 1987. *Fears, Phobias, and Rituals: Panic, Anxiety, and their Disorders.* New York: Oxford University Press.

Patton, J. Q. 2000. Reciprocal altruism and warfare: A case from the Ecuadorian Amazon. In *Adaptation and Human Behavior: An Anthropological Perspective.* L. Cronk, N. Chagnon and W. Irons, eds. New York: Aldine de Gruyter.

Prentice, A. M., T. J. Cole, F. A. Foord, W. H. Lamb, and R. G. Whitehead. 1987. Increased birthweight after prenatal dietary supplementation of rural African women. *American Journal of Clinical Nutrition* 46(6):912–925.

Profet, M. 1992. Pregnancy sickness as adaptation: A deterrent to maternal ingestion of teratogens. In *The Adapted Mind: Evolutionary Psychology and the Generation of Culture,* J. Barkow, L. Cosmides and J. Tooby, eds. Pp. 327–366. New York: Oxford University

Riley, A. P., J. L. Samuelson, and S. L. Huffman 1993. The relationship of age at menarche and fertility in undernourished adolescents. In *Biomedical and Demographic Determinants of Reproduction,* R. H. Gray, H. Leridon, and A. Spira, eds. Pp. 50–64. Oxford: Clarendon.

Rozin, P., and A. Fallon. 1987. A perspective on disgust. *Psychological Review* 94:23–41.

Rozin, P. L. Millman, and C. Nemeroff. 1986. Operation of the laws of sympathetic magic in disgust and other domains. *Journal of Personality & Social Psychology* 50:703–712.

Rutherford, M. D., J. Tooby and L. C. Cosmides. 1996. Adaptive sex differences in reasoning about threat. Paper presented at the Human Behavior and Evolution Society, June, Evanston, IL.

Schwartz, S. M., M. E. Wilson, M. L. Walker, and D. C. Collins. 1988. Dietary influences on growth and sexual maturation in premenarcheal rhesus monkeys. *Hormones and Behavior* 22:231–251.

Sugiyama, L. S. 1999. Patterns of pathology among the Shiwiar of Ecuadorian Amazonia. Informal presentation at risk preference roundtable, Risk Research Initiative, Economics Preferences Group, MacArthur Foundation. University of Utah, Salt Lake City.

Sugiyama, L. S. 1998. Evolutionary Ecology of Native Amazonians. Paper presented at the Institute for Latin American Studies, Post-graduate lecture series on "Biological Studies in Latin America," University of Austria, Vienna.

Sugiyama, L. S. 1996. *In search of the adapted mind: A study of human cognitive adaptations among the Shiwiar of Ecuador and the Yora of Peru.* Ph.D. dissertation. Ann Arbor: UMI.

Sugiyama, L. S. and R. Chacon. 1993. Yora dry season hunting, fishing, and horticultural activities. Paper presented at the Annual Meetings of the American Anthropological Association, November, San Francisco.

Sugiyama, L. S. and M. Scalise Sugiyama. 1997. Cultural Production as a Risk Buffering Strategy. Paper presented at the Annual Meetings of the Human Behavior and Evolution Society, June, Tuscon.

Tooby, J. and L. Cosmides 1996. Friendship and the banker's paradox: Other pathways to the evolution of adaptations for altruism. *Proceedings of the British Academy,* 88:119–143.

Tooby, J. and L. Cosmides 1988. Tooby, J., and Cosmides, L. The evolution of war and its cognitive foundations. Institute for Evolutionary Studies Technical Report #88-1.

Trivers, R. L. 1971. The evolution of reciprocal altruism. *Quarterly Review of Biology* 46:35–57.

Trinkaus, E. 1983. *The Shanidar Neandertals.* New York: Academic Press.

Truswell, A. S. and J. D. L. Hansen. 1976. Medical Research among the !Kung. In *Kalahari Hunter-Gatherers: Studies of the !Kung San and Their Neighbors,* R. B. Lee and I. DeVore, eds. Cambridge: Harvard University.

Walker, P. L., 1989. Cranial injuries as evidence of violence in prehistoric Southern California. *American Journal of Physical Anthropology* 80:313–323.

Walker, P. L., L. S. Sugiyama, and R. Chacon. 1998. Diet, Dental Health, and Cultural Change among Recently Contacted South American Indian Hunter-Horticulturalists. In *Human Dental Development, Morphology and Pathology: Essays in Honor of Albert Dahlberg.* John Lukacs and B. E. Hemphill, eds. University of Oregon Anthropological Papers.

Winterhalder, B. 1990. Open field, common pot: Harvest variability and risk avoidance in agricultural and foraging societies. In *Risk and Uncertainty in Tribal and Peasant Economies,* E. Cashdan, ed. Pp. 67–87. Boulder: Westview Press.

18

Reciprocal Altruism in Yanomamö Food Exchange

RAYMOND HAMES

Simple foraging and horticultural societies, commonly known as bands and tribes (Service 1962), are typically characterized as being economically egalitarian. How economic egalitarianism is defined varies. In relation to food sharing, the focus of this chapter, economic egalitarianism may mean "all individuals of the same age and sex cohort have equal access to life sustaining resources" (Speth 1990:3). This formulation suggests that food consumption within a group will be equalized according to age and sex status, and differential productive capacities and needs as consumption varies between households or individuals will be compensated through the exchange system. Related to egalitarian exchange is Sahlins's well-known concept of generalized reciprocity, which "refers to transactions that are putatively altruistic, transactions on the line of assistance given, and, if possible, and necessary, assistance returned" (Sahlins 1965:193–194). These transactions tend to occur among close kin or among those who live in close residential proximity. The flow of food in such cases is "in favor of the have not"(Sahlins 1990:194). Again, we find that relative need and productive ability determine who gives and who gets. In his widely cited distinction between immediate- and delayed-return egalitarian societies, Woodburn notes that sharing, especially of large game, serves as a leveling mechanism to enforce an equality of consumption. In fact, he views egalitarian sharing as a kind of graduated tax system where the most successful are chronically required to give more than those who are less successful (Woodburn 1982:441–442). Aspelin (1979; and see below), in an admirably detailed analysis of food exchange among the Mamaindê, shows that the amount of food given to a household is directly proportional to household need as indexed by household size. Egalitarian exchange therefore means that food is distributed among households in direct proportion to a household's need and a household's ability to give (Dowling 1968:503), which may be simply indexed by the number of producers or consumers and, especially, the household's consumer-to-producer ratio.

A theoretical alternative to egalitarian exchange is the theory of reciprocal altruism (Trivers 1971), which suggests that food exchanges are strategic in nature and are designed to enhance the fitness of the individual engaged in exchange. In contrast to egalitarian models, resource needs or requirements of potential recipients of food resources are not relevant to exchange considerations. Instead recipients are chosen based on their likelihood and ability to reciprocate in the future. Two predictions derivable from reciprocal altruism theory can be tested with Yanomamö data. The first is that the scope of exchange should be inversely correlated with village size. As village size increases there should be an increasing number of families who do not share with one another. Theoretical justification for this prediction stems from the work of Boyd and Richerson (1988). Secondly, there should be a positive correlation between giving and receiving. By this I mean that a family that gives to another family should, in return, receive food from that family. In effect, exchange should be balanced through some degree of reciprocation.

Studies of food exchanges inspired by evolutionary theory show that food exchanges are not balanced. Research in hierarchical societies (Betzig 1988; Bird and Bird 1997) clearly shows that high-status households receive disproportionately more and give disproportionately less in food exchanges. In an egalitarian context, Kaplan and Hill's (Kaplan et al. 1984) research on the foraging Ache show that while inequalities in giving and receiving persist at the economic level, they are compensated for or balanced at the level of sexual access and reproduction.

With few exceptions (e.g., Aspelin 1979; Betzig 1988; Bird and Bird 1997; Hames 1990, 1996) most of the detailed empirical or quantitative accounts of food sharing focus on egalitarian foragers (Cashdan 1985; Henry 1951; Kaplan and Hill 1985; Marshall 1961). These studies have shown that food sharing within small bands is intense, widespread, and frequently does not appear to enhance the nutritional status of the person who acquired the resource or his or her immediate household. Other studies (Burch 1992; Damas 1975; Endicott 1992; Gould 1982) indicate that egalitarian sharing may be highly restricted. For example, Burch notes, "This raises the possibility that many, if not most, accounts of generalized sharing among hunter-gatherers have been based on studies of the internal dynamics of single local-household villages. To the extent that this is so, the accounts are not wrong, they simply tell only part of the story" (1992:109). This observation suggests that our characterizations of sharing depend on the size of the group or whether one is documenting sharing within families comprising large extended-household units.

The goal of this chapter is to contrast predictions made by what I will call the generalized sharing model of food exchange with a model based on reciprocal altruism. In doing so I will examine the roles of village size, exchange balance, and household demography as determinants of exchange patterns among the Yanomamö, an egalitarian horticultural people of the Venezuelan Amazon. I will endeavor to demonstrate that reciprocal altruism provides a perspective superior to that of generalized sharing to account for food exchange patterns among the Yanomamö.

METHODS

The method used to gather data on Yanomamö food exchanges follows a modified time-allocation technique first employed by Kaplan and Hill (1984) in their studies of Ache exchange. In the course of a time allocation study, whenever I observed someone eating I noted what was being eaten and asked who produced the food and who gave it to them. Information on household membership of food consumer and food giver was added later. These observations led to the creation of a series of matrices to quantify the flow of resources between households in a village. A facsimile of one of these matrices is presented in Figure 18.1. It should be read in the following way: household B gave food six times to household A; household B received food four times from household A, and household B gave food 44 times to itself. This technique differs from measurements of food exchange where weighed inflows and outflows of foods are sampled (see, e.g., Hames 1990). Four matrices of three villages (one village was studied in two different years) are the basis for most of the analyses that follow. Total food exchange observations for each village are as follows: Bisaasi-teri (1986), 217; Bisaasi-teri (1987), 741; Rakoiwä, 254; and Krihisiwä, 232. General ethnographic character-

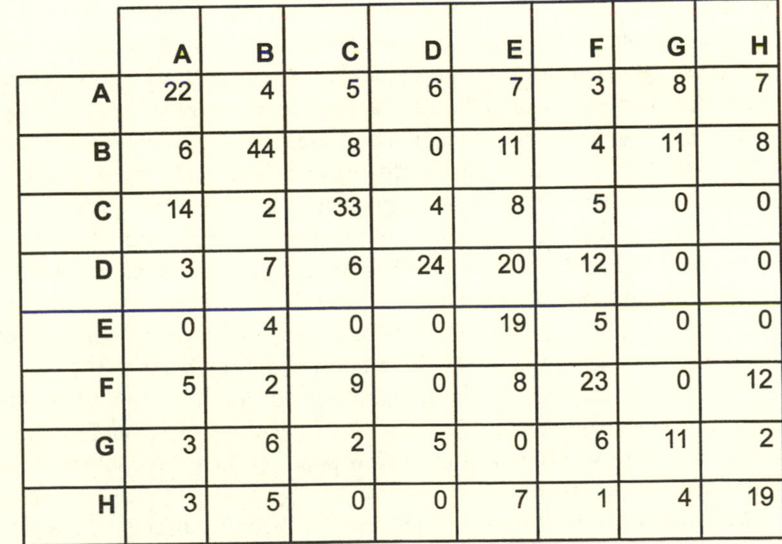

Gave \ Received	A	B	C	D	E	F	G	H
A	22	4	5	6	7	3	8	7
B	6	44	8	0	11	4	11	8
C	14	2	33	4	8	5	0	0
D	3	7	6	24	20	12	0	0
E	0	4	0	0	19	5	0	0
F	5	2	9	0	8	23	0	12
G	3	6	2	5	0	6	11	2
H	3	5	0	0	7	1	4	19

Figure 18.1. Facsimile of data table used to derive patterns of exchange between households.

istics of these villages and more detailed information on methods have been described elsewhere (Hames 1996).

ENTITIES IN EXCHANGE

General evolutionary models of reciprocal exchange focus on transactions between individuals. Nevertheless, attempts by anthropologists to evaluate these models in the context of food exchange among humans have tended to look at exchange between individuals who acquire resources and the families to which they gave food (Kaplan and Hill 1985; Hames 1990) or exchange between families (Hames 1996). This perspective is taken because humans live in households which, in part, are designed to pool resources acquired by members. As such, food flows not so much between individuals as between households. In a behavioral sense it is difficult for one individual to give another something for his or her sole consumption. For example, if an individual gives a raceme of plantains (approximately 20–30 kg of food) to another, the recipient carries it back to his or her place of residence, where all household members have access to the resource. Unlike many animals, the receiver does not consume it on the spot or run to a hiding place to consume it out of sight of family members. Characteristics of this sort of exchange are easily visible when one observes the distribution of medium-sized and large game animals in a Yanomamö village. The distributor calls out to individual households to fetch butchered and/or cooked meat, whereupon a boy or girl runs across the plaza, takes the meat from the distributor, and returns home with it. As I have noted elsewhere in the context of garden labor exchange (Hames 1987) this is a targeting problem: givers, in most cases, cannot easily give to individuals.

It should also be understood that the giver of a resource cannot easily or unilaterally decide which household or households will be the recipient(s). This is because other household members have the ability to influence which households receive food from their household. These constraints on individual choice in giving derive from a number of sources. Garden food, for example, is the result of joint labor by husband and wife. Therefore, they both have the ability to influence how garden products are distributed. In many other cases it is the consequence of competing interests in ensuring that family needs are met or that kin, affines, or social allies receive due consideration in distributions of resources collected by family members. As a consequence, in this paper exchange is analyzed in terms of food flows between families.

Households in this analysis are defined as collections of individuals who share a garden or set of gardens, a common hearth or set of hearths, collaborate extensively in food production, and are residentially distinct from other households. Households typically correspond to a variety of family forms such as extended (stem form) and nuclear polygynous and monogamous families. In some cases households are in transition which typically involves the dissolution of an extended family when, for example, a son-in-law completes his bride service.

THE FUNCTION OF EXCHANGE

Before making predictions about patterns in food exchange (i.e., who gets what and how much), we need to understand the function of exchange or what adaptive problem or problems it is designed to overcome. For the Yanomamö, what exchange is designed to accomplish is not completely clear. Based on previous research (Hames 1990), much exchange appears to be a strategy for risk reduction to insure low variance in food intake. On a day-to-day basis, the amount of food a household produces is not a simple function of the amount of effort or time its members puts into work. Unpredictable game encounters or localized thunderstorms that fell trees plantains laden with fruit can leave a household destitute for varying lengths of time. Sharing prevents such unhealthy periods of low food availability by directing flows of food from households who have a temporary excess of food to households who have a temporary deficit. Food storage, an alternative adaptation to the problem of risk, is extremely costly in the tropics. So too is a focus on less risky resources (Hames 1990) which would lower food-getting efficiency. Risk pervades foraging and gardening pursuits in different ways.

In terms of risk, hunting is the most variable of all subsistence pursuits. Compared to other food-getting activities, the possibility of complete failure is high and success can range from a 1 kg monkey to a 150 kg tapir. Widespread distributions of game appear to be one means of reducing variance in consumption of high-quality protein that is typically lacking in garden crops, which constitute more than 70% of the Yanomamö diet. There is a tendency to assume that gardening is a reliable food-getting activity. Indeed, to insure a continuous and reliable supply of plantains the Yanomamö stagger their planting. However, plantains are sensitive to a variety of environmental perturbations that make the production of a steady supply difficult to achieve. Since plantains cannot be stored for long periods of time, households are confronted with chronic problems of surplus and scarcity.

INTENSITY, SCOPE, AND BALANCE OF EXCHANGE

The vocabulary we use to describe patterns of food exchange in anthropology is poorly developed largely because quantitative accounts of the actual flow of food resources in a community are still in their infancy. In this section I will introduce several concepts to describe food exchange: intensity, scope, and balance. *Intensity* is a measure of what fraction of a household's food comes from other households. It directly measures the degree to which a household's consumption is a consequence of food resources from other households. In a sense, it is a measure of subsidy. The *scope of exchange* is a measure of the number of households from which a household receives food resources in a village. This concept is illustrated in Figure 18.2, which shows linkages (arrows) in exchange between households (solid circles) in a village. Exemplifying a narrow scope of exchange are three groups of households who intensively exchange food, but only among themselves. In contrast, a wide scope of exchange (shown in the right-hand side of the figure) indicates that each household has exchange relationships with nearly every other household in the village. In this example, there are no restricted exchange circles, and sharing is nearly coterminous with the entire village.

There is no obvious relationship between the intensity and scope of exchange among the Yanomamö. Although exchange is intensive among the Yanomamö, it tends to be limited to a small fraction of households in the village. Figure 18.3 shows the intensity of exchange in four Yanomamö villages for the four basic food resources. For example, nearly 39% of all the garden food consumed by a household was produced by other households in the village. Overall 40% of all food resources a household consumes was given to them by other households. Despite this relatively high degree of dependency on other households, the scope of exchange, measured by the number of households that actually engage in exchange, varies. This pattern is revealed in Figure 18.4, which shows that the number of household exchange partners in the four villages ranges from two to six. For example, on average, households in the village of Krihisiwä received or gave food to about four other households. Of course, the scope depends on the

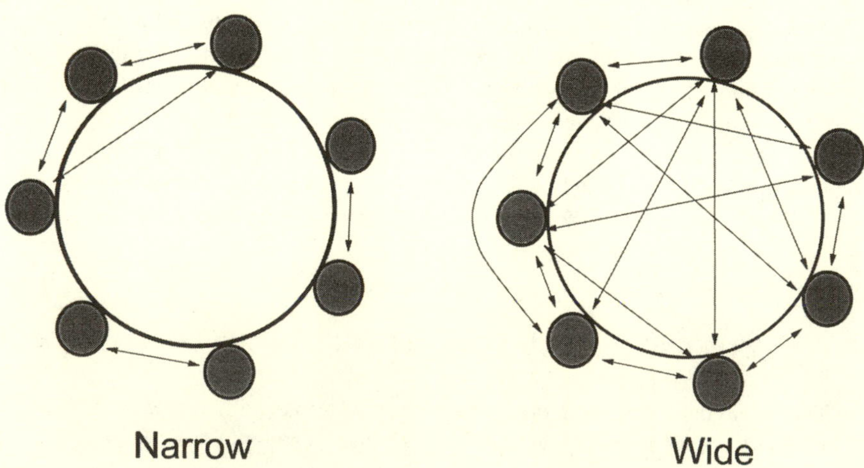

Figure 18.2. A graphical conceptualization of wide and narrow scopes of exchange in a Yanomamö village. The scope of exchange is considered wide if each family exchanges with many families; and scope is narrow if a family exchanges with few families.

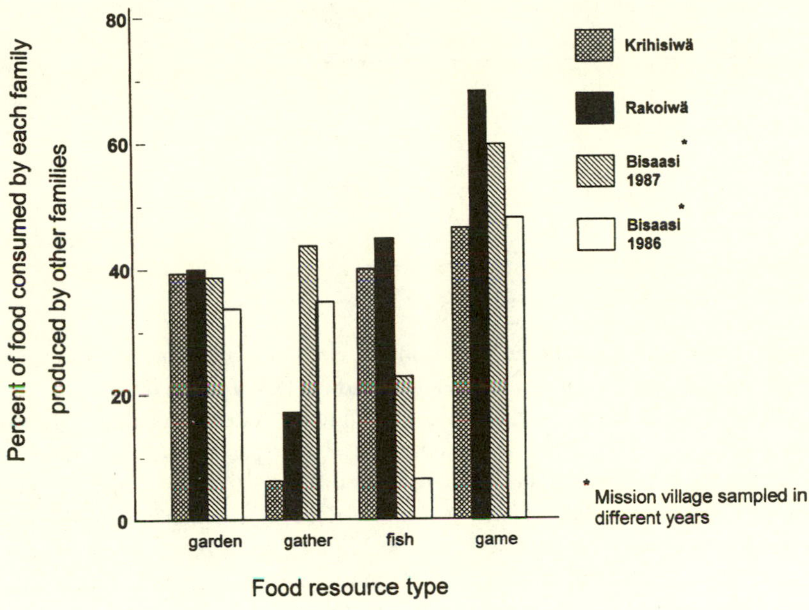

Figure 18.3. The intensity of exchange in four Yanomamö villages. Each bar measures the percentage of total food consumed by an average household (for each food type) that was given to them by other households in the village.

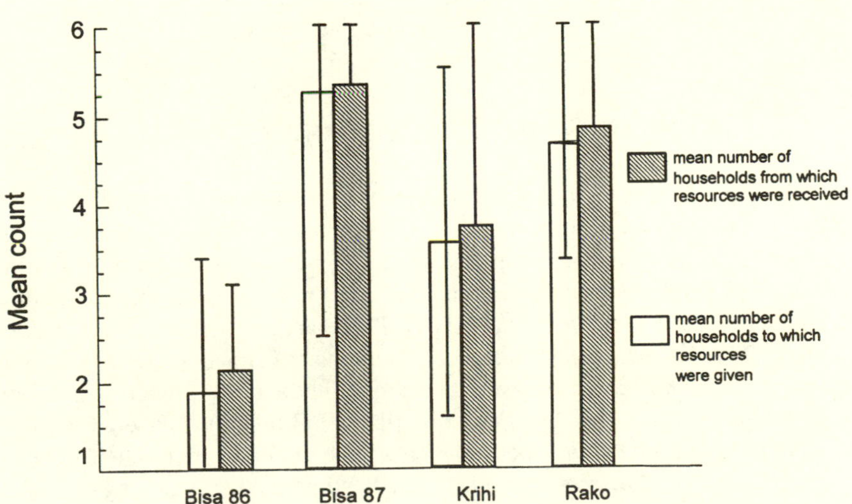

Figure 18.4. Mean number of exchange partners for each household in four Yanomamö villages.

Table 18.1. Percent of Households Participating in Exchange Dyads

Villages	*Households in exchange dyads*
Bisaasi-teri 1986	13%
Bisaasi-teri 1987	35%
Krihisiwä	34%
Rakoiwä	80%

number of households in a village. Accordingly, the households involved in food exchange range from 13% of available households to 80% (Table 18.1).

A final way in which to view exchange is through the concept of balance. There are two ways in which it can be calculated: general and specific. *General balance* is the amount received from in relation to the amount given to a household in comparison with all other households. It allows one to determine which households are net givers or receivers of food resources.[1] *Specific balance* refers to exchanges between individual households and enables one to determine whether there is a relationship between how much a household gave to and received from specific households in the village. Balance is quantified by a correlational analysis employing a matrix identical to the one portrayed in Figure 18.1. General balance is calculated by summing the row values (less giving to oneself) and correlating that figure with the sum of the column values (less receiving from oneself). Specific balance is calculated by comparing how much A gave to B and B gave to A, A gave to C and C gave to A, etc., for all household dyads in the village.

EXCHANGE AND HOUSEHOLD DEMOGRAPHY

As described above, there is a generalized belief that sharing in tribal societies is egalitarian. Although what amounts to an egalitarian pattern of sharing is not sharply defined, the general consensus is that all households tend to receive shares of food when distributions are made, and the amount received is proportional to the number of consumers in the household. For example, Aspelin's quantitative account (1979) provides clear evidence that among the Brazilian Mamaindê the amount of food a household received during distributions was proportional to its size (as measured by the number of normalized consumers). Conversely, large households should give more food than smaller households given their greater productive capacity. Reciprocal altruism makes no prediction regarding the relationship between household size and amount of food given or received.[2]

In a previous publication (Hames 1996) I provided quantitative evidence that household type was a determinant of an exchange pattern: polygynous households received proportionately more food from other village households than monogamous households. By this I mean that of the total food consumed by a polygynous household a greater proportion came from sources outside the household. Now I would like to consider the role of household demographic factors to determine if a generalized egalitarian pattern holds for the Yanomamö. If an egalitarian principle were at work, one would predict that household size and certain attributes thereof, such as number of producers, number of consumers, and consumer-to-producer ratios, should correlate with the amount of food given and received. Specifically, the number of consumers in a household should positively correlate with demand or the amount received; the number of producers should determine the amount given (ability to give); and the consumer-to-producer ratio should correlate positively with the amount of food received and negatively with the amount given. The reasoning is as follows. Households with a larger number of producers should be able to produce more and therefore have more to give to others, and households with a large number of consumers should have greater needs and therefore receive more than households with few consumers. Finally, the ratio of consumers to producers provides the best single measure of relative ability to give and need to receive. As the number of consumers relative to producers rises, individuals must work relatively harder to meet household demand. If there were an egalitarian principle designed to equalize work or insure adequate household consumption, then there should be a positive correlation between the amount of food received and the consumer-to-producer ratio. At the same time, consumer-to-producer ratios should negatively correlate with the amount of food given since households with few consumers relative to producers can give more easily. These predictions are a reflection of the old Marxian adage: from each according to his ability to work and to each according to his need.

Table 18.2 shows some support for the relationship between household size and total amount of food received: three of the four villages show a significant positive correlation between food received and household size. In addition, the village that does not show a statistically significant relationship fails to do so by the narrowest of margins. However, there is no correlation between household size and

Table 18.2. Receiving and Giving as a Function of Household Size in Four Yanomamö Villages

	Receiving		*Giving*	
Village	*Pearson's r*	*Significance (one-tailed)*	*Pearson's r*	*Significance (one-tailed)*
Rakoiwä	0.73	0.05	0.35	0.25
Krihisiwä	0.57	0.03	0.17	0.30
Bisaasi-teri 1987	0.58	0.02	0.28	0.16
Bisaasi-teri 1986	0.44	0.06	0.30	0.12

amount of food given. No data are presented on the relationship between number of consumers and giving and receiving and number of producers and giving and receiving because these factors correlate strongly with family size (Pearson's r in the range of 0.85 and 0.95 for all villages). However, see below for an analysis of consumer to producer ratios.

Table 18.2 can be interpreted to indicate that household size is correlated with the absolute amount of food received by a household. However, it does not mean that large households receive relatively more food resources than small households. To gain a relative measure of the relationship between household size and food received, one can divide the amount of food received by the number of times a household was observed eating. This normalized measure of consumption of food received from other households represents the percent of time individuals in a household were observed to eat food that was not produced by a household member. This measure is identical to that of household dependency or subsidy I made in a previous study linking food exchange and marriage form (Hames 1997). In none of the four villages is there a correlation between household size and percent of total food intake supplied by other households. These two results suggest that large households receive absolutely more food than small households but the amount they receive is not relatively greater.

Consideration of consumers and producers is common in economic anthropology as a consequence of long-term interest in Chayanovian analyses of households (e.g., Durrenberger 1984). Normally, estimates of full or fractional producers are not based on time allocation studies. Here the number of producers was based on Yanomamö time allocation statistics (Hames 1994). For Yanomamö men and women, labor time peaks between thirty and forty years of age and declines slightly thereafter. These individuals were counted as 1 producer each; all others were counted as a fraction of 1, depending on how closely they approximated the standard adult. To calculate consumers in a household, I used a similar procedure but relied on Kaplan's data on food consumption for all age and sex groups for the Machiguenga (Kaplan, in press), a people living in the Peruvian Amazon with an economic system very similar to that of the Yanomamö.

The results of these analyses (presented in Table 18.3) show no consistent relationship between amount of food received or given and consumer-to-producer ratio. In fact, one of the two statistically significant correlations (Bisaasi-teri 1986 "gave") is in the opposite direction of that predicted. If some sort of egalitarian principle were at work we would expect to see a positive correlation between consumer-to-producer ratios and amount of food received and a negative correlation between consumer-to-producer ratios and amount of food given.

VILLAGE SIZE AND SCOPE OF EXCHANGE

If the function of exchange were to reduce variance then one would not need to have more exchange partners than necessary to reduce variance in consumption

Table 18.3. Correlation (Pearson's r) between Consumer-to-Producer Ratios and Amount of Food Received and Given in Four Yanomamö Villages

Village	*Received*	*Gave*
Bisaasi-teri 1986	0.107	0.637*
Bisaasi-teri 1987	0.587*	0.065
Krihisiwä	0.236	–0.498
Rakoiwä	–0.563	0.204

*Correlation is significant at the 0.05 level (one-tailed)

to an acceptable level. In this regard, Winterhalder (1986; see also Winterhalder et al., this volume, for a more detailed analysis) has shown that exchange networks for hunters require no more than five or six households (assuming one hunter per household) to reduce hunting variance (the most risky of subsistence activities) to an acceptable level. This means that while additions to the sharing pool would further reduce variance in consumption the impact is minimal beyond five or six hunters. Although Winterhalder's model was designed to predict the size of groups whose rationale for grouping is to reduce variation in consumption, it is reasonable to hypothesize that the scope of exchange is partially a negative function of village size.

Reciprocal altruism theory predicts that chronic exchange should occur between individuals who have reason to believe that exchanges will occur indefinitely into the future and who have a means to insure that partners will not defect. Boyd and Richerson (1988) have shown that as sharing cliques or coalitions become larger, it becomes more difficult to deal with defectors. As a consequence, sharing among the Yanomamö should be restricted among a small circle of reliable reciprocators. Models of egalitarian exchange do not predict that exchangers should habitually limit their giving to a restricted circle of individuals.

If widespread sharing is more likely in small villages, we may be able to test this proposition for the Yanomamö by correlating the number of households in a village and the percent of household dyads who did not exchange food during the sampling period. For the four Yanomamö villages in this study, the number of households in a village ranged from 6 to 16 (or 24 to 102 people) who were present nearly 100% of the time.

To test this proposition a matrix of village households as givers and receivers of resources (shown in Figure 18.1) was produced for each of the four villages. The number of empty cells was counted for receivers and givers and expressed as a percentage of one half of the matrix less the diagonal cells. These measures as they relate to number of households in the village are represented in Figure 18.5. For example, in Krihisiwä approximately 60% of all possible household dyads neither gave food resources to nor received food resources from each other. Regression analyses of number of households against percent of dyads who nei-

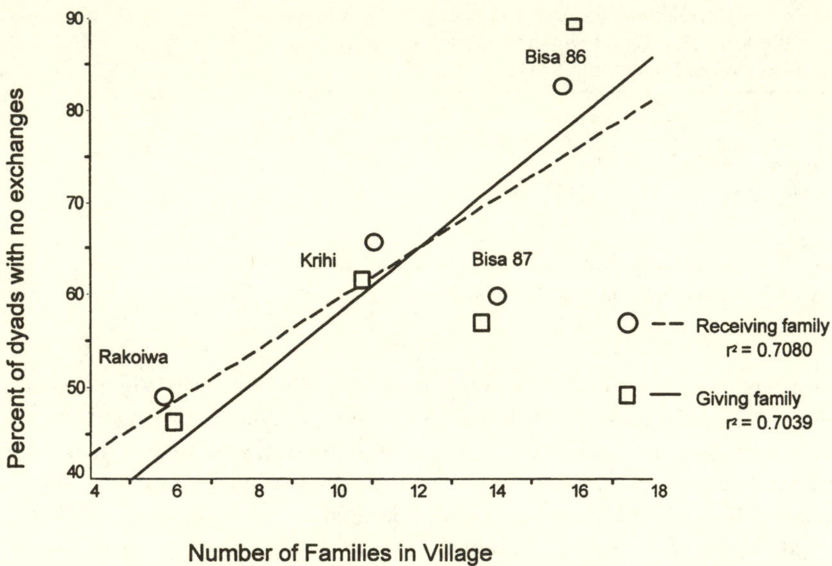

Figure 18.5. The relationship between number of families in a village and the percent of family dyads who did not exchange.

ther gave to nor received from one another show a strongly positive relationship in the predicted direction in both cases ($r^2 = 0.71$), but it falls short of statistical significance ($p = 0.08$, one-tailed; see Figure 18.5 for exact significance levels).

There is additional Yanomamö evidence that scope of sharing may be a function of village size. In an earlier publication John Saffirio and I (1983) described variation in sharing within five different Yanomamö villages in Brazil. My reanalysis of that data (presented in Figure 18.6) indicates that the scope of sharing, as measured by percent of village households who received gathered, hunted, or fished resources each time food was brought into the village, declines with village size. As Table 18.4 shows, the correlation coefficients for gathered foods and fish are highly significant, but not for game. Good (1987:136–137, tables 18 and 19) shows that after a Yanomamö village fissioned, reducing its size from 114 to 41 residents, the probability of a household *not* receiving a portion of a major animal kill went from 5% for tapir, 29% for white-lipped peccary, and 25% for collared peccary to 0% for all three species in the smaller village. Good uses these data to suggest that village fissioning is a consequence of members being unhappy with the distribution of game animals and leads to the formation of villages in which game is more widely shared. The analysis presented here suggests an alternative interpretation: food exchangers carefully limit their giving to a small set of partners whom the givers deem reliable, and the number they select is no larger than necessary to reduce variance in food intake.

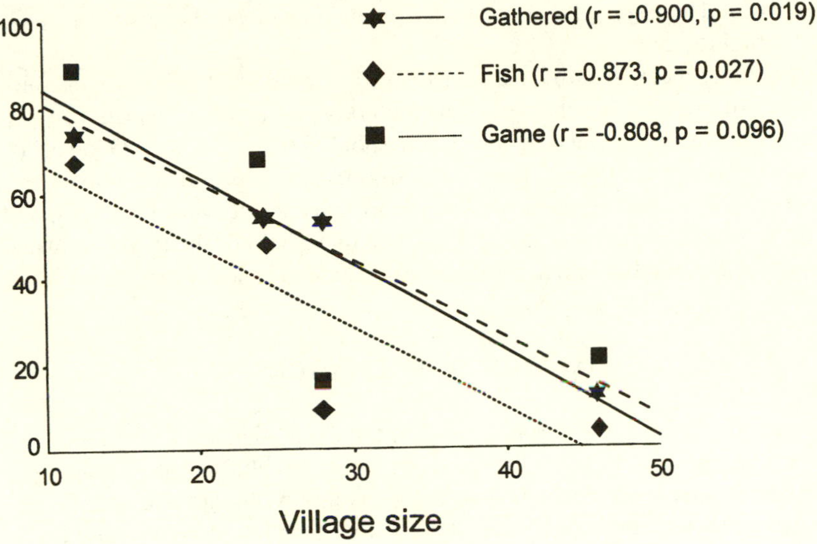

Figure 18.6. Percent of time food acquired through hunting, fishing, and gathering by a household was distributed to other households in the village in four Brazilian Yanomamö villages.

Table 18.4. Sharing Scope and Village Size in Five Brazilian Yanomamö Villages

Resource	*Pearson's r*	*Significance (one-tailed)*
Fish	–.873	0.027
Game	–.808	0.08
Gathered	–.90	0.019

In addition, there is some comparative evidence that scope of exchange is related to village size. Among the Mamaindê (or Nambiquara) of Brazil, 80% of the time five or fewer families were present in the village when food was distributed (Aspelin 1979:318). Of the 116 village-wide distributions recorded by Aspelin, present families were excluded from the distribution in five cases only. Significantly, perhaps, in four of these five cases of exclusion there were more than five families in the village.

Although my statistical analyses fail to achieve statistical significance at the 0.05 level, I am reluctant to accept the null hypothesis of no relationship between village size and scope of sharing for the following reason: The clear trend in the three independent research projects (those by Saffirio, Aspelin, and Good) is that village size and widespread sharing are negatively related, and my results are consistent with this pattern.

It should be kept in mind that the three studies described above measure exchange differently. My behavioral scan method measures the frequency of eating any food that was produced by one's household or that of another; Good measured the distribution of large game kills (those who did and did not receive portions of a kill); Saffirio measured the distribution of all wild resources; and Aspelin measured the portion received by each household of the total distributed in relation to the number of households present and household size.

BALANCE OF EXCHANGE

As mentioned above, a bivariate correlation of the amounts given and received between individual households compared for all households in the village will enable an assessment of general balance of exchange. With regard to specific balance, reciprocal altruism would predict a positive correlation between giving to and receiving from specific households. The amounts given and received are not expected to balance precisely over a period as short as the sampling frame of these studies (about two months in each village). Egalitarian models of exchange hold divergent views on balance. In one case, Sahlins (1965) predicts that balance of exchange is strongly influenced by closeness of kinship and residential proximity: the closer the degree of kinship and residential proximity between families, the more likely that exchanges will be unbalanced (i.e., those who are able to give, give to those who are in need). As residential and kinship distances increase, exchanges become more balanced, and as they further increase, exchanges become negatively balanced (i.e., households attempt to take advantage of one another; Sahlins 1965).[3] This model in some respects closely parallels simple kin selection models (Hames 1989) which predict that close genetic kin are more likely to be tolerant of imbalances in exchange than distant kin. However, Sahlins specifically disavows such an interpretation (Sahlins 1976) when he claims that closeness of kinship is defined culturally and not genetically. A different view is held by Aspelin (1979), who reasons that balance is likely to be an artifact of each individual family's ability to produce and need to consume. To some extent this proposition has already been evaluated in analyzing the relationship between amount received and given in relation to family demography.

In all four villages the correlation between giving and receiving within household dyads was positive and significant, but the correlations were weak to moderate (Table 18.5). The straightforward interpretation of this result is that households tend to limit their exchange relations to particular households. The strength of these associations is powerfully influenced by the fact that a significant number of households in all the villages did not exchange at all. For example, in Rakoiwä, which has the strongest correlation ($r = 0.50$), 12 of the 36 pairs did not exchange

Table 18.5. Specific Balance between Household Dyads in Four Yanomamö Villages

Village	*Pearson's r*	*Significance (one-tailed)*
Rakoiwä	0.50	0.001
Krihisiwä	0.29	0.019
Bisaasi-teri 1987	0.21	0.026
Bisaasi-teri 1986	0.16	0.026

at all. If these individuals are deleted from the sample, then the correlation coefficient diminishes to 0.25 ($p = 0.035$, one-tailed).

DISCUSSION

The analysis of Yanomamö exchanges presented here suggests that reciprocal altruism may be an important factor in food exchanges between families. Yanomamö tend to restrict their food exchange to a limited number of families, as seen in the analyses of village size and scope of exchange, and exchanges tend to be balanced. Although some support for the notion of egalitarian exchange is provided by the fact that large families received more food than small families, large families do not give more food relative to small families and they do not receive proportionately more food than small families.

Hawkes (1993) has suggested that lack of balance in giving and receiving is evidence against reciprocal altruism. The positive correlation between giving and receiving among Yanomamö families leads me to conclude that exchange among the Yanomamö is balanced. This positive relationship is strongly influenced by the fact that many families did not engage in exchanges. Although I have not done a detailed analysis of the balances, it is clear some families are in near perfect balance while others show moderate disparity. There are at least three different reasons for this lack of perfect balance. First, the short time period of the data collection may reveal imbalances that would be equalized over a long period of time. Second, as noted by Winterhalder (1996) and Gurven and colleagues (n.d.), marginal valuations as determined by resource type (meat vs. crops) or costs of giving or benefits of receiving may differ significantly from exchange to exchange owing to a variety of circumstances. For example, the benefit of receiving or cost of giving increases with the length of time one has gone without for both the giver and the receiver. Finally, ethnographers studying people as diverse as foragers (Mauss 1967) and Irish smallholders (Arensberg 1959) have long noted that attempts to balance exchanges are tantamount to ending exchange relationships. For these reasons I would conclude that a positive correlation between giving and receiving provides reasonable evidence that exchange is based on some form of reciprocal altruism. I believe the critical point demonstrated here is that exchange among the Yanomamö is strongly contingent such that families bias their giving to those who give to them. However, it is clear that a closer analysis of the nature of balances is required, especially in terms of the kinship and other social bonds that characterize families in exchange relationships.

Patterns of exchange found among the Yanomamö differ significantly from those found among foragers. Sharing among the Ache has a much wider scope: nearly all families receive portions of food brought into the camp, a pattern similar to what is found among the foraging-horticultural Mamaindê. To some extent these contrasts may be a simple function of group size since Yanomamö villages in this study ranged from about 50 to 100 residents compared with 30 to 40 found among the Mamaindê and Ache. As noted by Burch (1992), the widespread sharing we have come to expect among foragers may be an consequence of our observations being limited to small foraging groups. As groups become larger, the utility of widespread sharing may diminish, which may lead to sharing focused on subsets of families within a settlement.

These findings also suggest an alternative interpretation of Yanomamö village fissioning. As mentioned above, Good (1989) notes that as a village becomes larger, game animals are not as widely shared as they are in a small village.[4] My data and those of Saffirio show this effect for *all* food resources. Good argues that in large villages rancorous accusations of stinginess frequently accompany less-than-complete game distributions, and this ultimately leads to the village splitting into two smaller villages in which game is shared more widely. He argues that not being included in food distributions is an insult to one's status, and such insults lead to the creation of smaller villages where these insults have a lower probability of occurring. His model does not specify the function of game sharing other than to preempt accusations of stinginess regarding a scarce resource. This perspective seems to invoke motivations inherent in models of "tolerated theft" (Blurton Jones 1984) or what Peterson refers to as "demand sharing" (1993). Yanomamö can be extremely aggressive in their demands for resources, as Chagnon has documented (1974, 1992). Although my data also suggest that sharing may be more widespread (i.e., has greater scope) in small rather than large villages, I am unable to demonstrate a significant correlation between village size or number of families in a village and the intensity of sharing *any* (game, fish, garden, or gathered foods) food resources.[5] This means that the amount of food a family is likely to receive from all other families is independent of village size, and therefore fissioning to form smaller villages will not increase one's absolute intake of resources from other families. This is because sharing in large or smaller villages seems to be restricted to sets of families who form reciprocal sharing partnerships.

The apparent relationship between the scope of exchange and village size, and the finding that Yanomamö households appear to restrict their giving and receiving to specific households, have interesting implications for village structure. This pattern is further implicated by evidence for specific balance of exchange between households. These trends suggest that medium-sized and large villages may be economically subdivided into groups of households based on habitual sharing relationships. It would be interesting to determine whether these patterns parallel or replicate predictable lines of village fissioning that seem to be based on patterns of marital alliance and kinship, as documented by Chagnon (1981; Chagnon and Bugos 1979). It suggests that, in the absence of intense warfare, villages should be no larger than the minimum number of households needed to reduce subsistence risk. These small villages probably operate at an economic advantage because there is less competition for local resources. As warfare intensifies, villages must become larger for defensive and offensive purposes (Chagnon 1974), and villages begin to subdivide into groups of households who maintain intensive exchange relationships.

CONCLUSION

The Yanomamö are an egalitarian people, yet village-wide patterns of food sharing are not designed to channel food to households having difficulty meeting consumer demand by taking it from households that are able to meet consumer demand more easily. Instead, most sharing seems to be restricted to groups of households who preferentially share with one another. Within the sphere of habitually exchanging households it is possible that flows are not equal, and they may be based on relative need and productive ability. This restriction in scope leads to large and medium-sized villages being subdivided into a series of units that intensively share with one another and rarely share with households outside their group. An important future research issue is the identification of the nature of kinship and marital bonds that characterize congeries of households tied to each other through habitual and intensive sharing. In addition, it would be useful to determine whether other forms of economic and social interaction, ranging from cooperative labor to reciprocal childcare, also characterize these groupings.

NOTES

1. In an analysis of Nelson Graburn's Inuit exchange data, Pryor (1977:80) operationalizes balance as the amount received less the amount given divided by the sum of the amount given and received. The resulting measures range from 1.00, which means that the household always received and never gave, to 0.00, indicating that it gave as much as it received, to –1.00, meaning that it always gave but never received. This measure of balance is useful for understanding how factors other than exchange, such as household size or marital status, act as determinants of exchange balance. For example, Pryor (1977:84–85) found that marital status (married vs. unmarried) and sex were significant determinants.

2. However, recent research by evolutionary ethnographers at the University of New Mexico Sosis (1997) and Gurven et al. (n.d.) using bargaining theory and reciprocal altruism shows that family size is relevant to predicting the amount of food a family receives.

3. In a previous publication on Ye'kwana garden labor exchange I showed that, contrary to Sahlins's claim, closeness of genetic kinship was a powerful determinant of balance in garden labor exchange (Hames 1989). My colleague Napoleon Chagnon and I are currently analyzing whether or not closeness of kinship is a significant factor in Yanomamö food exchange balance.

4. Good provides no test results demonstrating that the change in sharing patterns is statistically significant.

5. Regression analyses of village size and number of families against intensity of sharing of all resources and of fish, game, gathered, and garden resources yielded a significant (one-tailed) correlation between village size and the intensity of sharing of gathered resources. Paradoxically, the correlation was positive.

REFERENCES

Arensberg, C. 1959. *The Irish Countryman: An Anthropological Study.* Gloucester, Massachusetts: P. Smith.

Aspelin, L. 1979. Food distribution and social bonding among the Mamaindê of Mato Gross, Brazil. *Journal of Anthropological Research* 35(3):309–327.

Betzig, Laura. 1988. Redistribution: Equity or Exploitation? In *Human Reproductive Behavior,* Laura Betzig, Monique Borgerhoff Mulder, and Paul Turke, eds. Pp. 45–60. Cambridge: Cambridge University Press.

Bird, Rebecca, and Douglas Bird. 1997. Delayed reciprocity and tolerated theft: The behavioral ecology of food sharing strategies. *Current Anthropology* 31:49–55.

Blurton Jones, N. 1984. A selfish origin for human food sharing: Tolerated theft. *Ethology and Sociobiology* 4:145–147.

Boyd, R., and P. Richerson. 1988. The evolution of reciprocity in sizeable groups. *Journal of Theoretical Biology* 132:337–356.

Burch, E. 1992. Modes of exchange in north-west Alaska. In *Hunters and Gatherers, 2: Property, Power, and Ideology.* T. Ingold, D. Riches, and J. Woodburn, eds. Pp. 95–109. New York: Berg.

Cashdan, E. 1985. Coping with risk: Reciprocity among the Basarwa of Northern Botswana. *Man* 20:454–474.

Chagnon, Napoleon. 1974. *Studying the Yanomamö.* New York: Holt, Rinehart and Winston.

———. 1981 Terminological kinship, genealogical relatedness and village fissioning among the Yanomamö Indians. In *Natural Selection and Social Behavior,* R. D. Alexander and D. W. Tinkle, eds. Pp. 490–508. New York: Chiron Press.

———. 1992. *Yanomamö: The Fierce People,* 4th ed. New York: Harcourt Brace Jovanovich.

Chagnon, Napoleon, and Paul Bugos. 1979. Kin selection and conflict: An analysis of a Yanomamö ax fight. In *Evolutionary Biology and Human Social Behavior,* N. A. Chagnon and W. Irons, eds. Pp. 213–238. North Scituate, Massachusetts: Duxbury Press.

Damas, David. 1975. Central Eskimo systems of food sharing. *Ethnology* 11:220–239.

Dowling, J. 1968. Individual ownership and the sharing of game in hunting societies. *American Anthropologist* 70:502–507.

Durrenberger, P. 1984. *Chayanov, Peasants, and Economic Anthropology.* New York: Academic Press.

Endicott, K. 1992. Property, sharing, and conflict among the Batek of Malaysia. In *Property, Power, and Ideology. Hunter-Gatherers,* vol. II, T. Ingold and D. Riches, eds. Pp. 110–127. Oxford: Oxford University Press.

Good, K. 1987. Limiting factors in Amazonian ecology. In *Food and Evolution,* M. Harris and E. Ross, eds. Pp. 407–426. Philadelphia: Temple University Press.

———. 1989. *Yanomami Hunting Patterns: Trekking and Garden Relocation as an Adaptation to Game Availability in Amazonia, Venezuela.* Ph.D. thesis, University of Florida.

Gould, R 1982. To have and have not: the ecology of sharing among hunter-gatherers. In *Resource Managers: North American and Australian Hunter-Gatherers,* N. Williams and E. Hunn, eds. Pp. 69–92. Boulder: Westview Press.

Gurven, M., K. Hill, H. Kaplan, A. Hurtado, and R. Lyles. n.d. Food sharing among Hiwi foragers of Venezuela: Tests and implications for reciprocity. Ms. in authors' possession, Department of Anthropology, University of New Mexico, Albuquerque.

Hames, Raymond. 1987. Relatedness and garden labor exchange among the Ye'kwana. *Ethology and Socbiology* 8:354–392.

———. 1989. Time, efficiency, and fitness in the Amazonian protein quest. *Research in Economic Anthropology* 11:43–85.

———. 1990. Sharing among the Yanomamö, part I: The effects of risk. In *Risk and Uncertainty in Tribal and Peasant Economies,* E. Cashdan, ed. Pp. 89–106. Boulder: Westview Press.

———. 1994. Yanomamö, varying adaptations of foraging horticulturalists. In *Anthropology,* C. Ember and M. Ember, eds. Pp. 103–131. New York: Prentice Hall.

———. 1996. Costs and benefits of monogamy and polygyny for Yanomamö women. *Ethology and Sociobiology* 17:181–199.

Hawkes, K. 1993. Why hunter-gatherers work: An ancient version of the problem of public goods. *Current Anthropology* 34:341–361.

Henry, Jules. 1951. The economics of Pilaga food distribution. *American Anthropologist* 53:187–219.

Kaplan, Hillard, and Kim Hill. 1985. Food sharing among Ache foragers: Tests of explanatory hypotheses. *Current Anthropology* 26:223–245.

Kaplan, Hillard, Kim Hill, Kristen Hawkes, and Ana Hurtado. 1984. Food sharing among Ache hunter-gatherers of eastern Paraguay. *Current Anthropology* 25:113–115.

———. 1990. Risk, foraging and food sharing among the Ache. In *Risk and Uncertainty in Tribal and Peasant Economies,* E. Cashdan, ed. Pp. 107–144. Boulder: Westview Press.

Marshall, Lorna. 1961. Sharing, talking, and giving: Relief of social tensions among the !Kung Bushmen. *Africa* 29:335–365.

Mauss, M. 1967. Essai sur le don. *The Gift: Forms and Functions of Exchange in Archaic Societies.* New York: Norton.

Peterson, Nicholas. 1993. Demand sharing: Reciprocity and the pressure for generosity among foragers. *American Anthropologist* 95:860–874.

Pryor, Fredric. 1977. *The Origins of the Economy: A Comparative Study of Distribution in Primitive and Peasant Economies.* Academic Press: New York.

Saffirio, G., and Raymond Hames. 1983. The forest and the highway. In *Working Papers on South American Indians 6 and Cultural Survival Occasional Paper 11 (joint publication),* K. Kensinger and J. Clay, eds. Pp. 1–52. Cambridge, Massachusetts: Cultural Survival.

Sahlins, Marshall. 1965. The sociology of primitive exchange. In *The Relevance of Models in Social Anthropology,* M. Banton, ed. Pp. 139–236. London: Tavistock.

———. 1976. *The Use and Misuse of Biology: An Anthropological Critique of Sociobiology.* Ann Arbor: University of Michigan Press.

Service, Elman. 1962. *Primitive Social Organization.* Random House: New York
Sosis, R., S. Feldstein, et al. 1997. Bargaining theory and cooperative fishing participation on Ifaluk Atoll. *Human Nature* 163–203.
Speth, J. 1990. Seasonality, resource stress, and food sharing in so-called "egalitarian" foraging societies. *Journal of Anthropological Archaeology* 9:148–188.
Trivers, R. 1971. The evolution of reciprocal altruism. *Quarterly Review of Biology* 46:35–57.
Winterhalder, Bruce. 1986. Diet choice, risk, and food sharing in a stochastic environment. *Journal of Anthropological Archaelogy* 5:369–392.
———. 1990. Open field, common pot: Harvest variability and risk avoidance in agricultural and foraging societies. In *Risk and Uncertainty in Tribal and Peasant Economies,* E. Cashdan, ed. Pp. 67–87. Boulder: Westview Press.
———. 1996. Social foraging and the behavioral ecology of intragroup resource transfers. *Evolutionary Anthropology* 5:22–24.
———. 1997. Gifts given, gifts taken: The behavioral ecology of nonmarket, intragroup exchange. *Journal of Archaeological Research* 5:121–167.
Woodburn, James. 1982. Egalitarian societies. *Man* 17:431–451.

19

Reciprocal Altruism and Warfare

A Case from the Ecuadorian Amazon

JOHN Q. PATTON

INTRODUCTION

Warfare is an aggressive act, but it also entails cooperation and alliance. As such, a comprehensive Darwinian approach to the study of warfare must address the "problem" of altruism. In this chapter, data collected among tribal people living in the Ecuadorian Amazon are presented and used to argue that reciprocal altruism plays an important role in the motivation of warriors to undertake the risks involved in war and feud, and that an analysis of reciprocal altruism with regard to tribal warfare provides an important tool in the study of tribal social structures.

Are Warriors Altruistic?

Among Wright's (1994) list of frequently asked questions and apparent puzzles for the Darwinian paradigm is "why do soldiers die for their country?" This puzzle can be rephrased: Why do warriors undertake the somatically risky behaviors associated with war when the benefits derived from the risks they take appear to be a public good, that is, group defense and the pursuit of coalitional goals? As Wright describes (1994, pp. 390–391), the most widely accepted solution to this puzzle has been kin selection (Hamilton 1964). It is argued that the social contexts for the evolution of human warfare were small patrilocal kin groups, and when warriors risked their lives they did so for close kin. Contemporary warriors in modern nations, as well as in many tribal societies, are seen as being motivated by a Pleistocene psychology operating within novel social and political settings where the group one defends is primarily made up of non-kin or of distant relatives. As a consequence, selection for inclusive fitness in the past has led to altruism in the present.

Although kin selection may help to explain the origins of warfare, defined here as intercoalitional violence,[1] it is an incomplete answer to the question of why warriors risk their lives. Many aspects of coalitional violence among humans, nonhuman primates, and other animals indicate that reciprocal altruism (Trivers 1971, Axelrod and Hamilton 1981, Axelrod 1984) is an important motivation for cooperation. Evidence of reciprocal altruism in primate coalitions has existed since Hall and DeVore's pioneering study of aggression and cooperation among male baboons (1965). Hall and DeVore presented data demonstrating that low-ranking members of the "central hierarchy" were allowed increased matings over higher-ranking non-members (i.e., they were compensated for their cooperation by higher-ranking coalition members). Since then, reciprocal altruism has commonly been used by primatologists to explain the motivation for the formation and maintenance of coalitions (see Harcourt and de Waal 1992). Chimpanzees (our nearest relatives) exhibit signs of complex coalitional decision-making based on reciprocal altruism (de Waal 1982; de Waal and Harcourt 1992) and the cognitive ability to triangulate political loyalties and predict mutual support during conflicts (de Waal 1982). Certainly at the beginning of the Pleistocene our ancestors were at least equally endowed with cognitive abilities for reciprocal altruism (see Trivers 1971:45), and since then we have evolved a human nature with a unique capacity for social intelligence and the ability to form non-kinship based alliances.

Reciprocal Altruism and Segmental Warfare

One characteristic of human warfare that appears to be a universal that we share with chimpanzees (Goodall 1986) and baboons (Kummer 1971), and offers evidence of reciprocal altruism, is the ability to form coalitions at different levels of political hierarchy, that is, the capacity for segmentary warfare (Boehm 1992). Segmentary warfare is the ability of groups to temporarily put aside conflicts in order to form larger political units in opposition to other similarly formed coalitions, and these in turn may unite against an even larger coalition, and so on, and so on. Political segmentation and the related principle of segmentary opposition is evident throughout different levels of human social complexity. In the recent history of human warfare this ability saw perhaps its greatest expression with the Allied and Axis coalitions during World War II, but it is also a defining characteristic of tribal societies (Sahlins 1961) and was first described for "acephalous," egalitarian societies in Africa (Evans-Pritchard 1940 for the Nuer, and Bohannan 1954 for the Tiv).

In tribal societies the joining of political segments is associated with widening degrees of kinship (Bohannan 1963, p. 137). This is in striking agreement with kin selection theory. Similarly, the concept of segmentary opposition is in agreement with Alexander's "balance-of-power" hypothesis (1979, p. 222), which holds that the primary function of human groups is to compete with other human groups and that the optimal size of human groups is determined by the need to maintain balances of power. Kin selection can easily explain the linking of lower-level political segments, but it is more difficult to explain cooperation at larger political levels where average degrees of relatedness are minimal or insignificant. At these levels reciprocal altruism provides a more reasonable explanation. Sahlins's (1965) model of "primitive" exchange illustrates this. His model resembles a bull's-eye target and consists of nested interaction sectors, with the household sector at the center surrounded sequentially by the lineage, village, tribal, and finally the intertribal sectors. Cross-cutting these sectors is a spectrum of reciprocity that goes from "generalized" (one-way gifts with no accounting of costs and benefits) at the household sector to "balanced" (equitable exchange, a balancing of costs and benefits) at the tribal sector and "negative" (cheating and theft) at the intertribal sector. Alexander (1979, p. 200) points out that Sahlins's generalized reciprocity and balanced reciprocity are strikingly similar to the concepts of kin selection and reciprocal altruism, respectively. As one moves from the household to the outer sectors in Sahlins's model, degrees of relatedness, and so the effectiveness of kin selection, diminish (Alexander 1979, p. 57), becoming insignificant by the time one reaches the tribal sector, which is characterized by balanced reciprocity (reciprocal altruism). Since warfare commonly takes place in these outer sectors, reciprocal altruism must play an important role in warfare (See Figure 19.1). At some point along this spectrum of social interaction sectors, motivations for cooperation in war and feud go from a combination of kin selection and reciprocal altruism at the center to reciprocal altruism as the major influence in the outer sec-

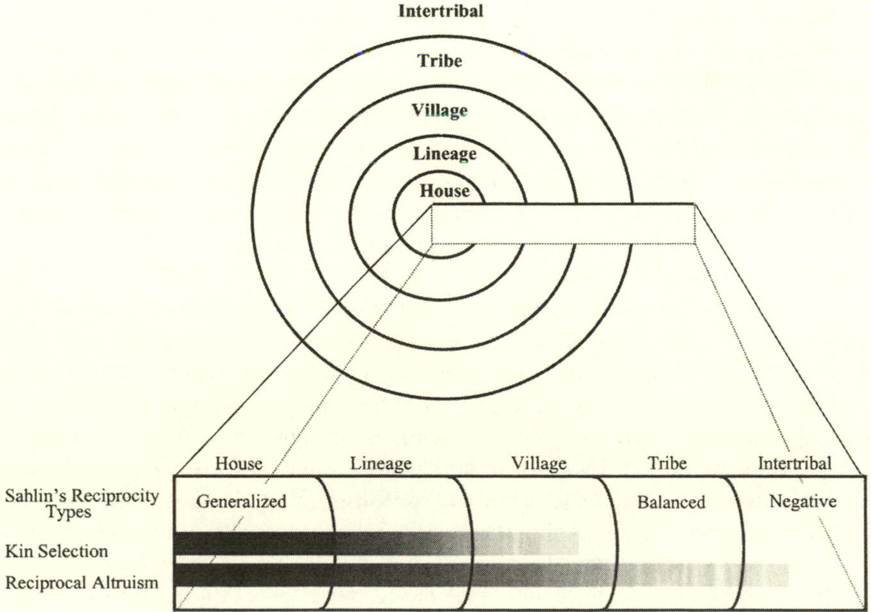

Figure 19.1. Spheres of Interaction, Kin Selection and Reciprocity.

tors. If this were not the case, segmentary warfare would be impossible to explain with our current Darwinian models of altruism.

Reciprocal Altruism and Status

Perhaps the most conclusive ethnographic data indicating that reciprocal altruism may play an important role in motivating warriors is Chagnon's (1988) reporting of a significant correlation between reproductive success (RS) and attaining the status of *unokai* among the Yanomamö. A man becomes *unokai* in a public ceremony designed to protect him from the spirit of a man he has killed or helped to kill. The vast majority of these killings occur during revenge raids on enemy villages. The *unokai* are not random killers, or murderers, but the Yanomamö equivalent of war heroes (Chagnon 1992, pp. 240–241). In addition to signaling a man's physical formidability, skill, and experience in successful warriorship, the *unokai* ceremony is also a public recognition of a man's willingness to take personal risk for the good of his coalition. The risk these men take for their coalitions appears to be reciprocated, as indicated by Chagnon's discovery that the *unokai* have on average two and a half times the number of wives and more than three times the number of offspring as do non-*unokai* (1988). Chagnon suggested that the *unokai*-RS correlation may be an example of culturally defined success leading to reproductive success (Irons 1979). If Chagnon is correct that the *unokai*-RS correlation is dependent on the proximate linkage of warriorship to status, Yanomamö warriors are not altruistic, but motivated by enlightened self-interest. That is, among the Yanomamö risks taken in war will be reciprocated with greater social status, which in turn leads to an increased ability to acquire wives. If warriors are motivated by the thought of receiving the benefits of higher status (and/or to avoid its loss) in proportion to the risks they take, their decision to participate in war or feud should conform to the logic of reciprocal altruism and should be amenable to cost-benefit analysis. Furthermore, a warrior's decision to undertake risks in war can be studied as a product of an evolved strategy for the use of violence for status gain within a coalitional context.

In egalitarian societies, status has been described as achieved rather than ascribed.[2] But status in egalitarian societies also has the following characteristics (among others): higher status for one coalition member comes at the cost of lower status for others (i.e., status is relative and status competition within coalitions is a zero-sum game); privileges of high status have appropriate limits; and dominance hierarchies can be overturned through coalitional readjustments limiting the power of would-be despots (Boehm 1993). Within egalitarian societies, high status is a social reward, something that is as much given or allowed by one's coalition members as it is achieved. Status is a product of social compromise.

If risks taken in coalitional violence are to be reciprocated in terms of social status and status is a product of social compromise, then strategies for the use of violence for status gain are dependent on the existence of shared psychological mechanisms for detecting and processing information concerning status and a man's willingness to take risks for his coalition.[3] These social decision-making mechanisms must be based on a shared logic of a social exchange contract for intercoalitional violence that implicitly defines the balancing of cost to benefits (i.e., individuals must keep score of risks taken and status gained or lost using the same rules for scorekeeping). If this were not the case, a warrior would have little or no confidence that others in his coalition would recognize their obligation to reciprocate in proportion to the risks he takes for them.

The Foci of This Study

The application of the theory of reciprocal altruism in the context of human warfare can be approached from multiple perspectives. This chapter focuses on two applications: (1) reciprocal altruism as it applies to a social contract for mutual defense, and (2) reciprocal altruism as a shared logic for the equitable distribution of status within coalitions.

Perhaps the most straightforward application of the theory of reciprocal altruism to human warfare is the argument that some expressions of intercoalitional violence are motivated by the prospects of reciprocal support in future conflicts. If this is so, as the nature of segmental warfare indicates, the cohesion of war-making coalitions composed of distantly or unrelated kin will be based on the perceived likelihood or trust that support in conflicts will be reciprocated in the future. In short, cooperation within such coalitions should be predicted by the model "$wb>c$" (Trivers 1971; Axelrod and Hamilton 1981; Axelrod 1984) predicting cooperation based on reciprocal altruism, where b is the value of support to the receiver, c is the risk incurred by the actor for the benefit of the receiver, and w represents the actor's expectation that he will receive support in the future as a consequence of c.

In game theory, the value w is defined as the number of times the game is played, such that the expectation of future support is a function of the number of opportunities for further cooperation. In an ethnographic context the measurement of w is more complex. Reciprocity need not be direct (Alexander 1987). Within coalitional settings, indirect reciprocity involving three or more individuals can be complex and general (Alexander 1987, p. 85). Coalitional boundaries are often volatile, and loyalties within and between coalitions are both nested and cross-cutting. A single conflict within a coalition may have dramatic effects on coalitional structure and composition, making the detection of group boundaries difficult and situational (Patton 1996, pp. 110–123). In this context, judgments concerning expectations for reciprocation may require calculating conflicting loyalties more than simply assessing opportunities for reciprocation. This makes judgments concerning the likelihood of reciprocal support (w) difficult. This difficulty underscores the complex social decision-making required of individuals acting within coalitions based on reciprocal altruism. It requires the cognitive ability de Waal refers to as "triadic awareness" (de Waal 1982). Triadic awareness is the ability to make judgments concerning one's own relationships while accounting for the relationships between others. This ability to triangulate political loyalties requires cognitive mechanisms for assessing relative values of *w* between individuals. It is this ability that allows individuals to make decisions concerning the strategic use of violence within coalitional settings, such as where on the political landscape violence must be avoided; where it will have the desired effect; how violence will restructure coalitional loyalties; and of most importance here, who will come to your aid during a conflict involving specific others.

The mathematical model for reciprocal altruism is structurally similar to the model for kin selection (Brown et al. 1982). The value *w* is comparable to Hamilton's *r* in the model "$rb>c$" (Hamilton 1964). Chagnon has demonstrated that among the Yanomamö, Hamilton's *r* provides a means for measuring social solidarity (1975) and predicting the location of political cleavages within communities during conflicts (Chagnon and Bugos 1979). In coalitions where cooperation is based on reciprocal altruism, measurements of *w* should likewise provide a means of describing coalitional solidarity and structure. Below, I describe a method for accessing relative measurements of *w* using a triangular awareness task and use these measurements to define coalitional boundaries and structure for Conambo.

The second approach taken in this chapter is to examine social decisions concerning status and a man's perceived value as a warrior, his warriorship, for signs of a shared logic for the equitable distribution of status within coalitions that conforms to the expectations of reciprocal altruism. As stated above, the *unokai*-RS correlation is dependent on the shared logic of a social contract, within the context of coalitional violence, that specifies the relationship between costs and benefits, that is, agreed upon "rules of the game."

Cosmides and Tooby have provided evidence that contracts for social exchange have an innate logic (Cosmides 1989, Cosmides and Tooby 1992). They argue for the existence of cognitive mechanisms for the detection of cheaters in social contracts, and by extension, that there is an innate logic specifying the exchange of costs and benefits in social contracts (i.e., an innate set of rules for scorekeeping). If the *unokai*-RS correlation requires a shared logic in the form of a social contract, it may be that the correlation is a product of innate cognitive mechanisms, based on reciprocal altruism, for making assessments concerning a social contract for intercoalitional violence. If such innate rules are in place, a man's social position within his coalition should in part be based on his value as a warrior to his coalition. There should be a positive correlation between warriorship and status. Just how important a variable warriorship is for determining status will depend on the relative importance of other status attributes.

In what follows, I will argue that in Conambo warriorship is perceived to be of utmost importance in determining a man's status, that coalitions of men are to a large extent based on reciprocal altruism, that values of *w* provide an useful tool for defining Conambo social structure, and that informants' judgments of status and warriorship provide evidence of a shared logic for a social contract for inter-coalitional violence based on reciprocal altruism.

Ethnographic Background and Site Description

The data presented in this chapter were collected during ethnographic fieldwork conducted from December 1992 to September of 1993 in the Ecuadorian Amazon among Achuar Jivaro and lowland Quichua speakers[4] living in the community of Conambo. The center of Conambo is located on the Conambo River at 76 degrees 52.76 minutes west longitude and 1 degree and 52.31 minutes south of the equator. No roads go to Conambo. Two days downriver from Conambo by canoe, the river joins the Rio Pindo at the Peruvian border to form the Rio Tigre. A short distance above Conambo the river is unnavigable. Below Conambo, river travel is closed at the border. The 185 people, give or take a few on any given day, who make up the community of Conambo live in 23 households spread along 3,000 m (as the crow flies but much further by foot) on both banks of the Conambo River.[5] With only a few exceptions, there is no line-of-sight between households, and it takes about an hour walking fast to travel from the house furthest downriver to the house furthest upriver. Both settlement and politics are remarkably decentralized (see Taylor 1981 for a discussion of Achuar settlement patterns).

The people of Conambo still live a relatively traditional lifeway and have only sporadic contact with nonindigenous peoples who fly in and out on small, six-passenger missionary aircraft. No missionaries or other nonindigenous people live in the community, but missionaries have established a primary school with two teachers who are indigenous people from other jungle communities.

The people of Conambo make their living through hunting, fishing, gathering, and swidden horticulture. They hunt with blowguns and curare-tipped darts, and with muzzle-loading shotguns (which are also the weapon of choice for homicide) for which they acquire shot, powder, and percussion caps through trade. Their subsistence strategies are very successful. Descola reports from a study conducted in the area that the average Achuar adult consumes 3,408 calories and 104.5 g of protein daily (1994, p. 210).[6] Conambo is in an area rich in game, and with 0.17 people/km[7] (Descola 1994) the Achuar have one of the lowest population densities in the Amazon. There is little reason in Conambo to risk one's life over hunting resources.

The people of Conambo have a strong egalitarian ethic, and politics are small-scale and flexible. Karsten noted that among Jivaroan peoples there is no "proper name for a chief" and that chieftainship exists only in times of war (1923, p. 7). Unlike the Yanomamö, among the Achuar there are no "headmen," nor is there a word that signifies such, but men of prominence are called *hundri,* which literally means "big man." The Achuar have no named lineages, and they reckon descent bilaterally. In terms of political organization, the Achuar resemble bands more than tribes (Ross 1988). This simple political organization is combined with matrilocal residence. Matrilocality leads to male coalitions that are to a large degree made up of distantly related or unrelated men. In Conambo, sets of brothers provide a nucleus for male coalitions, but the majority of men in Conambo are sons-in-law who have married in from other communities. Young men from Conambo more often than not leave the community to marry. This form of social organization is flexible and volatile. Kin terms have modifiers added to them that signify "real" or "branch" kin. The use of these modifiers is often manipulated according to one's political interests. This leads to a political structure in which kinship is an unreliable predictor of political support (Harner 1972). This uncertainty is no doubt the reason that would-be killers seek out counsel and prior permission from kinsmen and allies before taking action. Ross states that seeking counsel is an "important part of the protocol that characterized the pattern of Achuara hostilities," and it "behooves any Achuara contemplating revenge upon someone to discuss his plans with potential allies, aligning them in his camp in advance of his action" (1984, pp. 102–103). Jivaroan peoples are also known to employ spies during times of conflict (Harner 1972, p. 183).

This political landscape is less predictable than that found in most small-scale societies, and maneuvering through it requires very thoughtful warriorship (Patton 1996). It is also probably one reason why Achuar homicide rates are so high. The genealogical data for Conambo indicate that 50% of male forefathers were victims of homicide. Of the 30 immediate male ancestors of people currently living in Conambo for whom there were reported unambiguous causes of death, 15 died from shot gun blasts. In previous studies of homicide rates for the Achuar, Kelekna (1981) and Descola (1996) also report a rate of 50%, and E. Ross (1976) and J. Ross (1984, 1988) report a rate of 59% for Achuar men living on the Peruvian side of the border. Currently, homicides rates for Conambo are not as high as that figure would indicate. In the past 15 years or so, three men in Conambo have been killed in homicides. While this is still a relatively high rate of homicide for a community of this size, people recognize the present as a time of relative peace compared to the intense feuding that took place about 20 years ago and before. They refer to that time of intense feuding as "the time when we were ending." It is difficult to equate this level of homicide with notions of public good or group fitness. The history of the people of Conambo, typical for the Achuar, is one where issues of security, relative to subsistence, are overwhelmingly more important to environmental coping, and where social structure both influences and is a reflection of intercoalitional violence.

METHODS AND RESULTS

In this chapter, two separate data collection tasks and analyses are used to argue for the importance of reciprocal altruism as a basis for cooperation in war. The first involves a triadic awareness task to measure political loyalties, used in a description of Conambo coalitional structures. The second involves the collection of informants' judgments of men's status and warriorship, examined for signs of a shared social contract based on reciprocity.

Reciprocal Altruism and Social Structure

For this task, 38 informants (25 men and 13 women) were asked to make alliance judgments involving all 33 married men in Conambo. Each informant was shown photos of all of the men presented in random sets of three and asked "If there were a conflict involving these three men, which two would be most likely to unite against the third?" In essence, this was a triadic awareness task where informants were asked to make a judgment as to which of the possible coalitions represented in each triad was the strongest. Each triad represents three possible coalitional choices. If in a triad of individuals A, B, and C, the informant chooses the coalition A-B, the choice represents the judgment that the coalition A-B has more solidarity than coalitions A-C and B-C.

Each informant was asked to make comparative judgments of 99 dyadic coalitions for a total for all informants of 3,762 alliance judgments. Each of the men appeared in 228 possible coalitional choices and was compared with each of the other men an average of 7.13 times. Relative coalitional strengths for each of the hypothetical coalitions (each pair of men) were calculated by taking the number of times each coalition was chosen divided by the number of times each pair was presented as a choice, that is, the percentage of times the two men were judged to have the strongest alliance.

These relative alliance strengths were then tabulated in a matrix representing the relative strengths of all possible male dyadic coalitions. Alliance strengths alone may not predict who will side with whom in a conflict. Individuals with strong alliance ties may find themselves on opposite sides of a political divide because the bulk of their alliances may not overlap. In addition, not all alliances have the same value. One may be strongly allied with another, but it may be politically disadvantageous to side with them, depending on the coalitional context. The ability to make decisions as to who will side with whom requires more than political awareness of coalitional triads; it requires making alliance decisions with potentially as many dimensions as there are members within a group minus one. A better estimate of who will come to whose aid in a conflict can be made by assessing the degree to which individuals share the same set of allies (and enemies). To approximate this type of assessment, the matrix of alliance strengths was used to tabulate another matrix of alliance similarities. The cells of this matrix contained Pearson's correlation coefficients, which represent the degree to which each pair of men conform in terms of alliance strengths when compared with each of the other men in the sample, that is, the degree to which their sets of alliances correspond. This matrix of alliance similarities was used to detect Conambo men's coalitional boundaries, composition, and structure through the use of multidimensional scaling.

Multi-Dimensional Scaling (MDS) is commonly used by cognitive anthropologists and others to analyze informants' judgments concerning triadic comparisons and other similarity judgment tasks to uncover the "hidden structure" embedded in the data, and to describe and analyze systems of classification (Kruskal and Wish 1978). MDS takes informants' collective judgments concerning the similarity of objects and maps out in two dimensions a spatial representation of the data. Scales and axis labels are generally absent because they are arbitrary. The relationships among objects are represented by the relative distances between them, and in the detection of object clusters. In essence, MDS converts mental representations of the similarities between objects to spatial maps that can be used to reveal hidden relationships between objects in a form that makes intuitive sense. It is important to note that since the data used to generate MDS are derived from a number of different individuals, each with a slightly different perspective, the patterns in a MDS represent the degree to which informants share the same criteria for making similarity judgments of the items. If each informant has a different criteria for classifying items the arrangement of items in the MDS would appear random. The structure or strength of clustering in MDS, then, represents the degree to which informants' judgments and judgment criteria correspond.

Figure 19.2 is an MDS of the similarities in alliance of the 23 male heads of household in Conambo.[7] It represents a map of informants' mental representations of male alliances in Conambo, derived from a matrix of alliance similarities and based on judgments of who is likely to come to whose defense in a conflict. The

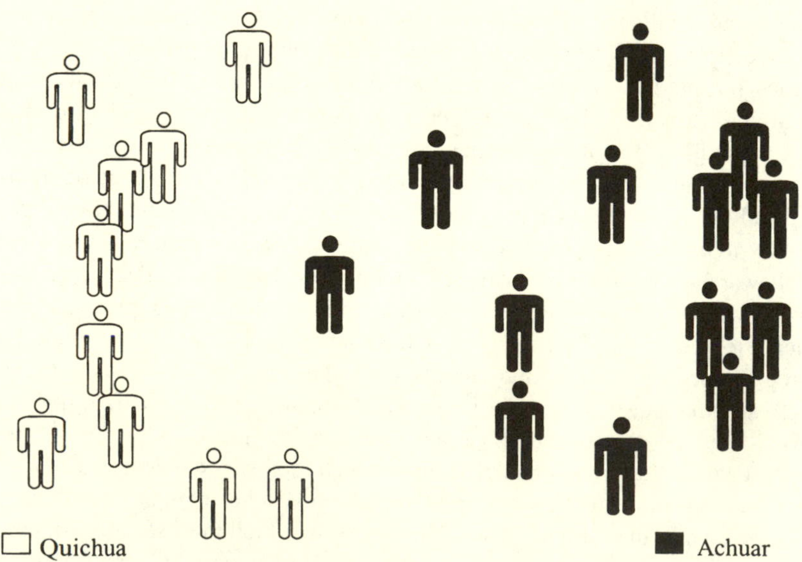

Figure 19.2. MDS of Alliance Similarities.

relative distance between the icons representing men in this figure is a relative measurement of the degree to which these men share alliance sets. A Tabu search technique (Glover 1989, 1990) was used to define the main political boundary separating the largest two alliance clusters, which are indicted in the figure as shaded and unshaded icons. These two alliances have been labeled Achuar and Quichua because these terms roughly correspond to the major ethnic divide within Conambo, but as used here they denote political rather than ethnic affiliation. Two-thirds (8 of 12) of the "Quichua" households have ethnically Achuar members in them and one-fourth (3 of 12) have ethnically Achuar male household heads. Most of the ethnic Achuar who are members of the Quichua alliance were at one time allied with the Achuar but defected to the Quichua alliance after homicides. One-third of the "Achuar" households have ethnic Quichua members (one is a male household head).

Figure 19.2 provides a map of the Conambo men's political landscape. An examination of this MDS of men's alliance similarities gives one an intuitive feeling for Conambo political divisions, where the line in the sand would be drawn in a community-wide conflict. But another advantage to this approach is that it allows for the examination of coalitional structures at different political levels or segments. Figure 19.3 is the MDS of the alliance similarities within the Achuar coalition without consideration of alliances across the coalitional boundary (i.e, ignoring the relationships between Achuar and Quichua men). Figure 19.3 depicts

Figure 19.3. MDS of Achuar Alliance Similarities.

factional structures within the Achuar coalition and provides a more appropriate illustration of who is likely to side with whom during a conflict within the Achuar coalition.

Status, Warriorship, and Reciprocal Altruism

For the second data task, informants' judgments of men's status and warriorship were collected. These data were then analyzed to determine if in fact informants' judgments of each man's status were positively correlated with how informants perceived his value as a warrior, providing evidence that informants' decisions were influenced by the logic of reciprocal altruism.

For this task 47 informants (26 from the Achuar coalition and 21 from the Quichua coalition)[8] were asked to rank all of the 33 married men in Conambo in terms of their status position within Conambo, using the same photos as in the task above presented in random sets of three. Each man was given two points for being chosen first in the triad, one point for second, and no points for third place. Status scores were calculated for each man by summing all points from all informants. Native terms for status were identified and used in this task. Warriorship scores for the same 33 men were collected from 34 informants (18 Achuar and 16 Quichua). Informants were asked "if there were a war today, which of these men would be the best warrior?" Warriorship scores were calculated using the same method used for calculating status scores.

Warriorship appears to be a very important determinant of men's status in Conambo (Figure 19.4), explaining 78.5% of the variation in men's status with very high confidence (Pearson's correlation coefficient of .785 with a two-tailed p of 0.000). Further analysis of the variation in informants' judgments also indicates a coalitional bias in judgments of status (Figure 19.5). Achuar informants on average judged Achuar men as having 16.24% greater status than Quichua men, while Quichua informants judged Quichua men as having on average 7.44% greater status (a difference of opinion of 23.68%). Judgments of warriorship showed less coalitional bias (Figure 19.6). Achuar informants on average judged Achuar men as being greater warriors by a margin of 36.94%. Quichua informants agreed that Achuar men were better warriors by a margin of 16.27% (a difference of opinion of 20.67%). Despite the variation in judgments due to coalitional bias, the correlation between warriorship and status remains strong and significant regardless of the coalitional membership of the informant and whether the judgments are made within or across coalitional boundaries (Table 19.1).[9]

DISCUSSION

The MDS of alliance similarities provides a means of estimating relative values of w. In the context of cooperation during conflicts, w is the discounted value

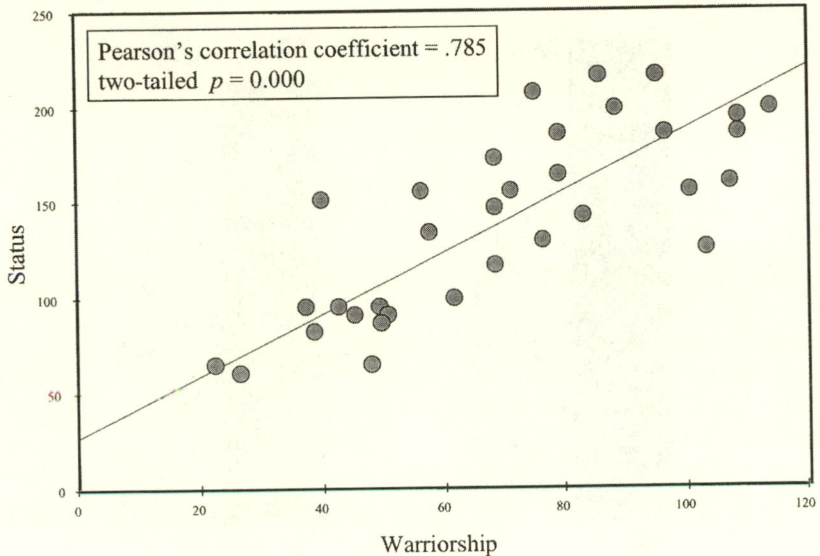

Figure 19.4. Plot Showing the Relationship between Status and Warriorship.

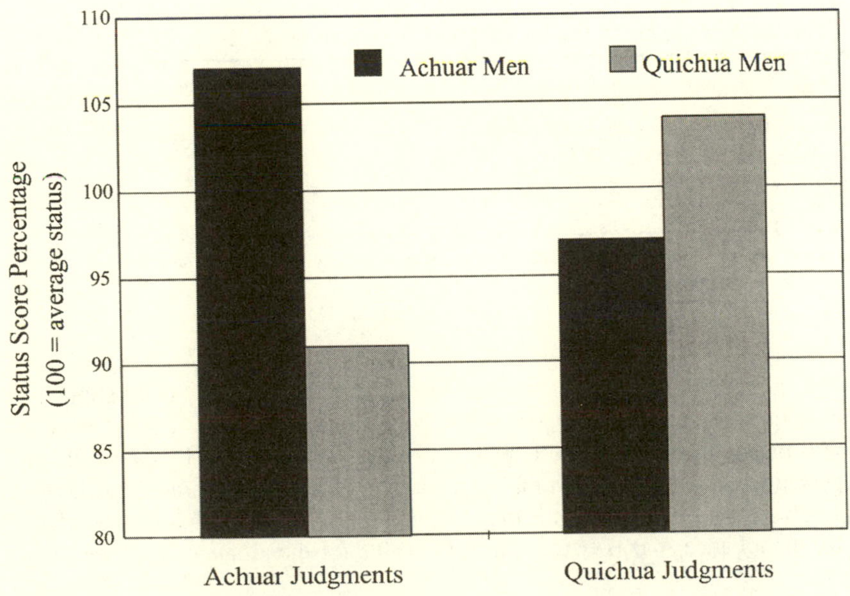

Figure 19.5. Coalitional Bias in Status Judgments.

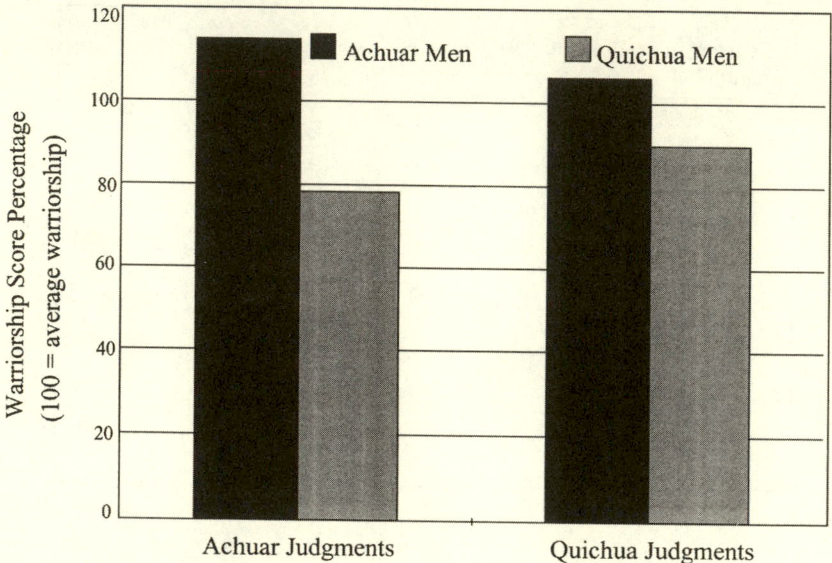

Figure 19.6. Coalitional Bias in Warriorship Judgments.

Table 19.1 Correlation Coefficients* for the Relationship between Status and Warriorship by Coalitional Membership and Bias

Judgements of:	*All Informants*	*Achuar Informants*	*Quichua Informants*
All Men	.785	.801	.727
Achuar Men	.770	.780	.738
Quichua Men	.903	.857	.827

*Pearson's correlation coefficients; all correlations were highly significant (two-tailed $p = 0.000$)

in the model for reciprocal altruism ($wb>c$) that represents the likelihood or expectation of reciprocal support in conflicts. If icon A is at half the distance to icon B than it is to icon C, these relative distances indicate that it is the collective expectation of informants that during a conflict, all else being equal,[10] A is twice as likely to come to the aid of B than to come to the aid of C, that is, the value of w for the alliance A-B is twice that of the value for the alliance A-C (see Figure 19.7).

Conambo's main political boundary, apparent in the MDS of alliance similarity (Figure 19.2), is also a boundary of ethnocentric coalitional bias. A description

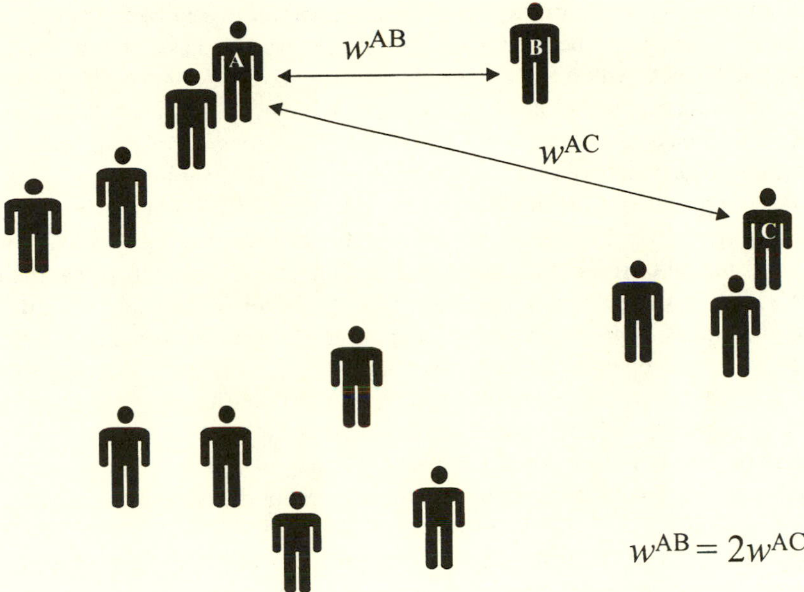

Figure 19.7. MDS of Achuar Alliance Similarities with relative values for *w*.

of alliance structures based on relative measurements of *w* (who is likely to reciprocate in a conflict) also describes a psychological boundary of in-group and out-group within Conambo. Members of a coalition emphasize the social importance of their men while de-emphasizing the social importance of men in the other coalition. This boundary in coalitional bias is independent evidence that the MDS in Figures 19.2 and 19.3 depicts actual coalitional structures. In coalitions with low average degrees of relatedness (*r*), and therefore weak kin selection motivations for cooperation, measurements of *w* provide a useful tool for the description of coalitional structures and a means of measuring relative degrees of coalitional solidarity at different levels of political segmentation.

Despite a coalitional bias, which represents an important source of variation in status judgments, the relationship between warriorship and status in Conambo remains strong and significant, and the logic of reciprocal altruism appears to hold throughout the status hierarchy as is evident by the strong, highly significant correlation between status and warriorship. Despite applying different scales in their judgment of a man's social importance, informants appear to share the same criteria for assessing status. These shared criteria fit the expectations of an evolved logic for social exchange based on reciprocal altruism. The people of Conambo appear to share a logic specifying the reciprocation of social status for a man's willingness to take risks in war. As stated above, the *unokai* correlation provides evidence that reciprocal altruism may play an important role in motivating warriors, and that status may be the reward for the risks warriors take. But, a system of costs and benefits within a coalitional context requires trust that others within your coalition recognize the same set of rules of reciprocity, as well as their obligation to reciprocate as specified by those rules. The strong correlation between status and warriorship, derived from the collective judgments of informants, indicates that the people of Conambo show a high degree of fidelity in making judgments concerning the relationship between status and warriorship, that is, they share the same set of rules. As a consequence, Conambo men can trust that their efforts will be rewarded, and indeed, men who are better warriors are rewarded with higher status. This proportional accounting of costs and benefits has the attributes of scorekeeping, which is the hallmark of reciprocal altruism as opposed to other possible forms of cooperation among non-kin such as group selection or byproduct mutualism (Mesterton-Gibbons and Dugatkin 1992).

Conambo politics are small-scale and have a history of violence. The people of Conambo, despite having only minimal cultural rules for defining social structure and minimal consanguineous relationships that bind men's coalitions, nonetheless appear to have a shared mental representation of the structure of men's alliances. Alliances appear to be based on reciprocal support in conflicts, and social hierarchy appears to be a product of a shared logic (a social contract) based on reciprocal altruism for rewarding better warriors with greater status. Together, the two data sets presented here offer support to the notion that within certain social contexts reciprocal altruism can be an important motivation for warriors and a basis for cooperation, solidarity, and social structure among male coalitions responsible for the management of violence.

SUMMARY

1. A triadic awareness task was used to measure relative alliance similarities between pairs of warriors, which indicate who is likely to reciprocate support during conflicts, providing an estimate of relative values of w in the model for reciprocal altruism ($wb>c$).

2. Relative values of w provide a useful tool for describing the structures and boundaries of coalitions of men where average degrees of relatedness are small.

3. Coalitional boundaries defined using values of w also define the psychological boundaries of ethnocentric bias.

4. The people of Conambo appear to have a shared logic based on reciprocal altruism which matches the expectations of an innate social contract for intercoalitional violence that specifies the reciprocation of costs (willingness to take risks) and benefits (social status).

5. In Conambo better warriors are rewarded with greater social status.

ACKNOWLEDGMENTS

I would like to thank John Tooby and Leda Cosmides whose Center for Evolutionary Psychology supported this study as part of the Human Universals Project. This study was also supported by grants from the James S. McDonnell Foundation to John Tooby (Cognitive Adaptations to Ancestral Environments), the National Science Foundation to John Tooby (BNS9157-449, Evolutionary Biology and Human Psychological Adaptation), and by the Chancellor's Post-Doctoral Fellowship for Academic Diversity at the University of Colorado at Boulder and its Department of Anthropology. I also would like to thank Brenda Bowser, Lee Cronk, and an anonymous reviewer for their thoughtful comments.

NOTES

1. Many definitions of warfare exist. For a review of anthropological definitions of war see Ferguson (1984:3–5). Ferguson argues that the underlying characteristic of war is that it is a "social activity" and defines war as "organized, purposeful group action, directed against another group that may or may not be organized for similar action, involving the actual or potential application of lethal force" (1984:5). Although this definition is more inclusive than most anthropological definitions of war, and allows for interspecies comparison, it is somewhat cumbersome. From an ethological perspective, de Waal and Harcourt define coalitions as "cooperation in an aggressive or competitive context" and as a "social tool to defeat others" (1992:2). The term "coalition" embodies the social characteristic of war in Ferguson's definition, and defining warfare as "intercoalitional violence" is just as inclusive and less cumbersome.

2. But see Maschner and Patton 1996 for a discussion of how lineage membership is an ascribed status in egalitarian societies where political power is in large part the result of lineage size.

3. Warfare is overwhelmingly a male activity. Therefore, this study focuses on men and male coalitions.

4. The Quichua speakers in Conambo fit Whitten's (1976) description of the Canelos Quichua. They are the last descendants of the Zaparos who, during the first half of the twentieth century, all but wiped each other out in feuds that were motivated by witchcraft accusations following a measles epidemic. The survivors of these "brujo" wars intermarried with Achuar who were expanding eastward to avoid the head-taking raids of the Jivaro studied by Harner (1972). Quichua, the Inca language, was the *lingua franca* and provided a common language for these intermarrying families. Most Achuar also speak Quichua, though only a few Quichua in Conambo were fluent in Achuar. In Conambo, apart from language, there is little difference in the lifestyle and politics between Quichua and Achuar households.

5. There are 23 households, excluding the teachers and defining households as independent economic units. Seven of these households have married in sons-in-law. For the purpose of this study, these young couples living under the same roof, or in the same household compound, of the bride's parents are not counted as separate households.

6. Philippe Descola and Ann Christine-Taylor visited Conambo for a short stay during fieldwork they conducted from November 1976 to August 1978. Most of this time they spent with an Achuar faction that had temporally moved upriver from Conambo to avoid conflict after a homicide. Descola (1996) provides a more complete description of Achuar life and feuding than is possible here. (For a more complete description of Conambo and the fieldwork that produced this study, see Patton 1996.)

7. The matrix of alliance similarities used for this MDS is derived from the relative alliance strengths as calculated from triadic comparisons among all 33 men.

8. The coalitional membership of informants was determined by the coalitional affiliation of the male head of the house in which they reside as determined by the previous data task.

9. The relationship between status and warriorship appears to be independent of age. Age is also a good predictor of status, but the data indicate that the relationship of status to age showed marked differences depending on the coalitional membership of the men. As compared to warriorship, age accounts for an additional 9.1% of the variation in Achuar men's status, but accounts for 13.9% less of the variation in Quichua men's status. An examination of outliers to the relationship between status and warriorship indicate that the majority of men who had higher status than predicted by their warriorship were shamans, and shamanism was another important source of status. The relationship of age to status, independent of warriorship, is most probably the result of higher status of shamans who were also older men. The Quichua coalition has fewer shamans than the Achuar. This may explain the greater correlation between status and warriorship among the Quichua.

10. In this case, if the potential risks to the actor and benefits to the receiver are equal. Status differences and differences in physical formidability between individuals undoubtedly change the conditions of risks and benefits within a conflict, but since the strengths for each hypothetical dyadic coalition was measured with comparison to a number of potential dyadic coalitions made up of individuals from throughout the range of status and formidability, the effects of these variables are mitigated to the degree possible within the confines of this study. For a comprehensive discussion of situations when conditions vary see Boyd 1992.

REFERENCES

Alexander, R. D. 1979. *Darwinism and Human Affairs.* Seattle: University of Washington Press.

Alexander, R. D. 1987. *The Biology of Moral Systems.* New York: Aldine de Gruyter.

Axelrod, R. 1984. *The Evolution of Cooperation.* New York: Basic Books.

Axelrod, R., and W. D. Hamilton. 1981. The evolution of cooperation. *Science* 211: 1390–1396.

Boehm, C. 1992. Segmentary "warfare" and the management of conflict: Comparison of East African chimpanzees and patrilineal-patrilocal humans. In *Coalitions and Alliances in Humans and Other Animals.* A. H. Harcourt and F. B. M. de Waal, eds. Pp. 137–173. Oxford: Oxford University Press.

Boehm, C. 1993. Egalitarian Behavior and Reverse Dominance Hierarchy. *Current Anthropology* 34:227–254.

Bohannan, P. 1954. *Tiv Farm and Settlement.* London: H. M. Stationery Office.

Bohannan, P. 1963. *Social Anthropology.* New York: Holt, Rinehart & Winston.

Boyd, R. 1992. The evolution of reciprocity when conditions vary. In *Coalitions and Alliances in Humans and Other Animals.* A. H. Harcourt and F. B. M. de Wall, eds. Pp. 473–489. Oxford: Oxford University Press.

Brown, J. S., M. J. Sanderson, and R. E. Michod. 1982. Evolution of Social Behavior by Reciprocation. *Journal of Theoretical Biology* 99:319–339.

Chagnon, N. A. 1975. Genealogy, solidarity, and relatedness: Limits to local group size and patterns of fissioning in an expanding population. *Yearbook of Physical Anthropology* 19:95–110.

Chagnon, N. A. 1979. Mate competition, favoring close kin, and village fissioning among the Yanomamö Indians. In *Evolutionary Biology and Human Social Behavior: An Anthropological Perspective.* N. A. Chagnon and W. Irons, eds. Pp. 213–238. North Scituate, Massachusetts: Duxbury Press.

Chagnon, N. A. 1988. Life Histories, Blood Revenge, and Warfare in a Tribal Population. *Science* 239:985–992

Chagnon, N. A. 1992. *Yanomamö: The last Days of Eden.* San Diego: Harcourt, Brace, and Javanovich.

Chagnon, N. A., and P. Bugos. 1979. Kin selection and conflict: An analysis of a Yanomamö ax fight. In *Evolutionary Biology and Human Social Behavior: An Anthropological Perspective.* N. A. Chagnon and W. Irons, eds. Pp. 86–132. North Scituate, Massachusetts: Duxbury Press.

Cosmides, L. 1989. The logic of social exchange: Has natural selection shaped how humans reason? Studies with the Wason selection task. *Cognition* 31:187–276.

Cosmides, L., and J. Tooby. 1992. Cognitive adaptations for social exchange. In *The Adapted Mind: Evolutionary Psychology and the Generation of Culture.* J. H. Barkow, L. Cosmides, and J. Tooby, eds. Pp. 163–228. New York: Oxford University Press.

Descola, P. 1994. Homeostasis as a cultural system: The Jivaro case. In *Amazonian Indians from Prehistory to the Present: Anthropological Perspectives.* A. Roosevelt, ed. Pp. 203–224. Tucson: University of Arizona Press.

Descola, P. 1996. *The Spears of Twilight: Life and Death in the Amazon Jungle.* New York: The New Press.

Evans-Pritchard, E. E. 1940. *The Nuer.* Oxford: Clarendon Press.

Ferguson, R. B. 1984. Introduction: Studying War. In *Warfare, Culture, and Environment.* R. B. Ferguson, ed. Pp. 1–88. New York: Academic Press.

Glover, F. 1989. Tabu Search—Part I. *ORSA Journal on Computing* 1:190–206.

Glover, F. 1990. Tabu Search—Part II. *ORSA Journal on Computing* 2:4–32.

Goodall, J. 1986. *The Chimpanzees of Gombe.* Cambridge, Massachusetts: Harvard University Press.

Irons, W. 1979. Cultural and biological success. In *Evolutionary Biology and Human Social Behavior: an Anthropological Perspective.* N. A. Chagnon and W. Irons, eds. Pp. 257–272. North Scituate, Massachusetts: Duxbury Press.

Hall, K. R. L. and I. DeVore. 1965. Baboon social behaviour. In *Primate Behaviour.* I. DeVore, ed. Pp. 53–110. New York: Holt, Rinehart and Winston.

Hamilton, W. D. 1964. The Genetical Evolution of Social Behavior, I & II. *Journal of Theoretical Biology* 7:1–52.

Harcourt, A. H. and F. B. M. de Wall. 1992. *Coalitions and Alliances in Humans and Other Animals.* Oxford: Oxford University Press.

Harner, M. J. 1972. *The Jivaro: People of the Sacred Waterfalls.* Garden City, New York: Anchor Press/Doubleday.

Karsten, R. 1923. *Blood Revenge, War and Victory Feasts Among the Jibaro Indians of Eastern Ecuador.* Smithsonian Institution, Bureau of American Ethnology, Bulletin 79.

Kelekna, P. 1981. Sex asymmetry in Jivaroan Achuara society: A cultural mechanism promoting belligerence. Ph.D. Dissertation, University of New Mexico.

Kruskal, J. B. and M. Wish. 1978. *Multidimensional Scaling.* Newbury Park, CA: Sage Publications.

Kummer, H. 1971. *Primate Societies: Group Techniques of Ecological Adaptation.* Chicago: Aldine Press.

Maschner, H. D. G. and J. Q. Patton. 1996. Kin selection and the origins of hereditary social inequality: A case study from the northern northwest coast. In *Darwinian Archaeologies.* H. D. G. Maschner, ed. Pp. 89–107. New York: Plenum Press.

Mesterton-Gibbons, M. and L. A. Dugatkin. 1992. Cooperation among unrelated individuals: Evolutionary factors. *The Quarterly Review of Biology* 67:267–281.

Patton, J. Q. 1996. Thoughtful warriors: Status, warriorship, and alliance in the Ecuadorian Amazon. Ph.D. Dissertation, University of California at Santa Barbara.

Ross, E. B. 1976. The Achuara Jivaro: Cultural adaptation in the upper Amazon. Ph.D. Dissertation, Columbia University.

Ross, J. B. 1984. Effects of Contact on Revenge Hostilities Among the Achuara Jivaro. In *Warfare, Culture, and Environment.* R. B. Ferguson, ed. Pp. 83–109. New York: Academic Press.

Ross, J. B. 1988. A balance of deaths: Revenge feuding among the Achuara Jivaro of the northwest Peruvian Amazon. Ph.D. Dissertation, Columbia University.

Sahlins, M. D. 1961. The segmentary lineage: Instrument of predatory expansion. *American Anthropologist* 63:322–345.

Sahlins, M. D. 1965. On the sociology of primitive exchange. In *The Relevance of Models for Social Anthropology*. M. Banton, ed. Pp. 139–236. London: Travestock.

Taylor, A.-C. 1981. God-wealth: The Achuar and the missions. In *Cultural Transformation and Ethnicity in Modern Ecuador.* N. Whitten, ed. Pp. 647–677. Urbana: University of Illinois Press.

Trivers, R. L. 1971. The Evolution of Reciprocal Altruism. *Quarterly Review of Biology* 46:35–57.

de Waal, F. B. M. 1982. *Chimpanzee Politics: Power and Sex Among Apes.* Baltimore: John Hopkins University Press.

de Waal, F. B. M., and A. H. Harcourt. 1992. Coalitions and alliances: A history of ethological research. In *Coalitions and Alliances in Humans and Other Animals.* A. H. Harcourt and F. B. M. de Wall, eds. Pp. 1–19. Oxford: Oxford University Press.

Whitten, N. E. 1976. *Sacha Runa: Ethnicity and Adaptation of Ecuadorian Jungle Quichua.* Urbana: University of Illinois Press.

Wright, R. 1994. *The Moral Animal. Why We Are the Way We Are: The New Science of Evolutionary Psychology.* New York: Vintage Books.

20

The Emergence and Stability of Cooperative Fishing on Ifaluk Atoll

RICHARD SOSIS

The evolution of cooperative hunting has been of immense interest to biologists and anthropologists. Biologists have observed cooperative hunting in numerous vertebrate and invertebrate species (see Packer and Ruttan 1988), and anthropologists have noted that human foragers often cooperate when hunting and fishing (see Hayden 1981). Cooperative hunting is frequently cited as a possible cause of sociality in humans and nonhuman species (e.g., Alexander 1974), although others have argued that cooperative hunting is a consequence rather than a cause of sociality (MacDonald 1983; Packer 1986; Packer et al. 1990). Anthropologists have suggested that cooperative hunting in hominids was a prominent factor in the evolution of human brain size and language (Washburn and Lancaster 1968), as well as the evolution of reciprocity in humans (Kurland and Beckerman 1985). Determining the ecological conditions under which selection pressures will favor cooperative food acquisition is essential for understanding the causes and consequences of cooperative foraging.

There are two components to the evolution of any cooperative behavior: emergence and stability. We can ask two questions to distinguish between the emergence and stability of cooperative hunting: When should a hunter join another hunter rather than hunt solitarily (emergence of cooperation)? and When should an individual free ride while others hunt cooperatively (stability of cooperation)? The goal of this paper is to test theoretical models of the emergence and stability of cooperative foraging using empirical data of cooperative sail-fishing activities on Ifaluk Atoll. Whereas prior models of the evolution of cooperative hunting have assumed that hunters share their returns equally among themselves or all group members (Boesch 1994; Packer 1988; Packer and Ruttan 1988), the models presented here will use empirically observed biases in the sharing patterns of fish in order to explain variance in male participation in cooperative fishing activities on Ifaluk.

EMERGENCE OF COOPERATIVE FORAGING

A number of factors are likely to influence the evolution of group foraging, such as resource defense (Crook 1972), vigilance and predator defense (Caraco and Pulliam 1984; Hamilton 1971), reproductive strategies (Wittenberger 1980), and foraging efficiency (Schoener 1971; see Pulliam and Caraco 1984; Slobodchikoff 1988; Smith 1981 for reviews of the benefits and costs of group foraging). Evolutionary ecologists have been particularly interested in determining the importance of foraging efficiency in the evolution of cooperative foraging, since natural selection is expected to produce foraging strategies that maximize the gain rate in time and energy limited organisms. Foraging return rates have been widely employed in optimal foraging models by anthropologists (see Kaplan and Hill 1992) and biologists (see Stephens and Krebs 1986) as a proximate currency that is assumed to be highly correlated with fitness. Two avenues for the evolution of cooperative foraging based in foraging efficiency have been proposed: variance reduction of average feeding rates (Caraco 1981; Clark and Mangel 1984; Real and Caraco 1986) and increase in average acquisition rates (Caraco 1987; Caraco and Wolf 1975; Pulliam and Millikan 1982). Greater attention has been given to the latter of these routes to cooperative foraging, and this paper will continue that trend.

Foragers are often expected to form foraging parties that maximize per capita net rate of energy capture. Following Smith (1981, 1983, 1985) we can algebraically define mean per capita net rate of energy capture as

$$R_n = \sum_{i=1}^{n} (E_a - E_e)/tn \tag{1}$$

where n is the foraging group size, t is the duration of the foraging acquisition event, and E_a and E_e are the energy acquired and the energy expended by each of the n members of the foraging group during time t.

A necessary condition for cooperative foraging to emerge is

$$R_n > R_1 \tag{2}$$

Thus, for cooperative foraging to emerge the mean per capita net return rate of n cooperative foragers must be greater than the mean per capita net solitary return rate.[1] Equation 2 assumes that individuals are free to decide whether to forage cooperatively or solitarily. Equation 2 does not need to hold for all n in order for cooperative foraging to be selected. In other words, the conditions for cooperative foraging to emerge may exist if there is a range of n (or only a single n) over which R_n is greater than R_1. For example, two fishermen on a large boat that they are not able to manage may have per capita fishing return rates much lower than if they were to fish alone on shore. However, the necessary conditions for cooperative foraging to emerge may exist if for some range, say 4–7 fishermen, the mean per capita net return rate of cooperative fishing is greater than the mean per capita solitary return rate.

Where cooperative foraging has emerged, there has been considerable interest in determining the optimal number of foragers in a foraging acquisition group (for reviews see Giraldeau 1988 and Smith 1991). Natural selection is expected to favor individuals who forage in groups of optimal size—in other words, groups that maximize mean resource acquisition rate and therefore genetic contribution (Pulliam and Caraco 1984). However, many studies have noted that the expectation to observe optimal group sizes among foragers may be unrealistic because of conflicts of interest between group members and individuals who want to join the group. Individuals are expected to join groups if they can increase their net benefits, which may result in a net decrease in benefits for those who are already group members (Clark and Mangel 1984; Hill and Hawkes 1983; Sibly 1983; Smith 1981). This insight has motivated researchers to determine the conditions under which cooperation is stable among a group of foragers.

STABILITY OF COOPERATIVE FORAGING

Even when the prerequisites for the emergence of cooperation are met, it is still necessary to determine the conditions under which cooperation will be stable (Axelrod and Hamilton 1981; Maynard Smith 1983). The ability of a free-riding strategy to invade a group of cooperators will determine the stability of cooperation. Two factors determine the success of a free riding strategy: the ability of cooperators to control a free rider's share of returns (e.g., Boesch 1994) and the ability of cooperators to impose costs on free riders (e.g., Boyd and Richerson 1992; Enquist and Leimar 1993; Hirshleifer and Coll 1988). Mesterton-Gibbons and Dugatkin (1992:270) have defined a "mechanism" for cooperation as a "principal effect whose removal would select for noncooperative behavior." Thus, the existence of a mechanism enabling cooperators to control a free rider's share of returns or impose costs on free riders is a necessary condition for the stability of cooperative foraging. Cooperation will be stable so long as the net benefits of participating (cooperating) in an acquisition event are greater than the net benefits of not participating (free riding).

As biologists have studied the conditions under which individuals cooperate, they have asked related questions concerning the stable coexistence of cooperator and noncooperator strategies. Producer-scrounger models have shown that producers (cooperators) and scroungers (noncooperators) can coexist in a stable environment as long as the net benefits received by scroungers are less than those of cooperators (Barnard 1984; Barnard and Sibly 1981; Vickery et al. 1991). These models suggest that cooperation will be evolutionarily stable when the average payoffs of pursuing cooperation are equal to the average payoffs of free-riding (cf. Higashi and Yamamura 1993; Rannala and Brown 1994).

The goal of this paper is to test theoretical models of the emergence and stability of cooperative foraging using empirical data of cooperative sail-fishing activities on Ifaluk Atoll. Following a brief ethnographic description, I will discuss the patterns and determinants of fish distribution on Ifaluk. Next I will evaluate whether cooperative fishing on Ifaluk meets the necessary conditions set in equation 2 for the emergence of cooperative foraging. Then, by assuming empirically observed biases in the fish distribution pattern, a model will be generated to predict the conditions under which an individual will join a cooperative pursuit. The model will be compared to observed fishing behavior on Ifaluk. The paper will conclude with a discussion of the results and directions for future inquiry.

ETHNOGRAPHIC BACKGROUND

Ifaluk is a small coral atoll (total land mass is 1.48 km^2 [Freeman 1951:237–238]) located in Yap State in the Caroline Islands of the Federated States of Micronesia.[2] Ifaluk consists of four atolls, two of which are inhabited: Falalop and Falachig. There are two villages on each of these atolls. Villages consist of 5–13 matrilocal compounds. The 36 compounds on Ifaluk range in size from 1 to 4 houses and 3 to 37 residents. Households are composed of either nuclear or extended families. The average number of residents on Ifaluk in 1995 was slightly more than 600.[3]

The residence pattern on Ifaluk is matrilocal. Although men reside at their wife's compound after marriage, they maintain a strong bond with the compound where they were raised, their natal compound. A man's bond to his natal compound is most prominently manifest in his responsibility to work for this compound. For example, as will be discussed below, men are expected to fish in cooperation with other men from their natal compound. Although men occasionally eat meals at their natal compound, they generally eat with their nuclear families at their residential compound.

METHODS

The data presented in this paper were collected from December 1994 through April 1995 on Ifaluk Atoll. During the field session I resided on Falalop atoll and collected observational data on fishing activities in Iyeur and Iyefang villages. I participated in 17 cooperative sail-fishing events, during which no quantitative data were collected. Table 20.1 presents the residential composition of compounds on Falalop.

The study population or risk set (i.e., those individuals who are at risk of participating in a cooperative sail-fishing event) consists of 60 males age 14 and older who either resided on Falalop atoll during the 1994–1995 field session or were raised on Falalop but resided on Falachig, typically as a result of marriage. The choice of excluding males younger than 14 from the risk set was not arbitrary.

Table 20.1. Residential composition and canoe ownership of Falalop compounds

village	*compound*	*number of males (≥14 yr.)*	*number of females (≥14 yr.)*	*number of children (<14 yr.)*	*own canoe*
Iyeur					
	Ilug	5	3	8	Y
	Harowchang	10	15	12	N
	Falichel	3	8	9	N
	Faligliow	1	7	3	Y
	Hawong	4	6	5	N
	village total:	**23**	**39**	**37**	
Iyefang					
	Imtaifou	3	4	2	N
	Woluwar	10	12	15	Y
	Falul	4	3	3	N
	Mataligob	2	5	6	Y
	Hapelmat	3	2	4	N
	Bwabwa	2	3	0	N
	Niwegitob	2	2	3	N
	village total:	**26**	**31**	**33**	
	atoll total:	**49**	**70**	**70**	

Although males younger than 14 often participate and contribute to cooperative fishing events, they are considered to be learning and not fully adult. They are never given any portion of the catch regardless of the distribution, and they are excluded from any men's feast.[4] There is a cultural precept that males are expected to fish on the canoe associated with the compound where they were raised (see below). Therefore, men who were raised in compounds on Falalop were included in the risk set since they are expected to fish on canoes owned by Falalop compounds, even if they currently reside on Falachig. Males that reside on Falalop who were raised on Falachig were also included in the risk set since they often fished on canoes from Falalop.

Observational data on solitary and cooperative sail-fishing were collected daily on Falalop from December 19 to April 5 with the exception of one week in March ($n = 98$ observation days). Every morning at 4:00 A.M. during this period I walked to the main canoe house on Falalop and waited for the men to commence cooperative fishing. I recorded which of the four canoes set sail, names of the fishermen on each canoe, and time of departure for each canoe. I was also at the canoe house when each canoe returned. I recorded the time of return for each canoe and the weight and species of each fish caught by canoe. Following the distribution of fish from the canoe house I reweighed all the fish and recorded where each fish was distributed. If inconsistencies were found between the first and second weighing, the fish were weighed a third time and the data were corrected accordingly. Sharon Feldstein monitored eight village-level (*felang*) and 24 compound-level (*shuliwa*) women's redistribution events. During her observations she recorded the names of the distributors, the weight and species of each share redistributed, and the name of the compound that received the share.

Solitary fishing activities occurred in the lagoon and were thus easily monitored because of their high visibility. Observation days were spent at one or several of the Falalop canoe houses that line the shore of the lagoon. All solitary fishing activities commenced from one of these canoe houses. Data collection activities that required me to leave the shoreline (e.g., spot observations) never caused me to lose sight of the lagoon for more than one half hour. Of 57 total solitary fishing events, data were missed during only 3 events. For each solitary fishing event I recorded the name of the solitary fisherman, the time of departure and return, and the weight and species of all fish caught. Data on the sharing patterns of solitarily acquired fish were recorded for 35 fishing events. I recorded the name of the recipient and the weight and type of species received.

The energetic costs of cooperative and solitary fishing were measured using the Energy Expenditure Prediction Program (EEPP) developed by the Center for Ergonomics at the University of Michigan. EEPP is a software program that predicts the energy expenditure of an individual engaged in an activity by calculating the metabolic energy expenditure of the sum of simple task elements of the activity (see Sosis 1997 for a more detailed description of EEPP and its use in this study). All statistical analyses were conducted using SAS.

RESULTS

Subsistence

The people of Ifaluk maintain a subsistence economy. The diet largely consists of pelagic and reef fish, taro, breadfruit, and coconut. Pigs, chickens, and dogs are also raised for consumption, but they are usually prepared only for bimonthly feasts. White rice is the most frequently purchased food product, although not all residents can afford it. There is no refrigeration on Ifaluk. Fish are occasionally smoked, but competition with the dogs, cats, and rats makes long-term storage difficult. For a more detailed description of subsistence on Ifaluk see Sosis 1997.

Fish is the primary source of protein and fats for the people of Ifaluk. Only males participate in fishing activities. Fishing on Ifaluk can be considered in two categories: solitary fishing and cooperative fishing. All solitary fishing methods exploit reef fish in Ifaluk's lagoon. During the observation period (n = 98 days), solitary fishing resulted in the capture of 62 different species of reef fish. The main type of solitary fishing during the trade wind season is line fishing with bait.[5] Octopus and land crabs are most frequently used as bait. Almost all males over 15 years of age own the solitary outrigger canoes used for line fishing. Spear and trap fishing were also observed during the trade wind season (see Burrows and Spiro 1957 for a description). During the observation period, only 15 of 45 males who stored their outrigger canoes on Falalop engaged in any form of solitary fishing, and their returns account for only 2.2% of the fish caught during this period.[6]

Cooperative sail-fishing accounts for 87.7% of all fish caught in the observation period (Sosis 1997). Most mornings during the trade wind season from October through May, males congregate at the central canoe hut on Falalop in preparation for the daily cooperative sail-fishing. After the canoes are prepared, all the males who are present help to push each canoe that will be sailing that morning into the lagoon. The canoes are then sailed outside the reef where the men fish for large pelagic fish such as yellow fin tuna, mahi mahi, and barracuda. Upon their return, the men throw their catch into a pile that is distributed by a divider after all the canoes have returned (see below).

There are four large sailing canoes on Falalop and eleven on Falachig. Each canoe is owned and maintained by a specific matriline, and hence compound. Each compound is historically associated with a particular canoe, and males are expected to fish on the canoe that is associated with the compound in which they were raised. Indeed, 86.4% (n = 815) of the observed time that males fished they sailed on the canoe that was associated with their natal compound. Although residence patterns are matrilocal, married men fished on the canoe associated with their wife's compound only 5.6% (n = 177) of the times they fished. Despite the consistency with which males adhere to cultural expectations, these rules appear flexible, especially when there are not enough males to man a particular canoe.

Distribution of solitarily acquired fish

Fish acquired by solitary means are the property of the fisherman. Some of the reef fish that men catch are taboo for women to eat. Often when these species are caught the fisherman will build a fire and cook the fish on the shore and invite any male over 14 years of age to join him in a small feast. During 54 observed solitary fishing events, 11 of the 62 species caught were taboo for women to eat, constituting 17.0% of the total weight of all solitarily acquired fish. An average of 76.8% (s.d. = 31.0%; n = 35) of fish caught by solitary means was consumed by the fisherman and his residential compound. During 19 of 35 observed sharing events, there was no sharing outside of the fisherman's residential compound.

Distribution of cooperatively acquired fish

There are a variety of distribution patterns for fish caught during cooperative fishing events. Betzig (1988) has previously described the fish distribution patterns on Ifaluk following cooperative net fishing, which occurs approximately once every two weeks during the summer. Here I will describe the fish distribution patterns following cooperative sail-fishing, which occurs exclusively in the trade wind season. Upon return from a morning's cooperative sail-fishing event, fishermen from each canoe throw their catch into a communal pile that is distributed after all the canoes return. On Falalop atoll, two men have the inherited responsibility of dividing the fish. The dividers determine the type of distribution and the amount of fish that is allocated to each recipient. During the 1994–1995 field session I observed five patterns of fish distribution following cooperative sail-fishing events on Falalop atoll. Multiple distribution types were often observed at the same distribution event. The five types are:

1. Canoe owner distribution (*shuliwa*): During a canoe owner distribution, compounds that own canoes receive the catch of their canoe. Table 20.1 shows which compounds own a canoe on Falalop atoll. A canoe-owning compound that receives fish subsequently redistributes the fish to other compounds, unless the catch is particularly small. Canoe-owning compounds retained an average of 59.7% (s.d. = 25.0%; *n* = 24) of the fish they produced. Redistributed fish are generally directed toward compounds where kin and men who fished on the canoe reside. Indeed, multiple regression analysis (Table 20.2) indicates that the number of males from a compound who fished on the canoe of the redistributing compound is a significant predictor of the amount of fish a compound receives from a canoe owner redistribution. Whether any resident of a compound is closely related to the matriarch or patriarch of the redistributing compound is a nearly significant predictor of the amount of fish received.
2. Village-level *ilet* distribution (*felang*): Villages on Ifaluk are composed of plots of land that are owned by the matriline of particular compounds. Plots of land each have an *ilet* value, which affects the flow of food resources contributed and received by the owners of the land. Plots are valued at 1 *ilet*, with the exception of two plots that are valued at 2 *ilet*. Ownership of land within a village is not restricted to compounds located in the village.

Table 20.2. Multiple regression analysis of the amount of fish (kg) received from canoe owner *re*distributions by compound
Full model F = 165.078, df = 3, p < .0001
$r^2 = .37$
n = 840 events

independent variable	*parameter estimate*	*standard error*	*p value*
number of fishermen from compound who fished on canoe of redistributing compound	1.2206	0.0643	<.0001
compound related*	0.0988	0.0585	0.0914
amount of fish (kg) initially distributed to canoe owning redistributing compound	0.001	0.0016	<.0001

*variable was input as 1 if anyone in the compound shared a coefficient of relatedness of 0.5 with the matriarch or patriarch of the redistributing compound, and 0 if nobody in the compound shared a coefficient of relatedness of 0.5 with matriarch or patriarch of the redistributing compound

Indeed, several compounds on Falachig atoll own land (and hence maintain *ilet*) within villages on Falalop atoll. On Falalop, compounds possess between one and three plots of land, and the total *ilet* maintained by compounds is also between one and three. Table 20.3 presents the number of *ilet* within Iyeur and Iyefang villages by compound and location of compound. There are 19 *ilet* in Iyeur (representing 184 residents) and 11 *ilet* in Iyefang (representing 135 residents). On Falalop, the number of *ilet* owned by a compound is positively correlated with the number of residents in the compound ($r = .72$, $p = .008$).

During a village-level *ilet* distribution fish are divided into two piles, one for Iyeur village and one for Iyefang village. From these piles each compound receives an amount of fish proportional to the number of *ilet* it possesses. The pile of fish for Iyeur village was typically slightly larger, but not proportional to the greater number of *ilet* or the greater number of residents represented by the *ilet* of Iyeur ($n = 17$ events, Iyeur mean = 69 kg, Iyefang mean = 63 kg).[7] One or two women from each compound that owns *ilet* within the village convene at their respective piles to cook and redistribute the fish. The eldest women present are in charge of the redistribution. The amount of fish that each compound receives is ideally deter-

Table 20.3. Number of *ilet* and compound location of compounds which possess *ilet* on Falalop Atoll

compound id number	*compound name*	*number of ilet in Iyeur*	*number of ilet in Iyefang*	*village of compound*
1	Imtaifou	1	1	Iyefang
2	Ilug	2	0	Iyeur
3	Harowchang	3	0	Iyeur
4	Falichel	2	0	Iyeur
5	Faligliow	2	0	Iyeur
6	Hawong	3	0	Iyeur
7	Woluwar	0	3	Iyefang
8	Falul	0	1	Iyefang
9	Mataligob	0	1	Iyefang
10	Hapelmat	0	1	Iyefang
11	Bwabwa	0	1	Iyefang
12	Niwegitob	2	0	Iyefang
13	Falfeliuw	1	0	Rawaii
14	Welipiye	1	0	Rawaii
15	Halingelou	1	0	Rawaii
16	Maiyefang	1	0	Mukulong
17	Hagotag	0	1	Rawaii
18	Hatibugot	0	1	Rawaii
19	Somat	0	1	Rawaii
	total:	19	11	

mined by the number of *ilet* that a compound possesses. Compounds that have 1 *ilet* expect to receive half as much fish from a redistribution as compounds that have 2 *ilet,* and one-third as much fish as compounds that have 3 *ilet.* For example, if a compound owns 2 *ilet* in Iyeur village, the compound expects to receive 2/19 of the total amount of fish received by Iyeur village.

As Figure 20.1 shows, the amount of fish that compounds actually received from observed village-level *ilet* distributions closely matches the amount of fish that compounds are predicted to receive. In other words, compounds with 2 *ilet* received roughly twice as much fish as compounds with 1 *ilet,* and compounds with 3 *ilet* received roughly three times as much fish as compounds with 1 *ilet.* In addition, only compounds that possess *ilet* within a village received fish from the redistribution. Compounds 1–12 are located on Falalop atoll and compounds 13–36 are located on Falachig atoll. These graphs show that compounds located on Falachig atoll tend to receive slightly less than predicted by a village-level *ilet* distribution and compounds located on Falalop atoll tend to receive slightly more than predicted by a village-level *ilet* distribution.

3. Atoll-level *ilet* distribution (*metalilet*): Similar to a village-level *ilet* distribution, in an atoll-level *ilet* distribution fish are distributed according to *ilet*. However, during an atoll-level *ilet* distribution fish are distributed directly from the canoe house to the compounds. Therefore, if as above a compound owns 2 *ilet* in Iyeur, the compound will receive 2/(19+11) or 1/15 of the total catch distributed via an atoll-level *ilet* distribution. Since Iyeur does not receive fish during a village-level *ilet* distribution proportional to the number of *ilet* in Iyeur (Iyeur on average receives 52.3% of the fish [n = 17] but maintains 63.3% of the *ilet*), compounds that have *ilet* located in Iyeur receive a greater proportion of the total catch during an atoll-level *ilet* distribution than during a village-level *ilet* distribution, whereas the converse is true of compounds that possess *ilet* in Iyefang village.
4. Fishermen distribution (*gagolagol*): Fish are distributed directly to males who fished on the canoe that caught the fish. Fish are subsequently cooked and consumed by the residential compound of the fisherman. Fishermen distributions apparently take two forms. In the first type fish are divided equally amongst all of the crew members (egalitarian distribution). In the second type fish are distributed separately to any residents of Falachig that participated in the fishing event (Falachig resident distribution).
5. Men's feast (*yafiileo/giubul*): Fish are cooked at the men's house and eaten by any male over 14 years old who desires to eat.

These distribution patterns can be classified as primary and secondary distribution types. The primary distribution types (canoe owner, village-level *ilet*, and atoll-

(a)

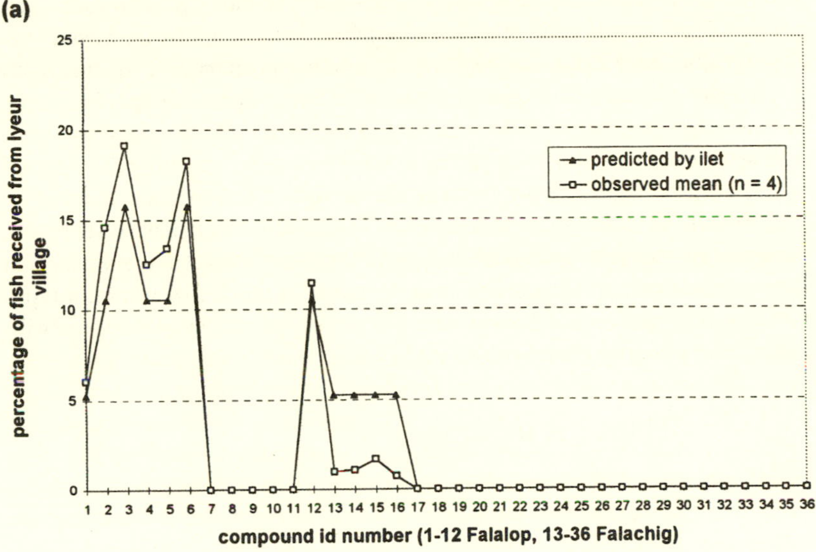

(b)

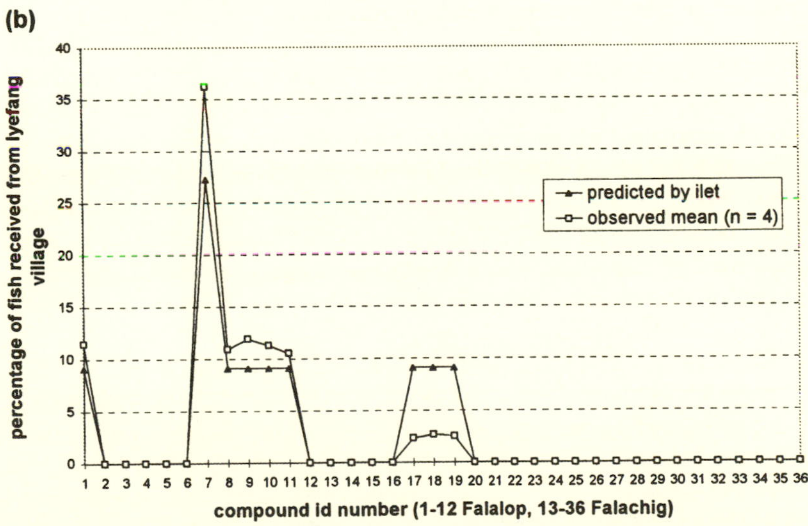

Figure 20.1. Predicted and observed percentage of fish received from village-level *ilet* redistribution to compounds from (a) lyeur village and (b) lyefang village.

level *ilet*) never co-occur, and nearly all distributions include one of these distribution types. The secondary distribution types (men's feast and fishermen distribution) generally occur in conjunction with one of the primary distribution types or with the other secondary distribution type. Table 20.4 presents the frequency that each distribution type was observed. The most frequently observed distribution type was the canoe-owner distribution, which occurred during 63.1% of all distribution events. Table 20.5 presents the percentage of fish that was distributed via each distribution type during the observation period. The primary distribution types account for more than 90% of the total fish distributed. Canoe-owner and village-level *ilet* distributions were clearly the most important distribution types observed. Together these distributions account for 80.9% of the total fish distributed and occur during 89.2% of all fish distributions.

Determinants of distribution of cooperatively acquired fish

Following a cooperative sail-fishing event, how do the dividers determine the distribution that will be used to disburse the catch? The most important determinant of distribution type appears to be the size of the catch. Figure 20.2 presents each distribution type by the total weight of fish caught.

Table 20.4. Frequency of fish distribution types observed on Falalop atoll following cooperative sail-fishing events

number of observation days = 98

		observed frequency
cooperative sail-fishing events		79
cooperative sail-fishing events with no catch		14
fish distribution events following cooperative sail-fishing		65
Distribution Types	*observed frequency*	*% of total distribution events*
canoe owner	23	35.4
canoe owner, men's feast	16	24.6
canoe owner, men's feast, Falachig resident	1	1.5
canoe owner, men's feast, egalitarian	1	1.5
village-level *ilet*	6	9.2
village-level *ilet*, men's feast	6	9.2
village-level *ilet*, men's feast, Falachig resident	4	6.2
village-level *ilet*, Falachig resident	1	1.5
men's feast	3	4.6
men's feast, egalitarian	1	1.5
atoll-level *ilet*, men's feast, Falachig resident	3	4.6

Table 20.5. Total amount of fish distributed following cooperative sail-fishing events by distribution type ($n = 65$ distribution events)

distribution type	*total amount distributed (kg)*	*percentage of total amount distributed*
canoe owner	1271.5	27.9
village-level *ilet*	2411.3	53.0
atoll-level *ilet*	445.4	9.8
Falachig resident	82.7	1.8
egalitarian	23.5	0.5
men's feast	316.8	7.0
total:	4551.2	100.00

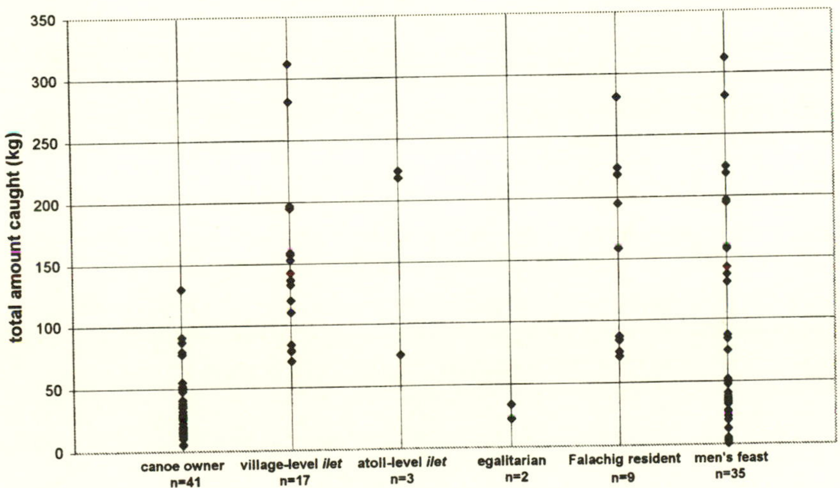

Figure 20.2. Total amount caught by distribution type (n = 65 distribution events).

Primary distribution types Figure 20.2 shows that when the catch is small, fish are distributed via canoe owner distributions, and when the catch is large, fish are distributed via *ilet* distributions. Table 20.6 presents the results of a logistic regression procedure where primary distribution type (canoe owner or *ilet*) is the response variable, and the total weight of the catch, number of fishermen, number of canoes that fished, and number of fish caught are predictor variables. The results show that the total weight of the catch is a significant predictor of whether a distribution is either a canoe-owner or an *ilet* distribution. The number of fishermen, number of canoes, and the number of fish caught do not have independent significant effects on the distribution type. Figure 20.3 indicates that the total amount caught is a function of the number of males who fish.

Table 20.6. Logistic regression analysis of the probability of a distribution type occurring dependent variable: distribution type
canoe owner distribution = 0
ilet distribution (village-level or atoll-level) = 1

independent variable	*parameter estimate*	*standard error*	*p value*
–2 log likelihood for model covariates = 56.2; $p < .0001$			
df = 4			
$n = 60$*			
total amount caught (kg)	0.0625	0.0238	**0.0085**
total number of fish caught	0.0858	0.0529	0.1051
number of canoes	0.6137	1.4381	0.6696
number of fishermen	–0.1434	0.3817	0.7071

*data on number of fishermen is missing for 1 event

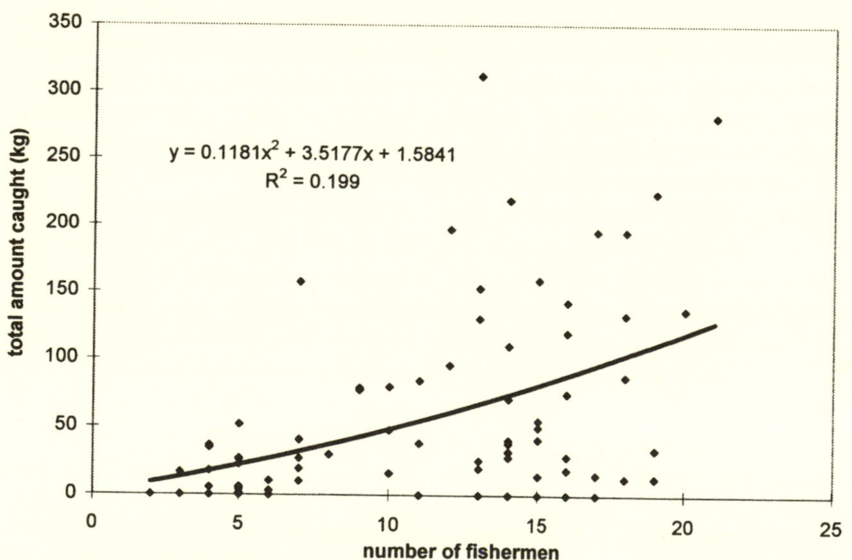

Figure 20.3. Total amount caught for 78 cooperative sail-fishing events by number of fishermen ($F = 9.34$, $p <.001$, df = 2).

Although the current data set does not show a significant difference in the size of the catch when village-level or atoll-level *ilet* distributions occur, I expect that with an increased sample size the data would show that the largest catches are distributed via atoll-level *ilet* distributions. However, the main distinguishing feature between village-level and atoll-level *ilet* distributions is the divisibility of the catch, i.e., the number of fish caught. The range of the number of fish caught when fish were distributed via village-level *ilet* distributions was 9–39 with a mean of 18.1 (n = 17 events), whereas the range of the number of fish caught when fish were distributed via an atoll-level *ilet* distribution was 52–267 with a mean of 126.3 (n = 3 events). If there are enough fish to distribute via an *ilet* distribution without any processing, fish are distributed by the men via atoll-level *ilet* distributions. If not, fish are cut, cooked, and distributed by the women via village-level *ilet* distributions.

Secondary distribution types Egalitarian distributions occur when the total weight of the fish caught is small, but the number of fish caught is large (i.e., prey size is small). The total weight of the catch for the two observed egalitarian distributions was 33.8 kg and 22.4 kg. If we consider all distributions where the total catch weighed 20–35 kg, it is clear that there is a significant difference between the number of fish caught when fish are distributed via egalitarian versus other distributions. The total number of fish caught during each of the egalitarian distributions was 48, whereas the total catch from the nine other distributions (20–35 kg each) ranged from 3 to 5 fish, with a mean of 3.7.

Falachig resident distributions occurred only when a male from Falachig fished and a large quantity of fish was caught. Eight of the nine Falachig distributions occurred in conjunction with an *ilet* type of distribution. In other words, Falachig resident distributions compensated Falachig fishermen for their fishing effort under conditions where they would otherwise not receive fish, since Falachig residents are unlikely to reside in compounds that possess *ilet* on Falalop.

Although Figure 20.2 shows that men's feasts occur for all catch sizes, they are more likely to occur when the total amount caught is large. Men's feasts occurred during 11 of 12 events (92%) where the total catch was >125 kg, and only 24 of 53 events (45%) where the total catch was ≤125 kg. When men's feasts occur, they account for only 10.0% (n = 35) of the fish distributed.

To summarize the primary distribution pattern, if few fish are caught, compounds that own canoes receive the catch of their canoe. These compounds typically retain most of the catch. Fish that are redistributed are primarily directed towards compounds where related kin and males who fished on the canoe of the redistributing compound reside. If the size of the catch is large, fish will be distributed throughout the atoll either via village-level or atoll-level *ilet* distributions. Regardless of whether or not an individual cooperatively fished, he (or more specifically, his residential compound) will receive a fixed percentage of the fish distributed. Secondary distribution patterns account for less than 10% of all fish distributed and appear to be aimed at rewarding those who fished (egalitarian and Falachig resident) as well as assuring that all men can eat a meal of fish regardless of their effort or fishing success (men's feast).

The fish distribution patterns following cooperative sail-fishing events are a mix of investment-based distribution types (canoe-owner, egalitarian, and Falachig resident), which reward men who fish, and population-wide distributions (*ilet*), which ensure that all residents, or at least all male residents (in the case of men's feasts), receive fish regardless of their participation in production. If fish are caught, men who fished ordinarily receive some of the catch. Free riders can only expect to receive fish for their families infrequently; population-wide distributions (village-level or atoll-level *ilet*) occurred in only 30.8% of all observed distributions. Thus, although there is potential for free riding when fish are distributed to all residents on the atoll, the investment-based distribution types limit the success of a free riding strategy.

EMERGENCE OF COOPERATIVE FISHING ON IFALUK

Sail-fishing on Ifaluk meets the necessary conditions set in equation 2 for the emergence of cooperative foraging. The mean per capita cooperative sail-fishing production rate is 1.57 kg/hr (36 individuals, 980 events) and the mean per capita solitary fishing (all types of solitary fishing) production rate is 0.86 kg/hr (12 individuals,[8] 54 events). The energetic costs of cooperative and solitary fishing were measured using the EEPP and calculated as 4.7 kcal/min and 4.9 kcal/min, respectively. There are 1,080 calories in 1 kilogram of raw yellow fin tuna (Genesis R&D Nutrition and Labeling Software), which was the primary species of fish caught cooperatively (89% of the total kilograms of fish caught cooperatively was yellow fin tuna [n = 79 events]). For solitary fishing, since there are 62 different species in my sample, an average of the caloric values of 5 species of reef fish (1,074 kcal) was used as an estimate of the caloric value of reef fish. Thus, the mean per capita net production rate of cooperative sail-fishing is 1,408.8 kcal/hr and the mean per capita net production rate of solitary fishing is 630.0 kcal/hr. This difference is significant ($t = 7.11$, df = 156.6, $p < .0001$). The mean per capita net cooperative sail-fishing production rate of the 12 solitary fishermen is 1,467.6 kcal/hr (355 events), which is also significantly higher than the mean per capita net solitary production rate of those men ($t = 5.79$, df = 300.5, $p < .0001$).

However, as a result of the biases in the distribution patterns described above, cooperation may not emerge if men who fish cooperatively have lower consumption rates than men who fish alone. By assuming the empirically observed distribution patterns, the consumption rates for cooperative and solitary fishing were calculated as the amount of fish received by ego's residential compound divided by the amount of time ego fished. Based on my personal observations, I am assuming that the within-compound sharing patterns are the same for fish caught cooperatively or solitarily. The mean per capita net consumption rate for cooperative fishing is –139.8 kcal/hr (36 individuals, 950 events) and the mean per capita net solitary fishing production rate is –254.6 kcal/hr (8 individuals, 35 events). This difference is significant ($t = 11.57$, df = 94.5, $p < .0001$). The mean per capita net cooperative sail-fishing consumption rate of the 12 solitary fishermen is –130.7 kcal/hr (397 events), which is also significantly higher than the mean per capita solitary production rate ($t = 9.94$, df = 193.3, $p < .0001$).[9]

STABILITY OF COOPERATIVE FISHING ON IFALUK

Cooperative fishing on Ifaluk will be stable as long as the net benefits of cooperation outweigh the net benefits of not cooperating. Given the bias in the sharing patterns on Ifaluk, these conditions will vary considerably between individuals. When a man decides whether or not to fish it is assumed that he makes this decision based on an evaluation of his expected payoff—in other words, the fitness gains that he can expect given the way that fish he produces will be distributed. In many cases this will be a monotonically increasing function of the net kilograms of fish that he and his close kin will consume as a result of his fishing effort. This assumption is adopted in the model below. Here I assume the sharing pattern and its determinants rather than try to explain it.

Fishing is a probabilistic activity with high variance in returns even for the most skilled fishermen. Environmental cues such as rainfall, wind patterns, strength of the tide, and the amount that was caught on the previous day can indicate better or worse fishing conditions; however, a fisherman does not know beforehand what his actual returns will be. Under the cooperative conditions of fishing on Ifaluk, environmental cues must also be coupled with knowledge of how others will respond to these cues for a fisherman to assess what his actual return rate will be.

For each male at risk to participate in a cooperative fishing event, there is an amount of fish that he expects to receive given the amount of fish that are caught, the distribution type, and whether or not he participated in the event. For each number of fishermen there is some probability that a specific distribution type will occur. Knowledge of these parameters will enable us to calculate a male's expected payoff in nutritional gains if he fishes or does not fish for each number of fishermen. We anticipate that when a male's expected payoff for cooperative sail-fishing is greater than his expected payoff for not cooperating he will fish cooperatively. Thus, we expect individual k to join a group of n fishermen if

$$Y_{ck}(n + 1) > Y_{dk}(n) \tag{3}$$

where Y_{ck} = individual k's net caloric gain from participating in a cooperative sail-fishing event and Y_{dk} = individual k's net caloric gain from not participating in a cooperative sail-fishing event. This model assumes that:

1. Individuals are free to decide whether or not to participate in any cooperative sail-fishing event.
2. Individual decisions to join or leave a group of fishermen are independent (i.e., the model is static).
3. Individual decisions to join or leave a group of fishermen are only based on an evaluation of individual caloric intake. The additional caloric benefits accrued by kin are not included in the model.
4. Individuals possess accurate knowledge of how their caloric payoffs vary with the number of participants in a cooperative fishing event.

This model additionally assumes that individuals know the number of members in the group they are deciding whether or not to join. Under the conditions of cooperative fishing on Ifaluk, this assumption appears to be violated; individuals do not know exactly how many men will be fishing until they arrive at the canoe house in the morning. However, it seems likely that the same ecological cues that indicate the quality of the fishing conditions are also used to determine how many others will fish on a given morning. Therefore, it is reasonable to assume that men can assess with some accuracy how many males will fish on a given day. For example, the total amount that was caught on the previous day appears to be an important determinant of individual fishing decisions. Table 20.7 presents the results of a logistic regression analysis where the dependent variable is whether or not an individual fished and the independent variable is the total amount of fish caught on the previous day. The results indicate that, controlling for participation on the previous day, the total amount caught on the previous day is a significant positive predictor of cooperative sail-fishing participation. In other words, if the catch on the previous day was large, it is probably a reliable indication that fishing returns will be favorable today. It is also probably one of many cues used to assess the number of men that will fish on a given day.[10]

Table 20.7. Logistic regression analysis of the probability of cooperative sail-fishing

independent variable	*parameter estimate*	*standard error*	*p value*
−2 log likelihood for model covariates = 871.3, $p < .0001$			
df = 2			
n = 4999			
total amount of fish caught (kg) on previous day	0.0042	0.0006	**<.0001**
fishing status on previous day	2.6224	0.0963	<.0001
participated in cooperative fishing event = 1			
did not participate in cooperative fishing event = 0			

The currency of this model is the net gain rate per day. The return rate per hour is often the currency of choice among evolutionary ecologists; however, if free riding is an available strategy (resources can be acquired without time investment), return rate per hour is not an interpretable currency. Therefore, the difference between output (caloric gains) and input (caloric expenditure) was used as a currency to measure individual fitness gains, which is simply the return rate per day.

Given knowledge of the distribution patterns as well as the frequency of distribution types across number of fishermen,[11] we can more accurately define equation 3 as

$$\sum_{s=c,v,a,r,m} [P_s(n+1) \times I_{sfk}(n+1)] \times T_k - E_k > \sum_{s=c,v,a,r,m} [P_s(n) \times I_{sdk}(n)] \times T_k \tag{4}$$

where:

P_s = probability of a distribution type occurring

I_{sfk} = caloric gains individual k's residential compound expects to receive from a distribution type if k fishes

I_{sdk} = caloric gains individual k's residential compound expects to receive from a distribution type if k does not fish

c = canoe owner distribution

v = village-level *ilet* distribution

a = atoll-level *ilet* distribution

r = Falachig resident distribution

m = men's feast

E_k = individual k's cooperative sail-fishing expected energy expenditure

T_k = consumer ratio, proportion of fish received by individual k's residential compound that individual k consumes

We can consider equation 4 in two parts. The left-hand side of the equation is individual k's expected payoff if he fishes and the right-hand side is k's expected payoff if he does not fish. The expected caloric gains if individual k fishes (LHS) is the probability of a distribution type occurring as a function of the number of fishermen if k fishes, multiplied by the expected caloric payoff of individual k for the distribution type, as a function of the number of fishermen if individual k fishes. Since fish are given to compounds and not directly to individuals (with the exception of the men's feast)[12] distribution types must be multiplied by the proportion of fish received by individual k's residential compound that k will consume, T_k, which is called the consumer ratio. It is assumed that food is shared equitably within a compound but that an individual will consume an amount of fish in relation to his or her age, sex, and weight.[13] The five distribution-type payoff probabilities are summed and the expected caloric expenditure of individual k is subtracted from this value. Individual k's expected payoff if he does not fish (RHS) is calculated as the probability of a distribution type occurring as a function of the number of fishermen if he does not fish, multiplied by the expected caloric payoff of individual k for the distribution type, as a function of the number of fishermen if individual k does not fish. As on the LHS of equation 4, the distribution payoff probabilities must be multiplied by k's consumer ratio and all five distribution-type payoff probabilities are summed.

Distribution type as a function of number of fisherman

In order to test the model presented for the stability of cooperation empirically it is necessary to calculate the hazard of a distribution type as a function of the number of fishermen. The hazard is simply the probability that an event will occur given that it is possible for the event to occur. Hazard functions were calculated for each distribution type using data from 78 observed cooperative sail-fishing events.[14] Figures 20.4a–e present the probability of a distribution type occurring by the number of men that participate in a cooperative sail-fishing event. Functions were calculated as the least squares fit for the data using a set of linear and second-order polynomial functions. Figure 20.4a shows that the probability of a canoe-owner distribution occurring decreases linearly as the number of fishermen increases. The function that depicts this trend, $y = -.0165x + .6977$, was put into equation 4 as $P_c(x)$, where x is the number of men who participate in a cooperative fishing event. Similarly, the function $y = .0263x – .0768$, which characterizes the probability of a village-level *ilet* distribution occurring by number of fishermen (see Figure 20.4b, was put into equation 4 as $P_v(x)$. Figures 20.4c–e present the functions that characterize the probability of atoll-level *ilet*, men's feast, and Falachig resident distributions occurring by number of fishermen, respectively. These functions were entered into equation 4 as $P_a(x)$, $P_r(x)$, and $P_m(x)$, respectively.

Mean share of returns by distribution type

Individuals from different compounds expect to receive a different share of the catch for a given distribution type. Using quantitative data on the amount distributed to each compound following cooperative sail-fishing events, a function was calculated for each residential compound of the 60 men in the risk set for each distribution type.

Canoe owner distribution Figure 20.5a presents the average amount of fish received by compound 4 from a canoe-owner distribution by number of fishermen. It was shown above (Table 20.2) that participation affects the amount of fish that an individual can expect to receive via a canoe-owner distribution. Therefore the data in Figure 20.5a are separated by whether or not any resident of the compound participated in the fishing event. The functions that describe the data shown in Figure

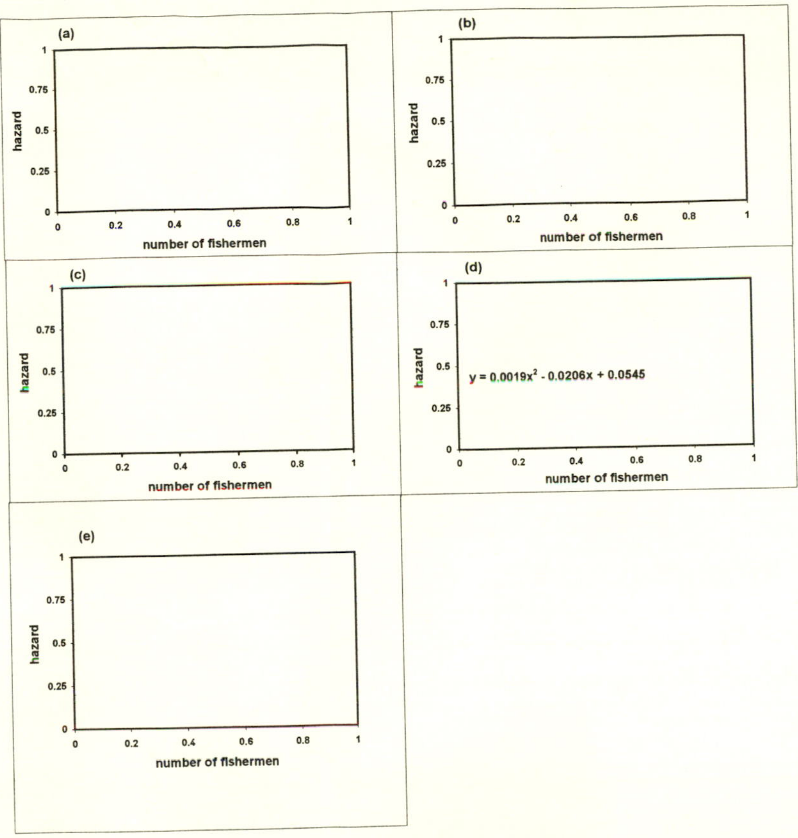

Figure 20.4. The hazard of a (a) canoe owner, (b) village-level *ilet*, (c) atoll-level *ilet*, (d) Falachig resident, and (e) men's feast distribution as a function of the number of men who participate in a cooperative sail-fishing event. These functions were put into equation 4 as $P_c(x)$, $P_v(x)$, $P_a(x)$, $P_r(x)$, and $P_m(x)$, respectively.

20.5a are curvilinear with a peak between ten and eleven fishermen. As more men participate in a cooperative fishing event, fish are not likely to be distributed via a distribution unless the catch is particularly small. The polynomial functions that characterize the data in Figure 20.5a (as well as the functions calculated for each compound, which are not presented here) were put into equation 4 as $I_{cfk}(x)$ and $I_{cdk}(x)$, respectively. Although the absolute amount of fish received from canoe-owner distributions by each compound varies, the shape of the functions that characterize the data (i.e., curvilinear with a peak around 10 fishermen) is similar for all compounds.

Because of a lack of data on fishing activity by residents of several compounds, canoe owner distribution data had to be averaged across a set of variables that

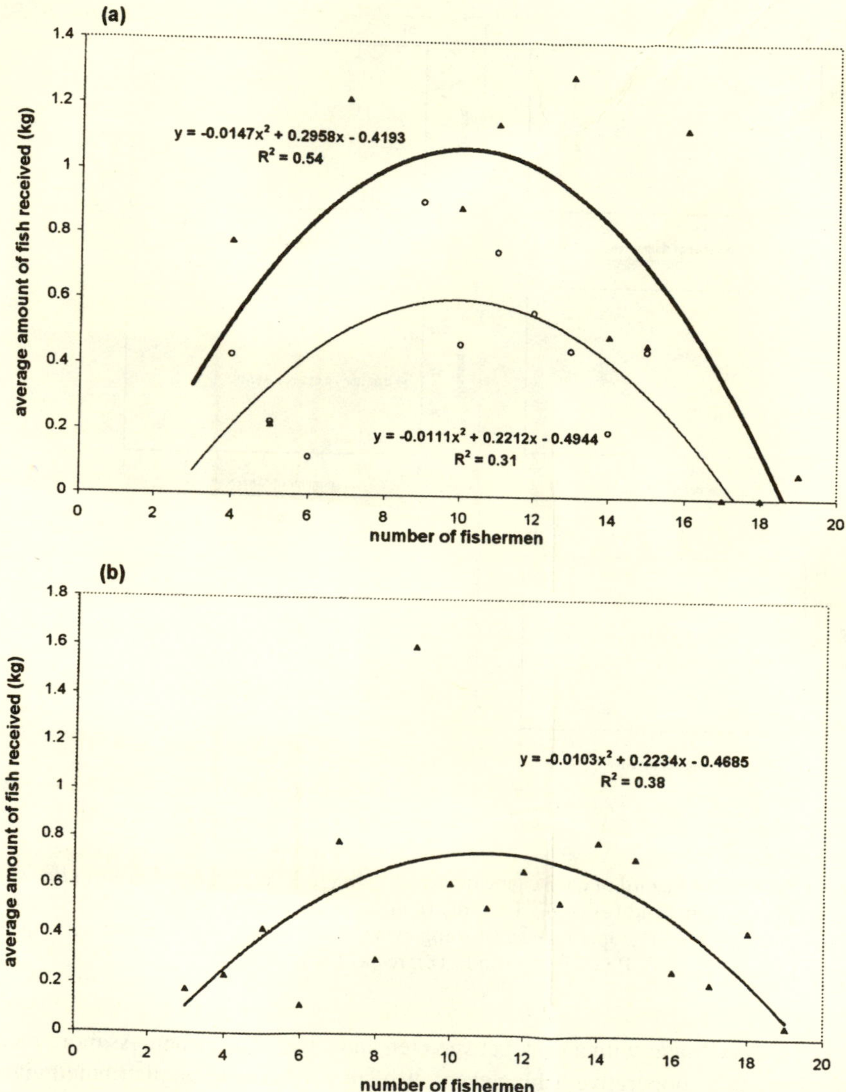

Figure 20.5. (a) Average amount of fish received by compound 4 from canoe owner *redistribution* by total number of fishermen. Data are separated by events when 1 or more men from compound 4 fished (solid triangles and thick line), and events when no men from compound 4 fished (open circles and thin line). (b) Average amount of fish received by non-canoe-owning compounds on Falalop from canoe owner *redistribution* if 1 or more males from compound fishes, by total number of fishermen.

characterize the compound. For example, no male residents of compound 8 ever cooperatively sail-fished. Therefore we do not know what function describes the relationship between expected returns of compound 8 and the number of fishermen when someone from compound 8 fishes. In this and similar circumstances data were combined across two variables: whether or not the compound owned a canoe, and location of compound, either Falalop or Falachig atoll. Compound 8 is a non–canoe-owning compound located on Falalop. Figure 20.5b presents the average amount of fish received by all non–canoe-owning compounds located on Falalop atoll when one resident from the compound participated in a cooperative sail-fishing event. The function $y = -.0103x^2 + .2234x - .4685$, which describes the combined data, was put into equation 4 for compound 8 as $I_{cfk}(x)$. This appears to be the most parsimonious solution to the problem of nonparticipation in estimating expected payoffs; individuals that never cooperatively fish can only know what their payoffs would be through knowledge of what others are receiving when they fish.

Village-level ilet *distribution* Figure 20.6a presents the average amount of fish received from a village-level *ilet* distribution by number of fishermen for compound 7. The data are characterized by the function $y = -0.004x^2 + 1.708 - 1.1$. For compound 7, this function was put into equation 4 as $I_{vfk}(x)$ and $I_{vdk}(x)$. The shape of the function that characterizes the data in Figure 20.6a is similar for all compounds, although each compound will have a distinct function that characterizes the amount of fish the compound receives during a village-level *ilet* distribution. It is not necessary to calculate separate functions that are dependent upon whether or not anyone from compound 7 cooperatively fished. Participation has no effect on the amount of fish that a compound will receive for village-level *ilet*, atoll-level *ilet*, or men's feast distributions (although the addition of one fisherman will increase the expected amount caught, and hence the amount distributed).

Atoll-level ilet *distribution* Atoll-level *ilet* distributions were only observed three times during the observation period. Therefore, the data are insufficient to determine what function characterizes the relationship between the amount received during an atoll-level *ilet* distribution and the number of fishermen. For each compound the mean percentage received of the total amount distributed via atoll-level *ilet* distributions was calculated and entered into equation 4 as $I_{afk}(x)$ and $I_{adk}(x)$.

Falachig resident distribution Males at risk of receiving fish from a Falachig resident distribution are assumed to receive equal amounts of fish as a function of the number of fishermen. In other words, in contrast to other distribution types, it was assumed that there is no variation in the amount received by residential compounds of Falachig fishermen via Falachig resident distributions. This assumption is necessary because of the small number of Falachig resident distributions (n =

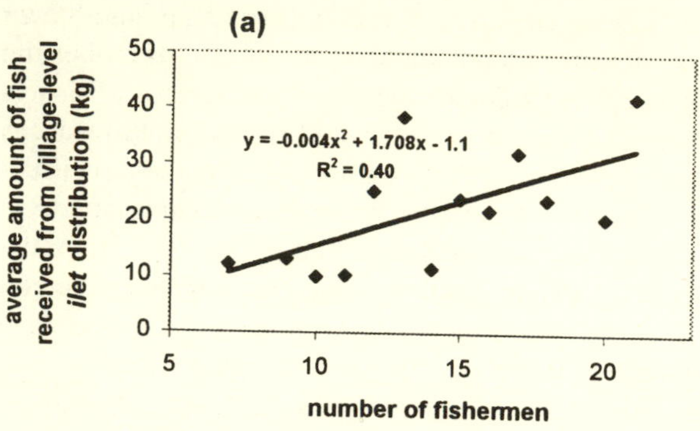

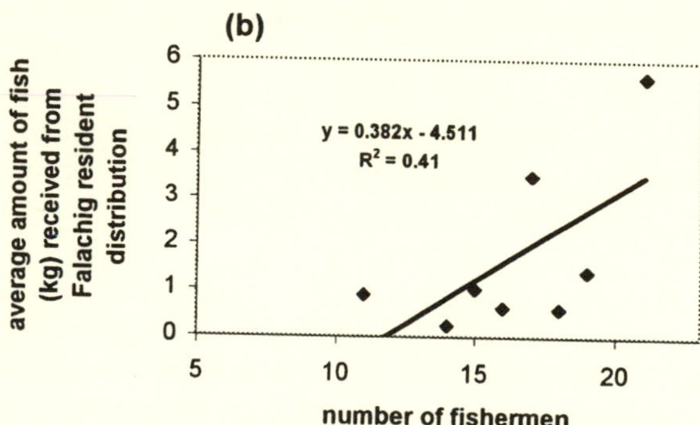

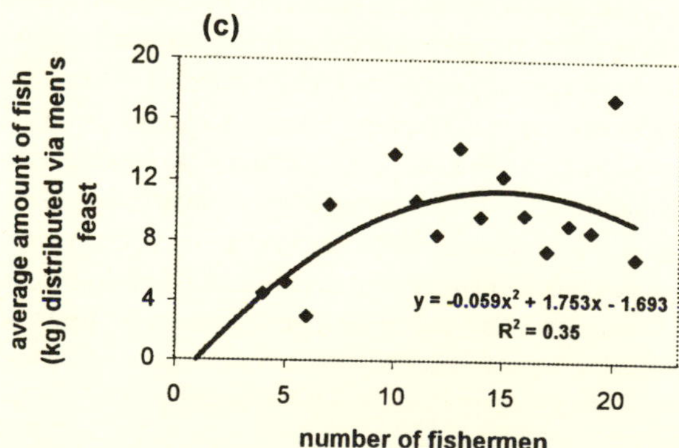

Figure 20.6. (a) Average amount of fish received from village-level *ilet* distribution by number of fishermen for compound 7 (n = 17 events). (b) Average amount of fish received from Falachig resident distribution by number of fishermen (n = 9 events). (c) Average amount of fish distributed via men's feast by number of fishermen (n = 35 events).

9), however, since there was no expectation of a systematic bias in the amount received by Falachig residents at the observed distributions (e.g., if two Falachig residents fished, their residential compounds would receive an equal quantity of fish), it is unlikely that an increased sample size of Falachig resident distribution events would affect this assumption. Figure 20.6b shows the average amount of fish received by a Falachig compound from a Falachig resident distribution by number of fishermen. The function, that characterizes this data, $y = 0.382x - 4.511$, was entered into equation 4 as $I_{rfk}(x)$ for those individuals at risk of receiving fish via a Falachig resident distribution. $I_{rdk}(x)$ is always zero since a Falachig resident must fish in order to receive fish via a Falachig resident distribution.

Men's feast. Figure 20.6c presents the relationship between the amount distributed via men's feasts and the number of participants in the fishing event. This function, $y = -0.059x^2 + 1.753 \times -1.693$, multiplied by the ratio $\frac{1}{N}$, where N is the total number of men at risk of partaking in a men's feast, was entered into equation 4 as $I_{mfk}(x)$ and $I_{mdk}(x)$ (see note 12). It was assumed that there is an equal probability of any male who is at risk of cooperative sail-fishing of partaking in a men's feast, regardless of whether or not they actually fished.[15]

Energetic Expenditure

As stated above, males on average expend 4.7 cal/min during cooperative sail-fishing. Males on average cooperatively sail-fished 179.7 minutes per event, thus expending 844.6 calories per event. In most traditional societies, protein is valued more than alternative calorie sources such as carbohydrates because of its scarcity or expense of acquisition. On Ifaluk we are able to determine precisely how much more protein is valued than carbohydrates because both can be assigned a monetary value. Parents of children enrolled at the Head Start program on Ifaluk can sell food for cash to Head Start (the option of providing food is rotated between parents). Food is sold raw and subsequently cooked by Head Start employees. The primary starch of the winter season is taro. Parents are paid \$0.65 /lb. of taro (485.3 kcal) and \$1.20 /lb. of fish (489.9 kcal). Thus, parents can receive one dollar for 408.2 kcal of fish or 746.6 kcal of taro. Therefore we assume that a unit of carbohydrate holds .547 the value of a unit of protein. Although males on average expend 844.6 kcal during a cooperative sail-fishing event, this must be multiplied by .547 when subtracted from gains in the currency of fish calories, owing to the higher value of fish relative to carbohydrate calories on Ifaluk.[16]

Results of the Model

Expected payoff curves were generated from equation 4 for each of the 60 males at risk of cooperative sail-fishing. Males from the same compound have similar expected payoff curves since fish are distributed to compounds and not directly to individuals, with the exception of men's feasts. However, the variance in expected payoffs of males from different compounds is high. Each individual at risk has two payoff curves: one if he fishes and one if he does not fish. Figure 20.7 shows a range of expected payoffs that males face. Notice that each set of payoff curves generates a different prediction concerning when a male will and will not fish. From Figure 20.7a we predict that male 209 from compound 7 will always fish since his payoff curve for fishing is always greater than his payoff curve for not fishing. Male 273 from compound 10 is predicted not to fish if fewer than 16 other males fish, but he should always fish if he expects that 16 or more males will fish (Figure 20.7b). Male 157 from compound 18 is never expected to fish (Figure 20.7c) and male 316 from compound 33 is predicted to fish only if he expects 17 or more others to fish (Figure 20.7d). We can also predict in Figures 20.7a–d that as the distance between the payoff curves increases a male's payoffs for alternative decisions will become less ambiguous, and hence motivation will increase to either fish, if the difference is positive, or not fish, if the difference is negative.

All payoff curves for the 60 males at risk of cooperative sail-fishing are monotonically increasing. This is important because it implies that over the observed range of fishermen (2–21) there is no conflict between joiners and members. A member will always expect to receive higher payoffs if another male wants to join the fishing party. This is consistent with my observations that no male was ever turned away from a fishing event, and once at the canoe house no male ever decided not to fish, as long as men took out a canoe.[17]

The model predictions can be compared with observed fishing behavior. Logistic regression analyses were conducted to test whether the model was a significant predictor of cooperative foraging decisions. The risk set for the analyses consists of the number of males at risk of participating in a cooperative sail-fishing event multiplied by the number of cooperative sail-fishing days. Over the 79 cooperative sail-fishing days, the number of males at risk (see "Methods") changed 11 times and ranged between 50 and 60 men as a result of individuals arriving and departing from Ifaluk. Thus, the total risk set consists of 4,083 person days. The dependent variable of the model is whether or not an individual fished. The independent variable was generated from the model as the difference in an individual's expected payoff curves between fishing and not fishing. As the difference between the payoff curves increases, males should have greater motivation either to fish, if the difference is positive, or to not fish, if the difference is negative. Results of the logistic procedure presented in Table 20.8 indicate that the model is a highly significant positive predictor of male cooperative fishing decisions. The effect on cooperative fishing participation of the expected difference between an individual's payoff curves is substantial. For example, if the difference in payoff curves is -250 kcal, the hazard of cooperative fishing is 0.06, whereas if the difference in payoff curves is 250 kcal the hazard is 0.39.

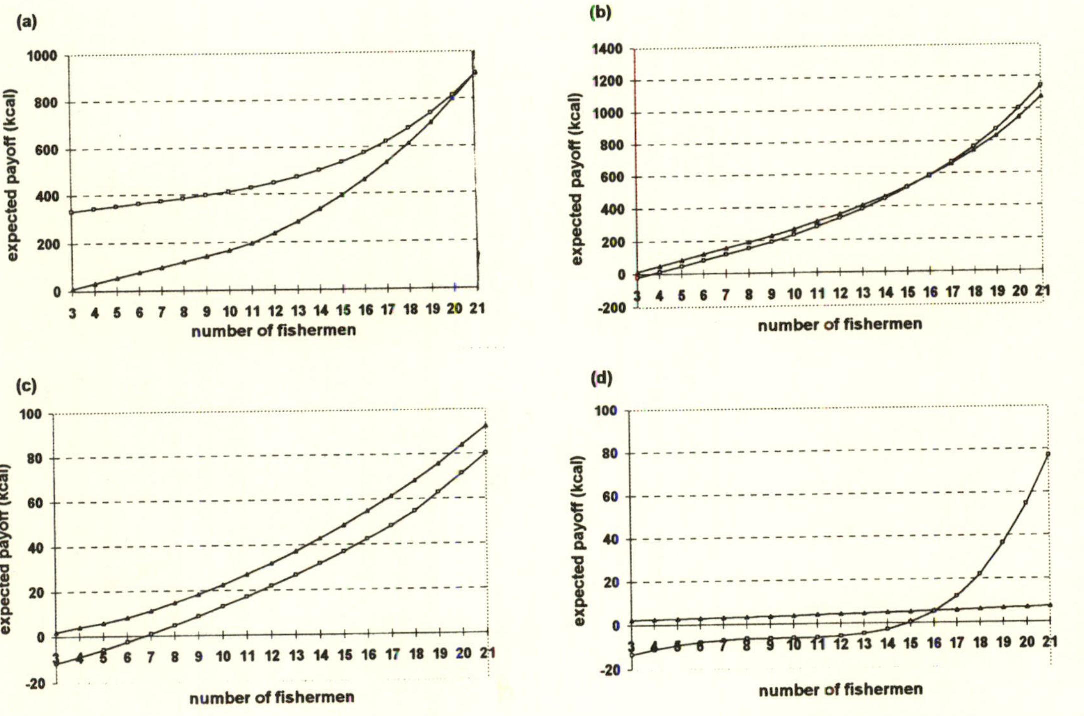

Figure 20.7. Expected caloric payoff by number of fishermen for (a) male id #209 of compound 7, (b) male id #273 of compound 10, (c) male id #157 of compound 18, and (d) male id #316 of compound 33. Expected caloric payoffs when only 2 men fish are not shown since they are identical for all males (no fish were ever caught when only 2 men fished). Solid triangles denote the payoffs for not fishing and open squares denote the payoffs for fishing. The scale of the y-axes are not the same in each graph.

Table 20.8. Logistic regression analysis of the probability of cooperative sail-fishing

independent variable	*parameter estimate*	*standard error*	*p value*
–2 log likelihood for model covariates = 167.06, $p < .0001$			
df = 1			
$n = 4083$			
difference between cooperative fishing and not fishing expected payoff (kcal)	0.0045	0.0004	**<.0001**

DISCUSSION

Emergence of Cooperative Fishing on Ifaluk

The simple model (equation 2) presented above as a necessary condition for the emergence of cooperative foraging is consistent with our observations of fishing on Ifaluk. The per capita net production and consumption rates of cooperative sail-fishing are significantly greater than the per capita net production and consumption rates of solitary fishing. Given the twofold difference between solitary and cooperative production rates, why does solitary fishing occur at all? First, the weather conditions necessary for the success of both production activities are mutually exclusive. Cooperative sail-fishing requires strong winds and tide, whereas solitary fishing can only occur when the winds and tide are calm. Thus, when the winds and tide are calm we expect the mean solitary fishing return rate to be much higher than the mean cooperative sail-fishing return rate. Second, only five males fished alone three or more times. Most males that attempted to solitary fish may have simply been trying their luck. Because schools of fish constantly move in and out of the lagoon where solitary fishing occurs, it may be worthwhile to occasionally assess the profitability of solitary fishing.

It is often argued that Western influences such as individualism and capitalism have negative effects on the cooperative social structure of traditional societies (e.g., Bethlehem 1975; Meeker 1970). In many cases this may be true. Within Yap State, Ifaluk is the only atoll where men still regularly fish cooperatively. The most obvious explanation for the breakdown of cooperative fishing on the other atolls is the introduction of motor boats and freezers, both of which the chiefs have prohibited on Ifaluk. Motor boats can be operated solitarily with very high return rates, and large catches can be stored in a freezer for long-term consumption. My results suggest, however, that westernization may actually have a positive effect on the prevalence of cooperative fishing on Ifaluk. Time constraints imposed by institutionalized schooling, a product of American colonialism in Micronesia, has probably resulted in a generation of males who are less skilled fishermen than their ancestors. Less time to invest in acquiring fishing skills is likely to have a greater impact on solitary fishing success than on cooperative fishing success, since solitary fishing is a skill-intensive activity. Certain roles in cooperative sail-fishing are also highly skilled, such as locating patches of fish and directing the canoe, but only one or two members of the crew need to perform these tasks. The remainder of the tasks involved in cooperative fishing require almost no skill. Indeed, the author, who had never fished a day in his life prior to visiting Ifaluk, proved to be a productive crew member simply by holding a fishing line. Although some boys skip school occasionally to fish, most boys fish only on the weekends and holidays. In addition, most males leave the atoll after the eighth grade to continue school on Woleai and then Ulithi, where the traditional fishing practiced on Ifaluk does not occur. Thus, with the introduction of Western schooling, males may not be acquiring the necessary fishing skills that would make solitary fishing a profitable winter activity. It is interesting to note that the individual who fished alone most frequently and maintained the highest mean solitary return rate had dropped out of school by second grade.

Technology also plays an important role in the emergence of cooperation on Ifaluk. The resource patch that is being exploited on Ifaluk consists of distinct, large packages typically weighing 5–20 kg. The most important technology utilized to exploit this patch is the sailing canoe, which requires cooperative participation. Operating a sailing canoe not only requires multiple individuals, it also necessitates a coordinated division of labor. Improvements in technology can also encourage cooperation by lowering the costs of acquisition. The recent transition from using heavy sails woven of palm fibers to lightweight American-made sails (purchased on Yap) has certainly lowered the energetic costs of cooperative sail-fishing on Ifaluk.

Stability of Cooperative Fishing on Ifaluk

Although the necessary conditions for cooperative foraging seem to hold on Ifaluk, these conditions are not sufficient for cooperation to be stable. Stability of cooperative foraging requires a mechanism that either controls a free rider's share of returns or imposes costs on free riders. The model presented here has specifically considered the first of these mechanisms. Concerning the latter mechanism, it may be that cooperative behavior is promoted through social controls such as the negative effect of gossip on reputation, although the costs in terms of reproductive fitness of a negative reputation are difficult to measure.

Unlike previous models of the evolution and stability of cooperation, which assume equal sharing among foragers or group members, the model presented here used empirically observed biases in the fish-sharing patterns on Ifaluk. The model has shown that the observed sharing patterns help us to predict the conditions under which an individual will join a cooperative pursuit. The sharing patterns appear to be the mechanism by which a free rider's share of returns is limited.

Although the model is a significant predictor of cooperative fishing participation, inclusion of at least two variables would improve the model's ability to approximate the conditions of production on Ifaluk. These elements will provide the basis for future research on the evolution of cooperative fishing on Ifaluk.

Opportunity costs One of the most notable shortcomings of the model is that the opportunity costs of cooperative sail-fishing have been ignored, primarily because of the difficulty in determining activities that were foregone. The most obvious consideration would be solitary fishing. However, the mutually exclusive weather conditions necessary for the success of these fishing activities makes this prospect unlikely. Another possibility is that the opportunity costs could be measured as a tradeoff between paternal care and cooperative fishing. However, the fitness benefits for men of, say, an hour of childcare may be much lower than the fitness benefits of an hour spent fishing, given an abundance of related female caregivers. Indeed, Sosis et al. (1998) found that the number of coresidential offspring was positively correlated with cooperative fishing participation. The most prominent type of male childcare observed consisted of boys joining their fathers or kin on a sailing canoe. If we consider what males who are not fishing are doing while others are out fishing, it is not obvious how the opportunity costs could be measured. Males who are not fishing in the morning are typically sleeping. Generally, males return from cooperative sail-fishing between 7:00 and 8:00 A.M., which is when males who do not fish usually begin their day. This may suggest that the opportunity costs to cooperative fishing could be measured as a tradeoff with somatic investment.

Relatedness The model would also be greatly improved if it accounted for the effect of a male's relatedness to the recipients of the catch on his fishing decisions. Preliminary analyses of a model that incorporates the amount of fish that a man expects his kin to receive into his payoff curves has yielded significant results (Sosis 1998). There are conditions under which the predictions of an inclusive fitness model differ from the predictions of a direct fitness model, such as the one presented above. For example, if the increase in foraging efficiency of joining a group is outweighed by the costs of lowering an individual's inclusive fitness by reducing the foraging efficiency of related group members, the individual is not expected to join the group (Rodman 1981; Smith 1985). However, this is not likely to be relevant to cooperative fishing on Ifaluk since the monotonically increasing payoff curves (see Figure 20.7a–d) suggest a lack of conflicts between joiners and members. One interesting consequence of including kin in the model is that the energetic costs of fishing become inconsequential. In other words, the addition of inclusive fitness benefits to the model would vastly increase an individual's benefits whereas energetic costs would remain the same as in the model presented above.

The importance of a man's relatedness to the recipients of his production is evident in the pattern of canoe use—namely, that men fish on the canoe of their natal compound rather than the canoe of their residential compound. If fish are distributed via a canoe-owner distribution, married men are largely acquiring fish for their sister's families rather than their own. When married men were asked why they do not fish on the canoes of their residential compound more often, they invariably communicate a sense of duty, claiming that they must "fish on the canoe that fed me when I was young." Whether the inclusive fitness benefits for a married man of fishing on the canoe of his natal compound are greater than the inclusive fitness benefits of fishing on the canoe of his residential compound needs to be further explored.

SUMMARY

1. This paper tests theoretical models of the emergence and stability of cooperative foraging using empirical data on cooperative sail-fishing activities on Ifaluk Atoll.
2. Consistent with a necessary condition for the emergence of cooperative foraging, it was found that the mean per capita net production and consumption rates of cooperative fishing are significantly greater than the mean per capita net production and consumption rates of solitary fishing.
3. Once cooperative foraging has emerged, a necessary condition for its stability is that the benefits of cooperation must outweigh the benefits of free riding. Two factors determine the success of a free riding strategy: the ability of cooperators to control a free rider's share of returns, and the ability of cooperators to impose costs on free riders.
4. The fish distribution patterns following cooperative sail-fishing events are a mix of investment-based distribution types, which reward men who fish, and population-wide distributions, which ensure that all residents, or all male residents, receive fish regardless of their participation in production. Although there is potential for free riding when fish are distributed to all residents on the atoll, the investment-based distribution types limit the success of a free riding strategy. The distribution patterns are a likely mechanism that enables the stability of cooperative fishing on Ifaluk.
5. By using empirically observed biases in the fish distribution pattern, a model was generated that predicts the conditions under which an individual will join a cooperative pursuit. Predictions from the model were compared with observed fishing behavior on Ifaluk. The results indicate that the difference in expected caloric payoff curves if an individual fishes or does not fish is a significant predictor of men's participation in cooperative sail-fishing.

ACKNOWLEDGMENTS

I wish to thank K. G. Anderson, Jim Boone, Barry Glazier, Mike Gurven, Kristen Hawkes, Kim Hill, Magdalena Hurtado, Hillard Kaplan, Charles Keckler, and Garnett McMillan for helpful discussions on the research presented here. Special thanks to Kim Hill for providing guidance at every stage of this project, as well as valuable comments on several drafts of the manuscript. I also thank K. G. Anderson, Lee Cronk, Mike Gurven, Magdalena Hurtado, and an anonymous reviewer for providing useful comments on various drafts of the manuscript. I am greatly indebted to Sharon Feldstein for her assistance during field work. This project was generously supported by the National Science Foundation (SBR9423070), L.S.B. Leakey Foundation, UNM Office of Graduate Studies, and UNM Department of Anthropology.

NOTES

1. Equation 2 is not a decision variable, such as the choice of whether to join a cooperative group or forage solitarily. Models of optimal group size, such as Smith's (1981) joiner's rule, assume that cooperation exists. The joiner's rule assumes that the decision variable that a forager faces is a choice between foraging solitarily or joining a *group of foragers*. Equation 2 does not assume that group foraging already exists, rather, it is an attempt to establish the conditions that must exist for cooperative foraging to emerge.

2. For a more detailed ethnographic description of Ifaluk see Burrows and Spiro (1957), Bates and Abott (1958), Turke (1985), Lutz (1988), and Sosis (1997).

3. During the 1994–1995 field session the movement of residents on and off the atoll were monitored for Falalop but not for Falachig atoll. Census data on Falachig were collected over a two-month period in which there were several opportunities for residents to return to and leave the atoll. No data were collected on the number of residents for all of Ifaluk at any specific point in time; thus the estimate of slightly more than 600 residents, rather than an exact figure.

4. Males under 14 years of age may of course receive fish within their own compound.

5. Informants claimed that solitary line fishing with bait was the main type of fishing (solitary or cooperative) during the season of calm winds (*lecheg*) from May to October.

6. These data refer to daytime solitary fishing. I did not collect systematic data on nighttime solitary fishing activities. However, casual discussions about solitary fishing indicate that nighttime solitary fishing occurred less frequently than daytime solitary fishing, and no individual exclusively fished at night.

7. On average Iyeur received 9.5% more fish than Iyefang during village-level *ilet* distributions, but it maintains 72.7% more *ilet* than Iyefang and the *ilet* represent 36.3% more residents (n = 17).

8. Fifteen males were observed fishing alone; however, data were not collected for three events that were the only solitary fishing events for three males.

9. It is not surprising that all consumption rates are negative given the wide distribution of fish on Ifaluk. In addition, these consumption rates do not account for the high value of fish calories, since it is the primary source of protein on Ifaluk (see below).

10. Whatever ecological cues individuals are using to assess the fishing conditions, they will never generate *exact* knowledge about the number of fishermen on a given day. Nor will an individual possess precise knowledge of his payoffs for a given number of fishermen. This is a problem that all deterministic models face; strategists rarely have perfect

knowledge of all the factors relevant to the outcome of their behavioral decision. A stochastic model that took into account errors in individual estimates of the number of participants would be more realistic, although considerably more complex than the model presented here.

11. Egalitarian distributions were not included in the following model since this type of distribution was only observed twice and accounts for less than 1% of the total fish distributed.

12. The caloric gains individual *k* expects to receive from a men's feast was calculated as the expected caloric value of a men's feast multiplied by the ratio $\frac{1}{N}$, where *N* is the total number of men at risk of partaking in a men's feast. In order to simplify equation 4, the men's feast was not designated by a separate variable from the other distributions. However, in generating predictions and testing the model, men's feasts were not multiplied by the consumer ratio as implied in equation 4.

13. Women's and children's weights were not measured. I have used Hillard Kaplan's calculation of consumer proportions by age, sex, and weight for the Piro (University of New Mexico, unpublished data) to estimate consumer proportions for Ifaluk residents. The Piro data were used because the physiques of the Piro and the people of Ifaluk are similar. Kaplan (1994) followed a procedure used by the World Health Organization (1985) and the National Research Council (1989a, Table 3-1; 1989b) for calculating the resting metabolic energy expenditure of individuals as a function of age, sex, and weight. The following table presents the consumer proportions that were used to determine the number of consumers in a compound on Ifaluk.

Proportion of Consumer

Age	Male	Female
0–2	0.3	0.3
3–5	0.5	0.5
6–8	0.6	0.6
9–11	0.7	0.7
12–14	0.9	0.8
15–17	1.2	0.9
18–20	1.1	0.9
21–24	1.1	0.9
25–39	1.1	1.0
40–49	1.1	0.9
50–59	1.1	0.9
>59	.8	0.7

14. Only 78 (rather than 79) cooperative sail-fishing events were used since data are missing on the number of fishermen for one fishing event.

15. Fish from a men's feast were generally left in the main canoe house for the duration of the day. Thus, any males over 14 years of age were able to consume this fish.

16. Ideally, to determine the value of a unit of protein and carbohydrate we would want to know the price that a kilogram of fish could be purchased on Ifaluk, not sold. However, these data are unavailable since individuals never purchased fish or taro from each other.

17. In contrast, Smith (1991) found that over the observed range of Inuit hunters in 16 hunt types, net return rates decreased at the largest group sizes for 15 of the hunt types analyzed, and thus there was expected to be a conflict of interest between joiners and members.

REFERENCES

Alexander, R. 1974. The evolution of social behavior. *Annual Review of Ecology and Systematics* 5:325–383.

Axelrod, R., and W. Hamilton. 1981. The evolution of cooperation. *Science* 211: 1390–1396.

Barnard, C. Editor. 1984. *Producers and Scroungers: Strategies of Exploitation and Parasitism.* London: Croom Helm.

Barnard, C., and R. Sibly. 1981. Producers and scroungers: A general model and its application to captive flocks of house sparrows. *Animal Behaviour* 29:543–550.

Bates, M., and D. Abbott. 1958. *Coral Island: Portrait of an atoll.* New York: Charles Scribner's Sons.

Bethlehem, D. 1975. The effect of westernization on cooperative behaviour in Central Africa. *International Journal of Psychology* 10:219–224.

Betzig, L. 1988. Redistribution: equity or exploitation? In *Human Reproductive Behavior: A Darwinian Perspective.* L. Betzig, M. Borgerhoff Mulder, and P. Turke, eds. Pp. 49–63. Cambridge: Cambridge University Press.

Boesch, C. 1994. Cooperative hunting in wild chimpanzees. *Animal Behaviour* 48:653–667.

Boone, J. 1992. Competition, Conflict, and the Development of Social Hierarchies. In *Evolutionary Ecology and Human Behavior.* E. Smith, and B. Winterhalder, eds. Pp. 301–337. New York: Aldine.

Boyd, R., and P. Richerson. 1992. Punishment allows the evolution of cooperation (or anything else) in sizable groups. *Ethology and Sociobiology* 13:171–195.

Burrows, E., and M. Spiro. 1957. *An Atoll Culture: Ethnography of Ifaluk in the Central Carolines.* Westport, Connecticut: Greenwood Press.

Caraco, T. 1981. Risk sensitivity and foraging groups. *Ecology* 62:527–531.

———. 1987. Foraging games in a random environment. In *Foraging Behavior.* A. Kamil, J. Krebs, and H. Pulliam, eds. Pp. 389–414. New York: Plenum Press.

Caraco, T., and H. Pulliam. 1984. Sociality and survivorship in animals exposed to predation. In *A New Ecology: Novel Approaches to Interactive Systems.* P. Price, C. Slobodchikoff, and W. Gaud, eds. Pp. 279–309. New York: Wiley.

Caraco, T., and L. Wolf. 1975. Ecological determinants of group sizes of foraging lions. *American Naturalist* 109:343–352.

Clark, C., and M. Mangel. 1984. Foraging and flocking strategies: Information in an uncertain environment. *American Naturalist* 123:626–641.

Crook, J. 1972. Sexual selection, dimorphism, and social organization in the primates. In *Sexual Selection and the Descent of Man, 1871–1971.* B. Campbell, ed. Pp. 231–281. Chicago: Aldine.

Enquist, M., and O. Leimar. 1993. The evolution of cooperation in mobile organisms. *Animal Behaviour* 45:747–757.

Freeman, O. Editor. 1951. *Geography of the Pacific.* New York: John Wiley and Sons.

Giraldeau, L. 1988. The stable group and the determinants of foranging group size. In *The Ecology of Social Behavior.* C. Slobodchikoff, ed. Pp. 33–53. San Diego: Academic Press.

Hamilton, W. 1971. Geometry for the selfish herd. *Journal of Theoretical Biology* 31:295–311.

Hawkes, K. 1992. Sharing and collective action. In *Evolutionary Ecology and Human Behavior.* E. Smith and B. Winterhalder, eds. Pp. 269–300. New York: Aldine.

Hayden, B. 1981. Subsistence and ecological adaptations of modern hunter-gatherers. In *Omnivorous Primates: Hunting and Gathering in Human Evolution.* G. Teleki and R. Harding, eds. Pp. 344–422. New York: Columbia University Press.

Higashi, M., and N. Yamamura. 1993. What determines animal group size? Insider-outsider conflict and its resolution. *American Naturalist* 142:553–563.

Hill, K., and K. Hawkes. 1983. Neotropical hunting among the Ache of Eastern Paraguay. In *Adaptive Responses of Native Amazonians.* R. Hames and W. Vickers, eds. Pp. 223–267. New York: Academic Press.

Hirshleifer, J., and J. M. Coll. 1988. What strategies can support the evolutionary emergence of cooperation? *Journal of Conflict Resolution* 32:367–398.

Kaplan, H. 1994. Evolutionary and wealth flows theories of fertility: Empirical tests and new models. *Population and Development Review* 20:753–791.

Kaplan, H., and K. Hill. 1992. The evolutionary ecology of food acquisition. In *Evolutionary Ecology and Human Behavior.* E. Smith and B. Winterhalder, eds. Pp. 167–201. New York: Aldine de Gruyter.

Kurland, J., and S. Beckerman. 1985. Optimal foraging and hominid evolution: labor and reciprocity. *American Anthropologist* 87:73–93.

Lutz, C. 1988. *Unnatural Emotions.* Chicago: University of Chicago Press.

MacDonald, D. 1983. The ecology of carnivore social behaviour. *Nature* 301:379–384.

Maynard Smith, J. 1983. Game theory and the evolution of cooperation. In *Evolution from molecules to man.* D. Bendall, ed. Pp. 445–456. Cambridge: Cambridge University Press.

Meeker, B. 1970. An experimental study of cooperation and competition in West Africa. *International Journal of Psychology* 5:11–19.

Mesterton-Gibbons, M., and L. Dugatkin. 1992. Cooperation among unrelated individuals: evolutionary factors. *The Quarterly Review of Biology* 1992:267–281.

National Research Council. 1989a. *Diet and Health.* Washington D.C.: National Academy Press.

———. 1989b. *Recommended Daily Allowances.* Washington D.C.: National Academy Press.

Packer, C. 1986. The ecology of sociality in felids. In *Ecological Aspects of Social Evolution: Birds and Mammals.* D. Rubenstein and R. Wrangham, eds. Pp. 429–451. Princeton: Princeton University Press.

———. 1988. Constraints on the evolution of reciprocity: lessons from cooperative hunting. *Ethology and Sociobiology* 9:137–147.

Packer, C., and L. Ruttan. 1988. The evolution of cooperative hunting. *American Naturalist* 132:159–198.

Packer, C., D. Scheel, and A. Pusey. 1990. Why lions form groups: Food is not enough. *American Naturalist* 136:1–19.

Pulliam, H., and T. Caraco. 1984. Living in groups: is there an optimal group size? In *Behavioural Ecology: An Evolutionary Approach.* J. Krebs and N. Davies, eds. Pp. 122–147. Sunderland, Massachusetts: Sinauer Associates.

Pulliam, H., and G. Millikan. 1982. Social organization in the nonreproductive season. In *Avian Biology.* D. Farner and J. King, eds. Pp. XX–XX. New York: Academic Press.

Rannala, B., and C. Brown. 1994. Relatedness and conflict over optimal group size. *Trends in Ecology and Evolution* 9:117–119.

Real, L., and T. Caraco. 1986. Risk and foraging in stochastic environments. *Annual Review of Ecology and Systematics* 17:371–390.

Rodman, P. 1981. Inclusive fitness and group size with a reconsideration of group sizes in lions and wolves. *American Naturalist* 118:275–283.

Schoener, T. 1971. Theory of feeding strategies. *Annual Review of Ecology and Systematics* 2:369–404.

Sibly, R. 1983. Optimal group size is unstable. *Animal Behaviour* 31:947–948.

Slobodchikoff, C. 1988. Cooperation, aggression, and the evolution of social behavior. In *The Ecology of Social Behavior.* C. Slobodchikoff, ed., Pp. 13–32. San Diego: Academic Press.

Smith, E. A. 1981. The application of optimal foraging theory to the analysis of hunter-gatherer group size. In *Hunter-Gatherer Foraging Strategies.* B. Winterhalder and E. Smith, eds. Pp. 36–65. Chicago: University of Chicago Press.

———. 1983. Anthropological applications of optimal foraging theory: A critical review. *Current Anthropology* 24:625–651.

———. 1985. Inuit foraging groups: Some simple models incorporating conflicts of interest, relatedness, and central-place sharing. *Ethology and Sociobiology* 6:37–57.

———. 1991. *Inujjuamiut Foraging Strategies.* New York: Aldine de Grutyer.

Sosis, R. 1997. *The Collective Action Problem of Male Cooperative Labor on Ifaluk Atoll.* Unpublished Ph.D. dissertation, Department of Anthropology, University of New Mexico.

———. 1998. *Explaining Variation in Cooperative Fishing Participation on Ifaluk Atoll.* Invited Lecture, Department of Anthropology, University of Connecticut, April 20.

Sosis, R., S. Feldstein, and K. Hill. 1998. Bargaining theory and cooperative fishing participation on Ifaluk Atoll. *Human Nature* 9:163–203.

Stephens, D., and J. Krebs. 1986. *Foraging Theory.* Princeton: Princeton University Press.

Turke, P. 1985. Fertility Determinants on Ifaluk and Yap: Tests of Economic and Darwinian Hypotheses. Unpublished Ph.D. dissertation, Department of Anthropology, Northwestern University.

Vickery, W., L. Giraldeau, J. Templeton, D. Kramer, and C. Chapman. 1991. Producers, scroungers, and group foraging. *American Naturalist* 137:847–863.

Washburn, S., and C. Lancaster. 1968. The evolution of human hunting. In *Man the Hunter.* R. Lee and I. DeVore, eds. Pp. 293–303. Chicago: Aldine.

Wittenberger, J. 1980. Group size and polygamy in social mammals. *American Naturalist* 115:197–222.

World Health Organization. 1985. *Energy and protein requirements. Report of a joint FAO/WHO/UNU expert consultation.* Technical Report Series 724. Geneva: World Health Organization.

PART VI

CONCLUSION

21

Twenty Years of Evolutionary Biology and Human Social Behavior

Where Are We Now?

J. PATRICK GRAY

WHERE WE ARE NOT

Closing the volume that resulted from the 1976 American Anthropological Association sessions on sociobiology, Chagnon wrote:

> We can imagine nothing more exciting or scientifically profound than the possibility that much of human behavior conforms to predictions from evolutionary biology—and nothing more legitimate as a field of anthropological inquiry. . . . Almost no explicitly sociobiological fieldwork in human societies has yet been accomplished. But, as the essays in this volume suggest, some existing data give us reason to believe that the return for such efforts will be great (1979:525–526).

This volume demonstrates that Chagnon's appraisal of the potential rewards for investing effort in sociobiological research was accurate. In the past twenty years, field workers guided by selectionist thinking[1] have revolutionized our views of many aspects of human sociality. The data gathered by these researchers have profoundly affected our understandings of human marriage and mating systems, parenting behaviors, social life in foraging societies, and many other topics. At a time when many cultural anthropologists have rejected the view that matters of fact are best established by systematic observation and measurement in favor of the idea that moral posturing and literary skills are better guides to reality, overestimating the value of the data produced by this group of field workers is difficult. The papers in this volume exhibit struggles with issues of how to operationalize variables, how to collect reliable information, and how to replicate results. These data will, therefore, be useful even to researchers who spurn a selectionist approach to human behavior.

Chagnon was also right about the excitement. The theoretical advances and empirical findings of the past twenty years have captured the imaginations of many scholars in the social sciences and humanities. Some lines of research have generated intense interest in the "pop intellectual" world of news magazines, talk shows, and general appeal books. The rapidity with which the topics of fluctuating asymmetry and mate selection, "sperm wars," or evolutionary explanations of (male) political power and sexual success found media exposure suggests that the public finds the application of evolutionary theory to certain aspects human social behavior to be of abiding interest. This media exposure is best characterized as a mixed blessing. While no one doubts the value of exposing the public to evolutionary theory and research (especially outside the creation/evolution debate so important in the United States), the publicity is marked by the loss of careful qualifications of the current limits of our knowledge, a feature characteristic of each chapter in this volume.

If we equate the scientifically profound with the practically important (as many funding agencies do), Chagnon was clearly right again. For example, the papers teasing apart the tangled relationships between reproductive success, pursuit of wealth, mortality rates, and social status have powerful implications for governments and agencies operating in a world where policies to affect population size are seen as urgently needed and yet frequently attacked as ineffective and as motivated by less than honorable intentions. New work on the tradeoffs women in postindustrial economies make between marriage, career, and reproduction, and on the dynamics of paternal investment in households where males are involved with children who are not their genetic offspring, raises significant questions for policies ranging from divorce law to welfare policy.

Unfortunately, Chagnon's claim that applying evolutionary theory to human behavior is a legitimate field of anthropological inquiry is still not widely accepted by cultural anthropologists. I attended both the 1976 and 1996 AAA meetings and left the latter feeling that exciting progress had occurred in the twenty years separating the two sessions. I did not feel that we had arrived at definitive answers for many questions raised at the 1976 meetings. Rather, I had the sense that the past twenty years had clarified some basic theoretical and methodological issues in how to apply selectionist thinking to human behavior. The sometimes heated debate among human behavioral ecologists, evolutionary psychologists, and dual inheritance theorists had highlighted differences in approaches that were not clear in 1976. The process of theoretical clarification has cast new light on the first generation of empirical studies and is stimulating ever more convincing research. Yet the 1996 meetings also produced a frisson of temporal disjointedness. While the sessions illustrated how a scientific paradigm had evolved and was continuing to evolve, I felt that the debate over the anthropological legitimacy of the paradigm had not advanced since the 1976 meetings. One reason for this feeling is clearly that many cultural anthropologists have explicitly moved away from the scientific model of analysis followed by selectionist thinkers. For some of this persuasion the theoretical and empirical results of the past twenty years need not be addressed—a blanket dismissal of the legitimacy of the scientific world view suffices to make the work worthy of attention only as another example of the inadequacy and danger of that world view. I will discuss this situation in the section on "where we are now."

The second reason for my temporal discomfort is more troubling. It appears to me that the responses of many who encounter evolutionary approaches to human behavior are still shaped by the highly polemical arguments that greeted sociobiology's debut on the stage of social science. For a large segment of the academic world the received wisdom is that sociobiology can be ignored, and should be avoided, because it is inherently racist, sexist, elitist, and genetically determinist. The sources cited for this opinion often include the first critical responses to sociobiology (especially Sahlins 1976 and Sociobiology Study Group of Science for the People 1976). Unfortunately, coining alternative (and more useful) labels for evolutionary approaches (human behavioral ecology, evolutionary psychology, etc.) does not seem to have changed how people regard such approaches. Selectionist thinking seems to have lost a vital public relations battle in cultural anthropology and other social sciences. This state of affairs requires that before we evaluate where we are now, refuting these charges by reviewing where we are not will be worthwhile.

If sociobiology is merely a reflection of "the socioeconomic prejudices" of its founders designed to legitimize existing social arrangements as "natural" (Sociobiology Study Group of Science for the People 1976:182), it must be judged to be a failure. At some point the paradigm seems to have escaped the control of its founders. A paradigm seeking to legitimize male domination of females, for example, should have continued to adhere to the "Man the (pair-bonded) Hunter" model popular at the time of the 1976 meetings. Instead we find many scenarios of human evolution that treat both males and females as active agents. In this volume Blurton Jones and colleagues (Chapter 4) and Hawkes and colleagues (Chapter 12) reevaluate the male provisioning explanation of pair bonds and suggest an alternative model focused on intergenerational bonds between females. I doubt that an inherently sexist paradigm could generate, much less consider seriously, models of human evolution incorporating the images of female primate sexuality in scenarios advanced by Hrdy (1997) and Smuts (1995). Should the datum that some women in pair-bonds synchronize extra-pair copulation with ovulation (Baker and Bellis 1995) be seen as feeding into male distrust of women, as promoting the view of women as active sexual agents, or just another facet of human behavior that makes sense in light our evolutionary history?

No doubt some individuals applying evolutionary theory to human behavior are sexist and some hypotheses and models they formulate are expressions of their prejudices. Nevertheless, the past twenty years have been marked by open debate over the role of the sexes in human evolution and over how much specific models have to say about the relations between the sexes among modern humans. At present, no one evolutionary scenario holds the assent of the majority of selectionist thinkers, and it is hard to find one in contention that somehow legitimizes the status quo as "natural." There is little agreement over how our evolutionary history affects the arrangement of sex roles in existing societies. Perhaps the only area of agreement is that the reproductive interests of men and women frequently conflict and that different environments result in different balances of costs and benefits for each sex. We have just started to tote up the relative costs and benefits in different societies. For example, Strassmann (Chapter 3) suggests that some polygynous Dogon males may achieve reproductive success at the expense of their wives. In contrast, male exploitation seems lower, or absent, in some cases discussed by Sellen and colleagues (Chapter 5).

There is also agreement that conflicts of interest over reproduction affect relationships between members of the same sex. Both Strassmann and Irons (Chapter 11) consider if Dogon and Yomut men increase their reproductive success at the expense of close male relatives. Investigations into the consequences of polygyny usually examine whether earlier wives achieve reproductive success at the expense of later co-wives. Wright (1994) provides a verbal model of conflicts of interest between females in societies with socially imposed serial monogamy and great skew in male resource control. Of course, we should not overlook the fact that frequently the interests of men and women are best served by cooperation, not conflict.

A review of the past twenty years clearly shows that sociobiology is not trapped in the position of attempting to legitimize male economic, political, personal, or sexual domination of women (see also Liesen 1995; Buss and Malamuth 1996). Researchers do not argue that such phenomena do not exist, but that they cannot be explained merely as the result of male bad faith. What is more important, they suggest that knowledge of the basic conflict of interests between the sexes and of how environmental variation affects the resolution of such conflicts provides the best base for designing policies to alter relations between the sexes. Also required, of course, is a selectionist analysis of how the alterations might affect the inclusive fitness of those promoting and resisting them.

The chapters in this volume are sufficient to refute the charge that selectionist theory is inherently racist. Human behavioral ecology does not suggest that the behavioral strategy sets of humans vary between "races." The Darwinian algorithms hypothesized by evolutionary psychologists are assumed to be common to all human populations. The definition of "culture" used by dual inheritance theorists sees cultural differences between populations arising out of historical and environmental, not biological, differences. Unfortunately, scholars critiquing explicitly racialist arguments such as *The Bell Curve* (Herrnstein and Murray 1994) often condemn all work relating human biology and behavior as a manifestation of racism. The only possible response to this tactic is to continue to stress that racial classifications play no role in selectionist theory. A more troubling situation occurs when authors use the vocabulary and principles of evolutionary theory to argue for racial differences (e.g., Rushton 1995). The most appropriate response here is not less biology, but better biology. Demonstrations of the misuses of evolutionary theory and of the superiority of explanations derived from human behavioral ecology are required (e.g., Mealey 1990).

The claim that sociobiology is inherently elitist is easily refuted by pointing to human behavioral ecology's concern with delineating how common goals and strategy sets get played out in different resource environments. Irons reports that he originally rejected the idea that Yomut striving for wealth was striving for reproductive success because "it painted a grim picture of winners and losers" (1997:48). A theory focused on differential success in obtaining resources necessary for reproduction must identify who wins and who loses. However, the theory does not necessarily predict that the winners have different evolved goals or strategies than the losers. All Yomut men probably strive for wealth, but some achieve it without too much effort because they are born into wealthy families while others fail to achieve it because of a poor starting condition or bad luck. Identification of winners and losers in one environment does not imply that the mix will stay the same if the environment changes. Nor does it force us to conclude that the social arrangement that helped to produce the current mix of winners and losers is either morally good or socially functional. Human behavioral ecology does not suggest that losers should passively endure social arrangements detrimental to their interests to secure a greater social good. In fact, by analyzing such cultural pronouncements as manipulative strategies winners use to increase their inclusive fitness (Alexander 1987; Cronk 1995; Wright 1994), selectionist thinking can provide losers with a more accurate critique of social settings characterized by high skew in resource control. Further, discovery of how winners become winners and losers become losers may help in devising strategies for changing the distribution of outcomes. Again, a selectionist analysis of the motives of those arguing for change and those resisting it is vital.

Finally, this volume shows that application of evolutionary theory to human behavior, especially in the human behavioral ecology tradition, is not about genetic determinism. Careful reading of these chapters reveals that no author hypothesizes genes for behavior. The route from gene to behavior is so tortuous that behavioral ecologists typically adopt the phenotypic gambit (see Smith, Chapter 2). There must be genetic underpinnings relevant to the potential strategy set possessed by members of a species. However, analysis of how different environmental contingencies (including other members of the species) affect the occurrence of behaviors in that strategy set and the payoffs for these behaviors can be analyzed without worrying about these underpinnings.

The heat generated by sociobiology's explosive introduction to the human sciences will continue to dissipate with the passage of time. With continued careful empirical research, and with rapid responses when evolutionary theory is misappropriated to further programs of sexism, racism, or elitism, it is possible the public relations war may yet be won.

WHERE ARE WE NOW?

This section is not intended as an overview of the current state of selectionist theory in cultural anthropology. Instead, I will first briefly discuss three important trends that I find to be exemplified by the papers in this volume: (1) a movement away from tests that pit selectionist hypotheses against null hypotheses generated by various types of cultural determinism; (2) increased theoretical and methodological sophistication; and (3) increasing awareness of the potential practical applications of selectionist thinking. I will then address the question from a second direction by discussing how selectionist thinking relates to the postmodernist moments ascendent in cultural anthropology during the past twenty years.

In their review of several classic papers in human behavioral ecology, Kacelnik and Krebs note that in early optimality studies models of optimization are usually pitted against the null hypothesis of random behavior (1997:23). Once the randomization hypothesis is rejected more sophisticated analyses of relations between currency and fitness, strategy sets and feedback functions can be conducted. Much selectionist social science is at the stage of demonstrating that selectionist-inspired hypotheses accord better with empirical data than do the null hypotheses generated by theoretical positions that eschew evolutionary theory. Chagnon and Bugos's paper in the 1979 volume showing that knowledge of degree of genetic relatedness could help predict sides in a Yanomamö axe fight is an excellent example of this type of argument. The null hypothesis here was simply that such knowledge would not help explain the distribution of fighters. In the current volume, Hames's demonstration that predictions from reciprocal altruism theory fit Yanomamö patterns of food exchange better than predictions from egalitarian exchange theory (Chapter 18) is a satisfying example of this mode of reasoning.

The resistance to selectionist thinking in cultural anthropology means that the pitting of evolutionary-based hypotheses against null hypotheses generated by theoretical positions emphasizing total cultural determinism will continue to be an important task for some time to come. However, most of the papers in the current volume (including Hames's) are already operating at the more sophisticated level identified by Kacelnik and Krebs. The authors analyze the predictions of different models generated from within the selectionist perspective, and the contrast between the perspectives of selectionist and nonselectionist cultural anthropology is either absent or left implicit.

The papers that assay the effects of polygynous marriage on female reproductive success (Strassmann, Sellen et al.) start with the assumption that human marriage systems can be analyzed using this currency and explore questions generated from the selectionist perspective. Both papers spotlight the potential conflicts between the sexes and emphasize the need to identify the environmental conditions that permit one sex to achieve its goal at the expense of the other. Each contributes information about possible feedback mechanisms between female reproductive success and marriage form. While previous studies have focused mainly on female fertility, these papers find an important role for child mortality. If we highlight feedback mechanisms affecting male reproductive success, we are led to question whether polygynous males achieve their increased reproductive success at the expense of their brothers or other close male relatives. Strassmann finds that while work group bosses gain more, subordinates also gain from polygynous marriage (see Irons on the Yomut situation). Finally, discovery of the various feedback mechanisms may allow us to predict shifts in the relative frequency of different strategies under conditions of environmental change (Borgerhoff Mulder 1996).

The section on the demographic transition provides a second example of this trend. The "obvious" null or negative correlation between wealth and reproductive success in societies that have undergone the demographic transition is often taken as a fact sufficient to prove that an evolutionary theory based on inclusive fitness considerations does not apply to human behavior (Vining 1986). A less extreme view hypothesizes a gulf between "us" of the demographic transition, where inclusive fitness theory does not apply, and "they" of traditional societies, where it does. Many commentators on Vining's paper noted that selectionist thinking can generate several models in which wealth was not related to reproductive success. Luttbeg and colleagues (Chapter 16) discuss three such models (quality/quantity tradeoff, indirect bias, and novel circumstances) and make a start toward examining their relevance to human behavior by determining if the marriage behavior of Kipsigis males is best explained by a decision rule that maximizes wealth passed to children or by one that maximizes reproductive success. The fact that the wealth maximization rule is the better predictor in this situation immediately leads to the problems of identifying (1) those environments in which wealth maximization demands fertility reduction, and (2) which variables affect the degree to which wealth maximization and reproductive maximization are in conflict. Kaplan and Lancaster's study of a skills-based competitive labor market economy (Chapter 14) provides one set of answers. They note that in this environment parents probably cannot detect diminishing returns for investment in a child until very high levels are reached. They also identify the balance between the time spent in infant care and the time required to feed family members as an important constraint on fertility in traditional societies. This constraint may have less of an impact on fertility decisions in societies where extrasomatic wealth is present.

The papers by Kaplan and Lancaster and by Luttbeg and colleagues close the gulf between demographic transition societies and traditional societies by suggesting that extrasomatic wealth and/or decision rules (and motivational structures) designed to maximize wealth per child are found in some traditional societies. Kaplan and Lancaster also argue that evolved proximate mechanisms might not respond to maximize fitness once extrasomatic wealth exists. Closing the gulf, however, raises some interesting questions about Irons's concept of the Adaptively Relevant Environment (ARE) and the relationship between cultural and reproductive success. Irons argues that socially imposed monogamy and widespread use of contraception do not belong to the ARE, and that we should not expect to find correlations between cultural and reproductive success in societies characterized by these features. Kaplan and Lancaster and Luttbeg and colleagues pose the question of whether or not inheritable extrasomatic wealth should be considered as part of the ARE. An exploration of this issue might involve some interesting research from the direction of evolutionary psychology. For example, does assuming that the strategy set open to foragers in the Environment of Evolutionary Adaptedness (EEA) lacked the option of maximizing extrasomatic wealth passed to offspring have significant implications for the Darwinian algorithms exhibited by the human mind? Mace (Chapter 13) notes that research on fertility behavior requires information on parental images of success for children, and Low (Chapter 15) remarks that we need more information how fertility decisions are related to absolute resource control and to images of perceived wealth trajectories. Again, this will be rich ground for research inspired by both the evolutionary psychology and dual inheritance perspectives.

This trend toward testing of alternative selectionist hypotheses is also found in Hewlett and colleagues' use in Chapter 8 of Draper and Harpending's and Blurton Jones's models to compare child rearing practices among the Aka, Ngandu, and Euro-Americans; in Blurton Jones and colleagues' exploration of the correlations between father-effect, fertility units per male, and divorce rate in four foraging societies (Chapter 4);[2] and in the comparisons of the grandmothering hypothesis and the male provisioning hypothesis of human evolution contained in papers by Hawkes and colleagues (Chapter 12). Finally, Sugiyama and Chacon (Chapter 17) argue that models generated from kin selection and reciprocal altruism theory are not adequate to explain how systems that buffer individuals against pathology risk evolve or are maintained in foraging groups, and thus turn to a selectionist theory based on social niche differentiation to solve their problem.

My comments on the second trend are more succinct. Most papers in this volume exhibit a methodological sophistication that is refreshing given much of cultural anthropology's resistance to quantification. An obvious example of that sophistication is the analysis of pitfalls in testing the relationship between wealth and reproductive success in societies stratified by wealth. The methodologies used by several authors are not widely known in cultural anthropology. I believe that the dynamic state modeling approach used by Mace and by Luttbeg and colleagues has great potential in cultural anthropology. Especially exciting is the idea that submitting such models to sensitivity analyses allows us to assign plausibility weights to suggested alternative explanations. When hypotheses are restricted to verbal arguments, discerning the sheer unlikeliness of some alternatives is often difficult. The values of time allocation studies are amply illustrated by several papers. Both dynamic state models and time allocation studies serve to examine intracultural variability in behavior, so I think it especially noteworthy that this volume contains two papers using multidimensional scaling techniques to investigate intracultural variation in cognitive structures. Most of the papers contain statements to the effect that we require more data on individual decision rules and perceptions if we are to increase our understanding of the phenomenon under analysis. Studies demonstrating how principles of behavioral ecology can be used to analyze the distribution and uses of cultural symbols certainly would increase the appeal of selectionist thinking to cultural anthropologists. The MDS techniques used by Jones (Chapter 7) and by Patton (Chapter 19) and Chagnon's work on Yanomamö kinship manipulation are excellent starts. These types of methodologies may also help move evolutionary psychology out of the laboratory and into the field, a move suggested by Smith.

The third trend I discuss will generate the most controversy. Several papers in this volume clearly show that selectionist-inspired research has the potential to make important contributions to public policy. Evolutionary medicine and evolutionary psychology will play important roles in the American subcultures of therapy. This, of course, is dangerous ground and threatens to rekindle the passions that greeted sociobiology's introduction to the public. For the taste of many, Wright (1994) may be too willing to derive policy implications from selectionist research, but his discussion of how such research can legitimately claim our attention is lucid. He argues that we cannot derive moral lessons from evolution. Once we have decided, on whatever grounds, that a given outcome is morally or practically desirable, however, selectionist research can legitimately enter the discussion by pointing to the potential costs and benefits of achieving that outcome. Selectionist analysis may also play a role in the debate over what is morally desirable by pointing out that moral claims may serve the inclusive fitness interests of those who make them. This will rarely shock the participants in a moral debate, although which interests are being served may occasion some surprise.

Wright is not alone in his willingness to draw pragmatic lessons from evolutionary research. After he places the human family system in evolutionary perspective, Emlen (1997; see also Davis and Daly 1997) suggests five steps to lower the risks of stepfamily dysfunctions. These are mainly educational, serving to warn participants and family therapists about potential problems (expect greater conflicts, understand the evolutionary basis of emotions, anticipate flashpoints of conflict). His recommendation that therapists should help alter the criteria used in selecting replacement mates could conceivably be implemented as public policy through training programs. His last recommendation, the signing of a stepfamily agreement, threatens to get lawyers involved, a sure sign of evolutionary theory's arrival on the American scene.[3] While some theorists may resist drawing policy implications from their research, we can be sure that individuals outside the field will do so. Coney and Mackey (1997), for example, do not discuss policy implications of their argument that social fathers serve as a deterrent to female "promiscuity," but as their research correlates rate of out-of-wedlock births with rates of sexually transmitted diseases its potential uses in public debates over policies are clear.

Should selectionist social science avoid the mine field of public policy? I believe that even if a retreat to academic journals and symposia were possible, it would be unwise (see Beckstrom 1993). The image of human nature offered by evolutionary theory is too important not to be placed alongside the images that currently dominate the social sciences and policy debates. As an example, consider the social "problem" of criminal behavior. Extreme cultural determinism, with its image of human nature as empty and as infinitely malleable, explains criminal behavior in terms of inadequate socialization into the norms of the social group. One can question the morality or fairness of those norms, but because humans are so pliable, socializing them into accepting norms that are unfair or even detrimental to their well-being should be possible. If "human needs and drives are indeterminate as regards their object because bodily satisfactions are specified in and through symbolic values" (Sahlins 1996:404), manipulating the symbol values to ensure compliance with any set of norms should be easy. Social policy based on this image of humans emphasizes education as the solution to criminal behavior. Children in social environments where hegemonic norms are not valued should be targeted for (counter-)educational programs that espouse such norms. Individuals caught in criminal activities should be reeducated into the conventional norms. I do not want to underestimate the impact of such programs, but their effectiveness and efficiency are questionable when they are used without programs that significantly affect the resource accumulation potential of individuals. The images of human nature derived from evolutionary theory (of "adaptation executors" or "fitness maximizers") can suggest when educational programs are likely to be effective and where behavior cannot be changed by moral suasion alone.

Another response to criminal behavior is to chalk it up to some form of innate depravity. It does not matter whether we see criminals as "evil" or as possessing "genes" for criminal behavior, this response sets them apart from the rest of the human community. The only effective action under this image of human nature is to remove the criminal from the community. In contrast, the perspective represented in this volume requires that we first hypothesize that criminals are individuals with the same evolved predispositions or Darwinian algorithms as all other humans. Their behaviors should be examined as adaptive responses to their resource environments. This formulation suggests that policies designed to lower rates of criminal behavior will be most effective when they alter the resource environments of individuals. Selectionist research can provide important clues about which aspects of the resource environment will be more effective in producing the desired changes. For example, Zhang (1997) finds that in the United States cash or in-kind welfare programs are negatively correlated with level of property crime, while Medicaid and school lunch programs exhibit no correlation with these offenses. He also notes that programs directed primarily at women and children (AFDC) have a smaller impact on property crime rates than general programs like public housing. Although Zhang operates from a simple economic model of criminal behavior, a selectionist perspective clearly has a great deal to contribute to the issues he discusses.

Daly and Wilson's use of evolutionary theory to elucidate the risks of child abuse in stepparent households offers another example of where a selectionist perspective would be helpful in producing more effective social programs. In their Canadian sample (Daly and Wilson 1997) the risk of abuse was negatively correlated with age of the mother. Social programs that teach maternal skills to young mothers probably will lower the rate of child abuse in this population. However, the finding that the stepparent effect on risk of abuse was independent of maternal age implies that programs only teaching mothering skills will not be as effective as programs that try both to improve maternal skills and to alter the calculus of the stepparent effect. Knowledge of the stepparent effect may be vital in explaining why educational programs sometimes fail to achieve their goals. A young mother may know perfectly well how to mother but may be trapped in a relationship where a potentially brighter reproductive future is purchased at the cost of permitting the abuse or neglect of her existing child(ren).

Each chapter in this volume contains material applicable to social policy. I can only briefly highlight one area. The papers on the demographic transition illustrate why the results of selectionist research must be brought into the debates over population control programs and environmental protection. Exploration of the evolved motivational structures relating reproductive success to material success is vital to understanding the possible ecological impacts of programs that effectively reduce fertility. The papers in this section suggest that one way to reduce fertility levels is to increase the resources required to produce children with high reproductive potential. As Low suggests, the possibility that lower fertility can be attained only through even greater per capita consumption of resources is a chilling thought for an environmental movement that tends to accept slower population growth as inherently good.

The complex relationships between sex differences in resource control, energy budgets, and fertility examined by Low and by Kaplan and Lancaster should be part of the intersecting dialogues on gender roles, family policies, and welfare that ignite passions in every country. Low (Chapter 15) notes that we have not yet collected the data necessary to conclude that fertility and wealth are negatively related in industrial societies, yet much social debate and many social programs assume that such a relationship exits. The successes and failures of social programs may be explained by the dynamics exposed by selectionist research. For example, in a sample of 22 industrialized countries Gauthier and Hatzius (1997) found that higher governmentally provided family benefits tend to elevate fertility, but that the effect was very small. As these countries exhibit the skill-based competitive labor market environment discussed by Kaplan and Lancaster, the small size of the effect should not surprise us. In a finding also relevant to Kaplan and Lancaster's paper Gauthier and Hatzius found that while in-kind and cash benefits affected fertility, maternity leave had no impact. Finally, selectionist thinking may help understand social dynamics in societies that are currently undergoing the demographic transition. For example, the Trivers-Willard hypothesis discussed in

Cronk's paper (Chapter 10) suggests that sometimes programs to reduce fertility will lead to an unbalanced sex ratio, perhaps by increasing female childhood mortality rates (see Das Gupta and Bhat 1997). Proponents of population limitation need to be aware of this possibility. Selectionist research may help design fertility limitation programs to counteract this scenario.

Because evolutionary theory's potential contribution to social policy is so great, its relationship to the postmodern moments in cultural anthropology is important. For many readers of this volume the first response to postmodernism may be to assume a live-and-let-live posture and to abandon a cultural anthropology that refuses to consider the impact of our evolutionary history on our social behavior. To the extent that such a response allows postmodernists to write sociobiological research out of cultural anthropology and aids in the general acceptance of their images of human nature, it limits the intellectual and social impact of the evolutionary perspective. Further, to the extent that postmodernism offers valuable insights into the realities studied by cultural anthropologists, such a response serves to buffer selectionist thinkers from important ideas. I do not labor under the delusion that a complete rapprochement between evolutionary and postmodern approaches to human behavior is possible, but I think it worthwhile to discuss whether the two positions are totally antithetical.

Some postmodernists argue that to define something is to engage in an act of force,[4] so I will not be so discourteous as to attempt a definition of postmodernism. Instead, I will discuss several strands of thought that people group under the label of postmodernism. I will take little time with the first strand, which makes scientific research impossible (see Kuznar 1997 for a more detailed analysis of postmodernism and science in anthropology). Positions that deny the existence of reality outside texts or those that state all truth claims are relative have little to offer evolutionary research. It should be noted, however, that theorists who hold such positions rarely demur from making pronouncements on social policy. One wonders from whence come their remedies for various social ills and how we could possibly judge their efficacy.

The strand of postmodernist thought responsible for debates on ethnographic authority, the crisis of representation, and the conditions for the production of knowledge has had a salubrious effect in cultural anthropology. I believe that much of this material eventually boils down the same lessons presented (with fewer literary flourishes) in any course in research methodology: alert yourself to your biases; recognize the limitations of your instruments; counter the human tendency to focus on events that confirm what you want to be the case and ignore those that do not; never forget that your results are abstractions from reality, not reality itself (see Cronk 1998). Another facet of this strand is the position that the origin and popularity of all scientific theories (except postmodernism?) must be traced to the social interests of the creators and users of the theory. Clearly, such a perspective aids in understanding the history of ideas. It will be vital in a science of memetics (Lynch 1996) that seeks to trace the distribution of ideas. Selectionist thinkers who view moral pronouncements as strategies in struggles over inclusive fitness, or who suggest that we analyze culture by studying how people use it to manipulate others, should not find this perspective too alien. Further, the recent history of selectionist thought in the social sciences raises some interesting questions along these lines. Is it coincidence that most models that assign a greater sexual agency to female primates were generated by women? Is it possible that the grandmothering hypothesis will gain wider currency because it allows aging baby-boomers to once again place their concerns at the center of the human story?

The major weakness of this position is that all too frequently the origin of an idea is taken as a measure of its validity. Explaining that an idea serves the class interest of the "elite" does not show it to be false, nor does the fact that an idea serves the interests of the "oppressed" mean it is correct. In the context of justification, it does not matter whether a man or a woman generated a model of a primate female sexual agency, all that matters is whether or not the model can be supported with empirical data. Having made this point, I do wish to note that the postmodern analysis does not become totally irrelevant. During periods when competing models coexist and the empirical evidence is not strong enough to eliminate all but one, we might expect adherence to one or the other model to be explained by personal interest.

Another strand of postmodern thought is illustrated by Sherry Ortner's (1995a) article on Sherpa shamanism. In the first part of the article she sketches an unpublished analysis of the decline of shamanism that she wrote in the mid-seventies. Her analysis was based on the binary opposition between individualism/relationism and situated the Sherpas in the "modernization narrative." She reexamines her analysis considering the lessons of feminist anthropology and postmodernism. She says of the modernization narrative and the binary oppositions (1995a:370):

> I do not want to say they are wrong, for I do not think they are, exactly. . . . I want to say, and show, that they are too simple, and that this simplicity is dangerous in all the ways that postmodern anthropology has recently brought to life: it feeds into a discourse of otherness in which the Other is either inferior or romantic, but either way excluded from equality of intercourse with us.

Ortner also notes (1995a:371) that a key lesson of feminist theory is that "a focus on oppositions encourages analysis in terms of 'essences' of the categories, rather than analysis in terms of the politics of the construction and deployment of the categories."

I suggest that because selectionist approaches to human behavior are firmly based in population thinking they tend not to fall victim to the kind of simplicity that worries Ortner. There is no tendency to mistake category names for essences. Typologies of various sorts do appear in hypothesis tests, of course, but they are usually proxies for difficult-to-measure variables. Tests comparing polygynous with monogamous societies, for example, are predicated on the hope that the contrast roughly captures variation in the operational sex ratio. Most of the papers in this volume discuss intrasocietal variation in individual strategies and emphasize the flexibility of such strategies in responding to changes in an individual's resource or social environment. The articles do not suggest that selectionist research is trapped in a grand narrative (except the narrative of evolution). The closest analogy with the modernization narrative cited by Ortner is probably the demographic transition. Yet the papers that focus on it do not assume all societies must undergo this process, nor do they assert that once the transition occurs it cannot be reversed. Again, a focus on the flexibility of strategies short-circuits any tendency to place selectionist research into a grand narrative.

Ortner suggests that if we abstain from thinking in essences and from inserting other societies into grand narratives we can avoid the discourse of otherness in which we define the Other to prevent him or her from engaging us as equals. I want to suggest that the evolutionary perspective is way ahead of the game here. Ortner is not clear on exactly how a relationship of equality is generated by the moves she suggests. In some strains of postmodernism once the Other is removed from the grand narratives of Western social science he or she is defined as living in a reality that is incommensurate with any Western narrative. If we resist the temptation to denigrate or romanticize this reality, we can grant equality only across a boundary of mutual incomprehension (although why we should do so is unclear). This is not the tack Ortner takes, however. She explores social dynamics that appear to be common to all societies (e.g., antagonists use the individualism/relationism dichotomy to maximize their advantage). In selectionist social science equality is granted by virtue of the fact that our evolved human nature is the same in all societies. Thus, the calculations involved in dividing life effort into somatic, mating, and parenting investment are panhuman. Certain standards of beauty are universal, as are Darwinian algorithms invoked by universal social situations (e.g., the need to detect cheaters).

I think that the assumption of an evolved human nature containing more than just a general "capacity for culture" casts brighter light on some discourses produced by postmodernism's introduction to cultural anthropology. The dialogue on resistance (Abu-Lughod 1990; Brown 1996; Ortner 1995b), for example, looks quite different if we assume an evolved human nature. During the conversation resistance has become more difficult to define. Some authors award the label only to cases when individuals consciously refuse hegemonic rhetoric and produce an antihegemonic discourse. For other theorists, any behavior or discourse that does not reproduce the hegemonic discourse exactly is seen as resistance. Thus, mistakes in performance, understanding, or minor variations in style become examples of resistance. What is under-theorized in this discourse is the grounding for resistance. If people are as easily inculcated as cultural determinism seems to argue, why should they resist the hegemonic discourse? To a selectionist thinker it makes sense that Bedouin women caught up in a system that frequently thwarts their reproductive interests sometimes lament their fate. Individuals with evolved motivational systems finely tuned to resource control, social contracts, and status differences will have plenty of grounds for resistance in any society. Because one's resource and/or social position can almost always be improved, resistance against those who stand in the way of improvement should be expected.

The selectionist notion of humankind also intersects with postmodernist discourse on political action and cultural anthropology (see D'Andrade 1995; Scheper-Hughes 1995). One place where the postmodernist rejection of essentialist thinking is most likely to break down is in its analysis of those who hold power and those who do not. The former are often seen as evil or immoral and the latter as good and moral. Some anthropologists have argued that anthropology's role should be to serve as a witness of the harms done to the opposed by the powerful and, if possible, to aid in the transformation of power relationships. Evolutionists will find it hard to buy into this romantic view of haves and have-nots. Those with power and those without bring the same set of evolved motivations and strategies to the table. We need to subject the world of the current winners to the same careful, and morally neutral, analysis that we use to understand the world of the losers. Analysis should be conducted in terms of winners and losers, not heros and villains. We should be aware that when the distribution of power changes, we will usually find many former "have-nots" adopting the same strategies of resource defense exhibited by the previous "haves." This viewpoint places evolutionists in the same camp with some postmodernist positions criticized as too extreme because they do not provide a grounding for the political agenda favored by the critic (Mascia-Lees et al. 1989; Scheper-Hughes 1995). Evolutionary theory will not tell us whom to identify with, nor who to root for, in the battle for just social arrangements. It is more likely to make us question the rhetoric of just social arrangements and to probe the motivations of those who push for different social formations. Once we have decided to take a position, however, selectionist research may prove invaluable in making sure our political activity is effective.

Comparing the portrait of humankind offered by evolutionary theory with the content-free image proffered by the extreme cultural relativism favored by much postmodernist thought, I find that the former is likely to be closer to reality, and a more useful guide to social action. Unfortunately, selectionist theory will probably not make much headway against the winds of postmodernism until it makes substantial progress in overcoming what cultural anthropologists see as its greatest weakness: the treatment of culture. With this thought, it is time to turn to the future.

WHERE SHOULD WE BE?

What should we aim for during the next twenty years? Some answers to this question are obvious. The public relations battle discussed in the first section will need continued attention. The rich tradition of sophisticated empirical research will continue to expand. With all due cautions, selectionist input into social policy will increase. As Smith notes, after having spent twenty years defining their differences, evolutionary psychology, human behavioral ecology, and dual inheritance theory must spend the next twenty producing an integrated selectionist approach to human social behavior.

I believe that the most important task in the next twenty years will be to incorporate "culture" into selectionist models of human behavior in ways more subtle than has been possible previously. While some theorists find the concept of culture unnecessary (Betzig 1997:17), most of the authors in this volume view it as vital to their research. Several authors call for more analysis of the decision rules individuals use in selecting among behavioral alternatives. I assume that such decision rules must be examined through the cultural logics in which they are embedded. The benefits of a new approach to culture do not flow only from cultural anthropology to evolutionary approaches to human behavior. The feedback between selectionist theory and cultural information may offer cultural anthropologists new insights into the dynamics of cultural systems.

Cronk's paper offers a glimpse into some possible rewards of adding "culture" to selectionist models. He notes that the Mukogodo are part of a larger cultural system with an expressed preference for males. His information on the stated preferences of Mukogodo women suggests either the absence of a preference or a slight bias toward males. However, these data were collected using prompts about desired family size and composition. It would be very interesting to have the same data for males and females gathered with several different prompts. Even more interesting would be an analysis of how variation in the culture of parenting behavior correlates with actual parenting behavior.

Borgerhoff Mulder's (1996) study of changes in Kipsigis bride-wealth provides another illustration of the types of questions that can be raised with selectionist thinking. Did the culture of bride-wealth (in Cronk's sense of a set of socially transmitted bits of information) contain several mutually exclusive notions at the start of the period covered by her research? Were these ideas known to all males, or were there differences in their distribution? Did the changes she describes result in the creation of many new cultural concepts, or mainly the re-weighting of the traditional ideas? Was it easy to switch from acting on one concept to another, so that switchers achieved success in both the old and new environments? Or, did the changes mean that those who had opted to act on a less successful concept in the traditional environment suddenly find themselves more successful in the new environment?

The incorporation of culture into selectionist models will be made easier by cultural anthropology's shift from emphasizing cultural homogeneity to analyzing intracultural variation. As noted in the second section, methodologies such as MDS and cognitive mapping can provide quantitative measurements of intracultural variation that can be easily integrated into selectionist research protocols. A very promising tool is the Culture as Consensus model developed by Romney and colleagues (1986). Such tools would be useful in distinguishing cases where behavioral differences are associated with cultural differences (perhaps indicating alternative strategies) from cases where behavioral differences exist without cultural differences (suggesting a "best of a bad job" situation).

A serious consideration of culture by evolutionary thinkers is required to meet two of the most important challenges to the perspectives advanced in this volume. One challenge comes from the perspective of cultural determinism, while the other comes from within the selectionist perspective.

Marshall Sahlins argues that selectionist social scientists are victims of the longstanding Western desire to explain all social reality as produced by the striving of individuals to fulfill pre-cultural biological needs. Sociobiology thus becomes another example of the Western cosmology trying to fit all other cultural realities into its tidy framework:

> One probably does not need much persuasion that our folk anthropology is disposed to these explanations of culture by nature. Ranging from racism in the streets to sociobiology in the universities and passing by way of numerous expressions of the common tongue, biological determinism is a recurrent ideology of Western society. Its ubiquity, I will argue, is a function of its transmission in anthropological traditions of cosmic dimensions: . . . the concept of man as a willful creature of need, especially as this notion has developed under the market economy, and, also, the theory of the human constitution inscribed in the Great Chain of Being, especially as linked to the antagonistic dualism of flesh and spirit of the Christian nightmare—the flesh as brutish, self-regarding animal nature underlying and overcoming the better inclinations of the human soul (1996:400).

On a superficial level, Sahlins restates the point that sociobiological ideas, like all other Western social science concepts, have their origin in Western social realities. As I noted above, the origin of scientific ideas ultimately has little to do with their validity. Sahlins has a more interesting point, one that forcefully demonstrates why selectionist thinkers need to grapple with the concept of culture. He sketches several cosmologies with social realities that are alien to the traditions of Western social science. What are we to make of his point that other societies conceptualize and explain social and physical reality with cultural logics different than Western cultural logic? One possible response is to suggest that selectionist theory need not consider how any group of people, including Westerners, sees its social reality. If selectionist theory can accurately predict behavioral outcomes without asking how people see their world, linking models derived from nonhuman animals to human behavior is made easier. In fact, listening to what people say is going on can frequently mislead. If Cronk had accepted Mukogodo statements about investment biases toward males, he might have missed the advantages females seem to accrue.

If we accept that selectionist social science needs to include "culture" in its explanations of human behavior, how can Sahlins's call for constant awareness of alternative cosmologies ("methodological cosmopolitanism") be incorporated into research? I see several possibilities that might apply to any particular case. Take the example of the free rider problem. Most selectionists assume that this problem is inevitable in any system with common goods and that actions must be taken against its destroying the system. One question to ask is whether people living in other cultural logics just not to conceptualize the free-rider problem, or do they conceptualize it differently than Westerners? A second question is: do people in other cultures act as if they were coping with the free rider problem even if they do not conceptualize it, or conceptualize it differently than Westerners? Theorists who find culture unnecessary assume that the answer to this question is yes. A third question is: is the free rider problem a trap of Western cosmology that would disappear if we changed our cultural logic? Might some alternative cultural logics sketched by Sahlins create a world where common goods exist and there is no need to deal with the possibility of free riders? This possibility is the one most desired by postmodernists most enamored of the idea that cultural logics are incommensurate.

As selectionists conduct research, they should seize opportunities to deepen our understanding of culture by engaging in methodological cosmopolitanism. Dwyer and Minnegal's (1997) analysis of reciprocal altruism and the free-rider problem among the Gwaimasi sago producers of New Guinea illustrates the potential for this type of research. A recent trend in Melanesianist cultural anthropology has been to emphasize the difference between Western and Melanesian social logics (see Strathern 1988, 1991), so Dwyer and Minnegal's finding that Gwaimasi hosts were less willing to permit free riding by guests when the probability of reciprocation disappeared is very interesting. Although Dwyer and Minnegal do not provide a full analysis of Gwaimasi social logic, their discussion of how discourse on relationships between guests, hosts, and resources changed as the probability for reciprocation declined illustrates the type of data necessary to meet Sahlins's challenge. They describe a host chopping down a tree planted by a guest and angrily demanding that the guests leave. It would be interesting to know the cultural logic he used in making this demand and how it related to the logic that had permitted guests free access to host land just a few months earlier.

The challenge to the perspective of this volume from within the selectionist perspective is the possible role of group selection in human evolution. After twenty years of debate, the issue of group selection is still not settled in evolutionary social science (see the debates in Boehm 1996; Palmer et al. 1997; Sober and Wilson 1998; Wilson 1998; Wilson and Sober 1994). I expect the next few years will see an increase in research designed to test competing hypotheses generated by group selectionist and lower level selectionist perspectives. There is little of group selection in the current volume, although Sugiyama and Chacon's use of Tooby and Cosmides (1996) foreshadows forthcoming debates. Tooby and Cosmides sketch pathways to altruism that do not involve kin selection or reciprocal altruism. Consideration of what role these pathways played in human evolution and whether they can be conceptualized in ways that do not require some form of group selection will be one of the most important tasks of the next few years.

In the 1979 AAA volume, E. O. Wilson predicted that "Anthropology will become more biological, and biology will become more anthropological. The seam between the two subjects will disappear, and both will be richer" (1979:521).

The papers in this volume are excellent illustrations of the mutual enrichment that is possible. Unfortunately, the two fields have not grown closer together during the past twenty years. Instead, a chasm has opened, threatening to isolate them from each other. We can only hope this was a temporary situation and that continued theoretical advancement and empirical research will eventually close the gap. There are signs that the postmodernist moment in cultural anthropology is waning and that younger researchers are more willing to consider evolutionary approaches to human social behavior. The next twenty years will be as exciting as the previous twenty.

NOTES

1. I personally find the label "sociobiology" useful for describing the types of research discussed in this volume. However, the phrase has now accumulated so much baggage that it is best to set it aside for a while. The phrases "selectionist social science" and "selectionist thinking" recommend themselves because they can accommodate each of the research traditions described by Smith without favoring one over the others.
2. See South and Lloyd (1995) for American data on this topic.
3. The lawyers can get some guidance from Beckstorm (1985, 1989).
4. Bourdieu and Passeron (1990:4) write, "every power which manages to impose meanings and to impose them as legitimate by concealing the power relations which are the basis of its force, adds its own specifically symbolic force to those power relations."

REFERENCES

Abu-Lughod, Lila. 1990. The romance of resistance: Tracing transformations of power through Bedouin women. *American Ethnologist* 17:41–55.

Alexander, Richard D. 1987. *The Biology of Moral Systems.* New York: Aldine de Gruyter.

Baker, R. Robin, and Mark A. Bellis. 1995. *Human Sperm Competition: Copulation, Masturbation, and Infidelity.* New York: Chapman and Hall.

Beckstrom, John H. 1985. *Sociobiology and the Law: The Biology of Altruism in the Courtroom of the Future.* Urbana: University of Illinois Press.

———. 1989. *Evolutionary Jurisprudence: Prospects and Limitations on the Use of Modern Darwinism Throughout the Legal Process.* Urbana: University of Illinois Press.

———. 1993. *Darwinism Applied: Evolutionary Paths to Social Goals.* Westport, Connecticut: Praeger.

Betzig, Laura. 1997. Introduction: People are animals. In *Human Nature: A Critical Reader.* L. Betzig, ed. Pp. 1–17. New York: Oxford University Press.

Boehm, Christopher. 1996. Emergency decisions, cultural-selection mechanics, and group selection. *Current Anthropology* 37:763–793.

Borgerhoff Mulder, Monique. 1996. Responses to environmental novelty: Changes in men's marriage strategies in a rural Kenyan community. *Proceedings of the British Academy* 88:203–222.

Bourdieu, Pierre, and Jean-Claude Passeron. 1990. *Reproduction in Education, Society, and Culture.* Newbury Park, California: Sage.

Brown, Michael F. 1996. On resisting resistance. *American Anthropologist* 98:729–749.

Buss, David M., and Neil M. Malamuth, eds. 1996. *Sex, Power, Conflict: Evolutionary and Feminist Perspectives.* New York: Oxford University Press.

Chagnon, Napoleon. 1979. Anthropology and the nature of things. In *Evolutionary Biology and Human Social Behavior: An Anthropological Perspective,* N. Chagnon and W. Irons, eds. Pp. 522–526. North Scituate, Massachusetts: Duxbury Press.

Chagnon, Napoleon A., and Paul E. Bugos, Jr. 1979. Kin selection and conflict: An analysis of a Yanomamö ax fight. In *Evolutionary Biology and Human Social Behavior: An Anthropological Perspective.* N. Chagnon and W. Irons, eds. Pp. 213–237. North Scituate, Massachusetts: Duxbury Press.

Coney, Nancy S., and Wade C. Mackey. 1997. Fatherhood as a deterrent against female promiscuity: a time to refurbish the Electra complex. *Mankind Quarterly* 38:3–23.

Cronk, Lee. 1995. Is there a role for culture in human behavioral ecology? *Ethology and Sociobiology* 16:181–205.

———. 1998. Ethnographic text formation processes. *Social Science Information/Information sur les Sciences Sociales* 37:321–349.

Daly, Martin, and Margo Wilson. 1997. Child abuse and other risks of not living with both parents. In *Human Nature: A Critical Reader.* L. Betzig, ed. Pp. 159–171. New York: Oxford University Press.

D'Andrade, Roy. 1995. Moral models in anthropology. *Current Anthropology* 36:399–408.

Das Gupta, Monica, and P. N. Mari Bhat. 1997. Fertility decline and increased manifestation of sex bias in India. *Population Studies* 51:307–315.

Davis, Jennifer Nerissa, and Martin Daly. 1997. Evolutionary theory and the human family. *Quarterly Review of Biology* 72:407–435.

Dwyer, Peter D., and Monica Minnegal. 1997. Sago games: Cooperation and change among sago producers of Papua New Guinea. *Evolution and Human Behavior* 18:89–108.

Emlen, Stephen T. 1997. The evolutionary study of the human family. *Social Science Information* 36:563–589.

Gauthier, Anne Héléne, and Jan Hatzius. 1997. Family benefits and fertility: an econometric analysis. *Population Studies* 51:295–306.

Herrnstein, Richard J., and Charles Murray. 1994. *The Bell Curve: Intelligence and Class Structure in American Life.* New York: Free Press.

Hrdy, Sarah B. 1997. Raising Darwin's consciousness: female sexuality and the prehominid origins of patriarchy. *Human Nature* 8:1–49.

Irons, William. 1997. Looking back two decades. In *Human Nature: A Critical Reader.* L. Betzig, ed. Pp. 46–49. New York: Oxford University Press.

Kacelnik, Alex, and John R. Krebs. 1997. Yanomamö dreams and starling payloads: the logic of optimality. In *Human Nature: A Critical Reader.* L. Betzig, ed. Pp. 21–35. New York: Oxford University Press.

Kuznar, Lawrence A. 1997. *Reclaiming a Scientific Anthropology.* Walnut Creek, California: AltaMira Press.

Liesen, Laurette. 1995. Feminism and the politics of reproductive strategies. *Politics and the Life Sciences* 14:145–162.

Lynch, Aaron. 1996. *Thought Contagion: How Belief Spreads Through Society.* New York: Basic Books.

Mascia-Lees, Frances E., Patricia Sharpe, and Colleen Ballerino Cohen. 1989. The post-modern turn in anthropology: Cautions from a feminist perspective. *Signs* 15:7–33.

Mealey, Linda. 1990. Differential use of reproductive strategies by human groups? *Psychological Science* 6:385–387.

Ortner, Sherry B. 1995a. The case of the disappearing shamans, or no individualism, no relationalism. *Ethos* 23:355–390.

———. 1995b. Resistance and the problem of ethnographic refusal. *Comparative Studies in Society and History* 37:173–193.

Palmer, Craig T., B. Eric Fredrickson, and Christopher F. Tilley. 1997. Categories and gatherings: group selection and the mythology of cultural anthropology. *Evolution and Human Behavior* 18:291–308.

Romney, A. Kimball, Susan C. Weller, and William H. Batchelder. 1986. Culture as consensus: a theory of culture and informant accuracy. *American Anthropologist* 88:313–338.

Rushton, J. Philippe. 1995. *Race, Evolution, and Behavior.* New York: Transaction.

Sahlins, Marshall. 1976. *The Use and Abuse of Biology.* Ann Arbor: University of Michigan Press.

———. 1996. The sadness of sweetness: The native anthropology of Western cosmology. *Current Anthropology* 37:395–428.

Scheper-Hughes, Nancy. 1995. The primacy of the ethical: Propositions for a militant anthropology. *Current Anthropology* 36:409–440.

Smuts, Barbara. 1995. The evolutionary origin of patriarchy. *Human Nature* 6:1–32.

Sober, Elliot, and David S. Wilson. 1998. *Unto Others: The Evolution of Altruism.* Cambridge: Harvard University Press.

Sociobiology Study Group of Science for the People. 1976. Sociobiology—another biological determinism. *BioScience* 26(3):182–186.

South, Scott J., and Kim M. Lloyd. 1995. Spousal alternatives and marital dissolution. *American Sociological Review* 60:21–35.

Strathern, Marilyn. 1988. *The Gender of the Gift.* Berkeley: University of California Press.

———. 1991. *Partial Connections.* Savage, MD: Rowman and Littlefield.

Tooby, John, and Leda Cosmides. 1996. Friendship and the banker's paradox: Other pathways to the evolution of adaptations for altruism. *Proceedings of the British Academy* 88:119–143.

Vining, D. R., Jr. 1986. Social versus reproductive success: The central theoretical problem of sociobiology. *Behavioral and Brain Sciences* 9:167–216.

Wilson, David S. 1998. Hunting, sharing, and multilevel selection. *Current Anthropology* 39:73–97.

Wilson, David S., and Elliot Sober. 1994. Re-introducing group selection to the human behavioral sciences. *Behavioral and Brain Sciences* 17:585–654.

Wilson. Edward O. 1979. Biology and anthropology: A mutual transformation? In *Evolutionary Biology and Human Social Behavior: An Anthropological Perspective.* N. Chagnon and W. Irons, eds. Pp. 519–521. North Scituate, Massachusetts: Duxbury Press.

Wright, Robert. 1994. *The Moral Animal: Evolutionary Psychology and Everyday Life.* New York: Random House.

Zhang, Junsen. 1997. The effect of welfare programs on criminal behavior: A theoretical and empirical analysis. *Economic Inquiry* 35:120–137.

Index